Water Law of the American West

Water Law of the American West

A Systems Approach

Dylan R. Hedden-Nicely
Professor of Law
Director of the Native American Law Program &
Natural Resources and Environmental Law Program
University of Idaho College of Law

Barbara A. Cosens
Distinguished Professor of Law, Emerita
University of Idaho College of Law

The Late Dale D. Goble
Distinguished Professor of Law, Emeritus
University of Idaho College of Law

Carolina Academic Press
Durham, North Carolina

Library of Congress Cataloging-in-Publication Data

Names: Hedden-Nicely, Dylan R., author. | Cosens, Barbara. | Goble, Dale, author.
Title: Water law of the American West : a systems approach / Dylan R. Hedden-Nicely, Barbara A. Cosens, and Dale D. Goble.
Description: Durham, North Carolina : Carolina Academic Press, 2024. | Includes bibliographical references and index.
Identifiers: LCCN 2024030906 | ISBN 9781531023027 (paperback) | ISBN 9781531023034 (ebook)
Subjects: LCSH: Water—Law and legislation—West (U.S.) | Water use—Law and legislation—West (U.S.) | Water rights—West (U.S.) | Water resources development—Law and legislation—West (U.S.) | Water-supply—Law and legislation—West (U.S.)
Classification: LCC KF5571 .H43 2024 | DDC 343.7309/240978—dc23/eng/20240714
LC record available at https://lccn.loc.gov/2024030906

Carolina Academic Press
700 Kent Street
Durham, North Carolina 27701
(919) 489-7486
www.cap-press.com

Printed in the United States of America

The authors dedicate this book to Dylan's daughter Minta Ardell as well as Barbara's grandchildren Claire, Rose, and Cal. Each of these young ones were born while this book was being conceptualized, planned, and written, and their future depends on the water lawyers and managers of the future who will learn from these materials. Do good work.

Contents

Preface

Water law is the law focused on development, allocation, use, and preservation of flow of fresh water. Basically, the non-navigational uses of surface and groundwater. Water law is designed to mediate interaction among humans seeking to use water and between humans and the water resource itself. The modern practice of water law requires not only an understanding of the judicial development of water law, but of the pervasive overlay beginning in the twentieth century of science-based agency administration, comprehensive water use statutory schemes, and adjudication. Practitioners of western water law must also understand that with an average of 50% of western lands in each state held by the federal government, including for Native American Tribes, and with the major development of dams on many western rivers undertaken by the federal government, water use and allocation is not merely a matter of state water allocation law. A modern water law practitioner must understand water law through the lens of the three sovereigns: State, Tribal, and Federal government, if they are to adequately represent water users and managers in the modern West. Finally, for those entering the practice of water law today, you enter at a time when many water sources are fully appropriated, yet demand is increasing due to population growth, and supply is less dependable due to climate change. Complicating this in the arid West is the late twentieth-century change in values that led to the late recognition of instream (or "environmental") flows as an important water use, and the evolving impact of climate change on water supply and water demand. To solve your clients' problems, you must not only understand water law, but the science of the water resource itself and the variety of competing worldviews of those who seek to use or protect it.

To resolve conflict, the modern water law practitioner must understand a water source as a connected part of a much larger system of surface and groundwater. The historical development of water law has been strongly connected to place, to the competing demands on a water source, and to the specific hydrology of that source. Thus, you will learn that the complexity of these interactions—and their emergent manifestations as problems that must be solved within the legal system—is context-specific. The emphasis on understanding climate, hydrology, society, and law and how they interact within a specific water basin is because these context-specific factors affect what may be the best legal solutions. To manage this complexity, the book focuses on the region of the Pacific Northwest, with notes concerning other areas where contrasting approaches are used. This region is dominated by the Columbia River and its tributaries. This focus forces you to study water law as part of a nested system that includes the resource itself, the varied and conflicting human values associated with the system, and the multiple jurisdictions that share the allocation and management of a connected system. By focusing on this systemic approach made possible by the focus on a single, very large water basin, and on the overlay of an administrative system on the common law, you will learn the processes and types of issues and solutions that will allow you to become a productive practitioner of water law in any arid western state. In short, *Water Law of the American West: A Systems Approach* is designed for the student entering the practice of water law in the twenty-first century.

The book is organized in six parts. Part I introduces you to the water resource, the demands on its use, and the challenges of supply. Chapter 1 begins with water by introducing you to the science of hydrology and the technology involved in the development of surface and groundwater and the dominant uses of western water—irrigation and environmental (instream) flows. Chapter 2 looks at the challenge posed by the impact of climate change on both water supply and demand. Chapter 3 introduces the human component by exploring the values and ways different societies understand water and the conceptual underpinnings of the approaches to resolving conflict over water use in the western United States. This chapter will address, but not solve, the dilemma that Native American tribes did not view their relationship with water as one of "owner" but more akin to one of "guardian," yet the legal system of the United States, including federal Indian water law, will be the lens through which this water law text is written. Chapter 4 turns to the basis of western water law by covering the sources of authority over water allocation found in the U.S. Constitution. This helps you begin with an understanding that both State and Tribal sovereignty over water are functions of federal law.

Part II focuses on the source of law for allocation of water by western states and its beginnings in common law. Common law is judicial law developed incrementally and followed within a jurisdiction as individual cases come before the courts. Chapter 5 covers the initial efforts of western state courts to determine what approach—riparian rights or prior appropriation—will apply to water allocation. Chapters 6–8 focus on prior appropriation and cover the common law attributes of a water right acquired by appropriation. Chapter 6 covers the act of diverting water, its relation to priority, and the varying approach of states to whether diversion is required or whether instream flow rights are possible at common law; Chapter 7 covers beneficial use and its role in determining the amount of water associated with a water right by prohibiting waste and how that evolves through time; Chapter 8 covers the concept of "use it or lose it," which provides for abandonment or forfeiture of all or a portion of a water right due to non-use. Chapter 9 addresses the common law of groundwater and the varying approaches of western states to its allocation and the problems that arose as the technology to pump large quantities of groundwater became available.

Part III turns to the "third sovereign" to cover Native American rights to water. Chapter 10 sets up the legal basis for aboriginal rights—rights held by Tribes from time immemorial, and reserved rights—water rights reserved by treaty, executive order, or act of congress. Chapter 11 covers the struggle to quantify reserved water rights. Chapter 12 covers the allotment of certain Native American reservations and the effect on water rights held for the tribe, tribal members, and by non-Indian water users. Chapter 13 covers the recent recognition that reserved water rights extend to groundwater.

Part IV addresses the role of the federal sovereign in western water. Chapter 14 introduces the variety of federal, non-Indian, reservations across the western United States and the law governing federal reserved water rights associated with these reservations. Chapter 15 covers the authority of the federal government over navigation stemming from the Commerce Clause of the Constitution, the transfer to states and reservations for Tribes of the beds and banks of navigable waterways, and the federal limitations on states' management and development of those submerged lands. Chapter 16 again turns to the Commerce Clause, this time as the source of authority for the massive federal development of western rivers for irrigation under the Reclamation Act, and a brief introduction to development of dams for flood control, under the Rivers and Harbors Act. Chapter 17 covers the federal role in interstate allocation of shared surface and ground water. Chapter 18 covers international customary law with respect to shared freshwater sources, the federal role in international law, and the development of treaties using the treaty between the United States and Canada on the Columbia River as an example.

Part V turns to the modern administrative overlay in which science-based agencies manage the water resource under comprehensive state water use acts that have both incorporated and altered the common law. Chapter 19 provides a brief introduction to administrative law for those students who lack that background, and to refresh the memories of those who do. Chapter 20 covers the development of permit systems to allow review of factors like water availability prior to water development. Chapter 21 explores flexibility in water rights through study of the change in water right process and the use of water banks to reduce the transaction costs of moving water to another user. Chapter 22 addresses statutory changes to the common law in three key areas: (1) the ability to permit a non-diversionary water right for the protection of environmental flows; (2) processes to allow growing municipalities to establish a quantification of water for future demand; and (3) regulations to slow or prohibit groundwater mining and changes to protections for well depth. Chapter 23 describes the setting we will use to understand administration of water. Chapter 24 looks at the emerging problem of management of surface and ground water as a single connected source—referred to as "conjunctive management." This provides an opportunity to learn about the complex roles of administrative agencies and the judiciary, and the interaction of law and science in solving emerging problems. Part V will focus on Idaho to provide an understanding of a comprehensive system and because it is the state among our four of focus that is farthest along in conjunctive management. It thus provides a look at how science-based agencies and modern courts approach some of the emerging water issues of our times. You will, nevertheless, also learn about emerging issues in other states that have not yet been addressed in Idaho, particularly on exempt domestic wells, as well as some of the novel approaches and solutions in Native American water right settlements.

Part VI covers the adjudication of water rights—a major undertaking by a number of western states in the latter half of the twentieth century—and concludes with a chapter on implementation. Adjudication was made necessary by the late development of administrative permit systems and the absence of a database for enforcement of pre-permit water rights. Adjudication gave rise to many court rulings on issues of first impression and on the overlay of water use acts on the common law. Because they took place once the West had access to a well-developed science of hydrology and water infrastructure technology, adjudication rulings often represent a more modern interpretation of water law. As a result of federal law, state adjudications also covered the quantification of Native American and federal water rights. On the one hand this forced Tribes into western state tribunals, and on the other hand it led to funding for water development on reservations and a quantification basis to seek enforcement in court. Chapter 25 covers the process of both private and general adjudication in state courts. Chapter 26 covers adjudication of Native American water rights in state courts, including the basis for state court jurisdiction over Native American and federal reserved water rights. Chapter 27 covers the divergence between litigation and settlement of Native American water rights and the factors that inform both. Chapter 28 covers the question of post-adjudication water management on Native American reservations and the struggle courts face with reservations that have significant non-Indian land ownership and water use as a result of allotment.

State common law rulings, water use acts, administrative systems, and adjudication processes and issues are highly context-specific and interrelated. Thus, Parts II and V focus heavily on a single state—Idaho. This is not merely attributable to the fact that all three of the authors of this text taught or teach water law in Idaho. In fact, the reason for the choice of Idaho is likely the same reason that all three of the authors were hired by the University of Idaho and can be found in the following facts:

- The high dollar value of irrigated agriculture in Idaho and southern Idaho is third only to the Central Valley (1) and Imperial Irrigation District (2) of California, in its annual crop value;
- Idaho is one of the fastest-growing states in the West;
- Recreation, focused on white water sports and fishing, is Idaho's fastest-growing industry;
- Idaho's primary surface water sources are highly connected to massive groundwater resources, with both heavily developed for agriculture;
- Idaho relies heavily on hydropower for its baseload energy supply; and
- Idaho has snow-fed surface watersheds that are increasingly becoming rain dominated due to climate change, altering the timing and temperature of runoff.

As a result of these factors, Idaho has been addressing many of the emerging water issues found across the West in recent decades. Nevertheless, the authors hope that, over time, faculty in other states will join us in posting online resources to allow comparative study of administrative systems and adjudication in other states.

By beginning with the water resource in Part I, this casebook reflects the need for students to understand not only the law, but the science of water resources and the society that seeks to use or protect it. Parts II–IV emphasize that each of the three sovereigns share the use and development of many western water sources. Parts V and VI bring in the overlay of the administrative system and the modern efforts to manage a scarce resource in the face of increasing demand, realization of the critical importance of ecosystem function, and the impacts of climate change. These concluding Parts also introduce the increasing role of diplomacy and development of novel solutions to solve modern water law problems. The co-authors hope that this approach will inspire a new generation of water law students to play a positive role in contemporary western water law.

Acknowledgments

The authors would like to acknowledge the outstanding group of legal scholars and practitioners who provided peer review on these Chapters: Professor Jason Robison, University of Wyoming, Associate Professor Burke Griggs, Washburn University, Professor Monte Mills, University of Washington, and Mark Cecchini-Beaver, United States Solicitor for the Department of the Interior. These pages truly stand on the shoulders of giants in their fields.

The authors would also like to acknowledge our amazing research assistants Jillian Greene, Sara Ajeti, Leilanee Taylor, Melissa Svancara, and Nicolette Clarke, each of whom were instrumental in the development of this casebook. We are so proud of what you have accomplished so far in your early careers and cannot wait to see what you do next. With you each at the helm, we are confident that our communities are in good hands as we move into an uncertain future.

Professor Cosens would also like to acknowledge her water law mentor from UC Hastings, Professor Brian Gray, stating: "He taught me in my first water law class that you need to understand a specific system (in that case, California), the law, the hydrology, the infrastructure, the people, the history, and get out on the ground if you are to understand water law. He also taught me that a good lawyer is a good storyteller."

For his part, Professor Hedden-Nicely acknowledges and honors his water law mentor (and co-author) Professor Barb Cosens. It was from Barb that I learned that the heart of every water law problem sits at the intersection of law, science, and society; only solutions that address all three remain durable through time. It is probably understating it to say that I would not be where I am but for your mentorship, quiet yet confident guidance, and advocacy.

Finally, we would like to acknowledge the water law students at the University of Idaho College of Law, who have beta tested this material and our approach to teaching law. Your enthusiasm and insights taught us so much and made this project a pleasure to develop.

About the Authors

Dylan R. Hedden-Nicely is a citizen of the Cherokee Nation of Oklahoma and was raised in the heart of the Columbia River Basin in Southwestern Idaho. Currently he serves as a professor of law and head of the University of Idaho College of Law's Native American Law Program.

Dylan earned his Bachelor of Science degree from the University of British Columbia in Honours Physical Geography and Geology (Honours Geomorphology). While there, he completed an Honours thesis that examined the integration of the Canadian Climate Model with snowmelt modeling techniques. Dylan attended law school and graduate school at University of Idaho, where he earned a Juris Doctor (magna cum laude) with an emphasis in Native American law, as well as in natural resources and environmental law. Concurrently, he earned a master's degree in water resources (science and engineering). His M.S. thesis focused on the development of a systems dynamics based water balance model to assess the impact of the physical and anthropogenic constraints placed upon Coeur d'Alene Lake in North Idaho. Much of Dylan's work continues to sit at the intersection of law and science, focusing in particular on the development of scientifically rigorous techniques to help evaluate complex legal questions.

After law school, Hedden-Nicely joined a Native American-owned law firm that focused exclusively on the representation of American Indian tribes. While in private practice, he focused on litigation and negotiation of issues related to Native American natural resources and water rights, and he continues to consult with tribes on these issues.

Dylan teaches a variety of courses, including Native American law, Native American natural resources law, tribal nation economics and law, and civil procedure. His research interests include Native American natural resources and water law, tribal treaty rights, tribal civil and regulatory jurisdiction, water rights law, the interrelationship of law and science with applications to natural resources law, tribal economic development and tribal governance, as well the underrepresentation of Native people in the legal profession.

Barbara A. Cosens is a University Distinguished Professor Emerita with the University of Idaho College of Law, where she taught for 16 years.

She holds a B.S. and M.S. in Geology from the University of California, Davis, and University of Washington respectively. She worked for almost a decade in the exploration and development of geothermal resources. She received her J.D. (magna cum laude) from the University of California, Hastings and an LL.M. in Environmental Law (summa cum laude) from Lewis & Clark Law School.

Barbara was instrumental in the development of the Program in Natural Resources and Environmental Law at the UI College of Law, and the development of the interdisciplinary Water Resources graduate program that included concurrent J.D./M.S. and J.D./Ph.D. degrees. Her teaching and research expertise is in water law, the law-science interface and water dispute resolution. She co-chaired the Adaptive Water Governance, project made possible through support from the NSF-funded National Socio-Environmental Synthesis Center, SESYNC, and spent spring 2015 at the Goyder Institute in Australia, comparing water law reform in the western United States and Australia during drought. Her research interests included the integration of law and science in water resource management and dispute resolution, water management and resilience, and the recognition and settlement of Native American water rights. She is a member of the Universities Consortium on Columbia River Governance.

Prior to entering the academy, Barbara served as lead negotiator for water right negotiations between the Montana Reserved Water Rights Commission and federal and tribal governments. In retirement she continues to be active in publication, serves in a senior advisory capacity on grants, and provides graduate student advising. In her outreach and engagement, she continues to provide education and expertise on the Columbia River Treaty as part of the Universities Consortium on Columbia River Governance. She is also working as a mediator on water disputes, particularly disputes among governments.

Dale D. Goble was a University Distinguished Professor and the Margaret Wilson Schimke Distinguished Professor of Law. He earned an A.B. in philosophy from Columbia College and a J.D. from the University of Oregon.

Following law school, he taught at Oregon for a year before joining the Solicitor's Office at the Department of the Interior in Washington, D.C., as an Honors Program Attorney. He left Interior to join the University of Idaho College of Law back in his home state.

During his time at the College of Law, Dale was also an adjunct faculty member of the Environmental Science, Bioregional Planning, Philosophy, and Water Resources Faculties at the University of Idaho. He was also a Member Scholar at the Center for Progressive Reform. He is co-author of the first casebook on Wildlife Law. The casebook brought together state law governing game management, conservation, and take with federal and international law focused on species protection under the heading of Wildlife Law to provide a more complete curriculum on biodiversity conservation, management, and take.

Dale is known at the University of Idaho for his work in bridging the science/law divide, developing a concurrent degree program between Environmental Science and Law, as well as his quest to insert as many cases as possible with potatoes into the Torts curriculum, which led to the student-created label of "Tater Torts." Dale taught Tater Torts to over 1500 students from 1982 to 2017 and was truly instrumental in shaping torts law in Idaho. Dale passed in 2022 while this book was in development. His contributions to this casebook and that of his co-authors is summarized below.

Several decades ago, while teaching Water Law at the University of Idaho College of Law, Dale Goble developed a supplementary electronic casebook for his students that reflected Idaho water law at the time and covered every major issue found in a water law casebook. He passed the materials onto Barbara Cosens when she joined the faculty in 2004. At that time, the Idaho adjudication of the Snake River Basin was in full swing, the Nez Perce Water Rights Settlement was in its final stages of negotiation, and the major battle over conjunctive management was underway in southern Idaho. In short, Idaho water law was in a period of rapid development. In her years working for the State of Montana, Barbara had learned that in states with science-based agencies implementing comprehensive water use acts, there is a complex relationship between statutes and the common law, and between law and science. All three must be understood to contribute to the modern practice of water law. She built on Dale's materials, adding major new cases, statutory changes to the common law, administrative practice of water law, adjudication, and litigation and settlement of reserved water rights, and used the materials to teach water law for the next 16 years. At the Festschrift in Honor of University of Idaho Distinguished Professor Emeritus Dale Goble held in 2019 after his retirement in 2017, Barbara promised to turn the materials into a published book. By that time, Dylan Hedden-Nicely had joined the faculty to head the Native American Law Program and would take over the teaching of water law on Barbara's retirement. Barbara and Dale invited him to join the casebook authorship and he raised the idea of giving equal voice to the water rights law of the three sovereigns—state, tribal, and federal. All three authors brought a strong background in law, interdisciplinary research, legal practice, and an appreciation for the importance of understanding the law-science intersection in resolving modern water disputes. The co-authors hope you will benefit from this collaboration.

During the writing of this book, our esteemed colleague and co-author, Dale Goble, passed. We dedicate this book to his memory, and Carolina Academic Press has graciously allowed us to retain him as co-author because his contribution was already substantial. We had the privilege of learning from and laughing with Dale as his mentees, colleagues, and friends. Thank you Dale for believing in both of us on this wonderful journey that is the academic life. We miss you.

Barbara Cosens

Dylan Hedden-Nicely

Water Law of the American West

Part I

The Physical, Climatic, Social, and Constitutional Backdrop for a Systems Approach to Western Water Law

The new challenges facing the modern practice of water law demand a deeper understanding of the resource itself and the society that relies on it. Practitioners must understand not only the law, but the social-ecological-technological system it resides in if they are to develop the innovations necessary to resolve conflict. Part I provides the foundations for developing a systems approach to western water law by examining: the unique physical characteristics of water; the climatic dependence of water supply and demand and the anticipated future with climate change; the value-based relation between society and water and its role in the development of water law; and the constitutional basis for western water law.

Water is essential for life. So much so that the presence of water in liquid form is the single most important factor in the search for extraterrestrial life. Water flows both above and below the ground, and jurisdictional boundaries generally ignore that reality.

The following water facts and related figures provide a background on water distribution, use, and scarcity.

- The distribution of water on earth is uneven and much of it is unfit for human consumption. Although 70% of the earth is covered with water, 97% is saltwater, 1.75–2% is frozen in glaciers, ice and snow, and 0.7–0.8% is stored as soil moisture or groundwater.[1] This leaves less than 0.01% present as fresh surface water in lakes, wetlands, rivers, and streams.

1. UNEP, *Vital Water Graphics: An Overview of the State of the World's Fresh and Marine Waters* (2d ed. 2008), https://www.grida.no/resources/5608.

- Groundwater represents about 90% of the world's readily available freshwater resources, and some 1.5 billion people depend upon groundwater for their drinking water.[2]
- Agricultural water use accounts for about 75% of total global consumption—mainly through crop irrigation—while industrial use accounts for about 20%, and the remaining 5% is used for domestic purposes.[3]
- Clean water supplies and sanitation remain major problems in many parts of the world, with 20% of the global population lacking access to safe drinking water. Around 1.1 billion people globally do not have access to improved water supply sources, while 2.4 billion people do not have access to any type of improved sanitation facility. About 2 million people die every year due to waterborne diseases from fecal pollution of surface waters; most of them are children less than five years of age.[4]
- It is estimated that two out of every three people will live in water-stressed areas by the year 2025. In Africa alone, it is estimated that 25 countries will be experiencing water stress (defined as water supply below 1,700 m^3 per capita per year) by 2025. Today, 450 million people in 29 countries suffer from water shortages.[5]
- In the United States, surface water is used more than groundwater.
- In the United States, water withdrawals for irrigation have leveled off in recent years as they have in other sectors.[6]
- The dominant water uses vary by state and are related to climate and economic base as will be discussed later in Part I. You will learn that withdrawals are not the same as the amount of water consumed. Thus, a small amount of water used for cooling in the thermoelectric process is evaporated, but most of the water is available for return to the source (albeit at a higher temperature). Consumptive water use varies by sector and is highest in the agricultural sector. Thus, in the Pacific Northwest, Idaho's agricultural industry is both the largest withdrawal of water and the largest consumptive use of water. Idaho is second only to California in irrigation water withdrawals.
- Access to indoor plumbing and safe drinking water also varies across the United States. A study reported in Nature Communications in 2021, concluded "[w]e find elevated levels of incomplete plumbing at the county level were significantly

---

2. *Id.*

3. UNEP, *Vital Water Graphics: An Overview of the State of the World's Fresh and Marine Waters* (2d ed. 2008), https://www.grida.no/resources/5626.

4. UNEP, *Vital Water Graphics: An Overview of the State of the World's Fresh and Marine Waters* (2d ed. 2008), https://www.grida.no/resources/5596; and https://www.grida.no/resources/5591.

5. UNEP, *Vital Water Graphics: An Overview of the State of the World's Fresh and Marine Waters* (2d ed. 2008), https://www.grida.no/resources/5625.

6. Noel Gollehon, *Agriculture Dominates Freshwater Use in the U.S.*, USDA Economic Research Service (Nov. 1, 2016), https://www.ers.usda.gov/amber-waves/2006/november/agriculture-dominates-freshwater-use-in-the-u-s/.

> ($p<0.05$) associated with older populations, lower income, higher poverty, greater portions of indigenous people (American Indian, Alaska Natives, Native Hawaiian, and Other Pacific Islanders), lower levels of education, and more rural counties."[7]

The variable distribution of water, variation in year to year and seasonal supply, and variation in human use are related to complex climatic, physiographic, and social factors. Thus, resolving disputes over water is both complex and context-specific. This book is designed to introduce you to that complexity and the way in which state, tribal, and federal legal systems resolve those disputes. Thus, a "systems approach" requires that we focus on a connected water system—in this case, the Columbia River Basin, and that we begin with a foundation on how the physical and social context impacts the law.

Part I introduces you to these social, legal, and physical complexities. Chapter 1 provides an introduction to hydrology and water use technology and seeks to explain why a basic understanding of these areas is important to the effective practice of water law. Chapter 2 covers the major challenge to water supply and demand that may dominate your careers—climate change—and the current understanding of how water resources in the Pacific Northwest will be affected. Chapter 3 looks at water and society to explore the differing views of the relationship between humans and water and how that may lead to different legal concepts. You will explore the western view of water as a common pool resource and the tension among property, regulatory, and collaborative approaches for its distribution. You will explore water through the Indigenous lens in which the relation of humans to water may be understood through the modern concept of guardianship. Chapter 4 explores the constitutional sources of authority to allocate, develop, regulate, and manage water, thus providing the legal framework within which water law has been adapted to its physical and social context.

---

7. J.T. Mueller & S. Gasteyer, *The Widespread and Unjust Drinking Water and Clean Water Crisis in the United States*, 12 Nat. Commun. 3544 (2021), https://doi.org/10.1038/s41467-021-23898-z.

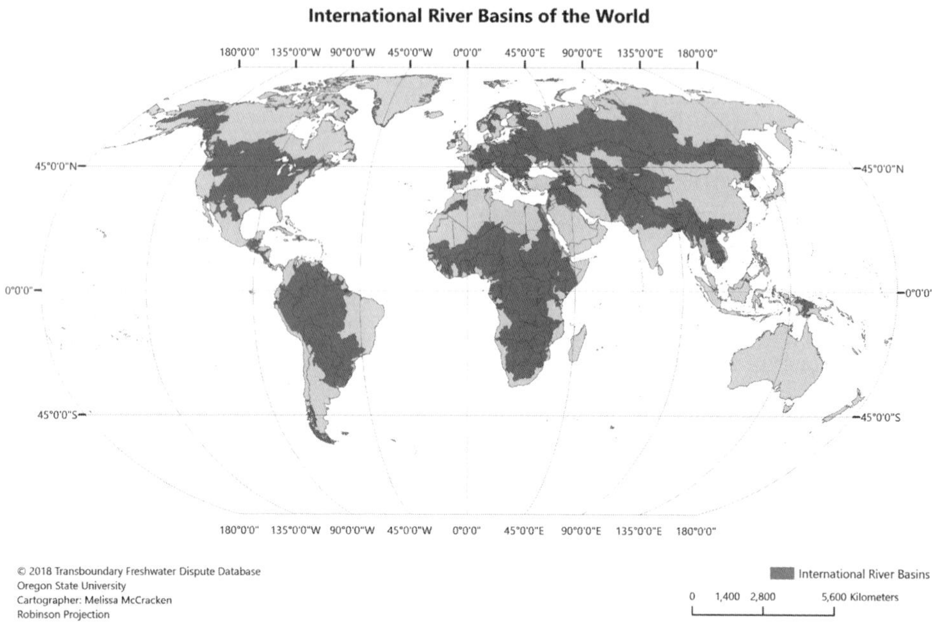

Figure I.1 The world's surface water basins, with over 300 shared across international borders. Source: Program in Water Conflict Management and Transformation, Oregon State University, International River Basins of the World—2018. https://transboundarywaters.science.oregonstate.edu/content/international-river-basins-world-2018.

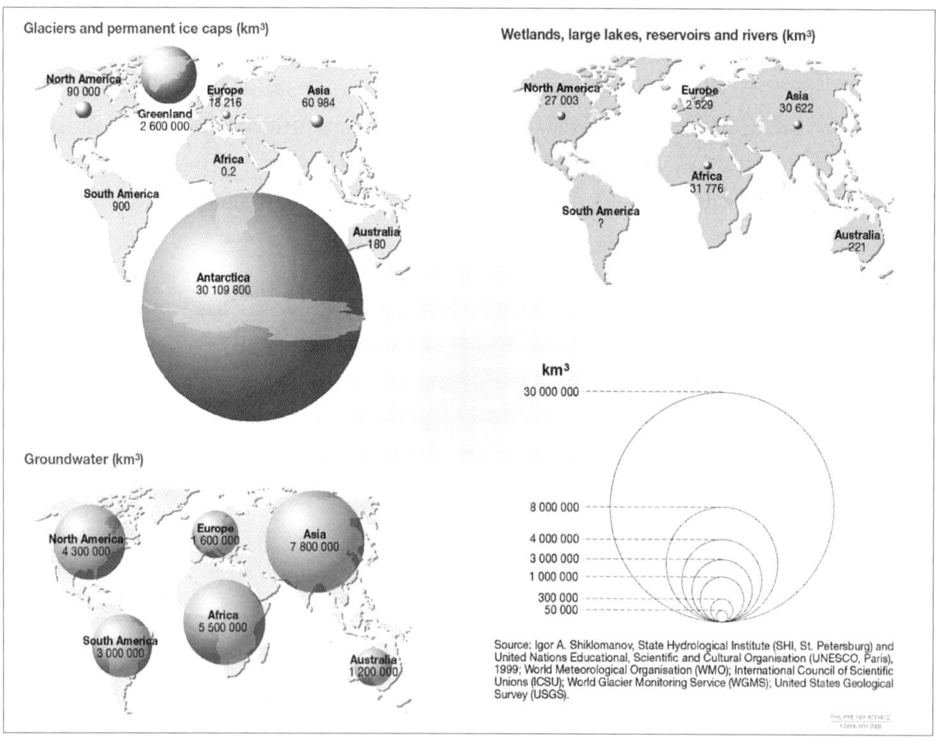

Figure I.2 Circles show relative volume of freshwater stored in ice, groundwater, and surface water sources. Source: Image includes source of data. Source of graphic: UNEP, *Vital Water Graphics: An Overview of the State of the World's Fresh and Marine Waters* (2d ed. 2008), graphic by Philippe Rekacewicz (2006), https://www.grida.no/resources/5608.

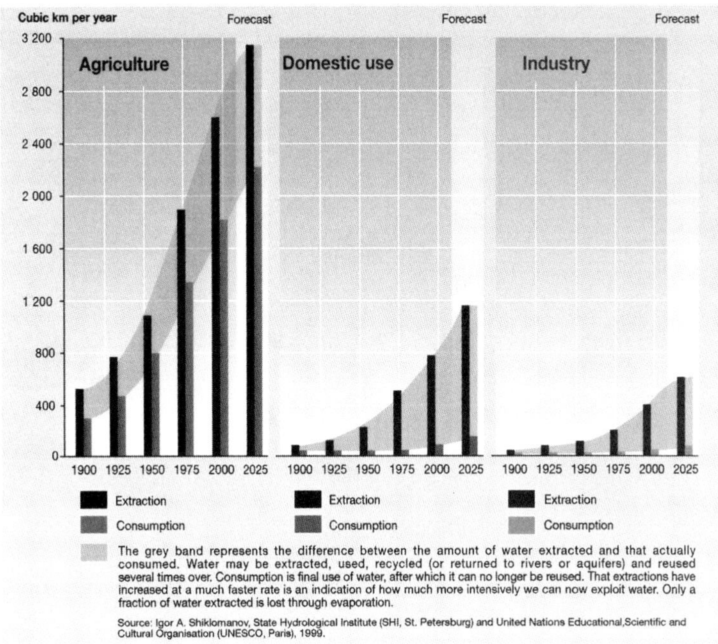

Figure I.3 Global water use by sector: Source: Image includes source of data. Source of graphic: UNEP, *Vital Water Graphics: An Overview of the State of the World's Fresh and Marine Waters* (2d ed. 2008), graphic by Philippe Rekacewicz (2006), https://www.grida.no/resources/5626.

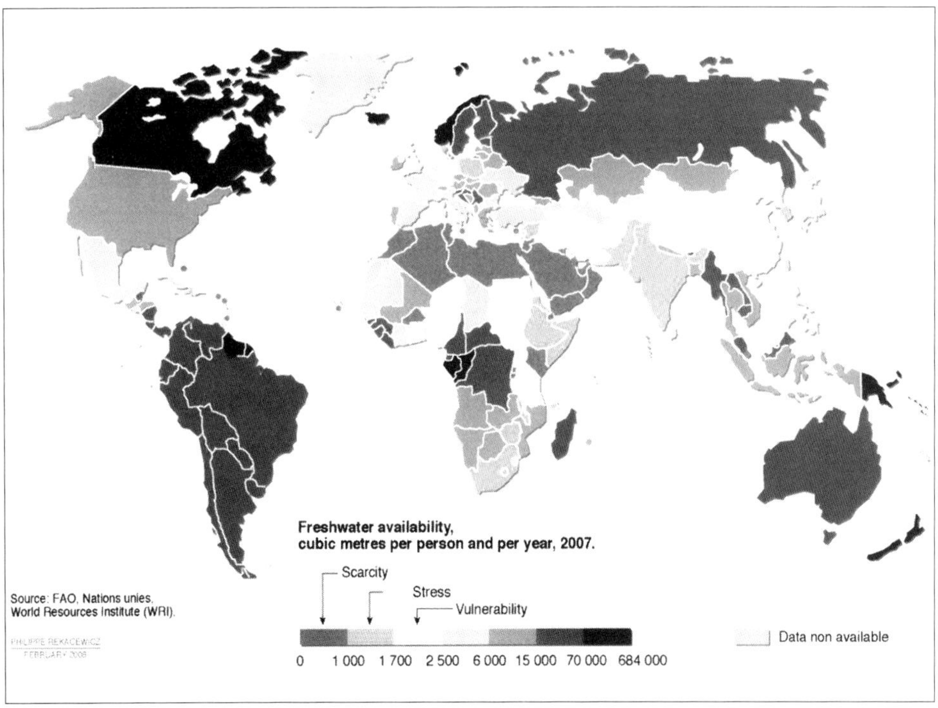

Figure I.4 Access to improved water source, cubic metres/person/year in 2004. Source: Image includes source of data. Source of graphic: UNEP, *Vital Water Graphics: An Overview of the State of the World's Fresh and Marine Waters* (2d ed. 2008), graphic by Philippe Rekacewicz (2006), https://www.grida.no/resources/5596.

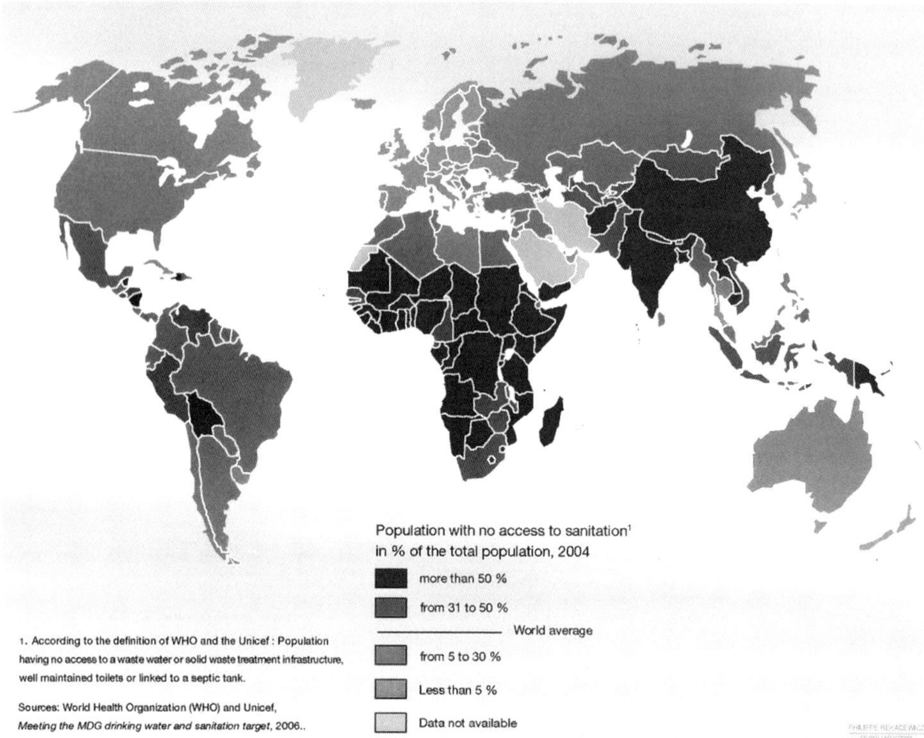

Figure I.5 Population with no access to sanitation by % of total population in 2004. Source: Image includes source of data. UNEP, *Vital Water Graphics: An Overview of the State of the World's Fresh and Marine Waters* (2d ed. 2008), graphic by Philippe Rekacewicz (2006), https://www.grida.no/resources/5591.

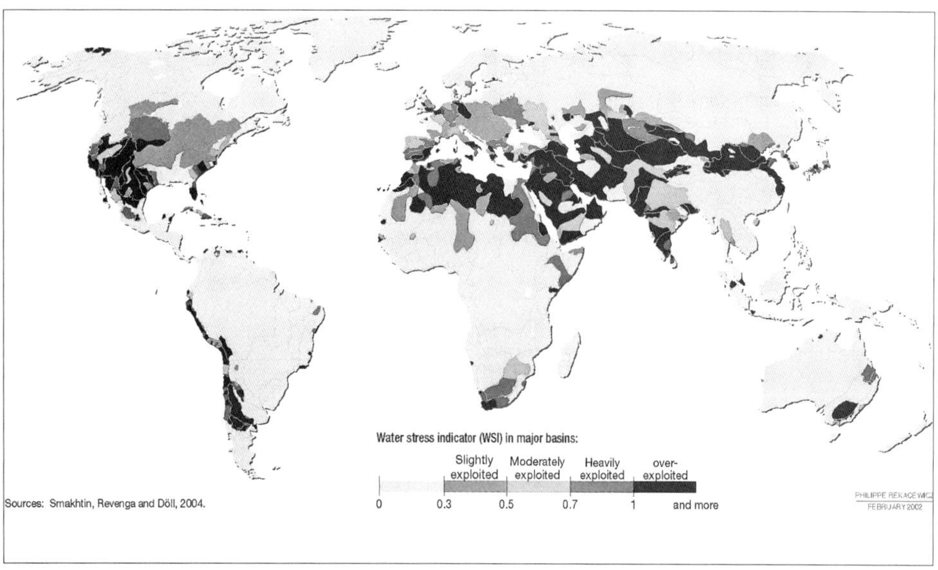

Figure I.6 Projection of water scarcity by 2050. Source: Image includes source of data. Source of graphic: UNEP, *Vital Water Graphics: An Overview of the State of the World's Fresh and Marine Waters* (2d ed. 2008), graphic by Philippe Rekacewicz (2006), https://www.grida.no/resources/5586.

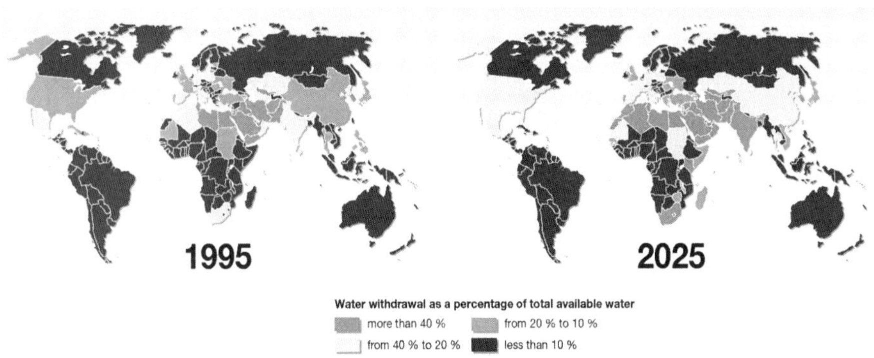

Figure I.7 Projection of water stress in 2025. With water demand defined as less than 1700 m3 per year per capita, the maps show relative water stress by calculating water withdrawal as a percentage of total available water. Source: UNEP, *Vital Water Graphics: An Overview of the State of the World's Fresh and Marine Waters* (2d ed. 2008), graphic by Philippe Rekacewicz (2006), https://www.grida.no/resources/5625.

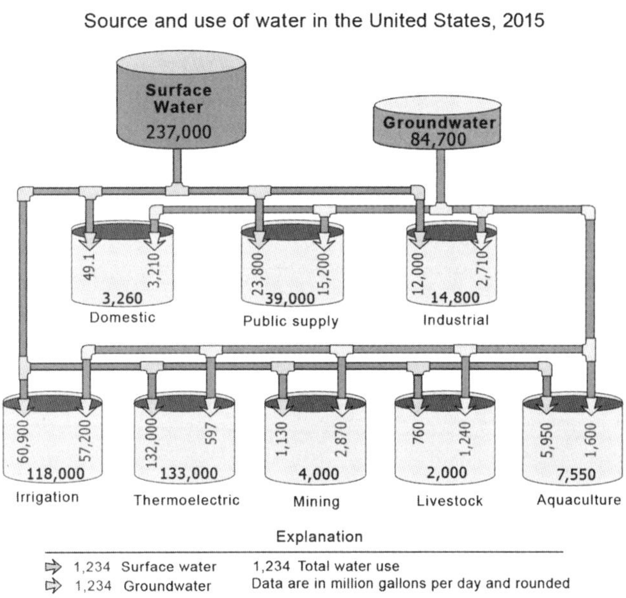

Figure I.8 Water withdrawals in the United States in 2015 by sector showing whether the source is ground or surface water. Withdrawals include both freshwater (87% of withdrawals, and saline water (13% of withdrawals). "The top row of cylinders represents where America's freshwater came from (source) in 2015, either from surface water, or from groundwater. Most of the water came from surface-water sources, such as rivers and lakes. About 26 percent of water used came from groundwater. The pipes leading out of the surface-water and groundwater cylinders on the top row and flowing into the bottom rows of cylinders show the categories of water use where the water was sent after being withdrawn from a river, lake, reservoir, or well. For example, the pipe coming out of the surface-water cylinder and entering the public supply cylinder shows that 23,800 Mgal/d of water was withdrawn from surface-water sources for public-supply uses (you probably get your water this way). Likewise, the pipe shows that public-suppliers withdrew another 15,200 Mgal/d of water from groundwater sources. Each cylinder below the sources represents a category of water use. The industrial cylinder, for instance, shows how much groundwater, surface water, and total water was used in the United States, each day, by industries." Source: USGS, *Total Water Use in the United States*, Water Science School (June 8, 2015), https://www.usgs.gov/media/images/source-and-use-water-us-2015.

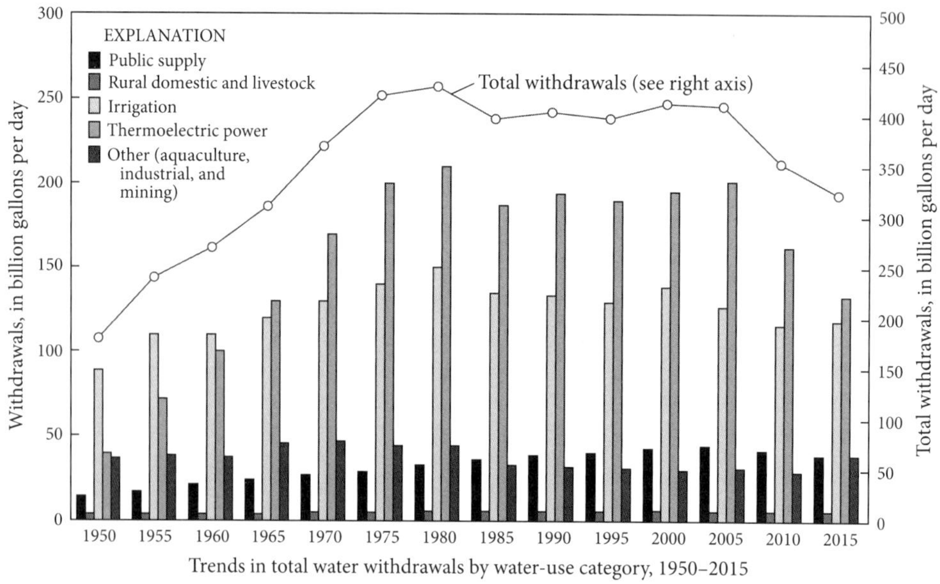

Figure I.9 Water withdrawals in the United States increased until the 1980s, leveled off between 1980 and 2005, and have declined in recent years. Source: USGS, *Total Water Use in the United States*, Water Science School (June 8, 2015), https://www.usgs.gov/media/images/trends-total-water-withdrawals-water-use-category-1950-2015-0.

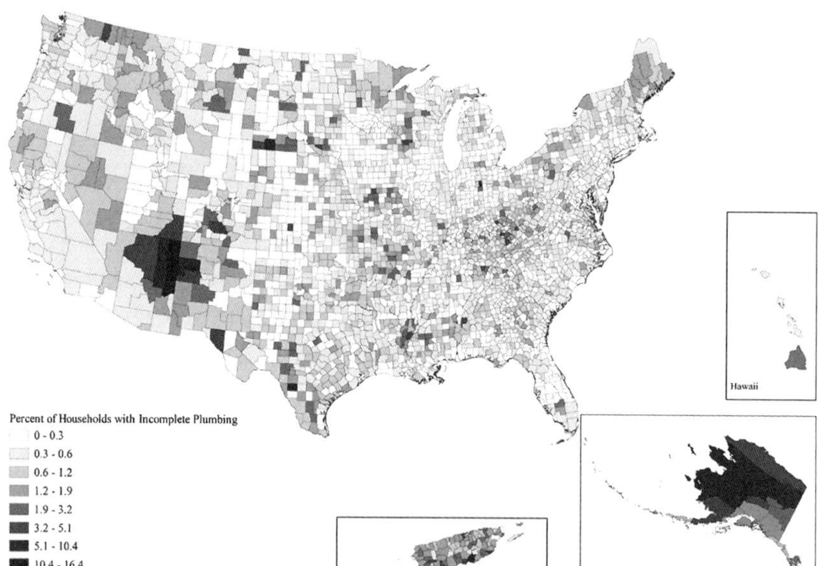

Figure I.10 Map of the percent of county households without full indoor plumbing as reported by the 2014–2018 American Community Survey. "Households are determined to have incomplete plumbing if they do not have access to hot and cold water, a sink with a faucet, a bath or shower, and—up until 2016—a flush toilet." Source: J.T. Mueller & S. Gasteyer, *The Widespread and Unjust Drinking Water and Clean Water Crisis in the United States*, 12 Nat. Commun. 3544 (2021), https://www.nature.com/articles/s41467-021-23898-z.

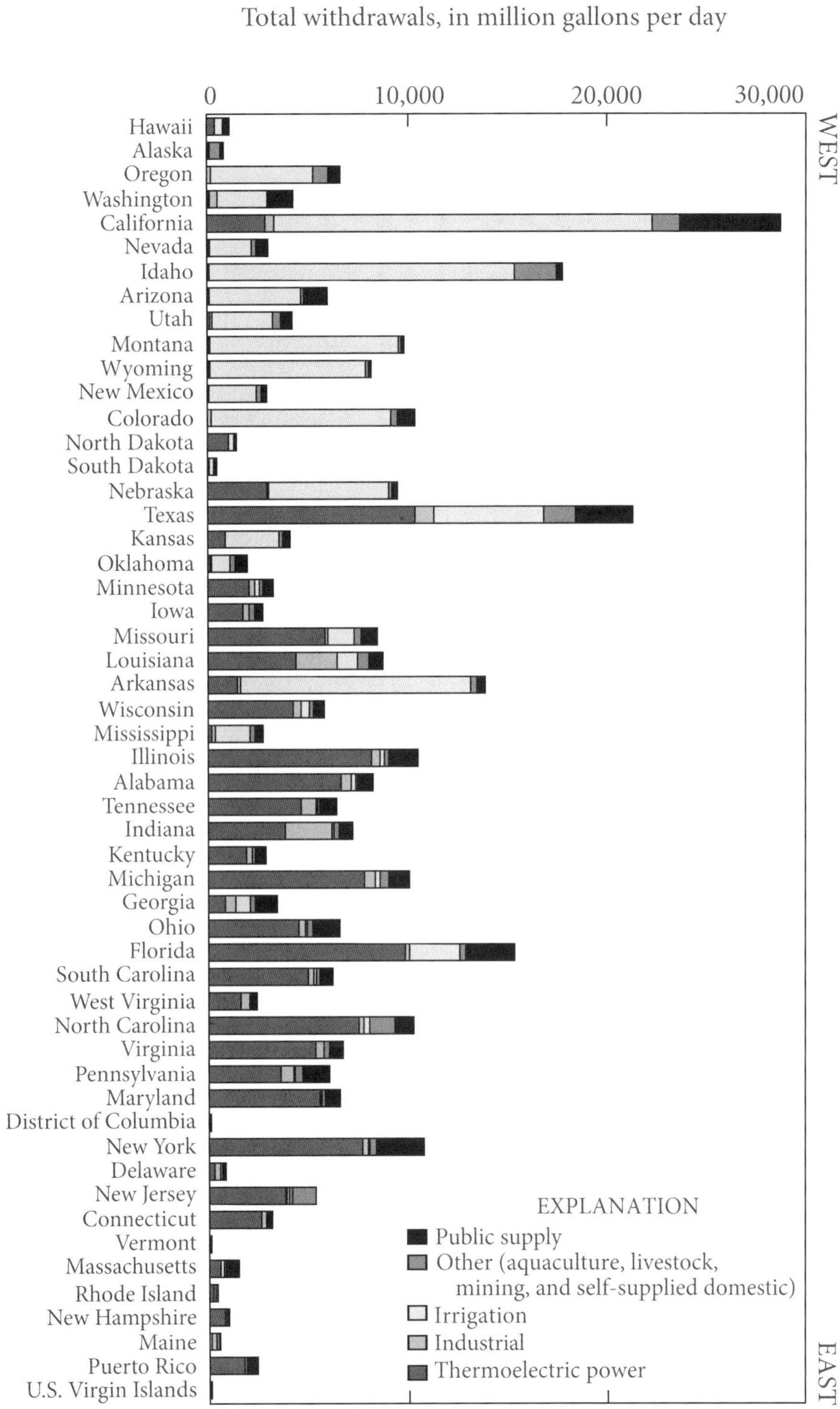

Figure I.11 Total water withdrawals in the United States by state and sector. Source: USGS, *Total Water Use in the United States*, Water Science School (June 8, 2015), https://www.usgs.gov/media/images/bar-chart-showing-use-water-2015-state-and-category-use.

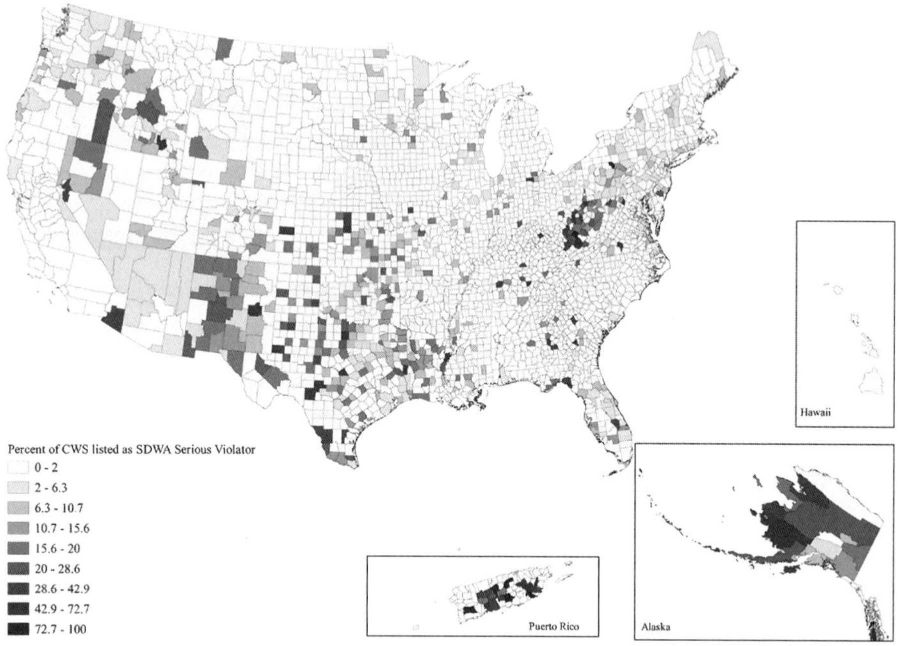

Figure I.12 Map of the percent of active county community water systems listed as "Safe Drinking Water Act (SDWA) Serious Violators." "Safe Drinking Water Act Serious Violators are those community water systems regarded by the Environmental Protection Agency as the most problematic due to violation and compliance history." Source: J.T. Mueller & S. Gasteyer, *The Widespread and Unjust Drinking Water and Clean Water Crisis in the United States*, 12 NAT. COMMUN. 3544 (2021), https://www.nature.com/articles/s41467-021-23898-z.

Chapter 1

An Introduction to Hydrology and Western Water Use Systems

Introduction

The modern practice of water law requires an understanding of the interrelationship between law, science, and society. This Chapter focuses on the science of water resources and their development. Concepts from the scientific field of hydrology and climatology take center stage in most water law and management problems. To a lesser degree, understanding the basics of geomorphology, geographic information systems, biology, soil science, and agricultural engineering can be important in particular situations. To the extent that a case requires scientific or engineering analysis, that work is done by technical experts. However, the lawyer remains the lead on the case. This role requires a working knowledge of the technical facets that underpin the legal issues at play. That understanding will help you use your experts more efficiently and may also allow you to develop innovative solutions that provide a better outcome for your client.

Historically, lawyers would learn these technical issues on the job as they arose in a particular case. The opportunity to constantly learn new concepts and ideas throughout their career is one of the more remarkable parts of the practice of water lawyers. Nonetheless, a basic understanding of some of these important scientific concepts will be helpful as you study and begin the practice of water law. Do not be intimidated if you have little background in science. Few lawyers do. The approach of this casebook is to help you begin the process of understanding how science affects the law and to formulate the types of questions at that interface that will optimize the use of your experts.

Terminology is important when working at the law/science interface. Under the USGS protocol (i.e., the protocol followed by scientists), "surface water" is two words, "groundwater" is one word, unless using the phrase "surface and ground water." Nevertheless, some state statutory schemes use "groundwater" and some use "ground water." To navigate these inconsistencies, when referring to the resource itself this book will use the USGS protocols; when referring to the law this book will use the form relied on in the statute or case in question. Also note that the term "data" is plural. By getting in the habit of saying "these data are" rather than "that data is" you will earn considerable credibility with the scientists you work with.

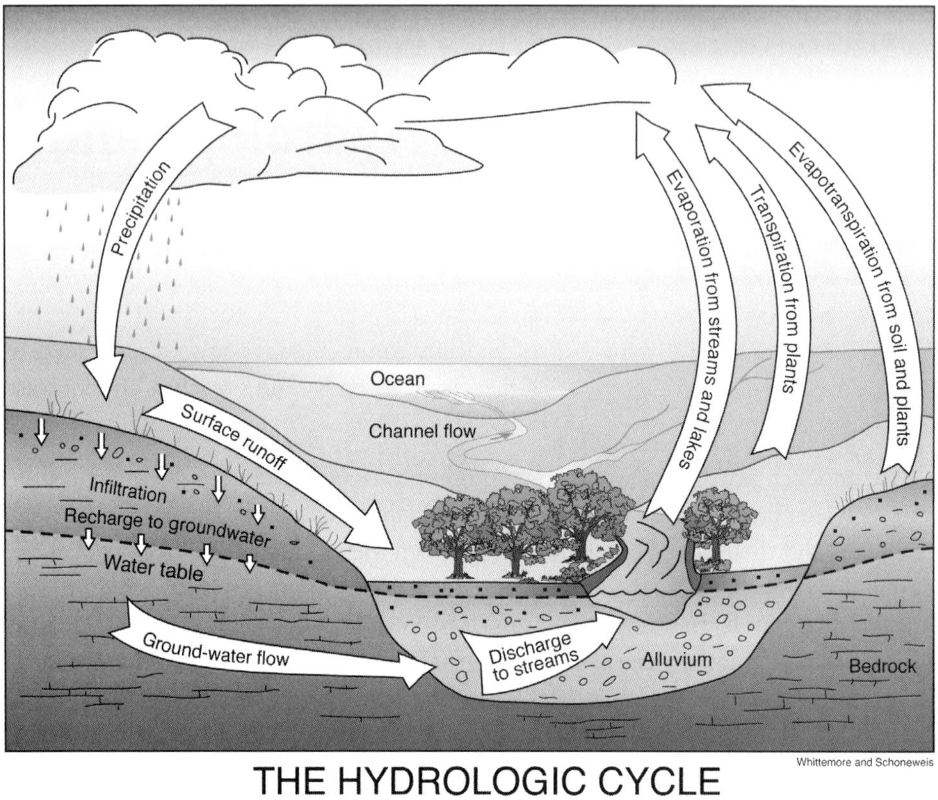

Figure 1.1 Graphic design by Melissa Svancara

This Chapter begins with a description of basic surface water hydrology followed by groundwater hydrology before finishing with a description of the water management system in Idaho's Eastern Snake Plain. This example exhibits many characteristics found in other regions of the irrigated West.

Surface Water Hydrology

Figure 1.1 illustrates that water moves over and through the earth in many ways. Initially, water falls to the earth in the form of precipitation—either rain or snow. Some of that precipitation is intercepted by plants and trees and is either consumed by plants or evaporated back into the atmosphere. The precipitation that reaches the earth can either infiltrate the ground or run over the surface. The portion that runs over the surface will eventually form into channels, find its way into a stream, and eventually flow into progressively larger rivers. Along the way, some portion may be taken up by plants, infiltrate into the ground, or evaporate back into the atmosphere. Several things may happen to the precipitation and/or surface water that infiltrates the ground. First, some of it may be taken up and consumed by plants through their root system.

Another portion, referred to as throughflow, may flow laterally near the surface and eventually spring back to the surface or into an adjacent stream. The final portion flows in a generally downward direction and recharges the underlying groundwater held in a permeable rock formation known as an aquifer.

Making matters more complex, ground and surface water are often interconnected. As mentioned above, surface water can often infiltrate the ground before reaching a perennial stream. Likewise, shallow groundwater often rises back to the surface at seeps and springs and then flows along the surface into adjacent streams. Even deep groundwater aquifers can be connected to surface water. Sometimes certain portions of a stream will gain water from hydrologically connected groundwater. Not surprisingly, these portions of the stream are referred to as "gaining reaches." In contrast, certain portions of a stream, referred to as "losing reaches" can also contribute water to a hydrologically connected aquifer. It is this complex movement of water that makes hydrology essential to the practice of water law.

The movement of surface water may be conceptualized as a series of stocks and flows. Stocks are hydrologic features that store water, such as ponds, reservoirs, lakes, and aquifers where water is accumulating and not readily moving at any given instant. In contrast, flows, as it sounds, are features such as streams, rivers, and manmade canals where water is flowing at a particular interval of time. For example, Figure 1.2 depicts a map of the Snake River as it flows into and out of Jackson Lake in Wyoming. That system can be simplified into a series of two flows—the Snake River as it flows into and out of Jackson Lake—and one stock, which is Jackson Lake reservoir.

Understanding the difference between these two types of hydrological features is important because they are measured differently. Water that is sitting in a stock such as a pond or lake is measured as a volume, which is defined as the product of the stock's length, width, and depth. Although we usually think of water volume in terms of liters or gallons, those units are not preferred when referring to large quantities of water. For example, when full, Jackson Lake contains approximately 276 *billion* gallons of water. Instead, water managers in the United States prefer to use the acre-foot as the unit for measuring volume; defined as the volume of water necessary to cover one acre of land with one foot of water. To visualize this, think of a football field, which is only slightly larger than an acre in size (Figure 1.3). Jackson Lake contains approximately 85,000 acre-feet of water.

Matters are somewhat more complex when water is flowing. Greek philosopher Heraclitus noted the complexity of flow, stating: "you cannot step in the same river twice." Flow requires that we measure a volume moving past a point over a unit of time. The most common unit of measurement in the United States for flowing water is the cubic foot per second. That unit is defined as one cubic foot of water moving past a point in one second. To visualize this, understand that a basketball has a volume of approximately one cubic foot. Thus, one cubic foot per second can be conceptualized as one basketball rolling past a point with a velocity of one foot per second. As shown

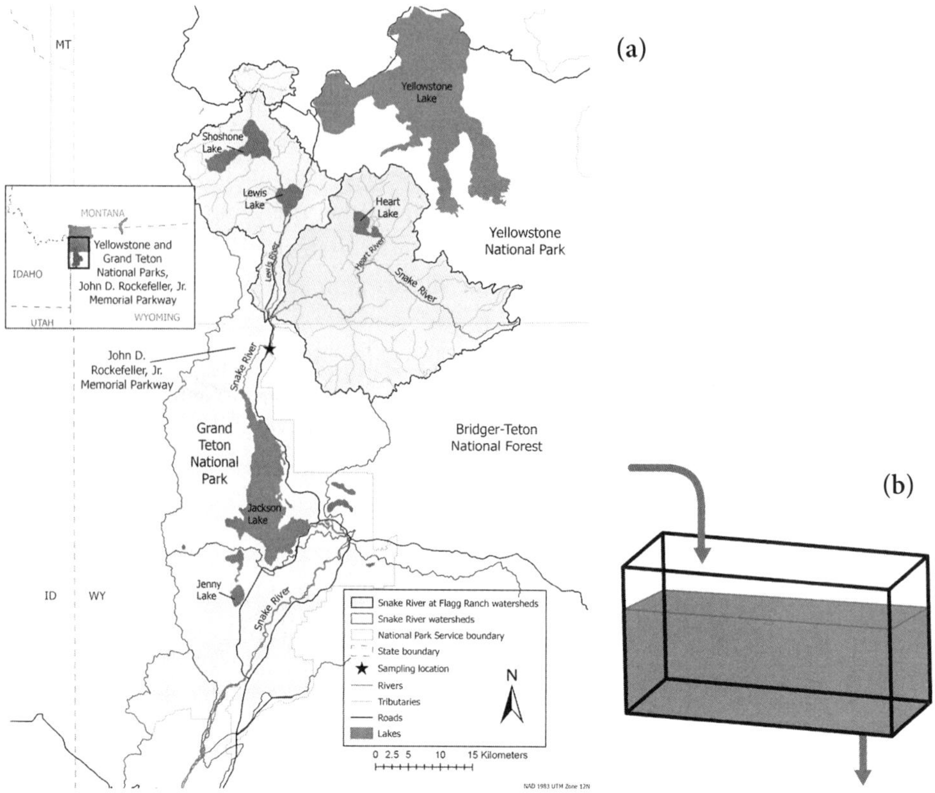

Figure 1.2 Illustration of movement of water through streams (flow) and lakes (storage): (a) Jackson Lake in the headwaters of the Snake River in Wyoming shows a real example of water storage with inflow and outflow. (b) The conceptual diagrams can be used to depict this type of water storage, or storage in an aquifer, a wetland, or the atmosphere. It resembles a bathtub with the arrows showing water in and water out, and the box showing storage. Source: (a) National Park Service, The Snake River at Flagg Rancy, Wyoming (Updated April 4, 2022), https://www.nps.gov/articles/000/snake-river-flagg-ranch.htm. Source (b) Graphic design by Leilanee Taylor.

in Figure 1.4, if the channel or conduit gets larger, the potential number of basketballs that may flow past that point likewise increases. In the case depicted in the second panel of Figure 1.4, the volume of water increases due to channel widening so that six basketballs pass a point each second. If the velocity remains at one foot per second, then the flow rate would increase to six cubic feet per second. Finally, the flow rate can also increase if the same volume of water is flowing at a higher velocity. For example, the slope of the third plate in Figure 1.4 is increased, causing the single basketball (i.e., one cubic foot) to now roll with a velocity of three feet per second. As a result, three basketballs flow past our hypothetical end point each second rather than one, resulting in an overall flow rate of three cubic feet per second.

As you read some of the older cases in Part II on state common law concerning water, you will see the term "miner's inches" used for the measurement of water flow. Unfor-

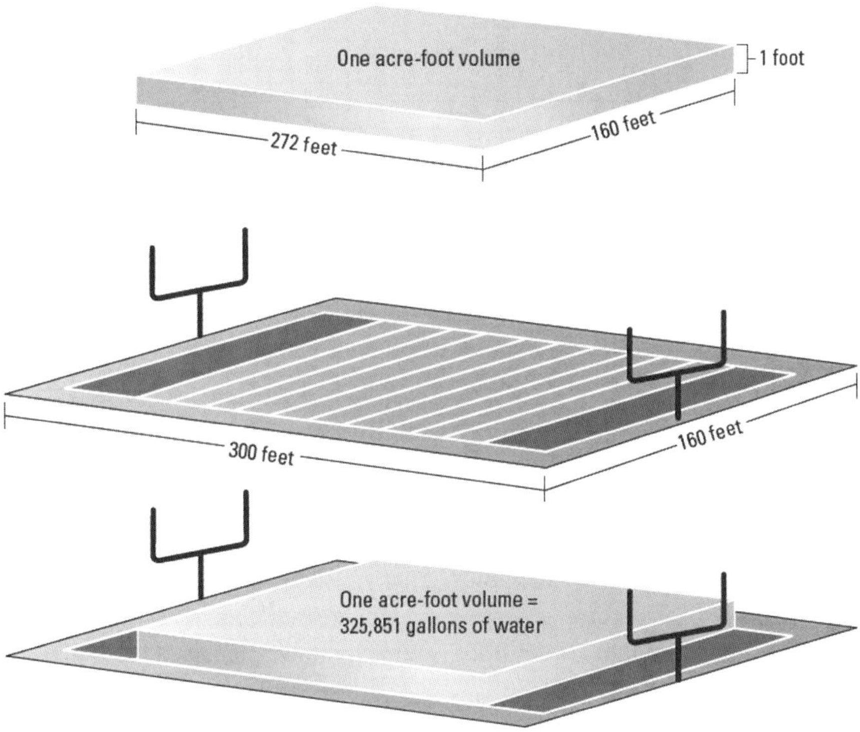

Figure 1.3 Illustrating the concept of the acre-foot as one foot of water over one acre of land. Source: Modified from Colorado State University, http//waterknowledge.colostate.edu/water-management-administration/water-uses/.

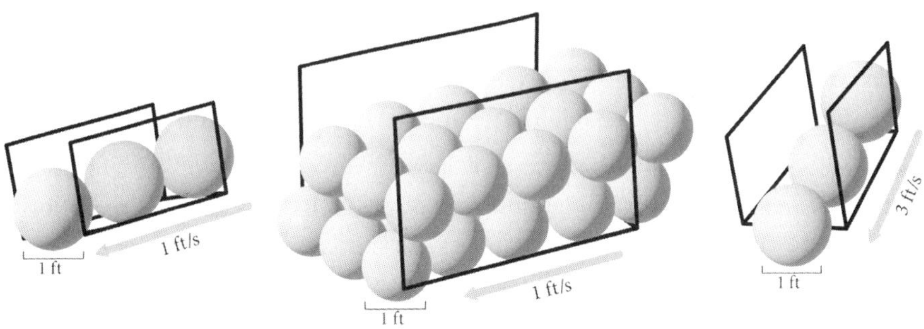

Figure 1.4 Cubic foot per second, or cfs, is a standard measure of the velocity of a fluid. It is the measure of cubic feet of water (illustrated by the basketballs) that move past a single point in one second. The water supply (basketballs), stream size, and stream gradient determine the velocity.

tunately, the measure of a miner's inch varied from state to state. Table 1.1 shows the conversion from miner's inches to cubic feet per second in the Columbia Basin states.

Streamflow data, as well as lake and reservoir storage data, are collected and inventoried by multiple federal, state, and private entities. Overwhelmingly, however,

Table 1.1

State	CFS Equivalent to 1 Miner's Inch	Miner's Inch Equivalent to 1 CFS
Idaho, Utah, Washington, Wyoming	0.020 cfs	50 Miner's Inches
Montana, Nevada, Oregon	0.025 cfs	40 Miner's Inches

the largest database of this information is with the United States Geological Survey (USGS), which collects these data at thousands of stream gage[1] sites throughout the United States.

Although each site collects different types of data, stream gages invariably include the collection of data related to water quantity. Stream gages will usually collect streamflow data (in cubic feet per second) every 15 minutes, while lake and reservoir gages are reported water volume data, while the data collected is usually the height of the water level above some datum (i.e., a fixed point of known elevation, usually taken to be sea level). If the shape of the lake or reservoir is adequately understood, then this height can readily be converted into an acre-foot volume by water managers.

Data reporting on hydrographs (a graph that shows change in flow over time) operate on a "water year" rather than a calendar year. The water year begins on October 1 and ends on September 30 of each year (when water law students should celebrate the Water New Year's Eve). Hydrologists use the water year for two reasons. First, most naturally flowing western streams reach their lowest point sometime around October 1 before rebounding as fall precipitation increases. Second, because much of the precipitation at higher elevations and latitudes in the West in late fall will be snow, the resulting water will not flow out until spring. If hydrographs were to operate on a calendar year, then precipitation that fell in the late fall of one year as rain would enter the river in one year, whereas that falling as snow is likely to melt and run off in the next year, making management and forecasting of water supply more confusing.

Using Figure 1.2 as an example, flow will also differ between the streamflow upstream and downstream of a storage (stock) such as Jackson Lake. Flow upstream of any dam is generally natural flow. The natural flow in the river increases as snow melts in the spring and then falls during the summer before rebounding again in the late fall. Streams in snowmelt-dominated watersheds throughout the West have similar behavior. A hydrograph of stream flow will have a peak during maximum spring runoff. In contrast, because outflow from Jackson Lake is controlled by a dam, the downstream flow is controlled and often reflects human demand for the water. Streamflow out of Jackson Lake is managed by the U.S. Bureau of Reclamation for flood control and irrigation purposes. With streamflow largely controlled by humans, the hydrograph will

1. Note that the use of the colloquial "gage" rather than the standard "gauge" is an artifact of USGS history.

have a random stepwise pattern that reflects sudden releases or water holdbacks conducted by the dam operators. Dam-controlled streams throughout the western United States that are operated for irrigation have similar hydrographs.

There is a strong interrelationship between the stocks and flows that make up our surface water hydrologic system. The change in volume for a stock such as a reservoir, lake, or pond during a particular period is equal to the amount of water flowing in (from upstream, or precipitation, or groundwater), minus the amount of water flowing out (in the outlet stream, by evaporation, or into groundwater). This simple "water balance" is shown in the conceptual bathtub-type drawing in Figure 1.2. You will be amazed at how often this simple concept of a water balance comes up in water management.

Once again using Jackson Lake from Figure 1.2 as our example, the change in the volume in that reservoir on June 1 is equal to the amount of water that flows into the reservoir over that 24-hour period minus the amount of water that flows out over the same period. Starting in the late winter and spring, snowmelt and precipitation generally cause inflow to exceed outflow, which in turn causes Jackson Lake Reservoir to increase in volume. Later in the summer, as the snowpack dwindles and precipitation generally decreases, inflow to Jackson Lake likewise decreases. At the same time air temperature increases, which increases evaporation as well as downstream anthropogenic consumptive uses of water for things such as irrigation, commercial, and industrial needs. As a result, outflow often outstrips inflow during this season, which in turn causes the volume of water in Jackson Lake to decline. This continues until autumn when temperatures fall, and precipitation returns to the region. This cycle repeats itself throughout the western United States and forms the foundation of western water management.

Groundwater Hydrology

Refer to Figure 1.1 to see that in addition to the surface, the second primary conduit for water movement is through the ground. Figure 1.5 shows a simplified but typical groundwater system, along with several terms that require definition. Water moves through aquifers, which are bodies of permeable rock or sediment that can hold and transmit water. On the other end of the spectrum are confining layers (or confining units), which are layers of rock or sediment with low permeability such that they either actively slow or prevent water movement and are largely unable to hold or transmit water. Aquifers that are sandwiched between two confining layers are referred to as "confined aquifers." Because they are confined, water pressure builds in these aquifers as water infiltrates into them. If tapped by a well, water will rise to the "potentiometric surface" of the confined aquifer, which is equal to the "water table" if the aquifer was unconfined. If the potentiometric surface is higher than the elevation of the ground, water will actively flow out of the well (called an "artesian" well). In other cases where the potentiometric surface is below the ground, water will rise to that level in the well, thereby reducing the amount of pumping necessary to retrieve the water.

Not surprisingly, aquifers that are not confined are referred to as "unconfined aquifers" (Figure 1.5). Water moves freely in an unconfined aquifer, which prevents the buildup of pressure. As a result, although unconfined aquifers serve as reservoirs of available water supply, the water must be actively pumped.

The final type of aquifer for our purposes are "perched" aquifers, which are accumulations of water that collect on top of relatively smaller impermeable layers of rock or sediment (Figure 1.5). Perched aquifers can be highly variable in size, sometimes supporting large uses of water while other times small enough to be insufficient for anything other than single-home domestic use.

The movement of water in an aquifer is a function of the hydraulic conductivity of the aquifer rock type ("lithology"), as well as the hydraulic gradient that is present within the aquifer. Hydraulic conductivity describes the ease with which a fluid (in our case, water) can flow through a porous medium. The hydraulic conductivity of many different types of rock and sediment have been determined through experiments. For example, gravel typically has a conductivity of between 85 feet per day and 8,500 feet per day, while clay aquifers can have a hydraulic conductivity as low as 0.000003 feet per day (Figure 1.6). Thus, clay is a common composition for a confining unit (Figure 1.5).

Although the hydraulic conductivity of an aquifer defines how easily a fluid can move through an aquifer, water does not move on its own. Instead, just as on the surface, groundwater must have some force acting upon it to move. The primary force causing surface water to move is gravity. Water moves from higher to lower elevations. Gravitational forces also operate underground, but pressure is an additional factor. The combination of these factors is referred to as the hydraulic head in the aquifer, and water moves from areas of higher hydraulic head to areas of lower hydraulic head. The difference in hydraulic head between two points within the aquifer forms the hydraulic gradient between those points. The higher that gradient, the more force is acting on the water within the aquifer to move from the point of high to low head.

In the confined layer in Figure 1.5, the hydraulic head will be higher on the left side of the aquifer relative to the middle. As a result, water will flow from that high point toward the middle of the aquifer. Of course, the other factor that will affect the rate at which that movement occurs is the hydraulic conductivity. If our hypothetical aquifer were composed of gravel or coarse sand, the water would move much more readily. If the aquifer were composed of clay or silt, the water would move slowly, under the same hydraulic gradient. This illustrates the proportional relationship between hydraulic conductivity and gradient; if our conductivity is low, a relatively higher gradient is needed to force the water to move at the same rate. Conversely, water flowing through a medium with a high hydraulic conductivity requires a lower hydraulic gradient to begin to move.

Like surface water, groundwater aquifers can be understood as a series of stocks and flows. Like surface water, the storage in an aquifer can be conceptualized using a water balance wherein the change in storage in the aquifer is equal to the amount of

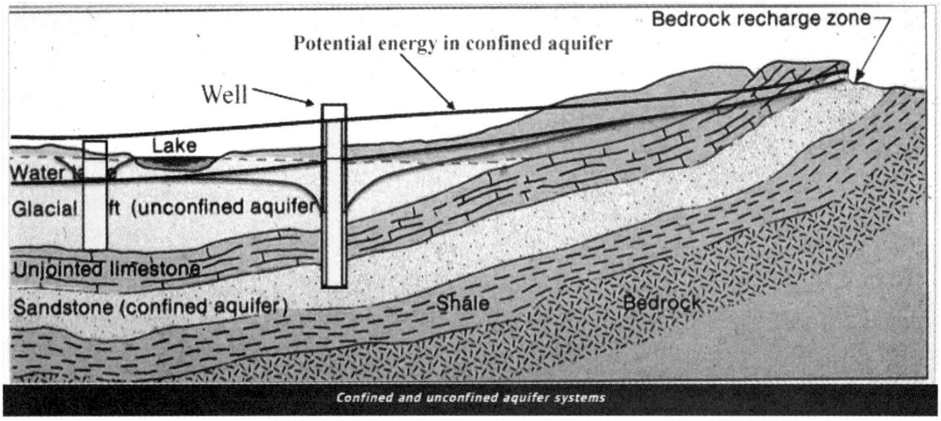

Figure 1.5 Hypothetical groundwater system showing both a confined and unconfined aquifer and two wells. The well on the right is called an "artesian well" because the water level is above the ground surface. Source: Maven's Notebook, California Water News Central, Groundwater Problems and Prospects, part 1: An overview of groundwater (March 12, 2015), https://mavensnotebook.com/2015/03/12/groundwater-problems-and-prospects-part-1-an-overview-of-groundwater/.

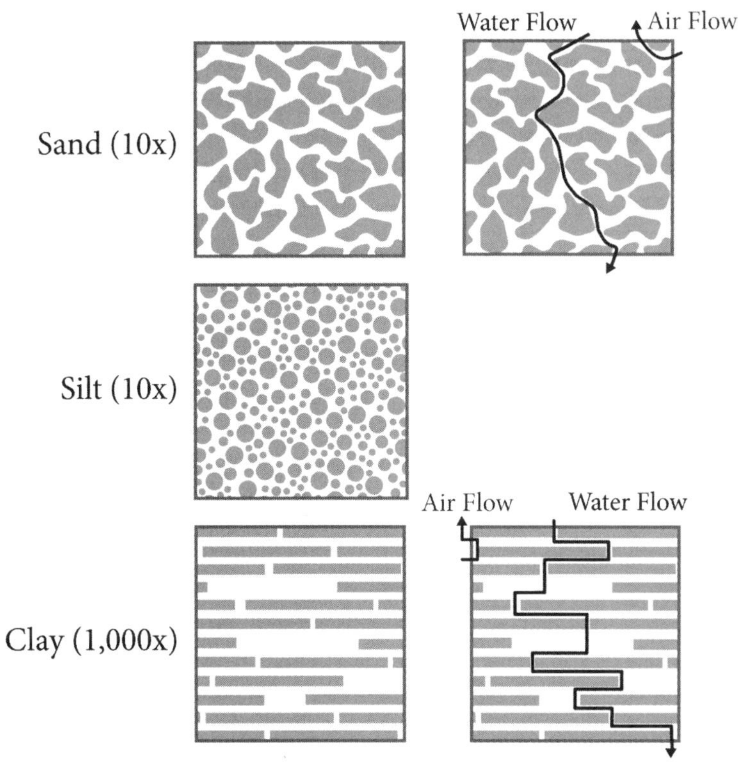

Figure 1.6 Differences in selected aquifer substrate (i.e., the rock or soil type water moves through) porosity (i.e., open space) and how those differences affect hydraulic conductivity (i.e., the ability of the water to move).

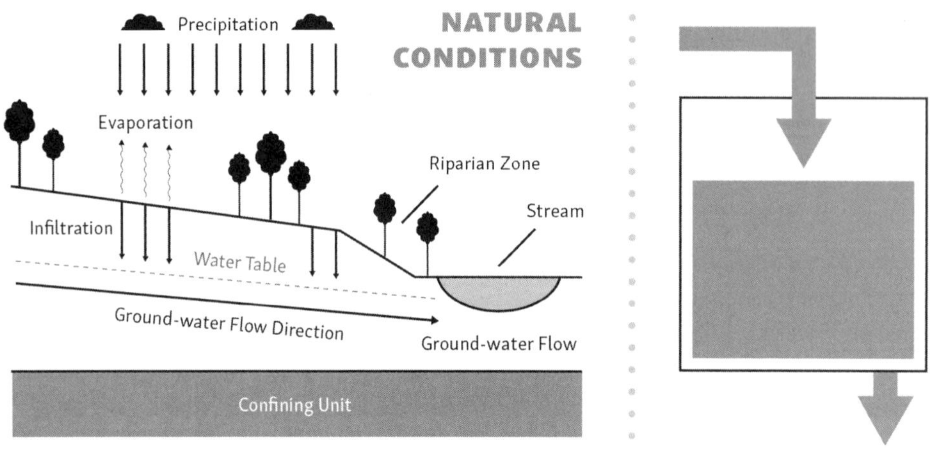

Figure 1.7 Conceptual model of water flow in an aquifer showing the contribution of water from groundwater to a surface water stream. The diagram shows the similarity between an aquifer and a surface water reservoir like Jackson Lake. Both store water and have inflow and outflow. Source: Michael Penzo, *The Principles of Groundwater Flow, Continuing Education for Professional Engineers*, https://pdh-pro.com/course/the-principles-of-groundwater-flow/.

water flowing into the aquifer minus the water flowing out. Referring to the conceptual model in Figure 1.7, water is flowing from the surface into the ground at the recharge area on the left of the image. In this area, water accumulates on the surface—either through precipitation or the melting of snow—and then some infiltrates the ground and seeps into the aquifer. Despite the fact that groundwater flows, it can be conceptualized as a stock like our lakes, ponds, and reservoirs, because it provides storage. In Figure 1.7, water flows out of the aquifer and into a surface water stream. Other sources of outflow may be springs, seeps, and wetlands. If the outflow is less than inflow, the aquifer will gain volume. Where the outflow exceeds inflow, aquifer volume will decrease. Under natural conditions, aquifers will reach a state of dynamic equilibrium in which, despite a mismatch in seasonal inflows versus outflows (i.e., inflow will be greater in the winter and spring but outflow will be greater in the summer and early fall in western states), annual outflow will generally match inflow. As we will explore in later chapters, that equilibrium is distorted when humans introduce a new outflow by extracting groundwater.

Recall that surface water is quantified in terms of volume (in acre-feet) and flowrate (in cubic feet per second). Because the geometry and physical characteristics of an aquifer are not perfectly known, volume quantification is only an approximation. Thus, it is impractical to quantify available groundwater in terms of volume. Groundwater is typically quantified in terms of the elevation of the water level in a well under static conditions (i.e., not being pumped) (Figure 1.8). Groundwater measurements are usually made in two ways.

First, as shown on the primary vertical axes (axes on the left of each graph) in Figure 1.8, groundwater is typically measured in terms of the depth from the surface to the point where water begins to fill the well. For example, in Figure 1.8(a), the top of the water in the aquifer at that location in March 2020 was approximately 43 feet below

(a)

(b)

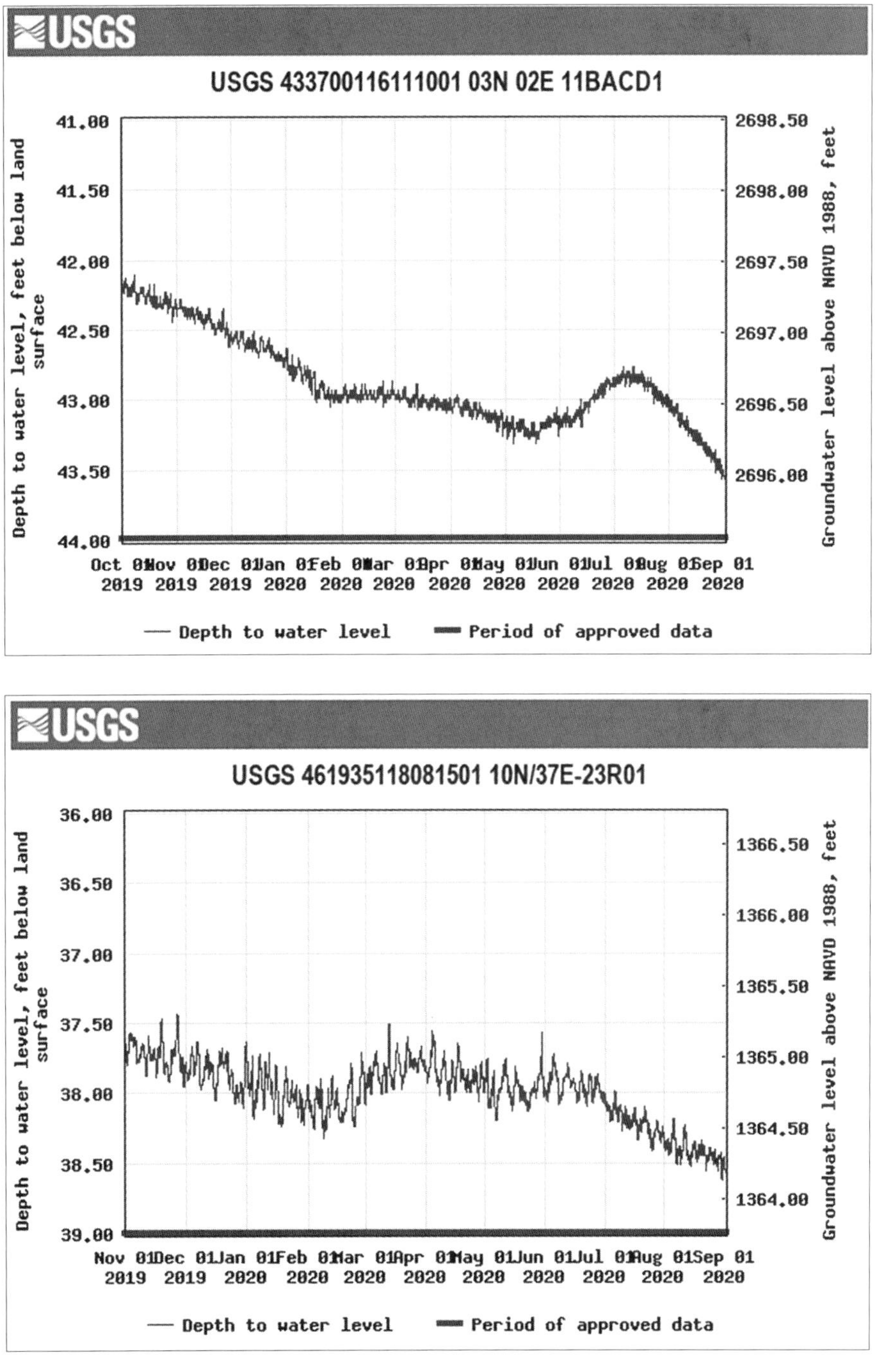

Figure 1.8 United States Geological Survey Measuring Station for Groundwater in (a) Ada County, Idaho; and (b) the Columbia River Basin in Washington State, showing seasonal variability in groundwater level from November 2019 to September 2020.

the surface. Although this measure is useful to understand how water availability is changing near a particular point, it does not allow for extrapolation to determine water availability throughout an aquifer because the surface elevation changes from location to location. As a result, measuring groundwater elevation relative to a fixed point is also necessary.

Thus, the second method relies on a fixed point against which water level is measured. The fixed point is generally mean sea level as shown on the secondary axis of the charts in Figure 1.8. Mean sea level, at least historically, remains relatively constant, which allows for water depths to be more readily compared in different locations throughout an aquifer. For example, looking to Figure 1.8(b), the water elevation at that site on March 1, 2020, was approximately 1367.75 feet above mean sea level. If you were to compare that to data from another wellsite within the same aquifer with an elevation of 1364 feet above mean sea level, you would know that the hydraulic gradient would cause water to generally move away from the first (higher elevation) site toward the second (lower elevation) site.

The assumption underlying the use of water level or elevation to understand volume is that dimensions of an aquifer are relatively fixed, which means that an increase in volume would lead to a proportional increase in the water level or elevation in the aquifer. Although imperfect, the technique allows water managers to spot trends in aquifer behavior. If, for example, managers see a steady decline in aquifer levels they can be confident that outflow is outpacing inflows (referred to as aquifer "mining") and can take corrective action by reducing anthropogenic withdrawals or begin managed aquifer recharge. Groundwater data is available from many private, state, tribal, and federal sources. The greatest single collector of groundwater data in the United States is likely the USGS, which collects data from nearly 17,000 wells scattered throughout the United States.

Groundwater pumps are typically sized in terms of their capacity in gallons per minute and this is generally the unit of measure for municipal and domestic wells. Once pumped out of the ground, the units of measure for irrigation wells remain the same for groundwater as for surface water. Thus, groundwater rights for irrigation are usually quantified in terms of the rate that water is pumped from the ground in cubic feet per second. Often groundwater rights are capped by a particular maximum rate of flow. For example, Idaho places a cap on the rate of flow for irrigation water at 1 cfs per 50 acres of land application.[2] Typically a water right will also have some annual volumetric cap, which is measured in acre-feet to reflect the fact that irrigation does not need to occur continuously. For example, irrigation water rights in southern Idaho are usually assumed to require a maximum of five acre-feet of water per acre cultivated each irrigation season.[3] As a result, if a farm in southern Idaho had 100 acres, their groundwater right would likely be for the flow necessary (capped at 2 cfs for 100 acres) to run their sprinklers over that 100 acres, up to a total volume of 500 acre-feet of water from the aquifer.

2. Idaho Code §§ 42-202(3), 42-220.

3. Idaho Code § 42-202(3).

Chapter 2

The Challenge of Climate Change

Introduction

Climate is both the primary driving factor in water supply and, to a lesser but significant degree, water demand. As a result, it also plays a major role in the choices societies have made in the development of doctrines to provide the legal framework for its allocation. Climate change throws a bit of a wrench in the system. This Chapter will cover the hydrologic system that western water users have come to rely on under historic climate conditions; the role those historic conditions have played in the development of water law; and the way in which climate change is upsetting that reliance.

The Hydrologic Cycle under Historic Climatic Conditions

Natural variability exists within the hydrologic cycle both from season-to-season and year-to-year. Nevertheless, the hydrologic cycle in the western United States has historically followed a consistent and predictable pattern for over a century. Although that predictability has been punctuated by intermittent periods of drought and abundance, it generally returns to its historic range. The seasonal variability is most easily explored through analysis of the hydrograph depicted in Figure 2.1.

Most western watersheds are said to be "snow dominated," which means that both the surface and ground water hydrology in these watersheds is primarily driven by the accumulation and melting of snow in a relatively consistent cycle each year. Starting on October 1, the beginning of the water year, Figure 2.1 shows that flows in the Salmon River are essentially at their lowest. The hydrograph variability during this time is the result of increased but random precipitation events that mostly run through the system. As a result of a random event, Figure 2.1 shows a small increasing trend in flows during the first month of the water year.

That trend reverses itself as fall turns to winter. During this time, much of the precipitation in the Salmon River Basin is falling as snow, which is stored throughout the landscape rather than finding its way to the river and flowing out of the system. The weather during this time is generally controlled by the position of the jet stream as it moves from west to east over North America. The jet stream is a narrow belt of high-altitude westerly winds that controls the general weather patterns in the western United States. In simplistic terms, it acts as a wall, blocking air and weather systems

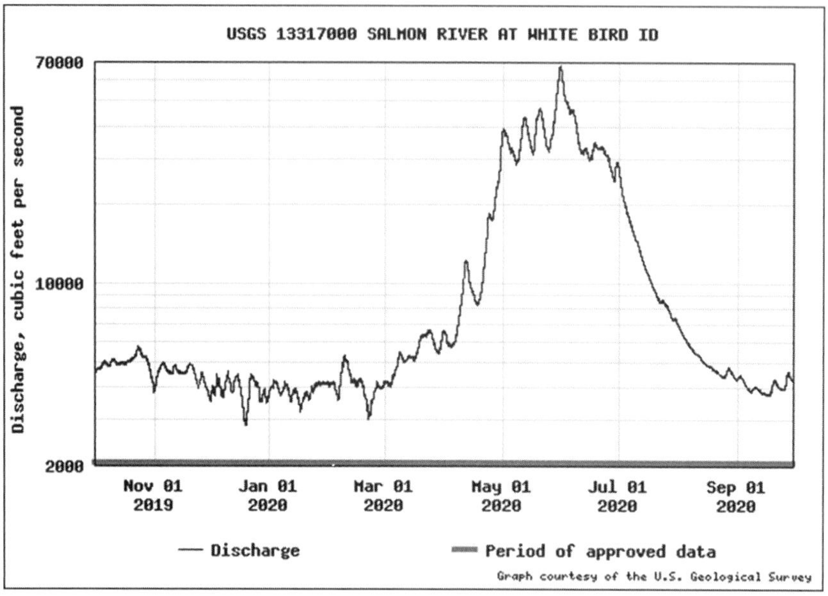

Figure 2.1 Hydrograph for the Salmon River at White Bird, Idaho, Water Year 2020. Source: USGS, Salmon River at White Bird ID—13317000; https://waterdata.usgs.gov/monitoring-location/13317000.

from moving past it. As a result, the air to the north of the jet stream is usually sourced from the Arctic, making it quite cold, while the air to the south usually comes off the Pacific Ocean, which is relatively warmer (Figure 2.2). Storms, which collide into but cannot readily move past the jet stream, tend to concentrate along the jet stream.

Not surprisingly, the position of the jet stream has a large influence on the amount of snowfall received in the West. Its position is influenced by ocean currents that are in turn influenced by the equatorial trade winds that drive warm water from South America toward Asia, allowing cold water to rise (upwell) along the west coast of the Americas in winter. Luckily, the wintertime position of the jet stream has historically followed a predictable pattern of variability. In many years, it exhibits a La Niña pattern (Figure 2.2(a) (top)), which is characterized by a jet stream that moves northward for the majority of the winter. Under those circumstances, the northwest and northern intermountain west exhibit a wetter but relatively warmer winter, while the southwest remains drier than normal. On the other hand, some years the jet stream exhibits an El Niño pattern (Figure 2.2(b) (bottom)) whereby it is primarily situated at relatively lower latitudes over North America. Contrary to the usual trend, this lower position allows for warm air from the Pacific Ocean to move north, and storms to concentrate farther south along the jet stream. This causes warm and dry winters for much of Canada and the northern United States. In contrast, the southwest and southern Rockies experience wetter winters during El Niño years.

Despite these general trends in climate, the day-to-day weather at any given point continues to fluctuate, providing a mixture of cold and warm days. That fluctuation in weather translates to the daily variability in the hydrograph. However, much of the

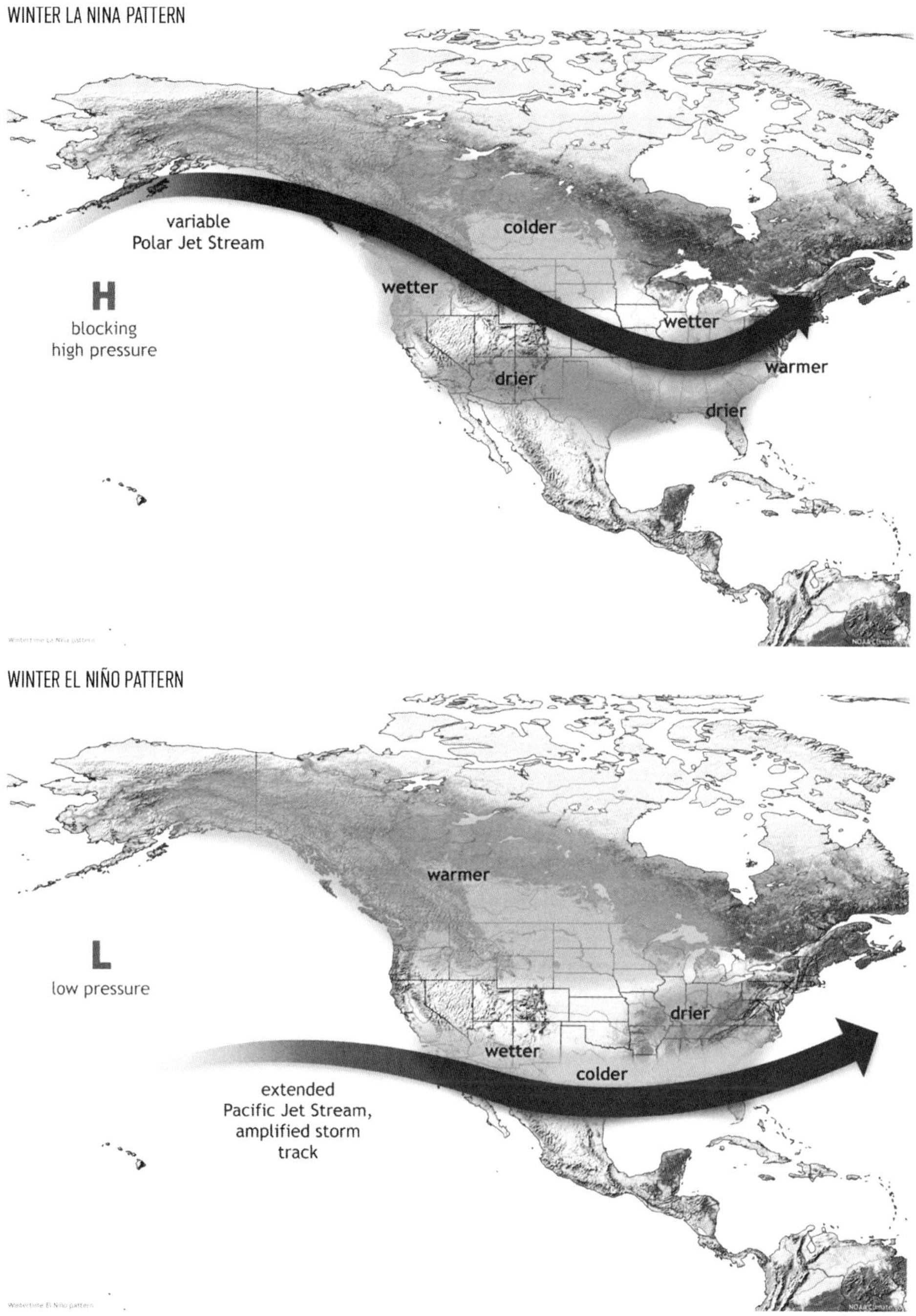

Figure 2.2 Typical jet stream position for La Niña (top) and El Niño (bottom) winters. Source: National Oceanic and Atmospheric Administration, *ENSO Winter Patterns* (2023), https://www.climate.gov/media/13112.

snow melted during these events infiltrates the ground rather than running off the landscape and into streams and rivers. As a result, winter also marks the time when groundwater in aquifers connected to surface water begins to be replenished.

Things change dramatically in the spring, as temperatures warm and precipitation begins to fall in the form of rain. Rain, and in particular rain-on-snow events, cause much of the water that was stored on the landscape in the form of snow to melt and begin to run through the system during this time. As you can see in Figure 2.1, runoff translates into significant increases in surface water discharge. This is also a time of groundwater recharge. The plants and animals that are native to the West have come to rely on this surface water discharge pattern each spring, with many fish species using the spring floods to migrate downstream. However, once it flows through the system it ceases to be available for local anthropogenic uses such as irrigation and domestic, commercial, municipal, and industrial uses. That becomes particularly problematic during the water short summer months (i.e., the primary growing season for crops).

Figure 2.1 depicts the typical summer-time hydrology for naturally occurring western streams. Once the snow has melted, streamflow decreases rapidly, eventually reducing to the stream's baseflow. Baseflow is defined as the portion of streamflow that does not result from precipitation (rain or snowmelt) but instead comes from delayed sources such as groundwater. Much of that drainage flows back out into streams, which allows them to flow much later in the year than would be possible if they relied solely on snowmelt. Nonetheless, baseflow is often not enough to satisfy the myriad consumptive uses of water by humans—storage is necessary to hold water for use later in the season. As a result, many streams throughout the West are dammed, allowing operators to store spring runoff for use in the summer.

Much of the West would be entirely undeveloped without this combination of natural storage as snowpack and artificial storage behind dams. Our water resources infrastructure depends on the relative stability of this hydrologic cycle. Climate change has and will continue to disrupt that stability.

The Relation between Historic Climate and Water Law

Before we introduce you to how climate is changing, it is important to understand the close relation between the development of water law and climate. Parts II, III, and IV will cover the historic development of state water law, federal law pertaining to Native American water rights, and federal law pertaining to federal water rights respectively. Your careers will be overshadowed by the effort to adapt that historic water law, management, and infrastructure to climate change, and you should always have the relation of this area of law to climate in the back of your mind as you learn today's system of water law.

Figure 2.3 illustrates the relation between water law and climate. Figure 2.3(a) illustrates the historic average annual precipitation in the United States in relation to the 100th Meridian. This demarcation is roughly the line that marks the part of the country to its west in which irrigation is necessary to grow crops. There are exceptions, such as the dryland wheat farming of the Palouse in northern Idaho and eastern Washington, and certain coastal valleys of the Pacific Northwest, but in general, throughout the

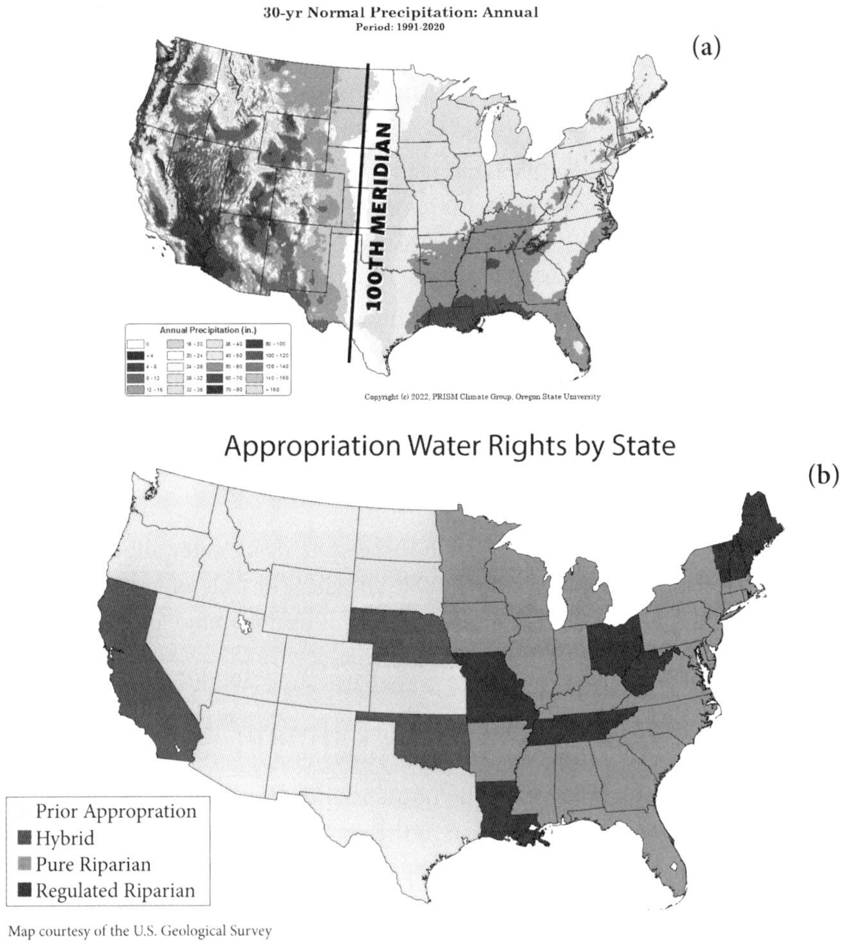

Figure 2.3 The relation between climate and water law: (a) shows mean annual precipitation in the United States in 1911. The line showing the 100th Meridian marks the area to the east in which crops can be grown without irrigation, and the area to the west (with certain coastal and northwest inland exceptions) in which irrigation is needed to grow crops; (b) shows the states that chose the prior appropriation doctrine (west of the 100th Meridian): those with either a mixture of prior appropriation and riparian, or a history of a mixture replaced by prior appropriation only, versus those to the east that chose the riparian doctrine. In relation to climate, the mixed or historically mixed states fall within the area spanning the 100th Meridian, or along the West Coast. Source (a) PRISM Climate Group, *30-yr Normal Precipitation: Annual, Period: 1991–2020* (2023), https://prism.oregonstate.edu/normals/. Source (b): JULIET CHRISTIAN-SMITH, A TWENTY-FIRST CENTURY U.S. WATER POLICY (2012).

regions of the Snake River, mid-Columbia, Sacramento, San Joaquin, Upper Klamath, Colorado, Rio Grande, Platte, and upper Missouri Rivers, irrigation is an essential aspect of growing crops.

Figure 2.3(b) shows the same demarcation in relation to the doctrine of water allocation adopted by states. To the east and in certain coastal states, the common law doctrine of riparian rights was adopted from England—a doctrine that focuses on shared use of a stream where it maintains much of its natural flow, large uses of water for irrigation and landscaping is not necessary, and it is not (or at least historically was not) necessary to transport water large distances to serve a particular use. To the west of this line, a new doctrine of prior appropriation was developed initially in the mining regions. It would allow movement of scarce water resources to places of use; complete appropriation of the flow of a stream; and protection for early water development to encourage settlement.

You will learn in Part III that a separate system of federal common law developed to protect the water rights of Native American tribes. Of importance to that system is the legal relation between the quantification of the water right and the purpose of the reservation. West of the 100th Meridian, most reservations have been interpreted to include an agricultural purpose that requires irrigation in the western climate. As you learned in the previous chapter, irrigation requires much more water than commercial, industrial, and municipal water uses. Thus, the potential exists for much higher quantification of Native American reserved rights in the western United States. Water scarcity drives a higher level of conflict over water in the western United States than in the east. You will learn in Parts III and VI that this has driven a greater effort to quantify reserved water rights in the West.

Climate change poses challenges to both these systems of water allocation and the infrastructure developed in reliance on a stable climate. The following section explains the relation between climate change and water supply and demand and focuses on the predictions for those changes in the Pacific Northwest.

Our Changing Climate

The reason the Earth is inhabitable by humans and most plant and animal life we are familiar with can largely be attributed to the existence of our atmosphere. Indeed, scientists estimate that without our atmosphere the average global temperature of the Earth would be around -18° Celsius or around 0° Fahrenheit. At that temperature, most, if not all water on Earth would be ice and while life could exist, it would not be in the form we are familiar with. In contrast, largely because of our atmosphere, the average global temperature has long hovered around a much more comfortable 14° Celsius or around 57° Fahrenheit.

The reason that the atmosphere is able to moderate the Earth's temperature is the greenhouse effect illustrated in Figure 2.4. The Earth draws its energy in the form of shortwave solar radiation from the sun. Some of that radiation is intercepted by the atmosphere and some is reflected into space by clouds and other reflective objects on Earth such as snow and ice. However, a majority of the sun's radiation is absorbed by the Earth itself, which in turn emits longwave radiation, which we feel as heat. Some of that longwave radiation escapes the atmosphere and some is absorbed by the atmosphere itself. A large portion of that longwave radiation is reflected back toward the Earth, causing the Earth to warm, and, like a greenhouse, keeping it warm at night when the sun goes down. How much longwave radiation the Earth is emitting is a function of the Earth's temperature. As the temperature increases, it emits more longwave radiation, and—under natural conditions—more is allowed to pass through the atmosphere into space, counteracting the heating effect. This negative feedback buffers the Earth's temperature, thereby keeping it in a relatively stable state of dynamic

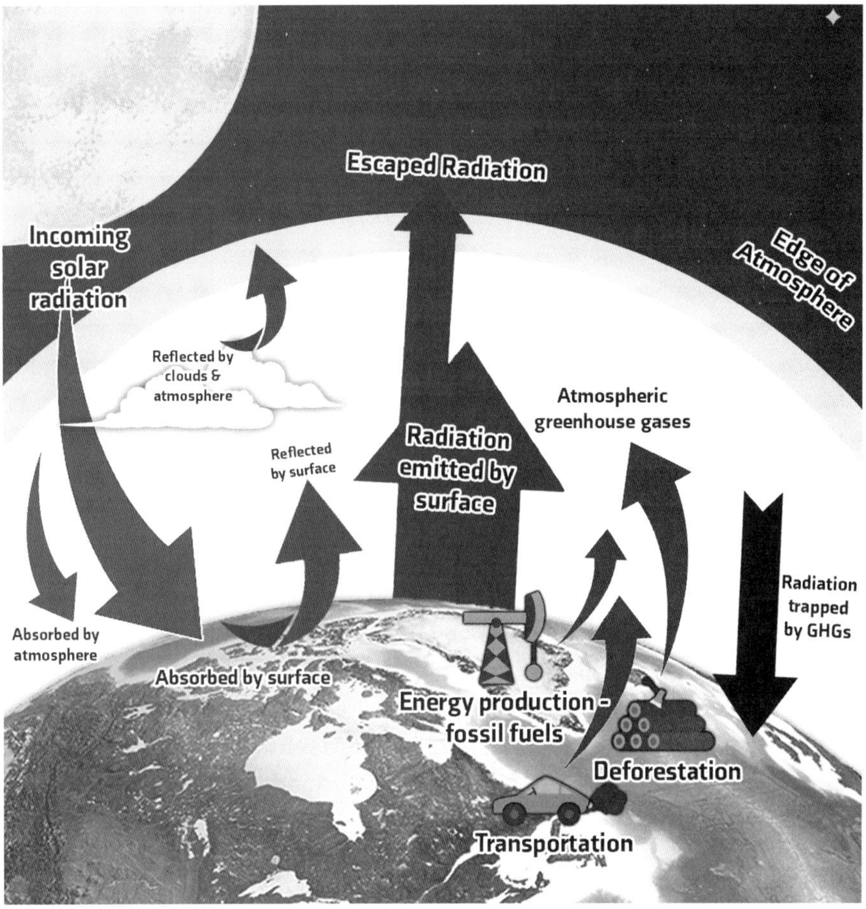

Figure 2.4 The Greenhouse Effect. Graphic design by Melissa Svancara.

equilibrium. But if something happens that allows a change in the energy trapped and radiated back to the Earth, that stability is threatened. Understanding how that change may occur requires understanding which gases in the Earth's atmosphere cause the greenhouse effect.

The atmosphere is composed of gases. Nitrogen and oxygen make up nearly 99% of the atmosphere. The atmosphere also contains what are known as greenhouse gases, the most important of which are carbon dioxide, methane, nitrous oxide, and ozone. Although these gases make up a tiny fraction of the atmosphere's composition, they are primarily responsible for the greenhouse effect. Even a small increase in the relative concentration of these gases in the atmosphere can have a large impact on the greenhouse effect. This increase in energy retained in the Earth's atmosphere and radiated back to earth influences the climate of the planet. The ocean buffers this process by absorbing some of the increase in greenhouse gases. This buffering, however, leads to ocean acidification and there is a limit to how much greenhouse gas the oceans can absorb. At the same time, the oceans are warming along with the rest of the planet. This alters currents, which in turn impacts climate.

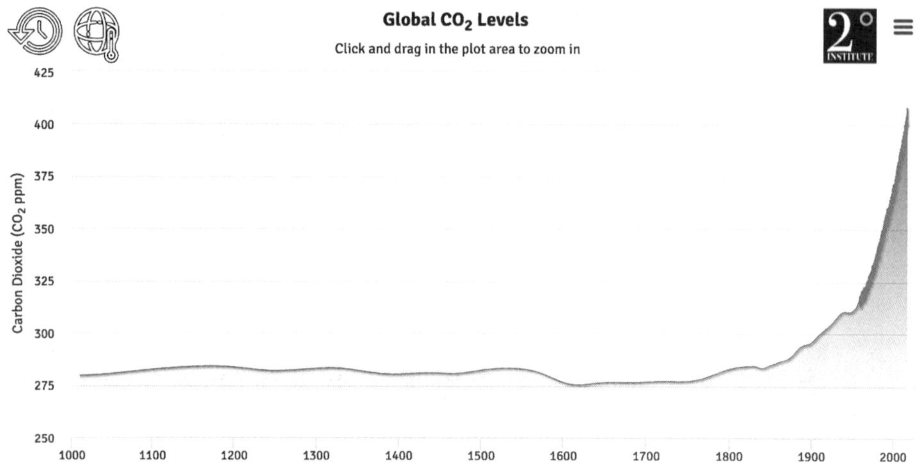

Figure 2.5 Global Atmospheric CO2 levels from 1000 to 2023. Graphic design by Melissa Svancara relying on data from NOAA Climate.gov.

Figure 2.5 shows that the concentration of greenhouse gases in the atmosphere was relatively stable for nearly 2,000 years of human history. Conditions changed dramatically in the 1800s with the onset of the industrial revolution. That revolution required relatively massive amounts of energy, primarily generated through the burning of fossil fuels such as coal and later oil and gas. These substances are called fossil fuels because they are derived from decomposing plants and animals that died long ago and were buried by sediment. As a result, they are composed largely of carbon, which is the primary building block of carbon dioxide and methane, two of the primary greenhouse gases. Burning fossil fuels, as well as deforestation and other disturbances to the environment, results in the emission of these gasses, which then build up in the atmosphere. As you'll see in the following section, the buildup of emissions from the burning of fossil fuels is directly correlated with increases in global temperatures, which in turn has resulted in significant changes to the hydrologic regime in the western United States.

The Hydrologic Cycle as the Climate Changes

Figure 2.6(a) demonstrates that average global temperatures closely track the composition of greenhouse gases in our atmosphere. At first, our oceans were able to absorb much of the heat being generated by the increased global temperatures, which is why we continued to have relatively cool years throughout the middle of the twentieth century. However, by the 1980s, global average warming began increasing in earnest, with the years 2010 through 2020 being the 10 warmest years on record.

Although an average global temperature increase of one and one-half degrees may not seem that significant, it has ripple effects throughout our environment. First, as shown in Figure 2.6(b), the warming is not uniform, with the poles warming much more significantly compared to the mid-latitudes. Although this may seem advanta-

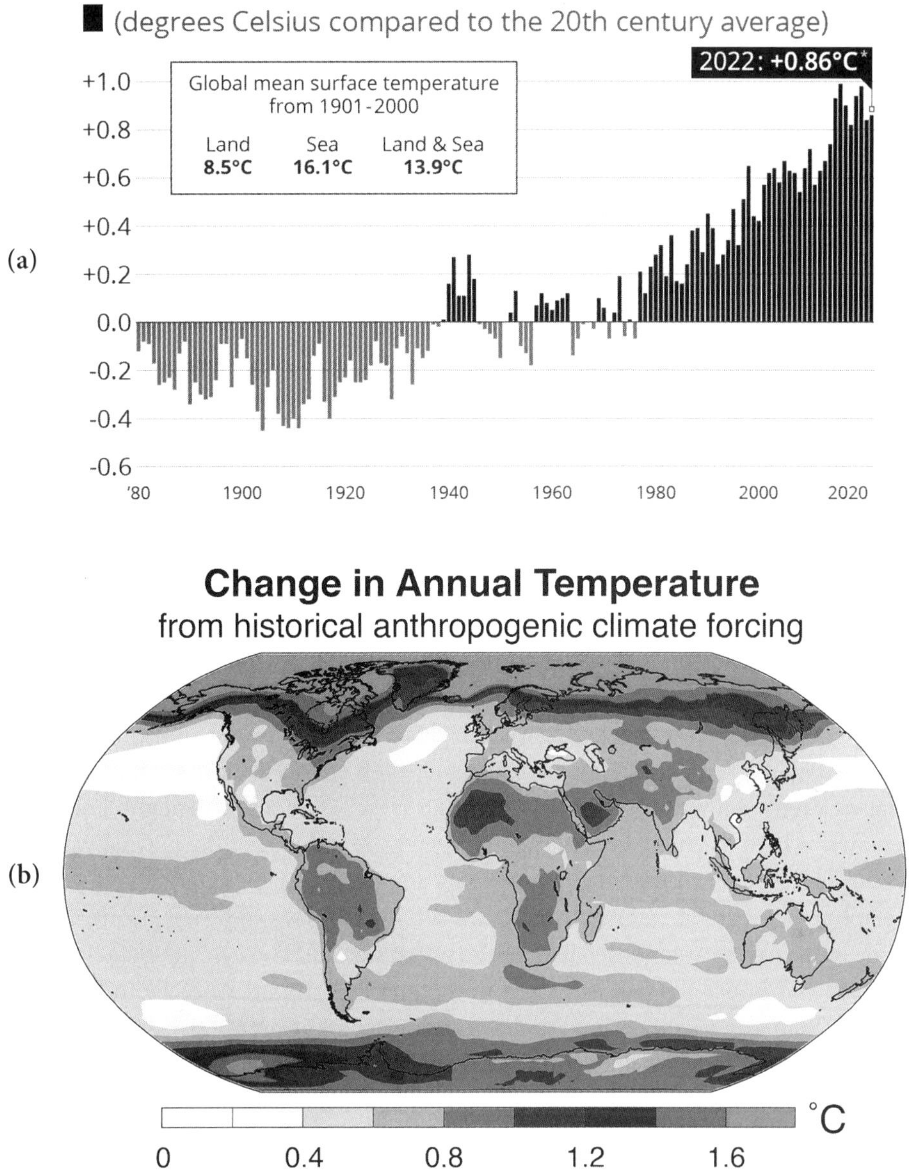

Figure 2.6 Global Annual Departure of Temperature from Average. Geographic Distribution of Global Temperature Increases. Source (a): Graphic design by Melissa Svancara relying on data from NOAA Climate.gov. Source (b): Joseph Garthwaite, Stanford News Service, *Climate Change Has Worsened Global Economic Inequality, Stanford Study Shows* (April 22, 2019); Image credit: Noah Diffenbaugh & Marshall Burke, https://news.stanford.edu/press-releases/2019/04/22/climate-change-wnomic-inequality/.

geous since most people live in the mid-latitudes, the poles play a central role in much of our weather and ocean current circulation, and they hold significant stores of water in the form of ice.

As a result of these and other feedbacks throughout our climatic system, we have already observed harms caused by climate change, including sea level rise and resulting land loss and a general drying in regions associated with the increased incidence of wildfire. The increase in energy in the atmosphere due to the increase in greenhouse gases also leads to greater variability, with more extremes in flooding and drought. These events are disruptive to humans, plants, and animals living on Earth, and cost the world economy billions of dollars each year.

These acute harms are likewise causing positive feedback loops (feedbacks that enhance rather than buffer a particular effect) that exacerbate climate change and the harms wrought by climate change. For example, the ice at the poles has a high reflectivity (called albedo), which helps to reduce warming caused by incoming solar radiation. However, as that ice melts it is replaced by darker landforms that more readily absorb the heat that was previously reflected, which results in an increase in ice melt. Likewise, climate change has led to an increased incidence of wildfire, which results in large emissions of greenhouse gases that further exacerbate climate change. These are just two examples of the myriad of positive feedbacks that exist. Importantly, there are many other positive feedbacks, each of which work together to result in more rapid climate change than predicted

Combined with these direct effects of the increase in energy in the atmosphere, ocean currents and corresponding atmospheric currents such as the jet stream appear to be changing. This may have dramatic impacts on the predictability of weather, reliable ocean currents (such as the Gulf Stream, which warms Europe), and the western La Niña and El Niño currents. The impacts of increased energy are also evident in extreme weather events—flooding, stronger hurricane seasons, extended drought. For the layperson it is hard to understand why these events are not part of the normal variability, particularly given the difficulty of attributing any one event to climate change. A useful metaphor is the use of steroids by athletes. While you may not be able to attribute any single home run by a star baseball batter to use of steroids, you can attribute the general increase in distance the ball is hit and in the number of home runs by that athlete to steroids. Similarly, scientists look to the likelihood that the number and size of extreme events in the past few decades would have occurred under historic conditions. While a decade ago they might have been able to say something like "more likely than not." Increasingly, as more events occur, it is becoming clear that many have a causal link to climate change by something that looks more like "beyond a reasonable doubt."[1]

Climate change is also causing more chronic changes in the hydrologic cycle for the western United States. Figure 2.7 shows that the decrease in winter and spring precipitation since 1955 is translating into decreasing snowpack.

---

1. Since 2011 the American Meteorological Society (AMS) has published a yearly special report in the Bulletin of the AMS (BAMS) on *Explaining Extreme Events from a Climate Perspective*, also referred to as BAMS EEE reports. The BAMS EEE reports reflect the increasing certainty in the causal link between anthropogenic climate change and extreme weather events, with the 2020 report reflecting a scientific consensus based on studies and modeling of individual events that the link exits. AMS, *Explaining Extreme Events from a Climate Perspective* (2023), https://tinyurl.com/2u7uu7bm.

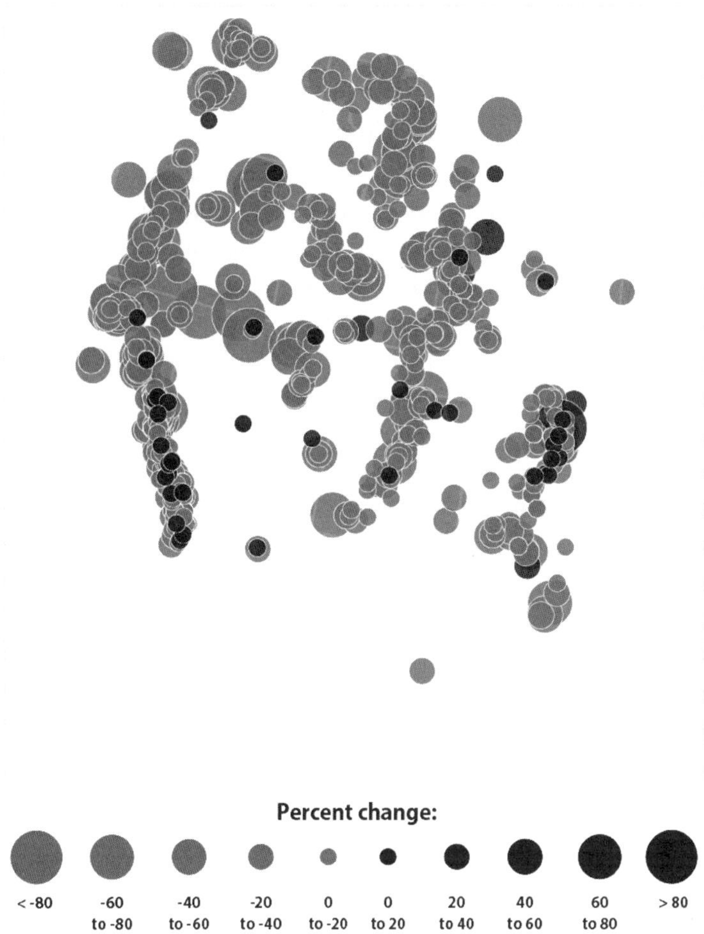

Figure 2.7 Observed Percent Change in Western United States Snowpack. Source: U.S. Environmental Protection Agency, Climate Change Indicators: Snowpack. Data source: USDA Natural Resources Conservation Service, 2022, https://www.epa.gov/climate-indicators/climate-change-indicators-snowpack.

In the Northwest, winter and spring precipitation are expected to increase. However, because of rising temperatures, more of that precipitation is falling as rain and rain-on-snow. Winter snow provides natural storage, but rain flows through the system and is unavailable during the water-short summer months. Rain-on-snow is worse, rapidly decreasing winter storage by melting the snowpack, which is then unavailable later in the season. Figure 2.7 shows that massive declines in snowpack are occurring throughout the Northwest.

Decreasing snowpack is directly correlated to decreasing streamflow in western rivers. Figure 2.8 shows that both spring and summer streamflow is expected to continue to decline in the major rivers of the Southwest, including the Colorado and Rio Grande, dropping by as much as 20% from historic average in the Rio Grande by the end of this century. The fact that we can already measure a decrease in snowpack since 1955 (Figure 2.7), however, means that we should already see the effects of reduced streamflow. Indeed, this is already evident in the southwest with Lake Mead and Lake Powell falling to their lowest levels on record in recent years.

Matters are once again more complex in the Northwest. Flows in the upper Columbia River Basin are expected to increase. That watershed is unique in the United States, however, in that its headwaters are relatively far to the north in the Canadian Rockies, where tributary watersheds are predicted to remain snow-dominated. This will contribute to relatively stable snowpacks and summer streamflows at the U.S./Canada border (note that the prediction in Figure 2.8 is for the river at Grand Coulee dam near the border). However, in northwest river systems, including the Columbia River downstream from the border, flows are expected to track closely with the precipitation, leading to deviation from the historic flow patterns. Winter and spring streamflow are expected to increase, consistent with the increasing rain and rain-on-snow events during these seasons. Peak runoff is already occurring earlier.[2] Consistent with the decline in snowpack combined with decreasing precipitation, late spring and summer streamflow are expected to decline by as much as 30% in this region by the end of the century.

Climate change is also stressing our groundwater supply. Many regions, particularly the Midwest, Arizona, Nevada, and North Idaho/Eastern Washington, rely extensively on groundwater for domestic, commercial, municipal, and industrial uses (DCMI) and irrigation needs. Earlier and more rapid snowmelt in the Northwest results in greater runoff earlier in the season when the soil is saturated and water cannot readily infiltrate into the ground. Matters are worse in the Southwest, where the overall decline in winter and spring precipitation simply means less water is falling on the ground during these times. As a result, groundwater recharge is declining throughout much of the West.

Climate change is also causing increases in water demand. Projections of estimated percent change in water demand from 2005 to 2060 without climate change predict relative stability in much of the United States with some increases on the coasts and southern United States.[3] In contrast, estimated percent changes in projected water demand from 2005 to 2060 with climate change predict increases in demand between 10 and 50% across most of the United States.[4] The primary driver is increased vegetative demand (crops and native vegetation) due to increased temperature.

By far, the largest consumer of water in the West is irrigation for agriculture. As a result, increases in irrigation crop water demand will be a primary driver of water stress from climate change in the West. Much of the West will likely see some increase

---

2. I.T. Stewart, D.R. Cayan & M.D. Dettinger, *Changes Toward Earlier Streamflow Timing Across Western North America,* 18 J. CLIMATE 1136; Hamlet et al., *20th Century Trends in Runoff, Evapotranspiration, and Soil Moisture in the Western U.S.,* 20 J. CLIMATE 1468 (2007).

3. U.S. Global Change Research Program, Fourth National Climate Assessment (2017), https://nca2018.globalchange.gov/.

4. *Id.*

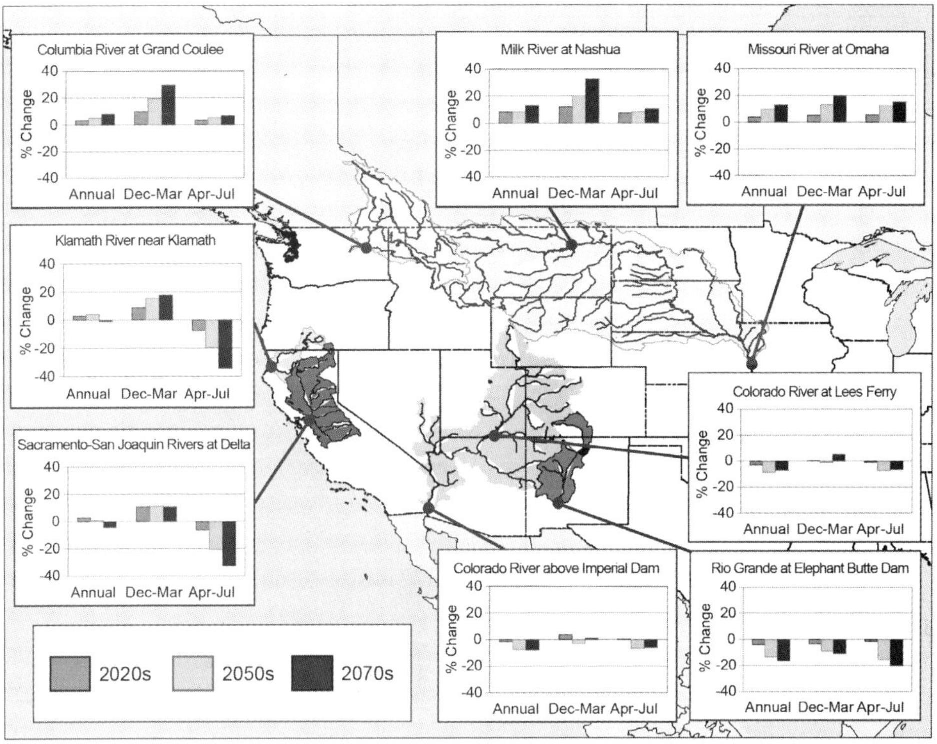

Figure 2.8 Expected Seasonal Change in Streamflow for Major United States River Systems. Source: U.S. Global Change Research Program, Third National Climate Assessment 74 (2017), https://www.globalchange.gov/our-work/third-national-climate-assessment#.

in the amount of water necessary to achieve the same historical crop yield. Some regions, such as the Inland Northwest and the Northern Rockies, will experience demand increases of as much as 50%. Irrigation demand is also projected to change at over 30 Indian Reservations located in agricultural regions throughout the West. Adjustment will be even more acute in places such as the Southern Plains, which has historically been farmed without irrigation but will likely experience large increases in crop water demand that will likely require the installation of expensive irrigation infrastructure.

Increased reliance on groundwater since the 1950s along with recent shifts to water stored as groundwater during drought is resulting in large groundwater declines in many parts of the West (Figure 2.9). Decrease in recharge as a result of climate change will exacerbate this problem.

Climate change also affects water quality. Although water quality is not generally a topic of water allocation law, it may become so if quality decreases below the level needed for existing beneficial water use, in particular for instream uses. For example, temperature is considered a component of water quality. With global warming, stream temperatures are expected to increase congruently with air temperature. Those tem-

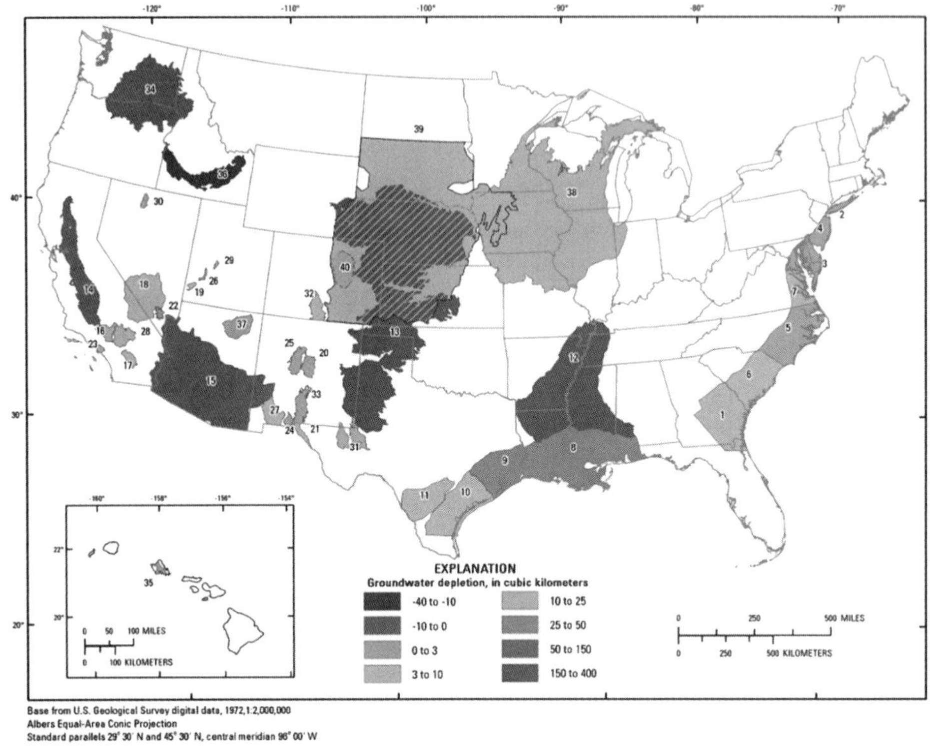

Figure 2.9 Map showing groundwater depletion in major aquifers in the United States (1900–2088). Source: Leonard F. Konikow, USGS, Science for a Changing World, Scientific Investigations Report 2013-5079, http://pubs.usgs.gov/sir/2013/5079.

perature increases are extremely detrimental to fish and other aquatic species, all of which have evolved for millennia under a relatively stable stream temperature regime. Just a slight increase in air temperature has a dramatic effect on the amount of habitat available to brown and rainbow trout, steelhead, and salmon, and the areas in which they will find lethal water temperatures are increasing.

In addition, many western soils are unable to absorb the precipitation generated by extreme weather events, which leads to increased stormwater runoff into western streams. That runoff contains large amounts of sediment and nutrients, both of which are components of water quality. Fine sediment can remain suspended in the water column, which increases stream turbidity and makes it more difficult for aquatic animals to breathe and for plants to photosynthesize. Coarse sediment can coat the bottom of a stream, which interferes with fish spawning and reduces habitat for myriad aquatic species. The combination of increasing levels of nutrients and temperatures promotes plant and algae growth. Those aquatic plants consume oxygen, reducing the level of dissolved oxygen in the water that is available for other aquatic species.

These water quality concerns are exacerbated in areas that have recently experienced wildfire, an increasing problem throughout the West as the climate changes. Recently burned soils that have lost their organic matter cannot readily hold water. That, combined with the loss of vegetation caused by wildfires, causes precipitation in burned areas to run off much more readily than unburned areas. That runoff causes erosion, taking recently burned soils into streams. Further, because it has lost the shade that trees provide, snow in recently burned areas melts much more quickly in the spring. These factors combine with the shifting winter and spring precipitation patterns noted above to cause spring runoff to occur even earlier in the season.

While we know that climate change is causing water supply to decline, water demand to increase, and water quality to change throughout most of the West, the question for water lawyers is: what do we do about it? Can the water laws and water infrastructure that currently exist in the western United States address these issues or will they need to be adjusted to make our communities sufficiently resilient to climate change? The answer is complex and uncertain, and begins by understanding the current law, management, and development of the waters of the West. Consider as you read this text where the flexibility in the law and its implementation lie and how you might use that to help water users adapt. The next chapter will begin by framing the different values that shape the way society mediates the relation between humans and water.

Chapter 3

Water and Society

Introduction

The manner in which a society determines whether and how to allocate and/or protect water is a complex function of values, history, culture, and climate, as well as the connected, renewable, and dynamic nature of water on and beneath the surface of the earth. In many cultures and religions, water plays a role in the sacred. In many Indigenous societies, the ecosystem value of the use of water *in situ* (meaning in its natural place) has long been recognized, while this recognition is relatively recent in western societies. This Chapter will begin by exploring the relation between water and society through the western classification of water as a *common pool resource* and conclude by viewing that relation through an Indigenous lens in which water is part of the living environment and *guardianship* is increasingly viewed as the human role in that relationship.

The Western Lens: Water as a Common Pool Resource[1]

Common pool resource is defined as a "resource system that is sufficiently large as to make it costly (but not impossible) to exclude potential beneficiaries from access to its use."[2] Water is considered a common pool resource. The use of the term "resource" in both the phrase and its definition makes implicit the western notion that the importance of water is in its use by humans.[3] The term "resource" includes:

> a: a source of supply or support . . .
>
> b: a natural source of wealth or revenue . . .
>
> c: a natural feature or phenomenon that enhances the quality of human life

---

1. Portions of the section are adapted from Barbara Cosens, *Water Law Reform in the Face of Climate Change: Learning from Drought in Australia and the Western United States*, 33 Envt'l. & Plan. L.J. 373 (2016).

2. E. Ostrom, Governing the Commons: The Evolution of Institutions for Collective Action 30 (1990).

3. Merriam-Webster Online Dictionary, *Resource* (05/04/2022), https://www.merriam-webster.com/dictionary/resource.

d: computable wealth ...

e: a source of information or expertise[4]

Garrett Hardin used the example of grazing of a common area to describe the inevitable tragedy of human exploitation of common pool resources because the benefit goes to the livestock owner alone and the cost in rangeland degradation is shared by all. The logical result, assuming people do not collaborate, is overuse. He identified government regulation, and private property as alternative means to avoid this "tragedy of the commons."[5]

Hardin's first alternative, division of a common pool resource into private property, has the advantage of connecting benefits and costs and is thought to incentivize stewardship.[6] Enforcement is made less costly by the existence of clearly defined rights.[7] In the context of water, flexibility to accommodate change over time may be provided through the development of water markets with low (i.e., government-supported) transaction costs. Nevertheless, a property approach may also lead to spill-over effects that reflect a shifting of costs to neighboring property (these costs are referred to as externalities). Unfortunately, the fact that water flows means that spill-over costs tend to represent the rule, rather than the exception, making privatization of the water resource a problematic approach if not combined with other measures.[8]

Hardin's second alternative, government regulation of the use of common pool resources, allows prospective adjustment of allocation as circumstances change, thus, informing investment. In states with a science-based administrative system (that you will learn about in Part V) it also allows a process of scientific investigation of possible secondary impacts of management actions. Nevertheless, limited resources and restraints on regulation that are intended to assure uniform implementation of environmental laws often prevent contextualization to local conditions and lead to dissatisfaction with the command-and-control approach.[9] If used alone, government regulation of a resource with the size and complexity of a water basin requires perfect knowledge and widespread enforcement—the costly nature of which are captured in the definition of a common pool resource. Thus, like property rights, regulation alone may prove inadequate for management of common pool resources.

Nobel laureate Elinor Ostrom documented a third approach to avoiding overuse of a common pool resource when she systematically studied the self-organization of local interests, including water districts, to maintain the sustainability of resources

4. *Id.*

5. G. Hardin, *The Tragedy of the Commons*, 162 Science 1243 (1968).

6. *Id.*

7. E. Ostrom, Governing the Commons: The Evolution of Institutions for Collective Action 30 (1990).

8. *Id.*

9. For a concise summary of the criticisms of command-and-control environmental regulation in the United States, see Eric W. Orts, *Reflexive Environmental Law*, 89 N.W.U. L. Rev. 1227 (1995).

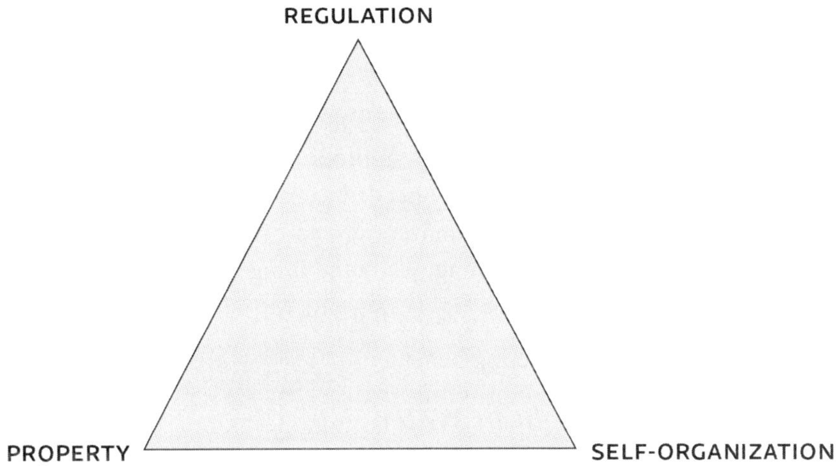

Figure 3.1 The three approaches thought necessary to manage a common pool resource. Most western systems of water law plot somewhere within the triangle—relying on a mix of all three approaches.

they rely on.[10] Self-organization provides for the contextualized local knowledge necessary to tailor solutions to resource allocation issues. Nevertheless, in the absence of external pressure, local governance may prove inadequate in the face of scarcity. In addition, local collaborative processes are thought to have a high risk of corruption and exclusion of marginalized populations.[11] Nesting local self-organization within a system of governance that provides access to capacity building and checks to ensure accountability and lack of corruption may be necessary.[12]

Despite the heavy emphasis on the property aspect of water in western politics, you will learn that western states apply a complex mix of all three approaches to management of water (Figure 3.1). The use of a system of property rights based on use (the doctrine of prior appropriation, covered in Part II) to allocate water in the western United States is nested within a regulatory system (covered in Part V) in which states (via their constitutions) assert ownership and regulatory authority over the water itself. Capacity for local self-organization is often government supported, with water irrigation districts providing the prime example. Water markets within districts function with low transaction costs and provide tailored flexibility to respond to variable water supply. State government-regulated water supply banks (covered in Part V) provide

---

10. E. Ostrom, GOVERNING THE COMMONS: THE EVOLUTION OF INSTITUTIONS FOR COLLECTIVE ACTION 30 (1990); E. Ostrom, *A General Framework for Analyzing Sustainability of Social-Ecological Systems*, 325 SCIENCE 419 (2009).

11. E. Ostrom, *A General Framework for Analyzing Sustainability of Social-Ecological Systems*, 325 SCIENCE 419 (2009).

12. Barbara Cosens et al., *Governing Complexity: Integrating Science, Governance, and Law to Manage Accelerating Change in the Globalized Commons*, 118(36) PNAS (2021), https://doi.org/10.1073/pnas.2102798118.

more formal mechanisms for water markets at larger scale and reduce the transaction costs of finding an exact match between buyer and seller.

A deep understanding of this complex mix of approaches will be necessary for present and future generations of water lawyers to help their clients navigate climate change. Because the core principle in prior appropriation of property rights is often identified as an obstacle to the flexibility needed as climate change unfolds, the following section focuses on the difficult concept of a so-called *usufructuary* right—i.e., a property right to the use of something, while the thing itself is owned by another. Understanding the concept of a use right is essential to identifying the underlying flexibility in western water law.

The Nature of a Use Right in Water

A *usufruct* for purposes of U.S. civil law is defined as:

> The right of enjoying a thing, the property of which is vested in another, and to draw from the same all the profit, utility and advantage which it may produce, ... Usufructs are of two kinds; perfect and imperfect. Perfect usufruct, which is of things which the usufructuary can enjoy without altering their substance, though their substance may be diminished or deteriorated naturally by time or by the use to which they are applied; as a house, a piece of land, animals, furniture and other movable effects. Imperfect or quasi usufruct, which is of things which would be useless to the usufructuary if we did not consume and expend them, or change the substance of them, ...[13]

Thus, the right to use water for consumptive uses in the western United States is an "imperfect usufruct." Ownership of the water itself remains with the sovereign. In the United States, as a matter of federal law, that ownership may be by the state or federal government or federal government on behalf of a tribe (the following chapter will cover this). Using state law as an example, many states recognize state ownership and authority to regulate water in their state constitutions. Thus, the Idaho Constitution states:

> USE OF WATERS A PUBLIC USE. The use of all waters now appropriated, or that may hereafter be appropriated ... is hereby declared to be a public use, and subject to the regulations and control of the state in the manner prescribed by law.[14]
>
> Montana's Constitution states:
>
> ... (2) The use of all water that is now or may hereafter be appropriated ... shall be held to be a public use.

---

13. John Bouvier, *Usufructuary Right*, A Law Dictionary, Adapted to the Constitution and Laws of the United States (2022), https://legal-dictionary.thefreedictionary.com/Usufructuary+Right.

14. Idaho Const., Art. XV, s. 1.

> (3) All surface, underground, flood, and atmospheric waters within the boundaries of the state are the property of the state for the use of its people and are subject to appropriation for beneficial uses as provided by law.
>
> (4) The legislature shall provide for the administration, control, and regulation of water rights....[15]

In contrast, and likely due to the greater rainfall in their more populous regions, Oregon does not address water in its constitution and Washington's treatment of water is limited to:

> PUBLIC USE OF WATER. The use of the waters of this state for irrigation, mining and manufacturing purposes shall be deemed a public use.[16]

Despite state ownership of water, courts have struggled with the nature of a use right in the context of Constitutional Takings analysis. In doing so, courts have given use rights greater protection from regulation by the government that owns the water than they give to outright private land ownership in issues such as zoning. By failing to understand the connection between a use right and its use, the U.S. Federal Circuit Court reasoned that any reduction in the object of a right (i.e., reduction in water) that is limited to use "Takes," or is a "Taking" of, that right.[17] This led to the conclusion that any government reduction in water delivery by a water right holder is a physical taking requiring compensation. In contrast, a regulatory taking would connect the water to its use and require a substantial diminishment in, for example, the crop yield, to be considered a Taking.

In fairness to the federal court, there is little precedent defining the nature of a use right. Idaho statutes set forth the understanding of this use right created in private parties that is consistent with the definition of a usufruct (above) by connecting the usufruct to its use:

> Nature of property in water. Water being essential to the industrial prosperity of the state ... its control shall be in the state ... *All the waters of the state, when flowing in their natural channels, including the waters of all natural springs and lakes within the boundaries of the state are declared to be the property of the state*, whose duty it shall be to supervise their appropriation and allotment to those diverting the same therefrom for any beneficial purpose ... and the right to the use of any of the public waters which have heretofore been or may hereafter be allotted or beneficially applied, *shall not be considered as being a property right in itself, but such right shall become the complement of, or one of the*

15. Mont. Const., Art. IX, s. 3.

16. Wash. Const., Art. XXI, s. 1.

17. Casitas Municipal Water District v. United States, 543 F.3d 1276 (D.C. Cir. 2008); in determining the amount of compensation, the court softened the impact of its ruling with a finding that the water district must show loss of beneficial use, not just paper loss, to receive compensation, Casitas Municipal Water District v. United States, 708 F.3d 1340 (D.C. Cir. 2013).

> *appurtenances of, the land or other thing to which, through necessity, said water is being applied* ... [emphasis added][18]

The current federal court interpretation of a use right as subject to physical takings analysis coincides with the increase in water demand for a growing population and changes in water supply due to climate change. The interpretation has a chilling effect on the assertion of government management and regulation to address emerging problems. Part of the career of future water lawyers will be to find flexibility despite those limitations.

Finding Flexibility in Western Water Allocation

A starting point for flexibility is to look to each of the three prongs for management of a common pool resource for areas of flexibility (Figure 3.1). First, are there regulatory tools for short-term reallocation of water? Governments have greater authority to regulate without paying just compensation in response to an emergency.[19] During its prolonged drought, California's (then) Governor Brown declared a state of emergency, allowing greater exercise of regulatory flexibility.[20] Emergency powers, however, may not be appropriate to address long-term climate change impacts. States have begun looking to the requirement (that you will learn about in Part II) that a water right only extends to what is reasonable and that what is reasonable evolves as technology and demand change.[21] Reasonable use does not alter the priority system, but provides assurance that junior water users will not be cut off from water supply if a senior water user is wasting water.

Government regulation also commonly relies on planning. This approach, however, is extremely difficult when facing the increased variability and unpredictability of water supply due to climate change. Professor Craig Anthony Arnold has called for adaptive planning in the face of uncertainty, stating:

> Adaptive planning is an iterative and evolving process of identifying goals and making decisions for further action that are flexible, contemplate uncertainty and multiple possible scenarios, include feedback loops for frequent modification to plans and their implementation, and build planning and management capacity to adapt to change.[22]

---

18. Idaho Code § 42-101.

19. Robin Kundis Craig, *Adapting Water Law to Public Necessity: Reframing Climate Change Adaptation as Emergency Response and Preparedness*, 11 Vt. J. Envt'l L. 709 (2010).

20. Gov. Edmund G. Brown Jr., *A Proclamation of a State of Emergency* (17 January 2014), https://www.gov.ca.gov/news.php?id=18368.

21. *See, e.g.*, American Falls Reservoir District No 2 v. Idaho Department of Water Resources, 154 P.3d 446, 449 (Idaho 2007). You will study this case in the context of modern water management in Part VI.

22. Craig Anthony Arnold, *Adaptive Watershed Planning and Climate Change*, 5 Envt'l & Energy L. & Pol'y J. 417, 440 (2010).

Second, where do property systems find flexibility? The short answer is: through the use of markets. Western states in general allow transfers of water separate from land or the use it is applied to under strictly controlled governmental processes (that you will learn about in Part V). Using Idaho as an example, water users seeking to change the type, period, or place of use or diversion must comply with a process overseen by the Idaho Department of Water Resources.[23] The Department's investigation, as well as the basis for objection by interested parties, includes whether the change will impact existing water rights, including those junior to the right being changed (the "no-injury rule"), and whether the change is in the public interest.[24]

The individual water transfer approach is inadequate to match those with excess water with those in need on a large enough scale to adapt during drought.[25] Thus, some states have developed state-facilitated water banks. Water right holders may deposit water in the water bank and others may withdraw it, eliminating the need for an exact match. Because the withdrawal is a "loan" rather than a transfer of the use right, the lengthy transfer process is avoided.[26] Water banks are, nevertheless, heavily regulated. The creation of a water bank in Idaho, under the oversight of the Idaho Water Resources Board, provides an example:

> WATER SUPPLY BANK CREATED. The water resource board shall have the duty of operating a water supply bank. The water supply bank shall make use of and obtain the highest duty for beneficial use from water, provide a source of adequate water supplies to benefit new and supplemental water uses, and provide a source of funding for improving water user facilities and efficiencies.[27]

The Idaho Statutes go on to provide the Board with authority to establish rules for operation of the water bank.[28]

Third, how does self-organization play a role in water allocation flexibility? Nobel laureate Elinor Ostrom focused her Ph.D. dissertation on the governance of groundwater basins and returned to that work in the context of management of common pool resources in the 1980s.[29] Her Ph.D. student, William Bloomquist, studied how lawsuits can trigger self-organization among groundwater districts, providing a catalyst for innovative solutions that are then institutionalized as settlements.[30] You will see

---

23. Idaho Code 42-222.

24. Idaho Code 42-222(1).

25. *See, e.g.*, B.G. Colby, *Transaction Costs and Efficiency in Western Water Allocation*, 72(5) Am. J. Agric. Econ. 1184 (1990); L.J. MacDonnell et al., The Water Transfer Process as a Management Option for Meeting Changing Water Demands, Vol. I (1990).

26. *See generally* Clifford et al., Analysis of Water Banks in the Western States (2004), https://apps.ecology.wa.gov/publications/documents/0411011.pdf.

27. Idaho Code § 42-1761.

28. Idaho Code § 42-1762.

29. Fabien Locher, *Historicizing Elinor Ostrom: Urban Politics, International Development and Expertise in the U.S. Context (1970–1990)*, 19 Theoretical Inquiries L. 533, 552 (2018).

30. William Blomquist, *Getting out of the Trap: Changing an Endangered Commons to a Managed Commons* (Aug. 17, 1987) *in* William Blomquist, Dividing the Waters: Governing Groundwater in Southern California (1992).

excellent examples of innovative settlement in your case studies on conjunctive management of surface and ground water, and on Native American water right settlements in the context of adjudication, in Part VI.

Ecosystem Services: The Forgotten Use in the Prior Appropriation System

The scientific recognition that environmental (or "instream") flows support the ecosystems on which we rely for everything from timber to fisheries to crops, and the change in values that caused people to increasingly seek environmental flows for both recreation and aesthetic value, arrived late in the system of priority. You will learn in Part V that, despite the common law requirement of a diversion for establishment of a prior appropriation water right, statutory schemes in the second half of the twentieth century began to allow establishment of water rights for environmental flows. Like any new water right, environmental flows are junior to all water rights in existence before them. Thus, water markets and voluntary actions (i.e., self-organization) are the current legal tools to obtain environmental flows in systems already heavily allocated by the mid-twentieth century. The following section on the Indigenous lens on water tells a very different story.

The Indigenous Lens: The Guardianship Model and Water as a Living Being[31]

Cultural linguistics views language as "a reflection of a thought world."[32] In an article on the importance of understanding the meaning underlying words used in treaties with Native American tribes, Indigenous scholar Dr. Sammy Matsaw and coauthors Cosens and Hedden-Nicely discuss the study of the relation between culture and meaning stating:

> Cultural linguistics looks at the emergent aspects of language including: 1) how language is used to form mental models of what is observed in time and space in the world around us as well as our own practices as a community of people and reflects the shared assumptions about the meaning of language; 2) how language is used to reflect classification of concepts reflecting the broader meaning associated with a single word; and 3) how metaphors may reflect cultural understanding of ourselves and our place in space and time [citations omitted].[33]

---

31. Note that this section relies heavily on quotes out of respect for the Indigenous voice and the dangers of trying to paraphrase concepts from a different worldview.

32. Sammy Matsaw et al., *Cultural Linguistics and Treaty Language: A Modernized Approach to Interpreting Treaty Language to Capture the Tribe's Understanding*, 50 Envt'l L. 415, 446 (2020).

33. *Id.* at 435.

The authors go on to state: "We do know that Indigenous languages are usually bounded by a particular place. They are also verb-based because there was/is more interest in processes and relationships (the use of past tense reflects the extinction/endangerment of Indigenous languages happening today)."[34] This worldview is captured in the quote "... all of nature is in me, and a bit of myself is in all of nature."[35] In the words of Sammy Matsaw, who is of both Shoshone-Bannock and Lakota descent:

> To me when the more I talked with my own generation about the ideas in *tygi* or *hoawai*, the Shoshone or Bannock word for "to hunt," respectively, it seems there was so much more to our language. Language for Shoshone and Bannock peoples, and Indigenous peoples of North America, are made up of mostly verbs whereas English and Latin based languages are made up of nouns.[36] ...
>
> In the Lakota language, there is more interest in the processes of energy than there is in the object per se[37] ... we were once more interested in the *is*, the *beingness* of life, our connection and fluidity between us and us between all of creation.[38]

Matsaw quotes Viola Faye Cordova, the first Native American woman to receive a Ph.D. in philosophy:

> They saw themselves as existing in a web of highly interrelated and interdependent "substances": air, water, other beings, and land. They maintained their life force by ingesting the life force of other beings. No less respect was due a wild onion than a deer. "Eat it," my father would say to us, "we took its life that we might continue our own." Eating was a holy sacrament; a thanksgiving to the creatures that provided us life.[39]

This worldview of interdependence and interrelationship leads to an environmental ethic that governs the relation between humans and the environment. This is captured in the authors' discussion of Indigenous Knowledge, Traditional Ecological Knowledge (TEK), and storytelling.

Indigenous Knowledge cannot be defined and shouldn't be. Scholars James Youngblood Henderson and Marie Ann Battiste offer a conceptualization as such:

> Perhaps the closest one can get to describing unity in Indigenous knowledge is that knowledge is the expression of the vibrant relationships between people, their ecosystems, and other living beings and spirits that share their lands.... All aspects of knowledge are interrelated and cannot be separated from the traditional territories of the people concerned.... To the Indigenous

34. *Id.* at 439.

35. John (Fire) Lame Deer & Richard Erdoes, Lame Deer, Seeker of Visions 137 (1973).

36. Sammy Matsaw et al., *Cultural Linguistics and Treaty Language: A Modernized Approach to Interpreting Treaty Language to Capture the Tribe's Understanding,* 50 Envt'l L. 415, 437 (2020).

37. *Id.* at 439.

38. *Id.* at 440.

39. *Id.* at 440 (quoting Viola Faye Cordova, *Time, Culture, and Self, in* How It Is: The Native American Philosophy of V.F. Cordova 171, 173 (Kathleen Dean Moore et al. eds., 2007)).

> ways of knowing, the self exists within a world that is subject to flux. The purpose of these ways of knowing is to reunify the world or at least to reconcile the world to itself. Indigenous knowledge is the way of living within contexts of flux, paradox, and tension, respecting the pull of dualism and reconciling opposing forces.... Developing these ways of knowing leads to freedom of consciousness and to solidarity with the natural world.[40]
>
> ...
>
> TEK *is* a relationship with land and Creation, not just *about* a relationship with land and Creation. Gregory Cajete, Tewa Indian from the Santa Clara Pueblo and Professor of Native American Studies and Language Literacy Sociocultural Studies at the University of New Mexico, where he is a leading expert on the integration of Indigenous knowledge in education and science states:
>
>> Native people traditionally lived a kind of communal environmental ethics that stemmed from the broadest sense of kinship with all life. The underlying aim of the science of ecology, therefore, the understanding of the web of relationships with the "household" of Nature, is not modern science's sole property. Understanding the relationship scientifically is not enough—living and nurturing these relationships is the key. This is the ecology of the Native community.[41]
>
> Regardless of the different tribal nations of the authors represented here in the above quotes, there is a distinction, *is/about*, as relationships with ecosystems are viewed differently, shaping a different worldview from European thinking.[42]
>
> ...
>
> Indigenous peoples of Turtle Island tell stories about the roles of plants and animals for their survivance and adaptively in the twenty-first century in a formation of red pedagogy upon highly modified landscapes to riverscapes from continued settlement. These stories are "contracts" between Indigenous peoples and life forms, and the environment (water, land, and sky) they rely upon. Within the agreements human beings are to take care of them as they sacrificed themselves to take care of Indigenous peoples. Because of the "contractual" relationship, Indigenous peoples *remember to remember* at intervals within the seasons to pay homage to life forms and the environment. The seasonal ceremony can begin in spring paying homage to "Traditional Foods," also known as "First Foods" in the Pacific Northwest, through varying customs and traditions, usually dependent on the bounded space of each tribe [citations omitted].[43]

---

40. *Id.* at 441 (quoting Deborah McGregor, *Coming Full Circle: Indigenous Knowledge, Environment, and Our Future*, 28 Am. Indian Q. 385, 390 (2003)).

41. *Id.* at 442 (quoting Deborah McGregor, *Coming Full Circle: Indigenous Knowledge, Environment, and Our Future*, 28 Am. Indian Q. 385, 390 (2003)).

42. *Id.*

43. *Id.* at 444–445.

It is only recently, with the rising voice of Indigenous peoples globally, that efforts have begun to honor a worldview that is foreign to the western view of nature as a source of resources, within the western legal system. The following paragraphs summarize the evolution of these efforts. They began with the initial efforts to recognize Rights of Nature and arose through the environmental movement, generally without participation from indigenous leaders and generally with limited success in implementation. More recently the concept of Rights of Nature has been integrated with the overlay of guardianship, often led by indigenous leaders, and appears to have both greater efficacy in implementation, and greater possibility of adherence to an indigenous worldview.[44]

In 1972, USC Law Professor Christopher Stone published an article titled "Should Trees Have Standing? Toward Legal Rights for Natural Objects."[45] Stone argued that by granting judicial standing to natural objects three improvements in environmental protection could be realized. First, cases could be brought (by lawyers on behalf of the natural objects) simply for harm to the river overcoming the hurdle of Standing. Second, the case could seek a remedy for intrinsic harm to the river or forest itself and the ecosystem it serves, regardless of any harm to a human being. Third, damages from such a suit would not only reflect the full extent of that harm regardless of the economic harm to human use, but would go to the natural object, thus directly funding its restoration. He noted that the concept of "personhood" has evolved over time to include other non-human entities such as corporations.

That same year, 1972, Justice Douglas cited Stone in his dissenting opinion in *Sierra Club v. Morton*, stating "[c]ontemporary public concern for protecting nature's ecological equilibrium should lead to the conferral of standing upon environmental objects to sue for their own preservation."[46] The case involved an effort by an NGO, Sierra Club, to prevent the U.S. Forest Service from granting a special use permit to Walt Disney Enterprises, Inc. to develop a ski resort in Mineral King Valley in Sequoia National Forest, California. The case was dismissed because the Sierra Club had only alleged a general injury to the type of environment its mission is to protect—not injury to specific members of the club, and thus failed to establish standing. Although Disney never built the resort, this requirement of harm to an identified person remains in the judicial requirement of standing to bring suit today.

---

44. The discussion of standing, personhood, and guardianship in this chapter relies heavily on the research of former University of Idaho M.S. student Dakota Goodman for her Thesis: "Protecting the Footprints of Rivers in the United States during the Anthropocene: A Personhood Proposal for the Columbia River Watershed and a Recognition of Genius Loci in Water Resources Management." The discussion of the Public Trust Doctrine and the case of *Juliana v. United States* relies heavily on the research of former University of Idaho J.D./Ph.D. student Bronson Pace for his Dissertation: "It's About Time: A Sociolegal Approach to Intergenerational Climate Justice in the United States, with Developments in Environmental Justice Scholarship, Climate Change Litigation, and Climate Adaptation Law."

45. Christopher D. Stone, *Should Trees Have Standing? Toward Legal Rights for Natural Objects*, 45 S. Cal. L. Rev. 450 (1970).

46. Sierra Club v. Morton, 405 U.S. 727, 741–742 (1972)

In 1970, University of California-Berkeley Professor Joseph Sax published an article titled "The Public Trust Doctrine in Natural Resource Law: Effective Judicial Intervention."[47] Sax argued that the Public Trust Doctrine (PTD), which requires the government to act as trustee of certain natural resources, at that time limited to the beds and banks of navigable waterways, should be extended to public resources (such as a national forest or a navigable river) because it meets three important criteria for a much-needed tool for environmental protection. First, it includes the "concept of a legal right in the general public." Second, it would "be enforceable against the government." Third, the evolving judicial interpretation of the PTD renders it "capable of an interpretation consistent with contemporary concerns for environmental quality."[48] You will learn about the PTD in Part IV. It is enough for our purposes here to know that the PTD, while still important in protecting public use of and access to navigable waterways, has only been extended to require ongoing governmental oversight of water allocation beyond statutory requirements in California, and has not been extended to other natural objects.

In 2014, University of Oregon Law Professor Mary Wood published a book titled *A Nature's Trust: Environmental Law for a New Ecological Era*, seeking to catalyze renewed interest in the PTD, particularly in application to environmental harm as greenhouse gas emissions threaten the Earth's atmosphere and the resulting climate change threatens the Earth's ecosystems.[49] In 2015 suit was filed on behalf of 21 children, members of the nonprofit Our Children's Trust, to compel the government to reduce the emission of greenhouse gases to the atmosphere.[50] The suit sought to redress the harm to future generations, but by detailing the harm to the 21 plaintiffs, the problem in *Sierra Club v. Morton* was avoided. The U.S. District Court denied the government's motion for dismissal, finding the children to have standing, and accepted the application of the PTD. The Ninth Circuit reversed, finding that the suit did not meet the redressability requirement of standing, stating: "it is beyond the power of an Article III court to order, design, supervise, or implement the plaintiffs' requested remedial plan. As the opinions of their experts make plain, any effective plan would necessarily require a host of complex policy decisions entrusted, for better or worse, to the wisdom and discretion of the executive and legislative branches."[51]

If these failed attempts that turn on the nuances of "injury" and "redressability" seem far removed from the indigenous worldview presented above, you would not be alone in your assessment.[52] It is increasingly recognized that self-determination

---

47. Joseph L. Sax, *The Public Trust Doctrine in Natural Resource Law: Effective Judicial Intervention*, 68(3) Mich. L. Rev. 471–566 (1970).

48. *Id.* at 474.

49. Mary C. Wood, A Nature's Trust: Environmental Law for a New Ecological Era (2014).

50. Juliana v. United States, 217 F. Supp. 3d 1224 (D. Or. 2016).

51. Juliana v. United States, 947 F.3d 1159, 1171 (9th Cir. 2020).

52. *See, e.g.*, Gabriel Eckstein et al., *Conferring Legal Personality on the World's Rivers: A Brief Intellectual Assessment*, 44 Water Int'l 1 (2021).

by indigenous peoples is the ethical, and possibly the only, pathway to give voice to indigenous values.[53]

In 2014, the government of New Zealand passed legislation granting personhood to the Te Urewera (a forested area formerly designated as Te Urewera National Park),[54] and in 2017 also granted personhood to the Te Awa Tupa (Whanganui River).[55] The following focuses on the 2017 Act.

In the English and Maori, the Te Awa Tupa (Whanganui River Claims Settlement Act) states:

> Tupua te Kawa comprises the intrinsic values that represent the essence of Te Awa Tupua, namely—
>
> *Ko Te Kawa Tuatahi*
>
> (a) *Ko te Awa te mātāpuna o te ora*: the River is the source of spiritual and physical sustenance:
>
> Te Awa Tupua is a spiritual and physical entity that supports and sustains both the life and natural resources within the Whanganui River and the health and well-being of the iwi, hapū, and other communities of the River.
>
> *Ko Te Kawa Tuarua*
>
> (b) *E rere kau mai i te Awa nui mai i te Kahui Maunga ki Tangaroa*: the great River flows from the mountains to the sea:
>
> Te Awa Tupua is an indivisible and living whole from the mountains to the sea, incorporating the Whanganui River and all of its physical and metaphysical elements.
>
> *Ko Te Kawa Tuatoru*
>
> (c) *Ko au te Awa, ko te Awa ko au*: I am the River and the River is me:
>
> The iwi and hapū of the Whanganui River have an inalienable connection with, and responsibility to, Te Awa Tupua and its health and well-being.
>
> *Ko Te Kawa Tuawhā*
>
> (d) *Ngā manga iti, ngā manga nui e honohono kau ana, ka tupu hei Awa Tupua*: the small and large streams that flow into one another form one River:
>
> Te Awa Tupua is a singular entity comprised of many elements and communities, working collaboratively for the common purpose of the health and well-being of Te Awa Tupua.[56]

---

53. Self-Determination is embodied in the UN Declaration on the Rights of Indigenous People (UNDRIP), *available at*: https://social.desa.un.org/issues/indigenous-peoples/united-nations-declaration-on-the-rights-of-indigenous-peoples. *See also* Robison et al., *Indigenous Water Justice*, 22 Lewis & Clark L. Rev. 841 (2018).

54. Te Urewera Act 2014, Public Act 2014 No. 51.

55. Te Awa Tupua (Whanganui River Claims Settlement) Act 2017, Public Act 2017 No. 7.

56. *Id.* at Part 2, Subpart 2, Clause 13.

The Act established a guardian, the Te Pou Tupua, to "be the human face of Te Awa Tupua and act in the name of Te Awa Tupua."[57] The guardian has two members, one appointed by the government of New Zealand, and one appointed by the iwi (Maori with interests in the River). While some criticize the Act for not leaving guardianship exclusively to the Maori, and for not recognizing aboriginal title in the River,[58] it is currently the furthest any western government has gone in establishing guardianship for rivers and landscapes that cross indigenous jurisdictional boundaries.

You will learn as you study the approaches to settlement of Native American water rights, and administration of those rights in Parts VI, that diplomacy (via settlement) remains the primary means to reflect self-determination in the existing western legal system. Only by representing their own interests have indigenous peoples been able to fully reflect their worldview in the relation between humans and water.

---

57. *Id.* at Part 2, Subpart 3, Clause 18.

58. *See* O'Donnell et al., *Conferring Legal Personality on the World's Rivers: A Brief Intellectual Assessment*, 44 Water Int'l 1 (2021).

Chapter 4

The Constitutional Basis for Western Water Law

Introduction

Without water the original settlement of western lands by Native Americans or Europeans would not have been possible. Whether by its sustenance of the salmon fisheries of the Pacific Northwest, the grasslands of the plains that fed the bison, or the irrigated agriculture of the Pueblos of the Southwest, water was essential to indigenous survival on the land. Whether to extract and process gold, irrigate farms and water livestock, provide interior navigation, or serve growing cities, water was essential to European development of the West. Thus, it is not surprising that history has affected how water law has developed.

To understand western water law today requires a dive into history. In Chapter 2 you learned about the relation between climate and water law and the fact that arid western states chose the doctrine of prior appropriation over the eastern approach to riparian rights. You also learned that the purpose of a Native American reservation determines the quantity of its water right and that purpose is strongly influenced by climate. But the leap to understanding how states and tribes have the legal authority to define water rights raises a number of foundational legal questions. How did states acquire the authority to own, allocate, and regulate water? How do Native American water rights, though only widely recognized in the latter half of the twentieth century, date back to the Treaties signed with tribes by the federal government? How can these two very different types of water rights—one based on economic development, one based on establishment of homelands; one based on state law, one based on federal law—exist side by side on shared water courses? What, if any, is the continuing role of the federal government?

Exploring these questions in their historical context is important because it informs today's tension between states and the federal government, and states and Native American tribes over who controls water. Despite all the myths surrounding western water law, you will learn in this Chapter that both state authority to allocate water and modern recognition of Native American water rights are functions of federal law. In the last Chapter you learned that water rights are not inviolate property rights, but a use right of a resource owned by a sovereign. Thus, the states, the United States in the case of federal reservations, and the United States and Native American beneficiaries in the case of Indian reservations, own the water itself. Water users hold a mere use right. This Chapter explores the federal, constitutional source of that sovereign ownership.

Federal Law Governing State Allocation of Water for Private Use

As noted by co-author Dale Goble in his article on *Prior Appropriation and the Property Clause*, "[w]ater plays a key role in the founding myth of the West," focused on the rugged individual and the customary development of a system of order in mining camps and along water courses that rewarded hard labor and the development of land, mineral, timber, and water resources for human use."[1] But that history could never have been institutionalized without the colonization of the West through federal acquisition of territory from other European countries, followed by acquisition and taking from Native Americans. As a result, current private rights to land and water use and state authority over water begin with federal ownership.

By the middle of the nineteenth century, the federal government held the lands that now comprise the western United States as against other settler nations (Figure 4.1). Congress had yet to enact the statutes that would allow large portions of this land to pass into private ownership through homesteading and establishment of mineral locations. Much of this land was held by sovereign tribes, with treaties on land cessions yet to be negotiated. And yet westward movement was in full swing following the discovery of gold in California in 1848. While no claim to ownership of the public lands could be asserted against the federal government, custom for the resolution of disputes developed first among trespassers on federal lands over mining claims and was then extended to disputes over water in California.[2] In doing so, they developed the custom of "first in time, first in right" (i.e., the doctrine of prior appropriation). The path from this use of local custom to allocate mineral claims and water among trespassers to today's system of western water allocation runs through the development of federal policy and legislation to handle the disposition of western public lands.

State authority to allocate and regulate water finds its source in the federal authority to determine the management of public lands found in the Property Clause of the United States Constitution, stating that "The Congress shall have Power to dispose of and make all needful Rules and Regulations respecting the Territory or other Property belonging to the United States."[3]

---

1. Dale Goble, *Prior Appropriation and the Property Clause: A Dialogue of Accommodation*, 71 Or. L. Rev. 381, 382 (1992). This important article in setting out the accommodation between federal ownership of the West in the early 1800s and the customary practices among those who trespassed upon that land prior to the Homestead and Mining laws of 1866 and 1872, will be relied on heavily to explain the development of state-based water rights in the West.

2. *Id.* at 384.

3. U.S. Const., art. IV, s. 3, cl. 2.

Figure 4.1 The location and timing of territorial acquisitions by the United States. Source: National Atlas of the United States, https://en.m.wikipedia.org/wiki/File:U.S._Territorial_Acquisitions.png.

Delegation of this authority over water to the states has been interpreted by the U.S. Supreme Court to arise from three statutes providing for the disposition of public lands to private interests. As noted by co-author Dale Goble:[4]

> Responding to the need for revenue to pay the Civil War debt, Congress in 1864 began a debate on disposition of the publicly owned mineral lands. This debate led to the enactment in 1866 of the first of three statutes that Congress adopted over the next twenty years that dealt obliquely with western water rights. This first statute was the 1866 version of what has come to be known as the General Mining Law.[5] Section 9 of the Act provided,
>
> > [W]henever, by priority of possession, rights to the use of water for mining, agriculture, manufacturing, or other purposes, have vested and accrued, and the same are recognized and acknowledged by the local customs, laws, and decisions of courts, the possessors and owners of such vested rights shall be maintained and protected in the same.[6]

---

4. Dale Goble, *Prior Appropriation and the Property Clause: A Dialogue of Accommodation*, 71 Or. L. Rev. 381, 388 (1992).

5. Act of July 26, 1866, ch. 262, 14 Stat. 251 (codified as amended at 30 U.S.C. § 51 and 43 U.S.C. § 661 (1988)).

6. § 9, 14 Stat. at 253. The debate in the Congress makes no mention of the water law provisions of the Act. *See* Cong. Globe, 39th Cong., 1st Sess. 3225–37, 3451–54, 314142, 4021–22, 4048–54 (1866).

> In 1870, Congress amended the Mining Law and extended the priority water rights to all public lands affected by this act; and all patents granted, or pre-emption or homesteads allowed, shall be subject to any vested and accrued water rights, or rights to ditches and reservoirs used in connection with such water rights, as may have been acquired under or recognized by the [1866] act.[7]

> The third statute was the Desert Land Act of 1877.[8] In addition to authorizing the sale of desert lands, this act provided that all unappropriated waters of nonnavigable streams on the public domain "shall remain and be held free for the appropriation and use of the public ... subject to existing rights."[9]

In 1879, the Court held that the Act of 1866 merely recognized rights that had been encouraged by the federal government, thus even pre-1866 appropriation of water would be protected. In doing so, the Court stated:

> It is the established doctrine of this court that rights of miners, who had taken possession of mines and worked and developed them, and the rights of persons who had constructed canals and ditches to be used in mining operations and for purposes of agricultural irrigation, in the region where such artificial use of the water was an absolute necessity, are rights which the government had, by its conduct, recognized and encouraged and was bound to protect, before the passage of the act of 1866. We are of opinion that the section of the act which we have quoted was rather a voluntary *recognition of a pre-existing right of possession*, constituting a valid claim to its continued use, than the establishment of a new one.[10]

This provided clear recognition of rights to existing use under local custom and law. With respect to future water development, the United States Supreme Court would later clarify that these Acts:

> effected a severance of all waters upon the public domain, not theretofore appropriated, from the land itself. From that premise, it follows that a patent issued thereafter for lands in a desert land state or territory, under any of the land laws of the United States, carried with it, of its own force, no common-law right to the water flowing through or bordering upon the lands conveyed.... Congress intended to establish the rule that for the future the land should be patented separately; and that all nonnavigable waters thereon should be reserved for the use of the public under the laws of the states and territories named.[11]

---

7. Act of July 9, 1870, ch. 235, § 17, 16 Stat. 217, 218 (codified as amended at 30 U.S.C. § 52 and 43 U.S.C. § 661 (1988)).

8. Act of Mar. 3, 1877, ch. 107, 19 Stat. 377 (codified as amended 43 U.S.C. §§ 321–339 (1988)).

9. *Id.* § 1. The debate on the bill was extremely perfunctory and makes no mention of the water law provisions, which were added in the Conference Committee. *See* 5 Cong. Rec., 2156, 2225 (1877).

10. Broder v. Water Co., 101 U.S. 274, 276 (1879).

11. California Oregon Power Co. v. Beaver Portland Cement Co., 295 U.S. 142 (1935).

Despite the language in the Acts and cases on non-navigable waters, this "recognition of a pre-existing right of possession" and allocation under local custom or laws, extended to all waters, not just the non-navigable waters of the public lands referred to in the 1877 statute. This is clarified in the case of the *Rio Grande Dam and Irrigation Co.*[12] To understand the importance of that case, it is first necessary to understand the legal distinction between navigable and non-navigable waters under federal law.

The common law of England recognized title to navigable waters, defined as waters subject to the ebb and flow of the tide, as held by the King (i.e., the sovereign) for use as public highways. This definition would cover harbors, estuaries, and near shore areas of the ocean, but did not extend to rivers inland from their tidal influence. In 1870, the U.S. Supreme Court held that:

> The doctrine of the common law as to the navigability of waters has no application in this country. Here, the ebb and flow of the tide do not constitute the usual test, as in England, or any test at all of the navigability of waters. There, no waters are navigable in fact, or at least to any considerable extent, which are not subject to the tide, and from this circumstance tidewater and navigable water there signify substantially the same thing. But in this country, the case is widely different. Some of our rivers are as navigable for many hundreds of miles above as they are below the limits of tidewater, and some of them are navigable for great distances by large vessels which are not even affected by the tide at any point during their entire length.[13]

The Court then articulated a new test that would extend the concept of navigable waters to the major rivers of commerce in the United States:

> Those rivers must be regarded as public navigable rivers in law which are navigable in fact. And they are navigable in fact when they are used or are susceptible of being used in their ordinary condition as highways for commerce over which trade and travel are or may be conducted in the customary modes of trade and travel on water. And they constitute navigable waters of the United States within the meaning of the acts of Congress, in contradistinction from the navigable waters of the states, when they form in their ordinary condition by themselves, or by uniting with other waters, a continued highway over which commerce is or may be carried on with other states or foreign countries in the customary modes in which such commerce is conducted by water.[14]

This language ties the federal authority to maintain these navigable waterways for the public to the Commerce Clause.[15] In 1899, the Court in *United States v. Rio Grande Dam & Irrigation Co.*[16] addressed the distinction between allowing state control of appropriation of non-navigable waters from public land (not reserved for a specific

12. 174 U.S. 690 (1899).
13. The Daniel Ball, 77 U.S. 10 Wall. 557, 563 (1870).
14. *Id.* at 563.
15. U.S. Const., art. I, § 8, cl. 3.
16. 174 U.S. 690 (1899).

purpose) and limitations on that state authority with respect to navigable waters. In reference to the interpretation of the Mining and Desert Lands statutes as allowing appropriation under state law, the Court stated:

> Obviously, by these acts, so far as they extended, congress recognized and assented to the appropriation of water in contravention of the common-law rule as to continuous flow. To infer therefrom that congress intended to release its control over the navigable streams of the country, and to grant in aid of mining industries and the reclamation of arid lands the right to appropriate the waters on the sources of navigable streams to such an extent as to destroy their navigability, is to carry those statutes beyond what their full import permits. This legislation must be interpreted in the light of existing facts,—that all through this mining region in the West were streams, not navigable, whose waters could safely be appropriated for mining and agricultural industries, without serious interference with the navigability of the rivers into which those waters flow.... To hold that congress, by these acts, meant to confer upon any state the right to appropriate all the waters of the tributary streams which unite into a navigable water course, and so destroy the navigability of that water course in derogation of the interests of all the people of the United States, is a construction which cannot be tolerated.[17]

The Court went on to explain that this limitation on appropriation to prevent destruction of navigability is not confined to diversion from the navigable portion of the river but extends to diversion from non-navigable headwaters and tributaries if it would destroy downstream navigability.[18]

Thus, by the close of the nineteenth century, we have clear direction from the U.S. Supreme Court that under federal law, states may allocate water from both navigable and non-navigable waters within their borders and, in doing so, may replace the common law rule of riparian rights with a doctrine of appropriation. The first limitation being that a state may not do so in a manner that destroys the (federally defined)[19] navigability of a waterway. In 1907 the Court announced one additional limit on state authority to allocate water when that water crosses state lines.

Watercourses do not respect state boundaries or, probably more to the point, despite the admonition of John Wesley Powell to draw western state boundaries on a water basin basis because water, and specifically its limitations, would control their development,[20] society ignored basin boundaries in determining state boundaries. This set the stage for disputes among states over water. The U.S. Constitution provides that "The

---

17. United States v. Rio Grande Dam & Irr. Co., 174 U.S. 690, 706 (1899).

18. *Id.* at 708–709.

19. You will learn when we discuss stream access that is a matter of state law, that state definition of *navigable waters* often includes smaller streams than those considered navigable under federal law.

20. John Wesley Powell, *Report on the Lands of the Arid Region of the United States*, USGS Unnumbered Monograph (2d edition 1879).

judicial Power [of the Supreme Court] shall extend to all Cases ... between two or more States. ..."[21] Under this Article III authority, a state may go directly to the U.S. Supreme Court when it is harmed by the allocation of water on a shared water course by a neighboring state. We will explore the nuances of the federal common law developed to decide these disputes in Part IV, but for our purposes here, it is important that the first case heard by the Court between two states, *Kansas v. Colorado*, established the guiding principle that would limit state allocation of water on shared water courses—the doctrine of equitable apportionment.[22] As the name implies, the doctrine did not use priority or concepts of common law riparianism, but instead turned to an equitable balancing of the needs of each state, thus limiting aggressive development by upstream states to the detriment of those downstream or, conversely, the assertion of priority through the early development of downstream states.[23]

While federal authority to limit state allocation of water to the extent it adversely affects navigability has its roots in the Commerce Clause, and equitable apportionment flows from the Article III jurisdiction of the U.S. Supreme Court, we must return to the Property Clause and the Treaty Clause to understand the authority for another area of water allocation separate from the authority afforded states—Native American water rights.

Federal Law Governing Native American Waters

Native American tribes held all the land and waters of the United States at the time of European Contact (Figure 4.2). When the Euro-American settlers crossed the 100th Meridian, they entered a land containing a complex web of independent indigenous nations. The people of these nations had long been using water according to their own laws and customs. The settlers had little respect for the ways of the people native to North America. Instead, they set out to claim and develop the landscape, and to dominate or remove the people indigenous to it. In the context of water use, that dominance was systemized through the development of the prior appropriation doctrine's emphasis on *the use* of water, often resulting in degradation of the ecosystem services indigenous people relied on. Although we will learn about many positive aspects of the concept behind beneficial use of water, its application to tribal people was detrimental in at least two ways. First, non-Indian judges and policymakers were the ones to decide what types of water uses were "beneficial." In so doing, they privileged Euro-American conceptions of beneficial use—uses that required development of water for economic gain. They refused to recognize a right to water for non-consumptive instream uses that supported traditional tribal subsistence practices such as hunting, fishing, and

---

21. U.S. Const., art. III, § 2, cl. 1.
22. Kansas v. Colorado, 206 U.S. 46 (1907).
23. *Id.*

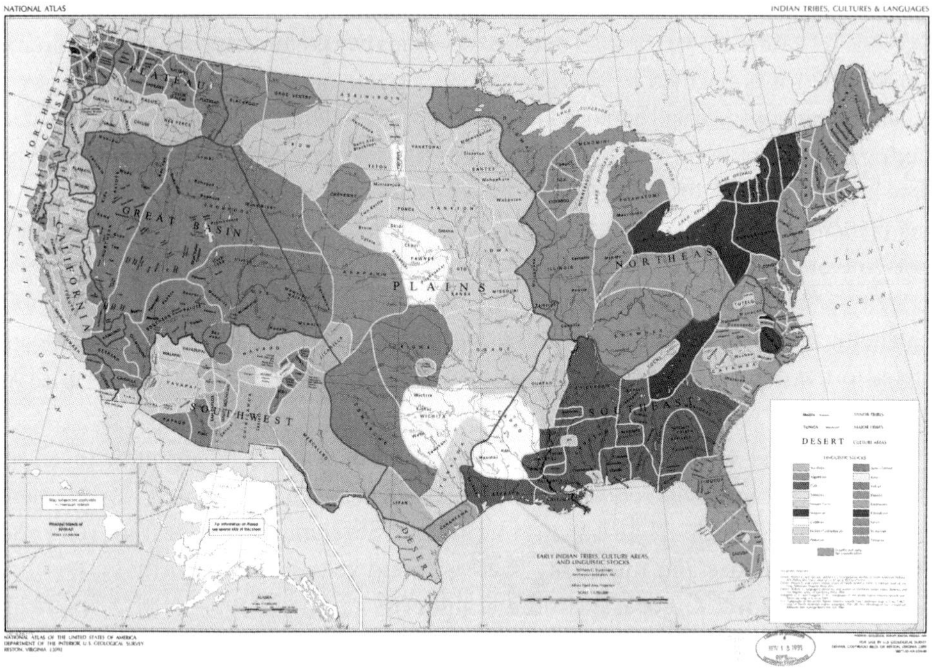

Figure 4.2 Map showing the territories of early tribes, cultural areas, and linguistic areas. William Sturtevant, *National Atlas. Indian tribes, cultures & languages [United States]* (1991). Available from the Library of Congress, https://www.loc.gov/resource/g3701e.ct003648r/.

gathering. Second, non-Indians systematically excluded Native people from lands that contained easily accessible sources of water. Without access, tribal people could not divert water and put it to beneficial use and therefore were largely excluded from acquiring water rights consistent with state law.

This exclusion began to change in the twentieth century as federal common law developed to recognize Native American water rights with legal title held by the United States, and beneficial title by certain Indian Tribes. But before we turn to the common law of what came to be called "reserved water rights," it is essential to understand the early development of law surrounding the relationship between the United States and the indigenous peoples of North America. To thoroughly understand the legal development, students should take a course in Native American Law. For our purposes, we will briefly discuss the competing theories on where in the U.S. Constitution lies the authority for federal plenary power over Tribes, including the exclusive power as against states and private parties to negotiate land (and water) cessions.

Article IX of the Articles of Confederation granted Congress the "sole and exclusive right and power of ... regulating the trade and managing all affairs with the Indians."[24] Whether the incorporation of this concept in the Commerce Clause of the U.S. Constitution stating "Congress shall have Power ... [t]o regulate Commerce with foreign

24. Articles of Confederation of 1781, art. IX, para. 4.

Nations, and among the several States, *and with the Indian Tribes ...*" (emphasis added)[25] was intended to provide for as broad a concept as "managing all affairs" as stated in the original Articles, remains an area of debate today.[26] Rather than engage in that debate, we turn to the early pronouncements by the U.S. Supreme Court on the relations among Tribes, States, and the Federal government. Three early cases (known as the Marshall Trilogy after their author—Chief Justice John Marshall) are critical to the development of a much broader understanding of federal authority stemming from federal constitutional power over war, commerce, and treaties.[27]

The first of these cases is the 1823 case of *Johnson v. M'Intosh*,[28] in which Justice Marshall found the United States (as opposed to private citizens) to have the exclusive power to enter land transactions with Indian tribes. The second is the 1831 case of *Cherokee Nation v. Georgia*,[29] which set the stage for the interpretation that Indian tribes did not have status as international actors and that the federal government had plenary power over them in dicta, stating: [Indian tribes] may, more correctly, perhaps, be denominated domestic dependent nations.... Their relation to the United States resembles that of a ward to his guardian."[30] The third is the 1832 case of *Worcester v. Georgia*,[31] finding that despite the concept of diminished power articulated in *Cherokee Nation v. Georgia*, Tribes retained sovereignty vis-à-vis states and that state laws do not apply within Indian reservations.[32] In doing so, Justice Marshall discusses the source of federal power over Indian tribes, stating in reference to the language quoted above from Article IX of the Articles of Confederation:

> The correct exposition of this article is rendered unnecessary by the adoption of our existing constitution," he wrote. "That instrument confers on congress the powers of war and peace; of making treaties, and of regulating commerce with foreign nations, and among the several states, and with the Indian tribes. These powers comprehend all that is required for the regulation of our intercourse with the Indians.[33]

Through war, disease, and decimation of food sources, the indigenous geography has been reduced from that shown in Figure 4.2 to that shown in Figure 4.3. These land cessions negotiated by the federal government with the Indigenous peoples of North America are memorialized in Treaties, Acts of Congress, and Executive Orders.

25. U.S. CONST., art. I, § 8, cl. 3.

26. Gregory Ablavsky, *Beyond the Indian Commerce Clause*, 124 YALE L. J. 882 (2014).

27. *Id.*

28. *Johnson v. M'Intosh*, 21 U.S. 543 (1823).

29. *Cherokee Nation v. Georgia*, 30 U.S. 1 (1831).

30. *Id.* at 13.

31. *Worcester v. Georgia*, 31 U.S. 515 (1832).

32. The Roberts Court has begun to chip away at this almost 200-year-old foundational principle for federal/tribal relations in the recent ruling in *Oklahoma v. Castro-Huerta*, 597 U.S. 629 (2022) (granting states the power to prosecute crimes against a non-Indian in Indian country).

33. Worcester v. Georgia, 31 U.S. 515, 559 (1832); *see also* Gregory Ablavsky, *Beyond the Indian Commerce Clause*, 124 YALE L. J. 882 (2014).

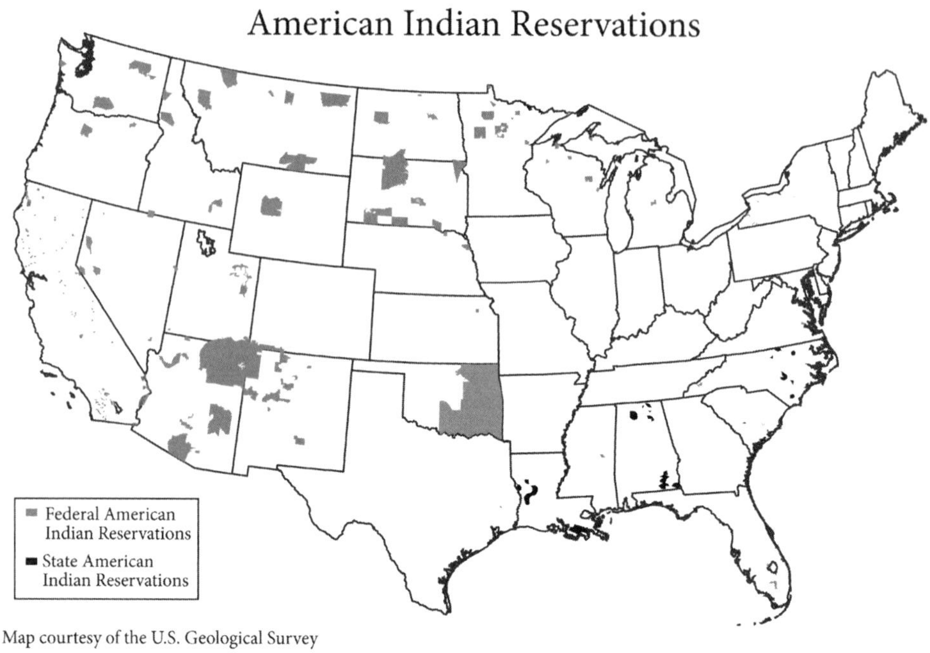

Figure 4.3 Current location of American Indian Reservations and Tribal Jurisdictions in the contiguous United States. Source: USGS.

These agreements, entered into by the United States following negotiation with Native American Tribes, are silent on the status of water associated with Treaty rights. In 1908, the United States Supreme Court, in the landmark case of *Winters v. United States*[34] (a case you will study in Part III), held that a Treaty right that could not be fulfilled without water carried with it an implied reservation of water. The Court very clearly grounded its ruling in the tenets of treaty interpretation, but also referenced the authority of the federal government to reserve water. This twofold basis is important because you will learn in Part IV that so-called "reserved water rights" also extend to federal lands withdrawn from the public lands and reserved for a specific purpose (e.g., military facility or national park). Both types of reserved rights represent water rights not governed by state ownership and jurisdiction to allocate water. Federal reserved rights, however, arise from the authority of the federal government over public lands found in the Property Clause, and will primarily be covered in Part IV, The Federal Role in Western Water. In contrast, while Congress and the Executive must still have the authority stemming from the Property Clause to reach agreements to acquire or reserve western lands with Native American tribes, they are not the only sovereign involved. Native American reserved rights have their source in negotiated agreements with Indian tribes and, as a result, their scope, purpose, and quantification are governed by rules pertaining to the interpretation of treaties. From Cohen's *Handbook of Federal Indian Law*:

34. Winters v. United States, 207 U.S. 564 (1908).

> The Supreme Court has stated: "[T]he standard principles of statutory interpretation do not have their usual force in cases involving Indian law." The basic Indian law canons of construction require that treaties, agreements, statutes, and executive orders be liberally construed in favor of the Indians and that all ambiguities are to be resolved in their favor. In addition, treaties and agreements are to be construed as the Indians would have understood them, and tribal property rights and sovereignty are preserved unless Congress's intent to the contrary is clear and unambiguous.[35]

You will read cases such as *United States v. Winans* (Part III) that call on the "canon of construction" that treaties must be interpreted as the tribe(s) would have understood them. While characterized as a requirement of the special relation between the federal government and Indian tribes, this canon also has roots in international law that requires ambiguity in the language of a treaty memorialized in a language that is not the primary language of one of the parties to be interpreted in favor of that party. The Court in *Winters,* the landmark U.S. Supreme Court case recognizing Native American reserved water rights, makes the implementation of this canon abundantly clear and implies that to hold otherwise would represent such overreaching as to invalidate the very treaties that western development was dependent on when it states:

> The case, as we view it, turns on the agreement of May, 1888, [the Fort Belknap Treaty] resulting in the creation of Fort Belknap Reservation. In the construction of this agreement there are certain elements to be considered that are prominent and significant. The reservation was a part of a very much larger tract which the Indians had the right to occupy and use, and which was adequate for the habits and wants of a nomadic and uncivilized people. It was the policy of the Government, it was the desire of the Indians, to change those habits and to become a pastoral and civilized people. If they should become such, the original tract was too extensive; but a smaller tract would be inadequate without a change of conditions. The lands were arid, and, without irrigation, were practically valueless. And yet, it is contended, the means of irrigation were deliberately given up by the Indians and deliberately accepted by the Government. The lands ceded were, it is true, also arid; and some argument may be urged, and is urged, that with their cession there was the cession of the waters, without which they would be valueless, and "civilized communities could not be established thereon." And this, it is further contended, the Indians knew, and yet made no reservation of the waters. We realize that there is a conflict of implications, but that which makes for the retention of the waters is of greater force than that which makes for their cession. The Indians had command of the lands and the waters—command of all their beneficial use, whether kept for hunting, "and grazing roving herds of stock," or turned to agriculture and the arts of civilization. Did they give up

35. Newton et al., Cohen's Handbook of Federal Indian Law § 2.02 (2012) (internal citations omitted).

> all this? Did they reduce the area of their occupation and give up the waters which made it valuable or adequate? And, even regarding the allegation of the answer as true, that there are springs and streams on the reservation flowing about 2,900 inches of water, the inquiries are pertinent. *If it were possible to believe affirmative answers, we might also believe that the Indians were awed by the power of the Government or deceived by its negotiators.* Neither view is possible [emphasis added].[36]

The Supremacy Clause of the U.S. Constitution renders the Treaties (including those negotiated with Indian tribes) as well as the laws (including congressional acts establishing reservations) and Executive Acts (including Executive Orders establishing reservations) part of the Supreme Law of the Land;[37] thus, the Indian reserved water right expressed or implied in a treaty, congressional act, or executive order is defined by federal law. Indian reserved water rights should be thought of not as a limitation or exception to state ownership and control of water, but a separate and coequal source of authority for allocation of water to which state jurisdiction does not apply.

---

36. *Winters* at 575–576.

37. U.S. Const. Art. VI, cl. 2 provides: "This Constitution, and the Laws of the United States which shall be made in Pursuance thereof; and *all Treaties* made, or which shall be made, under the Authority of the United States, shall be the supreme Law of the Land; and the Judges in every State shall be bound thereby, any Thing in the Constitution or Laws of any State to the Contrary notwithstanding" (emphasis added).

Part II

The Common Law Development of the Water Law of Western States

Part II focuses on the source of law for allocation of water by western states with its beginnings in common law. To introduce the chapters in Part II, it is essential to first explore the question: what is the common law?

Common law is judicial law developed incrementally as individual cases come before the courts. While customary law specific to a locale was recognized long before, the concept of common law courts and a recording of the law to be applied across England followed the Norman Conquest in 1066. The concept was to have law that applied uniformly across courts in a specific jurisdiction and that was developed through reliance on precedent.[1] Common law is thought to further the goal of certainty and equity by having similarly situated people treated the same. In its case-by-case development, the common law had some degree of flexibility and could evolve as times and circumstances changed. At the same time, following precedent provided a degree of stability and predictability to the law. In general, U.S. states adopted the body of common law developed in England upon joining the union,[2] then began their own incremental adjustment case-by-case.

The common law of England recognized riparian rights as the right of those owning land along a water course to the natural flow undiminished by other riparian owners. Any shortage was shared. Following adoption in the eastern United States, the courts modified the common law rule of riparian rights to allow reasonable use, but retained the concept of shared shortage. For an excellent discussion of the evolution of riparian

1. Black's Law Dictionary. For a history of the development of the common law, *see* John H. Langbein et al., History of the Common Law: The Development of Anglo-American Legal Institutions (2009).

2. Dale Goble, *Prior Appropriation and the Property Clause: A Dialogue of Accommodation*, 71 Or. L. Rev. 381, 384 (1992).

rights in the United States to modern regulated riparianism, see Joseph W. Dellapenna, *Global Climate Disruption and Water Law Reform*, 15 WIDENER L. REV. 409 (2010). Except for noting the initial adoption of riparian rights in the Columbia Basin states of Washington and Oregon, this casebook will focus on the adoption of prior appropriation in the West. This history is important to understanding western water law for four reasons.

First, as gold miners and settlers moved west it became apparent that mineral deposits and arable land (land with soil quality sufficient for crops) were not necessarily located along water courses.[3] Thus, as different customs developed in which water was transported by ditch over long distances, the courts would need to decide whether the law would protect this new type of use and, if so, under what authority they could deviate from the existing common law.

Second, once federal courts held (as discussed in Part I) that states could deviate from the common law of England and that federal law provided that authority, western states began the process of developing their own common law of prior appropriation with variations by state. Thus, to understand the doctrine of prior appropriation, it is necessary to examine its case-by-case development for the state you practice in. This text provides a roadmap for how to do that from a system perspective by highlighting the issues and how their resolution relates to other aspects of the system; it does not provide you with what the law actually is in each state.

Third, while the development of water law by the courts was supplemented by legislation in the early twentieth century in some cases, early statutory schemes were generally procedural, providing a means for notice of water development, recording, and in some states, an administrative system for resolution of disputes (with appeal to the judiciary). Comprehensive water use acts (discussed in Part V) that altered the common law were not widespread until after the middle of the twentieth century in most states. Nevertheless, the common law still applies to the meaning of terms, gap filling, and understanding intent in statutory schemes. Without clear indications of when the legislature intended to do so, these comprehensive statutory schemes both incorporated and altered the common law. Recognizing when and how they did so requires first understanding the common law. This casebook is organized to help you understand the common law backdrop (Part II) before moving to the modern administrative and statutory systems for state water allocation and management (Part V). The separation between Part II (state common law) and Part V (state statutory law) reflects the historical fact that the law pertaining to Native American water rights (Part III), and the law pertaining to the continuing role of the federal government in western water law (Part IV) developed before states developed comprehensive administrative systems.

Finally, the common law also provides fundamental principles that you may find yourself coming back to when facing a new problem that lacks precedent. The case

3. JOHN WESLEY POWELL, A REPORT ON THE LANDS OF THE ARID REGION OF THE UNITED STATES, WITH A MORE DETAILED ACCOUNT OF THE LANDS OF UTAH (1876).

study on conjunctive management covered in Part VI illustrates how lawyers draw analogies from the common law to suggest legal rules in situations of first impression for the judiciary.

Part II focuses on the common law basis of state-based water allocation and, in particular, the western doctrine of prior appropriation. This Part relies heavily on cases from Idaho to help you understand how a specific state's policies may affect multiple issues that arise in the allocation of water. This is critical to this casebook's systems approach. While historically it has been important in law to memorize the minority and majority approaches to an issue, as water scarcity increases, it will be more important for the practitioner to understand the relation between the issue and the human and physical system it arises in. This requires a systems approach to learning water law.

Chapter 5 will cover the initial efforts of western state courts to determine what approach, riparian rights or prior appropriation, will apply to water allocation. Chapters 6 through 8 will cover the common law attributes of a water right acquired by appropriation. Chapter 6 covers the act of diverting water, its relation to priority, and the varying approach of states to whether it is required diversion or whether instream flow rights are possible at common law. Chapter 7 covers beneficial use and its role in determining the amount of water associated with a water right by prohibiting waste and how that evolves through time. Chapter 8 covers the concept of "use it or lose it" that provides for abandonment or forfeiture of all or a portion of a water right due to non-use. Part II concludes with Chapter 9 addressing the common law of groundwater and the varying approaches of western states to its allocation and the problems that arose as the technology to pump large quantities of groundwater became available. This chapter will go beyond the Columbia River Basin states to illustrate the full range of doctrines across the West, because the types of issues that arise are often different when a different doctrine of allocation is used.

Chapter 5

The Common Law Beginnings of State-Based Western Water Law

Introduction

On statehood, states generally followed the practice of eastern states and adopted the common law of England as a general body of law.[1] While we saw in Part I that the U.S. Supreme Court ultimately clarified the principle that states may change provisions of the common law concerning water right allocation, this clarification was not available when early disputes began to arise. Thus, states and territories in the West faced the need to decide in their own courts whether to recognize the common law doctrine of riparian rights as part of their general adoption of English common law, or to sanction the new customary approach, which came to be known as prior appropriation and was developed first in the mining camps of California.

This Chapter addresses the early steps of state courts to identify the appropriate doctrine for allocation of water in the West including the initial development of prior appropriation in California and Colorado. By the time this issue reached the state supreme courts in the Pacific Northwest, California and Colorado had recognized the doctrine of prior appropriation. California also allowed for riparian rights.

Riparian Rights

You will first learn about those states in the Columbia River basin that initially allowed both riparian and appropriative rights. As noted in the discussion of the relation between climate and water law in Part I, it is no accident that the two states (Washington and Oregon) adopting a combination of riparian and appropriative rights (alongside a third, California) have western coastal portions in which rain and water sources are abundant. This Chapter begins with greater treatment of riparian law than covered in other casebooks on western water law, due to this climatic complexity of the Pacific Northwest and its impact on the law. This is part of the systems approach. You must learn to follow the history of water law in the state you practice in to understand how courts today address the complexities of history and climate, all operating on the same connected, multi-jurisdictional watercourse.

---

1. Dale Goble, *Prior Appropriation and the Property Clause: A Dialogue of Accommodation*, 71 Or. L. Rev. 381, 384 (1992).

Washington courts initially recognized riparian rights, reasoning that riparian rights are incidents of land ownership, and at least with respect to riparian land already acquired, cannot be taken by an act of the government without compensation. You will first read the case of *Crook v Hewitt* (1892),[2] in which the Washington Supreme Court attempted to adopt the common law of riparian rights as the sole doctrine applicable in the state. Notice that the sources cited are British. This case is also chosen because it articulates the American modification to the English rule of riparian rights that called for maintenance of the natural flow of the water source. The American modification allows reasonable use of the water. What is reasonable is a question of fact.

Crook v. Hewitt

Supreme Court of Washington
31 P. 28 (Sept. 17, 1892)

Opinion

DUNBAR, J. [Defendants/respondents Hewitt et al. are developing a project that will divert water away from land riparian to Wood's Creek along which Plaintiff/appellant Crook owns land. The diverted water would be piped to a nearby town. Unused (also referred to as "wastewater") would be returned to a different stream. When return flow is delivered to a different watershed, the diversion is entirely consumptive from the viewpoint of the water source.]

In this case, after the testimony of the appellant [Crook] was in, the respondents [Hewitt et al.] moved to dismiss the action on the two following grounds: (1) "That no interest whatever to this plaintiff in and to the stream known as 'Wood's Creek' has been shown in the testimony now before the court." (2) "That no evidence has been introduced before this court showing that the Everett Land Company or Henry Hewitt is intending to, or about to, divert a sufficient quantity of water from that stream to in any way prevent this plaintiff from having sufficient water to irrigate that land." The motion was sustained, and the cause dismissed. We have examined all the authorities presented by both appellant and respondents, and it seems to us that the law is uniformly settled that every proprietor of lands on the bank of a river has naturally an equal right to the use of the water which flows in the stream adjacent to his lands, as it was wont to run, without diminution or alteration. No proprietor has a right to use the water to the prejudice of other proprietors above or below him, unless he has a prior right to divert it, or a title to some exclusive enjoyment. He has no property in the water itself, but a simple usufruct while it passes along. *Aqua currit et debit currere ut currere solebat*[3] is the language of the law. Though he may use the water while it runs over his land, he cannot unreasonably detain it, or give it another direction, and he must return it to its ordinary channel when it leaves his estate. This is the law as pronounced by

2. 31 P. 28 (Wash. 1892).

3. [The phrase means: "water runs and ought to run as it was accustomed to run." Fellmeth AX and Horwitz, Guide to Latin in International Law (2021)].

Chancellor Kent, in 3 Kent, Comm. . . . , and, without particularizing, it is substantially the law as announced by all the text writers and courts. All the modification of the rule that there has been is to allow a reasonable use; because, as is said by many of the courts, to hold that there can be no diminution whatever of the water would be to deny any valuable use of it, and, therefore, the injury that is incidental to a reasonable enjoyment of a common right can demand no redress. Indeed, this can scarcely be called a modification of the text, but rather a construction which has always been recognized; and the reasonableness of the use is a question of fact, to be passed upon by the court or jury. But it must be borne in mind that this liberal condition attaches only to the use of the water as an incident to the land, and not to the diversion of the water from the land. A riparian proprietor may divert the water from the stream, as it passes through his own land, without license from the proprietors above him if he does not obstruct the water from flowing as freely as it was wont, and without license from the lower proprietors if he restores the water to its natural channel before it enters their land, and does not materially diminish its flow. The distinction is to be observed between the right to divert or change the course of the stream itself so as to turn it away from a lower proprietor, and the right to take water from the stream. The first is wholly unlawful; the second may be exercised to a reasonable extent.

. . .

The case must be reversed, with instructions to overrule the motion to dismiss. . . .

Notes & Questions

1. What evidence would be required to support the reasonableness of the water use of the riparian? Choose as many options as you want.
    a. Type and amount of use made by the riparian water user?
    b. Flow rate of the water source?
    c. Economic value of the use made by the riparian water user?
    d. Population and other water needs downstream of the riparian water user?
2. Washington and Oregon recognized both appropriative and riparian rights in their early common law. In a case between a riparian water user and an appropriator, what principles might guide the court in determining who prevails? This is the subject of the next case.

By 1897, a case in the more arid Yakima basin of Washington pitted riparian landowners against those seeking to divert water away from riparian land as allowed by the Mining and Desert Lands statutes. This forced the court in *Benton v. Johncox* to consider the relative rights of riparian landowners versus appropriators. This case also illustrates how common law adapts as new facts present problems to the court—in this case the problem of water allocation for very arid lands of eastern Washington that had been acquired under the federal public land laws. By the time of *Benton v. Johncox* these public land laws had been interpreted to allow for prior appropriation as discussed in Part I.

In *Benton v. Johncox*,[4] the court used the same concept later applied to reserved water rights, that the riparian right arises on acquisition of a patent to riparian land, regardless of use. If this acquisition occurs prior to the appropriation of water, even though not developed, the riparian owner is entitled to the continued flow of the river.

Benton v. Johncox

Supreme Court of Washington
49 P. 495 (1897)

Opinion

ANDERS, J. [Benton and other riparian water users seek to restrain Johncox and others who have diverted water to land away from the Ahtanum River in Yakima County, Washington. Johncox and the other appropriators allege that the land is arid and cannot produce crops without irrigation. The lower court held that while Washington allows appropriation of water, the rights of riparian water users who occupied the riparian land prior to the appropriation prevail.]

But it is most earnestly insisted by the learned counsel for appellants that the common-law doctrine touching riparian rights is not applicable to the arid portions of the state, and especially to Yakima county.... The legislature of the territory of Washington in the year 1863 enacted that "the common law of England, so far as it is not repugnant to, or inconsistent with, the constitution and laws of the United States and the organic act and laws of Washington territory, shall be the rule of decision in all the courts of this territory." ... Now, the common-law doctrine declaratory of riparian rights, as now generally understood by the courts, is not, in our judgment, inconsistent with the constitution or laws of the United States or of this state....

"By the common law," says the court in *Lux v. Haggin*, "the right of the riparian proprietor to the flow of the stream is inseparably annexed to the soil, and passes with it, not as an easement or appurtenance, but as part and parcel of it. Use does not create the right, and disuse cannot destroy or suspend it. The right in each extends to the natural and usual flow of all the water, unless where the quantity has been diminished as a consequence of the reasonable application of it by other riparian owners for purposes hereafter to be mentioned." And one of the purposes thereafter mentioned was irrigation....

While the doctrine announced by the foregoing authorities has never, so far as we are advised, been directly denied, it has been apparently ignored by the courts in some of the Pacific states and territories, on the theory that the principles and rules of the common law respecting the rights of private riparian owners were inapplicable to the condition and necessities of the people of the particular localities where the causes of action arose. But how it can be held that that which is an inseparable incident to the ownership of land in the Atlantic states and the Mississippi valley is not such an incident in this or any other of the Pacific states, we are unable clearly to comprehend.

4. 49 P. 495 (1897).

It certainly cannot be true that a difference in climatic conditions or geographical position can operate to deprive one of a right of property vested in him by a well-settled rule of common law....

...

... in the later case of *Sturr v. Beck*, the question as to the rights of the riparian proprietor as against an appropriator of the water did arise, and was determined by the court.... The learned chief justice, in delivering the opinion of the court, after referring to the act of congress of July 26, 1866 and the amendatory act of 1870, ..., said: "When, however, the government ceases to be the sole proprietor, the right of the riparian owner attaches, and cannot be subsequently invaded. As the riparian owner has the right to have the water flow *ut currere solebat*, undiminished except by reasonable consumption of upper proprietors, and no subsequent attempt to take the water only can override the prior appropriation of both land and water, it would seem reasonable that lawful riparian occupancy with intent to appropriate the land should have the same effect." ... While the court fully recognized the doctrine of prior appropriation of water on the public lands, in accordance with the local customs, laws, and decisions of courts, it announced and established the just and equitable rule that the riparian rights of a patentee of the government attach, by relation, at the very inception of his title, and will be protected as against subsequent appropriation of the water naturally flowing over the land. That case, it would seem, settles the law adversely to the contention of the appellants in this case....

The trial court in this case followed the rule laid down in the case of *Sturr v. Beck*, and other cases above referred to, and in so doing, we think, committed no error.

... A careful consideration of all the questions raised on this appeal discloses no error, and the judgment is therefore affirmed.

Notes & Questions

1. Similar to the *Crook* case, evidence presented in this case would need to address the reasonableness of water use of Benton and the other riparians. Which of the following is an additional issue of fact given the rule articulated in this case?
    a. The dates on which the riparian and appropriative users began using water.
    b. The dates on which the riparian landowners and appropriative water users acquired land.
    c. The dates on which the riparian landowners acquired riparian land, and the dates on which the appropriative water users began using water.
    d. The feasibility of sharing shortage among riparian and appropriative water users.
2. While this recognition of both riparian and prior appropriation rights complicates enforcement of water rights, it can be considered a natural outcome of climate. The Cascade Mountains divide the state into a relatively wet western portion and a relatively arid east. The appropriateness of both doctrines follows.

3. In 1910, the Washington Supreme Court made it clear that *Benton* is limited to situations in which the party asserting the riparian land acquired the land prior to any appropriation on the shared water course.[5] In 1917, the Washington legislature adopted the doctrine of prior appropriation as the sole means of obtaining new water rights.

Oregon initially recognized riparian rights. The case we have chosen to illustrate Oregon's version of riparian water rights, *Jones v. Conn*,[6] begins with a thorough explanation of the doctrine of riparian rights in Oregon. The case is also useful for the issue it addresses—whether a riparian owner who acquires additional non-riparian land adjacent to its original riparian lands may extend irrigation to those lands. Oregon chooses the rule that allows extension of the riparian right to other contiguous land once it is owned by the riparian owner. This approach encourages further development of land. An alternative approach taken in some riparian states is to limit riparian use to the original riparian land. This approach limits riparian water use and is appropriate in areas in which, although not arid, water scarcity is possible.

Jones v. Conn

Supreme Court of Oregon
64 P. 855 (1901)

Opinion

BEAN, C.J. (after stating the facts).... This is a controversy between riparian proprietors upon a natural water course....

[Jones has shown no damage from Conn's use of water, thus the issue before the court is whether Conn is using the water on riparian land. The court begins with a thorough explanation of the doctrine of riparian rights in Oregon.]

It is common learning that every person through whose premises a stream of water flows has a right to its use and enjoyment as it passes through his land; but, as all other proprietors have a similar right, it necessarily follows that one cannot use or divert the water to the injury of another. The right of each must be exercised in subordination to that of all the others. Within these limits, each proprietor is entitled to such use of the stream as may be conformable to the usages and wants of the community. It is often said that a riparian proprietor has a right, inseparably annexed to the soil, to have the water of a stream flow down to his land as it is wont to run, undiminished in quantity and unimpaired in quality; and that, if an upper proprietor takes it from the stream, he must return substantially the same quantity again before it leaves his premises. This rule, however, is subject to the limitation now well established that each proprietor is entitled to a reasonable use of the water for domestic, agricultural, and manufacturing purposes, and such use is not to be denied him on account of the loss necessarily consequent upon its proper enjoyment. In short, he has a right, in the language of

5. Avery et al. v. Johnson et ux., 109 P. 1028 (Wash. 1910).
6. 64 P. 855, 54 (Or. 1901).

Vice Chancellor Bacon in Earl of Sandwich v. Railway Co., 10 Ch.Div. 707, 712, "to make all the use he can—to derive every benefit he can—from the stream, provided he does not abstract so much as prevents other people from having equal enjoyment with himself"; or, as said by Lord Kingsdown in *Miner v. Gilmour,* 12 Moore P.C. 131, 156: "By the general law applicable to running streams, every riparian proprietor has a right to what may be called the ordinary use of the water flowing past his land; for instance, to the reasonable use of the water for his domestic purposes and for his cattle, and this without regard to the effect which such use may have, in case of a deficiency, upon proprietors lower down the stream. But, further, he has a right to the use of it for any purpose, or what may be deemed the extraordinary use of it, provided that he does not thereby interfere with the rights of other proprietors, either above or below him. Subject to this condition, he may dam up the stream for the purpose of a mill, or divert the water for the purpose of irrigation. But he has no right to interrupt the regular flow of the stream, if he thereby interferes with the lawful use of the water by other proprietors, and inflicts upon them a sensible injury." The right of a riparian proprietor to the use of the water of a stream flowing through his premises, and its limitations, are well expressed in a Maryland case, where the court say: "The right of every riparian owner to the enjoyment of a stream of running water in its natural state in flow, quantity, and quality is too well established to require the citation of authorities. It is a right incident and appurtenant to the ownership of the land itself, and, being a common right, it follows that every proprietor is bound so to use the common right as not to interfere with an equally beneficial enjoyment of it by others. This is the necessary result of the equality of right among all the proprietors of that which is common to all. As such owner, he has the right to insist that the stream shall continue to run *uti currere solebat*; that it shall continue to flow through his land in its usual quantity, at its natural place, and at its usual height. Without a grant, either express or implied, no proprietor has the right to obstruct, diminish, or accelerate the impelling force of a stream of running water. Of course, we are not to be understood as meaning there can be no diminution or increase of the flow whatever, for that would be to deny any valuable use of it. There may be, and there must be allowed to all of that which is common, a reasonable use; and such a use, although it may, to some extent, diminish the quantity, or affect, in a measure, the flow, of the stream, is perfectly consistent with the common right. The limits which separate the lawful from the unlawful use of a stream it may be difficult to define. It is, in fact, impossible to lay down a precise rule to cover all cases, and the question must be determined in each case, taking into consideration the size of the stream, the velocity of the current, the nature of the banks, the character of the soil and a variety of other facts. It is entirely a question of degree, the true test being whether the use is of such a character as to affect materially the equally beneficial use of the stream by others." It is accordingly now quite generally held in this country and in England that, after the natural wants of all the riparian proprietors have been supplied, each proprietor is entitled to a reasonable use of the water for irrigating purposes. The doctrine, as applied to the arid regions of the West, is thus stated by Mr. Justice McFarland in *Harris v. Harrison*: "According to the common-law doctrine of riparian ownership as generally declared in England and in most of the American states, upon the facts in the case at bar the plaintiffs would be entitled to have the waters of Harrison cañon continue to flow to and upon their land as they were naturally accustomed to flow, without any substantial deterioration in quality or diminution in quantity. But in some of the western and southwestern states and territories, where the year is divided into one wet and one dry season, and irrigation is necessary to successful cultivation of the soil, the doctrine of riparian ownership has by judicial decision been modified, or, rather, enlarged, so as to include the reasonable use of natural water for irrigating the riparian land, although such use may appreciably diminish the flow down to the lower riparian proprietor. *** Of course, there will be great difficulty in many cases to determine what is such reasonable use; and 'what is such reasonable use is a question of fact, and depends upon the circumstances appearing in each particular case.' *** The larger the number of riparian proprietors whose rights are involved, the greater will be the difficulty of adjustment. In such a case the length of the stream, the volume of water in it, the extent of each ownership along the banks, the character of the soil owned by each contestant, the area sought to be irrigated by each,—all these and many other considerations must enter into the solution of the problem; but one principle is surely established, namely, that no proprietor can absorb all the water of the stream so as to allow none to flow down to his neighbor." For the protection of the rights of the several riparian proprietors it has even been held that a court of equity may in a proper case apportion the flow of the stream, after the natural wants of the several proprietors have been satisfied, in such a manner as may seem equitable and just under the circumstances....

The plaintiffs admit the rule that, after the natural wants of all the riparian proprietors have been supplied, each is entitled to a reasonable use of the water for irrigating purposes, but insist that the exercise of the right must be limited to the tract of land through which the stream flows as first segregated and sold by the government of the United States, and that, even in such a case, where there are natural barriers within the tract which would prevent a portion of the land from deriving any benefit from the flow of the stream, the portion lying beyond the barrier should be excluded. But, as we understand the law, lands bordering on a stream are riparian, without regard to their extent. After a considerable search, we are unable to find any rule determining when part of an entire tract owned by one person ceases to be riparian. The discussions in the books are restricted to a definition of riparian proprietors and their respective rights. A riparian proprietor is one whose land is bounded by a natural stream, or through whose land it flows, and riparian rights are those which he has to the use of the water of the stream. They are derived entirely from the ownership of the land, and not from its area or the source of its title ... Mr. Long, in his recent work on Irrigation, in discussing this question, says: "Some questions have been raised as to what lands are to be considered riparian, within the sense of the preceding section. Literally, of course, riparian lands are lands bordering upon a stream, but it is sometimes a question as to how far back from the stream the land may be considered riparian. There is very little judicial authority on the question. It is plainly not possible to define the distance to which the riparian proprietor's right to use the water for irrigation or other purposes extends, but this will depend upon the circumstances of each case. The only general rule that can be laid down is that the distance and use should be reasonable." It would seem, therefore, that any person owning land which abuts upon or through which a natural stream of water flows is a riparian proprietor, entitled to the rights of such, without regard to the extent of his land, or from whom or when he acquired his title. The fact that he may have procured the particular tract washed by the stream at one time, and subsequently purchased land adjoining it, will not make him any the less a riparian proprietor, nor should it alone be a valid objection to his using the water on the land last acquired. The only thing necessary to entitle him to the right of a riparian proprietor is to show that the body of land owned by him borders upon a stream. This being established, the law gives to him certain rights in the water, the extent of which is limited and controlled less by the area of his land than by the volume of water and the effect of its use upon the rights of other riparian proprietors. By virtue of the ownership of land in proximity to the stream, he is entitled to a reasonable use of the water, which is defined as "any use that does not work actual, material, and substantial damage to the common right which each proprietor has, as limited and qualified by the precisely equal right of every other proprietor." In the determination of what will be considered such a use in a particular case, the character and extent of the land, its location, and the time of acquiring the title may all become, and are, no doubt, important factors to be considered; but they are not controlling, and each case must depend entirely upon its own facts and circumstances. The case of *Boehmer v. Irrigation Dist.* would seem to make the extent of riparian rights depend upon the source of title, rather than the fact of title; but in *Water Co. v. Hancock*, 85 Cal. 219, 24 Pac. 645, it was expressly held that all land bordering upon a stream which is held by the same title—in that instance consisting of 1,280 acres—is riparian, and no distinction was made on account of the source of title. Again, in *Wiggins v. Water Co.*, supra, and *Bathgate v. Irvine*, the right of a riparian proprietor to use the waters of a stream for irrigation was limited to the water shed. But, as we understand these cases, the court in each instance was determining the rights of the parties then before it, and not attempting to lay down an inflexible rule as a guide in all cases. Nothing more was held or decided than that under the claim alone of riparian rights the owner of land cannot, to the injury of another riparian proprietor, take the water beyond the water shed, or onto lands held by a title different from the title of those through which the stream flows; and this all will concede. The right to make a reasonable use of the water of a stream is a right of property, depending on the ownership of the land abutting on or through which the stream flows; and whether a given use is reasonable or not is a question of fact, to be determined under the circumstances of each particular case. The right to use the water belongs to the owner of the land, and the extent of its exercise is not to be determined by the area or contour of his land, but by its effect upon other riparian proprietors.

...

It is apparent, therefore, that the rule, so often stated and reiterated in the books, that a riparian proprietor is entitled to have the entire flow of the stream come down to his premises, is subject to the important limitation that an upper riparian proprietor may make such a use thereof as does not work any actual, material, and substantial damage to the common right which each proprietor has; and, whether a proposed use is of the character referred to, and therefore reasonable, does not depend so much upon the area of the land of the offending proprietor, or the place of the use, as upon the effect it has upon the correlative rights of the other proprietors. Under this doctrine the defendant was not a wrongdoer when he used the waters of the stream for the purpose of irrigation, nor does the fact that his land lies above the level thereof, so that it cannot be irrigated by means of ditches wholly on his own premises, affect his right to the use of the water, although it might have a material bearing upon the reasonableness of the use, if that question was here for decision. But there is no reason shown by this record why the defendant should be confined in the use of the water to any particular portion of his land. The amount of water taken and used by him before the trial was not sufficient to materially injure the plaintiffs, or to interfere in any substantial way with their rights as riparian proprietors.... The plaintiffs, therefore, were not entitled to an injunction restraining the defendant from using the waters of the stream for the purpose of irrigation, because such use was no injury to them....

It is suggested that the court ought to ascertain and determine the rights of the respective parties, and fix them in the decree, so that hereafter there may be no controversy concerning the matter. In the very nature of things, however, it is impossible in a case of this character to make such a decree. The rights of the several riparian proprietors are equal, each being entitled to but a reasonable use of the water for irrigating purposes, and what constitutes such use must necessarily depend upon the season, the volume of water in the stream, the area and character of the land which each riparian proprietor proposes to irrigate, and many other circumstances; so that it seems to us there is no basis upon which the court could frame any other decree than one enjoining and restraining the defendant from diverting the water from the stream to the substantial injury of the present or future rights of the plaintiffs, and, as the decree of the court below is to that effect, it will be affirmed.

Notes & Questions

1. The court in *Jones* rejects the notion that there is a bright-line rule for determining the quantity of a riparian right and specifically details the factual evidence that will be relevant to determine the reasonableness of the riparian use for irrigation. It includes (choose all that apply):
    a. Evidence showing the economic value of the use for irrigation;
    b. Evidence that may vary over time, including: season, flow of the stream;
    c. Evidence that may vary among riparians including: nature of the land and soil;
    d. Evidence of use in relation to that of other riparians, including: material injury to the other riparian.
2. What problems might occur with a rule that allows all the land acquired and added to a riparian track over time to be considered riparian?

3. Oregon limited riparian rights after passage of the federal Desert Lands Act of 1877 (discussed in Part I). In *Hough v. Porter*,[7] the Oregon Supreme Court held that the following language of the Act:

> ... all surplus water over and above such actual appropriation and use, together with the water of all lakes, rivers and other sources of water supply upon the public lands and not navigable, shall remain and be held free for the appropriation and use of the public for irrigation, mining, and manufacturing purposes subject to existing rights"[8]

limited riparian rights on lands acquired under the Act to domestic and stock uses and that any irrigation water rights (or other use enumerated in the Act—i.e., mining or manufacturing) must be developed under the doctrine of prior appropriation.[9] Oregon followed this with adoption of prior appropriation as the sole means of development of a water right in passage of a comprehensive water use act in 1909.

Prior Appropriation

The dominant approach to water allocation by western states is the doctrine of prior appropriation. The remainder of Part II will focus on the details of this common law doctrine. Under the doctrine of prior appropriation, a water use right is obtained by an individual or entity once they have diverted water and applied it to a beneficial use. It is not dependent on riparian ownership of land. Appropriated water could be transported many miles by ditch and used in a watershed that is not connected to the original source. This legal capacity to move water away from a water source was critical to development in a land with miles between sources of water and with mineral deposits or arable soil not necessarily confined to riparian locations. In times of shortage, water is allocated in order of priority based on who developed first, thus creating a stark contrast to the shared shortage of riparian rights.

In Part I we discussed the relation between this doctrine and the arid nature of the western lands and the concern that shared shortage would render all economic use of water impossible in times of drought. Certainly, the ability to move water away from riparian areas was critical to the development of the West and you will see that aspect emphasized in the cases chosen. You will also see that the concept of allocation in order of priority was discussed as essential at the time. You will learn in Part IV (covering the massive development of storage in the West by the federal government), and in Part VI (covering some physical solutions to the inconvenience of priority administration), that the West never really lived by this harsh aspect of the doctrine once the dominant use of western water moved from the mining camps to agricultural communities. Nevertheless, the harsh prospect of priority administration has served as a catalyst for many innovative solutions.

---

7. 98 P. 1083 (Or. 1909).
8. 19 Stat. U.S. 377.
9. *Id.* at 403–404.

Furthermore, it is unclear the degree to which the aridity of the West led to the initial development of the priority aspect of the doctrine or whether it developed as a mere accident of history stemming from the fact that the first cases to recognize the doctrine were associated with mining. The doctrine developed through custom in the mining districts in which the first to stake a claim had priority over others seeking to "jump" the claim. From there, it was a small step to apply the same concept to the water used to develop the mine. The California case of *Irwin v. Phillips*[10] is the first case to take this approach. Note that this case takes place prior to the Mining and Desert Lands Acts discussed in Part I that allowed public lands to go into private ownership. Thus, it applies to miners who are trespassers on public lands. Although it resolved the water dispute as between the miners, it establishes no right against the owner of the land—the federal government.

Irwin v. Phillips

Supreme Court of California
5 Cal. 140 (1855)

Opinion

HEYDENFELDT, J. ... [T]he whole merit of the case depends really on a single question, ... whether the owner of a canal in the mineral region of this State, constructed for the purpose of supplying water to miners, has the right to divert the water of a stream from its natural channel, as against the claims of those who subsequent to the diversion take up lands along the banks of the stream, for the purpose of mining. It must be premised that it is admitted on all sides that the mining claims in controversy, and the lands through which the stream runs, and through which the canal passes, are a part of the public domain, to which there is no claim of private proprietorship, and that the miners have the right to dig for gold on the public lands was settled by this Court in the case of Hicks *et al, v.* Bell *et al.,* 3 Cal., 219.

It is insisted by the appellants that in this case the common law doctrine must be invoked, which prescribes that a water course must be allowed to flow in its natural channel. But upon an examination of the authorities which support that doctrine, it will be found to rest upon the fact of the individual rights of landed proprietors upon the stream, the principle being both at the civil and common law that the owner of lands on the banks of a water course, owns to the middle of the stream, and has the right in virtue of his proprietorship to the use of the water in its pure and natural condition. In this case the lands are the property either of the State or of the United States, and it is not necessary to decide to which they belong for the purposes of this case. It is certain that at the common law the diversion of water courses could only be complained of by riparian owners, who were deprived of the use, or those claiming directly under them. Can the appellants assert their present claim as tenants at will? To solve this question it must be kept in mind that their tenancy is of their own creation, their

10. 5 Cal. 140 (1855).

tenements of their own selection, and subsequent, in point of time to the diversion of the stream. They had the right to mine where they pleased throughout an extensive region, and they selected the bank of a stream from which the water had been already turned, for the purpose of supplying the mines at another point.

Courts are bound to take notice of the political and social condition of the country, which they judicially rule. In this State the larger part of the territory consists of mineral lands, nearly the whole of which are the property of the public. No right or intent of disposition of these lands has been shown either by the United States or the State governments, and with the exception of certain State regulations, very limited in their character, a system has been permitted to grow up by the voluntary action and assent of the population, whose free and unrestrained occupation of the mineral region has been tacitly assented to by the one government, and heartily encouraged by the expressed legislative policy of the other. If there are, as must be admitted, many things connected with this system, which are crude and undigested, and subject to fluctuation and dispute, there are still some which a universal sense of necessity and propriety have so firmly fixed as that they have come to be looked upon as having the force and effect of *res judicata* Among these the most important are the rights of miners to be protected in the possession of their selected localities, and the rights of those who, by prior appropriation, have taken the waters from their natural beds, and by costly artificial works have conducted them for miles over mountains and ravines, to supply the necessities of gold diggers, and without which the most important interests of the mineral region would remain without development. So fully recognized have become these rights, that without any specific legislation conferring, or confirming them, they are alluded to and spoken of in various acts of the Legislature in the same manner as if they were rights which had been vested by the most distinct expression of the will of the law makers; as for instance, in the Revenue Act "canals and water races" are declared to be property subject to taxation, and this when there was none other in the State than such as were devoted to the use of mining. Section 2 of Article IX of the same Act, providing for the assessment of the property of companies and associations, among others mentions "dam or dams, canal or canals, or other works for mining purposes." This simply goes to prove what is the purpose of the argument, that however much the policy of the State, as indicated by her legislation, has conferred the privilege to work the mines, it has equally conferred the right to divert the streams from their natural channels, and as these two rights stand upon an equal footing, when they conflict, they must be decided by the fact of priority upon the maxim of equity, *qui prior est in tempore potior est in-jure* [he who is earlier in time is stronger in the law]. The miner, who selects a piece of ground to work, must take it as he finds it, subject to prior rights, which have an equal equity, on account of an equal recognition from the sovereign power. If it is upon a stream the waters of which have not been taken from their bed, they cannot be taken to his prejudice; but if they have been already diverted, and for as high, and legitimate a purpose as the one he seeks to accomplish, he has no right to complain, no right to interfere with the prior occupation of his neighbor, and must abide the disadvantages of his own selection.

It follows from this opinion that the judgment of the Court below was substantially correct, upon the merits of the case presented by the evidence, and it is therefore affirmed.

Notes & Questions

1. As between the people making use of the land and water, the court applies the concept of first-in-time, first-in right to both mining claims and water development. From the following list, choose any that support the court's choice of a "winner takes all" rule as opposed to a rule allowing for shared shortages:
   a. The cost and magnitude of the infrastructure needed to divert the water away from the water course.
   b. The location of mineral deposits away from water.
   c. The ability of newcomers to the water course to visually see how much water is left (i.e., notice).
   d. The fact that mining is purely an economic endeavor, unlike at least some historic notions of farming as the development of a family home, business, and community.
2. The court makes it clear that it is not addressing the rights of riparian owners of the land, since the land is owned by state or federal government. Under the reasoning in *Benton*, would the outcome be different if those asserting the riparian right had actually owned the land?

Colorado was the first state to consider the doctrine of prior appropriation in the context of irrigation. The case of *Coffin v. Left Hand Ditch Co.*, 6 Colo. 443 (1882), is historic not only as the first, but because it presents clear facts for the choice between the doctrines of riparian rights and prior appropriation. The diversion by Left Hand Ditch Co. moved water out of the watershed of St. Vrain Creek (Figure 5.1). Coffin owns riparian land on St Vrain Creek downstream of the diversion. The doctrine of prior appropriation would protect the diversion by Left Hand Ditch Co., whereas the riparian doctrine would protect a right of Coffin to the natural flow of the river diminished only by reasonable use. The water rights in question were acquired before the Colorado Constitution of 1876 recognized prior appropriation. Thus, the court must approach the issue as a question of common law. The Court adopted the doctrine of prior appropriation, reasoning that:

> It is contended by counsel for appellants that the common law principles of riparian proprietorship prevailed in Colorado until 1876, and that the doctrine of priority of right to water by priority of appropriation thereof was first recognized and adopted in the constitution. But we think the latter doctrine has existed from the date of the earliest appropriations of water within the boundaries of the state. The climate is dry, and the soil, when moistened only by the usual rainfall, is arid and unproductive; except in a few favored sections, artificial irrigation for agriculture is an absolute necessity. Water in the various

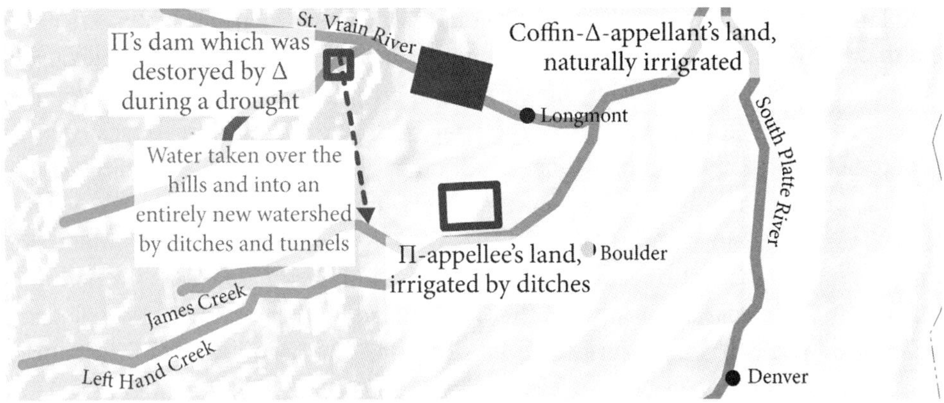

Figure 5.1 The diversion from St. Vrain Creek to the Left Hand Creek watershed is located upstream of Coffin's riparian land. Water flows from the bottom left (southwest) to the top right (northeast) in this illustration. Source: Andrew Kull, University of Texas Law School, Property Visual Syllabus, http://propertykull.weebly.com/coffin-v-left-hand-ditch-company.html. Source: Design by Leilanee Taylor.

streams thus acquires a value unknown in moister climates. Instead of being a mere incident to the soil, it rises, when appropriated, to the dignity of a distinct usufructuary estate, or right of property. It has always been the policy of the national, as well as the territorial and state governments, to encourage the diversion and use of water in this country for agriculture; and vast expenditures of time and money have been made in reclaiming and fertilizing by irrigation portions of our unproductive territory. Houses have been built, and permanent improvements made; the soil has been cultivated, and thousands of acres have been rendered immensely valuable, with the understanding that appropriations of water would be protected. Deny the doctrine of priority or superiority of right by priority of appropriation, and a great part of the value of all this property is at once destroyed.

... we hold that, in the absence of express statutes to the contrary, the first appropriator of water from a natural stream for a beneficial purpose has ... a prior right thereto, to the extent of such appropriation.

Notes & Questions

1. The court says nothing about the fact that the ruling may have the result of rendering the lands along St Vrain Creek downstream of the diversion valueless. Is it likely in the economic hierarchy of the time that those able to put money into an inter-watershed diversion may have substantially greater wealth than those simply seeking to turn water onto their adjacent fields? Does prior appropriation give greater protection to the wealthy? Or, once articulated, would it protect the poor farmers on St Vrain Creek if they had diverted the water first? Thus, is a bright-line rule more likely to be applied with a blind eye to who wins?

Many western courts would adopt Colorado's view that riparian rights were never an incident of land ownership in their state or territory. First, the Supreme Court of Montana Territory applied the rule of prior appropriation in *Thorp v. Woolman*, 1 Mont. 168, (1870), but did not have the issue of prior appropriation versus riparian rights before it. The Supreme Court of Montana later unequivocally affirmed that prior appropriation was the guiding principle of Montana water law in *Mettler v. Ames Realty Co.*, 61 Mont. 152, 201 P. 702 (1921). *Mettler* was a case of first impression for the Supreme Court of Montana in which a claimant was seeking affirmation of their rights as a riparian proprietor, the Court stated that "the common law doctrine of riparian rights has never prevailed in Montana," and found instead for the prior appropriator.

Idaho's Territorial Supreme Court followed its sister states and territories in 1890 when it decided *Drake v. Earhart*. The case is a good example of the issues a court would have struggled with in considering whether to choose prior appropriation as the sole state doctrine for allocation of water. As in *Left Hand Ditch*, the Idaho Court was asked to address the relative rights of a prior appropriator versus an owner of riparian land to water from a small stream named Quigley Creek in southern Idaho. In 1879, Quigley took possession of unsurveyed land at the mouth of a gulch near Hailey, Idaho, and appropriated the water in the stream flowing out of the gulch. He posted a notice at his point of diversion, claiming 600 inches from a stream that flowed only 150 inches. Drake and Covert subsequently acquired Quigley's interests in the land and water. In addition to irrigating a parcel of land, Drake and Covert sold surplus water from that appropriated to a railway line for its station in Hailey. Earhart and other defendants subsequently settled on lands directly adjacent (i.e., riparian) to Quigley Creek and upstream from Drake (Figure 5.2), acquired a federal patent for those lands, and began to use water from the stream. Because there was insufficient water flow to satisfy everyone's use, Drake and Covert sought an injunction to restrain Earhart and the other defendants from using water from Quigley Creek upstream from their diversion. Drake claimed he was the prior appropriator and therefore entitled to a paramount right to his entire appropriation of water. The basis of Earhart's defense was that, as a riparian owner, he enjoyed the right to a reasonable use of the stream and that shortage should be shared between himself and other users of the stream. The trial court sided with Drake and Earhart appealed.

The court articulates similar justifications for rejection of riparian rights to that used by the Colorado court—climate and necessity. Then, as now, state/territorial courts look to the rulings of other states when faced with a case of first impression (i.e., one in which the court has not made a ruling). But remember, a case from another state can be persuasive, but is not binding precedent. Thus, rather than cite the case from another state as controlling, the court will explain its reasoning and why that applies (or does not apply) in this state or territory. In this case, the rulings in other states are also used for another reason—to illustrate custom. Pay attention to the state opinions used in this way. The dissent is included in this excerpt to make it clear that the doctrine of

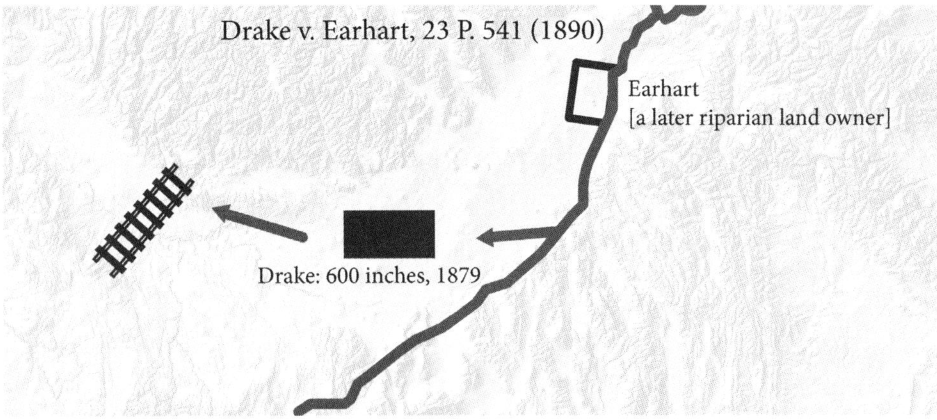

Figure 5.2 Conceptual Map with the Relative Location of Drake and Earhart's Properties Shown. Earhart is upstream from Drake. Source: Design by Leilanee Taylor.

prior appropriation that we take as commonplace now, was by no means inevitable at the time. In 1890 in Idaho, this decision could have gone either way.

Drake v. Earhart

Idaho Territorial Supreme Court
23 P. 541 (1890)

BEATTIE, C.J.—The important question, for the settlement of which this appeal was chiefly brought, is what, if any, rights the appellant [Earhart] has to any of that water as a riparian proprietor. His claim is not based upon prior or any appropriation under our territorial laws, but upon the fact that the stream in question flows by its natural channel through his land; hence, that he is entitled to the use thereof allowed by the common law. This doctrine of riparian proprietorship in water as against prior appropriation has been very often discussed, and nearly always decided the same way by and almost every appellate court between Mexico and the British possessions, and from the shores of the Pacific to the eastern slope, of the Rocky mountains, as well as by the supreme court of the United States. But for the fact that it has elsewhere repeatedly appeared in the same court, it would seem surprising that it should now be seeking another solution in this. While there are questions growing out of the water laws and rights not fully adjudicated, tiffs phantom of riparian rights, based upon facts like those in this case, has been so often decided adversely to such claim, and in favor of the prior appropriation, that the maxim, "first in time, first in right," should be considered the settled law here. Whether or not it is a beneficent rule, it is the lineal descendant of the law of necessity. When, from among the most energetic and enterprising classes of the east, that enormous tide of emigration poured into the west, this was found an arid land, which could be utilized as an agricultural country, or made valuable for its gold, only by the use of its streams of water. The new inhabitants were without law, but they quickly recognized that each man should not be a law unto himself. Accustomed, as they had been, to obedience to the laws they had helped make, as the settlements increased to such numbers as justified organization, they established their local customs and rules for their government in the use of water and land. They found a new condition of things. The use of water to which they had been accustomed, and the laws concerning it, had no application here. The demand for water they found greater than the supply, as is the unfortunate fact still all over this arid region. Instead of attempting to divide it among all, thus making it unprofitable to any, or instead of applying the common-law riparian doctrine, to which they had been accustomed, they disregarded the traditions of the past, and established as the only rule suitable to their situation that of prior appropriation. This did not mean that the first appropriator could take all he pleased, but what he actually needed, and could properly use without waste. Thus was established the local custom, which pervaded the entire west, and became the basis of the laws we have today on that subject. Very soon these customs attracted the attention of the legislatures, where they were approved and adopted, and next we find them undergoing the crucial test of judicial investigation. As far back as 1855, the supreme court of California, in *Irwin v. Phillips,* 5 Cal. 145, and in *Tartar v. Mining Co.,* 5 Cal. 397, distinctly held that the prior appropriator of water should hold it against tile riparian claim of the owner of land through which it flowed, and, also, that in all branches of industry the prior appropriator of land, water, and easements would be protected. Not only had such become the law by custom, by the legislative will, and the decisions of the courts, without dissent, but the general government, for many years, without protest, acquiesced in such occupation and use of its lands and waters by its citizens, while valuable properties and industries were building upon this principle. To put the question beyond uncertainty, to approve and adopt what already existed as the common law of the west, the congress, by its act of July 26, 1866, § 9, provided "that whenever, by priority of possession, rights to the use of water for mining, agricultural, manufacturing, or other purposes have vested and accrued, and the same are recognized and acknowledged by the local customs, laws, and the decisions of courts, the possessors and owners of such vested rights shall be maintained and protected in the same." It will be observed that the act is based upon the existence of local customs, laws, and decisions of courts....

It has been said that in the case at bar no custom has been shown. It is not necessary it should be; for, prior to the beginning of appellant's claim, the superior rights of prior appropriation were acknowledged by our territorial law of 1881, and by the decisions of our courts. By a practically unbroken line of decisions the rule of the cases above referred to in 5 Cal. has been followed, and is now established by so many and such high authorities that it would seem this theme of discussion is exhausted. Brief reference, however, may be made to some of the leading cases. *Basey v. Gallagher,* 20 Wall. 681, 682, clearly indorses the superior right of prior appropriation between agricultural claimants in the following explicit language: "In the late case of *Atchison v. Peterson,* 2 Idaho 507, we had occasion to consider the respective rights of miners to running waters on the mineral lands of the public domain; and we there held that, by the custom which had obtained among miners in the Pacific states and territories, the party who first subjected the water to use, or took the necessary steps for that purpose, was regarded, except as against the government, as the source of title in all controversies respecting it; that the doctrines of the common law declaratory of the rights of riparian proprietors were inapplicable, or applicable only to a limited extent, to the necessities of miners, and were inadequate to their protection; that the equality of right recognized by that law among all the proprietors upon the same stream would have been incompatible with any extended diversion of the water by one proprietor, and its conveyance, for mining purposes, to points from which it could not be restored to the stream; that the government, by its silent acquiescence, had assented to and encouraged the occupation of the public lands for mining; and that he who first connected his labor with property thus situated, and open to general exploration, did, in natural justice, acquire a better right to its use and enjoyment than others who had not given such labor; that the miners on the public lands throughout the Pacific states and territories, by their customs, usages, and regulations, had recognized the inherent justice of this principle, and this principle itself was at an early period recognized by legislation, and enforced by the courts of those states and territories, and was finally approved by the legislation of congress in 1866. The views there expressed, and the rulings made, are equally applicable to the use of water on the public lands for purposes of irrigation. No distinction is made in those states and territories, by the custom of miners or settlers or by the courts, in the rights of the first appropriator from the use made of the water, if the use be a beneficial one." In this case it is said: "The right of the first appropriator, exercised within reasonable limits, is respected;" that it "is not unrestricted. It must, be exercised with reference to the general condition of the country, and the necessities of the people." This language has been seized upon as justifying the equitable, if not equal, division of the water among all desiring or needing it, regardless of the claim of the prior appropriator. Such a construction is not justified, ... It is evident that all the court means by this language is that the first appropriator shall not be allowed more than he needs for some useful purpose; that he shall not, by wasting or misusing it, deprive his neighbor of what he has not actual use for. In 98 U.S. 461, *supra,* the court says: "The owners of a mining claim and the owner of a water-right enjoy their respective properties from the dates of their appropriation,—the first in time being the first in right; but, where both rights can be enjoyed without interference with or material impairment of each other, the enjoyment of both is allowed." It clearly follows, as the courts have certainly held, that when all cannot use the water without injury to the prior appropriator the other must yield to his superior right. The claim having been asserted that, when a party procured a patent for land, he would be entitled to the use of all waters flowing through the same, was put at rest by the act of congress of July 9, 1870, as follows: "Sec. 17. All patents granted, or pre-emption or homesteads allowed, shall be subject to any vested and accrued water-rights or rights to ditches," etc. Since this act the rulings have been uniform that the patentee of land has no claim upon the water flowing through the same as against a prior appropriator.

While there are numerous questions growing out of the water law, we have aimed to confine this discussion to that involved in this case, which is simply a contest between a prior appropriator of the water of a stream, all of which he claims, has used, and needs for a useful purpose, and a party who, since such appropriation, has entered and patented some of the land through which such water, by its natural channel, flows, and who claims its use as a riparian proprietor. In accord with the authorities, as well as with our local law on this subject, it must be held that the judgment of the lower court should be affirmed; and it is so ordered.

BERRY, J., *dissenting.*

... No custom as to the use of water is alleged or found, and the appellant contends that these facts are insufficient to sustain a judgment for the plaintiffs. He says that custom, and custom alone, where right exists to use water for irrigating purposes on the public domain, must be shown as the basis of that right; that it must be alleged and shown, and, of course, must be found. That is the law. Custom is indispensable to the plaintiffs' right. Such right is rounded on custom and user. 14 Stat. 253, § 9; *Basey v. Gallagher,* 20 Wall. 683. But nothing of the kind exists here.

....

3. The majority opinion pronounces the claim of a person whose lands lie upon a stream as resting on the "phantom of riparian rights." I deny that under the laws of this territory "riparian rights" are a "phantom," unless unlawfully and unjustly made so. The doctrine of riparian rights is a part of the common law; and the common law is the law of this territory, except as the statute steps in, and repeals or changes it. Section 18 of the Revised Statutes so declares. It provides that "the common law of England, so far as it is not repugnant to or inconsistent with the constitution or laws of the United States, in all cases not provided for in these Revised Statutes, is the rule of decision in all the courts in this territory." The United States statutes have in some respects modified the common-law rule of riparian rights on the public domain where customs are shown to exist, and not otherwise. No customs are pretended here. Indeed, all customs are studiously ignored. The statutes of the territory previous to 1881 had no provision whatever on the subject of water-rights. But in 1881 what are equivalent to common-law water-rights were in some respects expressly affirmed, only those rights were enlarged. Section 3180, Rev. St., provides that "all persons, companies, and corporations owning or claiming any lands situated on the banks or in the vicinity of any stream are entitled to the use of the waters of such stream for the purpose of irrigation, the land so held or claimed." In the preceding chapter of the statutes it is provided that by complying with certain conditions (not one of which is pretended to be compiled with in this case) a party may entitle himself to superior rights in the use of water. No one denies this fact. But it nowhere provides that any one may entitle himself to ownership of a stream, or to entirely exclude others "on the banks or in the vicinity of a stream" from some use of the water, as provided in section 3180, above quoted. Our statute is a little more comprehensive—a little stronger, in some respects, in favor of those needing water—than the common law of riparian rights; but it leaves many of those rights intact. It is wrong,

then, to designate these common-law rights as a "phantom." They are real, and the interests of our territory demand that they should be recognized.

4. By the common law, running water is not the subject of ownership. No statute of Idaho, nor of congress, either, makes it such. By custom, when that is shown, a person in its prior use may not be disturbed in its use, providing, as Mr. Justice FIELD says in *Basey v. Gallagher,* the custom and claim under it are reasonable. But that is as far as it goes,—as far as any statute of the United States or of this territory goes. Our own statutes are in accord with that view. Rev. St. Idaho, § 3188. In *Basey v. Gallagher,* 20 Wall. 683, Mr. Justice FIELD says that "in all such cases the right of the first appropriator, exercised within reasonable limits, is respected and enforced. We say within reasonable limits; for this right to water, like the right by prior occupancy to mining ground, *** is not unrestricted. It must be exercised with reference to the general condition of the country and the necessities of the people, and not so as to deprive a whole neighborhood or community of its use, and to vest an absolute monopoly in a single individual."

What does this judgment do, but to violate every provision of the foregoing, severally and as a whole? Is it reasonable to appropriate all the waters of a stream, even if it contains 1,000 inches, or whatever it may be, to irrigate "a piece" of land, with no intimation of its description or amount? Is it reasonable to allow absolute and "unrestricted" ownership in water diverted for purposes of irrigation, only, to be used, as in this case, for sale to railroads and brick-yards, or other purposes than irrigation, and still deny to others their natural, lawful, statutory rights in any of it? Where are the "reasonable limits" of such a claim? Is such a claim in accord with "the conditions of the country and necessities of the people," when those people are famishing for water, and precluded from using a drop, though an abundance runs past their doors? Does not this judgment establish "an absolute monopoly" of the waters of this stream? Every one of these questions carries with it its own answer. I do not propose to pursue this argument, and show that a great majority of the cases relied on to establish this doctrine of absolute ownership and exclusive monopoly in streams do not relate to the use of water for agricultural purposes at all, but that those cases relate to diversions or use for mining purposes only. That fact may be easily shown, or else that the cases where they relate to irrigation are based upon mining cases. There are few of them that are not so founded, even of those cited in the majority opinion. The doctrine of those cases would prevent the settlement upon lands depending on our natural streams, and as in the case at bar, would drive away half or more of the settlers who have already settled there. This is not for the interest of the territory, and to allow the example of this case to obtain will prove detrimental in other ways than in decreasing our population. The suffering settlers will very soon resort to the demoralizing aid of the ever present "Winchester" or revolver. People will not tolerate such unlawful claims; and the sooner they are abandoned, or reduced within reasonable bounds, the better will it be for all. This judgment should be reversed.

Notes & Questions

1. Following *Drake* and statehood, the Idaho Supreme Court reversed the next three decisions of the trial court for having failed to determine the rights of the parties according to the priority of their respective appropriations. *See Kirk v. Bartholomew*, 29 P. 40 (Idaho 1892); *Geertson v. Barrack*, 29 P. 42 (Idaho 1892); *Hillman v. Hardwick*, 26 P. 438 (Idaho 1891). It did so in *Hillman* in particularly scathing language:

    > We ... have this anomalous condition of affairs: A creek or stream flowing one hundred inches of water, with appropriations of that water to the amount or extent of eight hundred inches, in addition to the prior appropriation by the plaintiff of all the waters in the creek and its tributaries. To the ordinary mind, this might, and perhaps does, present a somewhat difficult problem for judicial solution, unaided by the statutes; but the learned district judge found no difficulty whatever in reaching a conclusion as unique as it is unprecedented. We say unprecedented, because this question, under statutes identical with that of Idaho, has been decided so often in favor of the prior appropriator that it has generally been considered, both by professionals and profanes, as a settled question; as instance, the question had been decided up to 1889 twice by the supreme court of the United States, seventeen times by the supreme court of California, five times by the supreme court of Colorado, six times by the supreme court of Nevada, twice by the supreme court of Montana, once by the supreme court of New Mexico, once by the supreme court of Oregon, and repeatedly by the supreme court of Idaho. In fact, the decision of the learned district judge in this case stands alone. We have been unable, by the most diligent search to find precedent of parallel for it. Heroically setting aside the statute, the decisions and the evidence in the case, he assumes the role of Jupiter Pluvius, and distributes the waters of Gooseberry creek with a beneficent recklessness, which makes the most successful efforts of all the rain wizards shrink into insignificance, and which would make the hearts of the ranchers on Gooseberry dance with joy, if only the judicial decree could be supplemented with a little more moisture. The individual who causes two blades of grass to grow where but one grew before is held in highest emulation as a benefactor of his race. How, then, shall we rank him who, by judicial fiat alone, can cause four hundred inches of water to run where nature put one hundred inches? *Hillman v. Hardwick*, 26 P. 438 (Idaho 1891).

2. The prior appropriation doctrine is often characterized by the maxim "first in time is first in right." Water rights are ranked according to the date of their appropriation. The older the water right, the more senior it is. In times of scarcity, water is allocated from the most senior uses to junior uses until water supply has been exhausted. A key goal of this system is certainty. Development of the West required water, which was scarce and expensive to capture and use. Those that made the large investment of time and money necessary to acquire the water needed to be certain that they would continue to be able to use it as the region continued to grow and competing users

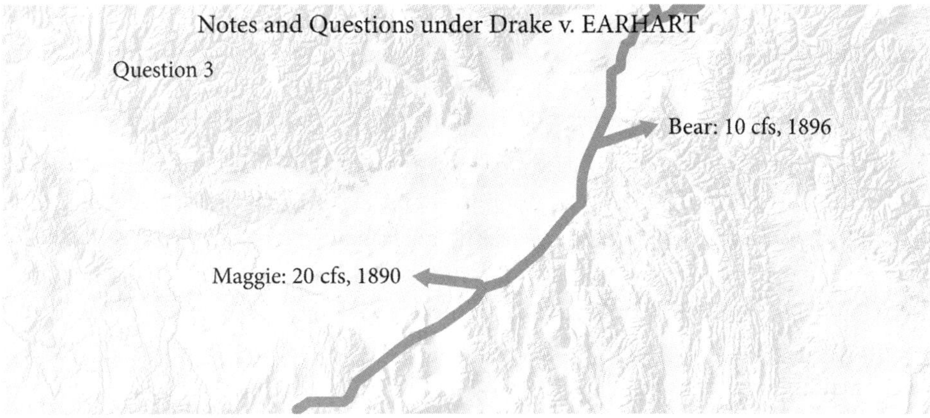

Figure 5.3 Map of fact pattern for Question 3 following *Drake v. Earhart*. The water is flowing from the top to the bottom of the slide (i.e., Bear is upstream). Source: Design by Leilanee Taylor.

moved in. The common law riparian doctrine, which is premised on shared shortage, provided no such certainty. Because water supplies are so scarce in the West, an incremental reduction in use could result in a total failure of everyone's beneficial use. Hence, the priority system was born.

3. The following problem is the simple case of two people who have developed appropriative water rights for irrigation. Bear is upstream, needs 10 cfs, and his priority date is 1895. Maggie is downstream, needs 20 cfs, and her priority date is 1890. If we assume no gain or loss of water in the stream between Bear and Maggie's headgate and the water falls to 15 cfs, who gets the water?[11]

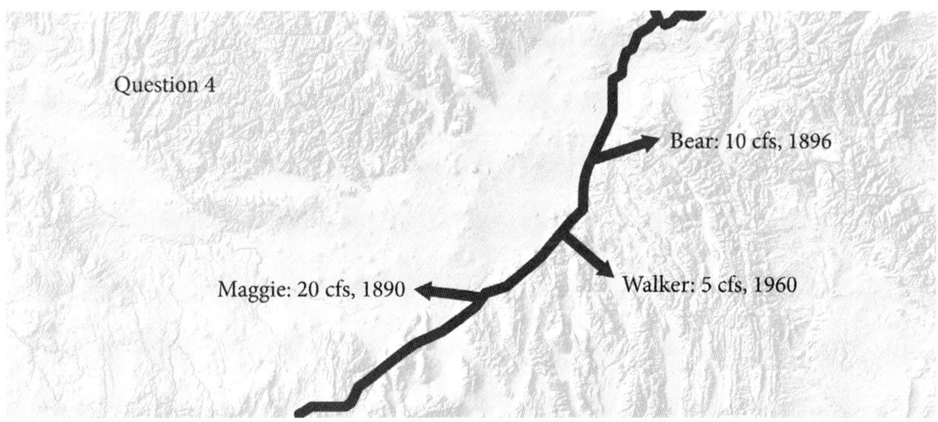

Figure 5.4 Map of fact pattern for Question 4 following *Drake v. Earhart*. The water is flowing from the top to the bottom of the slide (i.e., Bear is upstream). Source: Design by Leilanee Taylor.

4. This is the same as the problem above, but with the addition of a much more junior irrigator, Walker, downstream. This asks you to think about what is actually happen-

11. Hint: Professors Cosens and Hedden-Nicely use their current and former dogs as the appropriators in these scenarios. When in doubt, Professor Cosens' dogs win.

ing physically in the watershed that might on the one hand make the problem more complicated, and on the other hand, allow more water use. Remember from the introduction to hydrology that irrigation is not 100% efficient—meaning that of the water placed on a field, only a percentage (representing the efficiency) will be consumed in evapotranspiration, and the rest may come back to the stream as return flow (provided the diversion did not remove the water from the watershed). It turns out that even though Bear had to let all the 15 cfs in question 3 flow past his headgate, a much more junior user may take advantage of return flow. Thus, Walker may take up to 5 cfs if available. This would also be the case if another tributary enters the stream between Maggie and Walker's headgates.

5. In a typical year, the base (or minimum) flow of Big Creek occurs near the middle of August. During that time, the average flow is approximately 10 cfs. The following users have properly appropriated a water right from Big Creek:

   - User A: 3 cfs with a 1915 priority date;
   - User B: 2.5 cfs with a 1950 priority date;
   - User C: 5 cfs with a 1890 priority date;
   - User D: 2.5 cfs with a 1980 priority date.

   As happens on many western streams, a watermaster begins measuring water as flow drops to a level that administration is necessary and has the authority to open and close headgates. You are the watermaster.

   a. To whom is User A "senior?" To whom is User A "junior?"

   b. Who receives water in August in an average water year?

   c. What happens if the flow drops to 7 cfs?

   d. What happens if the flow drops to 4 cfs?

   e. What happens if Big Creek has a greater than average flow in August of 15 cfs?

Chapter 6

Common Law Attributes of State-Based Water Rights—Diversion

Introduction

Prior to the development of recording and permit systems, a water right under the doctrine of prior appropriation was acquired by the physical act of diversion and application to a beneficial use. This Chapter addresses the question of whether a physical diversion from the water course is necessary to create a right to water and, if so, what constitutes a diversion. It then explores the importance of the physical act of diversion as providing the evidentiary basis for establishing the priority date of the water right. Finally, it will consider whether the means of diversion, a key attribute of a prior appropriation water right, is actually protected as part of the usufructuary property right it establishes. This Chapter begins with cases determining the necessity of a diversion.

The Necessity of a Diversion

We begin our inquiry with two cases that explore the question of whether a diversion is strictly necessary to initiate a water right. The split in these cases between Idaho and Montana is illustrative of the range of possible outcomes. Idaho took the view that a physical diversion is essential to a water right unless otherwise authorized by statute (in Part V you will learn that Idaho now has a statutory system for protecting instream flows). Montana took the view that a diversion is not necessary as long as intent to appropriate can be shown.

For those states considering diversion as essential to creation of a common law water right, diversion served three important policies. First, it provided notice of the development to current and aspiring users of water from the same source. A general maxim in western water law is that a person has the right to take the stream as they find it. The presence of a physical diversion places subsequent water users on notice of the location and size of the senior water rights, thus providing a degree of certainty regarding the availability (or not) of additional water. They can then ascertain for themselves if it is worth investing in their own water infrastructure. Posting and permit systems would later fill this need for notice, but in the early development of the common law, new water users developed at their own risk and had to rely on their own efforts to ascertain the state of development on the water course.

Second, diversion demonstrated the requisite intent to appropriate a water right. Courts around the West required intent to appropriate as a prerequisite for a valid water right. Without the legal infrastructure or system for memorializing intent until permit and recording systems were developed, courts had little evidence of whether a person who was using water in a natural stream had intended to acquire a water right for its continued use. A physical diversion, therefore, was consistent with the overall goal of certainty because clearly the expense of installing diversionary works would not be undertaken if the developer did not intend to acquire a right to the continued use of the water diverted. As a result, most courts were willing to presume intent where a diversion works had been installed. *See, e.g., Wheat v. Cameron*, 210 P. 761 (Mont. 1922). For states recognizing non-diversionary rights, more direct evidence was necessary to show intent.

Third, diversion fulfilled the nineteenth-century policy that water be "used" in a manner that ensured the continued development of the West. The western economy during this time was driven by industries such as agriculture, grazing, and mining; all of which required the diversion and use of large quantities of water. Western courts privileged the uses that required diversion while simultaneously excluded instream uses as "wasted" water. Little value was placed on things that required water to remain *in situ* such as fish and wildlife, recreation, or aesthetics.

The Idaho case that considers diversion as essential to creation of a water right at common law is part of the Snake River Basin Adjudication which you will learn about in Part VI. You will learn in Part VI that the United States waived its sovereign immunity to be joined in a general adjudication, thus allowing the following case to be heard in state court. The case concerns the claims of the United States to instream flows for Minidoka National Wildlife Refuge (Figure 6.1).

State v. United States

Supreme Court of Idaho
134 Idaho 106, 996 P.2d 806 (2000)

KIDWELL, J.—This Court granted permissive appeal from an interlocutory order of the Snake River Basin Adjudication (SRBA) district court. The SRBA court ... held that diversion was not required to perfect the water right the United States claimed under Idaho's constitutional method of appropriation. We reverse, holding that the United States may not utilize Idaho's constitutional method of appropriation to claim a non-diversionary water right for purposes other than stock watering.

I. FACTS AND PROCEDURAL BACKGROUND

Water from Smith Springs and its associated seeps (Smith Springs) flows from the banks of the Snake River into a bay of Lake Walcott Reservoir above Minidoka Dam in Blaine County. Smith Springs are within the boundaries of Minidoka National Wildlife

Figure 6.1 A spring flowing into the reservoir at Minidoka National Wildlife Refuge. Source: Speck, *Minidoka National Wildlife Refuge Idaho* (2012), https://www.deviantart.com/speck2/art/Minidoka-National-Wildlife-Refuge-Idaho-324079672.

Refuge (Minidoka NWR). Minidoka NWR, originally the "Minidoka Reservation for Protection of Native Birds," was established by Executive Order of President Theodore Roosevelt in February 1909. The Executive Order expressly anticipated a reservoir site and specified that the reservation was set apart as a "preserve ... and breeding ground... for native birds." The land comprising the reservoir site and Minidoka NWR was condemned for use of the United States on May 17, 1915.

In the SRBA, the United States filed a claim, No. 36-15452, for 1.16 cubic feet per second (c.f.s.) based on the constitutional method of appropriation, for the waters from Smith Springs.[1] The United States claimed the appropriation for the non-consumptive beneficial use of wildlife from January 1 until December 31 of each year, with a priority date of May 17, 1915. The claim observed that Smith Springs provided a source of fresh water to the bay, maintained wetlands when the reservoir was drawn down, and kept areas of the bay open during winter, thereby providing important habitat for over-wintering birds. The United States acknowledged that there were "[n]o developed diversion works" at Smith Springs.

The Idaho Department of Water Resources (IDWR) Director's Report for Basin 36, filed in November 1992, recommended that the United States' claim be disallowed on the basis that a valid appropriation required a physical diversion.

Within required deadlines, the United States filed an objection and IDWR filed a response to the objection. The claim was designated a subcase and assigned to a special master....

1. The "constitutional" method of appropriation in Idaho law was a misnomer that you will explore in more detail in looking at the development of permit systems in Part V. For our purposes here, it simply refers to the common law appropriation of water.

... On March 11, 1996, the special master recommended that the United States be adjudicated a constitutional appropriation for an instream water right with a priority date of May 17, 1915 for 1.16 c.f.s. from Smith Springs for the beneficial use of wildlife. The State ... filed notices of challenge contesting the special master's recommendations.

After hearings, the SRBA court issued its order on October 10, 1997. It affirmed ... the special master's decision that a diversion was not required for an appropriation under the constitutional method....

This Court granted permission to appeal on January 20, 1998....

II. ANALYSIS

....

B. The United States May Not Claim an Instream Water Right for a Purpose Other Than Stock Watering Under Idaho's Constitutional Method of Appropriation.

Before us is the narrow question of whether the United States may utilize Idaho's constitutional method of appropriation to claim a non-diversionary water right for purposes other than stock watering. This presents a question of law, over which we exercise free review.

Until 1971, appropriations of water in Idaho could be made two ways. One method, "the statutory method," required applying for a permit under provisions of Title 42 of the Idaho Code. Under the other method, usually referred to as the "constitutional method of appropriation," a water user could make a valid appropriation without a permit, most commonly by diverting the water and putting it to beneficial use. A "constitutional appropriation" is an appropriation made under this latter method.

Idaho water law generally requires an actual diversion and beneficial use for the existence of a valid water right. Only two exceptions to the diversion requirement exist. No diversion from a natural watercourse or diversion device is needed to establish a valid appropriative water right for stock watering. In addition, State entities acting pursuant to statute may make non-diversionary appropriations for the beneficial use of Idaho citizens.

Neither of these exceptions covers the United States' claim. Although the stock-watering exception applies to appropriations made under the constitutional method, it applies only to watering livestock and does not extend to beneficial use for wildlife habitat. This limited exception to the diversion requirement is also recognized in other appropriation doctrine states.

...

III. CONCLUSION

.... United States may not utilize Idaho's constitutional method of appropriation to claim a non-diversionary water right for purposes other than stock watering. Therefore, the order of the SRBA court is ... reversed....

Notes & Questions

1. If you were arguing this case on behalf of those opposing development of a water right without a diversion, how would you distinguish *in situ* stockwatering rights (allowed in Idaho) from *in situ* fish and wildlife rights?

2. Recreation is currently the fastest growing industry in Idaho. Its iconic steelhead runs for sport fishing and its world class whitewater rafting drive much of this growth. What role should our changing values as a society play in changing the laws surrounding the diversion requirement? Should the common law evolve over time as it did in the next case in Montana? Or should legislative acts be the sole source of change?

While our next case was decided after Montana had developed statutes allowing water rights for instream flow, it seeks to answer whether it was possible to have a water right without a diversion before the statutes were enacted. In 1969, the Montana Legislature passed legislation allowing Department of Fish Wildlife and Parks to establish minimum instream flow rights on 12 identified streams and these rights were referred to as "Murphy's Rights." With passage of the 1973 Montana Water Use Act, Montana adopted a much broader system for the establishment of instream flows, which will be covered in Part V. In a 1988 case, referred to below as the *Bean Lake* case, the Montana Supreme Court held that no water right for fish and wildlife was recognized under Montana Law before 1973 with the exception of Murphy's rights. This case revisits the issues in the *Bean Lake* case. Similar to the Idaho case, the issue arose in the context of Montana's general stream adjudication, however in this case it is the state agency, not the United States seeking a water right for fish and wildlife.

In the Matter of the Adjudication of the Existing Rights to the Use of All the Water, Both Surface and Underground, Within the Missouri River Drainage Area, Including All Tributaries of the Missouri River in Broadwater, Cascade, Jefferson and Lewis and Clark Counties, Montana (Basin 41I)

Supreme Court of Montana
55 P.3d 396 (2002)

Opinion

Justice W. WILLIAM LEAPHART delivered the Opinion of the Court.—The Montana Department of Fish Wildlife and Parks (DFWP) appeals a ruling by the Chief Water Judge on five pre-1973 water rights claims in the Missouri River basin. The five claims are based on diversions of water for purposes of fish, wildlife or recreation. The Water Court ruling refers to *In the Matter of Dearborn Drainage Area* (1988), 234 Mont. 331, 766 P.2d 228 (*Bean Lake*) in remarking on the potential invalidity of the claims

...

DISCUSSION

Was *Bean Lake* correct in its holding that "under Montana law before 1973, no appropriation right was recognized for recreation, fish and wildlife, except through a Murphy right statute?"

...

The common law elements of a valid appropriation are intent, notice, diversion and application to beneficial use. However, in Montana, as in many western states, the flexibility of the prior appropriation doctrine has allowed acquisition of the right to use a specific amount of water through application of the water to a beneficial use. A. Stone, *Montana Water Law* (1994). Judicial opinions and scholarly commentators have repeatedly stated the rule that application to a beneficial use is the touchstone of the appropriation doctrine. *See, e.g.,* A. Stone, *Selected Aspects of Montana Water Law* 30 (1978); *Thomas v. Guiraud* ("[t]he true test of appropriation of water is the successful application thereof to the beneficial use designed, and the method of diverting or carrying the same, or making such application, is immaterial").

Bean Lake

Bean Lake involved a claim for in-lake water rights for fish, wildlife and recreation purposes in a natural pothole lake. In *Bean Lake* this Court stated, "[i]t is clear therefore that under Montana law before 1973, no appropriation right was recognized for recreation, fish and wildlife, except through a Murphy right statute."

The *Bean Lake* decision appears to be inconsistent with earlier case law in which the Court recognized appropriations for fish, wildlife and recreation. In holding that no appropriation right was recognized for fish, wildlife and recreation, the *Bean Lake* Court ignored *Osnes* and misread *Paradise Rainbows.* The *Osnes* Court ruled that an earlier diversion of water, even if used only to maintain a swimming pool or fish pond, had priority over a later appropriation and stated, "it is not clear that such a use [swimming pool or fish pond] would not be a beneficial use and hence the basis of a valid appropriation."

In *Paradise Rainbows,* the Court again recognized the diversion of water for fish ponds as a valid appropriation of water....

The majority of briefs submitted in this case concur that the *Bean Lake* decision is fraught with internal inconsistencies. In *Bean Lake,* the Court acknowledged that beneficial use is the touchstone of a valid appropriation right.

In seeming conflict with these findings that (1) beneficial use is the test of a valid right, and (2) fish, wildlife and recreation uses are beneficial uses, the Court concluded that "no Montana legal authority, deriving from common law or statute, acknowledged that recreational, fish or wildlife uses, even though beneficial, gave rise to any water rights by appropriation under Montana law" and therefore "under Montana law before 1973, no appropriation right was recognized for recreation, fish and wildlife...."

...

A. Did the Bean Lake Court correctly hold that prior to 1973 Montana did not recognize water rights for recreation, fish and wildlife purposes under the appropriation doctrine?

In *Bean Lake,* the Court cited and discussed *Paradise Rainbows,* in which this Court specifically recognized as a valid appropriation a diversion of water for fish propagation.... Prior to 1973, Montana explicitly recognized water rights for fish, wildlife and recreation uses. Montana was not alone in recognizing as beneficial the use of water for fish, wildlife and recreation purposes. *See, e.g., Faden v. Hubbell* ("[i]t is self-evident that water diverted and employed for the propagation of fish is devoted to a useful purpose, and all of the parties completed their appropriations of water by its application to the beneficial use designed"); *State ex rel. State Game Commission v. Red River Valley Co.* ("we are unable to find authority, or justification in reason, to support the claim that the 'beneficial use' to which public waters, as defined in this and other jurisdictions, may be put, does not include uses for recreation and fishing").

To the extent *Bean Lake* suggests that fish, wildlife and recreation are not beneficial uses, it simply misstates Montana precedent and is hereby overruled....

B. Does *Bean Lake* correctly hold that claims for the non-diversionary use of water for fish, wildlife and recreation are not recognized in Montana law under the prior appropriation doctrine?

In arguing this matter to the Court, DFWP has strenuously contended that, since the five water right claims which are the subject of the Department's appeal all involve diversions of water, the Court should correct the language in *Bean Lake* as it applies to diversionary rights but should leave the *Bean Lake* holding in tact as it applies to non-diversionary claims. The dissent also argues that the Court, in addressing non-diversionary uses, is going outside the issues and should confine itself to diversionary rights. We determine that such a restricted clarification would be inconsistent with the fact that the *Bean Lake* remark which has given rise to this appeal is being applied by the Water Court to both diversionary and non-diversionary pre-July 1, 1973, claims, and that the *Bean Lake* decision itself arose out of DFWP's claim for an instream, non-diversionary claim to the water in a natural pothole lake....

... To resolve the confusion engendered by *Bean Lake,* we now determine whether a valid appropriation of water may be established without a diversion where no diversion is physically necessary for the intended use.

While most traditional uses necessitated a diversion of water for application to beneficial use, the appropriation doctrine's history of flexibility and practicality support a holding that a diversion is not required where the application to beneficial use does not physically require a diversion. Common sense rebels against a rigid diversion requirement that would refuse to recognize an acknowledged beneficial use simply because application to the use does not require removal from and depletion of the water source. In accordance with the doctrine's flexibility, we find that a diversion is not a requisite element of an appropriation when it is not a physical necessity for application to a beneficial use.

More than one commentator has warned against the strict adherence to traditional elements, such as diversion, when the element no longer serves its original purpose. These scholars also note that beneficial use is the only essential element of a valid appropriation. *See, e.g.*, Tarlock, *Appropriation For Instream Flow Maintenance: A Progress Report on "New" Public Western Water Rights,* 1978 Utah L.Rev. 211, 221 ("Most western water experts agree that the actual diversion requirement serves no function that cannot be served by other water law doctrines and statutory procedures. Thus the real issue is whether these uses are beneficial"); Christine A. Klein, *The Constitutional Mythology of Western Water Law,* 14 Va. Envtl. L.J. 343, 351 (1995) ("Rigid adherence to the diversion requirement has increasingly restricted the traditional flexibility of the ideas of beneficial use and waste. Although appropriation to beneficial use is the true measure of a water right, diversion has frequently been substituted as the constitutional requirement").

Under prior appropriation, a diversion traditionally served dual purposes providing notice of a user's intent to appropriate water, and defining the extent of the use. In *Wheat v. Cameron* this Court explained that intent to appropriate is to be determined from the specific facts and circumstances pertaining.

...

In accordance with the historical flexibility of the doctrine of prior appropriation, the *Wheat* Court held that although intent could be *presumed* from actual diversion, intent could be proven through other facts and surrounding circumstances. Similarly, in *Bean Lake,* the Court noted that diversion could provide notice or proof of an intent to appropriate. These decisions do not require a diversion for proof of intent. To the contrary, the opinions suggest that although a diversion may provide proof, intent is the essential element and may be proven through means other than a diversion. In other words, a diversion, although sufficient to prove intent, is not necessary.

Decisions from this Court have not consistently required diversions for water appropriations.... *See, e.g., Donich v. Johnson* (appropriation recognized for instream reservoir); *Axtell v. M.S. Consulting* (domestic use recognized without a diversion). Those cases that do suggest that a diversion is an essential element of an appropriation involve uses that, of practical necessity, require a diversion for the application to beneficial use. *See, e.g., Warren v. Senecal* (diversion by ditch for use in mining and irrigation); *Sherlock v. Greaves* (diversion by pipes and flumes from ditch for irrigation and domestic use).

Justice Rice in his dissent states that, in recognizing instream uses prior to 1973, we are rewriting Montana history. Justice Rice's protestations to the contrary, Montana has a legendary history of cattle and sheep ranching. No doubt Montana's stockgrowers would be surprised to learn, as the dissent suggests, that Montana law would not have recognized a right to water stock directly from a stream, lake, pond or slough without a man-made diversion.... [T]he Montana Legislature recognized that pre-1973 claims for stock use and individual use *based upon instream flow* were valid. Such non-diversionary, instream claims were exempted from the mandatory filing requirement of Title 85, Chapter 2. ("Every person... asserting a claim to an existing right to the use of water arising prior to July 1, 1973, is ordered to file a statement of claim to that right with the department no later than June 30, 1983. Claims for stock and individual as opposed to municipal domestic uses *based upon instream flow* or ground water sources are exempt from this requirement; however, claims for such uses may be voluntarily filed." Section 85-2-212, MCA (emphasis added).

The fact that there are no Montana decisions establishing such an instream right merely reflects the fact that that issue was not litigated, not that such a right was beyond the pale of Montana prior appropriation doctrine....

The non-recognition of instream uses prior to 1973 would likewise have been a shock to Montana's early loggers and railroaders who used Montana stream flows to float logs and railroad ties. *See Montana Coalition for Stream Access v. Curran* where we recognized that the Dearborn River was used in 1887, two years before Montana statehood, to float approximately 100,000 railroad ties....

...

Ample case law depicting the evolution of the prior appropriation doctrine, and emerging from throughout the west, supports a conclusion that the doctrine should not rigidly demand a diversion where unnecessary to achieve the intended beneficial use. *See, e.g., Empire Water & Power Co. v. Cascade Town Co.* ("[i]f nature accomplishes a result which is recognized and utilized, a change of process by man would seem unnecessary"); *In re Water Rights in Silvies River* ("[w]hen no 'ditch, canal, or other structure' is necessary to divert the water from its natural channel, the law does not vainly require such works, prior to an appropriation"); *Town of Genoa v. Westfall* (("It is not necessary in every case for an appropriator of water to construct ditches or artificial ways through which the water might be taken from the stream in order that a valid appropriation be made. The only indispensable requirements are that the appropriator intends to use the waters for a beneficial purpose and actually applies them to that use"); *State, Dept. of Parks v. Idaho Dept. of Water Admin.* (Bakes, J., concurring) ("[w]here an appropriative water right does not require a diversion to make it effective and beneficial, in the absence of a statute requiring a diversion there appears to be no practical reason why a diversion should be required").

...

Only two short months after our *Bean Lake* decision, the Nevada Supreme Court decided a nearly identical controversy. In *State v. Morros,* the Nevada Court considered whether "Nevada law absolutely requires a physical diversion of water to obtain a water right" in a controversy involving an inlake appropriation claim for recreation purposes. After noting that the common law had evolved to allow appropriations for stock watering without a diversion when there was no practical need for a physical diversion, the

Nevada Court validated an inlake appropriation for recreation purposes. In protecting the inlake water right, the court held that just as the common law "conformed to the practical demands of stockwatering," so should it reflect the fact that "[d]iversions are not needed for and are incompatible with many recreational uses." We find the Nevada Court's reasoning persuasive.

...

Because beneficial use rather than diversion is the touchstone of the prior appropriation doctrine; because Montana has long recognized as beneficial the use of water for fish, wildlife and recreation; and because Montana has validated non-diversionary appropriations, we now hold that Montana law prior to 1973 did not absolutely require a diversion for a valid appropriation of water.

...

For the foregoing reasons, we overrule the *Bean Lake* conclusion that Montana, prior to 1973, did not recognize fish, wildlife and recreation appropriations of water, whether diversionary or non-diversionary. We hold that Montana recognized fish, wildlife and recreation uses as beneficial and that valid instream and in-lake appropriations of water existed in Montana prior to 1973 where the intended beneficial use did not require diversion, and when the facts and circumstances indicate that notice of the appropriator's intent had been given.

...

Notes & Questions

1. Suppose a company built a health spa and retreat directly adjacent to a beautiful natural waterfall. The reason for the spa's location is to provide clients with the beautiful view and soothing sounds from the falls. Under the differing approaches taken by the Idaho and Montana state courts, could the spa appropriate a water right for the continued flow of the waterfall in the absence of a statute allowing them to do so?
2. Suppose a rancher owns a meadow that is directly next to a stream. They use this meadow to feed their livestock. Every spring, the stream floods into the meadow, causing the meadow to become saturated with water. As a result, the grass in the meadow grows into the summer months. Without that flooding event, the meadow would cease to be usable for livestock grazing much earlier in the year. Under the differing approaches taken by the Idaho and Montana state courts, could the rancher appropriate a water right for that overflow? For the states where they couldn't, what would they have to do in order to acquire a water right?
3. In the absence of a diversion, what type of evidence would be necessary to show intent to appropriate?

What Constitutes a Diversion?

The next case looks at whether a "diversion" requires a structure that actually removes water from the stream channel. In this case, the question of diversion arises in the context of a dam built for flood control and hydroelectric power generation. Figure 6.2 illustrates that this type of dam is intended to cause the water level of the stream to be artificially raised or held at a higher level so that the force of the water as it drops to river level may run a turbine. The water-powered turning of the turbine creates energy for society. The next case asks whether this use of water, which depends on the instream impoundment of water behind a dam, has a valid diversion under Idaho law.

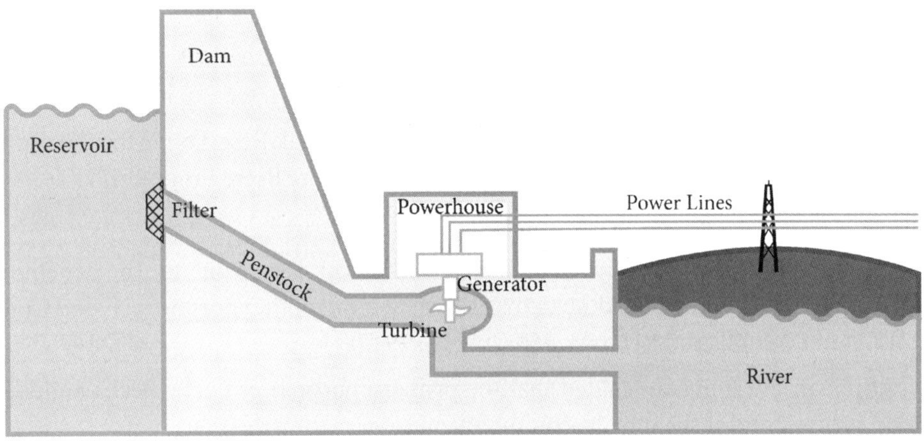

Figure 6.2 Schematic of a hydroelectric system. Source: Design by Leilanee Taylor.

In the District Court of the Fifth Judicial District of the State of Idaho, in and for the County of Twin Falls
In re SRBA

Subcase: 63-03618 (2008)
(Lucky Peak Reservoir)

MEMORANDUM DECISION AND ORDER ON CROSS-MOTIONS FOR SUMMARY JUDGMENT

RE: BUREAU OF RECLAMATION STREAMFLOW MAINTENANCE CLAIM

...

II. PROCEDURAL BACKGROUND

The water right claim in this case pertains to Lucky Peak Reservoir and Dam which are part of the Boise Project on the Boise River. At issue are two of the recommended purposes of use pertaining to streamflow maintenance....

The United States Bureau of Reclamation ("BOR" or "United States") claimed, and the Idaho Department of Water Resources ("IDWR") recommended, year 'round stream-flow maintenance storage and streamflow maintenance from storage in the amount of 152,300.00 AFY. The streamflow maintenance is for the channel of the Boise River downstream from Lucky Peak Dam to the confluence with the Snake River. The recommendation is based on and consistent with the license issued by IDWR in 2002 for this claim.

...

In general, the Objectors argue that the streamflow maintenance purpose of use cannot be decreed because under Idaho law only the Idaho Water Resource Board can hold a minimum instream flow claim....

...

IV. FACTUAL HISTORY

The facts in this subcase are not in dispute.... Lucky Peak Reservoir is the third and farthest downstream of the three on-river reservoirs of the Boise Project....

...

Congress authorized the construction of Lucky Peak Reservoir "for the benefit of navigation and the control of destructive flood waters and other purposes." Flood Control Act of 1946, 60 Stat. 641, 643, 650 (July 24, 1946).

Although the study concluded that the primary purpose of Lucky Peak would be flood control, one of the other recommended uses was for irrigation...

...

On December 18, 1957, the BOR filed permit application R-35086 with the Idaho Department of Reclamation [now Department of Water Resources] "To Construct a Reservoir and Appropriate and Store the Public Waters of the State of Idaho." The application was for 307,000 acre feet total capacity with 278,000 acre feet useable storage. The purpose of use stated was for "irrigation and power for irrigation pumping." ... Pursuant to publication notice, the last day to file timely protests to the approval of the application was January 27, 1958.... A protest was filed by the State of Idaho on behalf of the Idaho Department of Fish and Game.... Closures of the outlet of the dam during periods of annual maintenance resulted in low flows on the Boise River which caused problems for fish and wildlife.... As a result, the Idaho Department of Fish and Game made application for a 100 cfs water right from Lucky Peak and wanted a determination of its permit application prior to approval of the BOR's permit application....

...

Ultimately, the BOR resolved the protests through the filing of an amendment to the permit application. The application was amended to provide that "Lucky Peak stored waters will be utilized in the Boise Valley on presently irrigated lands for supplemental irrigation water" and also to include the following remark:

> This permit is issued on condition—That the yield of water from 50,000 acre feet of space be available for maintaining winter time flow in the Boise River below Boise Diversion dam under a release pattern established from time to time by the Director of the Idaho Fish and Game Department.

...

VII. DISCUSSION

...

B. The Idaho Minimum Stream Flow Act does not apply to the Streamflow Maintenance Claim.

The arguments raised by the Objectors rest on the assumption that the streamflow maintenance claim at issue is in all respects a minimum streamflow claim as defined by the Idaho Minimum Stream Flow Act, I.C. § 42-1501 *et seq.* ("IMSFA" or "Act"). The Respondents argue that because the claim involves a diversion, namely the dam, the IMSFA does not apply.... There are colorable arguments on both sides of the issue. While on one hand there is a diversion, the place of use is still located within the natural channel of the river. On the other hand, the entire flow of river is diverted and then artificially released. In other words, the claim does not involve the appropriation of a natural flow within the channel....

[The court provides a lengthy analysis, concluding that a dam is a diversion and thus the Act does not apply. The analysis is based on the language and legislative history of Idaho's Minimum Stream Flow Act; and the practice of the state agency in implementing the Act. You will study the Act in Part V. For purposes of this Chapter, the key information in determining that a dam is a diversion is that "the entire flow of river is diverted and then artificially released."

Notes & Questions

1. Under the reasoning in the Lucky Peak Reservoir case, would the developers of a hydropower dam be able to acquire a water right for hydropower production?

The Role of Diversion in Establishing the Priority Date

You have learned that priority is a key element of a prior appropriation water right. Thus, clear rules on the exact requirements for establishing priority are important to avoid conflict. The general rule is that the priority date is established by diversion and application to a beneficial use. Application of this rule is relatively straightforward in the case of small uses of water that take a small amount of time to develop, and thus there is no real difference between the date of diversion and the date of application to a beneficial use. However, larger diversions can take years to develop, and water use may be brought online incrementally as construction is completed. Should users who have expended significant time and capital in developing their water right lose their seniority to smaller uses of water that take less time to develop? Should large water developments face a race to complete, thus wasting the investment of one (and creating a disincentive to invest for all)? This is the issue in our next case. The timeline in Figure 6.3 will help you follow the sequence of events. You will also see that there were some administrative systems to allow (but not require) recording of rights in existence by the time of this case. You will learn about administrative systems for obtaining permits in Part V. Posting of notice of intent to appropriate preceded an early permit system in Idaho. Neither system was exclusive, meaning that water rights could still be obtained by mere diversion and application to a beneficial use.

Sand Point Water & Light Co. v. Panhandle Development Co.

Supreme Court of Idaho
83 P. 347 (1905)

AILSHIE, J. Prior to hearing this case on its merits, the respondent filed and presented a motion to dismiss the appeal, and also a motion to strike from the transcript the appellant's statement on motion for a new trial. We have carefully examined the record and affidavits used on the hearing of these motions and have concluded that both motions should be overruled, and it is so ordered.

This action was commenced by the respondent corporation [SPWL] to restrain the appellant corporation [PHD] from diverting and appropriating the waters of Sand creek and Switzer creek in Kootenai county, and to restrain and enjoin the defendants [PHD] from interfering with or diverting the waters of those streams in any way or manner that would interfere with the rights and appropriation of the plaintiff [SPWL]. The case went to trial upon complaint and answer, and resulted in a judgment for the plaintiff, from which judgment and an order denying a motion for a new trial, the defendant has appealed.

The substance of the trial court's findings of fact is that the plaintiff's grantor was the prior appropriator of the waters of Switzer creek and the west branch of Sand creek, situated in Kootenai county, and that such appropriation dates from September 26, 1903, the date on which respondent's grantor made his application to the State Engineer for a permit to divert, appropriate, and use the waters of those streams to the extent of 20 cubic feet per second. The court finds that plaintiff and its grantor had performed all the acts and requirements necessary or imposed by the statute for the protection of its appropriation, and had diverted the waters and applied them to a beneficial use in supplying the village of Sand Point and its inhabitants with water for domestic uses and fire purposes. The court also finds that the respondent's appropriation was and is prior to that of the appellant and so ordered and decreed. The appellant contends that the undisputed facts as disclosed by the evidence and appearing upon the record show clearly and beyond question that the court's findings are unsupported by the evidence,

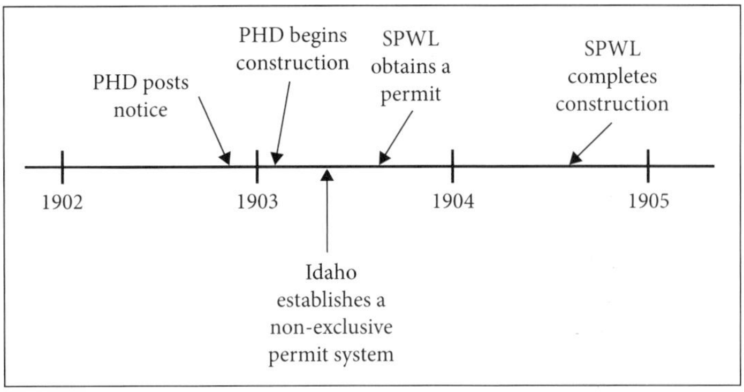

Figure 6.3 Timeline showing the order of actions to divert water and apply it to beneficial use in the case of *Sand Point Water & Light Co. (SPWL) v. Panhandle Development Co.*

and that he should have found that appellant's water right from these streams is prior and superior to the rights of respondent, and that the findings of the court in this respect are wholly unsupported. The facts as they appear from the record upon this point are substantially as follows:

On December 16, 1902, appellant's grantors located a water right on West Sand or Mill creek in Kootenai county, and the location notice thereof was posted and duly filed and recorded in the office of the county recorder of Kootanai county, and thereafter, in due time, was filed in the office of the State Engineer at Boise city. Within a few days thereafter the same parties duly and regularly made two additional locations on these streams. On the 14th day of January, 1903, and about 29 days after making the first location, work was commenced, which consisted in cutting out a trail up the canyon, and making a survey for flumes and ditches. Work was continuously prosecuted from that time until the date of the trial of this cause, with at least one man on the ground all the time engaged in building a road, and a flume and ditch through which to carry the waters of these streams, and the general work incident to the construction of the diverting work for carrying out the purposes for which the appropriation was being made. The fact stands upon the record practically undisputed, that on the 29th day of September, 1903, the date on which respondent's grantor obtained his permit from the State Engineer to divert and appropriate the waters of these streams, the appellant was actively engaged in the construction of its diverting works, and had at that time expended from \$700 to \$800 in the prosecution of the work.

It should be observed that appellant's location and the prosecution of its work was made under the act of February 25, 1899 (Sess. Laws 1899, p. 380), while the respondent's right was initiated under act approved March 11, 1903 (Sess. Laws 1903, p. 223). By the latter act a permit is obtained from the State Engineer to divert and appropriate the waters of any of the public streams of the state, while under the act of 1899, notice was required to be posted and a copy thereof filed and recorded with the county recorder, and a duplicate thereof filed with the State Engineer. By section 6, p. 381, of the act of 1899, under which appellant initiated its right, it is provided: "Within sixty days after the notice is posted, the claimant must commence the excavation or construction of the works by which he intends to divert the water, and must prosecute the work diligently and uninterruptedly to completion, unless temporarily interrupted by snow, rain, or cold weather." Respondent claims that the appellant failed to show that it had prosecuted the construction of its diverting works with the diligence required by section 6, supra, and for that reason, if for none other, the judgment was properly entered against appellant. It seems to us, however, when we consider that this work was being prosecuted in a mountainous section of the state where there is a heavy snow fall and a long winter season with much rough and stormy weather which would interrupt and delay the character of work that was being carried on, that the amount and kind of work which is shown to have been done evidences good faith, reasonable diligence, and a purpose to complete the work and apply the waters to the beneficial use designated. Saying nothing of the record notice which the respondent had, the work upon the ground and its continued prosecution was ample actual notice to respondent, or any other subsequent claimant to these waters, as to the nature of the claim asserted by appellant.

It seems to us that the real difficulty in this case has arisen from a wrong construction and misapplication of the word appropriate as used in our statutes. Section 8 of the act of February 25, 1899, provides that where an appropriator has complied with the preceding sections in the posting and recording of notices and the commencement and prosecution of work, "the claimant's right to the use of water relates back to the time the notice was posted." Section 7 of the act provides that by a completion of the work "is meant conducting the waters to the place of intended use." A person desiring to appropriate the waters of a stream may do so either by actually diverting the water and applying it to a beneficial use, or he may pursue the statutory method by posting and recording his notice and commencing and prosecuting his work within the statutory time. In the latter case his appropriation will be entitled to date from the time of posting his notice and any intervening locator or claimant of the waters will be treated as subsequent both in time and right. In such case the appropriation is initiated by the posting of the notice, and an inchoate right thereby arises which may ripen into a legal and complete appropriation upon the final delivery of the waters to the place of intended use. In other words, by pursuing the successive steps prescribed in the statute, and completing his diverting works, and applying the water to a beneficial purpose, the appropriation is completed. The only difference between an appropriation initiated by posting notice and one initiated by diversion and application of the waters is that the appropriator, who claims under notice, is allowed the extra 60 days within which to commence his work, and reasonable time thereafter in which to complete the same.

It appears that the lower court proceeded on the theory that the appropriation, regardless of the posting of notice, dates from the actual diversion of the water, and its application to the use intended, and the court accordingly finds that "the plaintiff did on or before the 14th day of August, 1904, complete its water system and did actually appropriate the waters flowing in the said stream described in the complaint, and has ever since said date actually appropriated and used all the waters in said stream described in the complaint in supplying the inhabitants of the village of Sand Point with water for domestic uses and fire purposes." This theory is incorrect as applied to appellant, so long as appellant continued to prosecute its work with reasonable diligence. So long as it did so, it was entitled to have its appropriation relate back to the posting of its notice; and, in that event, appellant would be entitled to protection as a prior appropriator as against the respondent. Some importance seems to have also been attached to the fact that the appellant was cognizant of the work being done by respondent, and the large expenditure being made by it in constructing its diverting works and water system, and that it should have made some demonstration or taken some action sooner to prevent respondent further prosecuting its work. This position, however, is without merit. The appellant was also prosecuting its work at the same time and for a similar purpose, but in the meanwhile neither one was actually diverting the water to the detriment or damage of the other, nor was there any apparent reason why appellant could or should have prevented respondent carrying on its work. There is no contention made in this case but that respondent has a valid water right and appropriation, and would be entitled to whatever of the waters of those streams the appellant fails to use or at any such times as the appellant fails to use and apply those waters. The only difficulty is that upon the undisputed facts of the case, respondent's right is subsequent and subordinate to appellant's right. On the facts as presented by this appeal, the trial court should have found that the defendant, the Development Company, had a prior and superior right to that of plaintiff, the Water & Light Company, and that defendant had prosecuted the construction of its diverting works with reasonable diligence.

The judgment is reversed, and cause remanded, with instructions to the trial court to make findings of fact in accordance with the views herein expressed, and enter judgment in accordance therewith. Costs awarded to appellant.

Notes & Questions

1. The rule from *Sand Point Water & Light* is that "so long as [a water user] continue[s] to prosecute its work with reasonable diligence ... it was entitled to have its appropriation relate back to [the time it began developing its water right]; and ... [is] entitled to protection as a prior appropriator as against the respondent." Similar to priority, this rule protects the investment of the person who acts first and avoids the waste of a race to complete. This applies only if the appropriator proceeds with due diligence. An earlier case in Idaho had addressed the question of what constitutes due diligence in the context of development of irrigation on land that has been homesteaded. The court in *Conant v. Jones,* 3 Idaho 606, 32 P. 250 (1893) states:

    > The appropriator would no doubt be entitled to a reasonable time in which to get his land in cultivation, and to make such application. If that be true, it follows that what constitutes reasonable time is a question of fact dependent upon the circumstances of each particular case. No inflexible rule should be made by which to decide what constitutes reasonable time in this matter. We are of the opinion that a person who complies with the law as to locating and conducting

> the water to the point of intended use has such time as he may need or require, using ordinary diligence in getting his land into cultivation, to make application of such water to the intended use; such time, at least, as is reasonable under all of the circumstances of the case.
>
> Poor men, as a rule, have settled upon the arid lands of this state, and taken them under the laws of congress, many of them under the homestead law, and are able to clear but a small portion of such lands of sage brush from year to year, and put it in condition for raising a crop; and it will take years for many of them to prepare their entire farms for cultivation, and to make application of the water appropriated thereto.

2. Choose each of the following that might be useful evidence in the effort prove due diligence:
   a. The type of beneficial use as it relates to the amount of infrastructure required;
   b. The scope of the permitting and land acquisition process to develop the project in relation to the start of work on the ground;
   c. The climate and topography of the project in relation to when work is performed;
   d. The time taken to complete other similar projects in similar terrain and climate.
3. The protection for an investment in water development prior to perfecting a claim to a right has its parallel in the common law concept of the *pedis possessio* doctrine in mining law. Under the General Mining Law you learned about in Part I, discovery of a valuable mineral deposit was necessary to obtain a patent (fee simple title) to the land. Due to a similar problem of the time it takes to determine if a valuable mineral deposit is present, the *pedis possessio* doctrine protected the original possessor of a mining claim during the period of exploration.

Finding Flexibility in Western Water Law—Means of Diversion

In addressing disputes among water users, changes to the means of diversion can sometimes allow more water to flow to junior water users, thus avoiding the harsh consequences of enforcement of priority. The question that arises is: can the government require a water user to change their means of diversion to allow water development for other users, or does the means of diversion have absolute protection as a property right? You learned in Part I that there is considerable confusion and debate about what it means to have a property right in a use. Here you explore whether that "use" right extends to protection for the means of diversion.

The case of *Schodde v. Twin Falls Land & Water Co.*[2] came before the U.S. Supreme Court because of the involvement of the U.S. Bureau of Reclamation. It addressed the question of whether government may require a change in means of diversion. The

2. 224 U.S. 107 (1912).

Reclamation dam would back water up beyond the location of a water wheel used by irrigators on the bench above the Snake River in Idaho to lift water out of the canyon for conveyance to their lands. The water wheel was powered by the flow of the river, which ceased when the dam was built. The issue, therefore, was whether a water right includes the right to the continued means of diversion, even when its current configuration renders it necessary to use the entire flow of the river. The Court's answer is no.

Schodde v. Twin Falls Land & Water Co.

Supreme Court of the United States
224 U.S. 107 (1912)

Opinion

Mr. Chief Justice White delivered the opinion of the court:— ... The court below summarized the averments of the three counts of the complaint, and as that summary accurately and sufficiently states the case, we adopt and reproduce it, as follows:

> 'Plaintiff's complaint contains three counts. Briefly stated, the cause of action as set out in the three counts of the complaint is as follows: ... In the year 1889 plaintiff's predecessors in interest, and in 1895, the plaintiff himself, appropriated certain quantities of water of the flow of Snake river for use on said lands.... The aggregate of water appropriated as alleged in the three counts is referred to in the briefs as 1,250 miner's inches. Soon after this water was appropriated the parties in interest erected water wheels in the river to lift the water to a sufficient height for distribution over the land. Nine of these wheels were erected opposite or near the tracts on the south side of the river, and two near the tract on the north side of the river. These wheels vary in height from 24 to 34 feet. The parties also constructed wing dams in the river, adjoining or in front of the lands owned by them, for the purpose of confining the flow of the water of the river, and raising it at such points above the natural flow of the river, so that the current would drive the water wheels and cause them to revolve and carry the water in buckets attached to the wheels to a height where it would be emptied into flumes and distributed over the lands by ditches, and used thereon to irrigate and cultivate the agricultural land and work the mining ground.... In the year 1903, while plaintiff was using the appropriated water of the river upon the described premises, the defendant commenced the construction of a dam across Snake river at a point about nine miles westerly from and below the lands of the plaintiff. The work was prosecuted on said dam until its completion in March, 1905. This dam is so constructed as to impound all the water of Snake river flowing at said point, and to raise the water about 40 feet in height. It is alleged that when defendant's dam was filled with water, the water was turned into a canal known as the 'Twin Falls canal,' owned by the defendant and located on the north side of the river; ... It is alleged that by reason of this dam the waters of Snake river have been backed up from said dam and to and beyond plaintiff's premises,

> and have destroyed the current in the river by means of which plaintiff's water wheels were driven and made to revolve and raise the water to the elevation required for distribution over plaintiff's lands. It is alleged that it is now impossible for plaintiff to so arrange or change his said dams or water wheels or flumes, or to build or construct other dams or water wheels or flumes that will raise any water whatever from said stream that can be used upon the plaintiff's lands, and by reason thereof plaintiff has not been able to irrigate said lands or any part thereof, or to raise profitable crops thereon, or to use the same as pasture lands, and will not in the future be able to irrigate said lands or to raise profitable crops or any crops thereon as long as defendant's dam is maintained; that there is no other supply of water available for use upon said lands except the waters of Snake river; …

…

The trial court recognized fully the right of the plaintiff to the volume of water actually appropriated for a beneficial purpose. It nevertheless dismissed the complaint on the ground that there was no right under the Constitution and laws of the state of Idaho to appropriate the current of the river so as to render it impossible for others to apply the otherwise unappropriated waters of the river to beneficial uses. The court did not find it necessary to deny that power might be one of the beneficial purposes for which appropriations of water might be made, but in substance held that to uphold as an appropriation the use of the current of the river to the extent required to work the defendant's wheels would amount to saying that a limited taking of water from the river by appropriation for a limited beneficial use justified the appropriation of all the water in the river as incident to the limited benefit resulting from the use of the water actually appropriated. The court said:

> 'It is conceded and is beyond question, that the statute law as well as judicial authority directly protects plaintiff in all the water he has actually appropriated, diverted, and used; but there is no statute, nor, so far as known, any judicial rulings, protecting him in the establishment and in the use of his water wheels, as he claims to, and must, use them for the diversion of water to his land.'

Again:

> 'As by art. 15, § 3, Constitution of Idaho, all unappropriated waters are subject to appropriation, it follows that all water that plaintiff has legally appropriated belongs to him, but all other is subject to appropriation. It is unquestioned that what he has actually diverted and used upon his land, he has appropriated; but can it be said that all the water he uses or needs to operate his wheels is an appropriation? As before suggested, there is neither statutory nor judicial authority that such a use is an appropriation. Such use also lacks one of the essential attributes of an appropriation,—it is not reasonable.'
>
> …

The court of appeals, in affirming the decree of dismissal, did so for substantially the reasons which controlled the trial court....

After elaborately reviewing the general principles upon which the law of appropriation rested, and referring to provisions of the Constitution and statute law of Idaho, and the decisions interpreting and enforcing the same, it was held that the extent of beneficial use was an inherent and necessary limitation upon the right to appropriate. Pointing out the disastrous results which would follow from any other view, the court said:

...

> 'There is, furthermore, the general principle that the right of appropriation must be exercised with some regard to the rights of the public. It is not an unrestricted right. In *Basey v. Gallagher* the Supreme Court of the United States said: 'Water is diverted to propel machinery in flour mills and saw mills, and to irrigate land for cultivation, as well as to enable miners to work their mining claims; and in all such cases the right of the first appropriator, exercised within reasonable limits, is respected and enforced. We say within reasonable limits, for this right to water, like the right by prior occupancy to mining ground or agricultural land, is not unrestricted. It must be exercised with reference to the general condition of the country and the necessities of the people, and not so as to deprive a whole neighborhood or community of its use, and vest an absolute monopoly in a single individual.'
>
> 'In *Fitzpatrick v. Montgomery* the supreme court of the state of Montana, after referring to what has been just quoted from *Basey v. Gallagher*, said: 'While any person is permitted to appropriate water for a useful purpose, it must be used with some regard for the rights of the public. The use of water in this state is declared by the Constitution to be a public use. U.S. Const. art. 3, § 15. It is easy to see that, if persons, by appropriating the waters of the streams of the state, became the absolute owners of the waters, without restriction in the use and disposition thereof, such appropriation and unconditional ownership would result in such a monopoly as to work disastrous consequences to the people of the state. The tendency and spirit of legislation and adjudication of the northwestern states and territories have been to prevent such a monopoly of the waters of this large section of the country, dependent so largely for prosperity upon an equitable, and, as far as practical, free, use of water by appropriations."

We have freely excerpted from the opinions of the courts below because, in our judgment, they so clearly portray the situation, and correctly apply the law to that situation as resulting from the Constitution and statutes of Idaho and the reiterated decisions of the court of last resort of that state, ... that we might place our decree of affirmance upon the reasons which controlled the courts below....

...

Affirmed.

Notes & Questions

1. *Schodde* sets up an important source of flexibility in western water law by allowing more use of water simply by adjustment to diversion infrastructure. As noted by water law scholar Dan Tarlock (2012),[3] the ruling has been used in recent decades as groundwater development has increased. Well depth is considered a "means of diversion" in groundwater development. See if you can find evidence for the policies against monopolies, and in favor of the greatest good for the public, prevalent at the time of the ruling. Keep this case in mind when you read about the concept of reasonableness in the context of quantity of water associated with a water right in the next Chapter.
2. What does the court of appeals (quoted in the opinion) mean when it states: "the general principle that the right of appropriation must be exercised with some regard to the rights of the public..."? Is there tension in the recognition of a private right to use water and the general rule (incorporated in many of the constitutions of western states) that the government holds ownership of the actual water for the benefit of the public?
3. Note that the Court does not provide information on where to draw the line. In *Schodde* the question is all or nothing: the water wheel requires the entire flow of the current; the dam stops the entire flow of the current. Based on *Schodde*, which of the following evidence might be useful in a case that is not so clear-cut but still involves the use of the current to carry water to or into the diversion:
    a. The amount of flow needed for the diversion relative to the amount of water put to beneficial use;
    b. The cost of a change to the diversion relative to the benefit of new water uses;
    c. The customary means of diversion in the area for similar uses;
    d. The priority date of the water right using the current for the diversion.

3. A.D. Tarlock, *The Legacy of* Schodde v. Twin Falls Land and Water Company: *The Evolving Reasonable Appropriation Principle*, 42 Envt'l Law 37, 63 (2012).

Chapter 7

Common Law Attributes of State-Based Water Rights—Beneficial Use

Introduction

The requirement of beneficial use is the most fundamental concept of the prior appropriation doctrine. Beneficial use is both a source of certainty in western water law and a source of flexibility. Thus, to understand this critical attribute of a prior appropriation water use right, this Chapter will provide additional background and discussion to help you understand beneficial use at common law, and how its interpretation at common law as the "measure" of the water right set the stage for the primary area of flexibility in the prior appropriation doctrine today.

As you learned in the last Chapter, most states required the acts of diversion and application to beneficial use to acquire a water right at common law. These acts also created a presumption that the third requirement, intent, was fulfilled. *Sand Point Water & Light Co. v. Panhandle Development Co.*, in the previous Chapter, provided the rule that a water right is perfected (i.e., meets all the legal criteria to progress from a claim to a property (use) right) only after diversion and application to a beneficial use. Provided the appropriator proceeds to complete the project with due diligence, the priority then relates back to the date of diversion (or posting or permit application once those systems were developed). As you learned in the last Chapter, in some states (like Montana) that did not require a diversion at common law, beneficial use was the sole act needed to perfect a water right provided intent could also be shown. Thus, beneficial use is a source of certainty in the law by providing a definite and generally visible means by which a right may be perfected.

Historically, the list of beneficial uses was short, focusing on uses that drove the nascent western economy. These uses generally included: domestic, agriculture, mining, manufacturing, and power. Instream uses other than hydropower, including uses of water *in situ* for fish, wildlife, recreation, and aesthetics, were generally considered not to be beneficial uses of water. *See, e.g.*, *Empire Water and Power Co. v. Cascade Town Co.*, 205 F. 123 (8th Cir. 1913) (stating: "complainant is not entitled to a continuance of the falls solely for their scenic beauty"). Nevertheless, caselaw considering whether the type of use is "beneficial" is rare. Instead, more focus is given to whether there is a hierarchy of types of use. You will learn about the interpretation of preferences specifically listed in the Idaho Constitution[1] in the case of *Montpelier Milling Co. v. City of Montpelier*.

In all states, the term "beneficial use" embodies much more than the mere purpose of the water right. Scholar Janet Neuman provides a concise statement of the common law role of beneficial use, stating "[b]eneficial use, without waste, is the basis, measure, and limit of a water right."[2] Beneficial use provides flexibility because it determines the measure and limit of the water right. Water right quantity is capped by what is generally a fact-based inquiry into the amount reasonably necessary for the particular beneficial use of water. This inquiry turns on the physical, economic, and social context in which the water will be used. The water right is limited to what is "reasonable" for the particular beneficial use, and no right is acquired for water used wastefully (i.e., in excess of what is reasonable). Today, the concepts underlying beneficial use as the measure and limit of a water right provide the potential for flexibility in the doctrine of prior appropriation. Theoretically, what is reasonable varies as water supply, water demand, technology, and the economics of water infrastructure evolve. But, as you will learn in Part V, states did not historically enforce the requirement of reasonable use to its full potential until administrative agencies were created and water scarcity began to impose limits on new water use.

This Chapter will first go directly to the concept of preferences for certain beneficial uses, particularly domestic use. This Chapter will conclude with the evolving concept of beneficial use as the measure and limit of the water right. Chapter 8 will continue with the attribute of beneficial use by exploring whether a water right must be actively and continuously put to a beneficial use to retain it—i.e., the use-it-or-lose-it concept.

Beneficial Use Preferences

While priority generally establishes the hierarchy of water use on a shared water course, some state constitutions and statutes lay out a hierarchy of preferred uses. This approach may be particularly important for drinking water. Note however, that drinking water is not the same as water for domestic purposes. Figure 7.1 shows the domestic use of water in the United States by state. Note the higher use is in the West. This is a reflection of the greater need for watering of traditional household landscaping west of the 100th Meridian. Contrast Figure 7.1 with Table 7.1, showing the amount of water considered necessary under the UN Declaration on the Human Right to Water, which primarily reflects water for drinking and sanitation.

1. Idaho Const. art. XV, s. 3.

2. Janet C. Neuman, *Beneficial Use, Waste, and Forfeiture: The Inefficient Search for Efficiency in Western Water Use*, 28 Envt'l Law 919 (1998). This concept is also codified in O.R.S. § 540.610(1), which states: "Beneficial use shall be the basis, the measure and the limit of all rights to the use of water in this state."

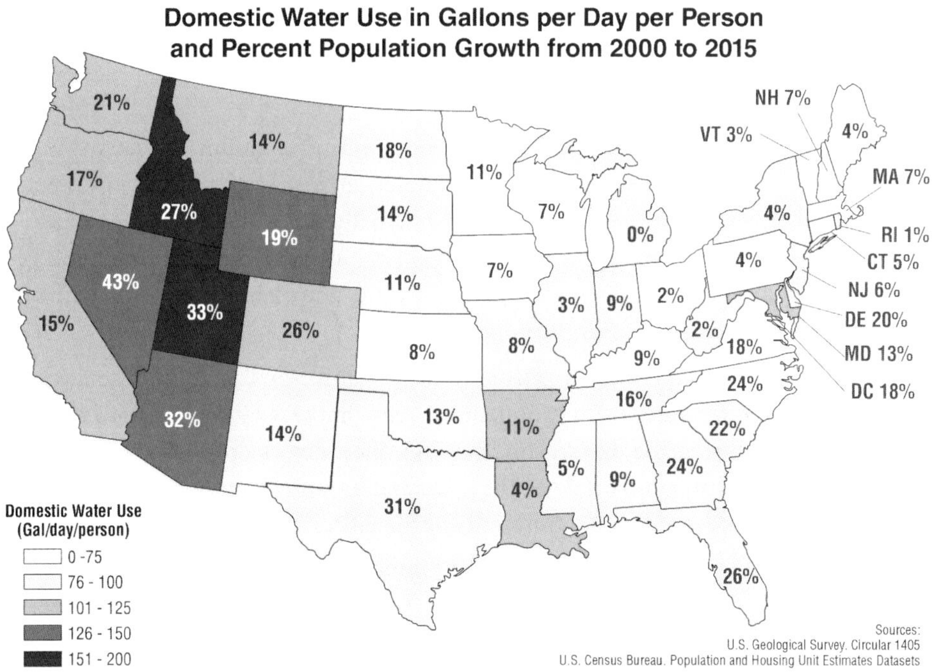

Figure 7.1 Domestic water use in the United States. Shades of gray show gallons per day per person. Percentage shown on each state corresponds to percent population growth from 2000–2015. Source: EPA, *How We Use Water* (2023), https://www.epa.gov/watersense/how-we-use-water.

Despite the relative abundance of domestic water in most of the United States (with notable exceptions including on the Navajo Reservation), the necessity of water for life tends to lead to greater protection for domestic use. The Idaho Constitution provides an example of a hierarchy of uses. Our next case addresses whether these preferences supersede the priority system that underpins the prior appropriation doctrine.

Requirements for the UN Declaration on the Human Right to Water

Sufficient	50–100 liters/person/day Equivalent to 13–26 gallons
Safe	Meets drinking water standards
Accessible	Requires no more than 1000 meter (equivalent to 0.6 miles) or 3 minute walk
Affordable	Costs no more than 3% of household income

Table 7.1 The UN Declaration on the Human Right to Water seeks access for all to water that is sufficient, safe, accessible, and affordable. The table defines those terms.

Montpelier Milling Co. v. City of Montpelier

Supreme Court of Idaho
113 P. 741 (1911)

STEWART, C.J.—This action is brought by the Montpelier Milling Company, a corporation, for the purpose of obtaining an injunction against the city of Montpelier, a municipal corporation, restraining the municipality from diverting the waters of Montpelier creek in Bear Lake county, Idaho. The cause was tried to the court and findings of fact made and a decree entered in favor of the plaintiff. The defendant, the city of Montpelier, appeals from the judgment.

[Plaintiff/respondent owned a grist and flour mill in the City of Montpelier. The mill was powered by water from Montpelier Creek that was diverted through a ditch and a pipeline. During the dry season, the Mill often diverted the entire flow of the creek. The Mill had a priority date of 1891. Defendant/appellant owned a waterworks system that supplied water to the residents of the city. The Mill alleged that In April, 1908, the City had begun diverting water from Montpelier Creek at a point about two miles above the Mill's point of diversion and that, as a result, the Mill was deprived of the water needed to run its mill.

[The trial court entered a decree in favor of the Mill, enjoining the City from diverting water so as to interfere with the flow of at least 10 second feet of water to the Mill's point of diversion.]

It is contended upon behalf of the appellant that the complaint fails to state a cause of action for the reason that it is alleged that the appropriation made by the respondent was for manufacturing and milling purposes, while the appropriation made by the appellant was for municipal and domestic purposes, and thus shows that the appropriation made by the appellant was superior in right to that of the plaintiff.

.... The contention of appellant is based upon a construction of section 3 of article 15 of the Constitution of this state. This section reads as follows:

> The right to divert and appropriate the unappropriated waters of any natural stream to beneficial uses, shall never be denied. Priority of appropriation shall give the better right as between those using the water; but when the waters of any natural stream are not sufficient for the service of all those desiring the use of the same, those using the water for domestic purposes shall (subject to such limitations as may be prescribed by law), have the preference over those claiming for any other purpose; and those using the water for agricultural purposes shall have preference over those using the same for manufacturing purposes. And in any organized mining district, those using the water, for mining purposes or milling purposes connected with mining, shall have preference over those using the same for manufacturing or agricultural purposes. But the usage by such subsequent appropriators shall be subject to such provisions of law regulating the taking of private property for public and private use, as referred to in section 14 of article 1 of this Constitution.

From the language thus used in this section appellant argues that it was the intention of the framers of the Constitution to make an appropriation of water for domestic uses a right superior to an appropriation made for manufacturing uses, without reference to the time or priority of such appropriations. In other words, appellant argues that the appropriation made by the respondent, being for manufacturing purposes, did not withdraw the water so appropriated from a subsequent appropriation made for domestic uses, and that the appropriation and use for manufacturing purposes conferred no right which could not be taken away and destroyed by an appropriation for domestic use. Applying this principle to the facts alleged in the complaint, it is claimed that the appropriation made by the respondent in the year 1891 for manufacturing and milling purposes, and the continuous use of such water from that date up to 1908, conferred no right upon the respondent which could not be defeated and subsequently acquired by the appellant upon an appropriation for domestic uses.

We do not think that the language thus used in the Constitution was ever intended to have this effect, for it is clearly and explicitly provided in said section that the right to divert and appropriate the unappropriated waters of any natural stream to beneficial uses shall never be denied; that priority of appropriation shall give the better right as between those using the water. This clearly declares that the appropriation of water to a beneficial use is a constitutional right, and that the first in time is the first in right, without reference to the use, but recognizes the right of appropriations for domestic purposes as superior to appropriations for other purposes, when the waters of any natural stream are not sufficient for the service of all those desiring the same. This section clearly recognizes that the right to use water for a beneficial purpose is a property right, subject to such provisions of law regulating the taking of private property for public and private use as referred to in section 14, art. 1, of the Constitution.

It clearly was the intention of the framers of the Constitution to provide that water previously appropriated for manufacturing purposes may be taken and appropriated for domestic use, upon due and fair compensation therefor. It certainly could not have been the intention of the framers of the Constitution to provide that water appropriated for manufacturing purposes could thereafter arbitrarily and without compensation be appropriated for domestic purposes. This would manifestly be unjust, and clearly in contravention of the provisions of this section, which declare that the right to divert and appropriate the unappropriated waters of any natural stream for beneficial use shall never be denied, and that priority of appropriation shall give the better right.

....

It is clear, therefore, that under the provisions of the above-quoted section of the Constitution, a municipality cannot take water for domestic purposes which has been previously appropriated for other beneficial uses without fully compensating the owner, and in this case it appearing that the respondent appropriated waters of Montpelier creek and applied the same to a beneficial use in 1891, the appellant had no right to interfere with such appropriation, to the injury of the respondent, without full compensation. There was no error in overruling the demurrer.

Notes & Questions

1. Assume that in 1915 User 1 diverted a large quantity of water to flood irrigate potatoes. Later, in 1920, User 2 diverts water from the same source and uses it for domestic purposes. In 1930 there is a shortage such that there is not sufficient water for both users. Under the rule from *Montpelier,* who gets the water?
2. Do you think that is an equitable outcome? Should a municipality be forced to turn off the taps so that others can continue to flood irrigate just because the irrigator happened to use the water first?
3. Is there anything that User 2 can do to prevent their home from going dry?
4. Note that the term "municipal use" includes more than just domestic use. As you learned in Part I, municipal use today generally includes DCMI (domestic, commercial, municipal, and industrial uses), depending on the nature of development in the municipality. In the case, the city of Montpelier was seeking water to serve domestic use.

Beneficial Use as the Measure of a Water Right: Reasonableness and the Prohibition on Waste

This section explores how beneficial use determines the cap on quantification of a water right. The basic rule in states following prior appropriation is that a water user is entitled to a water right for the amount of water they can put to a beneficial use. That amount is variously expressed as the amount that can be put to beneficial use without waste, the amount that constitutes reasonable use, and the amount that is necessary for the type of beneficial use. The prohibition of the wasteful use of water and the requirement of reasonable beneficial use serve as opposite sides of the same coin. On one side of the coin, courts have defined beneficial use as "limited to reasonable necessity and use, and none for waste."[3] On the other side, courts have articulated the definition from the point of view of waste wherein "[a]n excessive diversion of water, through waste, cannot be regarded as a diversion to beneficial use. . . ."[4]

At common law, the question of quantification was primarily developed in the context of irrigation water rights, due to their magnitude and thus impact on overall water supply. Irrigation is responsible for most of the water use in the West. Globally it is responsible for 70% of freshwater withdrawals,[5] and in Idaho, irrigation is responsible for 86% of water withdrawals.[6] Thus, many of the principles are developed by the courts in the context of irrigation, but are nevertheless more broadly applicable. The Idaho Supreme Court has held that:

---

3. Dern v. Tanner, 60 F.2d 626, 628 (D. Mont. 1932).
4. State ex. rel. Erickson v. McLean, 308 P.2d 983, 987 (N.M. 1957).
5. The World Bank, *Understanding Poverty: Water in Agriculture* (2023), https://www.worldbank.org/en/news/infographic/2023/07/26/water-in-agriculture.
6. Erin M. Murray, *Idaho Water Use,* in USGS: SCIENCE FOR A CHANGING WORLD (2015).

> [t]he lode star of utility of irrigation water is application to a beneficial use without waste, i.e., using no more than is necessary according to the standards and practices of good husbandry for the particular crop sought to be grown, soil and all other essential factors and conditions being taken into consideration, but it does not place any restriction on the kind of crops one may desire to raise.[7]

The Idaho Supreme Court's definition weaves together several important concepts we need to examine more closely. First, the court notes that built into the concept of beneficial use is a prohibition against waste. Notice how it defines when a use is wasteful or not. The court looks to objective, scientific "standards and practices. . . ." However, standards and practices of the type listed by the court in the quotation are not static. They will change over time and are generally relative to the unique circumstances of the use of each water right. In the context of irrigation, a water right may change across the landscape based upon "the particular crop sought to be grown, soil and all other essential factors and conditions being taken into consideration. . . ." Notice also that the quote disclaims consideration of the type of crop grown. The concept that water law will not dictate the type of crop to be grown remains true today. Consider the possibility that application of waste to crop type may change if climate change renders it wasteful to grow certain water-intensive crops in areas where they were formerly grown.

In the context of a domestic water right, reasonable use may include factors such as number of people in a household, size of the home, amount of lawn irrigation, whether the household also raises stock, etc. Commercial and industrial uses will likewise be based upon the amount of water necessary to fulfill the activity at issue. Regardless of the purpose of use the court will quantify the right based on the unique circumstances of each water right, taking expert testimony relevant to the amount of water reasonably necessary to achieve the water user's beneficial use.

States differ in the types of factors they will consider in identifying waste or determining reasonableness, and they also differ in the degree to which these limits on water quantity are enforced. Importantly, they also vary in the degree to which they allow reasonable use to evolve once the water right is issued. Those that allow what is reasonable to evolve may vary in whether they consider changes that include change in: technology; the economics of water use; and water supply and demand. The latter is of critical importance in the context of climate change.

Courts have clarified that the examination of waste applies not only to the final use of water, but begins at the point of diversion and extends through the conveyance system to the water's final application to the user's beneficial use. For example, the Idaho Supreme Court has held that "[a] water user is entitled to the allowance for only a reasonable loss in conducting his water from the point of diversion to the place of use."[8]

7. In re Robinson, 103 P.2d 693, 696 (Idaho 1940).
8. Basinger v. Taylor, 211 P. 1085 (Idaho 1922).

The court found then that the conveyance loss of 50% of the water diverted as a result of a poorly built canal was "unreasonable, excessive, and against public policy...."[9]

Because this concept of reasonableness/prohibition on waste offers the primary means for water use to evolve to address changing climate, demand, technology, and values, it is important to understand how the courts have approached these concepts, as well as how that approach has evolved with increasing scarcity. That evolution was traced by Professor Janet Neuman in her 1998 article, *Beneficial Use, Waste, and Forfeiture: The Inefficient Search for Efficiency in Western Water Use*,[10] which explores beneficial use as the potential source of increased efficiency of water use in the face of an evolving society but finds relatively little evolution in the concept at common law. For example, Neuman cites an early decision from the Oregon Supreme Court,[11] which failed to disallow the practice of using natural flooding for irrigation despite concluding that it was "obviously wasteful ... and should be sanctioned only until a fair opportunity is had to construct [the works necessary] to conserve the water and minimize the waste thereof."[12]

Instead, courts have generally determined reasonableness based on custom in the surrounding area (even, as Neuman points out, when the same custom has prevailed for 75 years), thus locking in inefficient practices. "Water use had to be completely out of line with local custom or blatantly inefficient to merit an actual finding of waste from a court."[13]

Importantly as noted above, the concept of "reasonableness" does not extend to determinations of which crops to grow, or how, absent a statutory or constitutional preference, one type of use should be balanced against another. Neuman points out in reference to the Newlands Project on the Truckee and Carson Rivers in Nevada, reasonableness is not a broad policy question of whether, for example, it is reasonable to divert "nearly the entire flow of two rivers to grow alfalfa in a region that receives five inches of annual natural precipitation, ... while destroying two native fish species in the process...."[14] Instead, as long as the use is within the definition of "beneficial," as irrigation is, it is merely a question of what is customary for irrigation in the area.

Nevertheless, as scarcity has increased, water law has begun to find the flexibility in beneficial use. Neuman quotes the California Supreme Court in the 1990 case of *Imperial Irrigation Dist. v. State Water Resources Control Bd. (IID I)*,[15] finding waste and stating:

> What is a beneficial use, of course, depends upon the facts and circumstances of each case. What may be a reasonable beneficial use, where water is present

---

9. *Id.*
10. 28 Envt'l Law 919 (1998).
11. In re Water Rights in Silvies River, 237 P. 322 (Or. 1925).
12. 28 Envt'l Law at 934.
13. *Id.* at 937.
14. *Id.* at 940.
15. *Id.* at 942, *quoting* 275 Cal. Rptr. 250 (Cal. Ct. App. 1990).

> in excess of all needs, would not be a reasonable beneficial use in an area of great scarcity and great need. What is a beneficial use at one time may, because of changed conditions, become a waste of water at a later time.[16]

The California court goes on to state:

> It is time to recognize that this law is in flux and that its evolution has passed beyond traditional concepts of vested and immutable rights.... In affirming this specific instance of far-reaching change, imposed upon traditional uses by what some claim to be revolutionary exercise of adjudicatory power, we but recognize this evolutionary process, and urge reception and recognition of same upon those whose work in the practical administration of water distribution makes such change understandably difficult to accept.[17]

Finally, you will learn in Part V when you study conjunctive management that modern administrative law has begun to push the concept of reasonable use. The Idaho Department of Water Resources has adopted what is currently one of the strictest approaches to determining reasonable use or waste, and moves in the direction of a "technology forcing standard" that Neuman found lacking in existing application of the prohibition on waste in 1998, and closer to the "reasonable efficiency test" the Washington Supreme Court rejects in *Grimes* (below). The concept that multiple factors must be considered, that those factors go beyond the specific water use and consider the water supply and the needs of other water users, and that the amount considered reasonable will evolve over time, is set forth in Idaho's administrative rules for Conjunctive Management. Under these rules, the Department of Water Resources will not enforce the seniority of a water right unless it is being used reasonably. The Idaho Supreme Court upheld the constitutionality of these rules in *American Falls Reservoir v. Department of Water Resources*,[18] which you will read in Part V. The non-exclusive list of factors the Department will consider include:

> a. The amount of water available in the source from which the water right is diverted.
>
> b. The effort or expense of the holder of the water right to divert water from the source.
>
> c. Whether the exercise of junior-priority ground water rights individually or collectively affects the quantity and timing of when water is available to, and the cost of exercising, a senior-priority surface or ground water right. This may include the seasonal as well as the multi-year and cumulative impacts of all ground water withdrawals from the area having a common ground water supply.

---

16. *Id.* at 942, *quoting* 275 Cal. Rptr. at 265.
17. *Id.* at 942, *quoting* 275 Cal. Rptr. 267.
18. 154 P.3d 433 (Idaho 2007).

d. If for irrigation, the rate of diversion compared to the acreage of land served, the annual volume of water diverted, the system diversion and conveyance efficiency, and the method of irrigation water application.

e. The amount of water being diverted and used compared to the water rights.

f. The existence of water measuring and recording devices.[19]

The next case illustrates the factual basis for determining whether waste is occurring at common law. Note that the court actually uses two legal reasons to uphold the trial court award of a smaller amount of water than claimed by defendant Shaub. First, the historic use. In the next Chapter, you will learn that a water right, or portion of a water right, can be lost through non-use (although note that not all states will allow forfeiture of a portion of a water right). Second, reasonableness or waste. On both issues, the Idaho Supreme Court accepts the decision of the trial court on the facts in the face of conflicting evidence. As is standard with a factual finding, it does so as long as there is competent and substantial evidence supporting the finding of the trial court.

Glenn Dale Ranches, Inc. v. Shaub

Supreme Court of Idaho
494 P.2d 1029 (1972)

Opinion

MCQUADE, C.J.—This is a water rights case.... Plaintiff-respondent is an Idaho corporation which farms approximately 555 acres in Twin Falls County,.... In 1968, [Glenn Dale] brought an action to quiet its alleged title to 230 miner's inches of water from the stream, and to enjoin other users from diverting more than their alleged shares. Subsequently, it moved for an injunction temporarily restraining [Shaub] from diverting more than 10 inches from the stream. [Glenn Dale] conceded those 10 inches to [Shaub] by virtue of an agreement between the parties' early predecessors. However, [Shaub] counter-claimed for 50 miner's inches by prior appropriation, or by prescriptive right deriving from continuous diversion of that amount by his immediate predecessors for more than five years.

[Shaub] was temporarily enjoined from diverting more than 10 inches from the stream. At subsequent hearings, held to show cause why a permanent injunction should not issue and to determine the equities of the parties, [Shaub] adduced testimony that his predecessors had diverted up to 50 inches since 1936. [Glenn Dale's] evidence rebutted that claim and showed that each year, up to the year immediately preceding the first hearing, it had physically interfered with delivery of more than 10 inches to the Shaub farm when the water was needed at the Glenn Dale Ranches. [Glenn Dale] further claimed that 10 inches from the stream, combined with 60 inches which [Shaub] drew from the Twin Falls Canal Company system, were more than

19. IDAPA 37.03.11.42.01 (2022).

adequate for the 54 irrigated acres on his 80-acre farm. When the hearings terminated, the court permanently enjoined [Shaub] from diverting more than 10 inches.

....

[Shaub] charges that [Glenn Dale] failed to prove either its prior appropriative rights or [Shaub's] ability adequately to irrigate his farm without diverting more than 10 inches from the stream.

...

... [I]t does appear from the record that [Glenn Dale] has diverted and put to beneficial use the water it now claims, since it purchased the farm. [Shaub] asserts an earlier appropriation by a deceased predecessor, whose son claimed that since 1936 his father had diverted 50 inches or more from the stream. That statement conflicted with evidence of Fern Nipper, the widow of [Glen Dale's] predecessor, who recalled that [Shaub's] predecessor had diverted only 10 to 15 inches by permission of her late husband. From this conflicting evidence, the trial court found that [defendant] acquired no interest beyond 10 inches from his predecessor. That finding is supported by competent and substantial, though conflicting, evidence and will not be set aside.

Even if a prior appropriation were found, [Shaub] is not entitled to all the water diverted. [Shaub] testified that 80 inches of water were required adequately to irrigate his property. Other witnesses estimated that one inch per acre irrigated would be sufficient. The trial court found that [Shaub] could apply to beneficial use only the 60 inches received from the canal system and 10 inches from the stream. That finding of fact is supported by substantial and competent, though conflicting, evidence, and will not be disturbed on appeal. This Court has declared that "it is against the public policy of the state *** for a water user to take from an irrigation canal more water, of that to which he is entitled, than is necessary for the irrigation of his land ***." That policy logically applies also to a stream supplying several farms, and prohibits [Shaub] from diverting more water than necessary for the beneficial purpose regardless of alleged seniority in right through priority in time.

[Shaub] contends that he cannot apply the full 70 inches to his crops because nearly half is lost as it is conducted from the stream or canal to the place of use. As a result, he is required to draw some 40 more inches from the stream in order to deliver adequate water to the crops. However, the public policy against wasting water prohibits additional diversion to compensate for unreasonable loss. This Court has held that the appropriator must construct flumes, pipes, or other lining if necessary to prevent such unreasonable loss. Accordingly, waters appropriated will be measured for their sufficiency from the point of diversion, not at the place of use.

....

Judgment and decree affirmed.

Notes & Questions

1. The concept of reasonableness and prohibition on waste applies to which of these components of irrigation water use?
   a. The conveyance of water through the natural stream to reach the water user's diversion.
   b. The means of diversion
   c. The conveyance infrastructure
   d. The use of water on the land
2. The Idaho Supreme Court defers to the factual findings of the trial court as long as they are supported by competent and substantial evidence. The court does not discuss this deference. Nevertheless, it goes into detail and in fact cites its own precedent for the proposition that a water user may not take more water "than is necessary for the irrigation of his land." Why?
3. The concept of waste also comes up with the notion of a "futile call." A "call" occurs when a senior water user asks the agency or the court to curtail the use of an upstream junior to satisfy their senior right. An upstream water user need not let water run down to a senior appropriator if the conditions of the stream are such that the water will never reach the downstream diversion. The call is deemed "futile," and the junior may continue using the water. You will learn more about this important concept in the context of conjunctive management of surface and ground water in Part V. For purposes of this Chapter, it is important to understand that the same policy of avoiding waste with the goal of maximizing use leads to the concept of a futile call.

The next case, from Washington, illustrates a slightly more modern approach to determining reasonableness/waste and is chosen to expose you to the heavily technical and fact-based inquiry of reasonableness. Note the central role that geography plays in the court's decision. Marshall Lake is located in northeastern Washington State, a region that is densely wooded and relatively moist in comparison to the majority of the arid portions of the western United States. Also note the relatively small amount of agriculture taking place in the area. Pay attention to how these climatic and other physical factors play into the court's assessment of reasonableness. Also, pay close attention to the court's reliance on, and deference to, expert testimony in determining reasonable use.

Department of Ecology v. Grimes

Supreme Court of Washington
852 P.2d 1044 (1993)

SMITH, Justice.... In September 1981, the Department of Ecology [plaintiff/respondent] filed a petition in the Pend Oreille County Superior Court for clarification of existing rights to divert, withdraw, or otherwise make beneficial use of the surface and ground waters of the Marshall Lake and Marshall Creek drainage basin (Marshall Lake basin). Ecology investigated the Marshall Lake basin and the locality served by it and found that the interests of the public and users of the surface and ground waters would be served by an adjudication and determination of the relative rights of all claimants to the use of these waters.

...

The Grimeses [defendant/appellant] submitted five claims for water rights, only the first of which is at issue in this appeal. This claim was for the use of waters for domestic supply, irrigation and recreational purposes. The Grimeses requested an instantaneous flow rate of 3 cubic feet per second (c.f.s.) for irrigation purposes, and a storage right of 1,520 acre feet of water in the Marshall Lake reservoir. The referee recommended that this claim be confirmed, but limited it to an instantaneous flow of 1.5 c.f.s. during irrigation season, and a storage right of 183 acre feet plus 737 acre feet for evaporative loss, for a total storage right of 920 acre feet.

...

On January 5, 1990, after hearing testimony on the Grimeses' exceptions, the Superior Court entered its "Decree Adjudicating Water Rights Pursuant to RCW 90.03.200." The decree approved the "Report of Referee", as amended by the "Report of Referee Pursuant to Order on Exceptions of May 19, 1988."...

The Doctrine of Prior Appropriation

The law of prior appropriation was established in this state by the Territorial Legislature in 1873 and recognized by this court in 1897. This court in *Neubert v. Yakima-Tieton Irrig. Dist.* said that "[t]he appropriated water right is perpetual and operates to the exclusion of subsequent claimants." In that case we said appropriative water rights require that:

> Once appropriated, the right to use a given quantity of water becomes appurtenant to the land. The appropriated water right is perpetual and operates to the exclusion of subsequent claimants.
>
>> "The key to determining the extent of plaintiffs' vested water rights is the concept of "beneficial use" *** An appropriated water right is established and maintained by the purposeful application of a given quantity of water to a beneficial use upon the land."...

Beneficial use refers to the quantity of water diverted by the appropriator, not to its availability in the source of supply. "The underlying reason for all this constitutional, legislative and judicial emphasis on beneficial use of water lies in the relation of available water resources to the ever-increasing demands made upon them."...

"Beneficial use" is a term of art in water law, and encompasses two principal elements of a water right.

First, it refers to the purposes, or type of activities, for which water may be used. Use of water for the purposes of irrigated agriculture is a beneficial use. The Grimeses' use of water to irrigate alfalfa fields is not at issue in this case.

Second, beneficial use determines the measure of a water right. The owner of a water right is entitled to the amount of water necessary for the purpose to which it has been put, provided that purpose constitutes a beneficial use. To determine the amount of water necessary for a beneficial use, courts have developed the principle of "reasonable use". Reasonable use of water is determined by analysis of the factors of water duty and waste.

In his findings establishing the measure of the Grimeses' water right, the referee stated that:

> Quantification of the amount of water to which this right is entitled creates somewhat of a problem in that there has been no direct testimony regarding the amount of water placed to beneficial use other than a reference in the state's investigatory report that 56 sprinklers are utilized in the system.... Therefore, the Referee will allow the standard duty of water which would be 1.2 cubic feet per second plus an additional 25 percent for transportation loss, thus making an aggregate amount of 1.5 cubic feet per second identified with this right....
>
> A second element concerning this right is the amount of storage of water to which these claimants are entitled.... [T]hese waters also have recreational benefits, not only to the riparian owners around the lake but also to the general public through the use of resort facilities located on the lake.... Therefore, the Referee recommends that a related but separate right be confirmed to these defendants for the storage of 920 acre-feet in Marshall Lake for irrigation and recreation purposes. The priority shall be fixed as of July 13, 1906. The period during which waters may be stored shall be identified as those periods of the year which do not include the April 1 to October 31 irrigation season.

The Grimeses challenge the referee's "consideration of the evidence" and his application of the law in making these findings. We first consider the evidence used by the referee in establishing the factors of water duty and waste. We then consider the test of "reasonable efficiency" employed by the referee, and adopted by the Superior Court, to evaluate these factors.

Water Duty

"[Water duty] that measure of water, which, by careful management and use, without wastage, is reasonably required to be applied to any given tract of land for such period of time as may be adequate to produce therefrom a maximum amount of such crops as ordinarily are grown thereon. It is not a hard and fast unit of measurement, but is variable according to conditions."

The referee based his determination of the volume of water necessary for irrigation in the Marshall Lake basin on a Washington State University Research Bulletin entitled "Irrigation Requirements for Washington—Estimates and Methodology" (Irrigation Report), and on the expert testimony of Jim Lyerla, the District Supervisor for seven Eastern Washington counties, including Pend Oreille County, in the Water Resources

Program of the Department of Ecology. Mr. Lyerla testified that as a part of his work in assigning water quantities to new water permittees, he relied on the Irrigation Report to determine the "water duty" for a proposed use of water. The Irrigation Report provides information for water requirements for specific crops, given in inches per acre per irrigation season, in 40 locations around the state, including Newport, Washington, 5 miles south of Marshall Lake.

Based on the testimony of Mr. Lyerla and the Irrigation Report, the referee determined that an irrigated alfalfa crop grown in the Marshall Lake area requires 21 inches or 1.75 acre feet of water per acre during the irrigation season. The referee then applied an efficiency factor and increased this water duty to 2.5 acre feet per acre per year. The referee found this water duty to be "approximately commensurate with the duty utilized by the Department of Ecology in its quantity allocations in this geographic area under the water right permit system."

Because water rights are characterized in both total yearly allowance and instantaneous flow, the referee also established the maximum rate of diversion at 0.0166 c.f.s. per acre under irrigation. The referee first calculated a standard flow of 1 c.f.s. of water per 60 acres as a reasonable instantaneous flow for alfalfa irrigation in the Marshall Lake basin. In considering the Grimeses' claim, he determined that the Grimeses were entitled to sufficient flow to irrigate 73 acres, or a minimum of 1.21 c.f.s. He then calculated in an efficiency factor to increase this flow by 25 percent and awarded the Grimeses an instantaneous flow of 1.5 c.f.s.

The referee observed that a larger water duty could be awarded to any claimant with specific information proving a right to a larger amount. The 2.5 acre feet/0.0166 c.f.s. water duty was applied when "quantitative evidence of the rate and volume of a right was neither submitted nor made clear during testimony." The referee also observed that "the use of water under all irrigation rights is, however, limited to the amount of water that can be beneficially applied to that number of acres identified in the water right." The referee did not indiscriminately award this water duty to any claim for an irrigation right, but required claimants to prove the number of acres historically irrigated.

In water rights adjudications, the establishment of a water duty must not be disturbed in "the absence of very conclusive evidence contrary to the ... adjudication, showing arbitrariness on [the] part [of the adjudicator]...." The referee's determination of a generic water duty for irrigation of alfalfa in the Marshall Lake basin is supported by a preponderance of the evidence and will not be disturbed by this court.

...

Waste

From an early date, courts announced the rule that no appropriation of water was valid where the water simply went to waste. Those courts held that the appropriator who diverted more than was needed for the appropriator's actual requirements and allowed the excess to go to waste acquired no right to the excess.... A particular use must not only be of benefit to the appropriator, but it must also be a reasonable and economical use of the water in view of other present and future demands upon the source of supply.... The difference between absolute waste and economical use has been said to be one of degree only....

Appellant Clarence E. Grimes acknowledged in his testimony that his existing irrigation system required a water flow of up to 3 cubic feet per second in order to deliver 1 cubic foot per second to the field, ... and that this system was highly inefficient, causing one-half to two-thirds loss of water.... Mr. Grimes also testified that uncertainties and ongoing litigation concerning the stability and safety of the irrigation dam had prevented continuous irrigation of his alfalfa acreage... Other claimants testified concerning their use of the water claimed....

While an appropriator's use of water must be reasonably efficient, absolute efficiency is not required.... The referee determined that, pursuant to RCW 90.14.160, the uncertainties concerning the irrigation dam constituted sufficient cause not to find a complete abandonment of the Grimeses' water right. He resolved the conflicting testimony by limiting the irrigable acreage to the 73 acres recommended by Ecology. Relying on a standard efficiency factor for irrigation sprinkler systems found in the irrigation report, he confirmed in the Grimeses a water right with one-fourth conveyance loss for a total of 1.5 cubic feet per second.... There was at least sufficient evidence for the referee to determine the maximum acreage to which the Grimeses' water right applied, and in limiting the allowable loss for system inefficiency in establishing their instantaneous flow.

The Reasonable Efficiency Test

In limiting the Grimeses' vested water right, the referee balanced several factors, including the water duty for the geographical area and crop under irrigation, the claimants' actual diversion, and sound irrigation practices. In his report, the referee described his method of calculating the Grimeses' water right as a "reasonable efficiency" test....

Amici curiae argue that this test is contrary to judicial decisions which have recognized that the standard of reasonable beneficial use of water for irrigation is limited to consideration of the use of the established means of diversion and application according to the reasonable custom of the locality.... Respondent Ecology argues that the 3-part "reasonable efficiency" test cited by the referee provides "the balance sought by the courts between the competing needs of efficiency and maximum utilization of the water, and the existing physical and economic limitations in each situation."... Ecology asserts that local custom in irrigation practices is but one of several factors the court must consider in deciding whether a given use of water is reasonable, and, therefore, beneficial.

While the referee stated that he relied on this test, and while he did in fact consider some of its elements, he did not actually utilize the test in its entirety. Therefore, we will review the factors he did consider to determine whether his analysis remained within the boundaries of prior appropriation law. In his discussion of the basis for his recommendation concerning the Grimeses' claim, the referee stated that he would "balance [the water duty] against not only the actual amount of water diverted from the lake for irrigation purposes but also against the concepts of beneficial use of water and sound irrigation practices." ...

...

This court has consistently held that rights of users of water for irrigation purposes are vested rights in real property.... Amici curiae assert that the "local custom" test has been employed historically to determine whether given applications of water are wasteful, within the meaning of beneficial use, and that courts should now apply it in the setting of general adjudications. This is the established law in this state....

Decisions of courts throughout the western states provide a basis for defining "reasonable efficiency" with respect to irrigation practices.... While customary irrigation practices common to the locality are a factor for consideration, they do not justify waste of water.... As this court stated in a case predating the Water Code of 1917:

> [W]hen rights in such an important element as water is in the arid regions are to be measured by the courts, we cannot lay down a rule that would give to the user an arbitrary right to use water at will. [An irrigator's] rights are to be measured by his necessities ... and not by any fanciful notion of his own....
>
> ....
>
> ... [C]ustom can fix the manner of use of water for irrigation only when it is founded on necessity ... [and] an irrigator is entitled to use only so much as he can put to a beneficial use, for the public policy of the people of the United States will not tolerate waste of water in the arid regions....

Local custom and the relative efficiency of irrigation systems in common use are important elements, but must be considered in connection with other statutorily mandated factors, such as the costs and benefits of improvements to irrigation systems, including the use of public and private funds to facilitate improvements....

In limiting the Grimeses' water use by a requirement of reasonable efficiency, the referee properly considered the irrigation report, the Grimeses' actual water use, and their existing irrigation system. The referee alluded to a test incorporating factors that consider impacts to the water source and its flora and fauna.... While consideration of these impacts is consonant with the State's obligations under RCW 90.03.005 and 90.54.010(1)(a) and (2), these factors cannot operate to impair existing water rights. Other laws may, however, operate to define existing rights in light of environmental values....

There is some confusion in the record as to the legal standard used by the referee in determining beneficial use....

... But in a footnote the referee set forth a detailed "test of reasonable efficiency" which he purportedly used in determining beneficial use. That "test" is stated as follows:

> (1) [C]ustomary delivery and application practices in the area, (2) technology and "practices" improvements feasible and available to reduce water consumptions and financial needs associated with implementation thereof, and (3) impacts of improvements of existing facilities and practices, if initiated, upon (a) the water source from which the diversion takes place, (b) the existing flora and fauna within the area of diversion, conveyancy and actual uses, (c) other water rights from said water source, and (d) other water users on other water sources....

There is nothing in the record to support the referee's statement that he employed the reasonable efficiency test. Nowhere in the record does he discuss application of the elements of the so-called "test". If he had in fact applied the "test", it would be necessary for this court to reverse and remand. That test is without statutory authorization in an adjudication proceeding which relates exclusively to confirmation of water rights established or created under "other provisions of state law or under federal laws."...

Adjudication proceedings cannot be used "to lessen, enlarge, or modify the existing rights of any riparian owner, or any existing right acquired by appropriation, or otherwise."... The suggested test would be contrary to the vested rights of water users. "It has long been settled in this state that property owners have a vested interest in their water rights to the extent that the water is beneficially used on the land."... Included in the vested rights is the right to diversion, delivery and application "according to the usual methods of artificial irrigation employed in the vicinity where such land is situated."... The test is contrary also to long established principles of Western water law....

While we reject use of the specific test suggested by the referee, we affirm because (1) there is no indication in the record that he in fact applied the factors stated in the "test", and (2) he applied the actual beneficial use made by Grimes, taking into account the actual needs and use and the methods of delivery and application in the vicinity. The adjudication and confirmation of a water right in an amount less than claimed by Grimes does not result from application of the so-called test.

...

... [T]he referee ... confirmed the right by using a normal duty of water for the type of crops raised and specifically added 25 percent for transportation loss. Making the best of inadequate proof by the claimant, it appears from the record that the referee applied the usual methods of irrigation employed in the vicinity where the Grimeses' land is located.

Notes & Questions

1. You will learn in Part V that, since the establishment of permit systems, the quantification stated in the permit is considered the maximum water right, with "reasonable use" on any given day or season often being something less. This approach relies on the assumption that, over time, changes in technology will reduce the amount of water needed. This is one area of possible flexibility with climate change. Increasing

temperature results in increased evapotranspiration by both crops and natural vegetation and it is not yet clear how courts will address this increasing demand in the context of the quantification of a water right.

2. In Part IV you will read the interstate water dispute between Montana and Wyoming and learn that there is a tension between individual farm efficiency and system-wide efficiency. The result being that the drive toward increasing farm efficiency is not always the best approach for the system as a whole.
3. What aspect of the "test of reasonable efficiency" set forth by the referee does the court object to?
   a. customary delivery and application practices in the area
   b. technology and "practices" improvements feasible and available to reduce water consumptions and financial needs associated with implementation thereof, and
   c. impacts of improvements of existing facilities and practices, if initiated, upon:
      i. the water source from which the diversion takes place,
      ii. the existing flora and fauna within the area of diversion, conveyancy and actual uses,
      iii. other water rights from said water source, and
      iv. other water users on other water sources.
4. What is the court's definition of water duty?

Chapter 8

Common Law Attributes of State-Based Water Rights: Beneficial Use— Loss through Non-Use

Introduction

In the previous Chapter you learned that beneficial use furthers the policy of providing for the maximum utility of water by limiting each water user to only the amount necessary for their specific beneficial use. This Chapter explores another aspect of beneficial use with that same goal in mind—the principle of "use-it-or-lose-it." Put simply, water users may not retain the right to use water that they have not been putting to beneficial use. This ensures that unused water is available for others.

This principle of "use-it-or-lose-it" can take several forms. First, it can be expressed as a prohibition against speculation, which occurs when people attempt to acquire a water right to hold for possible future use or sale. The general policy of maximizing access to water use underlies the prohibition against holding water the appropriator cannot currently use. A secondary policy that may or may not apply to the particular facts is to prevent the appropriator from holding a water right to profit during a future time of scarcity. Municipal use enjoys the one major exception to the prohibition on holding water for future use. Because municipalities must serve those who move into their service areas, they are allowed to plan and to hold water rights for reasonably anticipated future needs. It is important to note that the concern with holding water to sell at a higher price is not likely to apply to a municipality. This Chapter will look at the common law exception for municipal providers, and Part V will look at modern statutes addressing this issue.

Second, water rights that were validly appropriated can be lost for nonuse if the water right holder ceases putting the water to beneficial use. At common law, the concept of "use-it-or-lose-it" was limited to situations where a water user is shown to have intent to abandon their water rights. Intent generally required proof of more than mere non-use and was thus difficult to prove. More recently, western legislatures have passed forfeiture statutes, which call for a presumption of forfeiture if the water right is not used for a requisite period of time. Although these doctrines are distinct, they often overlap. As a result, this Chapter will cover both abandonment and statutory forfeiture, as well as defenses that have been applied to both doctrines.

Scholars and water managers point to rules such as use-it-or-lose-it as powerful tools to bring flexibility to water allocation. Water users, however, seek certainty, which has primarily been attained by assigning property rights to the continued use of water. This tension is resolved legally because courts are clear that the suite of rights that make up a water right does not include the continued right to unused water. Accordingly, no taking occurs when the government moves to reduce the quantification of a water right by the amount of water not used.

Loss for non-use, as well as the evolving interpretation of beneficial use and waste are major issues in the modern practice of water law, particularly as water supply and demand continues to change in the face of shifting climate and socioeconomic conditions. In particular, application of "use-it-or-lose-it" can provide a perverse incentive to continue using the full water right even when not needed, if not balanced by enforcement of the prohibition on waste. As a result, finding new ways to apply these doctrines to incentivize water efficiency and encourage water reuse are relevant as water users seek to do more with less water. Take note of the tension that exists between the competing policies of providing certainty to water users and of maximizing use; see how the courts balance these policies and consider whether you think that balance continues to make sense in an era of climate change. This Chapter concludes with a look at how courts are grappling with this complex problem.

Speculation and Holding Water for Future Use

Is it possible to acquire a water right today, thus locking in the priority date, for water that will not be used until some point in the future? The general response: no. In fact, it is considered "speculation." Put another way, no right to water is perfected if the water is not put to beneficial use. Speculation, therefore, is the attempt to acquire a water right without the intent or the ability to put water to a beneficial use. Like other aspects of beneficial use, the policy behind this rule traces its roots back to the overall policy of the prior appropriation doctrine to maximize the utility of water. It does so by ensuring that no person is able to hoard water to the detriment of others. The idea of holding water to profit from its rising cost in times of scarcity is also contrary to the recognition by western states of water as a public resource. As pointed out by the Supreme Court of Colorado, the hoarding of water "grounded in no interest beyond a desire to obtain water for sale," would:

> as a practical matter discourage those who have need and use for the water from developing it. Moreover, such a rule would encourage those with vast monetary resources to monopolize, for personal profit rather than for beneficial use, whatever unappropriated water remains.[1]

1. Colorado River Water Conservation Dist. v. Vidler Tunnel Water Co., 594 P.2d 566, 568 (Colo. 1979).

Speculation is allowed with land, so why not water? This is an example of how the law recognizes water as a common pool, scarce resource that is essential to the public good. Speculation allows hoarding when others need water and to drive up the price of water during times of shortage. If speculation in water were allowed, then a person could appropriate *all* the water in a particular stream, thereby monopolizing its use and effectively controlling the development of the region.

The next case demonstrates that speculation can come in different forms, some that may not include the intent to sell water. It involves the water flowing in Box Canyon Creek, which is an amazing but small spring-fed creek. Water from Idaho's Eastern Snake Plain Aquifer emerges into a pool, which then forms Box Canyon Creek and runs just 1.25 miles to the Snake River. Box Canyon Creek forms part of Idaho's Thousand Springs complex, which is prized by aquaculture developers for its abundant cold, clean water that provides ideal conditions for trout and other cold-water fish to be raised for human consumption. This case illustrates that failure to apply water to a beneficial use with merely a hope of acquiring the land it is to be used on is prohibited as speculation.

Lemmon v. Hardy

Supreme Court of Idaho
519 P.2d 1168 (1974)

Opinion

MCQUADE, J.—This action arises out of a dispute over the priority to the use of certain waters of Box Canyon Creek in Gooding County, Idaho. On June 19, 1969, the appellants, George Lemmon and Norman Standal, filed an application ... to divert 400 cubic feet of water from Box and Blind Canyon Creek. The application stated that the purpose of the diversion was for fish propagation, and that the water would be applied to land leased from the Idaho Power Company and/or Magic Springs, Inc.... [R]espondent Richard M. Kaster filed a protest.

On October 8, 1969, the respondents, Earl M. Hardy and Richard Kaster, were declared the successful bidders on the same Idaho Power Company property which [Lemmon and Standal] had claimed as a leasehold in their application for a water permit. [Hardy and Kaster] filed an application for water permit ... on October 27, 1969, for the diversion of 300 cubic feet of water from Box Canyon Creek for fish propagation. The application stated that the water was to be applied to the land purchased from the Idaho Power Company. Protests to the application were filed by [Lemmon and Standal].

On November 26, 1969, [Lemmon and Standal] filed an "amended application" ... [changing] the point of diversion and place of use of the water. Protests against the amended application were filed by [Hardy and Kaster].

... [A] hearing was held before the Director of the Department ... [who] found that there was insufficient water available to satisfy both applications. The Director ordered that both applications be approved and water permits issued, but that the Lemmon and Standal's priority date to the use of the water be postdated from the date of their original application of June 19, 1969, to the date of their amended application of November 26, 1969. Hardy and Kaster's priority date remained October 27, 1969.

....

The Hardy and Kaster's protests were filed on the basis that the Lemmon and Standal's application for a water permit was not filed in good faith but for speculative purposes.

....

The Director quotes extensively from *Kinney* on irrigation and water rights in reaching the conclusion that it is not speculation to file an application for a water permit without possessing any legal right to the use of the property designated as the point of diversion and place of use. The quotations include the statement that "Even trespassers upon the lands owned by others may make valid appropriations of water* * * ." The Director concluded that trespassers may make valid appropriations of water in Idaho .... All [the cases the Director relied on] are limited on their facts to appropriations that were made on unsurveyed federally owned land. *Kinney* states that a "* * * settler upon the unsurveyed lands of the United States has never been regarded as a trespasser * * *." The cases clearly do not support the broad proposition that all trespassers may establish valid water rights.

Furthermore in the case of *Bassett v. Swenson* it was held that, "It is quite generally held that a water right initiated by trespass is void. That is to say, one who diverts water and puts it to a beneficial use by aid of a trespass does not, pursuant to such trespass, acquire a water right. Any claim of right thus initiated is void." The *Bassett* case involved a trespass upon land privately owned. The rule as to trespass and water rights in Idaho appears to be that a water right initiated on the unsurveyed public domain is valid, but a water right initiated by trespass on private property is invalid.

In the case at bar the land designated as the point of diversion and place of use in appellants' original application was private property not owned by the appellants and therefore no valid water right could be developed on it. Since no valid water right was possible, it can be concluded that the application was filed for speculative purposes, not for development of a water right.

The Director also relied on the cases of *Marshall v. Niagara Springs Orchard Co.* and *Bassett v. Swenson*, in holding that it was not speculation to file an application for the use of water on designated land without a possessory interest in the land. Both cases involved power companies that filed applications for the use of water before obtaining the land for the point of diversion and power facilities by condemnation. It was held that filing an application without land ownership did not invalidate the application as long as the description of the diversion works was not obtained through trespass. The *Marshall* and *Basett* cases are distinguishable from this action. The power companies possessed the power of condemnation which permitted them to acquire the necessary land. They were not seeking land upon which to beneficially use the water, but solely for the power site generation purposes. The appellants in this action had shown no means of acquiring the land stated in their original application.

Lemmon and Standal's filing an application for a water permit with no possessory right in the land designated as the place of use amounted to speculation in and of itself. It is required by I.C. § 42-202 that an application for a water permit set forth,

> 4. The location and description of the proposed ditch, channel or other work and the amount of water to be diverted and used.
>
> * * *
>
> The application shall be accompanied by a plan and map in duplicate of the proposed works for the diversion and application of the water to a beneficial use, showing the character, location and dimensions of the proposed reservoirs, dams, canals, ditches, pipe lines and all other works proposed to be used by them in the diversion of the water, and the area and location of the lands proposed to be irrigated. (Amended 1973).

Lack of a possessory interest in the property designated as the place of use is speculation. Persons may not file an application for a water right and then seek a place for use thereof.

The Director's order that the appellants' priority date be postdated to the date of their amended application of November 26, 1969, is correct and the order is affirmed.

Notes & Questions

1. Lemmon and Standal undoubtedly intended to use the water for a beneficial use (fish propagation). Why did the Court nonetheless determine that their attempted appropriation was speculative?
2. Which of the following meets the court's criteria for speculation?
   a. An unincorporated area is rapidly expanding with farmland converting to subdivisions. Seeing an opportunity, Walker purchases the water rights in the area and offers them to the highest bidder.
   b. The subdivision statutes in a particular state require that the developer show proof of a 100-year water supply before the subdivision plat can be approved. The developer, Bea, purchases water rights to fulfill this requirement before obtaining approval of the subdivision plat.
   c. A canal company acquires water rights that will be used on its members' lands, not on land owned in the name of the canal company.

While the prohibition on holding a water right for future use is the general common law rule, there is one notable exception—municipal providers of water. The rationale underlying the anti-speculation doctrine begins to break down in the context of municipal water rights. Municipal water rights are generally held by municipalities as a service to their public. Municipal authority is generally defined by statute and confined to its service area. In fact, municipalities may be required to serve new households and other water needs within their service area. Because municipalities acquire money through taxation and bonds, they are not considered "for-profit" entities. Thus, the courts view municipal water rights as being different from water rights for other purposes. As you read the following case, consider what makes these rights different.

Beus et al. v. City of Soda Springs

Supreme Court of Idaho
107 P.2d 151 (1940)

HOLDEN, Justice.—[Ledge Creek is a small stream about three miles in length. Its source is a group of springs located about three-quarters of a mile in a northeasterly direction from the City of Soda Springs. In 1920 the City of Soda Springs purchased previously decreed water rights with the source in Ledge Creek amounting to 4.22 cfs. The City constructed a pipe line to the springs for the purpose of piping the water to the City for the use of its inhabitants and municipal purposes generally. However, at the time of the suit, the City was only using approximately 80 miner's inches (1.6 cfs) for municipal purposes. It argued that it was applying the rest to irrigation. Beus argued that the City had abandoned all water claimed by it in excess of 80 miners inches. The City denied abandonment and alleged it had beneficially used all the water so purchased by it, for municipal and irrigation purposes.]

Before findings were made and filed and decree entered thereon, the City specially requested the court to find: That it purchased [its] water rights in order to provide sufficient water for municipal purposes and use of its inhabitants, and the balance for the irrigation of the lands so purchased; that a "change in the point of diversion by the City of Soda Springs from the intake of its ditch for irrigation uses to the intake of its municipal pipe line and the change in the character and manner of use of the water from irrigation to culinary and municipal uses has been without damage to any junior appropriator and that no junior appropriator or owner of any subsequent decreed right will be injured or damaged in the future by the City of Soda Springs using so much of its decreed water right as it might from time to time need in its municipal pipe line for the uses of its inhabitants and for municipal purposes, with the balance of said aggregate right used upon the lands owned by it and described in these findings for irrigation and domestic purposes; that the variation in quantity of use of said water from irrigation to municipal uses, from time to time, and as need arises, increased the beneficial use of said water without injury or damage to any other appropriator;" and that the City of Soda Springs might have an alternating use of its water decreed to it between the farm lands and its municipal water system in such quantities and at such times as the respective needs might require.

January 8, 1940, the court made findings of fact and conclusions of law and entered judgment thereon. The City appeals from a part of the judgment and respondents and cross-appellants from a part. In limine, it may be stated, and as will presently appear, respondent concedes the right of the city to divert 80 miners inches of water into the pipe line for municipal purposes. That at once presents the question, in so far as the appeal of the City is concerned, as to whether it could, as it earnestly insists, in acquiring water in 1920 to supply then existing needs, also acquire and hold additional water for the purpose of supplying future needs, and, from time to time, divert from Ledge Creek into its pipe line as much of the additional water as would be necessary to supply the growing needs of the City, provided no one was injured thereby.

...

We will first discuss the question as to whether a municipality may, when acquiring water to supply its existing needs, also acquire and hold additional water for the purpose of supplying future needs.

Section 49-1132, I.C.A., provides a municipal corporation has power to "acquire by purchase, or otherwise, waterworks systems or plants, ... and construct, enlarge, extend, repair, alter and improve such plants or either of them, or any parts thereof, and to supply the municipality and the inhabitants thereof with water,...." It will be observed the statute expressly empowers a municipality to supply its inhabitants with water—without which a municipality would be impossible. To supply the inhabitants of a municipality with water may require, and in this instance did require, either the purchase of water, and the construction of "works" by means of which it can be pumped and piped to the inhabitants, or the purchase of an existing waterworks system. In either case, a municipality is authorized under the statute "to enlarge and extend either plant." But one thing can make the enlargement of a waterworks system necessary—municipal needs which an existing system cannot supply. The statute does not limit the power of a municipality to supply water to present inhabitants—the power granted is general—*to supply its inhabitants with water*. Hence, if, at the time of the acquisition of water for the purpose of supplying existing needs, it is necessary to also acquire and hold an additional supply to take care of future needs, a municipality undoubtedly has power to do so, in that "Wherever a power is given by statute, everything lawful and necessary to the effectual execution of the power is given by implication of law."

In *Holt v. City of Cheyenne* the Supreme Court of Wyoming had before it the question as to whether a city could acquire water for the purpose of supplying the future demands of its population, the identical question presented in this case. The court held:

"A city's right to appropriate the waters of a stream is not limited to the needs of its citizens at the time of adjudication of its rights, but it is entitled to appropriate for the probable future demands of its population."

The court then reviewed numerous authorities holding that property may be held by a municipality for its future growth and development without being subject to adverse claims of others, and then continues: "Such, we think, is the better reasoning, and is supported by the great weight of authority and to which many courts have in later cases acceded, although a contrary doctrine has been announced in earlier decisions."

A municipality may purchase lands, if that be necessary, to acquire water for its municipal needs, but is not required, after purchase, to irrigate the lands or cause the same to be irrigated, to avoid a loss of the water on a charge of abandonment. To require that would amount to nullifying the power granted to a municipality to acquire and hold water for future needs—an absolute necessity to the life and existence of a municipality.

...

It follows from what has been said ... that the judgment must be, and hereby is reversed, with directions to the trial court to find (and if necessary, take evidence) whether a diversion of the city's excess water from Ledge Creek into its pipe line, from time to time as needed, would work an injury to any other user of the waters of the stream, and enter judgment in harmony with the views expressed in this opinion.

Notes & Questions

1. What is the rule announced in *City of Soda Springs*?
2. Why do you suppose the City of Soda Springs was using its excess water for irrigation? What was the City trying to avoid? In the end, did their efforts change the outcome of the case?
3. What evidence might be necessary to prove "probable future demands"?
   a. Current water supply and capacity of infrastructure
   b. Population growth rate: current and anticipated
   c. City plan showing areas of growth and types of growth
   d. Potential new industries moving into the area

Abandonment

Abandonment is defined at common law as the intentional relinquishment of a water right by the owner of that right. The common law doctrine of abandonment generally required: (1) intent to abandon the use of the water; and (2) a period of nonuse. Abandonment applies after the water right has been perfected and can be found even if the water right has been adjudicated and included in a court decree. Thus, beneficial use is not merely a requirement of creating a water right; the water user has a continuing obligation to beneficially use that water.

As you know from other areas of the study of law, intent is difficult to prove. As noted by the Ninth Circuit "Few water right holders say in front of witnesses, 'I intend to abandon my rights.' Therefore, indirect and circumstantial evidence must almost always be used to show abandonment."[2] You will see in the first case from Montana that some courts will allow nonuse for a long period of time to create a presumption of intent to abandon. Pay close attention to the timing of non-use and the timing of intent to use the water in this next case. The mismatch in timing between non-use and

2. United States v. Orr Water Ditch Co., 256 F.3d 953, 945 (9th Cir. 2001).

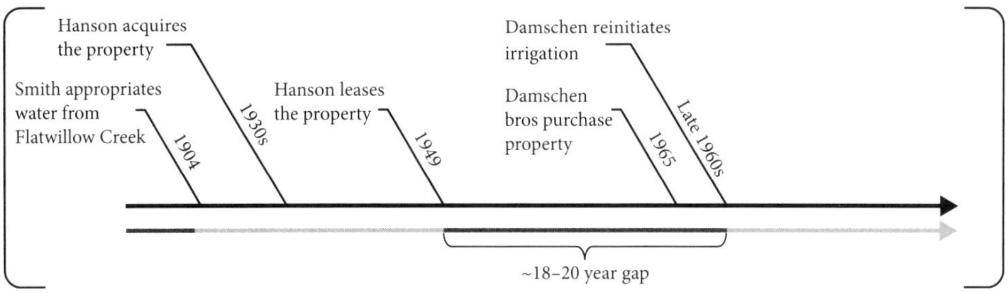

Figure 8.1 Timeline of actions taken in *Twin Creeks Farm & Ranch, LLC v. Petrolia Irrigation District.*

evidence regarding the water user's intent, as well as the fact that the case involved two different owners of the property is key to the Montana court's ruling. Figure 8.1 provides a timeline to help you understand the sequence of events in the facts.

Twin Creeks Farm & Ranch, LLC v. Petrolia Irrigation District

Supreme Court of Montana
461 P.3d 91 (2020)

Justice Beth Baker delivered the Opinion of the Court.—Petrolia Irrigation District ("PID") and Twin Creeks Farm & Ranch, LLC ("Twin Creeks") appeal the Water Court's rulings in adjudicating two of Twin Creeks' water rights claims. We affirm the Water Court's determination that Twin Creeks abandoned one claim by nonuse because the intent to abandon occurred concurrently with the nonuse. With respect to the second claim at issue, we conclude that the Water Court misapprehended the effect of testimony regarding its historical use and remand for further consideration.

FACTUAL AND PROCEDURAL BACKGROUND

[This case is part of Montana's state-wide adjudication. Each claim filed is examined by the Montana Department of Natural Resources and Conservation (DNRC). DNRC places "issue remarks" on any aspect of the claim that is not supported by the evidence filed or other evidence available to DNRC. DNRC then forwards the claim to the Montana Water Court—a trial court of special jurisdiction established for the purpose of the state-wide adjudication.]

... There were five Twin Creeks claims at issue before the Water Court.... [The Water Claim on Appeal is referred to as the 102 Claim]

On July 22, 1904, Samuel Smith filed a notice of appropriation for Flatwillow Creek and its tributary for 500 miner's inches to irrigate 45 acres ... on the Hansen property with a May 18, 1904 priority date.... Smith's desert-land entry documents support irrigation in the early 1900s.... Based on that evidence, the Water Court found the notice of appropriation was perfected and used on the 102 claim's place of use.

Damschen filed a statement of claim in 1982 for 45 acres on the Hansen property based on the 1904 Samuel Smith notice of appropriation. Damschen claimed 3,000 gallons per minute ("gpm"), or 6.68 cubic feet per second ("cfs"), based on pump capacity.

In 2005, DNRC examined the claims and reduced the flow rate to 1.70 cfs based on the agency's 17.00 gpm per acre standard. DNRC also inserted an issue remark based on the 1971 Water Resources Survey, … which identified zero acres irrigated. Twin Creeks's predecessors, the Taylors, objected to the flow rate and to the DNRC issue remark. PID filed an objection, asserting that the 102 claim was abandoned.

The Water Court found that nonuse of the claim between 1948 and 1971 showed a lack of intent to continue irrigating with the 1904 Samuel Smith water right; it thus found that the May 18, 1904 priority date was abandoned. The court found that Damschen began irrigating the field after the Damschens acquired the property in 1965. Based on the last evidence of nonuse—the 1971 Water Resources Survey—the court assigned a December 31, 1971 priority date for the 102 claim and restored the 3,000 gpm flow rate based on pump capacity. Twin Creeks appeals the 1971 priority date, asserting that the right had not been abandoned and that the 1904 priority date is correct.

…

DISCUSSION

The 102 [Claim]

Twin Creeks argues on appeal that the Water Court erred when it found the 1904 priority date for the 102 claim abandoned based on nonuse from 1948 to 1971 and Hansen's intent to abandon. It asserts that the court should have viewed intent through the actions of Damschen, not of Hansen, and that Twin Creeks successfully rebutted the presumption of abandonment because it demonstrated continuous use by Damschen and his successors. In response, PID urges this Court to affirm the Water Court's finding because Twin Creeks failed to present evidence sufficient to rebut the presumption of abandonment due to Hansen's nonuse.

Abandonment of a water right requires both nonuse and intent to abandon.… To find abandonment, there must be a "concurrence" of nonuse and intent.…

Whether a water right has been abandoned is a question of fact that depends on the conduct, acts, and intent of the parties claiming the use of the water.… Intent to abandon a water right may be inferred from all of the circumstances of the case and need not be proved directly.… A long period of continuous nonuse creates a rebuttable presumption of intent to abandon; the claimant must produce specific evidence excusing the nonuse to rebut this presumption.… Such evidence must relate to the specific nonuse on the property in question.… Determining abandonment requires weighing all of the relevant factual circumstances in the case.…

The Water Court heard evidence that the 102 claim's place of use was irrigated into the 1940s but was not irrigated when Hansen began to lease out the property. Witnesses familiar with the Hansen ranch from the 1940s to the 1970s testified at trial. Joe

Whisonant, Jacqueline Trump Whisonant, and Bill Solf all spent time on the Hansen property during the 1950s and 1960s. Jacqueline is Elliot Trump's daughter. Jacqueline testified that her family moved to the Hansen property in 1949 when her father leased it from Hansen and lived on the property until 1956. After she moved away, she and her husband, Joe, came back to the property frequently until 1965, when Elliot Trump retired and the Damschen brothers purchased the property.

Joe, Jacqueline, and Bill testified that the 102 claim's place of use was not irrigated when Elliot Trump leased the Hansen property. They testified that they did not recall any irrigation under the 102 claim until Damschen began irrigating the field in the late 1960s. Terry Sandman is a farmer in the Winnett area who spent time on the property. He testified that the field was irrigated into the 1940s but was not irrigated during the time Trump leased the property from Hansen.

Lee Yelin, a water rights expert, testified for Twin Creeks regarding his review of available information related to the 102 claim. He examined desert-land entry records and reviewed USDA aerial photos of the place of use. He testified that he did not see active irrigation in 1948 or 1954 based on the aerial photos. He confirmed active irrigation of 41.30 acres based on the 1979 aerial photo. The parties agree that once Damschen acquired the property the place of use was irrigated; they do not dispute that the property has been continuously irrigated since that time.

The Water Court found that the testimony, aerial photos, and 1971 Water Resources Survey showed no irrigation on the 102 claim's place of use. It found that the 102 claim was not used for twenty-three years, as Twin Creeks did not provide any credible evidence of irrigation for the 102 claim from 1948 to 1971. This long period of nonuse, the court reasoned, raised the presumption of intent to abandon the 1904 water right. It further found that this nonuse occurred when Hansen owned and leased the ranch and that Hansen's intent to abandon was more significant for the court's abandonment analysis than was Damschen's. The court found that seventeen years of continuous nonuse had elapsed by 1965, when Damschen took possession, raising the presumption of abandonment. The court found that Twin Creeks failed to provide specific evidence explaining or excusing this long period of nonuse and did not rebut the presumption of abandonment. The court thus held that the right had been abandoned.

Twin Creeks asserts that our decision in *Heavirland* requires the Water Court to consider the entire facts and circumstances of the case to determine evidence of intent to abandon. It asserts that the court erred when it limited the examination of intent to Hansen's and Trump's intent and did not consider Damschen's later intent and actions developing irrigation. We disagree.

In *Heavirland*, this Court examined the record of the intent and actions of the nonuser when it upheld the Water Court's ruling that the nonuser had not intended to abandon the water right. Reviewing whether the presumption of abandonment was overcome, the Court looked to: specific obstacles associated with irrigating the property; specific testimony regarding the nonuser owner's age and illness contributing to his decision to cease irrigating; the fact that the elderly nonuser installed power to the property in contemplation of one day running a pivot irrigation system; the financial hardships of the farm; and evidence that the nonuser's son actually filed and sold the water right at issue. *Heavirland*, ¶ 34. The supporting testimony from his son, who acquired the property and began irrigating once he installed a pivot irrigation system, informed our review of the nonuser's intent not to abandon concurrent with the non-use of the water. *Heavirland*.

Twin Creeks urges this Court to consider Damschen's intent when he expanded irrigation and continuously irrigated for forty-five years after acquiring the Hansen property. But Damschen's later intent to continue irrigating was not concurrent with the long period of nonuse at issue and the associated presumed intent to abandon the 102 claim.

Twin Creeks argues that the 102 claim's place of use on the Hansen property was remote and prone to flood damage, hindering irrigation. The Water Court found that the general obstacles on the Hansen property preventing irrigation such as being remote and being prone to flood damage were not specific to the water right or period of time at issue and were not enough to overcome the presumption of abandonment due to nonuse. We conclude that the Water Court did not err. It had sufficient evidence to find that the 1904 priority date was abandoned and to assign the December 31, 1971 priority date based on Damschen's use.

...

CONCLUSION

We affirm the Water Court's finding that the 102 claim was abandoned.

Notes & Questions

1. The court found a presumption of intent to abandon the use of water when evidence showed it had not been used for 23 years altogether and 16 years by the predecessor to Damschen's ownership. The court requires specific evidence to overcome the presumption. Which of the following types of evidence might it consider as sufficiently specific?
    a. testimony regarding the nonuser owner's age and illness contributing to his decision to cease irrigating;
    b. testimony indicating the farm is remote and prone to flood damage;
    c. testimony that the elderly nonuser installed power to the property in contemplation of one day running a pivot irrigation system;
    d. evidence of the financial hardships of the farm.
2. How long must the period of nonuse be to raise a presumption of intent to abandon? You will learn in the notes following the next case that statutes now specify a period of nonuse required to raise a presumption of forfeiture.

The next case, from Idaho, provides an opportunity to think about the type of evidence necessary to prove abandonment. It also addresses this in the complex context of variable water supply.

Union Grain & Elevator Co. v. McCammon Ditch Co.

Supreme Court of Idaho
240 P. 443 (1925)

Opinion

WM. E. LEE, J.—This is an action to quiet the title of plaintiff in and to 148 second feet of the waters of the Portneuf river in Bannock county for manufacturing purposes....

The trial court found:

> "That on the said 1st day of July, 1892, [the predecessor of Union Grain & Elevator Co.] diverted ... 97.55 cubic feet per second of time of the waters flowing [in the] Portneuf river, for the purpose of producing and generating sufficient power to run and operate [a] mill ..., and for the purpose of generating electricity with which to light the mill ..., and has ever since [that] date continuously and uninterruptedly, except when unlawfully hindered and interrupted by certain users ... above [the] point of diversion, used [the] amount of water.... That [the] amount of water so appropriated by said plaintiff was and is necessary for the successful operation of [the] mill...."

As a matter of law, the court concluded that the plaintiff—

> "* * * is entitled to the use at all times of 97.55 cubic feet per second of time of the waters of [the] Portneuf river, its right of appropriation to date from the 1st day of July, 1892, for the purpose of generating power to run and operate its mill. * * *"

...

[Distribution of the water with the river flowing at 207.96 cfs led to the result that:] the Portneuf Irrigating Company (with a right dating from 1889) would get 55 second feet, the McCammon Ditch Company (with a right dating from 1889) would get 50 second feet, appellant (with a right dating from 1892) would get 97.55 second feet, the McCammon Ditch Company (with a second right dating from 1901) would get 5.41 second feet, the remainder of the water, and that a large number of those who had theretofore been receiving water from the river and its tributaries and to whom rights had been decreed would receive no water whatever.... [Appeal to the court of the distribution determination led to an order restricting the timing of the right of Union Grain & Elevator Co. to use water from September 1 through July 9 of the following year, thus preventing use during the portion of the irrigation season from July 10 to August 31. Union Grain & Elevator Co. appealed.]

....

The first material inquiry is whether [the predecessor of Union Grain & Elevator Co.] ever acquired a right to any of the waters of the Portneuf during the dry season....

While the evidence shows that the mill was not operated continuously during the dry season of each and every year, that it was closed sometimes for one reason and sometimes for another, and that it was seldom, if ever, operated at night during the dry season, there can be no serious doubt that the evidence shows that the mill was operated in the dry season, and that appellant acquired a right to water from the stream for mill purposes. Mr. Whitehead, head miller from 1896 to 1906, probably respondent's best witness on this subject, said the mill "had been running pretty steady in the summer time up to 1900." While we are convinced that the evidence shows that [Union Grain & Elevator Co.] had acquired a right to a continuous flow of water during the dry season, we are equally certain that it was not, under the evidence, entitled to 97.55 second feet. As we read the evidence, the engineer, Burkett, during the first hearing, made measurements by which he determined that 97.55 second feet was the quantity of water required to keep the mill in operation. The measurements were not made when there was a scarcity of water but in December, 1920, while the elevators and machinery were all running and the mill was being run at its maximum capacity. From all the evidence we are satisfied that the mill was not run in the dry reason as it was running that day in December when it was measured by the engineer. Witness Whitehead, who was head miller from 1896 to 1906, and who worked at the mill later in 1916, testified that some changes were made in the machinery of the mill about 1900 by which the capacity of the mill was increased from 100 to 150 barrels per day. He said that it took about one-third as much water to operate the mill before the changes were made as it did after they were made. In 1916 other changes were made, according to Whitehead, that made it necessary to use "about twice as much" water. We are not relying solely on the evidence of Whitehead. From practically all the witnesses, testimony was elicited to the general effect that the mill did operate during the dry season, but that it was not operated 12 hours a day nor to its maximum capacity during the dry seasons, and that a right to a continuous 24-hour a day flow of 97.55 second feet during the dry season was never acquired.

It would appear that in such a case as this evidence should have been presented to the trial court from which it could have determined the quantity of water required to run the mill during the low-water periods prior to the time that the capacity of the mill was increased and prior to the time that subsequent rights to the waters of the river were acquired. It would not appear to one not versed in the operation of a flour mill by water power that as much water would be required to operate a mill of 100 barrels capacity as the same mill increased to 250 barrels capacity, that a mill at either capacity could be run with less water when grinding at normal than at maximum capacity, and that, by disengaging the machinery and appliances about the mill, as would naturally be done when the water was scarce, the work of grinding could be done on less than the maximum power testified to by the engineer. While appellant is entitled to have its rights protected by the court, it must not be awarded other or greater rights, as against other appropriators of the waters of the river, than it is entitled under the law. The right of appellant to the waters of the Portneuf river for mill purposes was limited to the quantity of water reasonably necessary to operate the mill. If the increases in the capacity of the mill in 1900 and 1916 required greater quantities of water, such requirements were ineffectual as against those who had acquired intervening rights.

After having strenuously insisted that [the predecessor to Union Grain & Electric Co.] never acquired a right to any of the waters of the river, some of the respondents insist that the right acquired to the use of certain of the waters of the stream during the dry season was abandoned by Harkness. This, they say, is established by the evidence that he frequently shut down the mill during the dry season and made statements to the effect that he would let the farmers have the water, and that, if the farmers did not raise any wheat, his mill would be of no use to him. Such actions and statements, if true, do not constitute abandonment. There can be no abandonment without an intention to abandon. In *Syster v. Hazzard*, 39 Idaho, 580, 229 P. 1110, this court said that "abandonment is a matter of intent coupled with corresponding conduct." And in *Joyce v. Murphy Land*, etc., Co., 35 Idaho, 549, 208 P. 241, it was said that abandonment "is the relinquishment of a right by the owner thereof without any regard to future possession by himself or any other person, but with the intention to foresake or desert the right." Abandonment may be shown by the facts and circumstances, but clear proof is required to make out a case. The proof here falls far short of abandonment. There is not the slightest evidence that Harkness, by permitting the use at times of water to which he had a prior right, intended thereby to abandon his right. The fact that he did operate his mill at times during the dry season, and that he "begged" water at times from some of those with prior rights, effectively negatives any intent to abandon his right.

From what has been said, it follows that the cause must be reversed and remanded to the trial court, with instructions to permit the parties to produce additional evidence to show the extent of the right of appellant prior to the time the capacity of the mill was enlarged and prior to the time that subsequent appropriators acquired their rights, ...

Notes & Questions

1. What is the key piece of evidence that negates a finding of intent in *Union Grain & Elevator Co.*?
2. In the 1944 case of *Carrington v. Crandall*, 65 Idaho 525, 147 P.2d 1009, the Idaho Supreme Court stated "that abandonment of a real property right can not be declared except upon *clear and convincing evidence.*" This high evidentiary standard applied to the type of evidence often unavailable in older water cases as illustrated by the *Union Grain* case makes it highly unlikely that a finding of abandonment will be made.
3. The difficulty of proving intent and the reluctance of courts to find abandonment except in extreme cases ultimately led legislatures to pass statutes providing for forfeiture after a specified period of nonuse without a need to show intent. The following

excerpt is from footnote 1 of a subsequent case in this Chapter—*State v. Hagerman,* 947 P.2d 400 (Idaho 1997):

> The statute in effect at the time *Albrethsen* was decided used the term "abandonment" not forfeiture. That statute provided:
>
> > All rights to the use of water acquired under this chapter or otherwise shall be lost and abandoned by a failure for the term of five years to apply it to the beneficial use for which it was appropriated, and when any right to the use of water shall be lost through nonuse or abandonment such rights to such water shall revert to the state and be again subject to appropriation under this chapter....
>
> *Albrethsen,* 231 P. at 421 (quoting C.S. § 5582 (1919)).
>
> The Legislature repealed a later version of this statute which also described loss of a water right in terms of "abandonment" and reenacted the statute using "forfeiture" language. Act of May 26, 1969, ch. 303, § 2, 1969 Idaho Sess. Laws 906.
>
> In the past, courts used the terms abandonment and forfeiture interchangeably. However, the two doctrines are separate and distinct [citing the next case of *Gilbert v. Smith*]. Abandonment is a common law doctrine involving intent to abandon and an actual surrender of the water right. *Id.* Forfeiture, on other hand, is predicated upon the statutory declaration that rights to water are lost where the appropriator fails to make beneficial use of the water for a continuous five year period....

The next case explores the difference between abandonment and forfeiture. Although the parties to this case are all diverting and using water in Idaho, the creeks run into the Bear River, an interstate river shared by Idaho and Utah. Thus, the prior decree was issued by the federal district court under its diversity jurisdiction in *Utah Power & Light Co. v. Last Chance Canal Co.* (unreported, U.S. Dist. Court, E.D. Idaho, July 14, 1920).

Gilbert v. Smith

Supreme Court of Idaho
552 P.2d 1220 (1976)

Opinion

SHEPARD, J.—This is an appeal from a declaratory judgment involving the water rights on three streams ... in Caribou County, Idaho. Involved are the waters of Birch Creek and Densmore Creek which, according to the testimony on behalf of all parties, are tributaries of and flow into Beaver Dam Creek which in turn is a tributary of Bear River....

[The decree awarded the predecessors in interest to Gilbert, a priority date of 1900 for water from Densmore and Birch Creeks, and Smith a priority date of May 1, 1882, for water from Densmore, Birch and Beaver Dam Creeks, that is diverted from Beaver Dam Creek below the confluence of Densmore and Birch Creeks].

... Between the point of confluence of the three creeks and the point of Smith's diversion, are a number of beaver dams and sump holes or sinks. Historically, those obstacles have caused losses of water and difficulty in obtaining water to satisfy the water rights of the respondents and their predecessors.

Between 1970 and 1973, appellant Gilbert gained possession of his property, increased the previous diversion for that property from Densmore and Birch Creeks and thereby increased the irrigated acreage of his land by some 60–80 acres. In 1973, [Smith's] desired to increase the water flow to their lands and completed a construction of a pipeline circumventing and avoiding the sump holes and beaver dams.

There is no claim herein to the water of Beaver Dam Creek. Rather, the substance of appellants' claim is that since the time of the 1920 decree the [Gilbert's] and their predecessors have diverted water from Densmore and Birch Creeks in excess of their decreed rights, have applied the same to beneficial use and are therefore entitled to such waters on the alternative grounds of abandonment and adverse possession. Following a court trial, Gilbert's claim was rejected and the court entered the following pertinent findings:

> 9. That none of the parties offered any proof as to the measurement of the waters used by each of them respectively in any of the years in dispute.
>
> 10. That [Gilbert] failed to prove use of the waters of Densmore Creek and Birch Creek in excess of their decreed right and [Gilbert] failed to prove use of any of the waters of Beaver Dam Creek.
>
> 11. That [Gilbert] failed to prove continuing, uninterrupted, open or adverse appropriation or use of any of the defendants' decreed waters of densmore (sic) and Birch Creek.
>
> 12. That any use of [Gilbert] of the decreed waters of [Smith] or their predecessors in Densmore Creek and Birch Creek was with the permission and consent of [Smith] or their predecessors in interest.

The court concluded that all rights as established by the Dietrich Decree should be reaffirmed and enjoined all the parties from interfering with those established rights. This appeal was brought on the basis that the judgment is not supported by the evidence.

The essential issues of this appeal have been argued to this Court in the context of the distinct doctrines of abandonment and adverse possession. While we think these issues do in fact arise in this dispute, we are also of the opinion in reviewing the arguments of the parties in light of the applicable law that an additional legal concept is presented by this appeal which necessitates independent consideration. Some confusion has resulted in this case due to misunderstandings of the exact elements of abandonment as they have been, and are intended to be, applied to water rights disputes. This confusion is largely understandable given the state of the case law in this jurisdiction. Although framed in the language of abandonment, appellants' principle argument in this appeal concerns not only the doctrine of abandonment but likewise the question of statutory forfeiture. This doctrine, although similar to abandonment, involves characteristics of significant difference which must be borne in mind in resolving this and similar disputes addressing the relinquishment of decreed water rights.

Abandonment is a common law concept involving the concurrence of an intention to abandon and the actual relinquishment or surrender of the water right.... It is not dependent necessarily upon length of time but upon the essential element of intent. Such intent may be evidenced by non-use for a substantial period of time but mere non-use is not per se abandonment.... In contrast, the doctrine of forfeiture is predicated upon a statutory declaration that all rights to use water may be lost where an appropriator fails to make beneficial use of the water for a statutory period regardless of the intent of the appropriator.... In Idaho this concept is set forth in I.C. § 42-222(2). The effect of that provision is that an appropriator who fails to apply his water right to a beneficial use for a continuous five year period is regarded as having lost all rights to the use of such water.... Although the terms abandonment and forfeiture have often been used by this Court interchangeably..., the case of *Carrington v. Crandall* makes it clear that they are distinct legal concepts and should be considered as such. We recognize that this Court has in the past failed to indicate this difference in addressing cases involving water rights disputes. Nevertheless, we deem it essential for this and other future cases of a similar nature to keep the concepts of abandonment and statutory forfeiture, and their application, distinct.

It is established that a water right in Idaho, although affirmed by a court decree, may be abandoned and subject to subsequent appropriation. One who seeks to alter decreed water priorities has the burden to demonstrate the elements of abandonment by clear and convincing evidence.

It is appellants' position that for the period of 53 years, from the time of the Dietrich Decree until the bypass pipeline was installed, the [Smiths] and their predecessors were unable to utilize the waters of Densmore and Birch Creeks. They assert that those waters would have been wasted had not the [Gilberts] and their predecessors diverted the water and applied it to beneficial use. It is thereby argued that because of their inability to utilize the water respondents effectively abandoned their rights and caused them to revert to the state. The implication is that respondents' failure to remedy the cause of the wasting is evidence of an intent to relinquish any right in the water.... Consequently, it is submitted that the diversion and use of the *entire* flow of Densmore and Birch Creeks by [Gilbert] and their predecessors constituted a new, lawful and superior appropriation of the rights.

As a rule, the law of water rights in this state embodies a policy against the waste of irrigation water. Such policy is not to be construed, however, so as to permit an upstream junior appropriator to interfere with the water right of a downstream senior appropriator so long as the water flowing in its natural channels would reach the point of downstream diversion. We agree that if due to seepage, evaporation, channel absorption or other conditions beyond the control of the appropriators the water in the stream will not reach the point of the prior appropriator in sufficient quantity for him to apply it to beneficial use, then a junior appropriator whose diversion point is higher on the stream may divert the water.... Nevertheless, it was [Gilbert's] burden here to show that neither the surface or underflow of Densmore or Birch Creeks, if uninterrupted, would reach the point of diversion of the [Smith's], as senior appropriators.... This the district court found the [Gilberts] had failed to do and we hold that the evidence sustains such a finding.

[The supreme court briefly reviewed the evidence and affirmed the district court:] The trial court on the basis of such conflict in testimony held that the appellants had failed to meet their burden. Such holding is supported by substantial, competent although conflicting evidence and therefore will not be disturbed on appeal....

With respect to statutory forfeiture, I.C. § 42-222(2) mandates a five year period during which respondents or their predecessors must have failed to apply their water right to the beneficial use for which it was appropriated. While there is evidence of continuous non-use in this case, the record does not identify any measurable five year period of non-use which would have supported the trial court in making the requisite finding to establish a statutory forfeiture. Forfeiture of water rights is not favored and all intendments are indulged in against a forfeiture.... Upon this record we hold that the trial court was correct in finding that no forfeiture occurred.

...

Appellants assert that the trial court erred in its finding that appellants' use of the waters was with the permission of the rightful owner. We may agree with appellants' assertion that there was insufficient evidence to sustain a finding that the use of the waters by the appellants and their predecessors was with the permission of the rightful owner. Nevertheless, as indicated by the aforesaid discussion, we find that the order of the trial court was correct, albeit based on partially erroneous grounds. Therefore it will be upheld by this Court.

... We have reviewed appellants' remaining assignments of error and find them to be without merit.

Notes & Questions

1. Which of the following are the key differences between abandonment and statutory forfeiture?
    a. Abandonment requires a showing of intent, forfeiture does not
    b. Abandonment requires no specific period of nonuse, but it is generally much longer than the five-year period in the Idaho forfeiture statute
    c. The burden of proof is higher for abandonment, which requires clear and convincing evidence.
2. The concept of "use it or lose it" is often pointed to as encouraging waste—e.g., an irrigator might apply more water than is reasonable to land to avoid a finding of abandonment. What aspect of the common law, if enforced, would counter this incentive to waste water?

The following case was of considerable importance in Idaho's Snake River Basin Adjudication (SRBA). You will learn about adjudication in Part VI. The SRBA was a process of determining the relative rights of all the water use in the basin making up about two-thirds of Idaho that required 27 years from inception to final decree in 2014. Today the process continues with the determination of late claims. For case management, the basin was divided into subbasins. However, when an issue that was likely to occur or have impacts in multiple basins arose, it could be certified as an "basin-wide issue."[3] This allowed all parties in the SRBA to participate and was thus binding on all. It also allowed the water court opinion to be considered an interlocutory order and thus could be immediately appealed to the Idaho Supreme Court. The issue in *State v. Hagerman Water Right Owners, Inc.* of whether a portion of a water right could be forfeited was basin-wide issue #10.

State v. Hagerman Water Right Owners, Inc.

Supreme Court of Idaho
947 P.2d 400 (1997)

SCHROEDER, J.:—

I. FACTS AND PRIOR PROCEEDINGS

...

On April 26, 1996, the district court issued a decision holding, as a matter of law, that water rights in Idaho are not subject to partial forfeiture for non-use. The SRBA court determined that the issue is one of first impression to be resolved by construing Idaho's forfeiture statute, I.C. § 42-222(2). That section provides in relevant part:

> *All* rights to the use of water acquired under this chapter or otherwise shall be lost and forfeited by a failure for the term of five (5) years to apply it to the beneficial use for which it was appropriated....

I.C. § 42-222(2) (1996) (emphasis added).

The district court focused on the word "all" in this section and reasoned that the plain and ordinary meaning of this provision is that "partial forfeiture is not provided for in this statute." ... This Court granted interlocutory appeal on August 5, 1996.

II. THE ISSUE OF WHETHER I.C. § 42-222(2) PERMITS PARTIAL FORFEITURE OF WATER RIGHTS HAS NOT BEEN RAISED PREVIOUSLY AS AN ISSUE ON APPEAL TO THIS COURT

The [plaintiffs] maintain that case law establishes this Court's recognition of statutory partial forfeiture. However, the question of whether part of a water right may be forfeited pursuant to I.C. § 42-222(2) has not been raised directly as the issue on appeal to this Court, ...

3. SRBA District Court Rules of Procedure, Rule 16, https://isc.idaho.gov/rules/SRBA_Rules_Of_Procedure.pdf.

In *Albrethsen v. Wood River Land Co.* Albrethsen brought an action to have a portion of the respondent Wood River Land Company's water right declared forfeited. [The right held by Wood River Land Company had been decreed as 5,595 inches.]... Albrethsen claimed that the evidence established that some 2,100 inches of the water right were not put to beneficial use between 1910 and 1914 and were allowed to flow back into the Wood River.... Albrethsen presented witnesses and evidence that Wood River's canal could not carry in excess of 3,850 inches. On rehearing, the Court concluded:

> We are of opinion that this statute intends that a right to the use of water, although based upon a decree of a court, may be lost by abandonment, ...
>
> One of the most conclusive methods of showing that an amount of water decreed to a particular system has not been beneficially used is to show that the canal or other diverting works through which the appropriation must be diverted ... does not have the required carrying capacity to divert and distribute the full amount of the appropriation....

... *Albrethsen* involved resolution of the factual inquiry of whether the canal in question could have ever delivered the quantity of water decreed, not whether the forfeiture statute provided for partial forfeiture. Nonetheless, the result was that a decreed water right was reduced by the amount of water that had not been applied to a beneficial use. Partial forfeiture, as a remedy, was assumed.

In *Graham v. Leek*, [Leek was decreed 3.2 cfs for use on the Lenman Tract. Graham claimed that he obtained a right to this water by adverse possession and that Leek had abandoned it.] The district court held for [Graham] and, with respect to abandonment, found that the Lenman Tract was dry farmed, that no attempt had ever been made to use any part of the water with one exception, and that use of the water was abandoned upon the Lenman Tract.... In this case, the Court addressed only whether the findings were supported by competent, although conflicting evidence, in the record.

...

Dovel v. Dobson in part dealt with the approval of the Director of the IDWR for the transfer of a water right in order to supply water for property not covered in an original water right. The water right covered three different fields, totaling ninety-six (96) acres. The third field was six (6) acres. Dobson objected to the transfer, arguing that approving the transfer would result in an enlargement because, he alleged, part of the water right had been forfeited for non-use. In approving the transfer, the Director concluded that the consumptive use appurtenant to the six-acre field had been forfeited through nonuse, but did not reduce the amount which had historically been diverted for the fields, concluding that the transfer would not change the amount of use authorized by the water right.... The district court concluded that the Director's decision was not clearly erroneous or an abuse of discretion. This Court affirmed,.... The decision in *Dovel* was limited to an examination of the facts and did not determine the issue of whether partial forfeiture is recognized under I.C. § 42-222(2) as a matter of law.

In sum, the issue of whether a water right may be partially forfeited pursuant to I.C. § 42-222(2) has not been directly addressed by the Court, although that principle has been assumed on occasions by both the Court and the litigants.

III. I.C. § 42-222(2) IS AMBIGUOUS

It is established that a water right in Idaho, although affirmed by a court decree, may be abandoned and subject to subsequent appropriation. The parties before this Court agree that the legislature intended I.C. § 42-222(2) to provide for total forfeiture when all of a water right has gone unused for the statutory period. The parties disagree as to whether I.C. § 42-222(2) contemplates partial forfeiture when part of the water right is unused for the statutory period.

In *Gilbert v. Smith,* the Court said that forfeiture of a water right is

> predicated upon a statutory declaration that all rights to use water may be lost where an appropriator fails to make beneficial use of the water for a statutory period regardless of the intent of the appropriator. In Idaho this concept is set forth in I.C. § 42-222(2). The effect of that provision is that an appropriator who fails to apply his water right to a beneficial use for a continuous five year period is regarded as having lost all rights to the use of such water.

Thus, in Idaho, forfeiture is a statutory concept well distinguished from the common law concept of abandonment.... The question of whether I.C. § 42-222(2) provides for partial forfeiture of a water right turns on interpretation of a statute, which is a question of law over which the Court exercises free review.... In applying I.C. § 42-222(2), if the statutory language is clear and unambiguous, the Court need merely apply the statute without engaging in any statutory construction.... Statutory interpretation begins with the words of the statute, giving the language its plain, obvious, and rational meanings....

The district court determined that I.C. § 42-222(2) unambiguously does not provide for partial forfeiture. This determination was incorrect.

Section 42-222 of the Idaho Code states in relevant part:

> (2) All rights to the use of water acquired under this chapter or otherwise shall be lost and forfeited by a failure for the term of five (5) years to apply it to the beneficial use for which it was appropriated and when any right to the use of water shall be lost though nonuse or forfeiture such rights to such water shall revert to the state and be again subject to appropriation under this chapter....

I.C. § 42-222(2) (1996). The district court determined that:

> "All" when used as an adjective means "the whole amount or quantity ... the whole number or sum of...." *Webster's Ninth New Collegiate Dictionary* 71 (9th ed.1991). Reviewing the plain and ordinary meaning of I.C. § 42-222(2), it is clear that partial forfeiture is not provided for within this statute....

I.C. § 42-222(2) has been amended numerous times without adding clarifying language providing for partial forfeiture as some other states have done.

Section 42-222(2) of the Idaho Code does not explicitly provide for partial forfeiture. In fact, the statute does not address any particular quantity of water at all that may be forfeited. The statute simply refers to "it" and "water."

Section 73-113 of the Idaho Code instructs that "[w]ords and phrases are construed according to the context and the approved usage of the language." I.C. §73-113. The word "all" is an adjective. In the ordinary use of the English language, adjectives precede or immediately follow the noun they modify. "All" in I.C. §42-222(2) modifies the word "rights." It does not modify the more distant word "water." Had the legislature intended the word "all" to modify "water," it could have easily constructed a sentence that conveyed such an intent. The use of the word "all" in I.C. §42-222(2) does not unambiguously close the door on the possibility of partial forfeiture.

IV. PARTIAL FORFEITURE IS AN ADMINISTRATIVELY RECOGNIZED CONCEPT WHICH IS IN ACCORD WITH THE ASSUMPTION MADE IN IDAHO CASE LAW

If it is necessary for the Court to construe a statute, then it will attempt to ascertain legislative intent.... In construing a statute this Court may examine the language used, the reasonableness of the proposed interpretations, and the policy behind the statute....

A. Administrative Practices and Policies

A basic rule of statutory construction is that the application of a statute is an aid to construction, especially where the public relies on that application over a long period of time. *Sutherland on Statutory Construction* (5th ed. 1992). As Sutherland explains:

> Statutes are documents having practical effects. It is therefore improper to construe them in the abstract, without taking into consideration the historical framework in which they exist.... Correlatively, such information is also relevant when deciding what the statute means to others because it is important to know how people affected by an act understand it.

Sutherland, §49.01 (footnotes omitted). "[W]here contemporaneous and practical interpretation has stood unchallenged for a considerable length of time it will be regarded as very important in arriving at the proper construction of a statute." *Id.* §49.07. In fact, "[o]ne of the soundest reasons sustaining contemporaneous interpretations of long standing is the fact that the public has relied on the interpretation...." *Id.* This Court has and continues to adhere to those tenets.

In *J.R. Simplot Co. v. Idaho State Tax Commission* the Court established a four-part test for when agency construction of a statute should be accorded deference. This Court summarized this test as follows:

> This four prong test states that an agency's construction of a statute will be given great weight if: (1) the agency has been entrusted with the responsibility to administer the statute at issue; (2) the agency's construction of the statute is reasonable; (3) the statutory language at issue does not expressly treat

> the precise question at issue; and (4) any of the rationales underlying the rule of deference are present.

There is no question that IDWR is entrusted with the responsibility to administer water resources in the state. I.C. §§42-1701 to -1778; §§42-1801 to -1806. Moreover, the statutory language does not "expressly treat the precise question at issue." As noted above, past cases from this Court indicate that partial forfeiture has been a recognized practice in Idaho....

The case of *Dovel v. Dobson* establishes that the practice of partial forfeiture has also been followed by the IDWR. The Director's finding in that case was that the "consumptive use appurtenant to the third field had been forfeited by nonuse...." IDWR's practice of interpreting I.C. §42-222(2) as allowing for a partial forfeiture is also apparent from its forms. The IDWR Application for Transfer of a Water Right asks applicants:

> 10. To your knowledge, has any portion of this water right undergone a period of five or more consecutive years of non-use?

Moreover, the record shows that some of those now opposing partial forfeiture advocated its use in their objections to the Director's report in the SRBA proceedings. A Hagerman water right owner filed an objection to a water right on the basis that the water right had been partially forfeited, stating:

> The recommendation is for a greater quantity of water than has been beneficially used since at least before 1970. Thus, the right to *anything more than 3.5 cfs does not exist.* It has been forfeited or abandoned and/or the claimant is estopped from claiming the unused portion pursuant to agreement between the claimant and this objector. (Emphasis added).

Case law and the record in this case show that the general public did indeed understand and depend upon the prior IDWR interpretation, policy and practice that partial forfeiture is a recognized concept in Idaho. That I.C. §42-222(2) allows for partial forfeiture is a reasonable interpretation and otherwise meets the standards for according this interpretation deference. The Court declines to "unsettle ... the repose of all those who have detrimentally relied on ... agency interpretations," and will accord IDWR's interpretation deference in this case.

B. Recognition of Partial Forfeiture Promotes Important Policy Goals

1. The Result of Reaching a Contrary Decision

If this Court were to find that I.C. §42-222(2) does not authorize partial forfeiture of a water right, once the amount element of a water right is decreed, a water user could hold the water against all subsequent appropriators by using only a part of the water. Such a scheme is inconsistent with Idaho water law, which provides that if a water right is abandoned or forfeited it reverts to the state, following which third parties may perfect an interest therein.... 'The governmental function in enacting ... the entire water distribution system under Title 42 of the Idaho Code is to further the state policy of securing the maximum use and benefit of its water resources." In *Kunz v. Utah Power 7 Light Co.* the Court commented:

> The water of this arid state is an important resource. Not only farmers, but industry and residential users depend upon it. Because Idaho receives little annual precipitation, Idahoans must make the most efficient use of this limited resource. The policy of the law of this [s]tate is to secure the maximum use and benefit, and least wasteful use, of its water resources.

Integral to the goal of securing maximum use and benefit of our natural water resources is that water be put to beneficial use. This is a continuing obligation.... Partial forfeiture makes possible allocation of water consistent with beneficial use concepts.

2. Recognition of Partial Forfeiture Promotes Economical Use of Water

Contrary to the water users' claims, the Court's decision does not promote uneconomical use of water in order to avoid forfeiture. A water user is not entitled to waste water. It follows that a water right holder cannot avoid a partial forfeiture by wasting that portion of his or her water right that cannot be put to beneficial use during any part of the statutory period. If a water user cannot apply a portion of a water right to beneficial use during any part of the statutory period, but must waste the water in order to divert the full amount of the water right, a forfeiture has taken place.

V. CONCLUSION

We reverse the decision of the district court determining that I.C. § 42-222(2) does not allow for partial forfeiture of water rights. This Court holds that partial forfeiture is provided for by I.C. § 42-222(2).

Notes & Questions

1. The court defers to IDWR in two very different ways. What are they?
2. Why would the issue of partial forfeiture be so important that it warranted certification as a basin-wide issue? In thinking about your answer, consider that the state was joined in its support of partial forfeiture by groundwater users—generally the most junior water users on Snake River plain—and a number of senior irrigation districts joined the defendants in arguing against partial forfeiture.
3. What policy toward water use is furthered by Idaho's approach to partial forfeiture? Many state courts are less likely to find forfeiture under similar circumstances. Oregon limited the application of a very similar forfeiture statute to partial forfeiture by an amended addition to the forfeiture statute (Oregon Revised Statutes Vol. 15, Title 45 § 540.610(3)). What policy is furthered by limiting partial forfeiture?

Under the common law concept of abandonment, a case did not necessarily end with a finding of intent to abandon and nonuse. There were numerous defenses, including that use had been resumed. The next case addresses the question of whether the defenses survived the enactment of statutory forfeiture and specifically looks at the complicated elements of resumption in use. As you read the case, consider why the same court that decided *Hagerman* in favor of tightening water use to make more water available to junior water users would now allow inroads through concepts like resumption in use.

Sagewillow, Inc. v. Idaho Department of Water Resources

Supreme Court of Idaho
70 P.3d 669 (2003)

Opinion

EISMANN, Justice.—This is an appeal from an order of the Idaho Department of Water Resources declaring that various water rights owned by Sagewillow, Inc., had been forfeited in whole or in part due to nonuse. Because the Department incorrectly applied the resumption-of-use defense raised by Sagewillow, we vacate the order and remand this case for further proceedings.

I. FACTS AND PROCEDURAL HISTORY

In 1989 and 1993, Sagewillow, Inc., purchased various parcels of real property, together with appurtenant water rights, located in Butte County....

The water rights originally appurtenant to the properties purchased by Sagewillow could irrigate 2,383 acres. For approximately twenty years, however, the land irrigated on those properties totaled 1,412 acres. After purchasing the properties, Sagewillow began increasing the number of acres irrigated. Sagewillow irrigated 2,000 acres in 1991, 2,100 acres in 1992, and 2,390 acres in 1993.

...

In 1994, Sagewillow filed seven more transfer applications with the Department seeking to change the places of use for its six groundwater rights. James Mays, Mays Land and Livestock, and the Blaine County Canal Company (herein collectively referred to as "Mays") filed protests to the requested transfers, and the proceeding was expanded to adjudicate whether Sagewillow's surface and ground water rights had been forfeited by nonuse.... Under the Department's order, Sagewillow would only be permitted to irrigate 1,412 acres....

II. ISSUES ON APPEAL

A. Did the Department of Water Resources correctly apply the doctrine of resumption of use?

...

III. ANALYSIS

A party aggrieved by a final order in a contested case decided by an agency may file a petition for judicial review in the district court. IDAHO CODE §§ 67-5270(3) (2001).... This Court does not substitute its judgment for that of the agency as to the weight of the evidence presented. *Id.;* IDAHO CODE § 67-5279(1) (2001). Rather, this Court defers to the agency's findings of fact unless they are clearly erroneous. The agency order may be overturned only where it: (a) violates statutory or constitutional provisions; (b) exceeds the agency's statutory authority; (c) was made upon unlawful procedure; (d) is not supported by substantial evidence in the record as a whole; or (e) is arbitrary, capricious, or an abuse of discretion....

A. Did the Department of Water Resources Correctly Apply the Doctrine of Resumption of Use?

Idaho Code § 42-222(2) provides:

> All rights to the use of water acquired under this chapter or otherwise shall be lost and forfeited by a failure for the term of five (5) years to apply it to the beneficial use for which it was appropriated and when any right to the use of water shall be lost through nonuse or forfeiture such rights to such water shall revert to the state and be again subject to appropriation under this chapter.

Idaho law has contained a similar provision since 1903.... This Court has held, however, that abandonments and forfeitures are not favored. Therefore, "although statutory abandonment did actually occur, the forfeiture is not effective if, after the five-year period, the original owner or appropriator resumed the use of the water prior to the claim of right by a third party." Sagewillow contends that it resumed use of its water rights during the period from 1989 to 1993. The parties disagree as to whether the resumption-of-use doctrine still applies, and, if so, how it should be applied in this case.

The Department contends that resumption of use only applies if there are no junior appropriators in the same or an interconnected water source. If there are junior appropriators, then the resumption of use will not apply. According to the Department, as a matter of law the resumption-of-use doctrine only applies to the most junior appropriator....

...

The requirement that junior appropriators have used the water is consistent with this Court's statement of the resumption-of-use doctrine that the prior use must be resumed "prior to a claim of right by a third party." Under the Department's argument, if the three most junior appropriators did not use their water rights for five years, the second and third most junior appropriators would forfeit their water rights, but the most junior appropriator would not. The most junior appropriator, by his mere existence, would be held to have made a claim of right to the water of the second and third most junior appropriators even though none of them used any water.

In the instant case, the Department did not make any finding that after the statutory period of nonuse and before resumption of use by Sagewillow and/or its predecessors, any junior appropriator used water that was available because of continued nonuse by Sagewillow and/or its predecessors.... The Department likewise did not make any finding that during such period any third party applied for and obtained a water right in the same or an interconnected watercourse....

Mays argues that the legislature has abolished the resumption-of-use doctrine by the portion of Idaho Code § 42-222 that provides as follows:

> Upon proper showing before the director of the department of water resources of good and sufficient reason for nonapplication to beneficial use of such water for such term of five (5) years, the director of the department of water resources

> is hereby authorized to grant an extension of time extending the time for forfeiture of title for nonuse thereof, to such waters for a period of not to exceed five (5) additional years.

This provision was first added to Idaho law in 1933. It does not by its terms expressly abrogate the resumption-of-use doctrine. Mays contends it did so by implication.

Although this Court has not previously addressed Mays' argument, in 1982 this Court stated that the statutory extension of the five-year period provided by Idaho Code § 42-222(2) and the doctrine of resumption of use were both viable defenses to forfeiture.

> Statutory forfeiture is based upon the legislative declaration in I.C. § 42-222(2) that water rights may be lost if they are not applied to a beneficial use for a period of five continuous years. Certain defenses to forfeiture have been recognized. Extension of the five year period may be made upon a showing of good cause, providing the application for extension is made within the first five-year period. I.C. § 42-222(2). Also wrongful interference with a water right or failure to use the water because of circumstances over which the water right holder has no control have been recognized as defenses. Further, if use of the water right is resumed after the five year period, but before any third parties make a claim in the water, then the courts will decline to declare a forfeiture.

The two defenses are not mutually exclusive. Both the statutory extension and the resumption-of-use doctrine can operate independently of each other.

... [The court reviews numerous cases in which forfeiture was found when another water user had initiated use of the forfeited water prior to resumption in use of the original appropriator.]

...

Under the resumption-of-use doctrine, statutory forfeiture is not effective if, after the five-year period of nonuse, use of the water is resumed prior to the claim of right by a third party. A third party has made a claim of right to the water if the third party has either instituted proceedings to declare a forfeiture, or has obtained a valid water right authorizing the use of such water with a priority date prior to the resumption of use, or has used the water pursuant to an existing water right. Because there can be a partial forfeiture of water rights by nonuse for five years, a resumption of use of only a portion of a water right prior to a claim of right by a third party will only prevent the forfeiture of that portion of the water right. The resumption of use must also be upon land to which the water right is appurtenant. Because the Department based its order upon an erroneous statement of the resumption-of-use doctrine, we must vacate the order and remand for further proceedings consistent with this opinion.

...

Notes & Questions

1. In addition to resumption of use, what other defenses to forfeiture does the court indicate it would be willing to consider?
   a. wrongful interference with use of the water right
   b. failure to use the water because of circumstances over which the water right holder has no control
   c. intent to resume use
2. Resumption of use is a valid defense to forfeiture if the resumption is made before there is a claim of right by a third party. IDWR interpreted a "claim of right" to be the acquisition of water rights from the same source by junior water users. How does that differ from the court's articulation of the defense? The court notes that IDWR's interpretation has the illogical result of allowing the defense to be used only by the most junior user on a stream. Why, nevertheless, might IDWR prefer its interpretation?

Chapter 9

State-Based Common Law of Groundwater

Introduction

During the early development of the common law, wells were generally hand-dug and used primarily for domestic purposes. Large-scale development of groundwater, particularly for irrigation, did not take place until the second half of the twentieth century, when drilling and pump technology from the oil industry and post-WWII rural electrification made it feasible. This means that even the earliest large groundwater rights generally came online decades after substantial appropriation of surface water rights in most locations.

During the early development of the common law of water, groundwater hydrology (or hydrogeology) was not understood. Instead, most courts considered it to be "secret, occult and concealed ... [making any] attempt to administer any set of legal rules ... practically impossible."[1] Courts, nevertheless, had to resolve disputes in the face of this uncertainty regarding the groundwater resource. As a result, early courts carved out a variety of rules for groundwater rights. Four approaches were developed. This Chapter covers multiple approaches, including those outside of the Columbia River basin, because the types of issues that arise and the approach to managing ground and surface water as a single resource (conjunctive management covered in Part V) differ depending on the approach chosen by a state. This contrasts with surface water, in which the common use of the prior appropriation for surface water in the West generally results in conflict over similar issues. By focusing on a subset of states for surface water, you learn how history, geographic and climatic setting, and human needs and values play into judicial decisions—i.e., the systems approach. The following paragraphs introduce the four approaches to groundwater allocation.

First, the common law developed in the eighteenth century in England viewed groundwater as an incident of land ownership. Under this theory, landowners had an absolute and unlimited right to use groundwater from a well on their land and

1. Houston & T.C. Ry. Co. v. East, 81 S.W. 279, 281 (Tex. 1904) (*quoting* Frazier v. Brown, 12 Ohio St. 294, 311 (1861)). In 1984, the Ohio Supreme Court overruled *Frazier*. Cline v. American Aggregates Corp., 474 N.E. 2d 324, 327 (Ohio 1984), stating: "[t]he 'mysterious and occult' description of ground water flows does not describe or recognize the present state of scientific advancement." *Id.* at 326. News of that advancement has not, apparently, reached the Texas courts.

there was no cause of action for injury resulting from that use. Considering the relative abundance of water in England and the fact that technology limited groundwater development to hand-dug wells for domestic use, this was probably an appropriate rule. In the first case you read in this Chapter you will see that Texas follows this approach.

Second, the adoption of the common law of England in the United States led to a modification allowing reasonable use when groundwater was developed as an incident of land ownership. Like the American rule of riparian rights for surface water, shortage must be shared. This rule was adopted in much of the eastern United States.

Third, a variation on "reasonable use" developed as the doctrine of correlative rights. Under this variation, reasonable use could still be made of groundwater, but shortage must be shared pro rata—i.e., according to the relative ownership of overlying land. The second case you read will illustrate this approach adopted by California.

Fourth, many western states adopted the doctrine of prior appropriation. The third case, from Idaho, will cover the adoption of prior appropriation for allocation of groundwater.

Complicating this list, some states mixed the doctrines, based on whether the groundwater amounted to an "underwater river" versus "percolating" groundwater versus artesian groundwater. These distinctions reflect the scientific uncertainty regarding groundwater that prevailed during its early development. Once wells were developed, the recognition of property use rights in groundwater made it difficult to alter this system, which had been based on a false understanding of hydrology.

At common law, the Supreme Courts of Washington, Oregon, and Montana applied different rules based on whether the groundwater amounted to an underground "river" versus "percolating groundwater." Each determined that if subsurface water is flowing in an ascertainable subterranean natural waterway then it is subject to appropriation the same as a surface water source. In 1912 the Montana Supreme Court stated "Subsurface water flowing in defined channels reasonably ascertainable is subject to the same rules as water flowing in surface streams."[2] In 1923 the Oregon Supreme Court stated: "[T]o render a subsurface stream subject to the rules of law applicable to the surface water courses, the existence and location of such stream must be reasonably ascertainable."[3] In 1935 the Washington Supreme Court stated: "Where a subterranean stream flows in a distinct, permanent, well-known and defined channel, it is governed by the same rules as apply to a natural watercourse on the surface."[4]

In contrast, all three state courts applied different rules to "percolating" water. In Washington the court found that all groundwater is presumed to be percolating and the existence of a watercourse must be clearly shown to overcome this presumption.[5] In Washington, percolating water is subject to the American rule of reasonable use,

2. Ryan v. Quinlan, 124 P. 512, 516 (Mont. 1912).

3. Hayes v. Adams, 218 P. 933, 935 (Or. 1923).

4. Evans v. City of Seattle, 47 P.2d 984, 985 (Wash. 1935).

5. *Evans*, 182 Wash. at 454.

meaning that a landowner may use their percolating groundwater in a reasonable manner upon their land.[6] In Oregon, if the water was deemed subterranean or percolating it was considered an incident of land ownership and could be put to any beneficial use the landowner saw fit—even to the injury of their neighbor.[7] The Supreme Court of Montana also held that "percolating water is not governed by the same rules that apply to running streams," and that a landowner may put their groundwater to beneficial use so long as it is done reasonably.[8] Statutory systems brought changes to the common law and all three states now apply the doctrine of prior appropriation to groundwater.

Should your career take you to Colorado, you will find a unique variation in which groundwater considered "tributary" to a stream followed the prior appropriation doctrine, and non-tributary groundwater is treated as a separate finite resource and must be developed according to a depletion plan. Colorado courts have imposed a presumption that all groundwater within a surface watershed is tributary since the mid-twentieth century.[9] With this approach, an application for a tributary groundwater right proceeds through the Colorado water courts along with surface water rights under the doctrine of prior appropriation, and nontributary groundwater was under the Office of the State Engineer.[10] The 1965 Colorado Groundwater Management Act retained the terms "tributary" and non-tributary water. The Act carved out a third category of "designated" groundwater defined as "groundwater which in its natural course would not be available to and required for the fulfillment of decreed surface rights, or groundwater in areas not adjacent to a continuously flowing natural stream."[11] Despite the increased clarity in definitions, the State Engineer and the Colorado judicial system had a difficult time addressing alleged interference between ground and surface water use as groundwater development increased (referred to as "conjunctive management," a concept you will study in Part V).[12] In 1969 the Act was amended, stating:

> (1)(a) It is hereby declared to be the policy of the state of Colorado that all water in or tributary to natural surface streams, not including nontributary groundwater ... originating in or flowing into this state have always been and are hereby declared to be the property of the public, dedicated to the use of the people of the state, subject to appropriation.... [I]t is the policy of this state to integrate the appropriation, use, and administration of underground water

---

6. *Id.*

7. *Hayes*, 109 Or. at 57.

8. *Ryan*, 124 P. at 516.

9. De Haas v. Benesch, 181 P.2d 453, 456 (Colo. 1947); Safranek v. Town of Limon, 228 P.2d 975, 977 (Colo. 1951).

10. For an excellent introduction to Colorado groundwater law, see David Harrison et al., *Intro to Ground Water Law in Colorado and Surface-Groundwater Conflicts in the South Platte, in* GROUNDWATER IN THE WEST (2004).

11. COLO. REV. STAT. § 37-90-103 (6)(a).

12. Fellhauer v. People, 447 P.2d 986 (Colo. 1968). In 1969 the Act was amended to protect existing wells from conjunctive management.

> tributary to a stream with the use of surface water in such a way as to maximize the beneficial use of all of the waters of this state.[13]

In 1985 the Act was amended to define "non-tributary" as groundwater that the "withdrawal of which will not, within one hundred years of continuous withdrawal, deplete the flow of a natural stream, including a natural stream."[14]

Before reading the cases, review the portions of Part I on the scientific underpinnings of groundwater hydrology.

The English Rule: Groundwater as an Incident of Land Ownership

Texas is the lone state (no pun intended) in the western United States following the English rule that groundwater is an incident of land ownership and there is no limit on extraction if the well and the use is on land owned by the water user. Pay attention to the court's rationale for following this rule.

Houston & Texas Central Railroad Co. v. East

Texas Supreme Court

81 S.W. 279 (1904)

Opinion

WILLIAMS, J.—This case is thus stated by the Court of Civil Appeals:

> 'This is a suit by W. A. East against the Houston & Texas Central Railroad Company for damages growing out of the alleged destruction by defendant of plaintiff's well....

[The plaintiff, East, dug a domestic well on his homestead that was about five feet in diameter and about 33 feet deep. Defendant, Houston & Texas Central Railroad Company, on land it owned, dug a well about 20 feet in diameter and 66 feet deep, placed a steam pump in the well, and produced about 25,000 gallons of water per day. Use of the well by the Houston & Texas Central Railroad Company dried up the well of East, despite studies done by the Railroad Company showing sufficient supply. The trial court found for the Houston & Texas Central Railroad Company. The Court of Civil Appeals reversed, finding the use of the groundwater by the Railroad Company unreasonable.]

...

... Since the dicision [sic] in the case of *Acton v. Blundell*, 12 Mees. & W. 324, the law as therein laid down, so far as it controls this case, has been recognized and followed

13. Colo. Rev. Stat. § 37-92-102

14. Colo. Rev. Stat. § 37-90-103 (10.5).

in the courts of England, and probably by all the courts of last resort in this country before which the question has come, except the Supreme Court of New Hampshire.... That doctrine is thus stated: 'That the person who owns the surface may dig therein and apply all that is there found to his own purposes, at his free will and pleasure; and that if, in the exercise of such right, he intercepts or drains off the water collected from the underground springs in his neighbor's well, this inconvenience to his neighbor falls within the description of *damnum absque injuria*, [loss or damage without injury] which cannot become the ground of an action.'... The practical reasons upon which the courts base their conclusions fully meet the more theoretical view of the New Hampshire court, and satisfy us of the necessity of the doctrine. Those reasons are thus summarized by the Supreme Court of Ohio in *Frazier v. Brown*: 'In the absence of express contract and a positive authorized legislation, as between proprietors of adjoining land, the law recognizes no correlative rights in respect to underground waters percolating, oozing, or filtrating through the earth; and this mainly from considerations of public policy: (1) Because the existence, origin, movement, and course of such waters, and the causes which govern and direct their movements, are so secret, occult, and concealed that an attempt to administer any set of legal rules in respect to them would be involved in hopeless uncertainty, and would, therefore, be practically impossible. (2) Because any such recognition of correlative rights would interfere, to the material detriment of the commonwealth, with drainage and agriculture, mining, the construction of highways and railroads, with sanitary regulations, building, and the general progress of improvement in works of embellishment and utility.' The mere quantity of water taken by the owner from his land has nowhere been held to affect the question. Exhaustion resulting from excavating and pumping for mining purposes has been considered in several cases to give rise to no liability. So the authorities generally state that the use of the water for manufacturing, brewing, and like purposes is within the right of the owner of the soil, whatever may be its effect upon his neighbor's wells and springs.

In Chasemore v. Richards, supra, the defendant, in supplying the wants of a town, used to such an extent the water which had percolated through his land into a water course as to reduce the water in the stream, and to leave the plaintiff's mill thereon without adequate power; and yet it was held that there was no liability.... If persons using lands in mining, manufacturing, and brewing may take therefrom all the water required in the prosecution of such businesses, what reason can exist why a railroad company may not do the same thing for such purposes as those to which it applies this well? We think none can be given....

...

... The defendant here is making a reasonable and legitimate use of the water which it takes from its own land, which use is not, in quality, different from, or in its consequences to plaintiff more injurious than, many upheld in the decisions....

The judgment of the Court of Civil Appeals is therefore reversed, and that of the district court affirmed.

Notes & Questions

1. Which of the following are among the reasons the court gives for adopting the English common law rule?
   a. The rule favors the higher economic use of new development
   b. Adjacent landowners may enter into contracts restricting use of water
   c. Groundwater is so poorly understood that administration under any rule recognizing relative rights to the water would be impossible
   d. Any other rule would interfere with any enterprise requiring excavation and resulting drainage of land
2. The court upholds a commercial use that eliminates domestic use of a well on a homestead that existed prior to the railroad development. The emerging international concept of the Human Right to Water seeks to avoid government action that would prevent access to water for basic needs for all. Basic needs are defined as: sufficient, meaning 15–100 liters/person/day (this equals 13–26 gallons); safe: meaning it meets drinking water standards; accessible: meaning within 1000 meters or a 30-minute walk (this is about 0.6 miles); and affordable: meaning no more than three percent of the household income. Does the Texas Supreme Court ruling in *Houston & Texas Central Ry. Co. v. East*, 81 S.W. 279, 281 (Tex. 1904), violate the concept of the Human Right to Water?
3. In 1995 the Texas legislature provided for the designation of groundwater management areas "in order to provide for the conservation, preservation, protection, recharging, and prevention of waste of the groundwater, and of groundwater reservoirs or their subdivisions, and to control subsidence caused by withdrawal of water from those groundwater reservoirs or their subdivisions, consistent with the objectives of Section 59, Article XVI, Texas Constitution..." Texas Water Code § 35.001. In 2012, the Texas Supreme Court held that local groundwater restrictions could result in a regulatory Taking of private property.[15] In 2013, the Texas Fourth Court of Appeals found a Taking in *Edwards Aquifer Authority v. Bragg* (421 S.W.3d 118 (Tex. Ct. App. 2013)) and in 2015 the Texas Supreme Court denied review. Thus, the legal authority over groundwater in Texas remains in flux.

The California Rule: Correlative Rights

The next case represents the adoption of the correlative rights doctrine in California. Pay attention to the reasons the court gives for deviating from the common law of England and note the similarities to the adoption of prior appropriation.

15. Edwards Aquifer Authority v. Day, 369 S.W.3d 814 (Tex. 2012).

Katz v. Walkinshaw

Supreme Court of California
74 P. 766 (1903)

Opinion

SHAW, J.—A rehearing was granted in this case for the purpose of considering more fully, and by the aid of such additional arguments as might be presented by persons not parties to the action, but vitally interested in the principle involved, a question that is novel, and of the utmost importance to the application to useful purposes of the waters which may be found in the soil.

...

... The complaint, in substance, states that the plaintiffs had wells upon their respective tracts of land, from which water flowed to the surface of the ground; that the water was necessary for domestic use and irrigation on the lands on which they were situate; that the defendant, by means of other wells and excavations upon on another tract of land in the vicinity prevented any water from flowing through the plaintiff's wells to their premises; and that this was done by drawing off the water through the wells of the defendant, taking it to a distant tract, and there using it....

... It is contended that the rule that each landowner owns absolutely the percolating waters in his land, with the right to extract, sell, and dispose of them as he chooses, regardless of the results to his neighbor, is part of the common law, and as such has been adopted in this state as the law of the land by the statute of April 13, 1850 (St. 1850, p. 219, c. 95) [adopting the common law of England], ...

The idea that the doctrine contended for by the defendant is a part of the common law adopted by our statute, and beyond the power of the court to change or modify, is founded upon a misconception.... The true doctrine is that the common law by its own principles adapts itself to varying conditions, and modifies its own rules so as to serve the ends of justice.... The question whether or not the rule contended for is a part of the common law applicable to this state depends on whether it is suitable to our conditions under the rule just stated.

It is necessary, therefore, to state the conditions existing in many parts of this state, which are different from those existing where the rule had its origin. In a large part of the state, and in almost all of the southern half of it, particularly south of the Tehachapi range of mountains, aside from grains, grasses, and some scant pasturage, there is practically no production by agriculture [sic] except by means of artificial irrigation. In a few places favored by nature crops are nourished by natural irrigation, due to the existence underneath the ordinary soil of a saturated layer of sand or gravel; but these places are so few that they are of no consequence in any general view of the situation. Irrigation in these regions has always been customary, and under the Spanish and Mexican governments it was fostered and encouraged. Even in the earlier periods of the settlement of the country after its acquisition by the United States, and while the population was sparse and scattered compared to the present time, the natural supply of water from the surface streams, as diverted and applied by the crude and wasteful methods then used, was not considered more than was necessary. As the population increased, better methods of diversion, distribution, and application were adopted, and the streams were made to irrigate a very much larger area of land. While this process was going on, a series of wet years augmented the streams, and still more land was put under the irrigating systems. Recently there has followed another series of very dry years, which has correspondingly diminished the flow of the streams. After this period began, it was soon found that the natural streams were insufficient. The situation became critical, and heavy loss and destruction from drouth was imminent. Still the population continued to increase, and with it the demand for more water to irrigate more land. Recourse was then had to the underground waters. Tunnels were constructed, more artesian wells bored, and finally pumps driven by electric or steam power were put into general use to obtain sufficient water to keep alive and productive the valuable orchards planted at the time when water was supposed to be more abundant.... But it is not yet demonstrated that the process is not in fact, for the most part, an exhaustion of the underground sources from which the surface streams and other supplies previously used have been fed and supported. In some cases this has been proven by the event. The danger of exhaustion in this way threatens surface streams as well as underground percolations and reservoirs. Many water companies, anticipating such an attack on their water supply, have felt compelled to purchase, and have purchased, at great expense, the lands immediately surrounding the stream or source of supply, in order to be able to protect and secure the percolations from which the source was fed.... Owing to the uncertainty in the law, and the absence of legal protection, there has been no security in titles to water rights. So great is the scarcity of water under the present demands and conditions that one who is deprived of water which he has been using has usually no other source at hand from which he can obtain another supply.

... there still remain large areas of rich soil which are dry and waste for want of water. This abundance of land, with the scarcity and high price of water, furnish a constant stimulus to the further exhaustion of the limited amount of underground water, and a constant temptation to invade sources already appropriated....

It is clear, also, that the difficulties arising from the scarcity of water in this country are by no means ended, but, on the contrary, are probably just beginning....

...

... [If the rule that groundwater is an incident of land ownership were adopted, groundwater users] will be constantly threatened with danger of utter destruction of the valuable enterprises and systems of waterworks which they control, and that all new enterprises of the same sort will be subject to the same peril. They will have absolutely no protection in law against others having stronger pumps, deeper wells, or a more favorable situation, who can thereby take from them unlimited quantities of the water, reaching to the entire supply, and without regard to the place of use....

The doctrine of reasonable use, on the other hand, affords some measure of protection to property now existing, and greater justification for the attempt to make new developments. It limits the right of others to such amount of water as may be necessary for some useful purpose in connection with the land from which it is taken. If, as is claimed in the argument, such water-bearing land is generally worthless except for the water which it contains, then the quantity that could be used on the land would be nominal, and injunctions could not be obtained, or substantial damages awarded, against those who carry it to distant lands. So far as the active interference of others is concerned, therefore, the danger to such undertakings in much less, and the incentive to development much greater, from the doctrine of reasonable use than from the contrary rule. No doubt there will be inconvenience from attacks on the title to waters appropriated for use on distant lands made by persons who claim the right to the reasonable use of such waters on their own lands. Similar difficulties have arisen and now exist with respect to rights in surface streams, and must always be expected to attend claims to rights in a substance so movable as water. But the courts can protect this particular species of property in water as effectually as water rights of any other description.

It may, indeed, become necessary to make new applications of old principles to the new conditions; and, in view of the novelty of the doctrine and the scope of argument, it is not out of place to indicate to some extent how it should be done, although otherwise it would not be necessary to the decision of the case. The controversies arising will naturally divide into classes. There will be disputes between persons or corporations claiming rights to take such waters from the same strata or source for use on distant lands. There is no statute on this subject, as there now is concerning appropriations of surface streams; but the case is not without precedent. When the pioneers of 1849 reached this state, they found no laws in force governing rights to take waters from surface streams for use on nonriparian lands. Yet it was found that the principles of the common law, although not previously applied to such cases, could be adapted thereto, and were sufficient to define and protect such rights under the new conditions. The same condition existed with respect to rights to mine on public land, and a similar solution was found.... The principles which, ... were applied to protect appropriations and possessory rights in visible streams, will, in general, be found applicable to such appropriations of percolating waters,.... Such rights are usufructuary only,.... In controversies between an appropriator for use on distant land and those who own land overlying the water-bearing strata, ... who have used the water on their land before the attempt to appropriate, ... the rights of the ... landowners are paramount to that of one who takes the water to distant land, but the landowner's right extends only to the quantity of water that is necessary for use on his land, and the appropriator may take the surplus.... Disputes between overlying landowners, concerning water for use on the land, to which they have an equal right, in cases where the supply is insufficient for all, are to be settled by giving to each a fair and just proportion...

...

With regard to the doctrine of reasonable use of percolating waters, we adhere to the views expressed in the former opinion.

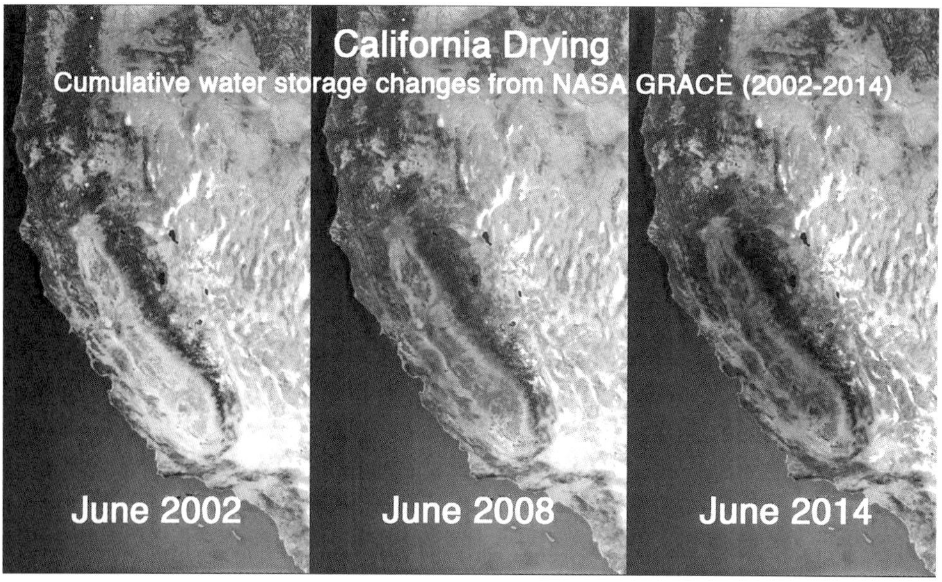

Figure 9.1 NASA GRACE data showing land subsidence from groundwater extraction in California's Central Valley. GRACE-FO, Jet Propulsion Laboratory, California Institute of Technology, *Water Storage* (2023), https://gracefo.jpl.nasa.gov/science/water-storage/.

Notes & Questions

1. Which of the following factors does the court list as important in determining whether the common law of England should be altered in application to California?
   a. The arid nature of the land and the need for irrigation
   b. Overdevelopment threatening depletion of the resource
   c. Increasing demand due to population growth and new technology
   d. The location of arable land at a distance from water supply
2. Which of the following is the rule articulated by the court for allocation of groundwater among owners of the overlying land? Which applies to allocation of groundwater to water users conveying the water away from the overlying land?
   a. Groundwater rights are an incident of land ownership and may not be conveyed away from the overlying land.
   b. Surplus water may be conveyed away from the overlying land and the rights of the owner of the overlying land are paramount.
   c. The rights of overlying landowners are shared equally and during shortage are shared proportionally.
   d. The rights of overlying landowners are allocated during shortage according to the date on which the land was settled.
3. The court was prescient with its statement: "It is clear, also, that the difficulties arising from the scarcity of water in this country are by no means ended, but, on the con-

trary, are probably just beginning." Although the correlative rights doctrine addresses how water will be shared in times of scarcity (i.e., pro rata), it does not address the fact that a large portion of a groundwater aquifer is storage and if pumping exceeds recharge, despite shared shortage, the aquifer will decline. Scarcity may not be an issue until the aquifer is depleted. This is referred to as aquifer mining and you will see how some states address it via statute in Part V. With the recent onset of long-term drought indicative of climate change, California farmers turned increasingly to groundwater—in fact, so much so that the depletion of groundwater sources was visible from space (Figure 9.1). In the face of declining groundwater levels, the California legislature passed the Sustainable Groundwater Management Act (SGMA), requiring those sharing a groundwater basin to develop plans to achieve sustainable use. At the time of writing of this book, those plans are under development.

Taking a Cue from Surface Water: The Doctrine of Prior Appropriation

The next case from Idaho illustrates the adoption of prior appropriation for groundwater. Pay attention to the reasons given by the court, particularly those influenced by what was known by 1931 about the science of groundwater. The dissent would have drawn a distinction between so-called "percolating" groundwater and water in a "subterranean stream." As you learned in Part I in the chapter on groundwater hydrology, scientists now understand that almost all groundwater is connected to surface water in some way. One of the modern water problems courts, water agencies, and legislatures are only beginning to address is the impact of groundwater development on surface water. States that chose the same doctrine for both surface and ground water have an advantage in addressing that problem.

Hinton v. Little

Idaho Supreme Court
296 P. 582 (1931)

GIVENS, J.—[The area that is the subject of the litigation is an artesian groundwater basin. Water under pressure is confined between two impervious layers so that when it is tapped it rises to the surface without pumping. The plaintiffs› engineer testified that the water entered this subterranean basin from high mountains lying to the south of the basin. There is some movement of the water into the basin from the south and laterally beneath the ground and between the different wells. Hinton has developed 18 wells from the artesian aquifer and Little has developed three. Hinton claim a prior right to the use of all artesian waters in the district on the theory of priority in appropriation and beneficial use]

[Hintons] contend that the same rule is to be applied to the appropriation of these subterranean waters as is applied to surface waters; namely, first in time is first in right. [Littles] contend on the other hand for either what is known as the English or common-law doctrine, that the owner of the surface of the ground owns all the water within his land, or the so-called American doctrine. It is evident that the English doctrine cannot be applicable, because, when any one of the landowners in question, so far as the evidence now shows, takes water from his well, it diminishes the flow in the other wells; hence it would seem apparent that he is taking, not alone that which belongs to him, as underlying his land, but is, in some measure at least, taking either directly or indirectly that which comes from underneath the land of other owners. Appellants contend for what is sometimes called the American, or the correlative use, doctrine, in effect this, that under circumstances as disclosed above each surface owner is entitled to take his proportionate share of the entire body of underground water, in the particular basin underlying the lands in question and affected by the different wells. There are numerous authorities which sustain the English doctrine, and there are authorities which define and sustain the American doctrine of correlative use, the first case probably clearly announcing the American doctrine being *Katz v. Walkinshaw,* 70 P. 663, 74 P. 766 (Cal. 1902). Without attempting to enumerate, cite, examine, or distinguish all of the decisions from the different jurisdictions, which have had occasion to touch upon this question, there are in this state four decisions which bear upon the question.

... It appears to be now fairly well settled that all underground subterranean waters are percolating waters, that is, that there is more or less movement, both perpendicular and horizontal, through the earth and rocks. Therefore, whether underground waters move in a well-defined channel, either in a generally confined direction as to the points of the compass or spread out laterally, is merely a question of difference or degree.

It would seem, therefore, that it is impossible to attempt to lay down one rule with regard to subterranean waters, existing more or less as a relatively stationary body of water under the ground, and subterranean waters in which there is a decided movement. In any event, the facts in the case at bar show that there is movement of the underground waters involved in this litigation, and we need pass herein on no other situation.

In *Le Quime v. Chambers,* a spring upon certain land, ... was appropriated ..., Chambers was given a preference right to file on the land, and tore up Le Quime's pipe, which he had theretofore used to convey the water in question to other lands. Chambers contended, as the appellants do herein, that the ownership of the land gave him the exclusive right to this water. Le Quime contended that the water was subject to appropriation, and he, being prior in point of time, was entitled to it....

It is ... apparent that this case clearly held that seeping percolating subterranean waters, though not in a well-defined stream, are the subject of appropriation, and that the rule of first in time, first in right, is applicable thereto.

...

Bower v. Moorman involved relative appropriation rights in adjacent wells where the taking of water from one well affected the flow in the other, the court stating the three pertinent questions to be considered as follows:

First, the right of a landowner to drive a well on his own land in order to obtain subterranean waters; second, to what depth and under what conditions may a well be driven before a permanent injunction will lie at the instance of an adjoining landowner, who is a prior appropriator of subterranean waters, for an interference with the flow of water in said adjoining landowner's well; third, are subterranean waters in this state subject to appropriation for a beneficial use.

The third and last of these considerations is the pertinent and decisive question herein, and was clearly, unequivocally, and decisively disposed of. After reviewing the so-called English doctrine and the reasonable use or correlative right doctrine, as announced in *Katz v. Walkinshaw,* and quoting section 3242 of the Rev. Codes to the effect that «the right to the use of waters of rivers, streams, lakes, springs and subterranean waters, may be acquired by appropriation,» and citing *Le Quime v. Chambers,* the court holds:

> "Any interference with a vested right to the use of water, whether from open streams, lakes, ponds, percolating or subterranean water, would entitle the party injured to damages, *and an injunction would issue perpetually restraining any such interference.*" *LeQuime (emphasis added).*

...

We then have a clear statement in *Bower v. Moorman,* to the effect that subterranean waters are the subject of appropriation. That being true, it follows that the judgment herein should be affirmed, since the waters here were appropriated by the respondents prior to the time that the appellants sought to take from their wells the amount of water now claimed by them.

BUDGE, J., DISSENTING:

...

The waters used by the parties derive from an underground source, being brought to the surface by means of wells piercing impermeable strata under which the waters are confined at varying depths.

[Hintons] allege, and, as a basis of the discussion to follow, the facts may be taken to show, that the appropriations by plaintiffs of water from their wells practically exhaust the supply, so that, if [Littles] increase the flow of water from their wells with which to irrigate new or additional lands, the pressure in plaintiffs' wells will be diminished and the flow from their wells thereby materially decreased.

The issue here is clear cut, viz. whether the artesian waters, the subject of this action, are private waters belonging to the respective owners of the freehold or are subject to appropriation as public waters under the Constitution and laws of the state.

....

Under the common-law or English rule, percolating waters are regarded as belonging to the owner of the freehold, like the rocks, soil, and minerals found there, and such owner may, in the absence of malice, intercept, impede, and appropriate such waters while they are upon his premises, and make whatever use of them he pleases, regardless of the fact that his use cuts off the flow of such waters to adjoining lands, and deprives the adjoining landowner of their use. However, this doctrine as to rights in percolating waters has been quite generally modified in this country by later decisions, the courts applying what has been called, variously, the rule of reasonable use, the rule of correlative rights, or the American rule—best expressed by the maxim that one must use his own as not to injure another—that each landowner is restricted to a reasonable exercise of his own rights and a reasonable use of his own property, in view of the similar rights of others. Thus, where two or more persons own contiguous tracts of land, underlaid by porous material extending to and communicating with them all, which is saturated with water moving with more or less freedom therein, it has been held each has a common and correlative right to the use of this water upon his land to the extent of a reasonable share thereof, if the supply is so scant that the use by one will affect the supply of the others....

While there is some authority to the contrary, it may be stated as a general rule that the rules of law applying to the appropriation of surface waters do not apply to waters percolating through the earth without a defined and known channel, and that such waters are not subject to appropriation.... In effect conceding the waters here in controversy are percolating waters, plaintiffs contend they are subject to the doctrine of appropriation and its incidents, the same as public surface waters.

....

Notes & Questions

1. Which of the following does the court use as reason(s) to refuse to make a distinction between water moving in an underground channel and "percolating" water?
   a. The economic cost of distinguishing between percolating water and an underground channel is prohibitive.
   b. It was understood by 1931 that underground water moves through rock and earth, thus the distinction between moving in a channel and percolating water is merely one of degree
   c. Prior Idaho cases applied prior appropriation to percolating, seeping water, and to subterranean water.
2. Which doctrine, prior appropriation or correlative rights subject to reasonable use, do you think is more resilient to climate change?

Means of Diversion

Groundwater management is made complex by the problem that aquifer boundaries may cross both land ownership and jurisdictional boundaries. Hydrologically connected groundwater may underlie land that is owned by different property owners. In that situation, if those landowners are all making use of groundwater, they are taking from a common source and are therefore in competition with one another for its use. When pumping from one well causes decline of water available from another well, the phrase "well interference" is the term used. Groundwater law generally addresses two different causes of well interference: aquifer mining and temporary interference from localized drawdown as a result of pumping. Common law addressed only the impact of well interference and did not provide any long-term solution for groundwater mining. In addition to the doctrines above that address means to allocate a diminishing supply, the drawdown of the water level, whether caused by mining or temporary interference, was addressed by rules pertaining to well depth. Well depth is considered part of the means of diversion. Both causes of lowering the water level will be introduced in the following section followed by a case illustrating the common law approach to well depth. You will see how groundwater mining is addressed by statute in Part V.

Groundwater Mining

Recall from Part I that the volume of water available in a groundwater basin is part storage and part flow-through. The volume changes according to the difference between the amount of water flowing into the basin and the amount of water flowing out. Under natural conditions, most groundwater basins have achieved what is referred to as dynamic equilibrium, meaning that although groundwater levels may change seasonally, their water level remains relatively stable over the long term. Groundwater pumping alters that equilibrium by increasing the amount of water flowing *out* of the groundwater basin. If that pumping causes long-term outflow to exceed the long-term amount of water flowing into the basin, then groundwater "mining" will occur and groundwater levels will decline.

Declining groundwater level may cause a variety of harm, but most relevant here is when the level declines to an elevation below one or more wells (Figure 9.2). Those wells will no longer be able to produce water. They are literally left "high and dry."

Without regulation, this arrangement creates a classic tragedy of the commons-type situation as discussed in Part I, whereby each user "[a]s a rational being ... seeks to maximize his gain. Explicitly or implicitly ... he asks 'what is the utility to me of [using more of the groundwater]." Garrett Hardin, *The Tragedy of the Commons,* 162 Science 1243, 1244 (1968). Each groundwater user benefits by maximizing their use of water. That benefit is not shared with any of the neighboring groundwater users. Just the opposite, each user loses out as others use the relatively finite resource. As a result, each user is incentivized to take as much water as they can as quickly as possible—"[e]ach man is locked into a system that compels him to increase his [use of the commons] without limit.... Ruin is the destination." *Id.*

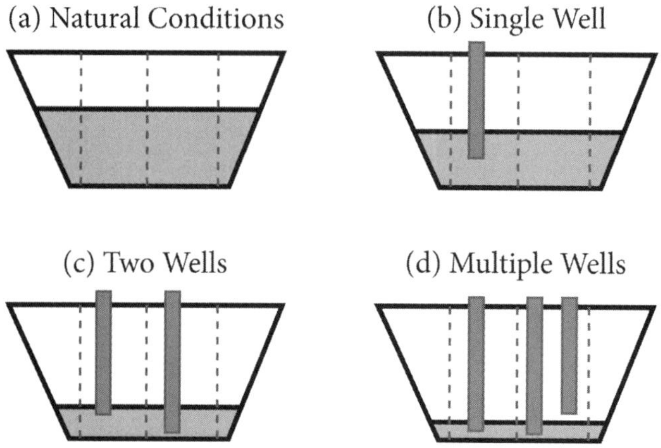

Figure 9.2 Diagram showing the shared aquifer problem—landowners with artificial surface boundaries are accessing a common source of groundwater below their property. As a result, one landowner's use of groundwater affects others using the common aquifer.

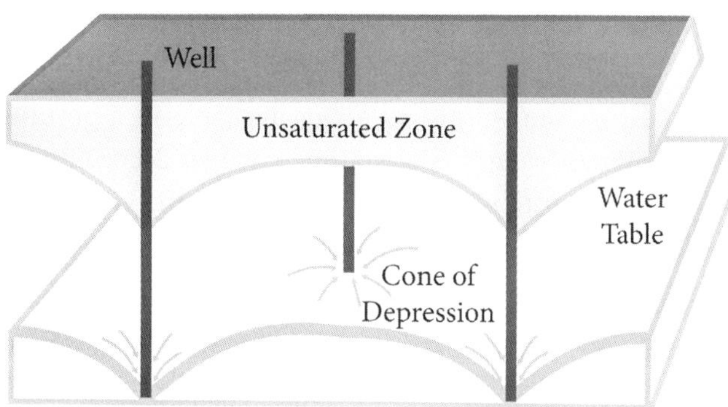

Figure 9.3 Cone of depression. Source: Design by Leilanee Taylor.

Temporary Depression of the Water Table Due to Pumping

Groundwater pumping can also have more localized effects. As shown in Figure 9.3, pumping from each well produces what is known as a "cone of depression" where pumping causes a depression in the groundwater level around the well. That depression is deepest right at the well, where the pump placed in the well is pumping water at a rate that exceeds the rate that water naturally flows into the well. The pumping effect diminishes with distance away from the well. If pumping of a well stops, the groundwater level rebounds. Thus, unlike groundwater mining, this is not a permanent depletion and generally only affects nearby wells. Often the wells affected are older, shallow, domestic wells. Although the shape of this depression can be conceptualized as an upside-down cone, the actual shape depends on the geologic composition of the aquifer material (i.e., the soil or rock formation the water is contained in). If the

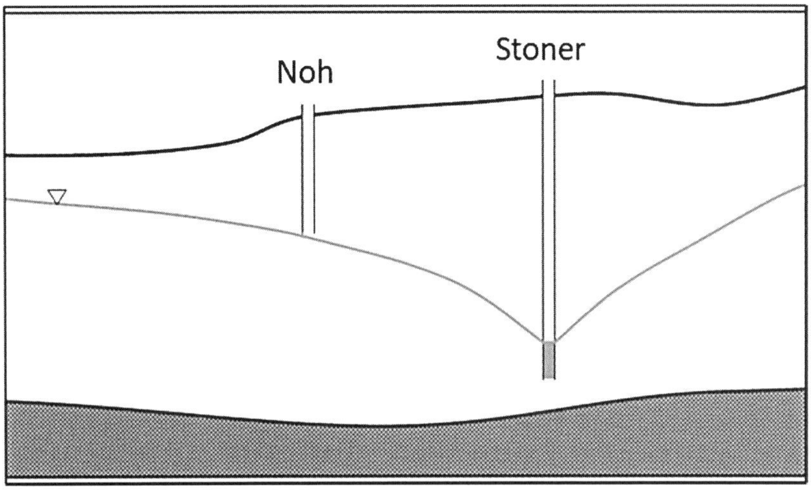

Figure 9.4: Well interference within a cone of depression.

material is more permeable in a particular direction, the well pump will draw more water from that direction, causing the cone to elongate in that direction.

The Common Law of Well Depth

The next case, *Noh v. Stoner*,[16] demonstrates the problem of well interference resulting from the localized effects of pumping. The case addresses the question of who should be responsible when one well interferes with another well and thus applies to both situations (with the caveat that statutes now address groundwater mining). Figure 9.4 depicts the situation from *Noh*. Noh was the prior appropriator, drilling his wells first, which, at the time they were drilled, were deep enough to produce a consistent supply of water. Later, Stoner drilled his own well on land neighboring Noh. That well was drilled to a lower depth and extracted a large enough quantity of water that it produced a cone of depression that dropped the water level to below the bottom of Noh's wells. As a result, Noh's wells went dry.

Noh v. Stoner

Supreme Court of Idaho
26 P.2d 1112 (1933)

GIVENS, Justice.—Respondents [Noh] sued for and were granted an injunction restraining appellants [Stoner], adjoining landowners, from further depleting an artesian basin tapped by respondents' two wells, drilled and operated prior to appellants' well. Both parties rely upon the proposition that subterranean waters of the nature herein are subject to appropriation and diversion as surface waters and are governed by the same rule of priority [citations omitted].

16. 26 P.2d 1112 (1933)

[Stoner] argue that the opening of [their] well did not cause all the depletion of the [Noh's] water supply, but that the loss in [Noh's] wells was somewhat occasioned by leaks in [Noh's] wells.

A careful study, however, of the record discloses that the evidence is sufficient to sustain the findings that because [Stoner] operated at a level below [Noh's] pumps, not because of leaks in [Noh's] wells, the water level in the artesian basin was lowered to such an extent that [Noh's] pumps were dry.

In other words, [Stoner] had pushed their point of diversion lower than [Noh's] point of diversion, and as a result there was no water at Noh's] point of diversion.

[Stoner] urge: "The necessity of a prior appropriation changing the methods or means of diverting water from the source of supply, by installing and employing, reasonable and average, but more powerful pumps and increased pumping depth, will not deprive a subsequent appropriator of the right to divert and use unappropriated subterranean water, and the prior appropriator must take the usual and reasonable measures to perfect such means."

This statement of the controversy is not quite correct; it is not altogether a question of unappropriated subterranean waters, since [Stoner] rely on the doctrine to the effect that, with subterranean or artesian waters, first in time is first in right....

[Stoner] contend that [Noh's] appliances are not sufficient, and that the duty rests on them to put in adequate pumps, meaning thereby that they should put their pumps at a lower point and perhaps also increase their capacity, relying on *Natoma Water & Min. Co. v. Hancock*, which, however, rests upon *Barrows v. Fox* and approves the doctrine therein to this effect: An earlier appropriator is not required to bear the expense incident or necessary to secure a flow of water to a later appropriator.

[Stoner] cite 26 Cal. Jur. § 311, p. 112: "A court of equity may, under proper circumstances, compel a prior appropriator to change the manner of his use so as to prevent unnecessary injury to those having subordinate rights." The text, however, has this in addition: "Of course, any interference with the rights of prior appropriators is actionable. Whether a subsequent use causes such interference is a question of fact."

Herein the court has found on substantial though conflicting evidence that [Stoner's] use interferes with [Noh's].

Walnut Irr. Dist. v. Burke allows a change of point of diversion only where there is no injury to the prior appropriator.

No cases are cited which are contra to *Barrows v. Fox, supra*, and other subsequent authority sustains the doctrine of that case.

...

In regard to surface water, it is statutory that an appropriator, prior or subsequent, may not change his point of diversion to the injury of another appropriator. And this principle is applicable herein.

[Testimony is quoted by the court on the cost of $1623.00 for deepening the level of Noh's pump, the court states:]

It is thus apparent that it is a controversy between [Stoner] and [Noh] as to who will bear the expense of lowering respondents' pumps so they will receive the same amount of water as before, and any expense involved herein for such purpose must fall on [Stoner] and not on [Noh].

In the instant case, the body of water tapped by [Noh's] and [Stoner's] wells is depleted perpendicularly by appellants' wells.

If [Stoner] may now compel respondents to again sink the well to a point below Noh's], to again receive the amount of water heretofore used, it would result ultimately in a race for the bottom of the artesian belt....

...

If subsequent appropriators desire to engage in such a contest the financial burden must rest on them and with no injury to the prior appropriators or loss of their water. Otherwise, if the users go below appellants and respondents were to go below them appellants would in turn, according to their theory, be deprived of their water with no redress.

...

Judgment affirmed in accordance with the opinion herein. Costs to respondents.

Notes & Question

1. The court quotes: "Of course, any interference with the rights of prior appropriators is actionable." Recall the case of *Schodde v. Twin Falls Land & Water Co.*, 224 U.S. 107, 32 S. Ct. 470 (1912), from Chapter 6, holding that means of diversion is not protected as a property right under the Takings clause of the United States Constitution, at least if it is not reasonable. Well depth is an aspect of "means of diversion" for groundwater development. Is the court holding that Noh's means of diversion is protected as part of the property right in groundwater?
2. Which of the following are types of evidence an attorney for a water user in Noh's position would want to prepare?
    a. Evidence of the seniority of their water right.
    b. Depths of their well and the well they are asserting as causing the problem.
    c. Pump depths and capacity in their well and the well they are asserting as causing the problem.
    d. Pump test done by running the pump in their well, noting flow rate, then noting the change in flow rate in their well during pumping of the other well and with the other well shut off.

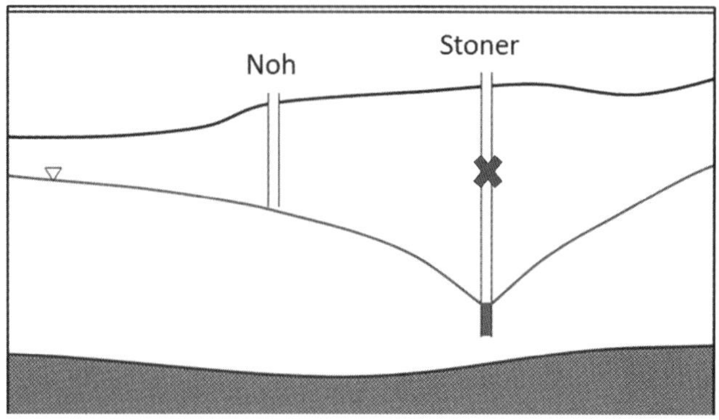

Figure 9.5 The result in *Noh v. Stoner*. Absolute protection for well depth of the senior water user may allow owners of senior shallow wells to hold the aquifer hostage—i.e., prevent new development for larger water uses.

3. States in the West took two primary approaches on the protection of well depth. The approach in *Noh*, which is considered absolute protection of senior water user well depth, is criticized by some as allowing small well owners to hold the aquifer hostage. Figure 9.5 showing the result in *Noh v. Stoner* demonstrates the result of absolute protection for well depth. The concern with this approach is that the senior shallow well owner may be able to hold the aquifer hostage from development by future enterprises.

   To address the concern with inability to develop an aquifer, some states gave no protection to well depth. This approach, however, could lead to a "race to the bottom" of the aquifer as each new appropriator drills a deeper well. Figure 9.6 illustrates the potential "race to the bottom" if no protection is given to well depth. Each party will need to keep deepening their well in a race against the other. Because the original owner receives no protection, when a new well is drilled that causes the original well to go dry, the original owner must deepen their well. If that then causes the newer well to go dry, that owner in turn must deepen their well. The race goes on until the water supply has been exhausted.

   Two potential solutions exist to this dilemma. First, consider that the court case merely sets up the balance of power in the subsequent negotiation. Thus, if you have new development of a large municipal, irrigation, or industrial well that will interfere with older shallow domestic wells, the rule chosen simply determines who pays to deepen the shallow well. Looked at in this way, it seems equitable that the large economic use should pay to deepen the domestic well. Unfortunately, it is not always such an easy David-versus-Goliath situation.

   Second, as you'll learn in Part V, states have adopted statutes that task their water management agencies with determining reasonable groundwater levels for aquifers throughout the state. In an effort to balance protection of the senior water right with ensuring the full economic development of the groundwater resource, these statutes

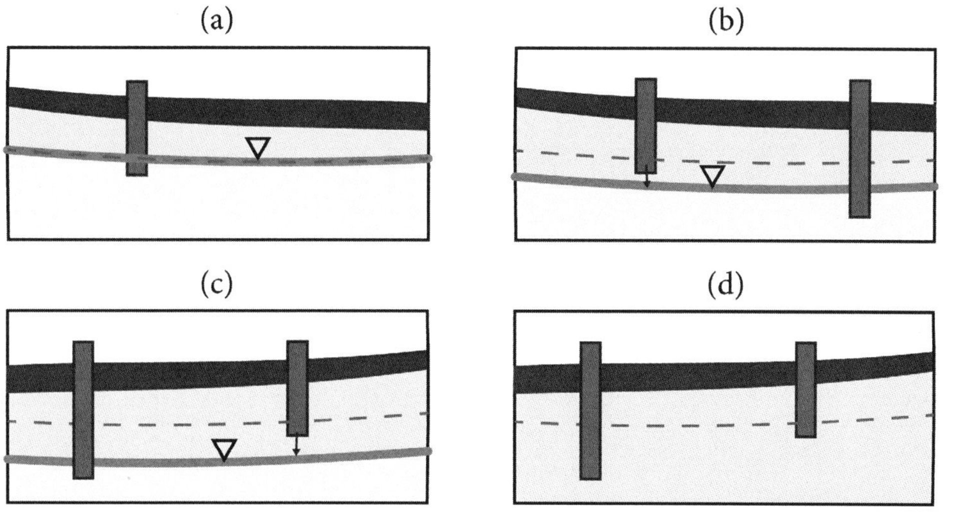

Figure 9.6 In states taking the opposite view to *Noh v. Stoner,* no regulation may lead to a race to the bottom: (a) the senior well is drilled just far enough to access the aquifer; (b) the junior well is drilled deeper than the senior and depletes the aquifer below the senior well; (c) the senior well is deepened and depletes the aquifer below the junior well; (d) the junior well is drilled deeper and depletes the aquifer for both.

require senior wells to be drilled at least to the depth determined to be "reasonable" by those agencies. If so, then their priority date is protected. If not, they are not entitled to seek priority administration until they deepen the well to the appropriate depth.

Part III

The Federal Common Law of Aboriginal and Reserved Water Rights: The Third Sovereign

Native American Tribes, the third sovereign alongside states and the federal government, relied on the use of water and the ecosystem services from the waters of what is now North America since time immemorial. Despite this critical reliance on water, treaties (as well as agreements memorialized as Congressional Acts or Executive Orders) between the United States and Tribes were, for the most part, silent on water. Pursuant to state law, substantial development of water by settlers had occurred before federal courts had occasion to address the water rights of Native American Tribes. Federal common law of reserved water rights did not begin to develop until the 1908 case of *Winters v. United States*,[1] covered in Chapter 10.

Regardless of who you ultimately represent, it will be essential to understand the different legal authority recognizing Native American water rights and appropriative water rights as well as their attributes if you are to play a positive role in solving the problems your clients face on the shared water courses of the West. Federal law determines the existence, nature, and scope of Native American water rights. Because federal law does not vary by state, the cases used in this Part originate all over the western United States.

You will learn about two types of Native American water rights in this Part—reserved and aboriginal rights. Both flow from the treaties, congressional acts, and executive orders establishing reservations and land cessions of Native American Tribes. The landmark case of *Winters* that you will read in Chapter 10, employs the principle you learned in Part I that these agreements with Tribes should be interpreted by federal

1. 207 U.S. 564 (1908).

courts as the relevant tribe would have understood them. *Winters* sets up the basis for both types of water rights:

> The Indians had command of the lands and the waters,—command of all their beneficial use, whether kept for hunting, 'and grazing roving herds of stock,' or turned to agriculture and the arts of civilization. Did they give up all this? Did they reduce the area of their occupation and give up the waters which made it valuable or adequate?[2]

First, the Court sets the stage for recognition of reserved water rights—those necessary to fulfill the purpose of the reservation as the tribe would have understood it (i.e., did they reduce the area of their occupation and give up the waters that made it valuable or adequate?"). In the case of *Winters*, the reduction in land base for the Gros Ventre and Assiniboine Tribes rendered subsistence on hunting impossible. Agriculture would be essential. On their reservation with only 14 inches of annual rain on average, irrigation would be the only means to make agriculture possible.[3] The reservation of waters in a treaty (or agreement by the executive with a Tribe later memorialized as an act of congress or executive order) occurs at the time of the agreement regardless of when the water is developed. Since land cessions from the Native Americans were a precursor to opening the western lands to settlement, Native American reserved water rights are generally the senior right on any shared water course. You will begin learning the details of these "reserved water rights," including their early priority date and the importance of their "purpose," in Chapter 10.

Second, while not at issue in *Winters*, the Court sets the stage for recognition of aboriginal water rights—those associated with Native practices that were not ceded by the language of the agreement (i.e., "The Indians had command of the lands and the water.... Did they give up all this?"). These rights may extend to domestic use, stock watering, agriculture in the southwestern United States, and to nonconsumptive water rights for traditional hunting, fishing, gathering, and other cultural and religious activities.[4] Note that courts have yet to resolve whether instream flow rights arise when associated with off-reservation fishing rights generally included in the treaties with Tribes in the Pacific Northwest, but the Ninth Circuit, which covers the Pacific Northwest, has recognized them within and adjacent to a reservation even when the reservation itself has been terminated. When recognized, these "aboriginal rights" date from "time immemorial." You will also learn about these rights in Chapter 10.

Chapter 11 will cover the quantification of reserved water rights. As an implied right, the water right is not quantified by the agreements with tribes and carries only the vague notion of federal common law that the quantity is the amount of water necessary for the purpose of the reservation or prior use. In Part VI, you will learn that the unquantified and undeveloped nature of Native American water rights made

---

2. Winters v. United States, 207 U.S. 564, 576 (1908).

3. Barbara Cosens, *A New Approach in Water Management or Business as Usual? The Milk River, Montana,* 18 J. Envt'l L. & Lit. 1 (2003).

4. *See, e.g.*, United States v. Adair, 723 F.2d 1394 (9th Cir. 1983).

them nearly impossible to protect against increasing non-Indian water development on shared water sources. At the same time, the senior status of these unquantified rights placed considerable uncertainty on the long-term efficacy of that non-Indian development. This led to considerable effort to define these water rights in the latter half of the twentieth century and continuing today. Part VI will cover the successful effort by the states to obtain jurisdiction to adjudicate Native American water rights and the variety of conflicting state interpretations on the nature of these water rights that resulted among states. You will also learn about the major push to move from litigation, which resulted in paper water rights, to settlement, which included means to develop tribal water while protecting existing state-based water uses. Settlement will also be covered in Part VI.

Chapter 12 will provide background on the important phase in the history of federal Indian law referred to as "allotment." During and following this phase, considerable land on certain reservations went into non-Indian ownership. Federal common law also addresses the water rights associated with both Indian-held allotments and non-Indian-owned land within the boundaries of an Indian Reservation. You will learn the term "Walton" rights for water associated with land acquired by a non-Indian from an Indian allottee.

The question of whether reserved water rights would extend to groundwater did not come before the federal courts until 2017. In *Agua Caliente Band of Cahuilla Indians v. Coachella Valley Water Dist.*, 849 F.3d 1262, 1269 (9th Cir. 2017), the Ninth Circuit Court of Appeals answered "yes" to this question and the U.S. Supreme Court denied certiorari in *Coachella Valley Water Dist. v. Agua Caliente Band of Cahuilla Indians*, 138 S. Ct. 468 (2017) and in *Desert Water Agency v. Agua Caliente Band of Cahuilla Indians*, 138 S. Ct. 469 (2017). You will read this important case in Chapter 13.

Chapter 10

The Federal Common Law Basis for Reserved and Aboriginal Water Rights

Introduction

Even though Indigenous people predate the European settlement of North America, Indigenous water rights were not recognized by the federal judiciary until the beginning of the twentieth century. By then, substantial development of surface water for private use had already taken place in the western United States, and the Reclamation Act of 1902 (covered in Part IV), which would lead to massive development of western rivers by the federal government, primarily for non-Indian water use, had already become federal law. Thus, the story of recognition and development of Native American water rights begins when scarcity was already a reality on western rivers.

The United States holds reservation land and resources in trust for the benefit of Native American tribes. Thus, as you learned in Part I, federal law controls the interpretation of the scope of Native American rights in land and water. As a result, development of the common law of Native American water rights took place in federal courts. In federal law there is no statutory overlay on the common law of reserved water rights, thus you will not find a Part devoted to federal statutory law to complement Part V on the state statutory overlay on the common law. Instead, you will learn in Part VI on adjudication that much of the effort to define, quantify, and settle the scope of Native American water rights has taken place in state court proceedings and settlement processes since the 1970s. Much of that effort has focused on the complex problem of how to protect and develop Native American water rights alongside state-based water rights on shared water sources. You will also learn in Part VI that the effort to resolve the scope of Native American water rights has led to the development of water codes by individual tribal governments.

This Chapter will introduce the common law development of reserved water rights by covering the foundation of the *Winters* Doctrine. It will then explore the range of reservation purposes (the basis for reserved water rights quantification) that have been recognized by federal courts. Finally, the Chapter will conclude by addressing water rights referred to as "aboriginal," because they reflect water use by Indigenous people prior to European contact that were never ceded to the United States.[1] To the extent possible, the structure of Part III parallels that of Part II to emphasize the focus on three separate sources of western water law based on the legal status of the three sovereigns.

Native American Reserved Water Rights

Native American reserved water rights flow from the treaties, executive orders, and acts of Congress that memorialize the agreements between tribes and the United States to cede land and establish reservations. In Part I we discussed the two sources of federal authority necessary to enter an agreement: (1) the authority to enter treaties with tribes stemming from the Treaty Clause; and (2) the authority (in relation to the states and citizens) over the land and resources in question via the Property Clause. You will find that the authority to reserve certain rights is not questioned in the following cases. Instead, the focus is on whether a right may be implied if not stated expressly in the agreement but is nevertheless necessary to fulfill the purpose of the agreement.

To focus on the source of the concept of implied rights you will first read the precedent followed in *Winters v. United States* (and authored by the same Justice), *United States v. Winans,* 198 U.S. 371 (1905). *Winans* teaches you two important points for understanding the common law of reserved water rights.

First, the United States Supreme Court's use of "canons of construction" for Native American Treaties (as well as agreements later memorialized as congressional acts or executive orders). The Court in *Winans* and later in *Winters* uses the canon requiring that the agreement be interpreted as the tribe(s) would have understood it. The principle itself stems from a principle of international law that when a treaty is negotiated and memorialized in the language of one sovereign, interpretations of ambiguous language will go against that sovereign. Underlying the principle is the assumption that the sovereign whose language dominates the agreement was likely to have the greater bargaining power. To understand the importance of this canon, consider that agreements with Native American Tribes were negotiated using translators who often understood only trade language and at times translations went through several translators before reaching the particular dialect of a tribe.[2] In a more recent case interpreting the scope of these same off-reservation fishing rights, the court states:

> The treaties were written in English, a language unknown to most of the tribal representatives, and translated for the Indians by an interpreter in the service of the United States using Chinook Jargon, which was also unknown to some tribal representatives. Having only about three hundred words in its vocabu-

1. Note that "aboriginal" water rights may also be referred to as "reserved" rights because they are rights the tribes reserved, rather than ceded, in agreements with the United States. This text uses the term "aboriginal" to distinguish these rights and the very different legal basis and analysis that accompanies their quantification.

2. *See, e.g.,* ALVIN N. JOSEPHY JR., THE NEZ PERCE INDIANS AND THE OPENING OF THE NORTHWEST 318 (1965).

Figure 10.1 Fish Wheel along the Columbia River, 1880s. Along with canneries to process the fish, by 1885 the fish wheels helped to harvest up to 45 million pounds of fish annually. Source: Oregon History Project, Columbia River Fish Wheel, URL: oregonhistoryproject.org/articles/historical-records/columbia-river-fish-wheel/.

> lary, the Jargon was capable of conveying only rudimentary concepts, but not the sophisticated or implied meaning of treaty provisions about which highly learned jurists and scholars differ.[3]

Second, in application of this canon, the Court concludes that the promise of a continued right to fish at customary off-reservation locations must carry with it an implied right to access the locations. The Court emphasizes the importance of a right to access fishing grounds implied by the right to fish, stating that access was "not much less necessary to the existence of the Indians than the atmosphere they breathed."[4] This concept of an implied right necessary to fulfill the rights written down in the treaty, whether or not associated with reserved land, is to become the key element in *Winters*.

United States v. Winans arose when Lineus and Audubon Winans refused Indian access across their land to a long-used fishing site on the Columbia River. The Winans brothers were also monopolizing the fishery in that location by using a fish wheel (Figure 10.1), a common method of obtaining large quantities of fish for canneries in the late 1800s. The brothers had a license from the State of Washington to operate this fish wheel. The United States claimed an implied right of access to fishing grounds recognized in the treaties of certain Columbia River Tribes and sought to enjoin the Winans brothers from blocking access to the fishing site. Caution—you may find the actual language used to express the understanding of the Tribe in *Winans* offensive.

3. United States v. Washington, 384 F. Supp. 312, 330 (W.D. Wash. 1974) (also known as "the Boldt Decision" after the judge who authored it).

4. 198 U.S. at 381.

United States v. Winans

Supreme Court of the United States
198 U.S. 371 (1905)

Mr. Justice McKenna delivered the opinion of the court: … The treaty is as follows:

'Article 1. The aforesaid confederated tribes and bands of Indians hereby cede, relinquish, and convey to the United States all their right, title, and interest in and to the lands and country occupied and claimed by them.…

'Article 2. There is, however, reserved from the lands above ceded, for the use and occupation of the aforesaid confederated tribes and bands of Indians, the tract of land included within the following boundaries: …

…

> 'The exclusive right of taking fish in all the streams where running through or bordering said reservation is further secured to said confederated tribes and bands of Indians, as also the right of *taking fish at all usual and accustomed places, in common with citizens of the territory*, [emphasis added]....

… 12 Stat. at L. 951.

[Winans] claim under patents of the United States the lands bordering on the Columbia river, and under grants from the state of Washington to the shore land which, it is alleged, fronts on the patented land. They also introduced in evidence licenses from the state to maintain devices for taking fish, called fish wheels.

At the time the treaty was made the fishing places were part of the Indian country,....

The pivot of the controversy is the construction of the second paragraph. [Winans] contend that the words 'the right of taking fish at all usual and accustomed places in common with the citizens of the territory' confer only such rights as a white man would have under the conditions of ownership of the lands bordering on the river, and under the laws of the state, and, such being the rights conferred, the respondents further contend that they have the power to exclude the Indians from the river by reason of such ownership....

… [I]t was decided that the Indians acquired no rights but what any inhabitant of the territory or state would have. Indeed, acquired no rights but such as they would have without the treaty. This is certainly an impotent outcome to negotiations and a convention which seemed to promise more, and give the word of the nation for more. And we have said we will construe a treaty with the Indians as 'that unlettered people' understood it, and 'as justice and reason demand, in all cases where power is exerted by the strong over those to whom they owe care and protection,' and counterpoise the inequality 'by the superior justice which looks only to the substance of the right, without regard to technical rules.' How the treaty in question was understood may be gathered from the circumstances.

The right to resort to the fishing places in controversy was a part of larger rights possessed by the Indians, upon the exercise of which there was not a shadow of impediment, and which were not much less necessary to the existence of the Indians than the atmosphere they breathed. New conditions came into existence, to which those rights had to be accommodated. Only a limitation of them, however, was necessary and intended, not a taking away. In other words, the treaty was not a grant of rights to the Indians, but a grant of right from them, a reservation of those not granted. And the form of the instrument and its language was adapted to that purpose. Reservations were not of particular parcels of land, and could not be expressed in deeds, as dealings between private individuals. The reservations were in large areas of territory, and the negotiations were with the tribe. They reserved rights, however, to every individual Indian, as though named therein. They imposed a servitude upon every piece of land as though described therein. There was an exclusive right of fishing reserved within certain boundaries. There was a right outside of those boundaries reserved 'in common with citizens of the territory.' As a mere right, it was not exclusive in the Indians. Citizens might share it, but the Indians were secured in its enjoyment by a special provision of means for its exercise.... The contingency of the future ownership of the lands, therefore, was foreseen and provided for; in other words, the Indians were given a right in the land, the right of crossing it to the river,—the right to occupy it to the extent and for the purpose mentioned. No other conclusion would give effect to the treaty. And the right was intended to be continuing against the United States and its grantees as well as against the state and its grantees.

The [Winans] urge an argument based upon the different capacities of white men and Indians to devise and make use of instrumentalities to enjoy the common right. Counsel say: 'The fishing right was in common, and aside from the right of the state to license fish wheels, the wheel fishing is one of the civilized man's methods, as legitimate as the substitution of the modern combined harvester for the ancient sickle and flail.' But the result does not follow that the Indians may be absolutely excluded. It needs no argument to show that the superiority of a combined harvester over the ancient sickle neither increased nor decreased rights to the use of land held in common. In the actual taking of fish white men may not be confined to a spear or crude net, but it does not follow that they may construct and use a device which gives them exclusive possession of the fishing places, as it is admitted a fish wheel does. Besides, the fish wheel is not relied on alone. Its monopoly is made complete by a license from the state....

The construction of the treaty disposes of certain subsidiary contentions of [Winans]. The Land Department could grant no exemptions from its provisions. It makes no difference, therefore, that the patents issued by the Department are absolute in form. They are subject to the treaty as to the other laws of the land.

It is further contended that the rights conferred upon the Indians are subordinate to the powers acquired by the state upon its admission into the Union. In other words, it is contended that the state acquired by its admission into the Union 'upon an equal footing with the original states,' the power to grant rights in or to dispose of the shore lands upon navigable streams, and such power is subject only to the paramount authority of Congress with regard to public navigation and commerce. The United States, therefore, it is contended, could neither grant nor retain rights in the shore or to the lands under water.

The elements of this contention and the answer to it are expressed in *Shively v. Bowlby*, 152 U.S. 1. It is unnecessary, and it would be difficult, to add anything to the reasoning of that case. The power and rights of the states in and over shore lands were carefully defined, but the power of the United States, while it held the country as a territory, to create rights which would be binding on the states, was also announced, opposing the dicta scattered through the cases, which seemed to assert a contrary view. It was said by the court, through Mr. Justice Gray:

> 'Notwithstanding the dicta contained in some of the opinions of this court, already quoted, to the effect that Congress has no power to grant any land below high-water mark of navigable waters in a territory of the United States, it is evident that this is not strictly true.
>
> 'By the Constitution, as is now well settled, the United States having rightfully acquired the territories, and being the only government which can impose laws upon them, have the entire dominion and sovereignty, national and municipal, Federal and state, over all the territories, so long as they remain in a territorial condition....

Many cases were cited. And it was further said:

> 'We cannot doubt, therefore, that Congress has the power to make grants of lands below high-water mark of navigable waters in any territory of the United States, whenever it becomes necessary to do so in order to perform international obligations, or to effect the improvement of such lands for the promotion and convenience of commerce with foreign nations and among the several states, or to carry out other public purposes appropriate to the objects for which the United States hold the territory.'

The extinguishment of the Indian title, opening the land for settlement, and preparing the way for future states, were appropriate to the objects for which the United States held the territory. And surely it was within the competency of the nation to secure to the Indians such a remnant of the great rights they possessed as 'taking fish at all usual and accustomed places.' Nor does it restrain the state unreasonably, if at all, in the regulation of the right. It only fixes in the land such easements as enable the right to be exercised.

The license from the state, which respondents plead, to maintain a fishing wheel, gives no power to them to exclude the Indians, nor was it intended to give such power. It was the permission of the state to use a particular device. What rights the Indians had were not determined or limited....

Decree reversed, and the case remanded for further proceedings in accordance with this opinion.

Mr. Justice White dissents.

Notes & Questions

1. In reference to the canon requiring the Court to interpret the Treaty as the Tribe would have understood it, the Court states: "How the treaty in question was understood may be gathered from the circumstances." Which of the following types of evidence and expertise might the attorneys for the Tribe develop if this case were brought today?
   a. Transcripts or other writings (diaries, etc.) of the treaty negotiations;
   b. Oral history from tribal elders on the importance of salmon to the Native diet and spiritual practices;
   c. Anthropologic testimony on the location of usual and accustomed fishing sites for this tribe and in relation to the location of the fish wheel;
   d. Testimony on the closest translation of the language "the right of taking fish at all usual and accustomed places, in common with citizens of the territory," into the language of the Tribe and what meaning that would have for the Tribe.
2. The right to access the usual and accustomed places recognized in *Winans* is an implied right. What does that mean and what must the Court find to recognize an implied right?
3. The Court states "the treaty was not a grant of rights to the Indians, but a grant of right from them, a reservation of those not granted." What does the Court mean by this language?
4. For a comprehensive history of the northwest tribes' heroic effort to vindicate their fishing rights, see Dupris, Hill & Rogers, *The Si'lailo Way: Indians, Salmon and Law on the Columbia River* (2006).

Winans was followed by *Winters v. United States*, 207 U.S. 564 (1908), the landmark U.S. Supreme Court ruling recognizing an implied right to water if necessary to fulfill the purpose of the treaty, executive order, or act of congress memorializing the agreement. Before reading the case, consider the setting and the arguments made in federal district court on behalf of the Gros Ventre and Assiniboine Tribes of the Fort Belknap Reservation. In keeping with a theme found throughout this textbook, notice that climate, hydrology, and social history matter just as they did in the development of the prior appropriation doctrine.

Co-author Cosens writes:[5]

> Thousands of years ago, ice pushed the Missouri River south into its present channel in Montana, leaving an empty river bed and a vast plain of glacial debris. A small stream that swells to a river in spring with runoff from the

---

5. Barbara Cosens, Chapter 1: *The Legacy of* Winters v. United States *and the* Winters *Doctrine, One Hundred Years Later, in* THE FUTURE OF FEDERAL AND INDIAN RESERVED WATER RIGHTS: THE WINTERS CENTENNIAL 2012 B. (B. Cosens and J. Royster eds., 2012) (*citing* JOHN SHURTS, INDIAN RESERVED WATER RIGHTS: THE WINTERS DOCTRINE IN ITS SOCIAL AND LEGAL CONTEXT 1880S–1930S, 35–36 (2000)).

Rocky Mountain front, began to carve its own path in the wake of the ancestral Missouri. Because of its load of suspended glacial silt, Meriwether Lewis called this stream the "Milk River." With its headwaters in the Rocky Mountain front in what is now Glacier National Park and the Blackfeet Indian Reservation, the river has high spring runoff. Flows in the Milk River prior to development of the Milk River Reclamation Project are estimated to have ranged from as high as 35,000 cubic feet per second (cfs) during spring runoff to as low as 5 cfs during late summer and early fall of a dry year. The Fort Belknap Reservation is located primarily in the valley of the Milk River, and was established for members of the Gros Ventre and Assiniboine Tribes. The river forms the reservation's northern boundary.

The Gros Ventre and Assiniboine Tribes have strikingly different histories. The Gros Ventre are thought to have separated from the Arapaho and became known as a division of the Blackfeet Nation in the mid-1700's. Gros Ventre were reported along the Milk River throughout the 1800's, and were party to the Blackfeet Treaty of 1855. The Assiniboine separated from the Sioux in the mid-1600's and were reported along the Upper Missouri River in the late 1700's and early 1800's. The Assiniboine were party to the 1851 Treaty of Fort Laramie designating their territory in the vicinity of the Missouri and Musсleshell Rivers. The Assiniboine Tribe was heavily reliant on the buffalo for sustenance and trade. Prior to the 1880's, the Milk River valley had abundant large game, including buffalo. Smallpox epidemics in 1780 and 1838 took their toll on the Assiniboine.

By the 1870's, the Gros Ventre and certain Assiniboine were known to inhabit an area along the Milk River near the Fort Belknap Agency. As the buffalo disappeared from the plains, the tribes were moved onto smaller and smaller reservations with the promise of agriculture by the federal government. Prior to May 1, 1888, the entire Milk River Basin within the United States lay within the larger reservation of the Blackfeet, Gros Ventre, and other tribes and groups of Indians, and the Fort Assiniboine Military Reservation (a smaller area wholly within the larger Indian Reservation). On May 1, 1888, the United States fragmented the larger reservation into three smaller reservations: the Blackfeet Reservation, Fort Belknap Reservation, and Fort Peck Reservation, with Fort Assiniboine remaining as a separate military reservation in the vicinity of what is now the Rocky Boy's Reservation.

The Acts of 1888 creating the Blackfeet, Fort Belknap, and Fort Peck Indian Reservations opened the remaining area in the Milk River Valley to settlement. Settlement began in earnest when the Great Northern Railroad was completed in 1890 along the north bank of the Milk River. Federal policy toward the western public lands at the turn of the twentieth century encouraged the development of small, family-owned, farms. The non-Indian irrigation development along the Milk River occurred with the encouragement of

> federal law. At the same time, federal Indian policy favored establishment of smaller reservations and conversion of Indian people to farmers. Unfortunately, insufficient water existed in the Milk River for implementation of both policies, and the basin became one of the sites of the earliest water disputes between appropriative and reserved water rights.
>
> In 1895, farmers began diverting water from the Milk River upstream from the Fort Belknap Reservation. Three years later, on July 5, 1898, the agency at Fort Belknap began diverting approximately 5000 miner's inches (approximately 125 cfs) of water from the Milk River for irrigation of reservation land. Although downstream irrigators both on and off the reservation saw diminished flows as more people settled in the upper Milk River valley, the development of farming proceeded until, as is inevitable in the Milk River Basin, severe drought struck in 1904–1905. As a result, water no longer reached the tribal diversion facilities. The United States filed suit in the United States Circuit Court for the District of Montana to enjoin diversion of water upstream from the Fort Belknap Reservation to the extent necessary to prevent interference with the flow of water to the reservation.
>
> ...
>
> U.S. Attorney Carl Rasch, who filed the *Winters* case on behalf of the United States and the Fort Belknap Reservation, argued several theories of the case as would any good attorney: (1) a factual argument based on prior appropriation which he knew he would lose if the court accepted the evidence of earlier diversion by irrigators upstream of the reservation; (2) a legal argument seeking recognition of riparian rights for a reservation with its northern border formed by the mid-line of the Milk River; and, as his primary argument, (3) a simple extension of precedent in the interpretation of treaty language reserving certain rights from the overall cession of territory by the tribes. Although many list the third theory as an afterthought which the Court adopted out of the blue, historian John Shurts points out that it was Attorney Rasch's primary argument and the one that most closely followed U.S. Supreme Court precedent.

This history of the filing of the case illustrates the way in which a good attorney in a case of first impression will begin with all possible arguments, even while holding to one that appears to most closely follow precedent. It is important to note as you read the case that the remedy sought in *Winters* was an injunction against upstream diversion to the extent it interfered with diversions on the Fort Belknap Reservation. The remedy sought was not a quantification of the water rights of the Fort Belknap Reservation, and the opinion does not discuss how these water rights should be quantified. One other note of history—the name of the first listed plaintiff was actually Henry Winter. This error is in the original case and follows through to the name of the *Winters* Doctrine.

Winters v. United States

Supreme Court of the United States
207 U.S. 564 (1908)

Opinion

Statement by Mr. Justice McKenna:—This suit was brought by the United States to restrain appellants and others from constructing or maintaining dams or reservoirs on the Milk river in the state of Montana, or in any manner preventing the water of the river or its tributaries from flowing to the Fort Belknap Indian Reservation.

...

The allegations of the bill, so far as necessary to state them, are as follows: On the 1st day of May 1888, a tract of land, the property of the United States, was reserved and set apart 'as an Indian reservation as and for a permanent home and abiding place of the Gros Ventre and Assiniboine bands or tribes of Indians in the state (then territory) of Montana, designated and known as the Fort Belknap Indian Reservation.' The tract has ever since been used as an Indian reservation and as the home and abiding place of the Indians....

Milk river, designated as the northern boundary of the reservation, is a nonnavigable stream.... It is alleged with detail that all of the waters of the river are necessary for all those purposes and the purposes for which the reservation was created, and that in furthering and advancing the civilization and improvement of the Indians, and to encourage habits of industry and thrift among them, it is essential and necessary that all of the waters of the river flow down the channel uninterruptedly and undiminished in quantity and undeteriorated in quality.

...

That all of said lands are situated within the watershed of the river, are riparian upon the river and its tributaries, but are arid and must be irrigated by artificial means to make them inhabitable and capable of growing crops.

[The defendants [Winter et al.] argued that] prior to the 5th day of July, 1898, and before any appropriation, diversion, or use of the waters of the river or its tributaries was made by the United States or the Indians on the Fort Belknap Reservation, [Winter et al.] entered upon the public lands in the vicinity of the river, made entry thereof at the United States land office, and thereafter settled upon, improved, reclaimed, and cultivated the same and performed all things required to acquire a title under the homestead and desert land laws, made due proof thereof, and received patents conveying to them, respectively, the lands in fee simple.

That all of said lands are situated within the watershed of the river, are riparian upon the river and its tributaries, but are arid and must be irrigated by artificial means to make them inhabitable and capable of growing crops.

That for the purpose of reclaiming the lands, and acting under the laws of the United States and the laws of Montana, the defendants ... commenced the construction of ditches and other instrumentalities, and completed them with diligence, and diverted, appropriated, and applied to a beneficial use more than 5,000 miners' inches of the waters of the river and its tributaries, of 120 cubic feet per second, irrigating their lands and producing hay, grain, and other crops thereon. The defendants and the stockholders of the defendant corporations have expended many thousands of dollars in constructing dams, ditches, and reservoirs, and in improving said lands, building fences and other structures, establishing schools, and constructing highways and other improvements usually had and enjoyed in a civilized community, and that the only supply of water to irrigate the lands is from Milk river. If defendants are deprived of the waters their lands cannot be successfully cultivated, and they will become useless and homes cannot be maintained thereon.

...

It is alleged that there are a large number of springs on the reservation and several streams from which water can be obtained for stock and irrigation purposes, and particularly these: People creek, flowing about 1,000 inches of water; *** That all of the waters of these streams can be made available for use upon the reservation, and that it was not the intention of the government to reserve any of the waters of Milk river or its tributaries. That the respective claims of the defendants to the waters of the river and its tributaries are prior and paramount to the claims of the United States and the Indians, except as to 250 inches used in and around the agency buildings, and at all times there has been sufficient water flowing down the river to more than supply these 250 inches

And it is again alleged that the waters of the river are indispensable to defendants, are of the value of more than $100,000 to them, and that if they are deprived of the waters 'their lands will be ruined, it will be necessary to abandon their homes, and they will be greatly and irreparably damaged, the extent and amount of which damage cannot now be estimated, but will greatly exceed $100,000,' and that they will be wholly without remedy if the claim of the United States and the Indians be sustained.

Mr. Justice McKenna delivered the opinion of the court:

...

The case, as we view it, turns on the agreement of May, 1888, resulting in the creation of Fort Belknap Reservation. In the construction of this agreement there are certain elements to be considered that are prominent and significant. The reservation was a part of a very much larger tract which the Indians had the right to occupy and use, and which was adequate for the habits and wants of a nomadic and uncivilized people. It was the policy of the government, it was the desire of the Indians, to change those habits and to become a pastoral and civilized people. If they should become such, the original tract was too extensive; but a smaller tract would be inadequate without a change of conditions. The lands were arid, and, without irrigation, were practically valueless. And yet, it is contended, the means of irrigation were deliberately given up by the Indians and deliberately accepted by the government. The lands ceded were, it is true, also arid; and some argument may be urged, and is urged, that with their cession there was the cession of the waters, without which they would be valueless, and 'civilized communities could not be established thereon.' And this, it is further contended, the Indians knew, and yet made no reservation of the waters. We realize that there is a conflict of implications, but that which makes for the retention of the waters is of greater force than that which makes for their cession. The Indians had command of the lands and the waters,—command of all their beneficial use, whether kept for hunting, 'and grazing roving herds of stock,' or turned to agriculture and the arts of civilization. Did they give up all this? Did they reduce the area of their occupation and give up the waters which made it valuable or adequate? And, even regarding the allegation of the answer as true, that there are springs and streams on the reservation flowing about 2,900 inches of water, the inquiries are pertinent. If it were possible to believe affirmative answers, we might also believe that the Indians were awed by the power of the government or deceived by its negotiators. Neither view is possible. The government is asserting the rights of the Indians. But extremes need not be taken into account. By a rule of interpretation of agreements and treaties with the Indians, ambiguities occurring will be resolved from the standpoint of the Indians. And the rule should certainly be applied to determine between two inferences, one of which would support the purpose of the agreement and the other impair or defeat it. On account of their relations to the government, it cannot be supposed that the Indians were alert to exclude by formal words every inference which might militate against or defeat the declared purpose of themselves and the government, even if it could be supposed that they had the intelligence to foresee the 'double sense' which might some time be urged against them.

Another contention of appellants is that if it be conceded that there was a reservation of the waters of Milk river by the agreement of 1888, yet the reservation was repealed by the admission of Montana into the Union, February 22, 1889, 'upon an equal footing with the original states.'

The language of counsel is that 'any reservation in the agreement with the Indians, expressed or implied, whereby the waters of Milk river were not to be subject of appropriation by the citizens and inhabitants of said state, was repealed by the act of admission.' But to establish the repeal counsel rely substantially upon the same argument that they advance against the intention of the agreement to reserve the waters. The power of the government to reserve the waters and exempt them from appropriation under the state laws is not denied, and could not be. *United States v. Rio Grande Dam & Irrig. Co.* 174 U.S. 702; *United States v. Winans*, 198 U.S. 371. That the government did reserve them we have decided, and for a use which would be necessarily continued through years. This was done May 1, 1888, and it would be extreme to believe that within a year Congress destroyed the reservation and took from the Indians the consideration of their grant, leaving them a barren waste,—took from them the means of continuing their old habits, yet did not leave them the power to change to new ones.

Appellants' argument upon the incidental repeal of the agreement by the admission of Montana into the Union, and the power over the waters of Milk river which the state thereby acquired to dispose of them under its laws, is elaborate and able, but our construction of the agreement and its effect make it unnecessary to answer the argument in detail. For the same reason we have not discussed the doctrine of riparian rights urged by the government.

Decree affirmed.

Notes & Questions

1. To what source of law does the Supreme Court look to determine whether the Tribes' water rights exist? Is this state or federal law?
2. According to the Court, what "conflict of implications" exists in this case? What two inferences could be drawn from the 1888 agreement's silence regarding water rights? How does the Court resolve that conflict? From this, can you develop a general rule for how courts must interpret treaties, congressionally ratified agreements, and executive orders related to tribes?
3. What was the purpose for the creation of the Fort Belknap Reservation? How did this drive the outcome of the case?
4. What priority date did the Court find for the Fort Belknap Reservation? What is it based on?
5. The Supreme Court spends little time on the question of the power of the federal government to reserve water, stating: "The power of the government to reserve the waters and exempt them from appropriation under the state laws is not denied, and could not be. *United States v. Rio Grande Dam & Irrig. Co.* 174 U.S. 702; *United States v. Winans*, 198 U.S. 371." This will be important in Part IV when you read about reserved water rights for federal non-Indian reservations.
6. Students of law should also consider what happened next in every case they read. A court ruling, even one by the highest court in the land, is not where the effort ends, at least not when an essential common pool resource is concerned. As in *Winters*, the court opinion articulates the rights and may alter the balance of power, but the underlying problem—in this case that of insufficient water supply—remains. Despite the arguments in court that loss of water to the settlers' upstream diversions would destroy their livelihoods, the newspaper articles along the Hi-line (the area along Montana's portion of the Milk River) told another story. Historian John Shurts explored the relation between the *Winters* case and the concurrent efforts to develop the Milk River Project, one of the first projects authorized under the 1902 Reclamation Act.[6] As you will learn in Part IV, the Reclamation Service (now the Bureau of Reclamation) required determination of existing relative rights to water prior to developing a project. The Fort Belknap Reservation represented one more cloud on

6. John Shurts, Indian Reserved Water Rights: The Winters Doctrine in its Social and Legal Context 1880s–1930s, Chapter 82 (2000).

water rights to the Milk River. While likely not representative of all views of the outcome of the *Winters* case, one editorial in the Milk River Valley News stated in reference to the Supreme Court opinion:

> *The decision was received in this city with much joy as we all know that this will have a tendency to hasten construction on diversion dams, latterals and storage reservoirs to hold and divert the unlimited flood waters of which there is enough going to waste every year to irrigate every foot of ground between here and Mondak.*[7] [Emphasis added in Shurts.]

Determining Purpose

The Court's decision in *Winters v. United States* made clear that the United States has the power to reserve new water rights necessary to satisfy tribal and federal purposes and objectives, and that it may have done so even if a water right was not expressly mentioned as long as water is necessary for the purpose of the reservation. The next case provides the analytical framework for identifying the purposes of the reservation and includes a new type of purpose: the continuation of traditional practices. These rights, often referred to as "aboriginal rights," are covered in more detail in the final section in this Chapter. The case of *Colville Confederated Tribes v. Walton*[8] addresses continuation of preexisting water uses to support a traditional fishery as a purpose of the Reservation. In this case it was no longer possible to access the traditional fishing grounds due to the development of dams. The court upholds the use of water rights for a replacement fishery at Omak Lake. While this is an interesting aspect of the case, it is more important that you pay attention to the evidence and reasoning the court uses to identify the purposes of the reservation.[9]

---

7. *Id.* (citing the January 9, 1908, edition of Harlem, Montana's *Milk River Valley News.*) Shurts also noted that Mondak was a town on the Montana/North Dakota border that no longer exists. *Id.* at n. 26.

8. 647 F.2d 42 (1981).

9. Note that the *Walton* case is primarily known for its treatment of the water rights of non-Indian allotment owners (referred to as Walton rights after the person claiming them in the case). You will learn about allotment and read that portion of the case in Chapter 12 of this Part. The case also refers to quantification of sufficient water to "permit irrigation of all practicably irrigable acreage on the reservation." This is a method of quantifying water for an agricultural purpose that the U.S. Supreme Court endorsed in *Arizona v. California*, 373 U.S. 546 (1963). You will learn about that later in this Chapter. For this case, focus on the range of purposes that could be associated with an Indian reservation.

Colville Confederated Tribes v. Walton

United States Court of Appeals, Ninth Circuit
647 F.2d 42 (1981)

Opinion

WRIGHT, Circuit Judge:— …

The Colville Confederated Tribes initiated this case a decade ago. They sought to enjoin Walton, non-Indian owner of allotted lands, from using surface and ground waters in the No Name Creek basin....

I. BACKGROUND

…

… President Grant created the Colville Reservation. Executive Order of July 2, 1872. Twenty years later, the northern half of the reservation was taken from the Indians and opened for entry and settlement.

In 1906, Congress ratified an agreement with the Colvilles that provided for distribution of reservation lands to the Indians pursuant to the General Allotment Act of 1887, 24 Stat. 388, and for disposition of the remainder by entry and settlement. The agreement was effectuated by Presidential proclamation in 1916.

In 1917, a row of seven allotments was created in the No Name Creek watershed. Walton, a non-Indian, now owns the middle three, numbers 525, 2371 and 894. He bought them in 1948 from an Indian, not a member of the Tribe, who had begun to irrigate the land by diverting water for 32 acres from No Name Creek. Walton immediately procured a permit from the state to irrigate 65 acres by diverting up to 1 cubic foot per second "subject to existing rights." He now irrigates 104 acres and uses additional water for domestic and stock water purposes.

The United States holds the remaining allotments in trust for the Colville Indians....

B.

The No Name Creek is a spring-fed creek flowing south into Omak Lake, which has no outlet and is saline. The No Name hydrological system, consisting of an underground aquifer and the creek, is located entirely on the Colville Reservation.

…

C.

Salmon and trout were traditional foods for the Colville Indians, but the salmon runs have been destroyed by dams on the Columbia River. In 1968, the Tribe, with the help of the Department of the Interior, introduced Lahonton cutthroat trout into Omak Lake. The species thrives in the lake's saline water, but needs fresh water to spawn. The Indians cultivated No Name Creek's lower reach to establish spawning grounds but irrigation use depleted the water flow during spawning season. The federal government has given the Indians fingerlings to maintain the stock of trout.

II. THE CASE BELOW

The trial court found that 1,000 acre feet per year of water were available in No Name Creek Basin in an average year. It calculated the quantity of the Colvilles' reserved water rights on the basis of irrigable acreage....

...

The court also held that the Indians were potentially entitled to use water to propagate trout, but refused to award water for that purpose. It concluded that spawning was unnecessary because fingerlings were provided free by the federal government.

...

III. THE TRIBE'S WATER RIGHTS

The Colvilles argue they have a right to use the waters of the No Name system under the implied-reservation, or Winters doctrine. We first consider the existence and the extent of that right.

A.

[The Court provides background on the *Winters* Doctrine.]

Congress intended to deal fairly with the Indians by reserving waters without which their lands would be useless. *Arizona v. California*, 373 U.S. at 600. We hold that water was reserved when the Colville Reservation was created.

B.

The more difficult question concerns the amount of water reserved. In determining the extent of an implied reservation of water for a national forest, the Supreme Court held:

> Where water is necessary to fulfill the very purposes for which a federal reservation was created, it is reasonable to conclude, even in the face of Congress' express deference to state water law in other areas, that the United States intended to reserve the necessary water....

United States v. New Mexico, 438 U.S. at 702.

... The specific purposes of an Indian reservation, however, were often unarticulated. The general purpose, to provide a home for the Indians, is a broad one and must be liberally construed. We are mindful that the reservation was created for the Indians, not for the benefit of the government.

To identify the purposes for which the Colville Reservation was created, we consider the document and circumstances surrounding its creation, and the history of the Indians for whom it was created. We also consider their need to maintain themselves under changed circumstances. See *United States v. Winans*, 198 U.S. 371, 381 (1905).

These factors demonstrate that one purpose for creating this reservation was to provide a homeland for the Indians to maintain their agrarian society. In a similar setting, the Supreme Court agreed with a Master's finding that water was reserved to meet future as well as present needs, and concluded "that the only feasible and fair way by which reserved water for the reservation can be measured is irrigable acreage." *Arizona v. California*, 373 U.S. at 600–01. We conclude that, when the Colville reservation was created, sufficient appurtenant water was reserved to permit irrigation of all practicably irrigable acreage on the reservation.

Providing for a land-based agrarian society, however, was not the only purpose for creating the reservation. The Colvilles traditionally fished for both salmon and trout. Like other Pacific Northwest Indians, fishing was of economic and religious importance to them. See *Washington v. Washington State Commercial Passenger Fishing Vessel Association*, 443 U.S. 658, 665 (1978); *United States v. Winans*, supra; (1871) Report of the Commissioner of Indian Affairs 277.

The Tribe's principal historic fishing grounds on the Columbia River have been destroyed by dams. The Indians have established replacement fishing grounds in Omak Lake by planting a non-indigenous trout.

We agree with the district court that preservation of the tribe's access to fishing grounds was one purpose for the creation of the Colville Reservation. Under the circumstances, we find an implied reservation of water from No Name Creek for the development and maintenance of replacement fishing grounds.

We note that the nature of a right to water for a replacement fishery is such that it cannot coexist with continuing rights to water for a fishery in the watershed where the fishery historically existed. Walton does not argue that the tribe has such rights. We affirm the district court's holding that the Colvilles have a reserved right to the quantity of water necessary to maintain the Omak Lake Fishery.

C.

The district court held that water for spawning could not be awarded at this time because the federal government provides the necessary fingerlings. We reverse this holding.

The right to water to establish and maintain the Omak Lake Fishery includes the right to sufficient water to permit natural spawning of the trout. When the Tribe has a vested property right in reserved water, it may use it in any lawful manner. As a result, subsequent acts making the historically intended use of the water unnecessary do not divest the Tribe of the right to the water.

…

I. CONCLUSION

On remand, the district court will calculate the respective rights of the parties. To the extent Walton's use of water exceeds his rights and interferes with the rights of the tribe, it will be enjoined.

REVERSED IN PART, AFFIRMED IN PART, AND REMANDED for proceedings in conformance with this opinion.…

Notes & Questions

1. Where does the court look to determine the purposes of the creation of the reservation? How do the canons of construction play into the court's analysis?
2. What does the court find the overarching purpose of reservation establishment to be? How do water rights to support the Tribes' fishery fit into that purpose?
3. Note the following language quoted from a case you will read in Part IV concerning federal reserved water rights for a National Forest:

    > Where water is necessary to fulfill the very purposes for which a federal reservation was created, it is reasonable to conclude, even in the face of Congress' express deference to state water law in other areas, that the United States intended to reserve the necessary water.

    United States v. New Mexico, 438 U.S. at 702, 98 S. Ct. at 3015.

    This language referring to the "intent" of Congress has led many down a rabbit hole of trying to discern that intent, including Idaho's state courts. But read that language in context—if "water is necessary to fulfill the very purposes for which a federal reservation was created, it is reasonable to conclude [even in the face of evidence to the contrary—or in *Winters* "a conflict of implications"] that the United States intended to reserve the necessary water." Necessity, not actual intent of Congress, is the focus of an inquiry into an implied reservation of water. As you learn from the Court's language in *Winters*, intent will be implied because to do otherwise when the purpose would be defeated implies deceit and would render the agreement establishing the reservation void: "If it were possible to believe affirmative answers, we might also believe that the Indians were awed by the power of the government or deceived by its negotiators. Neither view is possible."[10]

Reservation of Aboriginal Water Rights to Support Traditional Tribal Activities

"Aboriginal rights" refers to the suite of rights traditionally held by Native American tribes that were never ceded in any agreement with the federal government or taken by any act of the federal government. These rights address existing practices that were not ceded by the treaty, executive order, or act of Congress. The continuation of these practices was often confirmed through an express agreement with the tribe; but, similar to reserved water rights, the water right can also be implied due to the need for water if the practice is to continue. Because these rights were not included in language of cession, they are considered reserved by the tribe and protected by the agreement with the federal government. In contrast to reserved water rights that arise at the time

10. *Winters*, 207 U.S. at 576.

Figure 10.2 Salmon fishing on the Columbia River. Photo from early 1900s by Edward C. Curtis [public domain].

of reservation establishment, aboriginal rights are based on prior existing use, thus the priority date is "time immemorial."

The suite of aboriginal rights includes both consumptive and nonconsumptive water rights necessary to support traditional activities. As such, the scope and purpose of the right is based on the tribes' historical use. Examples of aboriginal rights include, but are not limited to, water for domestic use and spiritual practices, instream flows associated with the hunting and fishing practices, such as those of the tribes of the Pacific Northwest (Figure 10.2), and irrigation use associated with the farming, such as that practiced by the Pueblo Indians of the southwestern United States. *Colville* introduced you to these rights in the context of a replacement fishery. Now you will learn about the protection and continuation of the preexisting right.

While *Colville* addressed a replacement fishery, the case in the Ninth Circuit that followed in 1983, *United States v. Adair*, addresses historic fishing grounds. Note that, similar to *Colville*, the case discusses reservation purposes and treaty language just as it does for reserved water rights. This is important and indicates that one of the purposes of the reservation was to retain and protect these prior existing rights. This casebook and many scholarly writings, nevertheless, apply the term "aboriginal rights" to these rights. It is adopted here because it allows a clear distinction between water rights reserved for new uses at the time of the treaty, congressional act, or executive order, and rights retained by tribes and based on historic use. Pay attention to the differences between these rights and reserved rights arising at the time of creation of the reservation as you read the case. *United States v. Adair* takes place in the Klamath River basin, which is shared by numerous tribes and has its headwaters in southern Oregon and its terminus on the coast of California.

United States v. Adair

United States Court of Appeals, Ninth Circuit
723 F.2d 1394 (1983)

Opinion

FLETCHER, Circuit Judge: ...

I. BACKGROUND

A. History of the Litigation Area.

This suit concerns water rights in a portion of the Williamson River watershed. The Williamson River is part of the larger Klamath River watershed of Southern Oregon and Northern California. That part of the Williamson River watershed involved in this litigation drains an area of low, forested mountains, flat, grassy valleys and marshes east of the Cascade Range in south-central Oregon. The average rainfall in the area is low; summers are dry and winters are severe.

The major feature of the subject area is a large flat valley historically known as the Klamath Marsh. As the Williamson flows into the north end of this valley, it spreads out and soaks into the porous, pumice soil. During the wet months of the year, open water and aquatic vegetation cover the lower portion of the valley, the water to a depth of a few feet. The remainder of the valley is grassland. During dry summer months, as the water recedes, the grassland in the valley increases. This fluctuating marsh has been an important feeding and resting area for migratory ducks, geese and other waterfowl for thousands of years. In addition, the Marsh has always supported a variety of other indigenous wildlife. More recently, large parts of the Klamath Marsh have been used for grazing cattle.

The Klamath Indians have hunted, fished, and foraged in the area of the Klamath Marsh and upper Williamson River for over a thousand years. In 1864 the Klamath Tribe entered into a treaty with the United States whereby it relinquished its aboriginal claim to some 12 million acres of land in return for a reservation of approximately 800,000 acres in south-central Oregon. This reservation included all of the Klamath Marsh as well as large forested tracts of the Williamson River watershed. Treaty between the United States of America and the Klamath and Moadoc Tribes and Yahooskin Band of Snake Indians, Oct. 14, 1864, 16 Stat. 707. Article I of the treaty gave the Klamath the exclusive right to hunt, fish, and gather on their reservation. *Id.* Article II provided funds to help the Klamath adopt an agricultural way of life. 16 Stat. 708.

For 20 years, until 1887, the Klamath lived on their reservation under the terms of the 1864 treaty. In 1887 Congress passed the General Allotment Act, which fundamentally changed the nature of land ownership on the Klamath Reservation. Prior to the Act, the tribe held the reservation land in communal ownership. Pursuant to the terms of the Allotment Act, however, parcels of tribal land were granted to individual Indians in fee. Under the allotment system, approximately 25% of the original Klamath

Reservation passed from tribal to individual Indian ownership. Over time, many of these individual allotments passed into non-Indian ownership.

The next major change in the pattern of land ownership on the Klamath Reservation occurred in 1954 when Congress approved the Klamath Termination Act. Under this Act, tribe members could give up their interest in tribal property for cash. A large majority of the tribe chose to do this. In order to meet the cash obligation, in 1961, the United States purchased much of the former Klamath Reservation. The balance of the reservation was placed in a private trust for the remaining tribe members. In 1973, to complete implementation of the Klamath Termination Act, the United States condemned most of the tribal land held in trust. Payments from the condemnation proceeding and sale of the remaining trust land went to Indians still enrolled in the tribe. This final distribution of assets essentially extinguished the original Klamath Reservation as a source of tribal property.

Even though the Klamath Tribe no longer holds any of its former reservation, the United States still holds title to much of the former reservation lands. In 1958 the Government purchased approximately 15,000 acres of the Klamath Marsh, the heart of the former reservation, to establish a migratory bird refuge under the jurisdiction of the United States Fish and Wildlife Service. In 1961 and again in 1973, the Government purchased large forested portions of the former Klamath Reservation. This forest land became part of the Winema National Forest under the jurisdiction of the United States Forest Service. By these two purchases, the Government became the owner of approximately 70% of the former reservation lands. The balance of the reservation is in private, Indian and non-Indian, ownership either through allotment or sale of reservation lands at the time of termination.

B. Proceedings in the District Court

...

Pursuant to the terms of the Pretrial Order, the district court determined the priority of water rights among the litigants as follows: (1) the Klamath Tribe Indians have a water right, with a priority date of time immemorial, "to as much water on the Reservation lands as they need to protect their hunting and fishing rights," *United States v. Adair,* 478 F.Supp. 336, 345 (D.Or.1979); ...

III. WATER RIGHTS

...

A. A Reservation of Water to Accompany the Tribe's Treaty Right to Hunt, Fish, and Gather.

Article I of the 1864 treaty with the Klamath Tribe reserved to the Tribe the exclusive right to hunt, fish, and gather on its reservation. 16 Stat. 707, 708; *Kimball I,* 493 F.2d at 566. This right survived the Klamath Termination Act, 25 U.S.C. §§ 564–564w (1976). The issue presented for decision in this case is whether, as the district court held, these hunting and fishing rights carry with them an implied reservation of water rights.

...

1. Reservation of Water in the 1864 Treaty.

...

The question, therefore, is whether securing to the Indians the right to hunt, fish, and gather was a primary purpose of the Klamath Reservation. Resolution of this question, in turn, depends on an analysis of the intent of the parties to the 1864 Klamath Treaty as reflected in its text and the surrounding circumstances. *See Washington v. Fishing Vessel Ass'n,* 443 U.S. 658, 675–76 (1979); *United States v. Winters,* 207 U.S. at 575–76. The State and individual appellants argue that the intent of the 1864 Treaty was to convert the Indians to an agricultural way of life. The Government and the Tribe argue that an equally important purpose of the treaty was to guarantee continuity of the Indians' hunting and gathering lifestyle. Under the guidelines established in *Cappaert* and *New Mexico,* we find that both objectives qualify as primary purposes of the 1864 Treaty and accompanying reservation of land.

Article I of the Klamath Treaty expressly provides that the Tribe will have exclusive on-reservation fishing and gathering rights. 16 Stat. 708. This language has been interpreted to include, in addition, a grant of exclusive hunting and trapping rights. *Kimball I,* 493 F.2d at 566. As this court noted in *Kimball I,*

> The specific treaty provision reserving the Klamaths' exclusive right to fish could prompt the argument that their treaty excludes the right to hunt. However, in light of the highly significant role that hunting and trapping played (and continue to play) in the lives of the Klamaths, it seems unlikely that they would have knowingly relinquished these rights at the time they entered into the treaty.

In view of the historical importance of hunting and fishing, and the language of Article I of the 1864 Treaty, we find that one of the "very purposes" of establishing the Klamath Reservation was to secure to the Tribe a continuation of its traditional hunting and fishing lifestyle. This was at the forefront of the Tribe's concerns in negotiating the treaty and was recognized as important by the United States as well.

...

2. Effect of the Klamath Termination Act on the Tribe's Hunting and Fishing Water Rights

In 1954, Congress terminated federal supervision of the Klamath Tribe. 25 U.S.C. §§ 564–564w (1976). The state and individual appellants now argue that the Termination Act also abrogated any water rights reserved by the 1864 Treaty to accompany the Tribe's right to hunt and fish. Appellants' argument, however, overlooks the substantive language of the Termination Act, ... the canons of construction for legislation affecting Indian Tribes, and the implications of our decision in *Kimball I*. ... of the Termination

Act provides, "[n]othing in sections 564–564w of this title shall abrogate any water rights of the tribe and its members." … Because Congress in section 564m of the Termination Act explicitly protected tribal water rights and nowhere in the Act explicitly denied them, we can only conclude that such rights survived termination.…

…

3. Priority of the Water Right Reserved to Accompany the Tribe's Treaty Right to Hunt and Fish

The district court found that the Tribe's water right accompanying its right to hunt and fish carried a priority date for appropriation of time immemorial. *United States v. Adair,* 478 F.Supp. at 350. The State and individual appellants argue that an implied reservation of water cannot have a priority date earlier than establishment of the reservation.… We have been unable to find any decisions that squarely address this issue. We therefore begin our analysis by turning to well-established principles of Indian treaty interpretation and Indian property rights for guidance.

Foremost among these is the principle that "the treaty is not a grant of rights to the Indians, but a grant of rights from them—a reservation of those not granted." *United States v. Winans,* 198 U.S. 371 (1905).… Further, Indian treaties should be construed as the tribes would have understood them. *Choctaw Nation v. Oklahoma,* 397 U.S. 620, 631 (1970).… And any ambiguity in a treaty must be resolved in favor of the Indians. *Oliphant v. Suquamish Indian Tribe,* 435 U.S. 191, 208 n. 17 (1978).… A corollary of these principles, also recognized by the Supreme Court, is that when a tribe and the Government negotiate a treaty, the tribe retains all rights not expressly ceded to the Government in the treaty so long as the rights retained are consistent with the tribe's sovereign dependent status.…

In 1864, at the time the Klamath entered into a treaty with the United States, the Tribe had lived in Central Oregon and Northern California for more than a thousand years. This ancestral homeland encompassed some 12 million acres. Within its domain, the Tribe used the waters that flowed over its land for domestic purposes and to support its hunting, fishing, and gathering lifestyle. This uninterrupted use and occupation of land and water created in the Tribe aboriginal or "Indian title" to all of its vast holdings.… Aboriginal title is "considered as sacred as the fee simple of the whites." … The Supreme Court has specifically held that the Tribe had aboriginal title to timber on the Klamath Reservation *United States v. Klamath and Modoc Tribes,* 304 U.S. 119 (1938). The Tribe's title also included aboriginal hunting and fishing rights … and by the same reasoning, an aboriginal right to the water used by the Tribe as it flowed through its homeland.…

With this background in mind, we examine the priority date attaching to the Klamath Tribe's reservation of water to support its hunting and fishing rights. In Article I of the 1864 Treaty the Tribe expressly ceded "all [its] right, title and claim" to most of its ancestral domain. 16 Stat. 707. In the same article, however, the Tribe reserved for its exclusive use and occupancy the lands that became the Klamath Reservation, the same lands that are the subject of the instant suit. 16 Stat. 708. There is no indication in the treaty, express or implied, that the Tribe intended to cede any of its interest in those lands it reserved for itself.... Nor is it possible that the Tribe would have understood such a reservation of land to include a relinquishment of its right to use the water as it had always used it on the land it had reserved as a permanent home.... Further, we find no language in the treaty to indicate that the United States intended or understood the agreement to diminish the Tribe's rights in that part of its aboriginal holding reserved for its permanent occupancy and use. Accordingly, we agree with the district court that within the 1864 Treaty is a recognition of the Tribe's aboriginal water rights and a confirmation to the Tribe of a continued water right to support its hunting and fishing lifestyle on the Klamath Reservation.

Such water rights necessarily carry a priority date of time immemorial. The rights were not created by the 1864 Treaty, rather, the treaty confirmed the continued existence of these rights....

IV. CONCLUSION

...

As modified, the district court's opinion is AFFIRMED.

Notes & Questions

1. What are the primary differences between reserved and aboriginal rights?
2. Which of the following types of evidence might tribal attorneys present to prove aboriginal rights?
    a. Treaty/congressional act/or executive order language showing the tribe's intent to retain a historic right, and evidence that the right requires water.
    b. Oral history on the historic use of the claimed water right by the tribe.
    c. Anthropologic evidence showing historic use of the claimed water right by the tribe
    d. Absence of any cession of the right in agreement language and any subsequent acts of Congress or executive orders addressing the rights of the tribe.
3. What is the priority date of an aboriginal right?
4. Note that the court states: "Under the guidelines established in *Cappaert* and *New Mexico,* we find that both objectives qualify as primary purposes of the 1864 Treaty and accompanying reservation of land." These are the two cases that will be introduced in Part VI and are associated with federal, non-Indian reservations. It is the opinion of the authors that the courts that apply these cases to Native American water rights are inconsistent with U.S. Supreme Court precedent and its canons of construction for agreements with Native American tribes. This will be explained in Part VI.

Chapter 11

The Federal Common Law Attributes of Reserved Water Rights: Quantity, Future Use

Introduction

In this Chapter you will learn about the struggle to quantify implied reserved water rights. Although it would be 55 years following *Winters* before the U.S. Supreme Court addressed quantification of reserved water rights, federal common law continued to develop in the lower federal courts. The focus of early cases was on water for the purpose of irrigated agriculture. The United States filed suit in several situations in which upstream irrigation prevented diversion of water for irrigation projects on an Indian reservation. Since an implied reserved water right is identified by the language of the document establishing the reservation and not by use, these cases begin to grapple with the problem of quantification. You will see that lower courts began by simply leaving the decree open for claims as new uses arose. With the development of large-scale irrigation projects, including those authorized by the Reclamation Act (introduced in Part IV), pressure was on courts to issue a final decree allocating all the water of a system. It wasn't until the U.S. Supreme Court was called upon to allocate the water of a major river basin among states that the issue of allocation to the third sovereign was presented to the highest Court.

In 1963, the U.S. Supreme Court addressed, for the first (and only) time, the issue of quantification for agricultural purposes in a dispute between Arizona and California over apportionment of the Colorado River. The United States intervened to claim reserved water rights. Because agriculture is one of the largest uses, it was considered sufficient to quantify water rights for consumptive use for that purpose on most reservations with the understanding that it could then be changed to another use as former agricultural land was converted to uses like manufacturing. Methods for quantification of water for other large uses, such as instream flow for fish habitat, were developed later in the context of settlement, rather than as federal common law, and will be covered in Part VI. This Chapter will begin with the early lower federal court cases adjudicating all the water rights of a surface water system followed by the U.S. Supreme Court case of *Arizona v. California*. This Chapter will conclude with the consequences of the lower

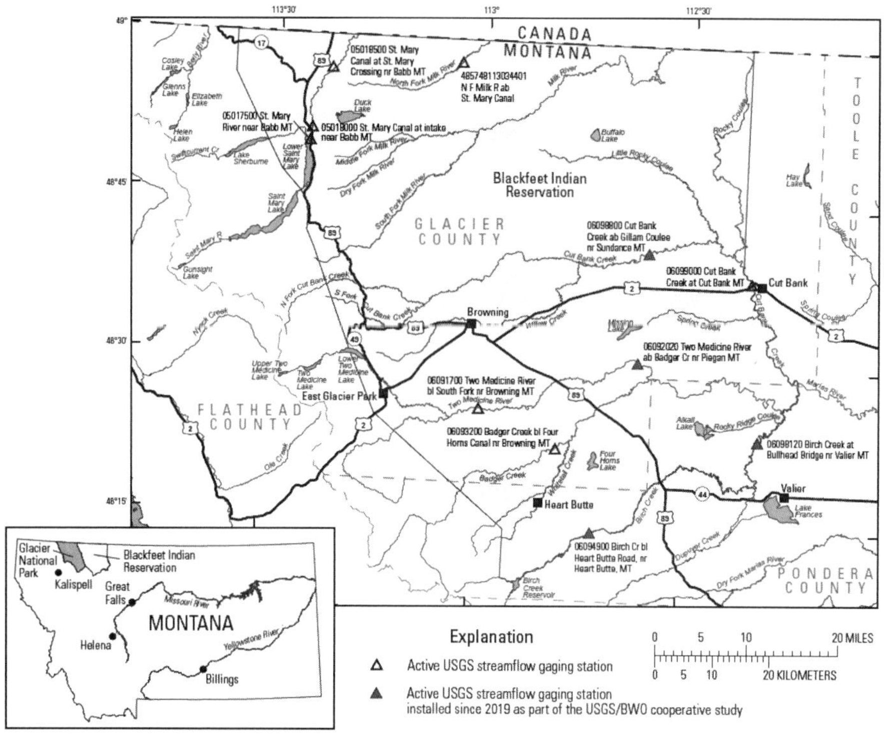

Figure 11.1 Blackfeet Reservation abuts Glacier National Park on the west, Canada on the north, and Birch Creek forms its southern boundary. The Reservation is across the continental divide, so the streams and rivers flow east into the Missouri River Basin, with the exception of the St. Mary River, which flows north into the drainage of the Saskatchewan River. Source: USGS, *Hydrologic Assessment of the Blackfeet Reservation* (Feb. 13, 2020), https://www.usgs.gov/centers/wyoming-montana-water-science-center/science/hydrologic-assessment-blackfeet-reservation.

court decrees in the early Reclamation era with the case of *Nevada v. United States*, 463 U.S. 110 (1983).

Future Use as Part of the Original Reserved Water Right

Conrad Inv. Co. v. United States, 161 F. 829 (9th Cir. 1908), was the first to follow *Winters* and had the issue before it of how to protect future use. Although filed before *Winters*, *Conrad* was issued by the Ninth Circuit just five months after the U.S. Supreme Court ruling in *Winters*.[1] The case involved similar facts. The United States filed suit against settlers with patents to land from the federal government who were diverting water from a stream shared with the Blackfeet Reservation (Figure 11.1).

1. For a good discussion of this history, see JOHN SHURTS, INDIAN RESERVED WATER RIGHTS: THE WINTERS DOCTRINE IN ITS SOCIAL AND LEGAL CONTEXT 1880s–1930s 76 (2000). Shurts notes that the *Conrad* case was filed prior to *Winters* but may not have been pursued as quickly because it addressed a potential rather than an existing threat to water supply for a reservation.

Of interest is the fact that the court, while issuing a decree that required the settlers to allow sufficient water for the current needs of the Reservation to flow down the creek, left the decree open to amendment. Thus, this immediate application of *Winters* as precedent in *Conrad Inv. Co. v. United States*, 161 F. 829 (9th Cir. 1908), clarifies that reserved water rights are those necessary to fulfill the purpose of the reservation, whether developed on its establishment, or later.

Conrad Inv. Co. v. United States

United States Court of Appeals, Ninth Circuit
161 F. 829 (1908)

Opinion

MORROW, Circuit Judge—This is an appeal from a decree entered in the United States Circuit Court for the District of Montana enjoining [Conrad Investment Co., defendant/appellant] from obstructing the flow of a stream of water to the extent of interfering with the rights of the Indians on the Blackfeet Indian reservation. The controversy relates to the right to the flow of water in Birch creek, an unnavigable stream whose middle line forms the southern and southeastern boundary of a tract of land in the county of Teton, in the state and district of Montana, reserved by the United States government for the permanent home and abiding place of certain tribes of Indians, under the name of the Blackfeet Indian reservation.

It is alleged by the complainant, and admitted by defendant, that large portions of the lands embraced within said reservation are well adapted for stock raising, and other large portions are susceptible of cultivation; that large herds of cattle and large numbers of horses, the property of the government and of the Indians, have been and are now 'pasturing and grazing upon said reservation and upon the lands within said reservation, being and situate along and bordering upon said Birch creek; that in order to make the lands productive beyond the growth of natural grass irrigation is necessary; that the defendant, a Montana corporation, in the year 1900 constructed a dam in the channel of said Birch creek for the purpose of diverting certain waters of said creek into a canal constructed by defendant ... the dam is capable of turning all the waters of Birch creek, beyond a small amount of seepage, into defendant's canal; and that the creek below defendant's dam was practically dry at certain points during at least a portion of each of the summers of 1904 and 1905, which seems to have been a condition before unknown.

In *Winters v. United States* the controversy involved the right of the United States and of the Indians residing upon the Belknap Indian reservation to the use of 5,000 inches of the waters of Milk river for useful and beneficial purposes.... A decree was entered in the Circuit Court for the District of Montana in favor of the [United States], and [*Winters* et al.] appealed. This court affirmed the decree, holding that the United States, by treaties with the Indians on the reservation, had impliedly reserved the waters of Milk river for the benefit of the Indians on the reservation to the extent reasonably necessary to enable them to irrigate their lands, and that grantees and settlers on public lands outside of the reservation could not acquire, under the desert land laws of the United States or the laws of the state of Montana relating to the appropriation of the waters of the streams of that state, the right to divert the waters of Milk river to the prejudice of the rights of the Indians residing upon that reservation. This decision has been affirmed by the Supreme Court of the United States in *Winters v. United States*.... In the course of the decision, the court said:

> 'The power of the government to reserve the waters and exempt them from appropriation under the state laws is not denied and could not be. United States v. Rio Grande Ditch & Irrigation Co., 174 U.S. 690, 702; United States v. Winans, 198 U.S. 371. That the government did reserve them we have decided, and for a use which would be necessarily continued through years.'

The present case is in many respects similar to the *Winters* Case. The act of Congress of May 1, 1888, which ratified an agreement with certain Indians and established the Ft. Belknap Indian reservation, with the middle of the main channel of Milk river for its northern boundary, established also the Blackfeet Indian reservation, with the middle of the channel of Birch creek for its southern and southeastern boundary, and in this case the diversion of the waters of Birch creek by means of a dam is the subject of controversy, as the diversion of the waters of Milk river by means of a dam was the subject of controversy in the *Winters* Case. The law of that case is applicable to the present case, and determines the paramount right of the Indians of the Blackfeet Indian reservation to the use of the waters of Birch creek to the extent reasonably necessary for the purposes of irrigation and stock raising, and domestic and other useful purposes. The government has undertaken, by agreement with the Indians on these reservations, to promote their improvement, comfort, and welfare, by aiding them to become self-supporting as a peaceable and agricultural people.

...

The ... Blackfeet Indian reservation covers a territory in the county of Teton, in the northwestern part of the state of Montana, about 40 miles east and west by 60 miles north and south, and containing about 900,000 acres. Portions of this land are suitable for grazing purposes, while other portions are adapted for agricultural purposes. The land is arid, and, where cultivated, requires water for irrigation....

Between Birch creek and Blacktail creek, and still north of Blacktail creek, there is a tract of land containing about 20,000 acres, 50 per cent. of which, or 10,000 acres, can be irrigated from Birch creek. In 1898 the government constructed a canal, about 5 1/2 miles long, from Birch creek onto the lands in the reservation adjoining the creek....

[Conrad Investment Co.], in its answer, admits the construction of a dam across the channel of Birch creek, as alleged in the complaint.... The evidence on the part of the complainant was in substance to the effect that the water of Birch creek allowed to escape over this dam was not sufficient to be depended upon for any kind of a practical use of the government ditch; that much of the time during the summers of 1904 and 1905 there was practically no water running in Birch creek at the head of the government ditch; that even the springs which had theretofore assisted in feeding the stream had diminished or disappeared, showing that they were fed by underflow of the stream from above and that their source had been cut off; . . .

Conceding that the defendant's enterprise is all that it claims, it is still subject to the rights of the Indians on the reservation in the diversion of the waters of Birch creek, and the question remains to be determined: What, under all the circumstances, is the government entitled to reserve for their uses? The court below in its decree does not direct the removal of defendant's dam from the channel of Birch creek, but has enjoined the defendant from in any manner or by any means impeding, preventing, or obstructing the waters of said creek to the amount and extent of 1,666 2/3 inches, or the equivalent of 33 1/3 second feet, from flowing down the natural channel of said creek and the points of diversion and places of use established by the complainant for the benefit of the Indians on the reservation. This decree does not at any time reserve all the waters of Birch creek for the [United States], but leaves a considerable flow of water to be retained by defendant's dam and used in its system of irrigation; and, after a careful examination of the evidence, we are of opinion that the decree of the Circuit Court is entirely reasonable and just, and should be affirmed in this respect.

. . .

It is further objected that the decree of the Circuit Court provides that, whenever the needs and requirements of the [United States] for the use of the waters of Birch creek for irrigating and other useful purposes upon the reservation exceed the amount of water reserved by the decree for that purpose, the complainant may apply to the court for a modification of the decree.

This is entirely in accord with complainant's rights as adjudged by the decree. Having determined that the Indians on the reservation have a paramount right to the waters of Birch creek, it follows that the permission given to the defendant to have the excess over the amount of water specified in the decree should be subject to modification, should the conditions on the reservation at any time require such modification.

. . .

The decree of the Circuit Court is affirmed.

Notes & Questions

1. Recall that the doctrine of prior appropriation does not allow water users (except for municipalities) to hold water for future use. According to the Ninth Circuit, may reserved water rights for Indian Reservations be held for future use?
2. Note that Carl Rasch, the U.S. Attorney who took the *Winters* case all the way to the U.S. Supreme Court in the name of the United States as trustee for the Tribes, is also the attorney who filed *Conrad*. How do you think the ruling in *Winters* shaped the ruling in *Conrad*?

Quantification: Incorporation in Federal District Court Decrees

Following *Conrad*, the United States continued to intervene, citing *Winters,* when upstream water use affected water diversion on a Reservation. This occurred on behalf of the Walker River Indian Reservation, located in Nevada and established in 1859. The headwaters of the Walker River are in California and the suit sought to adjudicate the water rights of private irrigators on both sides of the California-Nevada border. Thus, the basis for federal district court jurisdiction was diversity. The United States intervened because upstream water development in both California and Nevada was interfering with water use downstream on the Walker River Indian Reservation. The district court found that *Winters* had no application and awarded the United States water rights based on actual appropriation with a priority ranging from 1868 to 1886 based on actual diversion. The Ninth Circuit Court of Appeals reversed the finding that *Winters* did not apply and awarded a priority date of initial establishment of the reservation of 1859. The Reservation was determined to have approximately 10,000 acres of irrigable land, but the special master in the district court had determined that only 2100 acres were under irrigation at the time of the litigation, requiring a diversion of 26.25 cfs, and that the population on the Reservation was not increasing. The Government did not challenge this on appeal. The Ninth Circuit ordered entry of a decree:

> adjudging the United States to be entitled to the continuous flow of 26.25 cubic feet of water per second, to be diverted from Walker River upon or above Walker River Indian Reservation during the irrigation season of one hundred and eighty days for the irrigation of two thousand one hundred acres of land on the reservation, and the flow of water reasonably necessary for domestic and stock watering purposes and for power purposes to the extent now used by the Government, during the non-irrigating season, with a priority of November 29, 1859, and enjoining the defendants from preventing or interfering with the natural flow of the described quantities of water in the channels of the stream and its tributaries to and upon the reservation.[2]

The *Walker River* court said nothing about water for future use except for its reference to the lack of population growth on the Reservation. How that would be handled when a decree is issued with no statement that it is open to modification, as the court held in *Conrad*, is the subject of the case of *Nevada v. United States,*[3] at the end of the Chapter and briefly introduced in the next paragraph.

Following passage of the Reclamation Act in 1902 (which you will learn about in Part IV), development of federal water projects required a determination of water availability, including the extent of existing water appropriation. In cases where the

---

2. United States v. Walker River Irrigation District, 104 F.2d 334, 340 (9th Cir. 1939).
3. 463 U.S. 110 (1983).

water source crossed state lines and included Indian reservations along its path, as was the case on the Truckee and Carson Rivers flowing from California to Nevada (and located just north of the Walker River), adjudication occurred in federal district court. In the adjudication the United States claimed irrigation rights on behalf of the Pyramid Lake Paiute Indian Reservation, citing *Winters*. The Orr Ditch decree resulting from this litigation was issued in 1944 and included a settlement providing for irrigation of 5875 acres on the Reservation despite substantially more arable land. We will return to the problem of final decrees at the end of this Chapter in the 1983 case of *Nevada v. United States*, 463 U.S. 110. The case represents the attempt to reopen the Orr Ditch decree to provide for new and future uses on the Reservation. First, we cover the U.S. Supreme Court case on quantification, because you will only understand the magnitude of the impact of *Nevada v. United States* on the Pyramid Lake Paiute after reading *Arizona v. California*.

Quantification: The Practicably Irrigable Acreage Method

It was 55 years after the ruling in *Winters* before the Supreme Court addressed the quantification aspect of the *Winters* Doctrine in *Arizona v. California*. In the meantime, the United States, with the passage of the 1902 Reclamation Act (covered in Part IV), had begun developing the water resources of the western United States at an unprecedented rate. As a 1973 Report by the National Water Commission lays bare, that development:

> was pursued with little or no regard for Indian water rights and the Winters doctrine. With the encouragement, or at least the cooperation, of the Secretary of the Interior—the very office entrusted with protection of all Indian rights—many large irrigation projects were constructed on streams that flowed through or bordered Indian Reservations. With few exceptions the projects were planned and built by the Federal Government without any attempt to define, let alone protect, prior rights that Indian might have had in the water used for the projects.... In the history of the United States Government's treatment of Indian tribes, its failure to protect Indian water rights for use on the Reservations it set aside for them is one of the sorrier chapters.[4]

There is probably no better example of massive federal development for non-Indian water uses than the Colorado River—the site of the only U.S. Supreme Court opinion on quantification of Native American reserved water rights—*Arizona v. California*, 373 U.S. 546 (1963).[5]

---

4. NATIONAL WATER COMM'N, WATER POLICIES FOR THE FUTURE 474–475 (Jun. 14, 1973).

5. For excellent coverage of this case, see Lawrence MacDonnell, Arizona v. California*: Its Meaning and Significance for the Colorado River and Beyond after Fifty Years*, 4 ARIZ. J. ENVT'L L. & POL'Y 88 (2013).

Arizona v. California is an interstate water adjudication under the constitutional power of the U.S. Supreme Court provided by Article III Section 2, allowing it to extend the original jurisdiction of the Court "to Controversies between two or more States." The complex process of interstate allocation, including the details of *Arizona v. California* on that topic, will be covered in Part IV. For purposes of this Chapter, it is important to understand that the decision of the Court would allocate the entire flow of the Colorado River in its lower portion in the United States among state sovereigns. Located in the section of the river forming the border between Arizona and California are five Indian Reservations, two National Wildlife Refuges, and one National Monument (Figure 11.2). As a result, the United States intervened, asserting the rights for these Indian and federal reserved lands.

In addition to its interstate aspects, *Arizona v. California* is known for two important additions to the *Winters* Doctrine. First, after the long hiatus in Supreme Court development of the federal common law of reserved water rights, the Court reaffirmed the federal power to reserve land for a specific purpose. The Court confirmed that in doing so, it could reserve water rights by implication if necessary for that purpose(s). It then extended that to non-Indian federal reservations. You will see in Part IV that the Court wastes very little time in confirming the power of Congress to do so. Second, it endorsed a method of quantification for Native American reserved water rights when a purpose of the reservation was to develop agriculture in an area requiring irrigation. The case would need to address the entire allocation of water to the five Indian reservations. Thus, the Court must, for the first time, develop a method for quantifying not only current use, but future use for the reservations. This method is the aspect of the section that follows.

It is important to know first that in exercising its original jurisdiction, the Court will assign the case to a Special Master who will hear the case and forward to the Court the "Report of the Special Master" based on Findings of Fact and Conclusions of Law. The Court will then hear objections to the Report but will grant the Report a presumption of validity on the Findings of Fact. *Arizona v. California* is thus the Opinion of the Court following the hearing of objections to the Report of the Special Master. You will first read the Opinion of the Court relevant to quantification of Native American reserved water rights, then additional details from the Report of Special Master Simon Rifkind.

Arizona v. California

Supreme Court of the United States
373 U.S. 546, 83 S. Ct. 1468 (1963)

Mr. Justice Black delivered the opinion of the Court.—In 1952 the State of Arizona invoked the original jurisdiction of this Court by filing a complaint against the State of California and seven of its public agencies. Later, Nevada, New Mexico, Utah, and the United States were added as parties either voluntarily or on motion. The basic controversy in the case is over how much water each State has a legal right to use out of the waters of the Colorado River and its tributaries. [The case was referred to the

(a)

(b)

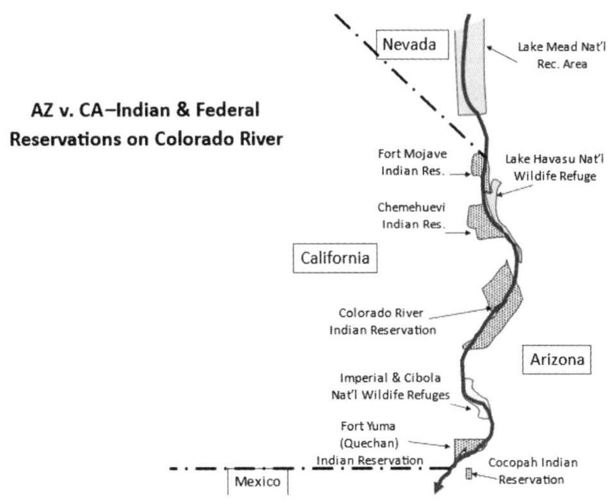

Figure 11.2 The Colorado River Basin in the United States showing (a) the upper and lower basin and the areas outside the basin that receive Colorado River water, and (b) the section of river forming the border between California and Arizona with the five Indian Reservations and additional federal reservations. U.S. Bureau of Reclamation, Colorado River Basin Water Supply and Demand Study 2 (2012), https://www.usbr.gov/watersmart/bsp/docs/finalreport/ColoradoRiver/CRBS_Executive_Summary_FINAL.pdf.

Special Master and now comes before the Court on objections to the Report of the Special Master.] ...

V. CLAIMS OF THE UNITED STATES.

In these proceedings, the United States has asserted claims to waters in the main river and in some of the tributaries for use on Indian Reservations, National Forests, Recreational and Wildlife Areas and other government lands and works. While the Master passed upon some of these claims, he declined to reach others, particularly those relating to tributaries. We approve his decision as to which claims required adjudication, and likewise we approve the decree he recommended for the government claims he did decide. We shall discuss only the claims of the United States on behalf of the Indian Reservations.

The Government, on behalf of five Indian Reservations in Arizona, California, and Nevada, asserted rights to water in the mainstream of the Colorado River. The Colorado River Reservation, located partly in Arizona and partly in California, is the largest. It was originally created by an Act of Congress in 1865, but its area was later increased by Executive Order. Other reservations were created by Executive Orders and amendments to them ranging in dates from 1870 to 1907. The Master found both as a matter of fact and law that when the United States created these reservations or added to them, it reserved not only land but also the use of enough water from the Colorado to irrigate the irrigable portions of the reserved lands. The aggregate quantity of water which the Master held was reserved for all the reservations is about 1,000,000 acre-feet, to be used on around 135,000 irrigable acres of land. Here, as before the Master, Arizona argues that the United States had no power to make a reservation of navigable waters after Arizona became a State; that navigable waters could not be reserved by Executive Orders; that the United States did not intend to reserve water for the Indian Reservations; that the amount of water reserved should be measured by the reasonably foreseeable needs of the Indians living on the reservation rather than by the number of irrigable acres; and, finally, that the judicial doctrine of equitable apportionment should be used to divide the water between the Indians and the other people in the State of Arizona.

The last argument is easily answered. The doctrine of equitable apportionment is a method of resolving water disputes between States. [You will learn about the balancing test of equitable apportionment in Part IV.] It was created by this Court in the exercise of its original jurisdiction over controversies in which States are parties. An Indian Reservation is not a State. And while Congress has sometimes left Indian Reservations considerable power to manage their own affairs, we are not convinced by Arizona's argument that each reservation is so much like a State that its rights to water should be determined by the doctrine of equitable apportionment. Moreover, even were we to treat an Indian Reservation like a State, equitable apportionment would still not control since, under our view, the Indian claims here are governed by the statutes and Executive Orders creating the reservations.

Arizona's contention that the Federal Government had no power, after Arizona became a State [this occurred on February 14, 1912], to reserve waters for the use and benefit of federally reserved lands rests largely upon statements in *Pollard's Lessee v. Hagan*, 3 How. 212 (1845), and *Shively v. Bowlby*, 152 U.S. 1 (1894). Those cases and others that followed them gave rise to the doctrine that lands underlying navigable waters within territory acquired by the Government are held in trust for future States and that title to such lands is automatically vested in the States upon admission to the Union. But those cases involved only the shores of and lands beneath navigable waters. They do not determine the problem before us and cannot be accepted as limiting the broad powers of the United States to regulate navigable waters under the Commerce Clause and to regulate government lands under Art. IV, § 3, of the Constitution [the Property Clause]. We have no doubt about the power of the United States under these clauses to reserve water rights for its reservations and its property.

Arizona also argues that, in any event, water rights cannot be reserved by Executive Order. Some of the reservations of Indian lands here involved were made almost 100 years ago, and all of them were made over 45 years ago. In our view, these reservations, like those created directly by Congress, were not limited to land, but included waters as well. Congress and the Executive have ever since recognized these as Indian Reservations. Numerous appropriations, including appropriations for irrigation projects, have been made by Congress. They have been uniformly and universally treated as reservations by map makers, surveyors, and the public. We can give but short shrift at this late date to the argument that the reservations either of land or water are invalid because they were originally set apart by the Executive.

Arizona also challenges the Master's holding as to the Indian Reservations on two other grounds: first, that there is a lack of evidence showing that the United States in establishing the reservations intended to reserve water for them; second, that even if water was meant to be reserved the Master has awarded too much water. We reject both of these contentions. Most of the land in these reservations is and always has been arid. If the water necessary to sustain life is to be had, it must come from the Colorado River or its tributaries. It can be said without overstatement that when the Indians were put on these reservations they were not considered to be located in the most desirable area of the Nation. It is impossible to believe that when Congress created the great Colorado River Indian Reservation and when the Executive Department of this Nation created the other reservations they were unaware that most of the lands were of the desert kind—hot, scorching sands—and that water from the river would be essential to the life of the Indian people and to the animals they hunted and the crops they raised. In the debate leading to approval of the first congressional appropriation for irrigation of the Colorado River Indian Reservation, the delegate from the Territory of Arizona made this statement:

> Irrigating canals are essential to the prosperity of these Indians. Without water there can be no production, no life; and all they ask of you is to give them a few

> agricultural implements to enable them to dig an irrigating canal by which their lands may be watered and their fields irrigated, so that they may enjoy the means of existence. You must provide these Indians with the means of subsistence or they will take by robbery from those who have. During the last year I have seen a number of these Indians starved to death for want of food.

Cong. Globe, 38th Cong., 2d Sess. 1321 (1865).

The question of the Government's implied reservation of water rights upon the creation of an Indian Reservation was before this Court in *Winters v. United States*, 207 U.S. 564, decided in 1908. Much the same argument made to us was made in *Winters* to persuade the Court to hold that Congress had created an Indian Reservation without intending to reserve waters necessary to make the reservation livable. The Court rejected all of the arguments. As to whether water was intended to be reserved the Court said:

> The lands were arid, and, without irrigation, were practically valueless. And yet, it is contended, the means of irrigation were deliberately given up by the Indians and deliberately accepted by the government. The lands ceded were, it is true, also arid; and some argument may be urged, and is urged, that with their cession there was the cession of the waters, without which they would be valueless, and 'civilized communities could not be established thereon.' And this, it is further contended, the Indians knew, and yet made no reservation of the waters. We realize that there is a conflict of implications, but that which makes for the retention of the waters is of greater force than that which makes for their cession.

The Court in *Winters* concluded that the Government, when it created that Indian Reservation, intended to deal fairly with the Indians by reserving for them the waters without which their lands would have been useless. *Winters* has been followed by this Court as recently as 1939 in *United States v. Powers*, 305 U.S. 527 [a case addressing allocation of water to allottees to be addressed in Chapter 12]. We follow it now and agree that the United States did reserve the water rights for the Indians effective as of the time the Indian Reservations were created. This means, as the Master held, that these water rights, having vested before the Act [the Boulder Canyon Project Act determined in the part of this case you will read under interstate allocation to allocate water among the lower basin states.] became effective on June 25, 1929, are 'present perfected rights' and as such are entitled to priority under the Act.

We also agree with the Master's conclusion as to the quantity of water intended to be reserved. He found that the water was intended to satisfy the future as well as the present needs of the Indian Reservations and ruled that enough water was reserved to irrigate all the practicably irrigable acreage on the reservations. Arizona, on the other hand, contends that the quantity of water reserved should be measured by the Indians' 'reasonably foreseeable needs,' which, in fact, means by the number of Indians. How many Indians there will be and what their future needs will be can only be guessed. We have concluded, as did the Master, that the only feasible and fair way by which reserved water for the reservations can be measured is irrigable acreage. The various acreages of irrigable land which the Master found to be on the different reservations we find to be reasonable.

...

VI. DECREE.

While we have in the main agreed with the Master, there are some places we have disagreed and some questions on which we have not ruled. Rather than adopt the Master's decree with amendments or append our own decree to this opinion, we will allow the parties, or any of them, if they wish, to submit before September 16, 1963, the form of decree to carry this opinion into effect, failing which the Court will prepare and enter an appropriate decree at the next Term of Court.

It is so ordered.

Notes & Questions

1. Arizona pointed out that, unlike the Milk River from *Winters*, the Colorado River was considered navigable on statehood. Why did Arizona think that mattered? Did it affect the Supreme Court's decision? Why or why not?
2. Many of the reservations at issue in *Arizona v. California* were set aside by executive order rather than a treaty or, like the Fort Belknap Reservation in *Winters*, by congressionally ratified agreement. Did that alter the outcome of the case in *Arizona v. California*?
3. According to Arizona, how should the tribal reserved water rights be quantified?
4. What quantification standard does the Court finally settle on? Why?
5. Is the quantity of the tribal water right limited to its current needs?

To find the details of the "Practicably Irrigable Acreage" method or PIA, it is necessary to turn to the 433-page Report of the Special Master setting forth the findings, conclusions, and recommended decree. The report includes details on the methodology, and the following excerpt covers its justification. When you study the modern era of quantification of reserved water rights in state general stream adjudications in Part VI, you will learn about the detailed approach to determining PIA and the science needed. Also not reproduced here is the reservation-by-reservation statement of how much irrigable land is available and the amount of water that would require.

Arizona v. California

Report of Simon H. Rifkind, Special Master
December 5, 1960

...

IV The Claims of the United States to Water in the Mainstream of the Colorado River

The United States claims, in addition to control of the mainstream by reason of the Boulder Canyon Project Act and its ownership and management of the various dams and works which regulate mainstream water, the use of water in the Lower Basin for a variety of its projects and needs. The United States urges that it has reserved water for the use of the various Indian Reservations,....

Indian Reservations

The United States argues that it has reserved water flowing in the Colorado River and its tributaries in the Lower Basin for the needs of all of the Indian Reservations located within the Lower Basin. Thus the United States claims that each Indian Reservation has the right to divert and consume the amount of water necessary to irrigate all irrigable acreage on the Reservation and to satisfy related needs, subject only to the priority of appropriative rights established before a particular Reservation was created and water reserved for its benefit.

...

... [W]herever I have found an intent to reserve water, I have inferred, absent evidence to the contrary, that the reservation was not limited to the needs of the population then resident upon the land, nor to the acreage being irrigated when the Reservation was created. I have concluded that enough water was reserved to satisfy the future expanding agricultural and related water needs of each Indian Reservation. Invariably the United States intended that the Indian tribes settled on a Reservation would remain there for generations, and the possibility that other Indians would be settled on the Reservation could not be excluded. Certainly the possibility of expanding populations, expanding agricultural development, and hence expanding-water needs must have been apparent at the time each Reservation was created. It is unreasonable to attribute to the United States an intention or an expectation that the Indians would remain stagnant or die out when they were settled on a Reservation. Since the Indians could remain on these Reservations and develop their society and economy only if water from the Colorado River was available to meet their future needs have found that the United States, when it reserved water, reserved it for all of such needs.

This conclusion comports with the holdings in the three cases decided by the Court of Appeals for the Ninth Circuit which are cited above. As that Court stated in *United States v. Ahtaimm Irrigation District,* 236 F.2d 321, 327 (9th Cir. 1956):

> "It is plain from our decision in the *Conrad Investment Co.* case, *supra,* that the paramount right of the Indians to the waters of Ahtanum Creek was not limited to the use of the Indians at any given date but this right extended to the ultimate needs of the Indians as those needs and requirements should grow to keep pace with the development of Indian agriculture upon the reservation."

The conclusion reached here is also consistent with the holding in the *Winters* case that the upstream farmers could not interfere with uses on the Indian Reservation which were initiated subsequent to the farmers' diversions.

The suggestion is unacceptable that the United States intended that the Indians would be required to obtain water for their future needs by acquiring appropriative rights under state law. The Indians were not an agricultural people and it was necessary for them to develop their agricultural skills after settling on the Reservations. It must have been apparent that if they were thrown into competition with the more advanced non-Indians in a race to acquire rights to water by putting it to beneficial use, they would have lost the match before it was begun. Rather than assuming that the United States intended to put the Indians in the position of having *to* leave their Reservations as their water needs increased if they were unable to satisfy these needs by acquiring appropriative rights under state law, I have concluded that reservations of water by the United States included enough to supply expanding needs regardless of state water law.

This brings us to the question of quantity. This is sharply debated, and many conflicting views have been advanced. I have concluded that the United States effectuated the intention to provide for the future needs of the Indians by reserving sufficient water to irrigate all of the practicably irrigable lands in a Reservation and to supply related stock and domestic uses. The magnitude of the water rights created by the United States is measured by the amount of irrigable land set aside within a Reservation, not by the number of Indians inhabiting it. At the times of the creation of the five Indian Reservations in question, it was impossible to predict the future needs of the Indians who might inhabit them. Indeed, in some instances it was not clear which Indian tribes would ultimately be settled on a particular Reservation. What the United States did, in withdrawing public lands for these Indian Reservations, was to establish areas that could be used in the indefinite future to satisfy the needs of Indian tribes in the United States as those needs might develop. It follows from this that the United States intended to reserve enough water to make the lands productive, in other words, enough to irrigate all of the practicably irrigable acreage. Only by reserving water in this manner could the United States ensure that the Reservation lands would be usable when needed to support an Indian economy. This conclusion is also supported by the fact that the irrigable land originally withdrawn for each of the five Indian Reservations was considerably more extensive than was necessary to support the Indians who inhabited the Reservations immediately after their establishment. The only explanation for this withdrawal of excess irrigable acreage is that the United States intended it to be utilized in the future. It must have been apparent that unless the United States reserved water for the land at the time of withdrawal, there might be no water left to appropriate at the time that the land was needed for the purposes *for* which it was withdrawn.

Arizona argues that the United States reserved water for the Indians themselves and not for the lands withdrawn for a Reservation. Arizona seems to envisage that the United States intended to create water rights in gross which would fluctuate in magnitude as the Indian population and needs fluctuated, the water right being measured by the amount of water needed at any particular time by the Indians actually inhabiting a particular Reservation. As pointed out above, the more sensible conclusion is that the United States intended to reserve enough water to irrigate all of the practicably irrigable lands on a Reservation and that the water rights thereby created would run to defined lands, as is generally true of water rights.

But even if Arizona were correct in her contention, the most feasible way to give full effect to the water rights created by the United States, as Arizona defines them, would be to decree to each Reservation enough water to irrigate all of the practicably irrigable acreage. It is clear that the water rights of the five Reservations in question cannot be fixed at present uses for this would defeat the basic purpose of reserving water to meet future requirements. Even if, as Arizona argues, the reservation of water was in gross for Indians and not Reservation lands, the Indians' needs may well increase in the future and these increased needs would have to be provided for. Thus, under the Arizona theory, there are two possible methods of framing the decree in this action, other than in terms of irrigable acreage.

One possibility would be to adopt an open-end decree, simply stating that each Reservation may divert at any particular time all the water reasonably necessary for its agricultural and related uses as against those who appropriated water subsequent to its establishment. However, such a limitless claim would place all junior water rights in jeopardy of the uncertain and the unknowable. Financing of irrigation projects would be severely hampered if investors were faced with the possibility that expanding needs on an Indian Reservation might result in a reduction of the project's water supply. Moreover, it would not give the United States any certainty as to the extent of its reserved rights, which would undoubtedly hamper the United States in developing them. Since, under the Arizona theory, United States water rights vary with changes in Indian population, the planning of works to serve future needs would be difficult because the United States could never know whether sufficient water to operate the works economically would be legally available.

The other possibility, which would avoid the serious disadvantage of creating uncertainty as to the extent of the reserved rights, would be to predict the ultimate needs of each Reservation and to decree that much water for its future uses. The shortcoming of this solution, however, lies in the difficulty of predicting the future needs of Indian Reservations. Failure to foresee expanding requirements would result in a forfeiture of the Indians' water rights and would stultify development of the Reservations. Whether it is ever possible accurately to predict the future needs of an Indian Reservation, it is clearly not possible in this case where the attention of the parties has been directed to a great many complex and important issues quite apart from those relating to the Indians. Whatever might be possible in a case involving solely the issue of the reserved rights of a single Indian Reservation, it would not be possible to predict future Reservation needs in this litigation.

Therefore, the most feasible decree that could be adopted in this case, even accepting Arizona's contention, would be to establish a water right for each of the five Reservations in the amount of water necessary to irrigate all of the practicably irrigable acreage on the Reservation and to satisfy related stock and domestic uses. This will preserve the full extent of the water rights created by the United States and will establish water rights of fixed magnitude and priority so as to provide certainty for both the United States and non-Indian users.

The amount of water reserved for the five Reservations, and the water rights created thereby, are measured by the water needed for agricultural, stock and related domestic purposes. The reservations of water were made for the purpose of enabling the Indians to develop a viable agricultural economy; other uses, such as those for industry, which might consume substantially more water than agricultural uses, were not contemplated at the time the Reservations were created. Indeed, the United States asks only for enough water to satisfy future agricultural and related uses. This does not necessarily mean, however, that water reserved for Indian Reservations may not be used for purposes other than agricultural and related uses. The question of change in the character of use is not before me. I hold only that the amount of water reserved, and hence the magnitude of the water rights created, is determined by agricultural and related requirements, since when the water was reserved that was the purpose of the reservation. Even in such cases, courts have not attempted to bind the Indian on the basis of a prediction as to future needs. See *Conrad Investment Co. v. United States*, 161 Fed. 829 (9th Cir. 1908).

The water rights established for the benefit of the five Indian Reservations and enforced in the recommended decree are similar in many respects to the ordinary water right recognized under the law of many western states: They are of fixed magnitude and priority and are appurtenant to defined lands. They may be utilized regardless of the character of the particular user. Thus Congress has provided for the leasing of certain Reservation lands to non-Indians, and these lessees may exercise the water rights appurtenant to the leased lands. *Skeem* v. *United States,* 273 Fed. 93, 96 (9th Cir. 1921). The measurement used in defining the magnitude of the water rights is the amount of water necessary for agricultural and related purposes because this was the initial purpose of the reservations, but the decree establishes a property right which the United States may utilize or dispose of for the benefit of the Indians as the relevant law may allow. See *United States* v. *Powers,* 305 U.S. 527 (1939).

Notes & Questions

1. The Special Master concludes that the reserved water right includes water for future needs and rejects two alternative approaches to handling those future needs. What are the two alternatives and why does the Special Master reject them?
2. What two interests is the Special Master attempting to balance when determining how to address the future needs of the tribes? Given what you know about the *Winters* Doctrine, does that balance seem appropriate?
3. You will learn in Part VI that state courts have taken different views on whether, once quantified using PIA, the reserved water right may be changed to other uses. The Appendix to the Final Consolidated Decree in *Arizona v. California,* issued in 1964 and amended in 2006 following settlement, states: "The foregoing reference to a quantity of water necessary to supply consumptive use required for irrigation, and as that provision is included within paragraphs (1) through (5) of Art. II(D) of this decree, shall constitute the means of determining quantity of adjudicated water rights

but shall not constitute a restriction of the usage of them to irrigation or other agricultural application."[6]

4. Fill in the following table comparing Indian reserved water rights and prior appropriation rights:

Attribute	Reserved Water Rights	Prior Appropriation
Priority		
Quantity		
Future Use		
Allocation during drought		

5. The Special Master drafted his report in 1960, well before climate change was well understood. How does the Special Master's approach of quantifying water rights for fixed quantities affect tribal certainty and water security now that climate change is affecting both water supply and demand?

The Quantification Consequences of a Final Decree

As you learned earlier in this Chapter, the process of adjudicating water rights in lower federal courts had the goal of entering final decrees. The focus was on individual irrigation water users across state lines and not on allocation among sovereigns. The effort to include Native American Reserved water rights included little attention to the future needs of the reservations. Following *Arizona v. California*, it was clear that the amount of water awarded in these decrees was woefully inadequate. The following case concerns the effort by the United States to reopen the Orr Ditch decree on the Truckee River, shared by California, Nevada, and the Pyramid Lake Paiute (Figure 11.3).

Nevada v. United States

Supreme Court of the United States
463 U.S. 110 (1983)

Opinion

REHNQUIST, Justice—In 1913 the United States sued to adjudicate water rights to the Truckee River for the benefit of the Pyramid Lake Indian Reservation and the planned Newlands Reclamation Project.... [I]n 1944, the United States District Court for the District of Nevada entered a final decree.... In 1973 the United States filed the present action in the same court on behalf of the Pyramid Lake Indian Reservation seeking additional water rights to the Truckee River. The issue thus presented is whether the Government may partially undo the 1944 decree, or whether principles of *res judicata*

6. Arizona v. California, 376 U.S. 340, Appendix (1964), and 547 U.S. 150, Appendix (2006).

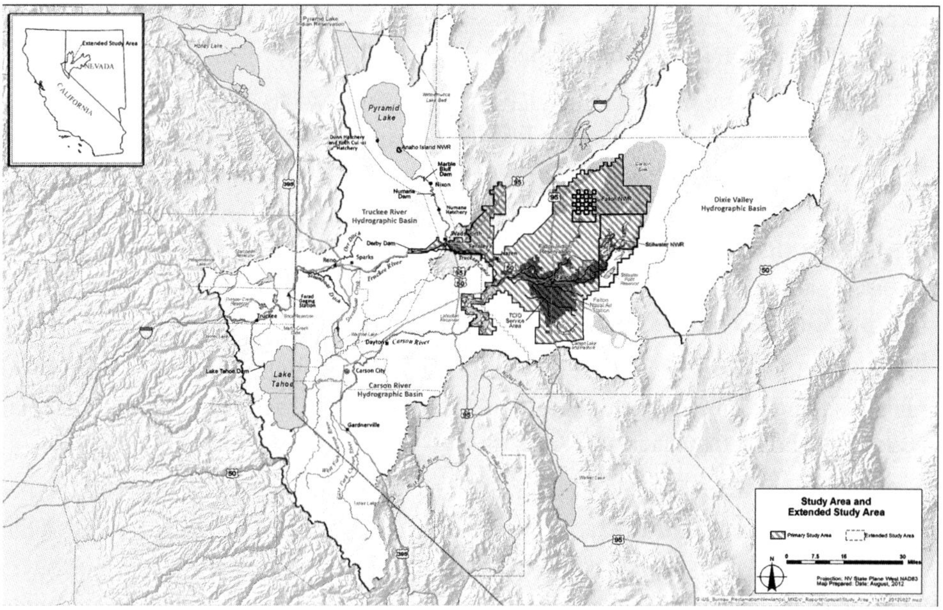

Figure 11.3 Truckee River Basin with its source in Lake Tahoe and its terminus in Pyramid Lake on the Pyramid Lake Paiute Indian Reservation. The map also shows the diversions to the Newlands Project, one of the first federal Reclamation projects. Source: Bureau of Reclamation Mid-Pacific Region Lahontan Basin Area Office, *Newlands Project Planning Study Special Report* (2013), https://www.circleofblue.org/wp-content/uploads/2013/04/Reclamation_Newlands-Project-Report.pdf.

prevent it, and the intervenor Pyramid Lake Paiute Tribe, from litigating this claim on the merits.

I

Nevada has, on the average, less precipitation than any other State in the Union. Except for drainage in the southeastern part of the State into the Colorado River, and drainage in the northern part of the State into the Columbia River, the rivers that flow in Nevada generally disappear into "sinks." … The present litigation relates to water rights in the Truckee River, one of the three principal rivers flowing through west central Nevada. It rises in the High Sierra in Placer County, California, flows into and out of Lake Tahoe, and thence down the eastern slope of the Sierra Nevada mountains. It flows through Reno, Nevada, and after a course of some 120 miles debouches into Pyramid Lake, which has no outlet.

It has been said that Pyramid Lake is "widely considered the most beautiful desert lake in North America [and that its] fishery [has] brought it worldwide fame. A species of cutthroat trout … grew to world record size in the desert lake and attracted anglers from throughout the world." S. Wheeler, The Desert Lake 90–92 (1967). The first recorded sighting of Pyramid Lake by non-Indians occurred in January of 1844 when Captain John C. Fremont and his party camped nearby. In his journal Captain Fremont reported that the Lake "broke upon our eyes like the ocean" and was "set like a gem in the mountains." 1 The Expeditions of John Charles Fremont 604–605 (1970).

Commenting upon the fishery, as well as the Pyramid Lake Indians that his party was camping with, Captain Fremont wrote:

> "An Indian brought in a large fish to trade, which we had the inexpressible satisfaction to find was a salmon trout; we gathered round him eagerly. The Indians were amused with our delight, and immediately brought in numbers; so that the camp was soon stocked. Their flavor was excellent—superior, in fact, to that of any fish I have ever known. They were of extraordinary size—about as large as the Columbia river salmon—generally from two to four feet in length." *Id.*, at 609.

When first viewed by Captain Fremont in early 1844, Pyramid Lake was some 50 miles long and 12 miles wide. Since that time the surface area of the Lake has been reduced by about 20,000 acres.

The origins of the cases before us are found in two historical events involving the Federal Government in this part of the country. First, in 1859 the Department of the Interior set aside nearly half a million acres in what is now western Nevada as a reservation for the area's Paiute Indians. In 1874 President Ulysses S. Grant by executive order confirmed the withdrawal as the Pyramid Lake Indian Reservation. The Reservation includes Pyramid Lake, the land surrounding it, the lower reaches of the Truckee River, and the bottom land alongside the lower Truckee.

Then, with the passage of the Reclamation Act of 1902, the Federal Government was designated to play a more prominent role in the development of the West....Accordingly, the Secretary withdrew from the public domain approximately 200,000 acres in western Nevada, which ultimately became the Newlands Reclamation Project. The Project was designed to irrigate a substantial area in the vicinity of Fallon, Nevada, with waters from both the Truckee and the Carson Rivers.

The Carson River, like the Truckee, rises on the eastern slope of the High Sierra in Alpine County, California, and flows north and northeast over a course of about 170 miles, finally disappearing into Carson sink. The Newlands Project accomplished the diversion of water from the Truckee River to the Carson River.... The combined waters of the Truckee and Carson Rivers impounded in Lahontan Reservoir are distributed for irrigation and related uses on downstream lands by means of lateral canals within the Newlands Reclamation Project.

Before the works contemplated by the Project went into operation, a number of private landowners had established rights to water in the Truckee River under Nevada law. The Government also asserted on behalf of the Indians of the Pyramid Lake Indian Reservation a reserved right under the so-called "implied-reservation-of-water" doctrine set forth in *Winters v. United States*, 207 U.S. 564 (1908). The United States therefore filed a complaint in the United States District Court for the District of Nevada in March, 1913, commencing what became known as the *Orr Ditch* litigation. The Government, for the benefit of both the Project and the Pyramid Lake Reservation, asserted a claim to 10,000 cubic feet of water per second for the Project and a claim to

500 cubic feet per second for the Reservation. The complaint named as defendants all water users on the Truckee River in Nevada. The Government expressly sought a final decree quieting title to the rights of all parties.

[A temporary decree was entered in 1926 and ultimately a settlement providing for irrigation of 5875 acres on the Reservation with a priority date of 1859 and irrigation of 232,800 acres within the Newlands Reclamation Project resulted in the District Court entering] ... a final decree adopting the agreement on September 8, 1944. No appeal was taken. Thus, 31 years after its inception the *Orr Ditch* litigation came to a close.

On December 21, 1973, the Government instituted the action below seeking additional rights to the Truckee River for the Pyramid Lake Indian Reservation; the Pyramid Lake Paiute Tribe was permitted to intervene in support of the United States. The Government named as defendants all persons presently claiming water rights to the Truckee River and its tributaries in Nevada. The defendants include the defendants in the *Orr Ditch* litigation and their successors, approximately 3800 individual farmers that own land in the Newlands Reclamation Project, and the Truckee-Carson Irrigation District. The District Court certified the Project farmers as a class and directed TCID to represent their interests.

In its complaint the Government purported not to dispute the rights decreed in the *Orr Ditch* case. Instead, it alleged that *Orr Ditch* determined only the Reservation's right to "water for irrigation," not the claim now being asserted for "sufficient waters from the Truckee River [for] the maintenance and preservation of Pyramid Lake, [and for] the maintenance of the lower reaches of the Truckee River as a natural spawning ground for fish." The complaint further averred that in establishing the Reservation the United States had intended that the Pyramid Lake fishery be maintained. Since the additional water now being claimed is allegedly necessary for that purpose, the Government alleged that the executive order creating the Reservation must have impliedly reserved a right to this water.

The defendants below asserted *res judicata* as an affirmative defense, saying that the United States and the Tribe were precluded by the *Orr Ditch* decree from litigating this claim. Following a separate trial on this issue, the District Court sustained the defense and dismissed the complaint in its entirety.

...

The Court of Appeals for the Ninth Circuit affirmed in part and reversed in part.... [T]he Court of Appeals found that the *Orr Ditch* decree did not conclude the dispute between the Tribe and the owners of Newlands Project lands. The court said that litigants are not to be bound by a prior judgment unless they were adversaries under the earlier pleadings or unless the specific issue in dispute was actually litigated in the earlier case and the court found that neither exception applied here.

The Court of Appeals conceded that "[a] strict adversity requirement does not necessarily fit the realities of water adjudications." Nevertheless, the court found that since neither the Tribe nor the Project landowners were parties in *Orr Ditch* but instead were both represented by the United States, and since their interests may have conflicted in that proceeding, the court would not find that the Government had intended to bind these nonparties *inter se* absent a specific statement of adversity in the pleadings. We granted certiorari in the cases challenging the Court of Appeals' decision, ... and we now affirm in part and reverse in part.

II

The Government opens the "Summary of Argument" portion of its brief by stating: "The court of appeals has simply permitted a reallocation of the water decreed in *Orr Ditch* to a single party—the United States—from reclamation uses to a Reservation use with an earlier priority. The doctrine of *res judicata* does not bar a single party from reallocating its water in this fashion...." Brief for United States 21. We are bound to say that the Government's position, if accepted, would do away with half a century of decided case law relating to the Reclamation Act of 1902 and water rights in the public domain of the West.

[The Court discusses its interpretation of the Reclamation Act which requires that state law be followed in appropriation of water and that the water acquired is appurtenant to the land irrigated by the project and the water rights are the property of the water users. You will learn about the Reclamation Act in Part IV and the debate over whether the United States holds legal title to project water and the water users hold beneficial interest; or whether the water rights are entirely the property of the water users. Justice Rehnquist seems to take both positions.]

In the light of these cases, we conclude that the Government is completely mistaken if it believes that the water rights confirmed to it by the *Orr Ditch* decree in 1944 for use in irrigating lands within the Newlands Reclamation Project were like so many bushels of wheat, to be bartered, sold, or shifted about as the Government might see fit. Once these lands were acquired by settlers in the Project, the Government's "ownership" of the water rights was at most nominal; the beneficial interest in the rights confirmed to the Government resided in the owners of the land within the Project to which these water rights became appurtenant upon the application of Project water to the land. As in *Ickes v. Fox* and *Nebraska v. Wyoming,* the law of relevant State and the contracts entered into by the landowners and the United States make this point very clear.

The Government's brief is replete with references to its fiduciary obligation to the Pyramid Lake Paiute Tribe of Indians, as it properly should be. But the Government seems wholly to ignore in the same brief the obligations that necessarily devolve upon it from having mere title to water rights for the Newlands Project, when the beneficial ownership of these water rights resides elsewhere.

... This Court has long recognized "the distinctive obligation of trust incumbent by the Government" in its dealings with Indian tribes, see, *e.g., Seminole Nation v. United States,* 316 U.S. 286, 296 (1942). These concerns have been traditionally focused on the Bureau of Indian Affairs within the Department of the Interior. *Poafpybitty v. Skelly Oil Co.,* 390 U.S. 365, 374 (1968). See 25 U.S.C. § 1.

But Congress in its wisdom, when it enacted the Reclamation Act of 1902, required the Secretary of the Interior to assume substantial obligations with respect to the reclamation of arid lands in the western part of the United States....

... [I]t may well appear that Congress was requiring the Secretary of the Interior to carry water on at least two shoulders when it delegated to him both the responsibility for the supervision of the Indian tribes and the commencement of reclamation projects in areas adjacent to reservation lands. But Congress chose to do this, and it is simply unrealistic to suggest that the Government may not perform its obligation to represent Indian tribes in litigation when Congress has obliged it to represent other interests as well. In this regard, the Government cannot follow the fastidious standards of a private fiduciary, who would breach his duties to his single beneficiary solely by representing potentially conflicting interests without the beneficiary's consent. The Government does not "compromise" its obligation to one interest that Congress obliges it to represent by the mere fact that it simultaneously performs another task for another interest that Congress has obligated it by statute to do.

With these observations in mind, we turn to the principles of *res judicata* that we think are involved in this case.

III

...

Simply put, the doctrine of *res judicata* provides that when a final judgment has been entered on the merits of a case, "[i]t is a finality as to the claim or demand in controversy, concluding parties and those in privity with them, not only as to every matter which was offered and received to sustain or defeat the claim or demand, but as to any other admissible matter which might have been offered for that purpose."

To determine the applicability of *res judicata* to the facts before us, we must decide first if the "cause of action" which the Government now seeks to assert is the "same cause of action" that was asserted in *Orr Ditch;* we must then decide whether the parties in the instant proceeding are identical to or in privity with the parties in *Orr Ditch.* We address these questions in turn.

A

[T]he only conclusion allowed by the record in the *Orr Ditch* case is that the Government was given an opportunity to litigate the Reservation's entire water right to the Truckee, and that the Government intended to take advantage of that opportunity.

...

The final decree in *Orr Ditch* clearly shows that the parties to the settlement agreement and the District Court intended to accomplish this purpose. The decree provided in part:

> "The parties, persons, corporations, intervenors, grantees, successors in interest and substituted parties hereinbefore named, and their and each of

> their servants, agents, attorneys, assigns and all persons claiming by, through or under them and their successors, in or to the water rights or lands herein mentioned or described, are and *each of them is hereby forever enjoined and restrained from asserting or claiming any rights in or to the waters of the Truckee River or its tributaries, or the waters of any of the creeks or streams or other waters hereinbefore mentioned except the rights, specified, determined and allowed by this decree....*" App. to Nevada Petn. for Cert a145 (emphasis added).

We need not, however, stop here. For evidence more directly showing the Government's intention to assert in *Orr Ditch* the Reservation's full water rights, we return to the amended complaint, where it was alleged:

> "16. On or about or prior to the 29th day of November, 1859, the Government of the United States, having for a long time previous thereto recognized the fact that certain Pah Ute and other Indians were, and they and their ancestors had for many years been, residing upon and using certain lands in the northern part of the said Truckee River Valley and around said Pyramid Lake ... and the said Government being desirous of protecting said Indians and their descendants in their homes, fields, pastures, fishing, and their use of said lands and waters, and in affording to them an opportunity to acquire the art of husbandry and other arts of civilization, and to become civilized, did reserve said lands from any and all forms of entry or sale and for the sole use of said Indians, and for their benefit and civilization. On, to wit, the 23d day of March, 1874, the said lands, having been previously surveyed, were by order of the then President of the United States, for the purposes aforesaid, withdrawn from sale or other disposition, and set apart for the Pah Ute and other Indians aforesaid.
>
> "The United States by setting aside said lands for said purposes and creating said reservation, and by virtue of the matters and things in this paragraph set forth, did on, to wit, the 29th day of November, 1859, reserve from further appropriation, appropriate and set aside for its own use in, on, and about said Indian reservation, and the land thereof, from and of the waters of the said Truckee River, five hundred (500) cubic feet of water per second of time." App. to Nevada Cert. Petn. a6–8.

This cannot be construed as anything less than a claim for the full "implied-reservation-of-water" rights that were due the Pyramid Lake Indian Reservation.

...

B

...

... The United States undoubtedly owes a strong fiduciary duty to its Indian wards.... It may be that where only a relationship between the Government and the tribe is involved, the law respecting obligations between a trustee and a beneficiary in private litigation will in many, if not all, respects, adequately describe the duty of the United States. But where Congress has imposed upon the United States, in addition to its duty to represent Indian tribes, a duty to obtain water rights for reclamation projects, and has even authorized the inclusion of reservation lands within a project, the analogy of a faithless private fiduciary cannot be controlling for purposes of evaluating the authority of the United States to represent different interests.

...

IV

In conclusion we affirm the Court of Appeals' finding that the cause of action asserted below and the cause of action asserted in *Orr Ditch* are one and the same. We also affirm the Court of Appeals' finding that the *Orr Ditch* decree concluded the controversy on this cause of action between, on the one hand, the *Orr Ditch* defendants, their successors in interest, and subsequent appropriators of the Truckee River, and, on the other hand, the United States and the Tribe. We reverse the Court of Appeals, however, with respect to its finding concerning the Truckee-Carson Irrigation District, and the Project farmers it represents, and hold instead that the *Orr Ditch* decree also ended the dispute raised between these parties and the plaintiffs below.

It is so ordered.

BRENNAN, Justice, concurring.

The mere existence of a formal "conflict of interest" does not deprive the United States of authority to represent Indians in litigation, and therefore to bind them as well. If, however, the United States actually causes harm through a breach of its trust obligations the Indians should have a remedy against it. I join the Court's opinion on the understanding that it reaffirms that the Pyramid Lake Paiute Tribe has a remedy against the United States for the breach of duty that the United States has admitted. See *ante,* at 2925, n. 16.

...

Notes & Questions

1. The Court in *Nevada v. United States* answers the question left open in *Walker River* of whether the United States may seek additional water on behalf of a Tribe once a water decree has been closed. What is the Court's answer? What is the legal basis for the answer?
2. Which of the following is true?
    a. The Court determined that the role of the United States as trustee for Indian Tribes represents a strict fiduciary duty that cannot be balanced against other interests of the United States.
    b. The Court determined that the United States has obligations both to Tribes and to water users who take water from a federal project and cannot act in the Tribes' interest alone.

3. It may be of interest to know that the Pyramid Lake Paiute Tribe found another legal avenue to protect their interests via the Endangered Species Act and today a settlement, 1990 Truckee-Carson-Pyramid Lake Water Rights Settlement Act, Pub. L. No. 101-618, Title II, leading to additional flow of water to Pyramid Lake at critical times. This has begun the recovery of the Lahontan cutthroat trout and the cui-ui.[7]
4. *Nevada v. United States* was the first case on reserved water rights issued by the Rehnquist Court. The tendency of the Rehnquist Court to reduce Native American rights in favor of states' rights and its failure to apply the canons of constructure for agreements between tribes and the United States led to the development of the Tribal Supreme Court Project "to strengthen tribal advocacy before the U.S. Supreme Court by developing new litigation strategies and coordinating tribal legal resources, and to ultimately improve the win-loss record of Indian tribes."[8] Activities include monitoring cases that might come before the U.S. Supreme Court and consulting with tribes on whether to seek Supreme Court review. While early rulings indicated a possible return to the long-established tenets of Federal Indian law (including the canons of construction), rulings under the Roberts Court beginning in 2022 suggest that the project will remain important to Native American tribes.

---

7. For those interested in learning about the settlement, *see* Barbara Cosens, *Farmers, Fish, Tribal Power, and Poker: Reallocating Water in the Truckee River Basin, Nevada and California,* 10 U.C. Hastings, West-Northwest: J. Envt'l L. and Pol'y 89 (2003).

8. Native American Rights Fund, *Tribal Supreme Court Project* (2023), https://sct.narf.org/.

Chapter 12

The Federal Common Law Attributes of Reserved Water Rights: Allotment and Priority

Introduction

You learned in *Winters* that the priority date of an implied reservation of water is the date of establishment of the reservation. In *Winters,* the Fort Belknap Agreement of 1888 was negotiated with the Tribes and ratified through an Act of Congress. In Chapter 1, you learned that the date of establishment applies whether by Executive Order (*Arizona v. California*) or by an act of an Executive department (such as the Department of the Interior) and later institutionalized by Executive Order (*Walker River*). You will now learn about the complication on many reservations caused by the General Allotment Act of 1887, also known as the Dawes Act, which resulted in substantial non-Indian ownership of land within certain reservations. This Chapter will begin with background on the Dawes Act, followed by federal cases that have addressed the measure, priority, and jurisdiction to administer water rights associated with allotted land in its various forms, including land that is reacquired by a tribe after going out of trust status.

The General Allotment Act of 1887: The Dawes Act

Indian reservations throughout the United States were generally set aside as a single parcel of land that was to be held in trust by the federal government for the common benefit of all members of the tribe. Land tenure was controlled by the tribal government. By the mid-1800s federal policy shifted from this communal land ownership with tribal nations living separately from the rest of U.S. society to assimilation. Assimilation in this context means to absorb a group of people "into the dominant culture of a society."[1] This occurs through the acquisition of "the basic habits, attitudes, and mode of life" of the dominant culture.[2] The federal government used a variety of means

1. Encyclopedia Britannica, *Assimilation Society* (2023), https://tinyurl.com/5bc8taat.
2. Merriam-Webster Online Dictionary, *Assimilation* (2023), https://tinyurl.com/5n8h842t.

to attempt assimilation, including boarding schools. Of primary importance to water rights is the effort to use the property ownership model of the dominant society to alter the relationship between tribal members and land. To accomplish this, the government converted land formerly held in common to individual allotments for tribal members through a reservation-by-reservation process. This approach would de-emphasize the role of tribal governments in favor of individual control of private property. It was thought that it would encourage tribal members to embrace the yeoman agricultural economy of the dominant society.

By the 1850s, certain treaties with Indian tribes included provisions for allotment of parcels of lands within a reservation to individual Indians. To make this approach more widespread, Congress passed the General Allotment Act (also referred to as the Dawes Act after the leading proponent in the Senate, Henry Dawes),[3] authorizing the Executive branch to survey existing Reservations for purposes of allotment of 40–160 acre parcels of land to individual Indians. Allotted land would initially remain in trust status, with the United States holding allotments in trust for the individual Indians. You will read about the water rights associated with trust allotments in *United States v. Powers*, 305 U.S. 527 (1939).

Over time, implementation of the Dawes Act on various reservations resulted in considerable loss of trust land (both tribal and individual). Until it ended with the passage of the Indian Reorganization Act in 1934,[4] the General Allotment Act resulted in the loss of 65% of tribal or individual trust land within the boundaries of Indian reservations. [5] This loss happened in three ways.

First, the General Allotment Act provided that after 25 years of beneficial ownership of a trust allotment, an Indian allottee deemed "competent" could receive a fee patent to the land. Fee patent land is private property and is both alienable and taxable. Many former allotments were sold due to tribal member unfamiliarity with state tax law, as well as the inability to pay taxes. Historical research shows that some of that land was lost to non-Indians through sharp practices, graft, and even murder.[6]

Second, through inheritance. Allotments often passed through intestate succession. Shares in land passing to descendants of allotees who were not tribal members (due to insufficient blood quantum) shifted to fee status. As a result, many allotments are held in what are referred to as "fractional interests." The term "fractional interest" does not refer to a physical fraction of land that could be separately sold. Instead, it refers to a frac-

---

3. 24 Stat. 388, ch. 119, 25 U.S.C. § 331.

4. Pub. L. 73-383. Under the Indian Reorganization Act, a fund was established to reacquire fee land within reservations and some progress was made. However, the fund was zeroed out with the onset of World War II. In recent years, certain tribes have made considerable progress in the reacquisition of land through funds obtained from casinos and other tribal business enterprises.

5. For an excellent summary of the General Allotment Act and its impacts, see Judith Royster, *The Legacy of Allotment*, 37 ARIZ. ST. L.J. 1 (1995).

6. *See* ANGIE DEBO, AND STILL THE WATERS RUN: THE BETRAYAL OF THE FIVE CIVILIZED TRIBES (1973). This history has recently been made common knowledge through the book and film: KILLERS OF THE FLOWER MOON, the book by David Grann, and film directed by Martin Scorsese.

tional ownership interest in the whole. Thus, former allotments now are held partially in trust and partially in fee. Other allotments have passed entirely to non-members and are held entirely in fee. You will read about the water rights associated with fee land owned by a non-Indian who acquired the land from an Indian allottee by sale or by succession in *Colville Confederated Tribes v. Walton*, 647 F.2d 42 (9th Cir. 1981).

Finally, on certain reservations "surplus" land left after allotment was opened to homesteading by non-Indians. You will read about the water rights associated with homesteaded land within an Indian Reservation that is subsequently reacquired by the tribe in *United States v. Anderson*, 736 F.2d 1358 (9th Cir. 1984). Reacquisition of both homesteaded land and former allotments initially took place through a fund established when the 1934 Indian Reorganization Act ended allotment. That fund was zeroed out with the onset of World War II. Over the past several decades, tribes across the country have engaged in large-scale land reacquisition programs to undo some of the devastating effects of allotment.

The Priority and Quantification of Water for Indian Allotments and Non-Indian Land within the Boundaries of a Reservation

The following sections address the water rights associated with allotments according to the following categories: (1) allotments held by tribal members; (2) allotments acquired by nonmembers from an allottee; and (3) former allotments reacquired by the tribe.

The Indian Allotment

United States v. Powers, 305 U.S. 527 (1939), is the first U.S. Supreme Court case to address the question of whether allotments carry with them a portion of the reserved water right for the Reservation. *Powers* originated on the Crow Reservation in south-central Montana. The Reservation has a complex patchwork of land ownership as a result of allotment. Shortly after the reservation was created, the United States developed an irrigation project for Indian lands using water from Lodge Grass Creek and the Little Bighorn River. By 1885, other members of the Tribe had built their own irrigation ditches, which ran from these same streams to irrigate lands outside the project area. Powers and other irrigators outside the project are Tribal members and hold allotted land in fee status.

The issue in *Powers* was whether any of the Crow Tribe's members holding allotments are entitled to a portion of the reserved water right for the reservation. The United States took the position that allotments did not acquire any of the reserved water right, thus diversion of water by allottees upstream of an Indian irrigation project developed by the United States on behalf of the Crow Tribe must be enjoined. You will see that the U.S. Supreme Court disagreed.

United States v. Powers

Supreme Court of the United States
305 U.S. 527 (1939)

Mr. Justice McREYNOLDS delivered the opinion of the Court—By this proceeding (begun in 1934) the United States seek to prevent further taking of water from certain non-navigable streams within the Crow Indian Reservation. This water is essential to the cultivation of [Powers et al.'] lands allotted more than twenty years ago to members of the tribe and presently held under properly acquired fee simple titles. The prayer of the bill is for a permanent injunction against 'maintaining or using said dams and ditches, as aforesaid, and from diverting by means of said dams and ditches or in any other manner any of the waters from Lodge Grass Creek or Little Big Horn River and their tributaries; * * *.'

The decree of the Circuit Court of Appeals dismissing the bill must be affirmed.

[The Crow Indian Reservation was established by Treaty on May 7, 1868, 15 Stat. 649, 650, 651. The Treaty allowed individual tribal members to select land for cultivation. The land would then no longer be held in common but in trust for the individual and their family. The Treaty is silent on water. Despite the provision allowing allotment, land was not allotted at this time. In 1882 an Act of Congress Ch. 74, 22 Stat. 42, 43, diminished the Reservation and provided for allotment of the remaining Reservation lands. Actual allotment did not occur until after passage of the Dawes Act.]

Commencing in 1901 allotments in severalty of tracts abutting or adjacent to the Little Big Horn River or Lodge Grass Creek were made to [Powers et al.'s] Indian predecessors. These culminated in the issuance of fee simple patents as provided by Act of May 8, 1906. Each patent undertook to convey the land 'together with all the rights, privileges, immunities and appurtenances, of whatsoever nature, thereunto belonging,' but contained no express provision concerning water rights. Respondents have succeeded to the interest of the original allottees either by mesne conveyances or by purchase at government sales of deceased allottees' lands.

The Little Big Horn River and its affluent, Lodge Grass Creek, under normal conditions may afford sufficient water to irrigate twenty thousand acres within the Reservation. Through private ditches [Powers et al.] and their predecessors have long conveyed water from these streams in order to irrigate their lands and thus render them susceptible of cultivation. It is not suggested that water therefor can be obtained from any other source.

[United States] maintain—

> That prior to 1885, the United States commenced construction of irrigation works intended to divert waters from the streams in question. These gradually developed into a system normally capable of carrying sufficient water to irrigate 20,000 acres. None of [Powers et al.'] lands lie within the ambit of these projects; and neither the original allotments nor the patents specifically granted the use of any water.

> That Congress gave the Secretary of the Interior control of Reservation waters. Irrigation projects initiated under his authority prior to allotments of respondents' lands sufficed to dedicate and reserve sufficient water for full utilization of these projects; rights acquired by the allottees were taken subject to this reservation.
>
> That because of drought during 1931 to 1934, and respondents' diversion of waters upstream from the projects so initiated, the available water became insufficient properly to irrigate some 8,000 acres lying therein and under cultivation. Accordingly the injunction should be granted; all waters from the two streams had been devoted to those and similarly situated lands so far as necessary for farming operations.

[Powers et al.] maintain that under the Treaty of 1868 waters within the Reservation were reserved for the equal benefit of tribal members and that when allotments of land were duly made for exclusive use and thereafter conveyed in fee, the right to use some portion of tribal waters essential for cultivation passed to the owners.

The [Powers et al.] claim to the extent stated is well founded.

Manifestly the Treaty of 1868 contemplated ultimate settlement by individual Indians upon designated tracts where they could make homes with exclusive right of cultivation for their support and with expectation of ultimate complete ownership. Without water productive cultivation has always been impossible.

We can find nothing in the statutes after 1868 adequate to show Congressional intent to permit allottees to be denied participation in the use of waters essential to farming and home making. If possible, legislation subsequent to the Treaty must be interpreted in harmony with its plain purposes.

The Secretary of the Interior had authority (Act 1887) [Dawes Act] to prescribe rules and regulations deemed necessary to secure just and equal distribution of waters. It does not appear that he ever undertook so to do. Certainly he could not affirmatively authorize unjust and unequal distribution. The statute itself clearly indicates Congressional recognition of equal rights among resident Indians.

Adoption by the Secretary of plans for irrigation projects to serve certain lands was not enough to indicate a purpose to exclude all other land from participation in essential water and thereby destroy the equal interest guaranteed by the Treaty. Subsequent allotments for farming followed by patents negative any such notion. The patented lands had no value for agriculture without water; they were selected for homes and individual farming.

The [United States has] shown no right to the injunction asked. We do not consider the extent or precise nature of [Powers et al.'s] rights in the waters. The present proceeding is not properly framed to that end.

The challenged decree must be affirmed.

Mr. Justice REED took no part in the consideration or decision of this case

Notes & Questions

1. The Court bases its decision that allottees are entitled to a portion of the reserved water rights of the Reservation on the following findings. Which of these findings are unique to facts relevant to the Crow Reservation and which are applicable to any reservation allotted under the Dawes Act?
   a. Congress authorized the Secretary "to prescribe rules and regulations deemed necessary to secure just and equal distribution of waters."
   b. "The Treaty of 1868 contemplated ultimate settlement by individual Indians upon designated tracts where they could make homes with exclusive right of cultivation for their support and with expectation of ultimate complete ownership. Without water productive cultivation has always been impossible."
2. The Court does not reach the question of how much water an Indian allottee is entitled to. You will learn in the next case the concept of awarding allottees a *pro rata* share (also referred to as "ratable" share) in proportion to the number of irrigable acres on the allotment. For example, if there were 100 practicably irrigable acres on a reservation and an allottee owned 10 practicably irrigable acres within their allotment, then they would be entitled to 10% of the total water reserved for irrigation on the reservation.

Non-Indian Land Acquired from an Allottee

Powers left unanswered the question of whether the allottee could pass their share of the reserved water right to a non-Indian. That issue became increasingly pressing as more tribal lands passed into non-Indian hands. Despite its importance, the U.S. Supreme Court has not had occasion to address the issue of non-Indian acquisition of allotted land within a reservation. Nevertheless, the Ninth Circuit Court of Appeals faced this issue in *Colville Confederated Tribes v. Walton*, 647 F.2d 42 (9th Cir. 1981), a case you have already seen in Chapter 10, focusing on the portion of the case addressing the purpose(s) of a reservation. That case originated in the No Name Creek Basin of the Colville Reservation in Northeastern Washington (Figure 12.1). Importantly, in the absence of a U.S. Supreme Court ruling, state courts and settlement processes that have addressed the issue of non-Indian water rights for a former allotment have followed the *Colville* case even outside the region of the Ninth Circuit. The following excerpt from an article by Professor Hedden-Nicely will refresh your memory on the setting of the *Colville* case.

> The Confederated Tribes of the Colville Reservation "traditionally fished for both salmon and trout," which were of "economic and religious importance to them." However, by the middle of the twentieth century "[t]he Tribe's principal historic fishing grounds on the Columbia River [had] been destroyed by dams." In response, the Colville Tribes set out to build a replacement fishery within the Colville Reservation. The Tribes and United States eventually determined to establish a Lahonton cutthroat trout fishery in Omak Lake. Lahon-

(a)

Figure 12.1: (a) Colville Indian Reservation showing the large areas of fee ownership of land due to allotment; (b) Map showing No Name Creek Basin on the Colville Reservation. Tribal allotments are shown in diagonal lines, and the allotments of Walton are shown in stippled pattern. Source: (a) Graphic design by Melissa Svancara; (b) Graphic design by Leilanee Taylor.

(b)

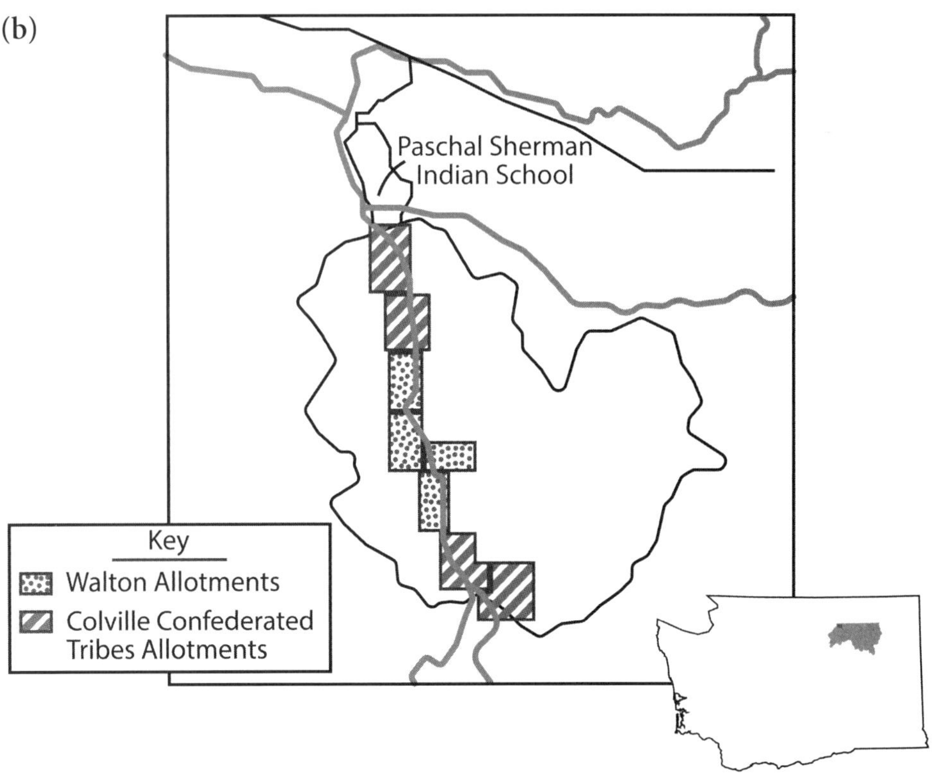

> ton trout evolved primarily within terminal saline lakes within the Great Basin of the United States. As a result, they spend the majority of their lives in saline lakes but then migrate into freshwater streams to spawn. Omak Lake within the Colville Reservation is a terminus lake, which causes it to be saline. A number of freshwater streams flow into Omak Lake, including No Name Creek. Resultantly, the Omak Lake/No Name Creek watershed provided ideal habitat for Lahonton trout.
>
> . . .
>
> [However,] The Confederated Tribes were not the only ones in need of water in the No Name Creek Basin. Boyd and Kenna Joan Walton acquired three allotments along No Name Creek in 1948 [*See* Figure 12.1(b)] and by the early 1970s they were irrigating 105 acres with water from groundwater wells that were hydrologically connected to No Name Creek. Additionally, the Waltons operated a dairy farm and used No Name Creek for stock watering. The impact on the Lahonton fishery was twofold. First, the Waltons, along with competing consumptive uses by the Confederated Tribes, caused there to be insufficient flows in No Name Creek during the irrigation season for trout migration, spawning, and rearing. Second, runoff from the Walton dairy feedlot caused the stream to become contaminated, which buried the spawning beds and suffocated the eggs. As a result, the Tribes and the United States brought suit against the Waltons, "seek[ing] to enjoin the Waltons' interference with tribal use of No Name Creek Basin Waters."[7]

The Waltons began diverting water and putting it to beneficial use in 1948, which would have been their priority date under state law. That date would be junior to the Colville Tribes' water rights for irrigation and instream flows, requiring the Waltons to curtail their use in times of shortage. Instead of claiming a state law water right, however, the Waltons claimed that they acquired the portion of the Tribes' reserved water right associated with the allotments they had purchased from an Indian allotee. Thus, the primary issue in *Walton* was whether allotee water rights run with the land. Stated from the viewpoint the court took in addressing the issue: may an Indian allottee alienate the portion of the reserved water right associated with an allotment to a non-Indian? This case also addresses the difficult issue of who has regulatory jurisdiction over the non-Indian water use on what is now fee land within the reservation. Pay particular attention to the specific facts that lead the court to its conclusion.

---

7. Dylan R. Hedden-Nicely, *The Historical Evolution of the Methodology for Quantifying Federal Reserved Water Rights for American Indian Tribes,* 50 Envtl. L. 205 (2019) (internal citations omitted).

Colville Confederated Tribes v. Walton

United States Court of Appeals, Ninth Circuit
647 F.2d 42 (1981)

Opinion

WRIGHT, Circuit Judge:—...

The Colville Confederated Tribes initiated this case a decade ago. They sought to enjoin Walton, non-Indian owner of allotted lands, from using surface and ground waters in the No Name Creek basin....

I. BACKGROUND

...

... President Grant created the Colville Reservation. Executive Order of July 2, 1872. Twenty years later, the northern half of the reservation was taken from the Indians and opened for entry and settlement.

In 1906, Congress ratified an agreement with the Colvilles that provided for distribution of reservation lands to the Indians pursuant to the General Allotment Act of 1887 and for disposition of the remainder by entry and settlement. The agreement was effectuated by Presidential proclamation in 1916.

[From the District Court opinion in this case: "Water from the No Name Creek basin presently serves seven parcels of land, all at one time allotted to individual Indians. The only lands within the basin presently held by non-Indians are the three allotments owned in fee by Waltons, each of which borders No Name Creek. The other four allotments in the basin are either held in trust by the United States for the heirs of the allottees and leased to the Tribe or are held in trust directly for the benefit of the Tribe. Historically, the two allotments to the north of Waltons were irrigated with surface waters from Omak Creek located on the northernmost allotment, while the two allotments south of Waltons were irrigated with waters diverted from No Name Creek." *Colville Confederated Tribes v. Walton*, 460 F.Supp. 1320 (E.D. Wash. 1978)]

....

B.

The No Name Creek is a spring-fed creek flowing south into Omak Lake, which has no outlet and is saline. The No Name hydrological system, consisting of an underground aquifer and the creek, is located entirely on the Colville Reservation.

...

C.

Salmon and trout were traditional foods for the Colville Indians, but the salmon runs have been destroyed by dams on the Columbia River. In 1968, the Tribe, with the help of the Department of the Interior, introduced Lahonton cutthroat trout into Omak Lake. The species thrives in the lake's saline water, but needs fresh water to spawn. The Indians cultivated No Name Creek's lower reach to establish spawning grounds but irrigation use depleted the water flow during spawning season. The federal government has given the Indians fingerlings to maintain the stock of trout.

...

III. THE TRIBE'S WATER RIGHTS

[This section on the quantification of the Tribe's water right was presented in Chapter 10.]

IV. THE GENERAL ALLOTMENT ACT OF 1887

We next consider Walton's rights as the fee owner of allotted land, and reverse the district court's judgment that he has no right to reserved water.

A.

The General Allotment Act provided that land on reservations could be allotted for the exclusive use of individual Indians. Remaining land was to be made available for homesteading by non-Indians. After holding allotted lands in trust for individual Indians for a 25-year period, the federal government could convey the land to the allottee in fee, "discharged of said trust and free of all charge or incumbrance whatsoever." 25 U.S.C. s 348.

Because the use of reserved water is not limited to fulfilling the original purposes of the reservation, Congress had the power to allot reserved water rights to individual Indians, and to allow for the transfer of such rights to non-Indians. Whether it did so is a question of Congressional intent.

The General Allotment Act represented the shift in federal objectives from segregation of Indians on reservations to assimilation of them in non-Indian culture and society. Its primary sponsor, Senator Dawes, explained that "the quicker (the Indian) is mingled with the whites in every particular the better it will be."

The Act was designed to encourage Indians to become self-supporting citizens by making them landowners. Allotted lands were held in trust for a 25-year period because of

> the desire to protect the Indian against sharp practices leading to Indian landlessness, the desire to safeguard the certainty of titles, and the urge to continue an important basis of governmental activity (on the Indians' behalf).

F. Cohen, Handbook of Federal Indian Law 221 (1940); U.S. Department of Interior, Federal Indian Law 788–89 (1958).

The only reference to water rights in the Act is found in section 7:

> In cases where the use of water for irrigation is necessary to render the lands within any Indian reservation available for agricultural purposes, the Secretary of the Interior is authorized to prescribe such rules and regulations as he may deem necessary to secure a just and equal distribution thereof among the Indians residing upon any such reservation; and no other appropriation or

> grant of water by an riparian proprietor shall be authorized or permitted to the damage of any other riparian proprietor.

25 U.S.C. s 381.

The Act was passed over 20 years before the Supreme Court announced the implied-reservation doctrine in *Winters*. There is nothing to suggest Congress gave any consideration to the transferability of reserved water rights. To resolve this issue, we must determine what Congress would have intended had it considered it.

B.

It is settled that Indian allottees have a right to use reserved water. *United States v. Powers,* 305 U.S. 527 (1939). "(W)hen allotments were made for exclusive use and thereafter conveyed in fee, the right to use some portion of tribal waters essential for cultivation passed to the owners." We must determine whether non-Indian purchasers of allotted lands also obtain a right to some portion of reserved waters.

(1)

The general rule is that termination or diminution of Indian rights requires express legislation or a clear inference of Congressional intent gleaned from the surrounding circumstances and legislative history.... Upon careful consideration, we conclude this principle supports the proposition that an Indian allottee may sell his right to reserved water.

The district court's holding that an Indian allottee may convey only a right to the water he or she has actually appropriated with a priority date of actual appropriation reduces the value of the allottee's right to reserved water. We think this type of restriction on transferability is a "diminution of Indian rights" that must be supported by a clear inference of Congressional intent.

By placing allotted lands in trust for 25 years, Congress evinced an intent to protect Indians by preventing transfer of those lands. But there is no basis for an inference that some restrictions survived beyond the trust period. Congress provided for extensions of the trust period, but directed that fee title be conveyed to the allottee when the period expired. We think the fee included the appurtenant right to share in reserved waters, and see no basis for limiting the transferability of that right.

This conclusion is supported by our decision in *United States v. Ahtanum Irrigation District*, 236 F.2d 321, 342 (9th Cir. 1956). Ahtanum held that non-Indian purchasers of allotted lands are entitled to "participate ratably" with Indian allottees in the use of reserved water....

(2)

In determining the nature of the right acquired by non-Indian purchasers, we consider three aspects of an allottee's right to use reserved waters.

First, the extent of an Indian allottee's right is based on the number of irrigable acres he owns. If the allottee owns 10% of the irrigable acreage in the watershed, he is entitled to 10% of the water reserved for irrigation (i.e., a "ratable share"). This follows from the provision for an equal and just distribution of water needed for irrigation.

A non-Indian purchaser cannot acquire more extensive rights to reserved water than were held by the Indian seller. Thus, the purchaser's right is similarly limited by the number of irrigable acres he owns.

Second, the Indian allottee's right has a priority as of the date the reservation was created. This is the principal aspect of the right that renders it more valuable than the rights of competing water users, and therefore applies to the right acquired by a non-Indian purchaser. In the event there is insufficient water to satisfy all valid claims to reserved water, the amount available to each claimant should be reduced proportionately.

Third, the Indian allottee does not lose by non-use the right to a share of reserved water. This characteristic is not applicable to the right acquired by a non-Indian purchaser. The non-Indian successor acquires a right to water being appropriated by the Indian allottee at the time title passes. The non-Indian also acquires a right, with a date-of-reservation priority date, to water that he or she appropriates with reasonable diligence after the passage of title. If the full measure of the Indian's reserved water right is not acquired by this means and maintained by continued use, it is lost to the non-Indian successor.

The full quantity of water available to the Indian allottee thus may be conveyed to the non-Indian purchaser. There is no diminution in the right the Indian may convey. We think Congress would have intended, however, that the non-Indian purchaser, under no competitive disability vis-a-vis other water users, may not retain the right to that quantity of water despite non-use. See *United States v. Adair*, 478 F.Supp. at 348–49; *United States v. Hibner*, 27 F.2d at 912.

C.

The district court's holding that Walton has no right to share in water reserved when the Colville reservation was created is reversed. On remand, it will need to determine the number of irrigable acres Walton owns, and the amount of water he appropriated with reasonable diligence in order to determine the extent of his right to share in reserved water.

...

V. STATE PERMITS

...

A.

State regulatory authority over a tribal reservation may be barred either because it is pre-empted by federal law, or because it unlawfully infringes on the right of reservation Indians to self-government.... Although these barriers are independent, they are related by the concept of tribal sovereignty. "The tradition of Indian sovereignty over the reservation and tribal members must inform the determination whether the exercise of state authority has been pre-empted by operation of federal law."

Indian tribes are unique aggregations possessing attributes of sovereignty over both their members and their territory....

A tribe's inherent power to regulate generally the conduct of non-members on land no longer owned by, or held in trust for the tribe was impliedly withdrawn as a necessary result of its dependent status. Montana v. United States, 450 U.S. 544 (1981). Exceptions to this implied withdrawal exist. A tribe retains the inherent power to exercise civil authority over the conduct of non-Indians on fee lands within its reservation when that conduct threatens or has some direct effect on the health and welfare of the tribe. Id. This includes conduct that involves the tribe's water rights.

A water system is a unitary resource. The actions of one user have an immediate and direct effect on other users. The Colvilles' complaint in the district court alleged that the Waltons' appropriations from No Name Creek imperiled the agricultural use of downstream tribal lands and the trout fishery, among other things. Cf. Montana, 450 U.S. at 544 complaint did not allege peril to subsistence or welfare of tribe from non-Indian hunting and fishing on fee lands).

Regulation of water on a reservation is critical to the lifestyle of its residents and the development of its resources. Especially in arid and semi-arid regions of the West, water is the lifeblood of the community. Its regulation is an important sovereign power.

Although we need not decide whether this power resides exclusively in the tribe or the federal government, or whether it may be exercised by them jointly, its importance forms the backdrop for our consideration of the pre-emption issue.

B.

We hold that state regulation of water in the No Name system was pre-empted by the creation of the Colville Reservation. The geographic facts of this case make resolution of this issue somewhat easier than it otherwise might be. The No-Name system is non-navigable and is entirely within the boundaries of the reservation. Although some of the water passes through lands now in non-Indian ownership, all of those lands are also entirely within the reservation boundaries.

The Supreme Court has held that water use on a federal reservation is not subject to state regulation absent explicit federal recognition of state authority. Federal Power Commission v. Oregon, 349 U.S. 435 (1955). Thus, in creating the Colville Reservation, the federal government pre-empted state control of the No Name system.

...

I. CONCLUSION

On remand, the district court will calculate the respective rights of the parties. To the extent Walton's use of water exceeds his rights and interferes with the rights of the tribe, it will be enjoined.

REVERSED IN PART, AFFIRMED IN PART, AND REMANDED for proceedings in conformance with this opinion....

Notes & Questions

1. What is the basis and where does the court look to determine if Walton, a non-Indian, acquired any of the Colville Reservation's reserved water rights on acquisition of an Indian allotment that had gone into fee status?
2. What is the measure, priority, and status of the water rights held by Walton? How does that differ from a state-based right under prior appropriation?
3. If the Waltons do not use the full amount to which they are entitled, who should be entitled to the use and control the balance of that reserved water right?
4. Do you agree with the Court's assessment that restricting the transferability of water rights affects a "diminution" of Indian allottees' rights? What about the diminution of the rights of the tribe as a whole that results from this rule?
5. The court holds that Walton's claims under state permits are not valid, because creation of the Colville Reservation preempted state jurisdiction. Which of the following, according to the court, informs this conclusion?
   a. The Tribe's inherent territorial sovereignty
   b. The presumption that non-Indians on non-Indian land within a reservation fall within state jurisdiction is overcome in this case by the exceptions to that rule. In this case, water is essential to the health and welfare of the Tribe.

c. Water is a unitary resource, thus the actions of one water user affects other water users.

Non-Indian Water Rights Associated with Land Homesteaded within the Reservation/Water Rights on Lands Reacquired by Tribes

On some of the larger reservations, land that could support a farm remained after allotment. This so called "surplus" land was opened to homesteading. Once again, the Ninth Circuit, in *United States v. Anderson*, 736 F.2d 1358 (9th Cir. 1984), addresses the water rights of homesteaders within the reservation. The issue comes up in the context of reacquisition of the land by the Tribe, so must also address the question of what sort of water right comes with the reacquired land. Pay attention to how the court distinguishes both the nature of the homesteaders' right and the regulatory jurisdiction over it from *Colville*. Similar to *Colville*, in the absence of a U.S. Supreme Court ruling, state courts and settlements have followed the Ninth Circuit ruling.

Anderson arose out of a water dispute on the Spokane Reservation, which is located directly across the Columbia River from the Colville Reservation in eastern Washington. Congress passed the Spokane Allotment Act in 1908, which allotted to each tribal member 160 acres of reservation land. Once each tribal member received their allotment, much of the land allotted ended up in non-Indian hands. The land remaining after each member received their allotment was declared "surplus" and made available to non-Indians for homesteading. By the time of the case, the Tribe had required many allotments that had been sold to non-Indians, as well as "surplus" lands that had been previously homesteaded by non-Indians. The primary issue the Ninth Circuit faced was whether these lands continued to have water rights associated with them and, if so, what their priority dates should be.

United States v. Anderson

United States Court of Appeals, Ninth Circuit
736 F.2d 1358 (1984)

Opinion

J. BLAINE ANDERSON, Circuit Judge:—The United States of America appeals a district court's determination that water rights appurtenant to certain reservation lands which passed out of trust status but which have subsequently been reacquired by the Spokane Tribe of Indians are entitled to a priority date as of the date of reacquisition by the Spokane Tribe. The Spokane Tribe also appeals, urging that the district court erred in holding that the State of Washington had regulatory jurisdiction over use of water by non-Indians on non-Indian land within the Spokane Indian Reservation. We affirm in part and reverse in part and remand for further proceedings in accordance with this decision.

I. BACKGROUND

This action was originally filed in 1972 by the United States, acting on its own behalf and as trustee for the Spokane Tribe of Indians (Tribe), pursuant to 28 U.S.C. § 1345 (1976). The Tribe was permitted to intervene as a plaintiff. Defendants include the State of Washington, acting in its governmental and proprietary capacities, and all other persons or corporations who might have an interest in the disputed water rights which were the subject of the litigation.

The plaintiffs sought an adjudication of water rights in the Chamokane Basin, a hydrological system including Chamokane Creek, its tributaries and its ground water basin. The waters of the Chamokane Basin are not wholly within the Spokane Indian Reservation; Chamokane Creek originates north of the reservation and flows south along the eastern boundary. The creek leaves the reservation by discharging into the Spokane River which, in turn, joins with the Columbia River and flows into the Pacific Ocean. A water master for the Chamokane Basin has been appointed, according to the terms of a judgment entered on September 12, 1979, by the Honorable Marshall A. Neill, United States District Judge.

The Spokane Indian Reservation is not exclusively owned and resided upon by Indians. Non-Indian settlement has occurred there, encouraged by various federal programs authorizing allotment of reservation lands to individual Indians and opening excess land to homesteading by non-Indians. Some land opened for homesteading was never claimed and was subsequently restored to the Tribe by the Act of May 19, 1958, 72 Stat. 121. Some of the reservation land was homesteaded by non-Indians and some former Indian allotments passed into non-Indian ownership; much of this property has been reacquired by the Tribe and returned to trust status pursuant to the Act of June 10, 1968, 82 Stat. 174, codified as amended at 25 U.S.C. § 487. This vacillation of land ownership provides a framework for the instant controversy.

II. DISCUSSION

Three general categories of reservation land are involved here: lands now owned in fee by non-Indians; lands which never left trust status; and lands removed from trust status which were subsequently reacquired by the Tribe and returned to that status. This later category, that of lands reacquired by the Tribe and returned to trust status, includes (1) lands opened to homesteading which were never claimed; (2) lands allotted to individual Indians who later sold their parcels to non-Indians; and (3) lands opened for homesteading which were acquired by non-Indians.

Changes in the ownership of lands within the Spokane Indian Reservation created doubts regarding the priority dates of the water rights appurtenant to those lands. Additionally, a question has arisen regarding the regulatory jurisdiction of the State of Washington concerning allocation of excess Chamokane Basin Water rights within the reservation and appurtenant to non-Indian lands.

A. *Priority Dates for Reacquired Lands.*

The district court awarded a priority as of the date of the creation of the reservation to those water rights appurtenant to land which never left trust status and those water rights appurtenant to lands opened for homesteading which were never claimed. This award was based on the doctrine of tribal reserved *Winters* rights and is not at issue here.

Those water rights appurtenant to lands reacquired by the Tribe following allotment and sale to non-Indians or homesteading were awarded a priority date as of reacquisition by the Tribe. The United States takes issue with this determination. We hold that those perfected water rights appurtenant to homesteaded lands will not have a priority as of the date of reacquisition of the property by the Tribe; instead, they will carry a priority as determined under state law. Homesteaded lands where the water right has not been perfected or the rights have been lost, will have a priority date as of the date of reacquisition, rather than an original, date-of-the-reservation priority. We hold that those water rights appurtenant to lands reacquired after allotment and sale to non-Indians carry a priority date, as to those water rights not lost to nonuse, as of the date of creation of reservation.

1. *The alloted lands.*

[The court follows the ruling in the preceding case of *Colville Confederated Tribes v. Walton,* 647 F.2d 42, 50 (9th Cir.1981) for the water right associated with allotted lands.]

...

The *Walton* decision makes it clear that reserved *Winters* rights do not cease to exist merely because the land passes out of Indian ownership. The Ninth Circuit held that the full quantity of water available to the Indian allottee thus may be conveyed to the non-Indian purchaser. It follows that upon reacquisition of these lands, the Tribe is equally entitled to an original priority date. We find, therefore, that *Winters* rights appurtenant to allotted lands conveyed to a non-Indian purchaser will pass with title upon reacquisition by the Tribe and will retain their original priority date.

The Ninth Circuit has restricted its rule concerning the transfer of reserved rights appurtenant to allotted lands. The first restriction is that "the non-Indian successor's right to water is 'limited by the number of irrigable acres [of former reservation lands that] he owns.'" The second restriction may be simply expressed as: use it or lose it. Pursuant to this restriction, a non-Indian successor acquires a right to that quantity of water being utilized at the time title passes, plus that amount of water which the successor puts to beneficial use with reasonable diligence following the transfer of title. Where "the full measure of the Indian's reserved water right is not acquired by this means and maintained through continued use, it is lost to the non-Indian successor." Consequently, on reacquisition the Tribe reacquires only those rights which have not been lost through nonuse and those rights will have an original, date-of-the-reservation priority.

2. *The homesteaded properties.*

The Supreme Court has determined that a homesteader acquires no federal water rights incident to the transfer of public lands into private ownership. *California Oregon Power Co. v. Beaver Portland Cement Co.,* 295 U.S. 142 (1935). Application of this rule to the case before us would terminate the availability of *Winters* rights on those reservation lands which have been declared public domain, opened to homesteading, and subsequently conveyed into private ownership. This result is supported by the fact that *Winters* rights were only intended to assist in accomplishing the needs of the reservation; where the land has been removed from the Tribe's possession and conveyed to a homesteader, the purposes for which *Winters* rights were implied are eliminated. Therefore, a homesteader is not entitled to rely on the *Winters* doctrine. The appropriation doctrine will serve as the source of his water rights. *See California Oregon Power Co.,* 295 U.S. at 164 (Desert Land Act gives sanction to appropriation doctrine, seeking to remove impediment to its successful operation).

It is a basic tenet of western water law that water rights perfected through appropriation and not subsequently lost to nonuse or abandonment will generally pass with transfer of title to real property and will carry a priority date as of their original application to beneficial use. We see no reason to depart from this rule as to the perfected water rights of homesteaders on reacquisition of the property by the Tribe. As to lands in this category, state law determines the priority date.

Where the homesteader has no perfected water rights or has lost rights which were perfected, there are no rights to be regained by the Indians on reacquisition of the property. This principle protects the intervening rights, if any, that may have been acquired in good faith by third party water users during the homesteading process and prior to reacquisition by the Tribe. On return of the property to tribal status, it becomes necessary to utilize the *Winters* doctrine to assure that the Tribe has sufficient water to "fulfill the very purposes for which [the] reservation was created." We treat these lands in a manner analogous to that of a newly created federal reservation and find that the purposes for which *Winters* rights are implied arise at the time of reacquisition by the Tribe.... Therefore, we hold that the Tribe is entitled to an implication of *Winters* rights with a priority for these rights as of the date of reacquisition, rather than an original, date-of-the-reservation priority....

III. CONCLUSION

For the foregoing reasons, we AFFIRM in part and REVERSE in part and REMAND for further proceedings in accordance with this decision.

Notes & Questions

1. What is the basis and where does the court look to determine if a non-Indian that has acquired a former allotment acquired any of the Spokane Reservation's reserved water right? What important limitation is placed on the right while in the ownership of the non-Indian? How do these results affect the right the Tribe is able to reacquire?
2. What quantity is a subsequent purchaser of a former allotment entitled to? What do you think should happen to the excess water if the subsequent purchaser has failed to use the full quantity of water they are entitled to under *Walton* and *Anderson*?
3. What is the basis and where does the court look to determine if a non-Indian homesteader acquired any of the Spokane Reservation's reserved water right?
4. What is the measure, priority, and status of the water right held by the homesteader?
5. What water rights does the Tribe have on reacquisition of allotted land? Homesteaded land?
6. What policy is the Court upholding in coming to these rules? Who do these rules privilege?
7. Is the Court's holding consistent with the Indian canons of construction and the usual presumptions against the abrogation of tribal treaty rights? Should it be Congress or the courts that develop the policy related to Indian affairs and rights? Can you find congressional intent to alter tribal water rights and priority dates?
8. The court holds that state jurisdiction applies to use of excess water by non-Indians on non-Indian-owned land within the reservation. Which of the following, according to the court, informs this conclusion?
    a. The Tribe's sovereignty over its reserved water right is protected.
    b. The presumption that non-Indians on non-Indian land within a reservation fall within state jurisdiction is not overcome in this case by the exceptions to that rule. In this case, the health, welfare, and political integrity of the Tribe will not be affected.
    c. The water source in question, unlike that in *Colville,* is not solely within the Reservation boundaries, and is navigable.

Chapter 13

The Federal Common Law Attributes of Reserved Water Rights: Groundwater

Introduction

The U.S. Supreme Court has never addressed the question of whether the reserved water rights doctrine extends to groundwater. Recall from earlier chapters in this Part that *Winters* addressed the question of water rights from the Milk River, *Arizona v. California* was an adjudication of water rights from the Colorado River, and *Nevada v. United States* concerned the Truckee River. Also recall from Part II that state common law struggles with the nature of the connection between surface and groundwater with the result being variable treatment of groundwater by states, and general treatment of it as a separate resource from surface water.

This Chapter begins with a review of statements by federal district courts followed by the Ninth Circuit, suggesting that federal law might treat groundwater the same as surface water, allowing either to be the source for a reserved water right. These cases, however, either did not require the courts to reach the question of whether the doctrine of reserved water rights extend to groundwater, were vacated after settlement, or are no longer precedent due to contrary law on another issue. This Chapter then turns to state court pronouncements on the issue. In Part VI, you will learn why state courts have jurisdiction to make a determination like this regarding rights recognized by federal law; however, a brief overview of the rulings on groundwater are relevant here to illustrate the confusion that may occur when an issue of federal law has not been decided. This Chapter concludes with the first Circuit Court case (again from the Ninth Circuit) with the question of a reserved right to groundwater directly before it—a ruling that was then denied cert by the U.S. Supreme Court.

Hints from the Federal District Courts

This section covers a sampling of federal district court statements on the reserved right to groundwater.

In *Tweedy v. Texas Co.*, 286 F. Supp. 383 (D. Mont. 1968), the federal district court for Montana had to decide whether state or federal law applied to a dispute over the impacts of oil and gas development on groundwater within the boundaries of the Blackfeet Reservation. In determining that federal law controlled, the court stated that although "[t]he *Winters* case dealt only with the surface water ... the same implications which led the Supreme Court to hold that surface waters had been reserved would apply to underground waters as well."[1] The land in question was an allotment and had passed out of Indian ownership and, while not entirely clear from the case, it appears the groundwater wells affected were developed after the land was in non-Indian ownership. The *Tweedy* case was decided before the 1981 case of *Walton* (a case you read in Chapter 12) determined that once the land passed out of Indian ownership, new development of water would take place under state law, thus the determination that federal law controlled in *Tweedy* was in error and the statement that *Winters* applies to groundwater was rendered unnecessary.

More recently, the Western District of Washington had the question of whether reserved water rights extend to groundwater directly before it. This ruling was *vacated* by agreement of the parties on approval of a settlement between the Lummi Nation and the State of Washington regarding groundwater, and thus carries no precedential value. Nevertheless, it is useful to look at the statements by the court. First, the court looks to one of the state court rulings covered later in this Part, and states:

> *In re General Adjudication of All Rights to Use Water in Gila River System & Source,* 989 P.2d 739, 748 (Ariz. 1999) ("*Gila River III* "), where the Court held that "[a] reserved right to groundwater may only be found where other waters are inadequate to accomplish the purpose of a reservation." The Court is unaware, however, of any federal precedent that would require adherence to *Gila River III*, permitting reserved groundwater rights only where surface waters are inadequate to provide for the needs of the Reservation. [fn 8]

United States v. Washington, 375 F. Supp. 2d 1050, 1068 (W.D. Wash. 2005). Thus, the court agreed with the Arizona Supreme Court that reserved rights extend to groundwater, but rejected the limitation that court applied that would allow it only if there is insufficient surface water.

Footnote 8 included the language of an earlier unpublished opinion on the same case between the Lummi Nation and the state of Washington. The footnote states:

> [This] Court ruled previously that "as a matter of law ... the reserved water rights doctrine extends to [Case Area] groundwater even if groundwater is not

1. *Tweedy*, 286 F. Supp. at 385.

connected to surface water," finding that federal reserved water rights law would not differentiate between surface and groundwater in identifying reserved waters. See Order, docket no. 304, at 8; see also Felix S. Cohen, Handbook of Federal Indian Law, at 585–86 (1982) ("Rights [to reserved water] should attach to all water sources-groundwater basins, streams, lakes, and springs ...").[2]

Hints from the Ninth Circuit Court of Appeals

The Ninth Circuit in *Colville Confederated Tribes v. Walton*, 647 F.2d 42 (9th Cir. 1981) (addressed in Chapter 12 in this Part), recognized that surface and ground water may be a single water source, stating:

> "The No Name Creek is a spring-fed creek flowing south into Omak Lake, which has no outlet and is saline. The No Name hydrological system, consisting of an underground aquifer and the creek, is located entirely on the Colville Reservation.
>
> "The aquifer lies under the Indians' northern allotments and the northern tip of Walton's allotment ..."

Walton, 647 F.2d at 45. Thus, the court recognizes the absence of a physical separation between surface and groundwater. However, the dispute in that case concerned the diversions affecting the waters of No Name Creek and Omak Lake—i.e., surface water resources.

The Ninth Circuit in *United States v. Cappaert,* 508 F.2d 313 (9th Cir. 1975) found that the water rights reserved for a federal, non-Indian reservation (the topic of federal non-Indian reservations is explored in Part IV, and you will read the U.S. Supreme Court opinion on the case) could be protected by an injunction against pumping of connected groundwater. The case involved a groundwater-fed pool exposed in a cave at Devil's Hole National Monument in Nevada, which was being drawn down by groundwater pumping for irrigation two miles from the Monument. The court states: "[i]n our view the United States may reserve not only surface water, but also underground water." *Cappaert,* 508 F.2d at 317. However, as you will learn in greater detail when you read the case in Part IV, the Supreme Court did not affirm that aspect of the Ninth Circuit opinion. Instead, it sidestepped the issue, finding that although it was hydrologically connected to groundwater, the pool of water that made up Devil's Hole was entirely surface water. Thus, the issue of whether a reserved right to groundwater was created on establishment of the Monument need not be reached. Nonetheless, the Court held that a reservation of a surface water resource can be protected from groundwater pumping that affects it by stating that "the United States can protect its

2. United States v. Washington, 375 F. Supp. 2d 1050, 1068, n. 8 (W.D. Wash. 2005).

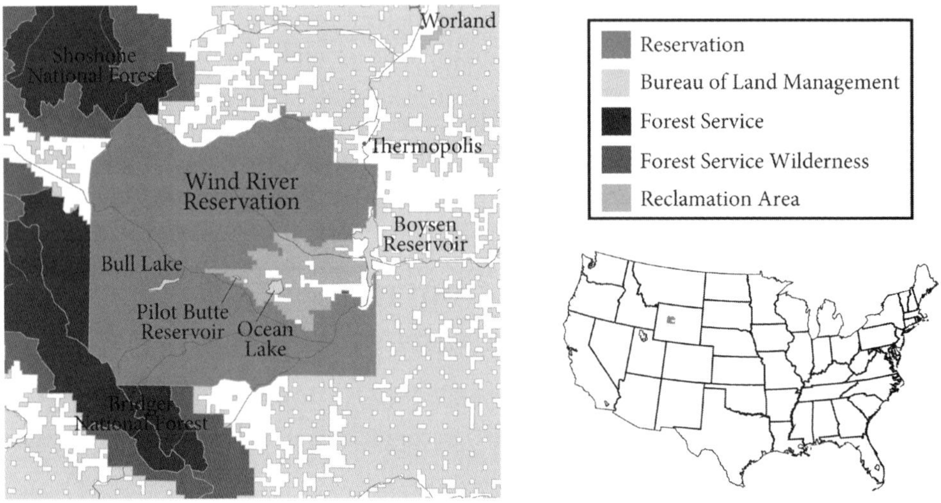

Figure 13.1 Wind River Reservation showing the major drainages and water bodies as well as a Reclamation project within the boundaries of the Reservation. The Big Horn River basin adjudication in Wyoming addressed the water rights for the Shoshone and Northern Arapaho Tribes of the Wind River Reservation. Source: Modified from USGS, Arapaho Tribe of the Wind River Reservation, Wyoming, nationalatlas.gov. https://data.nativemi.org/tribal-directory/Details/arapaho-tribe-of-the-wind-river-reservation-wyoming-198754.

water from subsequent diversion, whether that diversion is of surface or groundwater." *Cappaert v. United States*, 426 U.S. 128, 143 (1976).

State Court Pronouncements on Federal Common Law

As noted above, you will learn in Part VI that, due to a waiver of sovereign immunity by Congress, the United States may be joined in a general adjudication of water rights (one that involves all claims to water from a particular watershed) in state court. You will read the cases that determine this waiver extends to the United States in its role as the party who holds Indian land and resources in trust for the tribes. Thus, several state courts have had occasion to consider the issue of whether reserved water rights extend to groundwater.

With a single exception, state courts have universally held that reserved water rights may extend to groundwater. That exception comes from the Wyoming Supreme Court, which held that the reserved water doctrine does not extend to groundwater.

Wyoming

Wyoming's adjudication of the water rights in the Big Horn River basin included the reserved water rights of the eastern Shoshone and Northern Arapaho tribes of the Wind River Reservation (Figure 13.1). The Wyoming Supreme Court's decision that reserved water rights do not extend to groundwater seems to have been based primarily on the absence of U.S. Supreme Court precedent and, thus, the fear of being the first to extend the doctrine to groundwater. The struggle the court faced is evident in the following excerpt from the opinion. Note also the discussion of the cases mentioned in the previous section. The excerpt does not include the facts of the case and focuses only on the issue of whether a reserved right to groundwater is possible under federal law.

In re the General Adjudication of All Rights to Use Water in the Big Horn River System

Wyoming Supreme Court
753 P.2d 76 (1988)

Before BROWN, C.J., and THOMAS, CARDINE, and MACY, JJ., and HANSCUM, District Judge

. . .

A. *Groundwater*

The logic which supports a reservation of surface water to fulfill the purpose of the reservation also supports reservation of groundwater. See *Tweedy v. Texas Company,* 286 F.Supp. 383, 385 (D.Mont.1968) ("whether the [necessary] waters were found on the surface of the land or under it should make no difference"). Certainly the two sources are often interconnected. See § 41-3-916, W.S.1977 (where underground and surface waters are "so interconnected as to constitute in fact one source of supply," a single schedule of priorities shall be made); Final Report to the President and to the Congress by the National Water Commission, Water Policies for the Future 233 (1973) (groundwater and surface water "often naturally related"); *Cappaert v. United States,* supra 426 U.S. at 142–143 (citing additional authority to this effect).

Acknowledging the above, we note that, nonetheless, not a single case applying the reserved water doctrine to groundwater is cited to us. The ninth circuit indicated that groundwater was reserved in *United States v. Cappaert,* 508 F.2d 313, 317 (9th Cir.1974). The United States Supreme Court, however, found the water in the pool reserved for preservation of the pupfish was not groundwater but surface water, protected from subsequent diversions from either surface or groundwater supplies. *Cappaert v. United States,* supra 426 U.S. at 143. Nor have the other cases cited to us granted a reserved right in underground water. In *Colville Confederated Tribes v. Walton,* supra 647 F.2d 42, there is slight mention of the underground aquifer and of pumping wells, *Id.* at 52, but the opinion does not indicate that "their wells" are a source of reserved water or even discuss a reserved groundwater right. *Tweedy v. Texas Company,* supra 286 F.Supp. 383, did not recognize a reserved groundwater right. Pueblo water rights, which include not only surface water but also groundwater "interrelated to the surface water as an integral part of the hydrologic cycle," *State of New Mexico ex rel. Reynolds v. Aamodt,* 618 F.Supp. 993, 1010 (D.N.M.1985), do not apply here.

The district court did not err in deciding there was no reserved groundwater right. Because we hold that the reserved water doctrine does not extend to groundwater, we need not address the separate claim that the district court erred in determining that the State owns the groundwater. The State has not appealed the decision that the Tribes may continue to satisfy their domestic and livestock needs (part of the agricultural award) from existing wells at current withdrawal rates; therefore, we do not address that question.

Notes & Questions

1. You can see the struggle the court is facing. By 1988, the science had advanced to the point of understanding that most groundwater is connected to surface water. At the same time, the Justices were well aware that state law does not always recognize that connection—so why must federal law do so? This dilemma is a good lesson in the difficulty and types of reasoning you will need to argue when facing a question of first impression.
2. How does the court respond to this dilemma?
3. You will learn in Part VI that Wyoming's choice of litigation is often contrasted to what has become the preferred approach of settlement. Settlement allows for practical solutions. In the context of groundwater, states and tribes may come up with a plan to manage development and well interference in shared aquifers without addressing the legal issue of whether the doctrine of reserved water rights extends to groundwater.

Arizona

The Arizona Supreme Court applied basically the same reasoning as the Wyoming Supreme Court concerning the logic of applying *Winters* to both surface and ground water and came to the opposite conclusion. The Arizona case concerned the Gila River Indian Community (Figure 13.2) Note, however, the primary difference in the full application of *Winters* in this case. Again, the excerpt does not include the facts of the case and focuses on the issue of whether a reserved water right to groundwater exists.

In re the General Adjudication of All Rights to Use Water in the Gila River System and Source (Gila III)

Arizona Supreme Court
989 P.2d 739 (1999)

Opinion

FIDEL, Judge—

...

In *Cappaert,* the Court applied the reserved rights doctrine in a case that turned on the hydrological connection of surface water and groundwater. There, upon applica-

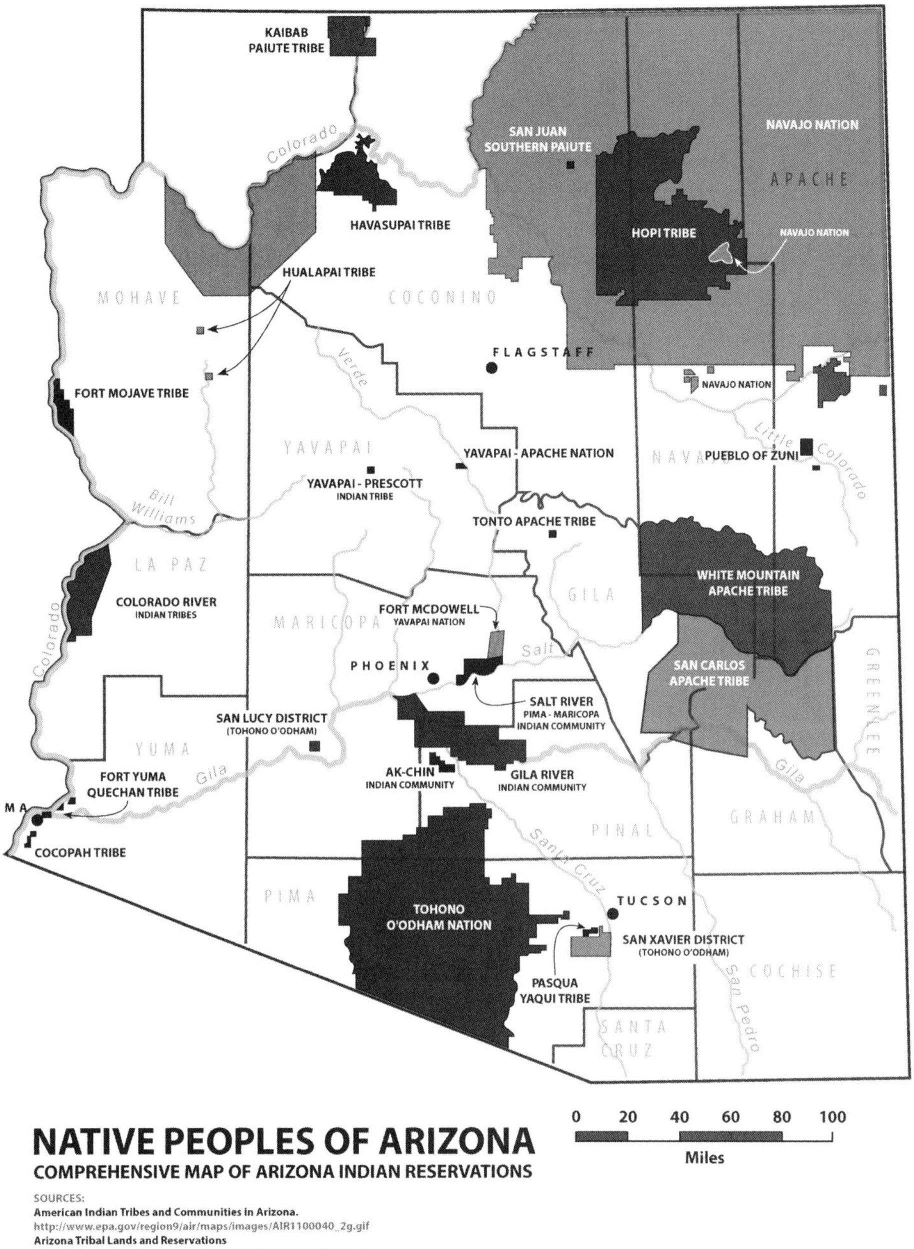

Figure 13.2 Reservations in Arizona, including the Gila River Indian Community on the Gila River. Source: University of Arizona, Native Peoples of Arizona, Comprehensive Map of Arizona Indian Reservations. https://universitysecretary.arizona.edu/sites/default/files/native_peoples_of_arizona_-map_0.pdf.

tion by the United States, a federal district court had issued, and the Ninth Circuit had affirmed, an injunction restricting pumping from wells drilled on private ranch land bordering the Devil's Hole National Monument. The wells drew water from the same underground source as a pool within the monument where lived an endangered breed of fish. One purpose of the monument was to preserve the pool and its rare fish. *Id.* at 141, 96 S.Ct. 2062. Upon evidence that pumping from the wells had lowered the pool's surface to a level that inhibited the spawning of the fish, the Supreme Court affirmed the district court's injunction, which restricted the ranch's pumping to the extent necessary to maintain the pool at a water level that sufficed to support the fish. *Id.*

Although the Ninth Circuit, in its *Cappaert* opinion, expressly determined that the reserved rights doctrine extends to groundwater, ... the Supreme Court found it unnecessary to reach that question, explaining that the water in the pool was surface water. *Cappaert,* 426 U.S. at 142. Yet upon evidence that "federal water rights were being depleted because ... the '[g]roundwater and surface water are physically interrelated as integral parts of the hydrologic cycle,'" the Court held that "the United States can protect its water from subsequent diversion, whether the diversion is of surface or groundwater."

In *Cappaert,* as before, the Supreme Court left the question of a reserved right to groundwater unresolved. The Court's decisions, however, provide guideposts toward our holding that such a right exists.

We find one guidepost in *Winters,* where the Court stressed that the arid lands of the Fort Belknap Reservation could not be made "inhabitable and capable of growing crops" without an implicit reservation of Milk River waters. We find a similar guidepost in *Arizona v. California,* where the Court declared it "impossible to believe" that those who created the Colorado River Indian Reservation "were unaware that most of the lands were of the desert kind—hot, scorching sands—and that water from the [Colorado River and its tributaries] would be essential to the life of the Indian people and to the animals they hunted and the crops they raised." The reservations considered in those cases depended for their water on perennial streams. But some reservations lack perennial streams and depend for present or future survival substantially or entirely upon pumping of underground water. We find it no more thinkable in the latter circumstance than in the former that the United States reserved land for habitation without reserving the water necessary to sustain life.

We find another guidepost to decision in the Supreme Court's association of surface and groundwater in *Cappaert* as "integral parts of the hydrologic cycle." True, the Court identified the waters to be protected as the surface waters of the pool in Devil's Hole. But in contrast to prior cases where the use to be enjoined was an upstream diversion of surface waters, in *Cappaert* the use to be enjoined was a pumping of groundwater from beneath adjoining land. The Court declined to differentiate one means of diversion from another. Instead, the Court held that "the United States can protect its water from subsequent diversion, whether the diversion is of surface or groundwater." That federal reserved rights law declines to differentiate surface and groundwater—that it recognizes them as integral parts of a hydrologic cycle—when addressing the diversion of protected waters suggests that federal reserved rights law would similarly decline to differentiate surface and groundwater when identifying the water to be protected.

In summary, the cases we have cited lead us to conclude that if the United States implicitly intended, when it established reservations, to reserve sufficient unappropriated water to meet the reservations' needs, it must have intended that reservation of water to come from whatever particular sources each reservation had at hand. The significant question for the purpose of the reserved rights doctrine is not whether the water runs above or below the ground but whether it is necessary to accomplish the purpose of the reservation.

...

For the foregoing reasons, we hold that the trial court correctly determined that the federal reserved water rights doctrine applies not only to surface water but to groundwater. We decide this issue in the abstract at this time as a necessary step in determining the scope of interests to be encompassed by this adjudication. We do not, however, decide that any particular federal reservation, Indian or otherwise, has a reserved right to groundwater. A reserved right to groundwater may only be found where other waters are inadequate to accomplish the purpose of a reservation. To determine the purpose of a reservation and to determine the waters necessary to accomplish that purpose are inevitably fact-intensive inquiries that must be made on a reservation-by-reservation basis.

Notes & Questions

1. The court uses *Winters* as a "guidepost" to determine that reserved water rights extend to groundwater. How does it use *Winters* to reach this conclusion?
2. The court finds a reserved water right to groundwater, but places a limitation on that right. What is that limitation? Is the limitation consistent with how the court applies *Winters*?

Montana

The Montana Supreme Court also concluded that reserved water rights extend to groundwater. The court had previously enjoined issuance of state water use permits within the Flathead Reservation until the Tribes' water rights were quantified in a process of negotiation underway at the time of the case. The prior cases concerned surface water. The next case arose when a non-Indian with fee land within the reservation sought a groundwater permit to produce bottled water for commercial purposes.

Confederated Salish & Kootenai Tribes of the Flathead Reservation v. Stults

Montana Supreme Court
59 P.3d 1093 (2002)

Opinion

Justice Terry N. Trieweiler delivered the Opinion of the Court—

[After noting that the prior cases only addressed surface water permits, the court goes on to state:]

Furthermore, the only federal authority which has been cited to this Court by either party supports the conclusion that there is no distinction between surface water and groundwater for purposes of determining what water rights are reserved because those rights are necessary to the purpose of an Indian reservation. In *Tweedy v. Texas Co.* (D.Mont.1968), 286 F.Supp. 383, 385, the U.S. District Court for the State of Montana stated as follows:

> When the Blackfeet Indian Reservation was created, the waters of the reservation were reserved for the benefit of the reservation lands. The *Winters* case dealt only with the surface water, but the same implications which led the Supreme Court to hold that surface waters had been reserved would apply to underground waters as well. The land was arid-water would make it more useful, and whether the waters were found on the surface of the land or under it should make no difference.

In *United States v. Cappaert*, the Ninth Circuit Court of Appeals likewise cited *Winters* for the proposition that so much water is reserved as is necessary to accomplish the purpose of a reservation and went on to conclude that the water reserved is not limited to surface water but may include underground water.

In *Cappaert v. United States*, the Supreme Court concluded that the groundwater at issue was physically interrelated with surface water before concluding that the federal government had reserved an interest in the groundwater. However, the Court then plainly stated that:

> Thus, since the implied reservation of water rights doctrine is based on the necessity of water for the purpose of the federal reservation, we hold that the United States can protect its water from subsequent diversion, whether the diversion is of surface or groundwater.

Cappaert, 426 U.S. at 143, 96 S.Ct. at 2071.

Finally, in the only state court decision cited by either party which includes any analysis of the issue, the Arizona Supreme Court ... held that:

> In summary, the cases we have cited lead us to conclude that if the United States implicitly intended, when it established reservations, to reserve sufficient unappropriated water to meet the reservations' needs, it must have intended that reservation of water to come from whatever particular sources each reservation had at hand. The significant question for the purpose of the reserved rights doctrine is not whether the water runs above or below the ground but whether it is necessary to accomplish the purpose of the reservation.

For those reasons, the Arizona Supreme Court held that the federal reserved water rights doctrine applies to not only surface but to groundwater. However, that Court did not decide, and we do not decide, whether the groundwater at issue was necessary to accomplish the purpose of the reservation. As stated by the Arizona Supreme Court:

> To determine the purpose of a reservation and to determine the waters necessary to accomplish that purpose are inevitably fact-intensive inquiries that must be made on a reservation-by-reservation basis.

We see no reason to limit the scope of our prior holdings by excluding groundwater from the Tribes' federally reserved water rights in this case. The Legislature has created the Montana Reserved Water Rights Compact Commission, a body charged with the difficult task of quantifying and negotiating Indian reserved water rights. Quantifying the amount of groundwater available to the Tribes is simply another component of that inquiry. If it cannot be done to the parties' satisfaction, then comprehensive water rights adjudication is the proper forum in which to make that determination.

Notes & Questions

1. What aspect of the Arizona Supreme Court ruling does the Montana Supreme Court find persuasive?
2. Does the Montana Supreme Court adopt the Arizona court's limitation allowing a reserved water right to groundwater only if other waters are not available?

Idaho

Most recently, the Idaho Supreme Court has extended the doctrine to groundwater in *United States and Coeur d'Alene Tribe v. Idaho,* 448 P.3d 322, 350 (Idaho 2019). The case was decided after the Ninth Circuit Court of Appeals' decision in *Agua Caliente* (covered in the next section), and the denial of certiorari in that case by the U.S. Supreme Court. The North Idaho Water Rights Group had argued "that there is no binding authority allowing federal reserved groundwater claims," and that the Wyoming ruling in *Big Horn* is persuasive. *United States and Coeur d'Alene Tribe v. Idaho,* 448 P.3d 322, 350 (2019). The Idaho Supreme Court rejected these arguments, stating that: "reliance on *Big Horn I,* in which the court admitted that logic supports the implied reservation of groundwater, does not undermine *Agua Caliente.* Thus, the district court did not err in allowing domestic use groundwater claims." *United States and Coeur d'Alene Tribe v. Idaho,* 448 P.3d 322, 351 (2019)

Resolution in the Ninth Circuit— *Agua Caliente*

The arid Coachella Valley (Figure 13.3) of California has limited surface water, except for that imported by canal from the Colorado River. Groundwater is the primary source of supply from within the valley. The valley contains, among other cities, Palm Springs and Palm Desert and is located just a few hours from both Los Angeles and San Diego. Despite the limited water supply, there is large and increasing demand for both a massive agricultural industry as well as domestic, commercial, municipal,

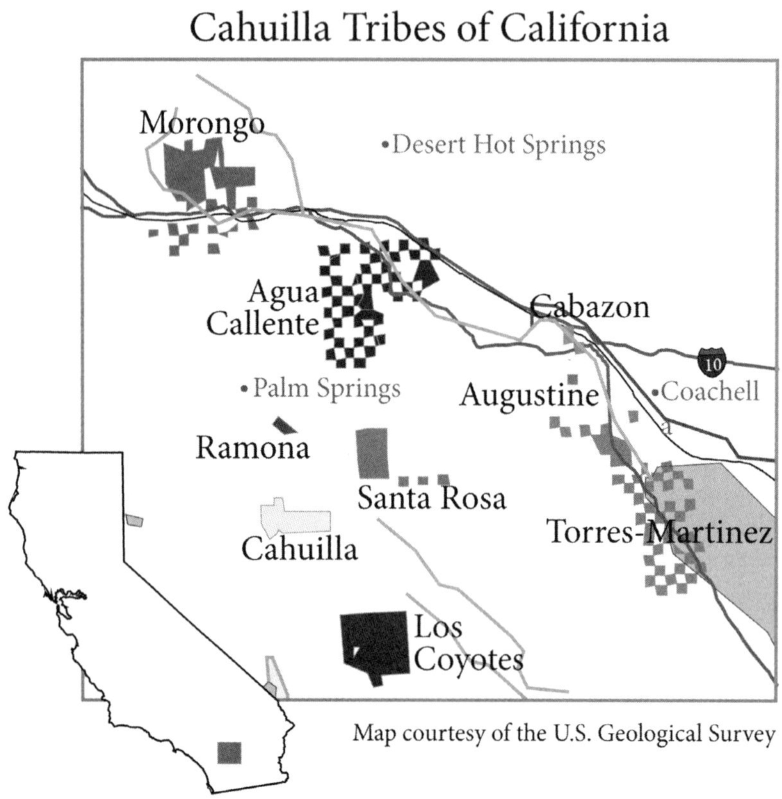

Figure 13.3 Lands of the Cahuilla Tribes of California. The lands of the Agua Caliente Band of Cahuilla Indians overlaps cities that include Palm Springs and Palm Desert. Source: USGS.

and industrial needs. The region is also the home of the Agua Caliente band of Cahuilla Indians, who have lived in the region since time immemorial.

As drought gripped California and the Colorado River Basin through the second decade of the twenty-first century, water users in the Coachella Valley increasingly turned to groundwater to satisfy increasing demand. That led to overdraft of the groundwater supply from the Coachella Valley, which in turn resulted in conflict between the Agua Caliente Band and the major non-Indian water suppliers, the Coachella Valley Water District and the Desert Water Agency. The Agua Caliente Band asserted an implied reserved right to groundwater, putting the question of whether the *Winters* Doctrine extends to groundwater squarely in front of the Ninth Circuit for the first time. Importantly, following the recognition of a reserved right to groundwater in this case, the U.S. Supreme Court denied certiorari. Settlement negotiations over the allocation/quantification of rights to the Coachella Valley Groundwater Basin among the Agua Caliente Band of Cahuilla Indians and various water districts and agencies are under way at the time of writing of this textbook.

Agua Caliente Band of Cahuilla Indians v. Coachella Valley Water District

United States Court of Appeals, Ninth Circuit
849 F.3d 1262 (2017)

TALLMAN, Circuit Judge:

"When the well's dry, we know the worth of water."
Benjamin Franklin (1706–1790), Poor Richard's Almanac

The Coachella Valley Water District ("CVWD") and the Desert Water Agency ("DWA") (collectively, the "water agencies") bring an interlocutory appeal of the district court's grant of partial summary judgment in favor of the Agua Caliente Band of Cahuilla Indians (the "Tribe") and the United States. The judgment declares that the United States impliedly reserved appurtenant water sources, including groundwater, when it created the Tribe's reservation in California's arid Coachella Valley. We agree. In affirming, we recognize that there is no controlling federal appellate authority addressing whether the reserved rights doctrine applies to groundwater. However, because we conclude that it does, we hold that the Tribe has a reserved right to groundwater underlying its reservation as a result of the purpose for which the reservation was established.

I

A

The Agua Caliente Band of Cahuilla Indians has lived in the Coachella Valley since before California entered statehood in 1850. The bulk of the Agua Caliente Reservation was formally established by two Presidential Executive Orders issued in 1876 and 1877, and the United States, pursuant to statute, now holds the remaining lands of the reservation in trust for the Tribe. The reservation consists of approximately 31,396 acres interspersed in a checkerboard pattern amidst several cities within Riverside County, including Palm Springs, Cathedral City, and Rancho Mirage.

The Executive Orders establishing the reservation are short in length, but broad in purpose. In 1876, President Ulysses S. Grant ordered certain lands "withdrawn from sale and set apart as reservations for the permanent use and occupancy of the Mission Indians in southern California." Exec. Order of May 15, 1876. Similarly, President Rutherford B. Hayes's 1877 Order set aside additional lands for "Indian purposes." Exec. Order of Sept. 29, 1877. These orders followed on the heels of detailed government reports from Indian agents, which identified the urgent need to reserve land for Indian use in an attempt to encourage tribal members to "build comfortable houses, improve their acres, and surround themselves with home comforts." Comm'r of Indian Aff., Ann. Rep. 224 (1875). In short, the United States sought to protect the Tribe and "secure the Mission Indians permanent homes, with land and water enough." Comm'r of Indian Aff., Ann. Rep. 37 (1877).

Establishing a sustainable home in the Coachella Valley is no easy feat, however, as water in this arid southwestern desert is scarce. Rainfall totals average three to six inches per year, and the Whitewater River System—the valley's only real source of surface water—produces an average annual supply of water that fluctuates between 4,000 and 9,000 acre-feet, most of which occurs in the winter months. In other words, surface water is virtually nonexistent in the valley for the majority of the year. Therefore, almost all of the water consumed in the region comes from the aquifer underlying the valley—the Coachella Valley Groundwater Basin.

The Coachella Valley Groundwater Basin supports 9 cities, 400,000 people, and 66,000 acres of farmland. *See* CVWD-DWA, The State of the Coachella Valley Aquifer at 2. Given the demands on the basin's supply, it is not surprising that water levels in the aquifer have been declining at a steady rate. Since the 1980s, the aquifer has been in a state of overdraft, which exists despite major efforts to recharge the basin with water delivered from the California Water Project and the Colorado River. In total, groundwater pumping has resulted in an average annual recharge deficit of 239,000 acre-feet, with cumulative overdraft estimated at 5.5 million acre-feet as of 2010.

...

III

...

A

For over one hundred years, the Supreme Court has made clear that when the United States "withdraws its land from the public domain and reserves it for a federal purpose, the Government, by implication, reserves appurtenant water then unappropriated to the extent needed to accomplish the purpose of the reservation."

In what has become known as the *Winters* doctrine, federal reserved water rights are directly applicable "to Indian reservations and other federal enclaves, encompassing water rights in navigable and nonnavigable streams." The creation of these rights stems from the belief that the United States, when establishing reservations, "intended to deal fairly with the Indians by reserving for them the waters without which their lands would have been useless." *Arizona v. California*, 373 U.S. 546, 600, (1963); *see also id.* at 598–99, 83 S.Ct. 1468 ("It is impossible to believe that when Congress created the great Colorado River Indian Reservation and when the Executive Department of this Nation created the other reservations they were unaware that most of the lands were of the desert kind—hot, scorching sands—and that water from the river would be essential to the life of the Indian people and to the animals they hunted and the crops they raised.").

Despite the longstanding recognition that Indian reservations, as well as other reserved lands, require access to water, the *Winters* doctrine only applies in certain situations: it only reserves water to the extent it is necessary to accomplish the purpose of the reservation, and it only reserves water if it is appurtenant to the withdrawn land.

Once established, however, *Winters* rights "vest ... on the date of the reservation and [are] superior to the rights of future appropriators."

...

B

... [W]e now determine the primary purpose of the Tribe's reservation and whether that purpose contemplates water use. To do so, we consider "the document and circumstances surrounding [the reservation's] creation, and the history of the Indians for whom it was created."

The Executive Orders establishing the Tribe's reservation declared that the land was to be set aside for "the permanent use and occupancy of the Mission Indians" or, more generally, for "Indian purposes." *See supra* Part I. While imprecise, such a purpose is not indecipherable. Our precedent recognizes that "[t]he specific purposes of an Indian reservation ... [are] often unarticulated. The general purpose, *to provide a home for the Indians*, is a broad one and must be liberally construed." Moreover, "[m]ost of the land in these reservations is and always has been arid," and it is impossible to believe that the United States was unaware "that water ... would be essential to the life of the Indian people."

The situation facing the Agua Caliente Tribe is no different. Water is inherently tied to the Tribe's ability to live permanently on the reservation. Without water, the underlying purpose—to establish a home and support an agrarian society—would be entirely defeated. Put differently, the primary purpose underlying the establishment of the reservation was to create a home for the Tribe, and water was necessarily implicated in that purpose. Thus, we hold that the United States implicitly reserved a right to water when it created the Agua Caliente Reservation.

C

While we conclude that the federal government envisioned water use when it established the Tribe's reservation, that does not end our inquiry. We must now determine whether the *Winters* doctrine, and the Tribe's reserved water right, extends to the groundwater underlying the reservation. And while we are unable to find controlling federal appellate authority explicitly holding that the *Winters* doctrine applies to groundwater, we now expressly hold that it does.

Apart from the requirement that the primary purpose of the reservation must intend water use, the other main limitation of the reserved rights doctrine is that the unappropriated water must be "appurtenant" to the reservation. Appurtenance, however, simply limits the reserved right to those waters which are attached to the reservation. It does not limit the right to surface water only. *Cappaert* itself hinted that impliedly reserved waters may include appurtenant groundwater when it held that "the United States can protect its water from subsequent diversion, whether the diversion is of surface or groundwater." If the United States can protect against groundwater diversions, it follows that the government can protect the groundwater itself.

Further, many locations throughout the western United States rely on groundwater as their only viable water source. *See, e.g.*, *In re Gen. Adjudication of All Rights to Use Water in Gila River Sys. & Source*, 989 P.2d 739, 746 (Ariz. 1999) ("The reservations considered in [*Winters* and *Arizona*] depended for their water on perennial streams. But some reservations lack perennial streams and depend for present and future survival substantially or entirely upon pumping of underground water. We find it no more thinkable in the latter circumstance than in the former that the United States reserved land for habitation without reserving the water necessary to sustain life."). More importantly, such reliance exists here, as surface water in the Coachella Valley is minimal or entirely lacking for most of the year. Thus, survival is conditioned on access to water—and a reservation without an adequate source of surface water must be able to access groundwater.

The *Winters* doctrine was developed in part to provide sustainable land for Indian tribes whose reservations were established in the arid parts of the country. And in many cases, those reservations lacked access to, or were unable to effectively capture, a regular supply of surface water. Given these realities, we can discern no reason to cabin the *Winters* doctrine to appurtenant surface water. As such, we hold that the *Winters* doctrine encompasses both surface water and groundwater appurtenant to reserved land. The creation of the Agua Caliente Reservation therefore carried with it an implied right to use water from the Coachella Valley aquifer.

D

The final issue we must address is the contours of the Tribe's reserved right, including its relation to state water law and the Tribe's existing water rights.

A "reserved right in unappropriated water ... vests on the date of the reservation and is superior to the rights of future appropriators." Further, reserved rights are not analyzed "in terms of a balancing test." *Id.* Rather, they are federal water rights that preempt conflicting state law. *See Walton*, 647 F.2d at 51–53; *see also New Mexico*, 438 U.S. at 715 ("[T]he 'reserved rights doctrine' ... is an exception to Congress' explicit deference to state water law in other areas."). Finally, the rights are not lost through non-use. Instead, they are flexible and can change over time.

Despite the federal primacy of reserved water rights, the water agencies argue that because (1) the Tribe has a correlative right to groundwater under California law and (2) the Tribe has not drilled for groundwater on its reservation, and (3) because the Tribe is entitled to surface water from the Whitewater River Decree, the Tribe does not need a federal reserved right to prevent the purpose of the reservation from being entirely defeated. Put differently, the water agencies argue that, because the Tribe is already receiving water pursuant to California's correlative rights doctrine and the Whitewater River Decree, a federal reserved right is unnecessary.

However, the water agencies' arguments fail for three reasons. First, state water rights are preempted by federal reserved rights. *See Walton*, 647 F.2d at 51; *see also Ahtanum Irrigation Dist.*, 236 F.2d at 329 ("Rights reserved by treaties such as this are not subject to appropriation under state law, nor has the state power to dispose of them."). Second, the fact that the Tribe did not historically access groundwater does not destroy its right to groundwater now. *See Walton*, 647 F.2d at 51. And third, the *New Mexico* inquiry does not ask if water is currently needed to sustain the reservation; it asks whether water was envisioned as necessary for the reservation's purpose at the time the reservation was created. *See supra* Part III.B. Thus, state water entitlements do not affect our analysis with respect to the creation of the Tribe's federally reserved water right.

IV

In sum, the *Winters* Doctrine does not distinguish between surface water and groundwater. Rather, its limits derive only from the government's intent in withdrawing land for a public purpose and the location of the water in relation to the reservation created. As such, because the United States intended to reserve water when it established a home for the Agua Caliente Band of Cahuilla Indians, we hold that the district court did not err in determining that the government reserved appurtenant water sources—including groundwater—when it created the Tribe's reservation in the Coachella Valley.

...

AFFIRMED.

Notes & Questions

1. What was the purpose for the creation of the Agua Caliente Reservation? What evidence does the Court use to determine the purpose of the reservation? Did that reservation include reserved water rights for groundwater?
2. Which of the following are factors the court relied on to reach its conclusion that the reserved water rights doctrine can extend to groundwater?
    a. While the Supreme Court opinion in *Cappaert* did not address the question, the court uses it to conclude: "If the United States can protect against groundwater diversions, it follows that the government can protect the groundwater itself."
    b. For many parts of the arid western United States, groundwater is the only source of water supply.
    c. The *Winters* Doctrine is focused on providing a sustainable land for Indian tribes. Without groundwater, the Aqua Caliente Reservation is not sustainable.
3. The Court noted that the United States is entitled to reserve water that is "appurtenant" to a reservation of land. How does the Court define "appurtenant"? Does the water have to physically touch the reservation?
4. The defendants in *Agua Caliente* argued that because the Tribe was entitled to groundwater under state law, the purpose of the Reservation would not be defeated in the absence of a federal reserved water right. Does the Court agree? Why or why not?

Part IV

The Federal Role in Western Water

Part IV addresses the role of the federal sovereign in western water. The following introduction to Part IV should begin the process of dispelling the myth that states have sole authority over water and that the role of the federal government is one of deference to state law. Instead, it is more accurate to think of the federal role as one of cooperation and assistance in areas relevant to commerce and navigation, and one of supremacy in areas relevant to the federal proprietary role over federal land and its associated resources. Thus, to develop a full understanding of the federal role, it is necessary to begin with the sources of federal authority.

Unlike the states, which have general authority to act on behalf of the health, safety, and welfare of their citizens, federal authority is limited to that granted by the U.S. Constitution. You may find it useful to review Part I on the constitutional sources of federal authority regarding water before reading the summary of that authority that follows.

Federal authority to own and regulate water stems from the Property and Commerce Clauses of the U.S. Constitution. The U.S. government acquired western lands and resources from Native American and European sovereigns. Those acquired lands and resources fall within the very broad authority of the Property Clause. As you learned in Part I, the federal government transferred the ownership and authority to allocate non-navigable and navigable waters, to the extent it did not compromise navigability, to the states. You also learned in Part I and in Part III that the federal government relied on that authority as well as its Indian treaty authority to enter agreements recognizing aboriginal water rights and reserving new water rights as necessary for the purpose of an Indian reservation. In Chapter 14, you will see that this authority over western lands and resources also allows the federal government to reserve water for its own purposes when it withdraws land from the public domain and reserves it for a federal purpose.

The Commerce Clause is the source of federal authority over navigable rivers. You will learn in Chapter 15 that even though the authority over the beds and banks of navigable rivers transferred from the federal to state governments on statehood, the states hold those lands in trust for the public. This places limitations on state authority to allow development that prevents public access. You will also learn that the California state courts have extended this concept of trusteeship to state water allocation that impacts the public trust values of downstream navigable waterways.

Chapter 16 turns to the massive federal development of western rivers for irrigation under the Reclamation Act, for flood control under the Rivers and Harbors Act, and for hydropower (hydropower was developed at federal dams and, under regulation authorized by the Federal Power Act, at other public and private dams). This development transformed the rivers and the economy of the Pacific Northwest. The primary era of dam building occurred during the first half of the twentieth century; much of it aimed at fueling, and (following the Depression), reviving the rural economies of the West. Dam building also had major impacts on riverine ecosystems and on Native American treaty rights (particularly fishing rights).

In Chapter 17 you will learn about the federal role in interstate allocation of water. The major river basins and many small watersheds and many aquifers of the United States are not confined to state boundaries (see Figures 17.1 and 22.1). You will learn about the three major means of resolving interstate disputes: (1) through litigation invoking the original jurisdiction of the U.S. Supreme Court provided in Article 3, Section 2 of the U.S. Constitution; (2) through a negotiated Compact among the relevant states and approved or authorized by Congress, as provided for by Article I, Section 10, Clause 3 of the U.S. Constitution; and (3) through an act of Congress under its Commerce Clause authority. In addition, you will learn about the ability of states and communities to enter informal cross-border agreements on water management.

Finally, in Chapter 18 you will learn about the sovereign authority of the federal government to enter treaties with foreign nations, including those concerning shared water courses with Canada and Mexico. Under the U.S. Constitution, the Executive has the authority to negotiate treaties, but ratification requires the consent of a two-thirds majority of the Senate (Article II, Section 2, Clause 2). You will explore this in the context of the Columbia River Treaty between the United States and Canada.

Chapter 14

Federal (Non-Indian) Reserved Water Rights

Introduction

In Part III, you learned about reserved water rights implied from agreements between the United States and Native American tribes. This Chapter turns to the extension of the *Winters* Doctrine to federal, non-Indian reservations. The link between the two types of reserved water rights—Indian and federal—lies in the authority of the government over federal property and associated resources via the Property Clause. As noted in Part III, however, the fact that Indian reserved water rights are created by an agreement with a tribe means that the interpretation of the intended purpose (from which the implied right flows) is governed by the canons providing for construction of the agreement as the tribe would have understood it. In contrast, federal reserved water rights are subject to the general rules of statutory construction—i.e., what does the plain language of the act reserving the land in question imply, and what do the surrounding documents tell us about the intent of Congress? Despite this important difference, the term "*Winters* Doctrine" is used to refer to both Indian and federal reserved water rights, creating some confusion in their interpretation. By separating the discussion of Indian reserved water rights in Part III from federal reserved water rights, covered in Part IV, we intend to highlight this important distinction.

Each of the three cases that follow was decided between 1963 and 1978, after a long hiatus in U.S. Supreme Court rulings on reserved water rights. Only the first, the 1963 case of *Arizona v. California*, also addresses Native American reserved water rights. You were introduced to that case in Part III in the context of quantification of Native American reserved water rights and will return to the case in Chapter 17 in the context of interstate allocation of water. The brief excerpt to follow is the Court's initial extension of the doctrine of implied reserved water rights to non-Indian federal reservations.

(a)

(b)

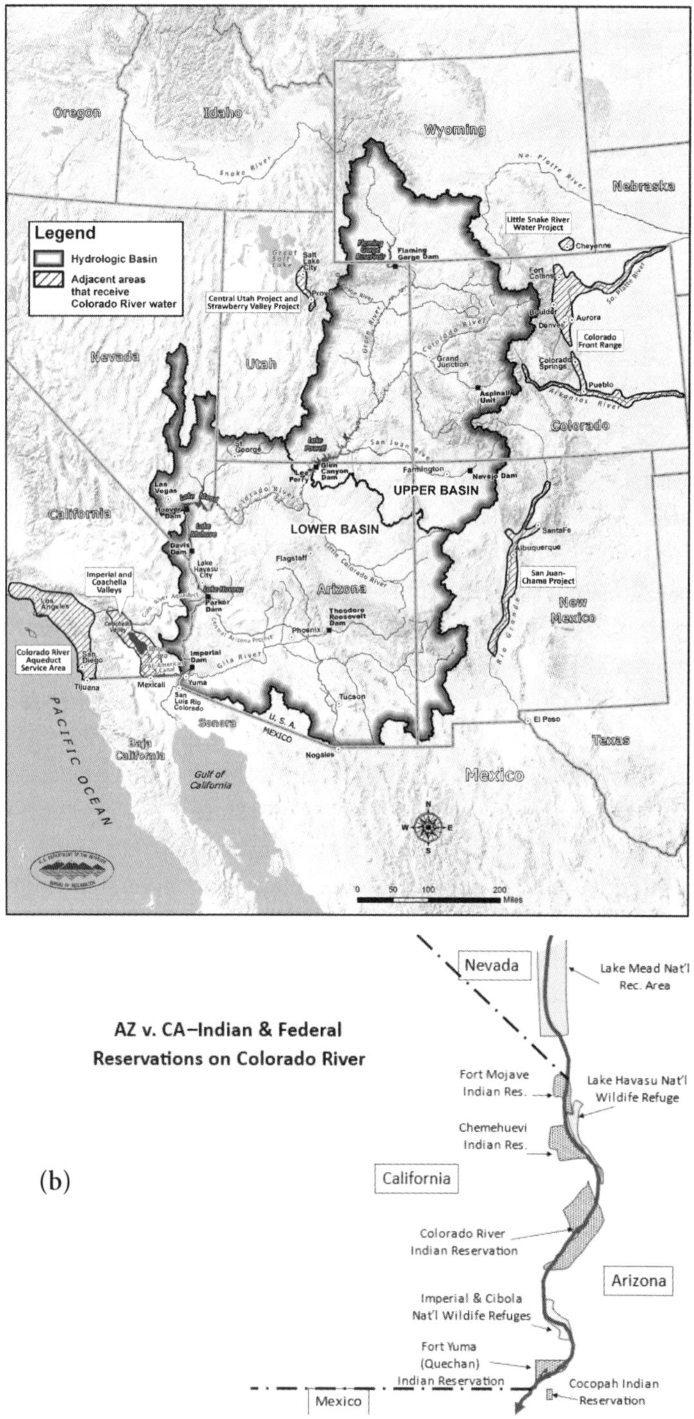

Figure 14.1 Colorado River Basin, showing (a) the upper and lower basin, the primary tributaries, and in hatched, use of River water outside the basin; and (b) the Indian and Federal Reservations along the California/Arizona border addressed in *Arizona v. California*. U.S. Bureau of Reclamation, Colorado River Basin Water Supply and Demand Study 2 (2012), https://www.usbr.gov/watersmart/bsp/docs/finalreport/ColoradoRiver/CRBS_Executive_Summary_FINAL.pdf.

Extension of the *Winters* Doctrine to Federal Reservations

Arizona v. California is an interstate water adjudication under the constitutional power of the United States Supreme Court provided by Article III, Section 2, providing that the original jurisdiction of the Supreme Court extends "to Controversies between two or more States." The dispute called for allocation of the entire flow of the Colorado River in what is referred to as the "lower basin." This portion of the river extends from Lee's Ferry just below Glen Canyon Dam to the U.S. border with Mexico (Figure 14.1). Located in the section of the river forming the border between Arizona and California are five Indian Reservations (leading to the endorsement of the PIA method of quantification you learned about in Part III), two National Wildlife Refuges, and one National Monument. As a result, the United States intervened, asserting the rights for these Indian and federal reserved lands.

In exercising its original jurisdiction, the Court assigns the case to a Special Master who will hear the case and forward to the Court the "Report of the Special Master" based on Findings of Fact and Conclusions of Law. The Court will then hear objections to the Report but will grant the Report a presumption of validity on the Findings of Fact. *Arizona v. California* is thus the Opinion of the Court following the hearing of objections to the Report of the Special Master. This case is important not for its detailed explanation of why reserved water rights also apply to non-Indian, federal reserved land, but for its quick dismissal of any possible argument that they do not apply.

Arizona v. California

Supreme Court of the United States
373 U.S. 546 (1963)

Mr. Justice Black delivered the opinion of the Court

In 1952 the State of Arizona invoked the original jurisdiction of this Court by filing a complaint against the State of California and seven of its public agencies. Later, Nevada, New Mexico, Utah, and the United States were added as parties either voluntarily or on motion. The basic controversy in the case is over how much water each State has a legal right to use out of the waters of the Colorado River and its tributaries. After preliminary pleadings, we referred the case to George I. Haight, Esquire, and upon his death in 1955 to Simon H. Rifkind, Esquire, as Special Master to take evidence, find facts, state conclusions of law, and recommend a decree, all 'subject to consideration, revision, or approval by the Court.' The Master conducted a trial lasting from June 14, 1956, to August 28, 1958, during which 340 witnesses were heard orally or by deposition, thousands of exhibits were received, and 25,000 pages of transcript were filled. Following many motions, arguments, and briefs, the Master in a 433-page volume reported his findings, conclusions, and recommended decree, received by the Court on

January 16, 1961. The case has been extensively briefed here and orally argued twice, the first time about 16 hours, the second, over six....

...

V. CLAIMS OF THE UNITED STATES.

In these proceedings, the United States has asserted claims to waters in the main river and in some of the tributaries for use on Indian Reservations, National Forests, Recreational and Wildlife Areas and other government lands and works. While the Master passed upon some of these claims, he declined to reach others, particularly those relating to tributaries. We approve his decision as to which claims required adjudication, and likewise we approve the decree he recommended for the government claims he did decide....

...

Arizona's contention that the Federal Government had no power, after Arizona became a State, to reserve waters for the use and benefit of federally reserved lands rests largely upon statements in *Pollard's Lessee v. Hagan*, 3 How. 212 (1845), and *Shively v. Bowlby*, 152 U.S. 1 (1894). Those cases and others that followed them gave rise to the doctrine that lands underlying navigable waters within territory acquired by the Government are held in trust for future States and that title to such lands is automatically vested in the States upon admission to the Union. But those cases involved only the shores of and lands beneath navigable waters. They do not determine the problem before us and cannot be accepted as limiting the broad powers of the United States to regulate navigable waters under the Commerce Clause and to regulate government lands under Art. IV, § 3, of the Constitution [the Property Clause]. We have no doubt about the power of the United States under these clauses to reserve water rights for its reservations and its property.

...

The Master ruled that the principle underlying the reservation of water rights for Indian Reservations was equally applicable to other federal establishments such as National Recreation Areas and National Forests. We agree with the conclusions of the Master that the United States intended to reserve water sufficient for the future requirements of the Lake Mead National Recreation Area, the Havasu Lake National Wildlife Refuge, the Imperial National Wildlife Refuge and the Gila National Forest.

... Finally, we note our agreement with the Master that all uses of mainstream water within a State are to be charged against that State's apportionment, which of course includes uses by the United States.

VI. DECREE.

While we have in the main agreed with the Master, there are some places we have disagreed and some questions on which we have not ruled. Rather than adopt the Master's decree with amendments or append our own decree to this opinion, we will allow the parties, or any of them, if they wish, to submit before September 16, 1963, the form of decree to carry this opinion into effect, failing which the Court will prepare and enter an appropriate decree at the next Term of Court.

It is so ordered.

...

Notes & Questions

1. What is the source of federal power to reserve water for federal land that is withdrawn from the general operation of the public land laws and reserved for a specific purpose such as a National Wildlife Refuge? Is that federal source of power the same as for reserved water rights held for the benefit of American Indian tribes?
2. Two quotes from the excerpt are all that the Court says of this extension of the *Winters* Doctrine to federal reservations:

   > *We approve his* [i.e., the Special Master] *decision as to which claims required adjudication, and likewise we approve the decree he recommended for the government claims he did decide.*

   And:

   > *The Master ruled that the principle underlying the reservation of water rights for Indian Reservations was equally applicable to other federal establishments such as National Recreation Areas and National Forests. We agree with the conclusions of the Master that the United States intended to reserve water sufficient for the future requirements of the Lake Mead National Recreation Area, the Havasu Lake National Wildlife Refuge, the Imperial National Wildlife Refuge and the Gila National Forest.*

   This was the first time a court had extended the *Winters* Doctrine to non-Indian federal reservations. The fact that the Court accepted this with no discussion emphasizes the clear power of Congress to create an implied reservation of water on federal land. Remember from Part I the broad source of federal power over federal lands stemming from the Property Clause. While that discussion also noted that the power to enter Treaties with Native American Tribes and thus how those Treaties will be interpreted is markedly different, the power of Congress to reserve the public lands, whether for Indian or federal purposes in relation to states and non-Indians remains this broad power under the Property Clause.

Prior to reading the cases that follow, it is important to understand an aspect of Federal Public Lands law that determines which federal lands the *Winters* Doctrine might apply to. In the second half of the nineteenth century, the western lands (except military reservations) were held by the United States as public lands subject to the various public land laws (including the Homestead Act, Desert Lands Act, and the General Mining Law discussed in Part I) that allowed transfer to private ownership. However, new policies developed concerning the use, preservation, and management of certain of the public lands that would require their retention in federal ownership. The process to do so required "withdrawal" of the lands from the application of the general public land laws, and reservation for a specific purpose or set of purposes. Today, the west has land still held as public land and managed by the Bureau of Land Management (BLM). But it also has lands withdrawn from the public land laws and reserved as National Parks, National Forests, National Wildlife Refuges, National Monuments, Military Reservations, National Laboratories, Wilderness Areas, lands reserved for a specific purpose such as development of a dam, and waters reserved as Wild and Scenic Rivers (Figure 14.2). Reserved water rights apply only to the lands withdrawn and reserved through a congressional act or through authority provided to the executive through a congressional act. Depending on the act, Congress may have expressly reserved water along with the reservation of land, but far more likely the water right will be implied because water is necessary for the purpose of the federal reservation.

The Scope of Federal Reserved Water Rights: Narrowing Purpose and Quantity

The next two cases, *Cappaert v. United States* and *United States v. New Mexico*, address non-Indian federal reservations (i.e., a National Monument and a National Forest) and explore the purposes and amount of water reserved. These two cases mark the only times the Supreme Court has substantively revisited the *Winters* Doctrine since *Arizona v. California*. The following case, *Cappaert*, concerns the impact of nearby groundwater pumping on a water feature in a cave at Devil's Hole National Monument in Nevada (Figure 14.3). The rare Desert Pupfish lives in that water. As you read, pay careful attention to any statement by the Court suggesting a limitation on the amount of water reserved. Consider whether the limitation is applicable when interpreting a reservation of water in an agreement that must be interpreted as the tribe(s) would have understood it. Also pay attention to: (1) whether the Court considers the water reserved in Devil's Hole to be groundwater; (2) whether the authority of the federal government to reserve water is limited to navigable waters, and (3) whether the reserved water right recognized is express or implied.

Cappaert v. United States

Supreme Court of the United States
426 U.S. 128 (1976)

Mr. Chief Justice BURGER delivered the opinion of the Court—The question presented in this litigation is whether the reservation of Devil's Hole as a national monument reserved federal water rights in unappropriated water.

Devil's Hole is a deep limestone cavern in Nevada. Approximately 50 feet below the opening of the cavern is a pool 65 feet long, 10 feet wide, and at least 200 feet deep, although its actual depth is unknown. The pool is a remnant of the prehistoric Death Valley Lake System and is situated on land owned by the United States since the Treaty of Guadalupe Hidalgo in 1848, 9 Stat. 922. By the Proclamation of January 17, 1952,

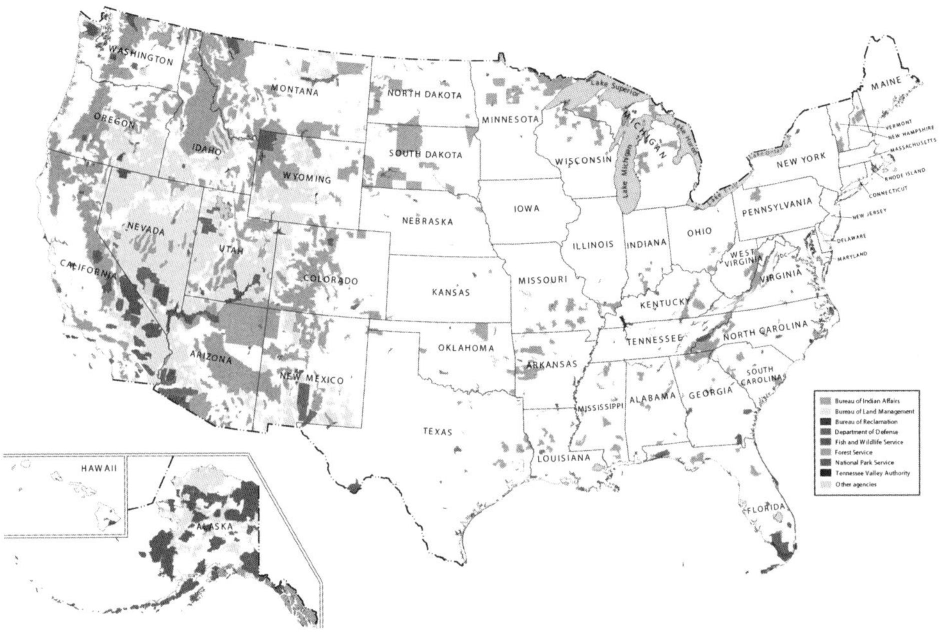

Figure 14.2 Federal and Indian Lands of the United States showing the federal agency with management authority. The light shade depicts the "public lands" managed by the BLM. These are not considered to be reserved lands. The remaining land colors depict "reserved lands" that may include express or implied federal reserved water rights. U.S. Dept. of the Interior, *Federal Lands and Indian Reservations* (2006). Source: GISGeography, Federal Lands of the United States Map, https://gisgeography.com/federal-lands-united-states-map/.

(a) (b)

Figure 14.3 (a) Devil's Hole rock formation showing the "underground pool." (b) Desert Pupfish, referred to by Travel Nevada as the rarest fish in the world. Source: Travel Nevada, *10 Things You Need to Know About Devil's Hole and the World's Rarest Fish* (2023), https://travelnevada.com/wildlife/10-things-you-need-to-know-about-devils-hole-and-the-worlds-rarest-fish/.

President Truman withdrew from the public domain a 40-acre tract of land surrounding Devil's Hole, making it a detached component of the Death Valley National Monument. Proclamation No. 2961, 3 CFR 147 (1949–1953 Comp.).... The Proclamation was issued under the American Antiquities Preservation Act, 34 Stat. 225, 16 U.S.C.

§431, which authorizes the President to declare as national monuments "objects of historic or scientific interest that are situated upon the lands owned or controlled by the Government of the United States...."

> The 1952 Proclamation notes that Death Valley was set aside as a national monument "for the preservation of the unusual features of scenic, scientific, and educational interest therein contained." The Proclamation also notes that Devil's Hole is near Death Valley and contains a "remarkable underground pool." Additional preambulary statements in the Proclamation explain why Devil's Hole was being added to the Death Valley National Monument:
>
> "WHEREAS the said pool is a unique subsurface remnant of the prehistoric chain of lakes which in Pleistocene times formed the Death Valley Lake System, and is unusual among caverns in that it is a solution area in distinctly striated limestone, while also owing its formation in part to fault action; and
>
> "WHEREAS the geologic evidence that this subterranean pool is an integral part of the hydrographic history of the Death Valley region is further confirmed by the presence in this pool of a peculiar race of desert fish, and zoologists have demonstrated that this race of fish, which is found nowhere else in the world, evolved only after the gradual drying up of the Death Valley Lake System isolated this fish population from the original ancestral stock that in Pleistocene times was common to the entire region; and
>
> "WHEREAS the said pool is of such outstanding scientific importance that it should be given special protection, and such protection can be best afforded by making the said forty-acre tract containing the pool a part of the said monument...."

...

The Cappaert petitioners own a 12,000-acre ranch near Devil's Hole, 4,000 acres of which are used for growing Bermuda grass, alfalfa, wheat, and barley; 1,700 to 1,800 head of cattle are grazed. The ranch represents an investment of more than $7 million; it employs more than 80 people with an annual payroll of more than $340,000.

In 1968 the Cappaerts began pumping groundwater on their ranch on land 2½ miles from Devil's Hole; they were the first to appropriate groundwater. The groundwater comes from an underground basin or aquifer which is also the source of the water in Devil's Hole. After the Cappaerts began pumping from the wells near Devil's Hole, which they do from March to October, the summer water level of the pool in Devil's Hole began to decrease. Since 1962 the level of water in Devil's Hole has been measured with reference to a copper washer installed on one of the walls of the hole by the United States Geological Survey. Until 1968, the water level, with seasonable variations, had been stable at 1.2 feet below the copper marker. In 1969 the water level in Devil's Hole was 2.3 feet below the copper washer; in 1970, 3.17 feet; in 1971, 3.48 feet; and, in 1972, 3.93 feet.

When the water is at the lowest levels, a large portion of a rock shelf in Devil's Hole is above water. However, when the water level is at 3.0 feet below the marker or higher, most of the rock shelf is below water, enabling algae to grow on it. This in turn enables the desert fish (Cyprinodon diabolis, commonly known as Devil's Hole pupfish), referred to in President Truman's Proclamation, to spawn in the spring. As the rock shelf becomes exposed, the spawning area is decreased, reducing the ability of the fish to spawn in sufficient quantities to prevent extinction.

In April 1970 the Cappaerts, pursuant to Nevada law, Nev.Rev.Stat. § 533.325 (1973), applied to the State Engineer, Roland D. Westergard, for permits to change the use of water from several of their wells....

In August 1971 the United States, invoking 28 U.S.C. § 1345, ... sought an injunction in the United States District Court for the District of Nevada to limit, except for domestic purposes, the Cappaerts' pumping from six specific wells and from specific locations near Devil's Hole.... On June 2, 1972, the United States filed an amended complaint, adding two other specified wells to the list of those to be enjoined.

The Cappaerts answered, admitting that their wells draw water from the same underlying sources supplying Devil's Hole, but denying that the reservation of Devil's Hole reserved any water rights for the United States....

On June 5, 1973, the District Court, by Chief Judge Roger D. Foley, entered a preliminary injunction limiting pumping from designated wells so as to return the level of Devil's Hole to not more than 3.0 feet below the marker.... The District Court found that the water from certain of the wells was hydrologically connected to Devil's Hole, that the Cappaerts were pumping heavily from those wells, and that that pumping had lowered the water level in Devil's Hole....

The District Court then held that in establishing Devil's Hole as a national monument, the President reserved appurtenant, unappropriated waters necessary to the purpose of the reservation; the purpose included preservation of the pool and the pupfish in it. The District Court also held that the federal water rights antedated those of the Cappaerts, that the United States was not estopped, and that the public interest required granting the injunction. On April 9, 1974, the District Court entered its findings of fact and conclusions of law substantially unchanged in a final decree permanently enjoining pumping that lowers the level of the water below the 3.0-foot level. 375 F.Supp. 456 (1974).

The Court of Appeals for the Ninth Circuit affirmed, 508 F.2d 313 (1974), ... in a thorough opinion by Senior District Judge Gus J. Solomon, sitting by designation, holding that the implied-reservation-of-water doctrine applied to groundwater as well as to surface water. The Court of Appeals held that "(t) he fundamental purpose of the reservation of the Devil's Hole pool was to assure that the pool would not suffer changes from its condition at the time the Proclamation was issued in 1952...." Id., at 318....

We granted certiorari to consider the scope of the implied-reservation-of-water-rights doctrine.... We affirm.

I. Reserved-Water-Rights Doctrine

This Court has long held that when the Federal Government withdraws its land from the public domain and reserves it for a federal purpose, the Government, by implication, reserves appurtenant water then unappropriated to the extent needed to accomplish the purpose of the reservation. In so doing the United States acquires a reserved right in unappropriated water which vests on the date of the reservation and is superior to the rights of future appropriators. Reservation of water rights is empowered by the Commerce Clause, Art. I, § 8, which permits federal regulation of navigable streams, and the Property Clause, Art. IV, § 3, which permits federal regulation of federal lands. The doctrine applies to Indian reservations and other federal enclaves, encompassing water rights in navigable and nonnavigable streams....

...

In determining whether there is a federally reserved water right implicit in a federal reservation of public land, the issue is whether the Government intended to reserve unappropriated and thus available water. Intent is inferred if the previously unappropriated waters are necessary to accomplish the purposes for which the reservation was created.... The Proclamation discussed the pool in Devil's Hole in four of the five preambles and recited that the "pool ... should be given special protection." Since a pool is a body of water, the protection contemplated is meaningful only if the water remains; the water right reserved by the 1952 Proclamation was thus explicit, not implied....

Also explicit in the 1952 Proclamation is the authority of the Director of the Park Service to manage the lands of Devil's Hole Monument "as provided in the act of Congress entitled 'An Act to establish a National Park Service, and for other purposes,' approved August 25, 1916 (39 Stat. 535; 16 U.S.C. §§ 1–3)...." The National Park Service Act provides that the "fundamental purpose of the said parks, monuments, and reservations" is "to conserve the scenery and the natural and historic objects and the wild life therein and to provide for the enjoyment of the same in such manner and by such means as will leave them unimpaired for the enjoyment of future generations." 39 Stat. 535, 16 U.S.C. § 1.

The implied-reservation-of-water-rights doctrine, however, reserves only that amount of water necessary to fulfill the purpose of the reservation, no more. *Arizona v. California*, supra, 373 U.S., at 600–601. Here the purpose of reserving Devil's Hole Monument is preservation of the pool. Devil's Hole was reserved "for the preservation of the unusual features of scenic, scientific, and educational interest." The Proclamation notes that the pool contains "a peculiar race of desert fish ... which is found nowhere else in the world" and that the "pool is of ... outstanding scientific importance...." The pool need only be preserved, consistent with the intention expressed in the Proclamation, to the extent necessary to preserve its scientific interest. The fish are one of the features of scientific interest. The preamble noting the scientific interest of the pool follows the preamble describing the fish as unique; the Proclamation must be read in its entirety. Thus, as the District Court has correctly determined, the level of the pool may be permitted to drop to the extent that the drop does not impair the scientific value of the pool as the natural habitat of the species sought to be preserved. The District Court thus tailored its injunction, very appropriately, to minimal need, curtailing pumping only to the extent necessary to preserve an adequate water level at Devil's Hole, thus implementing the stated objectives of the Proclamation.

Petitioners in both cases argue that even if the intent of the 1952 Proclamation were to maintain the pool, the American Antiquities Preservation Act did not give the President authority to reserve a pool. Under that Act, according to the Cappaert petitioners, the President may reserve federal lands only to protect archeologic sites. However, the language of the Act which authorizes the President to proclaim as national monuments "historic landmarks, historic and prehistoric structures, and other objects of historic or scientific interest that are situated upon the lands owned or controlled by the Government" is not so limited. The pool in Devil's Hole and its rare inhabitants are "objects of historic or scientific interest."

II. Groundwater

No cases of this Court have applied the doctrine of implied reservation of water rights to groundwater. Nevada argues that the implied-reservation doctrine is limited to surface water. Here, however, the water in the pool is surface water. The federal water rights were being depleted because, as the evidence showed, the "(g)roundwater and surface water are physically interrelated as integral parts of the hydrologic cycle." C. Corker, Groundwater Law, Management and Administration, National Water Commission Legal Study No. 6, p. xxiv (1971). Here the Cappaerts are causing the water level in Devil's Hole to drop by their heavy pumping.... It appears that Nevada itself may recognize the potential interrelationship between surface and groundwater since Nevada applies the law of prior appropriation to both. Thus, since the implied-reservation-of-water-rights doctrine is based on the necessity of water for the purpose of the federal reservation, we hold that the United States can protect its water from subsequent diversion, whether the diversion is of surface or groundwater.

III. State Law

Petitioners in both cases argue that the Federal Government must perfect its implied water rights according to state law. They contend that the Desert Land Act of 1877 and its predecessors ... severed nonnavigable water from public land, subjecting it to state law. That Act, however, provides that patentees of public land acquire only title to land through the patent and must acquire water rights in nonnavigable water in accordance with state law. *California Oregon Power Co. v. Beaver Portland Cement Co.*, 295 U.S. 142, 162 (1935).... This Court held in *FPC v. Oregon* that the Desert Land Act does not apply to water rights on federally reserved land....

...

We hold, therefore, that as of 1952 when the United States reserved Devil's Hole, it acquired by reservation water rights in unappropriated appurtenant water sufficient to maintain the level of the pool to preserve its scientific value and thereby implement Proclamation No. 2961. Accordingly, the judgment of the Court of Appeals is

Affirmed.

Notes & Questions

1. The Supreme Court lays out a bright line rule for determining when the federal government impliedly intended to reserve water in the absence of an express statement by Congress. What is the rule? Some scholars refer to *Cappaert* as an express reservation. Where do you think they find justification for that?
2. According to the Court, what is the constitutional basis that allows the United States to reserve water rights for its property? The Court has interpreted the Commerce Clause to allow federal regulation of navigable waters and their tributaries to the extent that an action affects navigability. Does this mean that federal reserved water rights are limited to water from navigable waters? Is the basis the exact same for water rights reserved for the benefit of Indian tribes?
3. What language in *Cappeart* limits the quantification of a reserved water right?
4. Does the Court find that reserved rights extend to groundwater? How does the Court address the fact that the injunction applies to groundwater wells?
5. Note that the Court also articulates a quantification by providing an injunction against drawing the underground pool below a specified level. Consider the steps of scientific proof you would need to go through to establish the information that allowed the Court to reach that conclusion: (1) the Cappaert wells are hydrologically connected to the underground pool that is expressly mentioned in the Proclamation; (2) the pupfish requires an algae-covered shelf in the pool to spawn; (3) if the water is drawn below -3 feet, the shelf is exposed and the pupfish cannot spawn.

Despite its limitation on the implied water right to "only that amount of water necessary to fulfill the purpose of the reservation, no more," the Court's decision in *Cappaert* to allow an injunction diminishing groundwater pumping sent a shock wave through western states. To them, the scope of the *Winters* Doctrine was a surprise and government leaders within the western states sounded the alarm. Because water is critical to the political integrity and economic security of states, as well as the health and welfare of its citizens, control over water has long been viewed as a critical component of governmental sovereignty. Although the Constitution expressly vests Congress with power over federal property (including water), years of congressional acquiescence to seemingly total state control over water law and policy had led to beliefs that states had total jurisdiction over the allocation of all water resources within their borders (despite *Winters*). While the first half of the twentieth century welcomed federal development of western water under the Reclamation Act covered in Chapter 16, the second half heralded a tension over who controls water. With the Court's decisions in *Arizona v. California* and *Cappaert*, states now faced the possibility that the federal government retained control over vast water rights appurtenant to those federal lands that had

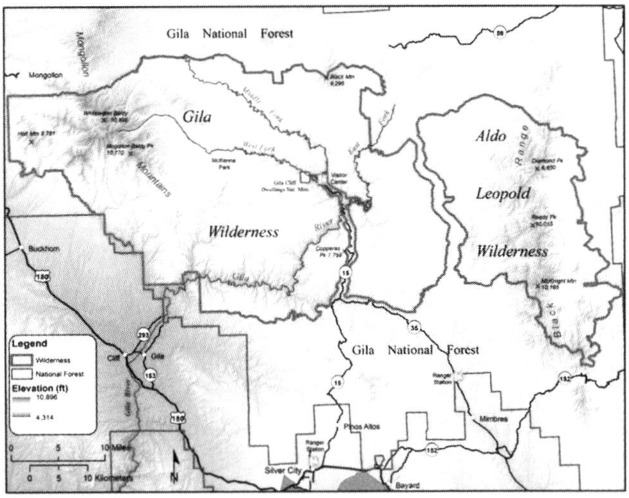

Figure 14.4 Gila National Forest and associated Wilderness Areas in New Mexico. The Rio Mimbres headwaters in the national forest and flows southeast through private land. Source: Molly E. Hunter et al., *Historical and Current Fire Management Practices in Two Wilderness Areas in the Southwestern United States*, USDA Report No. RMRS-GTR-325 (2014). https://www.fs.usda.gov/rm/pubs/rmrs_gtr325.pdf.

been withdrawn from the public domain and reserved for a specific purpose. As noted above, this would be all except the public lands managed by the Bureau of Land Management (Figure 14.2).[1] That was an untenable situation for many western states, which began to look for ways to limit the *Winters* Doctrine.

The next case addresses claims of the United States Forest Service for water rights appurtenant to the Gila National Forest (Figure 14.4). The case concerns an adjudication in state court of all the water rights from the Rio Mimbres. The river serves irrigation and mining interests on private lands and the United States filed claims for reserved water rights for the national forest. You will learn in Part VI why a state may adjudicate federal water rights. This case is one of the few results out of a state adjudication that has been granted certiorari on petition to the U.S. Supreme Court. As you read the case, consider how the Supreme Court balanced the competing sovereign interests of the states and the United States and how it limits the concept of reserved water rights. Again, consider whether the reasoning behind this limitation applies to Indian reservations. Also, consider why irrigators downstream from a National Forest would object to a reserved water right for instream flow on the forest land—i.e., a right that would require the water to be left in the stream until it flows off the forest where it would be available for their appropriation.

1. Note that BLM land also includes designated Wilderness Areas and Wild and Scenic rivers, which may have reserved water rights.

United States v. New Mexico

Supreme Court of the United States
438 U.S. 696 (1978)

Mr. Justice REHNQUIST delivered the opinion of the Court— ... The State District Court held that the United States, in setting aside the Gila National Forest from other public lands, reserved the use of such water "as may be necessary for the purposes for which [the land was] withdrawn," but that these purposes did not include recreation, aesthetics, wildlife preservation, or cattle grazing. The United States appealed unsuccessfully to the Supreme Court of New Mexico. We granted certiorari to consider whether the Supreme Court of New Mexico had applied the correct principles of federal law in determining petitioner's reserved rights in the Mimbres. We now affirm.

I

The question posed in this case—what quantity of water, if any, the United States reserved out of the Rio Mimbres when it set aside the Gila National Forest in 1899—is a question of implied intent and not power. In *California v. United States* [you will study this case in Chapter 16 when you learn about Reclamation Law], we had occasion to discuss the respective authority of Federal and State Governments over waters in the Western States. The Court has previously concluded that whatever powers the States acquired over their waters as a result of congressional Acts and admission into the Union, however, Congress did not intend thereby to relinquish its authority to reserve unappropriated water in the future for use on appurtenant lands withdrawn from the public domain for specific federal purposes [citing *Winters, Arizona v. California,* and *Cappaert*].

... Substantial portions of the public domain *have* been withdrawn and reserved by the United States for use as Indian reservations, forest reserves, national parks, and national monuments. And water is frequently necessary to achieve the purposes for which these reservations are made. But Congress has seldom expressly reserved water for use on these withdrawn lands. If water were abundant, Congress' silence would pose no problem. In the arid parts of the West, however, claims to water for use on federal reservations inescapably vie with other public and private claims for the limited quantities to be found in the rivers and streams. This competition is compounded by the sheer quantity of reserved lands in the Western States....

... While many of the contours of what has come to be called the "implied-reservation-of-water doctrine" remain unspecified, the Court has repeatedly emphasized that Congress reserved "only that amount of water necessary to fulfill the purpose of the reservation, no more." *Cappaert, supra*, at 141.... Each time this Court has applied the "implied-reservation-of-water doctrine," it has carefully examined both the asserted water right and the specific purposes for which the land was reserved, and concluded that without the water the purposes of the reservation would be entirely defeated....

This careful examination is required both because the reservation is implied, rather than expressed, and because of the history of congressional intent in the field of federal-state jurisdiction with respect to allocation of water. Where Congress has expressly addressed the question of whether federal entities must abide by state water law, it has almost invariably deferred to the state law. See *California v. United States*. Where water is necessary to fulfill the very purposes for which a federal reservation was created, it is reasonable to conclude, even in the face of Congress' express deference to state water law in other areas, that the United States intended to reserve the necessary water. Where water is only valuable for a secondary use of the reservation, however, there arises the contrary inference that Congress intended, consistent with its other views, that the United States would acquire water in the same manner as any other public or private appropriator.

. . .

[The State District Court appointed a Special Master who recommended water for: domestic-residential use, road-water, recreational, wildlife, stock watering and instream flow for fish preservation.] ...

The District Court of Luna County ... concluded that the United States had not established a reserved right to a minimum instream flow for any of the purposes for which the Gila National Forest was established, and that any water rights arising from cattle grazing by permittees on the forest should be adjudicated "to the permittee under the law of prior appropriation and not to the United States."

The United States appealed this decision to the Supreme Court of New Mexico. The United States contended that it was entitled to a minimum instream flow for "aesthetic, environmental, recreational and 'fish' purposes." ... The Supreme Court of New Mexico concluded that, at least before the Multiple-Use Sustained-Yield Act of 1960, national forests could only be created "to insure favorable conditions of water flow and to furnish a continuous supply of timber" and not for the purposes upon which the United States was now basing its asserted reserved rights in a minimum instream flow.... The United States also argued that it was entitled to a reserved right for stockwatering purposes. The State Supreme Court again disagreed, holding that stockwatering was not a purpose for which the national forests were created....

II. A

The quantification of reserved water rights for the national forests is of critical importance to the West, where, as noted earlier, water is scarce and where more than 50% of the available water either originates in or flows through national forests. When, as in the case of the Rio Mimbres, a river is fully appropriated, federal reserved water rights will frequently require a gallon-for-gallon reduction in the amount of water available for water-needy state and private appropriators. This reality has not escaped the attention of Congress and must be weighed in determining what, if any, water Congress reserved for use in the national forests.

The United States contends that Congress intended to reserve minimum instream flows for aesthetic, recreational, and fish-preservation purposes. An examination of the limited purposes for which Congress authorized the creation of national forests, however, provides no support for this claim. In the mid and late 1800's, many of the forests on the public domain were ravaged and the fear arose that the forest lands might soon disappear, leaving the United States with a shortage both of timber and of watersheds with which to encourage stream flows while preventing floods. It was in answer to these fears that in 1891 Congress authorized the President to "set apart and reserve, ... any State or Territory having public land bearing forests, in any part of the public lands wholly or in part covered with timber or undergrowth, whether of commercial value or not, as public reservations."

The Creative Act of 1891 unfortunately did not solve the forest problems of the expanding Nation. To the dismay of the conservationists, the new national forests were not adequately attended and regulated; fires and indiscriminate timber cutting continued their toll. To the anguish of Western settlers, reservations were frequently made indiscriminately....

Congress' answer to these continuing problems was three-fold. It suspended the President's Executive Order of February 22, 1897; it carefully defined the purposes for which national forests could in the future be reserved; and it provided a charter for forest management and economic uses within the forests. Organic Administration Act of June 4, 1897. In particular, Congress provided:

> *No national forest shall be established, except to improve and protect the forest within the boundaries, or for the purpose of securing favorable conditions of water flows, and to furnish a continuous supply of timber for the use and necessities of citizens of the United States;* ...

The legislative debates surrounding the Organic Administration Act of 1897 and its predecessor bills demonstrate that Congress intended national forests to be reserved for only two purposes—"[t]o conserve the water flows, and to furnish a continuous supply of timber for the people." ... 30 Cong.Rec. 967 (1897) (Cong. McRae). National forests were not to be reserved for aesthetic, environmental, recreational, or wildlife-preservation purposes.

> "The objects for which the forest reservations should be made are the protection of the forest growth against destruction by fire and ax, and preservation of forest conditions upon which water conditions and water flow are dependent. The purpose, therefore, of this bill is to maintain favorable forest conditions, without excluding the use of these reservations for other purposes. They are not parks set aside for nonuse, but have been established for economic reasons."

30 Cong.Rec. 966 (1897) (Cong. McRae).

Administrative regulations at the turn of the century confirmed that national forests were to be reserved for only these two limited purposes.

Any doubt as to the relatively narrow purposes for which national forests were to be reserved is removed by comparing the broader language Congress used to authorize the establishment of national parks. In 1916, Congress created the National Park Service and provided that the "fundamental purpose of the said parks, monuments, and reservations ... is to conserve the scenery and the natural and historic objects and the wild life therein and to provide for the enjoyment of the same ... unimpaired for the enjoyment of future generations." National Park Service Act of 1916, 39 Stat. 535, § 1, as amended, 16 U.S.C. § 1 (1976 ed.).

When it was Congress' intent to maintain minimum instream flows within the confines of a national forest, it expressly so directed, as it did in the case of the Lake Superior National Forest:

> "In order to preserve the shore lines, rapids, waterfalls, beaches and other natural features of the region in an unmodified state of nature, no further alteration of the natural water level of any lake or stream ... shall be authorized." 16 U.S.C. § 577b (1976 ed.).

National park legislation is not the only instructive comparison. In the Act of Mar. 10, 1934 Congress authorized the establishment within individual national forests of fish and game sanctuaries, *but only with the consent of the state legislatures....*

If, as the dissent contends, *post*, at 3025, Congress in the Organic Administration Act of 1897 authorized the reservation of forests to "improve and protect" fish and wildlife, the 1934 Act would have been unnecessary. Nor is the dissent's position consistent with Congress' concern in 1934 that fish and wildlife preserves only be created "with the approval of the State legislatures."

As the dissent notes, in creating what would ultimately become Yosemite National Park, Congress in 1890 explicitly instructed the Secretary of the Interior to provide against the wanton destruction of fish and game inside the forest and against their taking "for the purposes of merchandise or profit." Act of Oct. 1, 1890, § 2, 26 Stat. 651. Congress also instructed the Secretary to protect all "the natural curiosities, or wonders within such reservation, ... in their natural condition." By comparison, Congress in the 1897 Organic Act expressed no concern for the preservation of fish and wildlife within national forests generally. Nor is such a concern found in any of the comments made during the legislative debate on the 1897 Act.

...

C

In 1960, Congress passed the Multiple-Use Sustained-Yield Act of 1960, which provides

> "It is the policy of Congress that the national forests are established and shall be administered for outdoor recreation, range, timber, watershed, and wildlife and fish purposes. The purposes of sections 528 to 531 of this title are declared to be supplemental to, but not in derogation of, the purposes for which the national forests were established as set forth in the [Organic Administration Act of 1897.]"

The Supreme Court of New Mexico concluded that this Act did not give rise to any reserved rights not previously authorized in the Organic Administration Act of 1897. "The Multiple-Use Sustained-Yield Act of 1960 does not have a retroactive effect nor can it broaden the purposes for which the Gila National Forest was established under the Organic Act of 1897." While we conclude that the Multiple-Use Sustained-Yield Act of 1960 was intended to broaden the purposes for which national forests had previously been administered, we agree that Congress did not intend to thereby expand the reserved rights of the United States.

The Multiple-Use Sustained-Yield Act of 1960 establishes the purposes for which the national forests "*are* established and *shall* be administered." (Emphasis added.) The Act directs the Secretary of the Agriculture to administer all forests, including those previously established, on a multiple-use and sustained-yield basis. In the administration of the national forests, therefore, Congress intended the Multiple-Use Sustained-Yield Act of 1960 to broaden the benefits accruing from all reserved national forests.

The House Report accompanying the 1960 legislation, however, indicates that recreation, range, and "fish" purposes are "to be supplemental to, but not in derogation of, the purposes for which the national forests were established" in the Organic Administration Act of 1897.

...

As discussed earlier, the "reserved rights doctrine" is a doctrine built on implication and is an exception to Congress' explicit deference to state water law in other areas. Without legislative history to the contrary, we are led to conclude that Congress did not intend in enacting the Multiple-Use Sustained-Yield Act of 1960 to reserve water for the *secondary* purposes there established....

...

IV

Congress intended that water would be reserved only where necessary to preserve the timber or to secure favorable water flows for private and public uses under state law. This intent is revealed in the purposes for which the national forest system was created and Congress' principled deference to state water law in the Organic Administration Act of 1897 and other legislation. The decision of the Supreme Court of New Mexico is faithful to this congressional intent and is therefore

Affirmed.

Mr. Justice POWELL, with whom Mr. Justice BRENNAN, Mr. Justice WHITE, and Mr. Justice MARSHALL join, dissenting in part.

I agree with the Court that the implied-reservation doctrine should be applied with sensitivity to its impact upon those who have obtained water rights under state law and to Congress' general policy of deference to state water law....

I do not agree, however, that the forests which Congress intended to "improve and protect" are the still, silent, lifeless places envisioned by the Court. In my view, the forests consist of the birds, animals, and fish-the wildlife-that inhabit them, as well as the trees, flowers, shrubs, and grasses. I therefore would hold that the United States is entitled to so much water as is necessary to sustain the wildlife of the forests, as well as the plants. I also add a word concerning the impact of the Court's holding today on future claims by the United States that the reservation of particular national forests impliedly reserved instream flows....

...

Notes & Questions

1. For what purposes does the United States claim water rights in *New Mexico*? Can you counter the argument made by the Court that the language of the Organic Act for national forests only gives rise to two purposes?
2. To the Court, it is important that "[federal] claims ... inescapably vie with other public and private claims for [water]," and they "will frequently require a gallon-for-gallon reduction in the amount of water available for water-needy state and private appropriators...." According to the Court, how do these facts color congressional intent when it sets aside land? Is it true that an upstream instream flow requires "a gallon-for-gallon reduction in the amount of water available" for downstream private irrigation?
3. *New Mexico* gave rise to the primary-secondary purposes rule. What is that rule? How does the Court differentiate between primary and secondary purposes?
4. *New Mexico* marked a significant recalibration in the scope of the *Winters* Doctrine. Afterward, it was clear that the doctrine, at least as applicable to federal, non-Indian reservations, only allowed for the reservation of water rights necessary to fulfill the "primary" purposes of the federal reservation of land. And a purpose would only be considered a "primary" purpose if "water is necessary to fulfill the very purposes for which a federal reservation was created...." It is up to the courts to sift through the claimed purposes of any given reservation and anoint those it deems to be "primary." As a result, the primary-secondary purposes test has proven to be a powerful tool for courts, usually state courts, that are often under considerable political pressure to limit the scope of the reserved rights doctrine.[2] Does this primary-secondary test reasoning apply to Indian Reservations?
5. The "partial dissent" in *New Mexico* begins by stating: "I agree with the Court that the implied-reservation doctrine should be applied with sensitivity to its impact upon those who have obtained water rights under state law and to Congress' general policy of deference to state water law." This sentence gave rise to what is known as the "sensitivity doctrine." Justice O'Conner used this concept when she wrote what would have been the majority opinion in appeal of a major Native American water right case from Wyoming. She later recused herself due to family claims to water in the Gila River adjudication in Arizona. As a result, what would have been a 5–4 opinion became a plurality simply refusing to alter the state court decision. But the draft opinion became public on release of Justice Marshall's papers following his

2. *See, e.g.*, Sandra B. Zellmer and Justin Huber, *The Shallows Where Federal Reserved Water Rights Founder: State Derogation of the* Winters *Doctrine*, 16 U. Den. Water L. Rev 261, 283–89 (2013).

death. O'Connor would have required "sensitivity" to private development and reduced the quantification of the tribal water right if the irrigation projects proposed for calculation of PIA lacked a "reasonable likelihood" of being built. This approach has never been adopted, but is part of the debate over whether *New Mexico* should have any bearing on Native American reserved water rights. As you will learn in Part VI, Congress has allowed state courts to assert jurisdiction to adjudicate Native American and federal reserved water rights in comprehensive water adjudications.

Discerning the Purposes of the Federal Non-Indian Reservations

For reasons we will explore in Part VI, the federal courts have had limited opportunity to address type of use or quantification of reserved water right for non-Indian reservations. *Cappaert* and *New Mexico* are the only cases on the scope of federal non-Indian reserved rights to reach the U.S. Supreme Court. As a result, many questions regarding the scope of the *Winters* Doctrine remain to be answered.

To help you understand some of the questions that remain, we conclude this section with a district court opinion that analyzes the purposes for the creation of a number of wilderness areas within Colorado. Notably, this case was ultimately dismissed by the Tenth Circuit, which held that the issues were not ripe for review. *Sierra Club v. Yeutter*, 911 F.2d 1405 (1990). Nevertheless, the case remains instructive on how federal courts have interpreted the *Winters* Doctrine in application to federal (non-Indian) reservations since *Cappaert* and *New Mexico*.

In *Sierra Club v. Block,* the lower court found a reserved water right for instream flows to preserve the wilderness character of designated Wilderness Areas in Colorado. The Wilderness Act passed Congress in 1964, when the western map of the distribution of federal lands was already defined. It authorized the designation by Congress of Wilderness Areas within other land management categories including national forests, public lands, and national parks. The map of the Wilderness Areas in Colorado, the subject of the next case, illustrates this nesting of Wilderness Areas within lands with a broader purpose (Figure 14.5). Pay attention to where the court finds the purposes of the Wilderness Act. Consider how it handles the fact that the Wilderness Areas in question were created within National Forest land, thus no new "withdrawal" occurred on their creation. Consider the type of scientific evidence that would be necessary to establish the quantification of the instream flows (a topic you will learn about in Part VI). Note also that the court addresses the instream flow rights created under the original reservation as national forests *for the purpose of securing favorable conditions of water flows,* as found in New Mexico. The court also addresses concerns with existing water infrastructure projects located within newly designated wilderness areas.

Colorado National and Public Lands

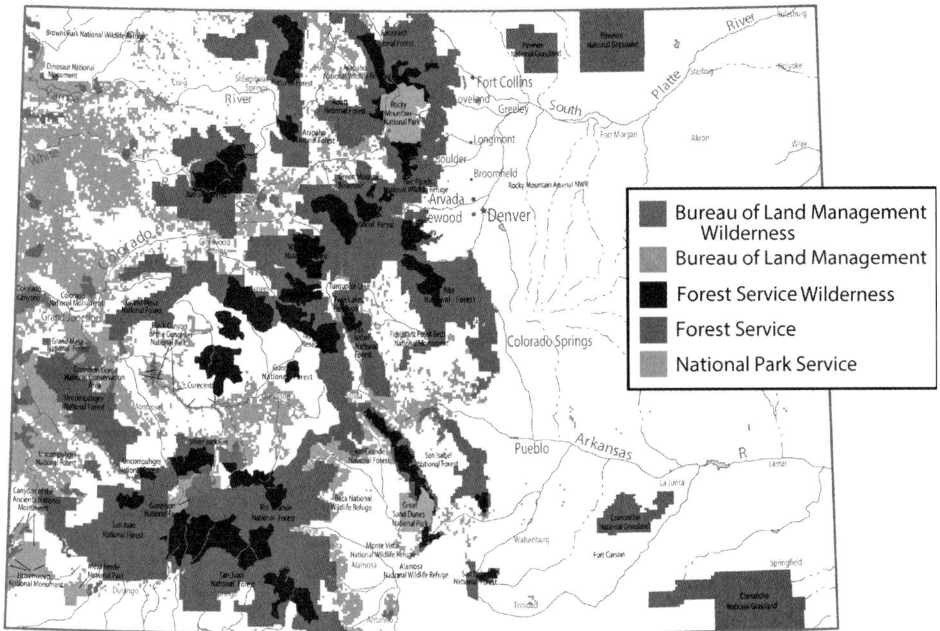

Map courtesy of the U.S. Geological Survey

Figure 14.5 Map of Colorado Wilderness Areas illustrating nesting within national forests, national parks and monuments, and public (BLM) lands. Source: USGS.

Sierra Club v. Block

United States District Court, D. Colorado
622 F. Supp. 842 (1985)

MEMORANDUM OPINION AND ORDER

KANE, District Judge—I. INTRODUCTION

Plaintiff Sierra Club brought this action seeking relief against the following federal officials: John Block, Secretary of Agriculture;....

Sierra Club contends that federal reserved water rights exist in each of the designated wilderness areas which federal defendants administer in Colorado, and that these reserved water rights are implied from the Wilderness Act, 78 Stat. 890, 16 U.S.C. §§ 1131 *et seq.* It is further asserted that federal defendants have failed to claim these reserved water rights....

Review of federal defendants' alleged inaction is sought under the Administrative Procedure Act (APA). Sierra Club requests that I enter a declaratory judgment, pursuant to the Declaratory Judgment Act to the effect that: 1) federal reserved water rights exist in each of the subject Colorado wilderness areas, and 2) the failure of federal defendants to claim those rights is arbitrary and capricious, constitutes unlawfully withheld agency action, and is a violation of the public trust. Sierra Club also requests an order requiring federal defendants to take such action as I deem necessary to protect reserved water rights in the Colorado wilderness areas....

...

III. BACKGROUND

As will become apparent, resolution of these issues, particularly that of whether federal reserved water rights exist in the Colorado wilderness areas, centers primarily on the legislative history and the specific provisions of the Wilderness Act....

From 1924 to 1939, the Secretary of Agriculture and the Chief of the Forest Service took it upon themselves to set aside certain primitive areas of the national forests as wilderness-type areas.... Although this action was widely approved, concern was expressed, beginning in the late 1940s and early 1950s, regarding the federal officials' unrestricted power over, and the tenuous status of, these wilderness-type areas....

This concern prompted the introduction of legislation in 1956 to give statutory recognition to, and congressional control over, the wilderness-type areas....

After eight years of debate and consideration of successive bills on the subject, Congress established the National Wilderness Preservation System by passing the Wilderness Act on September 3, 1964. Initially, the Wilderness Act gave "statutory designation as wilderness to all but one of the areas classified by the Department of Agriculture or the Chief of the Forest Service ... and provide[d] for their inclusion in [the] national wilderness preservation system."... Since 1964, however, Congress has designated many additional areas of federally-owned land as wilderness pursuant to the Act.

As the legislative history and the provisions of the Wilderness Act make abundantly clear, the primary motivation of Congress in establishing the wilderness preservation system was to "guarantee ... that these lands will be kept in their original untouched natural state." 110 Cong.Rec. 17448 (statement of Rep. Cleveland); *see* 16 U.S.C. § 1131(a)....

...

Regarding the administration of areas designated as wilderness, Congress provided that "the area shall continue to be managed by the Department and agency having jurisdiction thereover immediately before its inclusion in the ... [system] unless otherwise provided by Act of Congress." 16 U.S.C. § 1131(b). Under § 1133(b), "each agency administering any area designated as wilderness shall be responsible for preserving the wilderness character of the area ..." Specifically, Congress mandated that "wilderness areas shall be devoted to the public purposes of recreational, scenic, scientific, educational, conservation, and historical use." 16 U.S.C. § 1133(b).

In preserving the natural state of the wilderness areas, Congress prohibited or seriously limited most uses inconsistent with the protection of the wilderness, such as mining, timbercutting, road-building, and other commercial uses. *See* 16 U.S.C. § 1133(c) and (d). In this respect, wilderness areas differ greatly from the national forests, for example, where such uses are permitted. *See* S.R.Rep. No. 109, 88th Cong., 1st Sess. at 12–15 (1963).

...

IV. FEDERAL RESERVED WATER RIGHTS

... for the reasons stated below, I now explicitly hold, and enter final declaratory judgment, pursuant to 28 U.S.C. § 2201 and 5 U.S.C. § 706, that federal reserved water rights do exist in the designated Colorado wilderness areas.

A. Implied-Reservation-of-Water Doctrine

The doctrine of implied-reservation-of-water is judicially created. [The court reviews *Winters*] ...

The effect of *Winters* was to superimpose a judicially implied federal water right on a state system that based water rights on prior appropriation. The full implications of this decision were not apparent, however, until over fifty years later when the Court considered the application of the doctrine to non-Indian federal reservations in *Arizona v. California,* 373 U.S. 546, 83 S.Ct. 1468, 10 L.Ed.2d 542 (1963).

... [The court reviews *Cappaert* and *New Mexico*]

B. Withdrawal and Reservation

... [The court reviews the difference between public domain lands and reserved lands.]

Although often used interchangeably, the terms "withdraw" and "reserve" have different meanings. "Withdrawal" generally refers to the act of removing certain lands from the operation of federal mining, homestead or other disposal and use-related laws. "Reservation", on the other hand, as stated above, generally refers to the dedication of federal lands to a specific federal purpose.... The reason these terms are used interchangeably is that, usually, a reservation includes a withdrawal.

In the instant case, each of the subject wilderness areas was created from previously reserved national forest lands in Colorado....

Although wilderness designation was not the *original* withdrawal from the public domain and reservation of the land in this case, it does not follow that wilderness areas were not withdrawn and reserved or that the implied-reservation-of-water doctrine is not applicable. On the contrary, application of the definitions of "withdrawal" and "reservation" to this case, as well as legislative history of the Wilderness Act, clearly demonstrate that the wilderness areas were in fact withdrawn and reserved.

First, it is clear from the Wilderness Act itself that the wilderness areas designated pursuant to the Act were withdrawn from use-related laws. For example, 16 U.S.C. § 1133(d)(3) states that "the minerals in lands designated by this chapter as wilderness areas are *withdrawn* from all forms of appropriation under the mining laws and from disposition under all laws pertaining to mineral leasing and all amendments thereto" (emphasis added). Other provisions seriously limit additional uses inconsistent with wilderness preservation. Section 1133(c) provides that

> there shall be no commercial enterprise and no permanent road within any wilderness area designated by this chapter and, except as necessary to meet minimum requirements for the administration of the area for the purpose of this chapter (including measures required in emergencies involving the health and safety of persons within the area), there shall be no temporary road, no use of motor vehicles, motorized equipment or motorboats, no landing of aircraft, no other form of mechanical transport, and no structure or installation within any such area.

...

Additionally, the Wilderness Act specifies particular federal purposes to which the wilderness areas are dedicated....

Moreover, there are several instances in the legislative history of the Wilderness Act which demonstrate that Congress intended that the wilderness areas be withdrawn and reserved. First, the debates regarding the Wilderness Act reveal that it was the "outgrowth" of investigations and a report by the Outdoor Recreation Resources Review Commission.... After three years of investigation and research, the commission issued a report in January 1962. In that report, which members of Congress quoted from during the debate on the Wilderness Act, *see, e.g.*, 110 Cong.Rec. 5885 (statements of Sen. Anderson), the commission stated that

> [t]here is a widespread feeling, which the Commission shares, that the Congress should take action to assure the permanent *reservation* of these [wilderness areas] and similar suitable areas in national forests, national parks, wildlife refuges, and other lands in Federal ownership.

Outdoor Recreation Resources Review Commission, *Outdoor Recreation for America, A Report to the President and to the Congress* (1962) (emphasis added).

...

The fact that the Wilderness Act withdrew the designated wilderness areas from disposal or use-related laws and that it established specific purposes for the wilderness areas amply demonstrates that Congress intended that these areas be "withdrawn" and "reserved".... Accordingly, I hold that a withdrawal and reservation of these lands has been made.

Defendant-intervenors' contention that the Wilderness Act is merely a land management statute is similarly without merit. Defendant-intervenors attempt to liken the Wilderness Act to land management statutes such as the Federal Land Policy and Management Act (FLPMA), 90 Stat. 2744, ... the Multiple-Use Sustained-Yield Act of 1960 (MUSYA), 74 Stat. 215, ... Defendant-intervenors overlook the fact, however, that none of these land management statutes effect a withdrawal and reservation of lands as does the Wilderness Act....

In sum, the Wilderness Act does effect a withdrawal and reservation of wilderness areas to which the implied-reservation-of-water doctrine applies. Wilderness designation creates an entirely new category of lands dedicated to preservation and conservation. Wilderness is not simply a land-management status. Rather, wilderness areas are federal reservations whose status, as concerns the implied-reservation-of-water doctrine, is equal to that of other federal reservations such as national forests, parks, and monuments.

C. Congressional Intent and Purposes

...

The Wilderness Act contains several congressional statements of purpose for the National Wilderness Preservation System. Under 16 U.S.C. § 1131(a), wilderness areas are designated for the purpose of "preservation and protection in their natural condition, ... to secure for the American people of present and future generations the benefits of an enduring resource of wilderness." Wilderness is defined by 16 U.S.C. § 1131(c) to be "an area where the earth and its community of life are untrammeled by man, where man himself is a visitor who does not remain", and is further defined as "retaining its primeval character and influence, without permanent improvements or human habitation, ... [which] has outstanding opportunities for solitude or a primitive and unconfined type of recreation; ... [and] may also contain ecological, geological, or other features of scientific, educational, scenic, or historical value." Additionally, Congress mandated that the "wilderness areas shall be devoted to the public purposes of recreation, scenic, scientific, educational, conservation, and historical use." 16 U.S.C. § 1133(b).

These purposes were emphasized again and again during the hearings and debates on the Wilderness Act....

... Senator Hubert Humphrey, one of the earliest sponsors of wilderness legislation, stated that

> [o]f all the pieces of legislation that have been passed, in terms of looking to the future, in terms of providing for the recreational needs of our people, in terms of preservation of the great resources of America and the need of a growing population to know something of the great out of doors, untouched and unscathed, nothing is more significant than this piece of legislation.

110 Cong.Rec. 20602 (statement of Sen. Humphrey).

While these concerns and purposes were foremost in the minds of its members, Congress also sought to carry over and maintain the purposes for which the national forests had been established....

At first blush, it would appear that the purposes of conserving water flows and providing a continuous supply of timber conflict with the conservation and recreational purposes set forth in the Wilderness Act.... Defendant-intervenors' argument ignores, however, the legislative history of the Wilderness Act. Additionally, their reliance on *New Mexico* as dispositive of this issue is misplaced because *New Mexico* is distinguishable in several respects.

First, the legislative history establishes that Congress was indeed concerned with protecting the watersheds and preserving water flows for downstream irrigation and domestic use as well as preserving the character of the wilderness and providing for recreation:

> If we do not act now to conserve our vanishing wilderness, it will soon be lost forever. The wilderness not only is important to those who love the outdoor life and the sportsmen who hunt and fish there; it is equally needed for nature studies and general scientific inquiry, and for wise watershed and wildlife conservation.

110 Cong.Rec. 5942 (statement of Sen. Church) (emphasis added). It was further stated that

> one of the purposes of the proposed legislation is to prevent a further opening up of the area, which is what has occurred in past years, so that the scenic and wilderness values, which are the predominant values, can be preserved, and so that the wildlife and the *watershed* can be preserved as well.

110 Cong.Rec. 5895 (statement of Sen. Church) (emphasis added).

Congress was aware of the need to protect the watersheds in these mostly high alpine wilderness areas and, clearly, it intended to carry over and maintain this important purpose in the Wilderness Act. This purpose does not, however, conflict with the other purposes of the Wilderness Act. On the contrary, preservation of wilderness areas in their natural state actually enhances water quality and quantity....

...

New Mexico is distinguishable from the instant case in several respects. First, as stated above, unlike the MUSYA, the Wilderness Act is not a land-management statute....

Second, as discussed above, the conservation and recreation purposes of the Wilderness Act do not conflict with the purposes of conserving water flow. In fact, these purposes are completely compatible....

...

In sum, it is clear that Congress intended each of the purposes specified in the Wilderness Act to be primary, rather than secondary, in nature. For this reason, in addition to those stated above, *New Mexico* is inapposite.

Moreover, contrary to defendant-intervenors' assertions, Congress intended to reserve previously unappropriated waters in the wilderness areas to the extent necessary to accomplish these purposes. It is beyond cavil that water is the lifeblood of the wilderness areas. Without water, the wilderness would become deserted wastelands. In other words, without access to the requisite water, the very purposes for which the Wilderness Act was established would be entirely defeated. Clearly, this result was not intended by Congress. Accordingly, under the implied-reservation-of-water doctrine, it is implied from the Wilderness Act that Congress reserved water rights in the wilderness areas to the extent necessary to accomplish the purposes specified in the Act.

Thus, I now hold that federal reserved water rights do exist in previously unappropriated water in each of the Colorado wilderness areas designated as such pursuant to the Wilderness Act and managed by federal defendants.

Insofar as the purpose of conserving water flows was originally attached to creation of the national forests, the priority of reserved rights for that purpose dates back to the original forest reservation. *See United States v. City and County of Denver,* 656 P.2d 1, 30–31 (Colo. 1982). Reserved rights for the remaining primary purposes of the Wilderness Act vest on the date of the individual reservations or designations as wilderness....

On the other hand, it is important to note that these reserved rights will probably have little effect on prior appropriators. Nor did Congress intend to interfere with existing water projects. For example, with respect to the La Garita Wilderness, Congress stated that

> [w]ater diversion facilities exist within a portion of the proposed additions, and it is the committee's intention that wilderness designation not interfere with necessary operation, maintenance or repair of such facilities.

H.R.Rep. No. 617, 96th Cong. 1st Sess. at 9 (1979).

...

[The court goes on to find that the Wilderness Act "unequivocally imposes certain duties on the part of agencies and officials administering the wilderness areas." But that in the absence of a statutory duty to protect them through legal action, the court cannot find them in violation of the APA. However, the court does feel it necessary to ensure that the USFS will take some measure to protect the wilderness water rights, thus it states the following.]

...

I am still obligated, however, to insure federal defendants' compliance with statutory law....

As the briefs and the administrative record show, reserved water rights is only one of several tools available to federal defendants to meet their statutory duty to protect and preserve wilderness water resources....

Now that the issue of whether reserved water rights exist in these areas has been resolved, it is necessary to give federal defendants the opportunity to consider further the usefulness of these rights in complying with their statutory duty to protect wilderness water resources. These federal defendants are required to meet clear statutory obligations. How they meet this responsibility is a matter left to their discretion. Whether they must meet this responsibility is no longer subject to dispute. In remanding this action to the federal defendants, I order them to come forward with a memorandum explaining their analysis, final decision, and plan to comply with their statutory obligations regarding protection and preservation of wilderness water resources.

...

Notes & Questions

1. What is the purpose of the reservation in *Sierra Club v. Block*, and where does the Court find that purpose?
2. Since wilderness areas may be created within other federal lands, including those that have already been withdrawn from the public lands, does it matter if there is no new "withdrawal?" In other words, is the Wilderness Act merely a change in administration similar to the Multiple-Use Sustained Yield Act held by the Supreme Court to merely broaden administration of forests rather than create new purposes in *New Mexico*?
3. What questions would you need to have your experts explore to try to establish a quantification for the instream flows?
4. Pursuant to the order of the court, the Forest Service had to develop a "memorandum explaining their analysis, final decision, and plan to comply with their statutory obligations regarding protection and preservation of wilderness water resources." The court later found the report supplied by the Forest Service inadequate in *Sierra Club v. Lyng*, 661 F. Supp. 1490 (1987) stating:

> The plan submitted in response to this order is woefully inadequate and constitutes an insouciant disregard of the government's statutory responsibility to protect wilderness area federal reserved water rights. In violation of my order of November 25, 1985, the plan does not describe the actions of the agency on remand. I therefore have no way of ascertaining how the agency reached its cursory conclusions. In addition, as related above in detail, the plan gives short shrift to the possible advantages and disadvantages involved in a prompt adjudication of reserved federal water rights in Colorado's wilderness areas. The government has seen fit to adjudicate reserved federal water rights in many, if not all, of the reserved federal lands in Colorado *except* for wilderness areas.... This omission is entirely unexplained. Finally, the plan is completely deficient in the kind of detail necessary to conduct a satisfactory review of agency action. For example, no facts are provided about the location, date, extent, etc. of any of the individual absolute or conditional water rights mentioned in the plan. Remand is once again necessary, and the possibility of sanctions against the federal defendants now appears on the horizon.

The USFS report contained the following brief analysis of alternatives.[3] Consider how you might advise an agency in preparing a document like this at the request of a court.

> *Alternatives*
>
> As stated above, the Forest Service has not found any present threats of adverse effects upon wilderness water resources that would impair the intent of Congress for the identified wilderness areas in Colorado. However, as with the

3. United States Department of Agriculture, *Report on Methods for Protecting Wilderness Water Resources on Lands Administered by the Forest Service,* included as an addendum to *Sierra Club v. Lyng*.

management and protection of any of the lands and related resources administered by the Forest Service, there are various methods of resource protection available to the agency. Depending upon the factual circumstances presented, the Forest Service can protect wilderness water resources by one or more of the following:

1. Deny or impose protective conditions in any land use authorizations for any activity on National Forest System land outside of, but in a position to affect, water resources in any designated wilderness area.
2. Recommend to the President protective conditions in or the denial of any authorization for construction of water diversion or storage facilities in a designated Wilderness Area.
3. Recommend litigation to the Department of Justice in those situations where any activity not amenable to control by land use authorization threatens to adversely affect water resources in a designated Wilderness Area.
4. Acquire or seek authority to acquire land or water rights where necessary to eliminate any threat of adverse effect upon wilderness water resources.
5. Report to the President for transmission to the Congress, as provided for in the Wilderness Act, 16 U.S.C. 1136, any problems created by future water developments outside of the lands administered by the Forest Service that may adversely affect wilderness water resources.
6. Comment on and recommend the denial or conditioning of any permits, rights-of-way, or licenses issued by other federal agencies for water developments that may adversely affect wilderness water resources.

In addition, the Forest Service will maintain communication and coordination with the State of Colorado so that actions taken by the State of Colorado under authority of state water law may complement the protection of wilderness water resources provided by the Forest Service.

This Chapter has provided you with the primary federal court pronouncements on reserved water rights for federal non-Indian reservations. *Cappaert* and *New Mexico* introduced you to the concept of federal deference to states in water allocation and the resulting narrowing of the application of the *Winters* Doctrine. You will revisit this issue in Part VI when state courts consider whether this narrowing applies to Indian reserved water rights. The Wilderness water cases have given you a taste of the issues that arise in considering federal reserved water rights, but the major scientific issue of how to quantify the rights remains untested. Much of that work begins with state court adjudication and settlement covered in Part VI.

Chapter 15

The Commerce Clause: The Public Trust Doctrine and Public Rights

Introduction

In addition to the private rights to use water through state allocation and federal reservation, there are also certain public rights in this common pool resource and the land underlying it. This Chapter introduces you to the ancient concept of the public rights in the beds and banks of federally recognized navigable waterways (the Public Trust Doctrine or PTD), as well as the concept of public rights to access and use *in situ* (meaning in place) on state-recognized navigable waterways. This Chapter is included under Part IV, addressing the federal role in western water, despite its mixture of federal and state law because the legal basis begins with federal law. Nevertheless, keep in mind that the law presented here overlaps with state common law on water allocation found in Part II.

The basis for application of the PTD to a particular waterbody is whether the waterbody is "navigable." Confusing the question of navigability is the fact that federal and state tests differ. The federal test applies to issues of federal law (generally issues of what can be done with the beds and banks including issues such as development of dams, marinas, or harbors), and the state test applies if the issue is one of state law (generally access issues). The federal common law test for navigability determines: (1) who owns the beds and banks of a waterway; and (2) whether the Commerce Clause allows the federal government continuing regulatory jurisdiction over the waters and over waters tributary to a navigable water (note that the addition of tributary water provides a broader scope of waters subject to federal regulatory jurisdiction than those with government ownership of the beds and the banks). The state test for navigability determines whether the public has rights to access and use the water for activities such as fishing, boating, swimming, and recreation. State tests for navigability vary and generally apply to a broader range of waterbodies than the federal test.

This mixture of federal and state tests means that issues of public rights comprise a confusing area of water law. Which meaning to use for "navigability" depends on the question being asked. Complicating this is the fact that the scope of federal jurisdiction and the obligations of federal and state governments with respect to the trust are in flux. In recent years, state courts and legislatures have considered the intersection between the Public Trust Doctrine and water allocation with a variety of outcomes. To help guide you through the confusion, this introduction will walk you through the steps in the development of this area of law.

The concept in federal common law that certain waters are "public waters" that must remain open to the public for navigation has its roots in Roman law, but for our purposes begins with English common law. Under English common law, the beds and banks of navigable waterways are held by the sovereign. In addition to ownership of the beds and banks, the sovereign retains regulatory authority over the overlying waters to keep them open to public navigation—the so-called "navigational servitude." The applicable waters under English law were limited to waters subject to tidal influence.

Due to the vast freshwater rivers and lakes in the United States, the concept of navigable waters was extended to all waterways that "are navigable in fact when they are used, or are susceptible of being used, in their ordinary condition, as highways for commerce, over which trade and travel are or may be conducted in the customary modes of trade and travel on water."[1]

In formulating the new country following the Revolutionary War, the original states held the title to the beds and banks, while the federal government retained its regulatory authority for purposes of navigation. According to the United States Supreme Court, the original 13 colonies gained absolute ownership over those submerged lands upon their independence from Great Britain.[2] Less clear was whether new states would also own the submerged lands within their boundaries. Indeed, it was the United States that acquired those lands from the myriad Native American tribes that had owned them since time immemorial, and it was the United States that formed those lands into federal territories. Although the Constitution provided that new states could be created from territories, it was silent as to whether those states would acquire title to the submerged lands underlying navigable waters within their territory. The Supreme Court filled this gap by announcing the equal footing doctrine, wherein new states are admitted on "equal footing" to the original 13 states.[3] As a result, the U.S. Supreme Court concluded that the federal government held in trust the submerged lands underlying navigable waters within the territories, which presumptively pass to the new state upon statehood.[4]

State title to the beds and banks of navigable rivers differs from title to land. In the 1892 case of *Illinois Central Railroad Co. v. Illinois*, 146 U.S. 387, the first case you will read, the U.S. Supreme Court held that the states hold the submerged lands in trust for the people. What has become known as the Public Trust Doctrine (PTD) requires that the state not sell or permit development of submerged lands by private parties

1. The Daniel Ball, 77 U.S. 557, 563 (1870).
2. Martin v. Waddell's Lessee, 41 U.S. 367 (1842).
3. *Id.*
4. *Id.*

to the detriment of the public interest in access and use. In attempting to walk the line between state ownership, public interest, and the federal regulatory authority, the Court in *Illinois Central* states:

> It is the settled law of this country that the ownership of and dominion and sovereignty over lands covered by tide waters, within the limits of the several states, belong to the respective states within which they are found, with the consequent right to use or dispose of any portion thereof, *when that can be done without substantial impairment of the interest of the public in the waters, and subject always to the paramount right of congress to control their navigation so far as may be necessary for the regulation of commerce* with foreign nations and among the states.... [Emphasis added.][5]

It is also important to note that transfer to the states does not occur if the beds and banks have been reserved prior to statehood. Your second case, *Idaho v. United States,* 533 U.S. 262, will explore this topic by looking at reservation of a lakebed to a Native American tribe. This is one of several cases that make it clear that the equal footing doctrine does not alter agreements between the federal government and Native American Tribes.[6] To date, there are no court rulings determining whether these submerged lands reserved prior to statehood are subject to the PTD.

Once you have covered these foundational cases on the PTD and who owns the beds and banks, this Chapter turns to the intersection between these concepts and water use. It begins with public rights to *in situ* use of navigable waterways. This is an area of state authority derived both from ownership of the beds and banks of waterways that meet the federal definition of navigability at statehood, and from ownership of the overlying water on both public and private waterways. State ownership of the overlying water for the public benefit is often articulated in state constitutions in western states. Article IX, Section 3, Clause 3 of the Montana Constitution provides an example: "All surface, underground, flood, and atmospheric waters within the boundaries of the state are the property of the state for the use of its people and are subject to appropriation for beneficial uses as provided by law."

This dual source of authority has allowed states to develop their own definition of the waters subject to the rights of the public, but unfortunately the term "navigable waters" is still used. The definition of navigability varies by state. Some built on the federal concept of use for commerce by formulating a test such as capacity to float a six-inch log (a common way of getting timber to market in the nineteenth century). Others equate "navigable for public use" as applying to those waters susceptible to a public use. Recognized public uses have evolved over time, but today generally include fishing, boating, swimming, and other forms of recreation.

---

5. Illinois Central Railroad Co. v. Illinois, 146 U.S. at 435, citing Pollard's Lessee v. Hagan, 3 How. 212; Weber v. Commissioners, 18 Wall. 57.

6. *See, e.g.,* Herrera v Wyoming, 139 S. Ct. 1686 (2020).

The confusion among the federal and state definitions of "navigable" are generally dealt with by referring to the federal definition as "navigable for title" and the state definitions as "navigable for use." The Montana and Idaho cases you will read following the foundational federal cases on the PTD address the issue of when a stream is "navigable for use" and whether this differs from "navigable" for title in that state. These cases also discuss the types of public uses allowed in these waterways. You will see that these cases view public rights in terms of access to navigable waters rather than in terms of any obligation by the state to protect the flow or quality of the waters to maintain their suitability for public use.

Beginning with an article in 1970 by Professor Joseph Sax on *The Public Trust Doctrine in Natural Resource Law: Effective Judicial Intervention*, 68 MICH. L. REV. 471 (1970), and the 1982 California case, *National Audubon Society v. Superior Court of Alpine County,* 658 P.2d 709 (the *Mono Lake* case), states began to consider the relation between their public trust duties regarding the beds and banks of rivers and any similar duty regarding their allocation of the overlying waters. In other words, does the limitation on disposition of public trust resources to what "can be done without substantial impairment of the interest of the public in the water," from *Illinois Central*, apply to allocation of water for private use? Reading cases from California and Nevada, and legislation from Idaho, you will learn about three different ways states have approached this issue. Understanding this unsettled area of law and the rationale behind states' choice of different paths is of particular importance in light of the use of the PTD to assert a trust duty regarding the atmosphere in the *Juliana* climate change suit.[7]

Foundations of the Public Trust Doctrine

Illinois Central Railroad Co. v. Illinois, 146 U.S. 387 (1892), is considered the foundational case for the PTD and the duty imposed on states to manage the beds and banks of navigable rivers in a manner that does not impair the public's interest in access to and use of those rivers. It arose when the State of Illinois rescinded a law allowing for the sale of some of the submerged lands underlying Lake Michigan to a private railroad company, which was planning to fill those lands to expand the Chicago harbor in Lake Michigan, build a railroad station, and lay tracks out of the City of Chicago. The legal issue involves the validity of the original land transfer. If it was invalid because the state lacked authority to transfer the land, then there is no Taking resulting from the rescission.

From this case you will learn about the equal footing doctrine that results in transfer of the beds and banks of navigable waterways to states. Pay attention to the fact that it is the unique geography of the United States with its massive freshwater riv-

---

7. Juliana v. United States, 217 F. Supp. 3d 1224 (D. Or. 2016) and appeal, Juliana v. United States, 947 F.3d 1159 (9th Cir. 2020).

ers and lakes that justifies the extension of sovereign ownership of submerged lands beyond tide lands. You will also learn that the purpose of the public trust is to protect public rights in use of the land and waters. Pay attention to the uses the Court lists. In many ways the original transfer of land by the state to the railroad company is similar to the public/private collaborations popular today. The state and the city were unable to finance development of the harbor. The railroad presented an opportunity for private financing. How, according to the Court, does this harm the public? What would need to be present in a public/private partnership like this to satisfy the public trust doctrine?

Illinois Central Railroad Co. v. Illinois

Supreme Court of the United States
146 U.S. 387 (1892)

Opinion

Mr. Justice FIELD delivered the opinion of the court.

...

The object of the suit is to obtain a judicial determination of the title ... claimed by the company to the submerged lands, constituting the bed of the lake,.... The determination of the title of the company will involve a consideration of its right to construct, for its own business, as well as for public convenience, wharves, piers, and docks in the harbor.

...

The state of Illinois was admitted into the Union in 1818 on an equal footing with the original states, in all respects.... The boundaries of the state ... include [portions of] ... Lake Michigan....

It is the settled law of this country that the ownership of and dominion and sovereignty over lands covered by tide waters, ... belong to the respective states within which they are found, with the consequent right to use or dispose of any portion thereof, when that can be done without substantial impairment of the interest of the public in the waters, and subject always to the paramount right of congress to control their navigation so far as may be necessary for the regulation of commerce with foreign nations and among the states. This doctrine has been often announced by this court, and is not questioned by counsel of any of the parties. *Pollard's Lessee v. Hagan*, 3 How. 212; *Weber v. Commissioners*, 18 Wall. 57.

The same doctrine is in this country held to be applicable to lands covered by fresh water in the Great Lakes, over which is conducted an extended commerce with different states and foreign nations. These lakes possess all the general characteristics of open seas, except in the freshness of their waters, and in the absence of the ebb and flow of the tide.... At one time the existence of tide waters was deemed essential in determining the admiralty jurisdiction of courts in England. That doctrine is now repudiated in this country as wholly inapplicable to our condition....

... Some of our rivers are navigable for great distances above the flow of the tide,—indeed, for hundreds of miles,—by the largest vessels used in commerce. As said in the case cited [*The Genesee Chief*, 53 U.S. 443, 12 How. 443 (1851)]: 'There is certainly nothing in the ebb and flow of the tide that makes the waters peculiarly suitable for admiralty jurisdiction, nor anything in the absence of a tide that renders it unfit. If it is a public, navigable water, on which commerce is carried on between different states or nations, the reason for the jurisdiction is precisely the same....'

The Great Lakes are not in any appreciable respect affected by the tide, and yet on their waters, as said above, a large commerce is carried on, exceeding in many instances the entire commerce of states on the borders of the sea.... So also, by the common law, the doctrine of the dominion over and ownership by the crown of lands ... is not founded upon the existence of the tide over the lands, but upon the fact that the waters are navigable;.... The public being interested in the use of such waters, the possession by private individuals of lands under them could not be permitted except by license of the crown, which could alone exercise such dominion over the waters as would insure freedom in their use so far as consistent with the public interest. The doctrine is founded upon the necessity of preserving to the public the use of navigable waters from private interruption and encroachment.... We hold, therefore, that the same doctrine as to the dominion and sovereignty over and ownership of lands under the navigable waters of the Great Lakes applies which obtains at the common law as to the dominion and sovereignty over and ownership of lands under tide waters in the borders of the sea, and that the lands are held by the same right in the one case as in the other, and subject to the same trusts and limitations....

... [The Court discusses the rights of the Railroad Company as owner of riparian land, then goes on in the paragraphs included in the following to discuss the submerged lands and to articulate the public trust doctrine.]

We proceed to consider the claim of the railroad company to the ownership of submerged lands in the harbor, and the right to construct such wharves, piers, docks, and other works therein as it may deem proper for its interest and business. The claim is founded upon the third section of the act of the legislature of the state passed on the 16th of April, 1869, the material part of which [grants the submerged land to the Illinois Central Railroad Company in fee, but without the power to alienate]....

... On the 15th of April, 1873, the legislature of Illinois repealed the act. The questions presented relate to the validity of the [third] section cited, of the act, and the effect of the repeal upon its operation.

...

[The question the Court must ask to determine if the repeal is a Taking is] ... whether the legislature was competent to make a grant of the kind [in the first place].

The act, if valid and operative to the extent claimed, placed under the control of the railroad company nearly the whole of the submerged lands of the harbor, subject only to the limitations that it should not authorize obstructions to the harbor, or impair the public right of navigation, or exclude the legislature from regulating the rates of wharfage or dockage to be charged. With these limitations, the act put it in the power of the company to delay indefinitely the improvement of the harbor, or to construct as many docks, piers, and wharves and other works as it might choose, and at such positions in the harbor as might suit its purposes, and permit any kind of business to be conducted thereon, and to lease them out on its own terms for indefinite periods. The inhibition against the technical transfer of the fee of any portion of the submerged lands was of little consequence when it could make a lease for any period, and renew it at its pleasure; and the inhibitions against authorizing obstructions to the harbor and impairing the public right of navigation placed no impediments upon the action of the railroad company which did not previously exist. A corporation created for ... its own profit generally.

The circumstances attending the passage of the act through the legislature were on the hearing the subject of much criticism. As originally introduced, the purpose of the act was to enable the city of Chicago to enlarge its harbor, and to grant to it the title and interest of the state to certain lands adjacent to the shore of Lake Michigan, ... and place the harbor under its control;.... But during the passage of the act its purport was changed. Instead of providing for the cession of the submerged lands to the city, it provided for a cession of them to the railroad company....

The question, therefore, to be considered, is whether the legislature was competent to thus deprive the state of its ownership of the submerged lands in the harbor of Chicago, and of the consequent control of its waters;....

That the state holds the title to the lands under the navigable waters of Lake Michigan,.... But it is a title different in character from that which the state holds in lands intended for sale. It is different from the title which the United States hold in the public lands which are open to pre-emption and sale. It is a title held in trust for the people of the state, that they may enjoy the navigation of the waters, carry on commerce over them, and have liberty of fishing therein, freed from the obstruction or interference of private parties. The interest of the people in the navigation of the waters and in commerce over them may be improved in many instances by the erection of wharves, docks, and piers therein, for which purpose the state may grant parcels of the submerged lands; and, so long as their disposition is made for such purpose, no valid objections can be made to the grants.... But that is a very different doctrine from the one which would sanction the abdication of the general control of the state over lands under the navigable waters of an entire harbor or bay, or of a sea or lake. Such abdication is not consistent with the exercise of that trust which requires the government of the state to preserve such waters for the use of the public. The trust devolving upon the state for the public, and which can only be discharged by the management and control of property in which the public has an interest, cannot be relinquished by a transfer of the property. The control of the state for the purposes of the trust can never be lost, except as to such parcels as are used in promoting the interests of the public therein, or can be disposed of without any substantial impairment of the public interest in the lands and waters remaining.... A grant of all the lands under the navigable waters of a state has never been adjudged to be within the legislative power; and any attempted grant of the kind would be held, if not absolutely void on its face, as subject to revocation. The state can no more abdicate its trust over property in which the whole people are interested, like navigable waters and soils under them, ... than it can abdicate its police powers in the administration of government and the preservation of the peace. In the administration of government the use of such powers may for a limited period be delegated to a municipality or other body, but there always remains with the state the right to revoke those powers and exercise them in a more direct manner, ... [the trust property] cannot be placed entirely beyond the direction and control of the state.

The harbor of Chicago is of immense value to the people of the state of Illinois, in the facilities it affords to its vast and constantly increasing commerce; and the idea that its legislature can deprive the state of control over its bed and waters, and place the same in the hands of a private corporation, created for a different purpose,—one limited to transportation of passengers and freight between distant points and the city,—is a proposition that cannot be defended.

...

Any grant of the kind is necessarily revocable, and the exercise of the trust by which the property was held by the state can be resumed at any time. Undoubtedly there may be expenses incurred in improvements made under such a grant, which the state ought to pay; but, be that as it may, the power to resume the trust whenever the state judges best is, we think, incontrovertible....

...

This follows necessarily from the public character of the property, being held by the whole people for purposes in which the whole people are interested. As said by Chief Justice Taney in *Martin v. Waddell*, 16 Pet. 367, 410: 'When the Revolution took place the people of each state became themselves sovereign, and in that character hold the absolute right to all their navigable waters, and the soils under them, for their own common use, subject only to the rights since surrendered by the constitution to the general government.'...

...

In People v. Ferry Co., 68 N. Y. 71, 76, the court of appeals of New York said:

> 'The title to lands under tide waters, within the realm of England, were by the common law deemed to be vested in the king as a public trust, to subserve and protect the public right to use them as common highways for commerce,

> trade, and intercourse. The king, by virtue of his proprietary interest, could grant the soil so that it should become private property, but his grant was subject to the paramount right of public use of navigable waters, which he could neither destroy nor abridge. In every such grant there was an implied reservation of the public right, and so far as it assumed to interfere with it, or to confer a right to impede or obstruct navigation, or to make an exclusive appropriation of the use of navigable waters, the grant was void....'

...

The legislation of the state in the lake front act, purporting to grant the fee of the submerged lands mentioned to the railroad company, was considered by the court below, ... as a mere license ... that it was unable to perceive why it was not competent for the state, by subsequent legislation, to repeal the act...

...

The CHIEF JUSTICE, having been of counsel in the court below [for the City of Chicago], and Mr. Justice BLATCHFORD, being a stockholder in the Illinois Central Railroad Company, did not take any part in the consideration or decision of these cases.

Mr. Justice SHIRAS, dissenting with opinion. I am authorized to state that Mr. Justice GRAY and Mr. Justice BROWN concur in this dissent.

Notes & Questions

1. What is the doctrine that results in transfer of the beds and banks of navigable rivers from the federal government to the states?
2. What is the justification for extending sovereign ownership to freshwater lakes and rivers far from tidal influence?
3. What types of uses constitute the public rights to the beds and banks and overlying waters?
4. Would the Court have found the grant to the Railroad to be valid in any form? If so, what limitations would it need to have?

As noted in the introduction, the Court has long recognized that the United States may reserve the beds and banks of a navigable waterway prior to statehood, thereby maintaining federal ownership. You will see in the following case not only the recognition of this principle, but the process of determining: (1) whether submerged lands were reserved; and if so (2) did reservation take place before statehood? As you read the case, remember the rules of construction for Native American agreements. Also recall that in recognizing reserved water rights, the Court extends the doctrine to treaties, executive orders, and congressional acts reserving land. The case addresses the rights of the Coeur d'Alene Tribe to the beds and banks of Lake Coeur d'Alene within the Tribe's present Reservation (Figure 15.1).

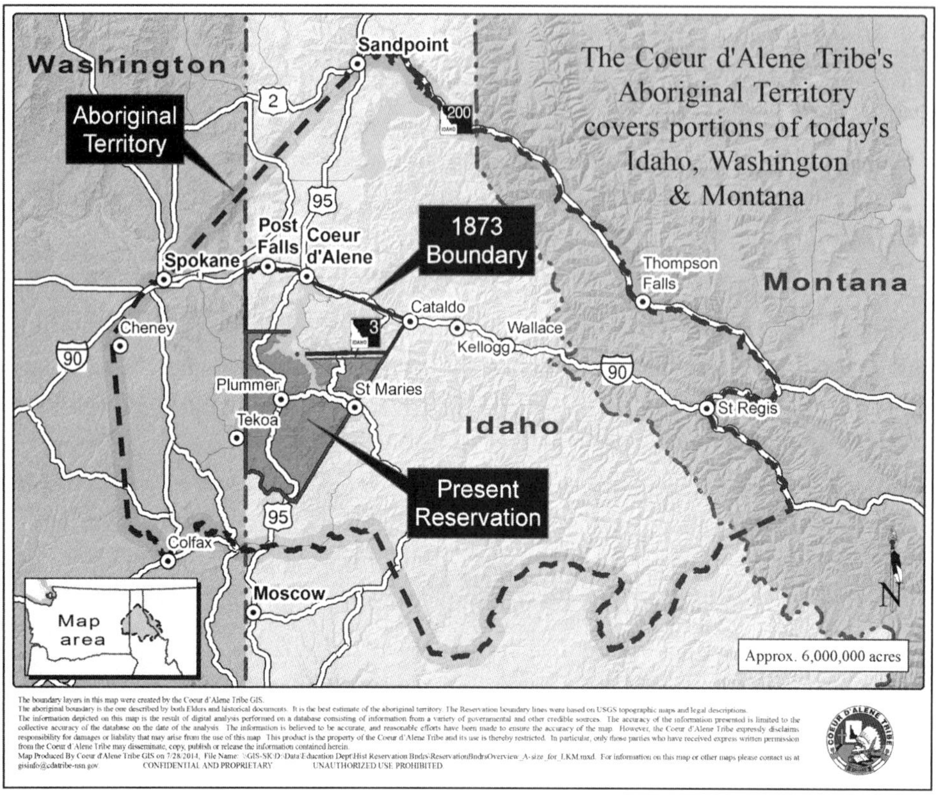

Figure 15.1 Map depicting (1) the Coeur d'Alene Tribe's aboriginal territory (dashed); (2) the 1873 Reservation (solid line); and (3) the present extent of the Tribe's Reservation (shaded). Map used with permission of Coeur d'Alene Tribe GIS Dept.

Idaho v. United States

Supreme Court of the United States

533 U.S. 262 (2001)

Justice SOUTER delivered the opinion of the Court.

The United States brought this quiet title action against the State of Idaho. The question is whether the National Government holds title, in trust for the Coeur d'Alene Tribe, to lands underlying portions of Lake Coeur d'Alene and the St. Joe River. We hold that it does.

I

The Coeur d'Alene Tribe once inhabited more than 3.5 million acres in what is now northern Idaho and northeastern Washington, including the area of Lake Coeur d'Alene and the St. Joe River.... Tribal members traditionally used the lake and its related waterways for food, fiber, transportation, recreation, and cultural activities.... The Tribe depended on submerged lands for everything from water potatoes harvested from the lake to fish weirs and traps anchored in riverbeds and banks....

Under an 1846 treaty with Great Britain, the United States acquired title to the region of Lake Coeur d'Alene, ... subject to the aboriginal right of possession held by resident tribes,.... In 1867, in the face of immigration into the Tribe's aboriginal territory, ... President Johnson issued an Executive Order setting aside a reservation of comparatively modest size,.... The Tribe found the 1867 boundaries unsatisfactory, due in part to their failure to make adequate provision for fishing and other uses of important waterways. When the Tribe petitioned the Commissioner of Indian Affairs a second time, it insisted on a reservation that included key river valleys because "we are not as yet quite up to living on farming" and "for a while yet we need have some hunting and fishing." ...

Following further negotiations, the Tribe in 1873 agreed to relinquish (for compensation) all claims to its aboriginal lands outside the bounds of a more substantial reservation.... The reservation boundaries described in the agreement covered part of the St. Joe River (then called the St. Joseph), and all of Lake Coeur d'Alene except a sliver cut off by the northern boundary....

Although by its own terms the agreement was not binding without congressional approval, later in 1873 President Grant issued an Executive Order directing that the reservation specified in the agreement be "withdrawn from sale and set apart as a reservation for the Coeur d'Alene Indians." ... The 1873 Executive Order set the northern boundary of the reservation directly across Lake Coeur d'Alene, which, the District Court found, was contrary "to the usual practice of meandering a survey line along the mean high water mark." ... An 1883 Government survey fixed the reservation's total area at 598,499.85 acres, which the District Court found necessarily "included submerged lands within the reservation boundaries." ...

As of 1885, Congress had neither ratified the 1873 agreement nor compensated the Tribe. This inaction prompted the Tribe to petition the Government again,.... In response, Congress authorized new negotiations to obtain the Tribe's agreement to cede land outside the borders of the 1873 reservation.... In 1887, the Tribe agreed to cede

> "all right, title, and claim which they now have, or ever had, to all lands in said Territories [Washington, Idaho, and Montana] and elsewhere, except the portion of land within the boundaries of their present reservation in the Territory of Idaho, known as the Coeur d'Alene Reservation."

The Government, in return, promised to compensate the Tribe, and agreed that

> "[i]n consideration of the foregoing cession and agreements ... the Coeur d'Alene Reservation shall be held forever as Indian land and as homes for the Coeur d'Alene Indians ... and no part of said reservation shall ever be sold, occupied, open to white settlement, or otherwise disposed of without the consent of the Indians residing on said reservation."

As before, the agreement was not binding on either party until ratified by Congress.

In January 1888, not having as yet ratified any agreement with the Tribe, the Senate expressed uncertainty about the extent of the Tribe's reservation and adopted a resolution directing the Secretary of the Interior to "inform the Senate as to the extent of the present area and boundaries of the Coeur d'Alene Indian Reservation in the Territory of Idaho," and specifically, "whether such area includes any portion, and if so, about how much of the navigable waters of Lake Coeur d'Alene, and of Coeur d'Alene and St. Joseph Rivers." S. Misc. Doc. No. 36, 50th Cong., 1st Sess., 1 (1888). The Secretary responded in February 1888 with a report of the Commissioner of Indian Affairs, stating that "the reservation appears to embrace all the navigable waters of Lake Coeur d'Alene, except a very small fragment cut off by the north boundary of the reservation," and that "[t]he St. Joseph River also flows through the reservation." S. Exec. Doc. No. 76, 50th Cong., 1st Sess., 3 (1888). Based largely, it appears, on this report, Idaho conceded in the Court of Appeals (as it does here) that the 1873 Executive Order reservation included submerged lands....

In May 1888, shortly after receiving the Secretary's report, Congress passed an Act granting a right-of-way to the Washington and Idaho Railroad Company "for the extension of its railroad through the lands in Idaho Territory set apart for the use of the Coeur d'Alene Indians by executive order, commonly known as the Coeur d'Alene Indian Reservation."... Notably, the Act directed that the Tribe's consent be obtained and that the Tribe alone (no one else being mentioned) be compensated for the right-of-way, a part of which crossed over navigable waters within the reservation....

Congress was not prepared to ratify the 1887 agreement, however, owing to a growing desire to obtain for the public not only any interest of the Tribe in land outside the 1873 reservation, but certain portions of the reservation itself....

But Congress did not simply alter the 1873 boundaries unilaterally. Instead, ... the 1889 Indian Appropriations Act included a provision directing the Secretary of the Interior "to negotiate with the Coeur d'Alene tribe of Indians," and, specifically, to negotiate "for the purchase and release by said tribe of such portions of its reservation not agricultural and valuable chiefly for minerals and timber as such tribe shall consent to sell."... Later that year, the Tribe and Government negotiators reached a new agreement under which the Tribe would cede the northern portion of the reservation, including approximately two-thirds of Lake Coeur d'Alene, in exchange for $500,000.... The new boundary line, like the old one, ran across the lake, and General Simpson, a negotiator for the United States, reassured the Tribe that "you still have the St. Joseph River and the lower part of the lake."... And, again, the agreement was not to be binding on either party until both it and the 1887 agreement were ratified by Congress....

On June 7, 1890, the Senate passed a bill ratifying both the 1887 and 1889 agreements.... On June 10, the Senate bill was referred to the House, where a parallel bill had already been reported by the House Committee on Indian Affairs....

On July 3, 1890, while the Senate bill was under consideration by the House Committee on Indian Affairs, Congress passed the Idaho Statehood Act, admitting Idaho into the Union "on an equal footing with the original States," Act of July 3, 1890, ch. 656, 26 Stat. 215. The Statehood Act "accepted, ratified, and confirmed" the Idaho

Constitution, ibid., which "forever disclaim[ed] all right and title to ... all lands lying within [Idaho] owned or held by any Indians or Indian tribes" and provided that "until the title thereto shall have been extinguished by the United States, the same shall be subject to the disposition of the United States, and said Indian lands shall remain under the absolute jurisdiction and control of the congress of the United States," Idaho Const., Art. XXI, § 19 (1890).

A little over a month later, on August 19, 1890, the House Committee on Indian Affairs reported that the Senate bill ratifying the 1887 and 1889 agreements was identical to the House bill that it had already recommended....

In 1894, Congress approved yet another agreement with the Tribe, this time for the cession of a lakeside townsite called Harrison, within the boundary of the ratified reservation....

The United States, acting in its own capacity and as trustee for the Tribe, initiated this action against the State of Idaho to quiet title (in the United States, to be held for the use and benefit of the Tribe) to the submerged lands within the exterior boundaries of the Tribe's current reservation, which encompass the lower third of Lake Coeur d'Alene and part of the St. Joe River.... The Tribe intervened to assert its interest in the submerged lands, and Idaho counterclaimed, seeking to quiet title in its own favor. Ibid. Following a 9-day trial, the District Court quieted title "in favor of the United States, as trustee, and the Coeur d'Alene Tribe of Idaho, as the beneficially interested party of the trusteeship, to the bed and banks of the Coeur d'Alene Lake and the St. Joe River lying within the current boundaries of the Coeur d'Alene Indian Reservation." 95 F.Supp.2d, at 1117. The Court of Appeals for the Ninth Circuit affirmed. 210 F.3d 1067 (2000). We granted certiorari, 531 U.S. 1050, 121 S.Ct. 653, 148 L.Ed.2d 557 (2000), and we now affirm.

...

II

Due to the public importance of navigable waterways, ownership of the land underlying such waters is "strongly identified with the sovereign power of government." *Montana v. United States,* 450 U.S. 544, 552 (1981).... In order to allow new States to enter the Union on an "equal footing" with the original States with regard to this important interest, "the United States early adopted and constantly has adhered to the policy of regarding lands under navigable waters in acquired territory ... as held for the ultimate benefit of future States." ... Therefore, in contrast to the law governing surface land held by the United States, *see Scott v. Lattig*, 227 U.S. 229, 244 (1913), the default rule is that title to land under navigable waters passes from the United States to a newly admitted State. *Shively, supra*, at 26–50. Specifically, although Congress has the power before statehood to convey land beneath navigable waters, and to reserve such land for the United States, "'[a] court deciding a question of title to the bed of navigable water must ... begin with a strong presumption' against defeat of a State's title." ...

Armed with that presumption, we have looked to Congress's declarations and intent when we have had to resolve conflicts over submerged lands claimed to have been reserved or conveyed by the United States before statehood....

The issue of congressional intent is refined somewhat when submerged lands are located within a tract that the National Government has dealt with in some special way before statehood, as by reserving lands for a particular national purpose such as a wildlife refuge or, as here, an Indian reservation. Because reserving submerged lands does not necessarily imply the intent "to defeat a future State's title to the land," Utah Div. of State Lands, supra, at 202, we undertake a two-step enquiry in reservation cases. We ask whether Congress intended to include land under navigable waters within the federal reservation and, if so, whether Congress intended to defeat the future State's title to the submerged lands....

Our most recent case of this sort, *United States v. Alaska*, supra, addressed two parcels of land initially reserved not by Congress but, as here, by the Executive Branch. We explained that the two-step test of congressional intent is satisfied when an Executive reservation clearly includes submerged lands,...

Here, Idaho has conceded that "the executive branch had intended, or by 1888 had interpreted, the 1873 Executive Order Reservation to include submerged lands." Brief for Petitioner 17. The concession is a sound one. A right to control the lakebed and adjacent waters was traditionally important to the Tribe, which emphasized in its petition to the Government that it continued to depend on fishing.... The District Court found that the acreage determination of the reserved area in 1883 necessarily included the area of the lakebed within the unusual boundary line crossing the lake from east to west.... In light of those findings and Idaho's concession, the parties here concentrate on the second question, of Congress's intent to defeat Idaho's title to the submerged lands....

In the Court of Appeals, Idaho also conceded one point covered in this second part of the enquiry. It agreed that after the Secretary of the Interior's 1888 report that the reservation embraced nearly "all the navigable water of Lake Coeur d'Alene," S. Exec. Doc. No. 76, 50th Cong., 1st Sess., at 3, Congress was on notice that the Executive Order reservation included submerged lands....

The District Court did not merely impute to Congress knowledge of the land survey, but also explained how the submerged lands and related water rights had been continuously important to the Tribe throughout the period prior to congressional action confirming the reservation and granting Idaho statehood. And the District Court made the following findings about the period preceding negotiations authorized by Congress:

> "The facts demonstrate that an influx of non-Indians into the Tribe's aboriginal territory prompted the Federal Government to negotiate with the Coeur d'Alenes in an attempt to confine the Tribe to a reservation and to obtain the Tribe's release of its aboriginal lands for settlement. Before it would agree to these conditions, however, the Tribe demanded an enlarged reservation that

> included the Lake and rivers. Thus, the Federal Government could only achieve its goals of promoting settlement, avoiding hostilities and extinguishing aboriginal title by agreeing to a reservation that included the submerged lands." Id., at 1107....

...

The manner in which Congress then proceeded to deal with the Tribe shows clearly that preservation of the land within the reservation, absent contrary agreement with the Tribe, was central to Congress's complementary objectives of dealing with pressures of white settlement and establishing the reservation by permanent legislation. The Tribe had shown its readiness to fight to preserve its land rights when in 1858 it defeated a force of the United States military, which it misunderstood as intending to take aboriginal lands.... The concern with hostility arose again in 1873 before the reservation boundaries were established, when a surveyor on the scene had warned the Surveyor General that "[s]hould the fisheries be excluded there will in my opinion be trouble with these Indians."...

Hence, although the goal of extinguishing aboriginal title could have been achieved by congressional fiat, *see Tee-Hit-Ton Indians v. United States,* 348 U.S. 272, 279–282 (1955), and Congress was free to define the reservation boundaries however it saw fit, the goal of avoiding hostility seemingly could not have been attained without the agreement of the Tribe. Congress in any event made it expressly plain that its object was to obtain tribal interests only by tribal consent. When in 1886 Congress took steps toward extinguishing aboriginal title to all lands outside the 1873 boundaries, it did so by authorizing negotiation of agreements ceding title for compensation. Soon after that, when Congress decided to seek a reduction in the size of the 1873 reservation itself, the Secretary of the Interior advised the Senate against fiddling with the scope of the reservation without the Tribe's agreement....

The facts, including the provisions of Acts of Congress in 1886, 1888, and 1889, thus demonstrate that Congress understood its objective as turning on the Tribe's agreement to the abrogation of any land claim it might have and to any reduction of the 1873 reservation's boundaries. The explicit statutory provisions requiring agreement of the Tribe were unchanged right through to the point of Congress's final 1891 ratification of the reservation, in an Act that of course contained no cession by the Tribe of submerged lands within the reservation's outer boundaries. Nor, it should be added, is there any hint in the evidence that delay in final passage of the ratifying Act was meant to pull a fast one by allowing the reservation's submerged lands to pass to Idaho under a legal presumption, by virtue of the Statehood Act approved eight months before Congress took final action on the reservation. There is no evidence that the Act confirming the reservation was delayed for any reason but comparison of the respective House and Senate bills, to assure that they were identical prior to the House's passage of the Senate version....

... The intent, in other words, was that anything not consensually ceded by the Tribe would remain for the Tribe's benefit, an objective flatly at odds with Idaho's view that

Congress meant to transfer the balance of submerged lands to the State in what would have amounted to an act of bad faith accomplished by unspoken operation of law....

...

In sum, Congress undertook to negotiate with the Coeur d'Alene Tribe for reduction in the territory of an Executive Order reservation that Idaho concedes included the submerged lands at issue here. Congress was aware that the submerged lands were included and clearly intended to redefine the area of the reservation that covered them only by consensual transfer, in exchange for the guarantee that the Tribe would retain the remainder. There is no indication that Congress ever modified its objective of negotiated consensual transfer, which would have been defeated if Congress had let parts of the reservation pass to the State before the agreements with the Tribe were final. Any imputation to Congress either of bad faith or of secrecy in dropping its express objective of consensual dealing with the Tribe is at odds with the evidence. We therefore think ... that Congress recognized the full extent of the Executive Order reservation lying within the stated boundaries it ultimately confirmed, and intended to bar passage to Idaho of title to the submerged lands at issue here.

Notes & Questions

1. The Court finds, and Idaho conceded, that the 1873 agreement setting aside the Coeur d'Alene Reservation reserved the submerged lands to the lake and river that are within the boundary of the Coeur d'Alene Reservation. What role did the 1873 Agreement play in the Court's analysis? What type of formal agreement was it from the viewpoint of the United States?
2. Once the 1873 agreement is discussed, the Court turns to the second part of its inquiry—whether Congress intended to defeat State title to the submerged lands. What is the test the Court uses to determine if submerged lands were reserved from transfer to the state? What does the Court focus on to determine that Congress intended to defeat State title? Note that the test for navigability did not come up in this case because the parties stipulated that the Lake and portion of the St. Joe River at issue are navigable.
3. A court addressing itself to the issue of whether submerged lands have been reserved for the benefit of an Indian tribe must grapple with conflicting presumptions. On the one hand, the Supreme Court has been clear that "[a] court deciding a question of title to the bed of navigable water must ... begin with a strong presumption' against defeat of a State's title." On the other hand, the Supreme Court applies canons of construction when construing treaties, agreements, executive orders, and other laws dealing with Indian tribes. As you know, those canons require that these laws be liberally construed in favor of the tribes, as the tribes would have understood them, and with ambiguities resolved in their favor. How does the Court address this conflict of presumptions, if at all? How should it, in your opinion? Note that no such conflict arises when the United States alleges that it reserved submerged lands for its own purposes. *See, e.g.*, *United States v. Alaska*, 545 U.S. 75 (2005).

4. Within the area of focus of the textbook, two other cases considered the issue of reservation of submerged lands to a Native American tribe in Montana. The Ninth Circuit has found reservation of submerged lands of Flathead Lake in Montana for the Confederated Salish and Kootenai Tribes, *Confederated Salish and Kootenai Tribes v. Namen*, 534 F.2d 1376 (9th Cir. 1976), *cert. denied*, 429 U.S. 929 (1976). In *Montana v. United States*, 450 U.S. 544, 101 S. Ct. 1245 (1981), the U.S. Supreme Court held that there is a strong presumption against defeating the title of a future state and that the beds and banks of the Big Horn River were not reserved for the Crow Tribe. The Court found no language in the Crow Treaty referring to the riverbed, and thus found state title had not been defeated.

Public Rights: The Public Trust Doctrine and Stream Use and Access

As noted in the introduction, the term "navigability" is used for both the federal test of which submerged lands are transferred to the states at statehood (navigability for title), and the state test of which waters are subject to public use (navigability for use). State law controls use for the same reasons states have jurisdiction to allocate water—i.e., the states own the water for the benefit of the people. The two cases in this section take a different approach to determining when the federal or state test is applied. The first case in this section, *Montana Coalition for Stream Access, Inc. v. Curran,* 682 P.2d 163 (1984), addresses both ownership of the beds and banks and public use of the overlying water and concerns the Dearborn River. See if you can spot which facts indicate (to this court) that both tests are at issue. Then identify the two tests—the federal and the Montana tests. The second case, *Southern Idaho Fish & Game Association v. Picabo Livestock, Inc.*, 528 P.2d 1295 (1974), considers the question of use for fishing, even when access requires standing on the stream bed, to be a question of the state test of navigability for use. Standing on the stream bed, or portaging around an obstacle, are merely incidents necessary to allow exercise of the public right for use.

Montana Coalition for Stream Access, Inc. v. Curran

Supreme Court of Montana
682 P.2d 163 (1984)

Opinion

HASWELL, Chief Justice— .... The District Court held that the public have a right to use waters and the streambed of the Dearborn River up to the high water mark as it flows through Curran's property and that the State of Montana owns the streambed between the low water marks.... We affirm.

The Dearborn River is approximately sixty-six miles long and originates along the east slope of the Continental Divide in west-central Montana. The river flows generally in a southeasterly direction from its source ... to the Missouri River.

...

The Coalition is a nonprofit Montana corporation formed to promote public access to Montana's rivers. Individual members of the Coalition use the stretch of the Dearborn running through Curran's property for recreational pursuits such as floating and fishing. Some members of the Coalition who have floated or attempted to float the Dearborn have experienced interference and harassment from Curran or his agents.

Curran and Curran Oil Co., of which he is a principal stockholder, have extensive land holdings in Lewis and Clark and Cascade Counties.... Approximately six to seven miles of the Dearborn flows through property owned or controlled by Curran....

Curran claims title to the banks and streambed of a portion of the Dearborn River and claims to have the right, as an owner of private property, to restrict its use.

The District Court essentially held that the Dearborn River is in fact navigable for recreation purposes under Montana law; that recreation access to it is determined by state law according to one criterion—namely, navigability for recreation purposes; and that the question of recreational access is to be determined according to state, not federal, law.

...

I

...

Curran maintains that the District Court erred by misconstruing the law to be applied in determining the navigability of the Dearborn at the time Montana was admitted to the Union.

The United States Supreme Court has held, and all parties agree, that federal law controls the issue of navigability for title purposes.

Federal law on navigability for title purposes provides that rivers are navigable in law which are navigable in fact. *The Daniel Ball* (1870), 77 U.S. (10 Wall.) 557. "And they are navigable in fact when they are used, or are susceptible of being used, in their ordinary condition, as highways for commerce,...." *The Daniel Ball,* supra, at 563. In 1874, the United States Supreme Court elaborated on its holding in *The Daniel Ball,* supra, and stated that "... the true test of navigability of a stream does not depend on the mode by which commerce is, or may be, conducted, nor the difficulties attending navigation...." *The Montello* (1874), 87 U.S. (20 Wall.) 430.

Navigability in fact under federal law can be determined by the log-floating test. *The Montello,* supra; ... *State of Oregon v. Riverfront Protection Association* (9th Cir.1982), 672 F.2d 792. In *Riverfront Protection Association,* supra, the McKenzie River was declared navigable despite the fact that log drives could only be conducted during April, May and early June.

The evidence in this case, supplied by the affidavits of two competent historians, demonstrates that the Dearborn River was used in 1887, two years before Montana statehood, to float approximately 100,000 railroad ties. Furthermore, in 1888 and 1889, one or two log drives per year were floated down the Dearborn. One drive in 1888 contained 700,000 board feet. Clearly, the Dearborn satisfied the log-floating test for navigability under the federal test of navigability for title purposes.

Since the Dearborn was navigable under the log-floating test at the time of statehood in 1889, title to the riverbed was owned by the federal government prior to statehood and was transferred to the State of Montana upon admission to the Union.

...

States admitted to the Union subsequent to the original thirteen succeeded to the same rights on the theory that the lands acquired by the United States from the original thirteen colonies or from foreign governments were held in trust for the new states in order that they might be admitted on an equal footing with the original states.

...

Of further importance to the issue of navigability for title is the Public Trust Doctrine. The theory underlying this doctrine can be traced from Roman Law through Magna Carta to present day decisions.

The Public Trust Doctrine was first clearly defined in *Illinois Central Railroad v. Illinois*. [The court refers to the controversy in Illinois Central and states:]

> "That the State holds the title to the lands under the navigable waters of Lake Michigan,.... It is a title held in trust for the people of the State.... *The State can no more abdicate its trust over property in which the whole people are interested, like navigable waters and soils under them, so as to leave them entirely under the use and control of private parties,* ... (Emphasis added.)

In summary, the "equal-footing" doctrine as set forth in *Pollard's Lessee,* supra, which held that the federal government retained title to navigable waters so that all states entering the Union subsequent to the original thirteen would enter on an "equal footing" and the Public Trust Doctrine, which provides that states hold title to navigable waterways in trust for the public benefit and use are two important doctrines to be considered in determining a navigability-for-title question. In this matter, the log-floating test was properly applied and the State found to hold title to the riverbed of the Dearborn. In this matter, where title to the bed of the Dearborn rests with the State, the test of navigability for *use* and not for title, is a test to be determined under state law and not federal law.

...

III

The third issue is whether the District Court erred in determining that recreational use and fishing make a stream navigable. We find no error.

The concept of determining navigability based upon public recreational use is not new. One of the earlier cases, decided in 1893, held:

> "... The division of waters into navigable and nonnavigable is but a way of dividing them into public and private waters,—a classification which, in some form, every civilized nation has recognized; the line of division being largely

> determined by its conditions and habits. In early times, about the only use—except, perhaps, fishing,—to which the people of England had occasion to put public waters, and about the only use to which such waters were adapted, was navigation,.... *But if, under present conditions of society, bodies of water are used for public uses other than mere commercial navigation, in its ordinary sense, we fail to see why they ought not to be held to be public waters, or navigable waters, if the old nonmenclature is preferred. Certainly, we do not see why boating or sailing for pleasure should not be considered navigation, as well as boating for mere pecuniary profit.* Many, if not the most, of the meandered lakes of this state, are not adapted to, and probably will never be used to any great extent for, commercial navigation; but they are used—and as population increases, and towns and cities are built up in their vicinity, will be still more used—by the people for sailing, rowing, fishing, fowling, bathing, skating, taking water for domestic, agricultural, and even city purposes, cutting ice, and other public purposes which cannot now be enumerated or even anticipated. *To hand over all these lakes to private ownership, under any old or narrow test of navigability, would be a great wrong upon the public for all time, the extent of which cannot, perhaps, be now even anticipated....*" (Emphasis added.)

Lamprey v. State (Metcalf) (1893), 52 Minn. 181, 53 N.W. 1139, 1143.

Since 1893, the concept expressed in *Lamprey* has been followed and the idea of navigability for public recreational use has spread to numerous other jurisdictions....

Navigability for use is a matter governed by state law. It is a separate concept from the federal question of determining navigability for title purposes.

> "... [the U.S. Supreme Court] established the basic test for public waters for the purposes of our federal system. But the problems of federalism are not the same as the problems which may arise entirely within a state; the federal test for land-title and federal jurisdiction does not have to be the test for state determinations of the waters that are public for various state purposes." 1 Waters and Water Rights (Clark Ed.) pgs 212–213, (1967). (Footnotes omitted.)

In 1961, the Wyoming Supreme Court supported public use of waters suitable therefor without regard to title or navigability....

In essence, the Wyoming court held that public recreational use of waters was limited only by the susceptibility of the waters for that purpose.

The Constitution of Montana provides:

> "All surface, underground, flood, and atmospheric waters within the boundaries of the state are the property of the state for the use of its people and are subject to appropriation for beneficial uses as provided by law."

Thus, Curran has no right to control the use of the surface waters of the Dearborn to the exclusion of the public except to the extent of his prior appropriation of part of the water for irrigation purposes, which is not at issue here. Curran has no right of ownership to the riverbed or surface waters because their ownership was held by the federal government prior to statehood in trust for the people. Upon statehood, title was transferred to the State, burdened by this public trust.

In essence, the question is whether the waters owned by the State under the Constitution are susceptible to recreational use by the public. The capability of use of the waters for recreational purposes determines their availability for recreational use by the public. Streambed ownership by a private party is irrelevant. If the waters are owned by the State and held in trust for the people by the State, no private party may bar the use of those waters by the people. The Constitution and the public trust doctrine do not permit a private party to interfere with the public's right to recreational use of the surface of the State's waters.

In sum, we hold that, under the public trust doctrine and the 1972 Montana Constitution, any surface waters that are capable of recreational use may be so used by the public without regard to streambed ownership or navigability for nonrecreational purposes.

X

We add the cautionary note that nothing herein contained in this opinion shall be construed as granting the public the right to enter upon or cross over private property to reach the State-owned waters hereby held available for recreational purposes.

[The court goes on to clarify] we hold that the public has a right to use the state-owned waters to the point of the high water mark except to the extent of barriers in the waters. In case of barriers, the public is allowed to portage around such barriers in the least intrusive way possible, avoiding damage to the private property holder's rights.

...

Affirmed.

Notes & Questions

1. In looking at the facts of the case, which uses by the Coalition members required use of the beds and banks (federal test) and which uses required use of the water (Montana test)?
2. What is the federal test according to the court, and how does the Dearborn meet it?
3. What is the state test pronounced by the court, and how is it met?

In the following case, pay attention to the different approach of the Idaho court, which finds only the state test for navigability at issue. Note, however, that the state test is identical to what the Montana court states as the federal test. Also, pay attention to the fact that Idaho has codified these public rights and consider which state recognizes broader public rights. The case takes place on Idaho's Silver Creek.

Southern Idaho Fish & Game Association v. Picabo Livestock, Inc.

Supreme Court of Idaho
528 P.2d 1295 (1974)

BAKES, J.—Plaintiff-respondent Southern Idaho Fish and Game Association, ... brought a declaratory judgment action to have the court determine the rights of [its members] and the members of the public similarly ... to the use of the waters of Silver Creek, and the bed, channels and banks thereof for fishing and recreational uses.

Silver Creek, with its headwaters in Blaine County, ... is renowned as one of the best fly fishing streams in the United States.

Appellant Picabo Livestock, Inc., ... owns land in Blaine County through which Silver Creek flows. On September 15, 1968, appellant, through its president, Mr. Leonard N. Purdy, ordered six members of respondent association to leave the creek stating that they were trespassing on private property. Three of the members were fishing from float rings and three were fishing from a boat. All of the fishermen entered the creek upstream from appellant's land and at all times stayed in the water except for a portage around Kilpatrick Dam....

On September 19, 1968, members of respondent floated nine logs with diameters in excess of 6 1/2 inches down Silver Creek....

... the trial court held that Silver Creek is navigable where it flows through the ranch lands.... The court further held that Silver Creek was a public highway up to the high water mark and that respondents and other members of the public have the right to use the waters of Silver Creek and the bed, channels and banks thereof, up to the high water mark, as a public highway for travel and passage, up or downstream, for business or pleasure, and to exercise the incidents of navigation—boating, swimming, fishing, hunting and all recreational purposes—so long as they can enter into the waters thereof by not crossing dry land owned by the defendant. The trial court also found that as a necessary incident to the use of Silver Creek as a public highway for travel and recreational uses, members of the public could remove themselves and their boats, floats, canoes, or other floating crafts, from the stream and walk or portage such crafts around irrigation dams which completely obstruct the navigation of the stream and which do not have connected therewith sluiceways, locks or sufficient fixtures so arranged as to permit timber or boats and other floating crafts to pass around, through or over said dams without unreasonable delay or hindrance, and then re-enter the stream immediately below said dams at the nearest point where it is safe to do so. From the judgment of the trial court appellant brings this appeal.

The basic issues before the trial court and this Court on appeal are whether Silver Creek is navigable and, if so, what are the rights of the public to use a navigable stream. Idaho Code §§ 36-901 and 36-907 provide as follows:

> "**36-901. Public waters highways for fishing.**—Navigable rivers, sloughs or streams within the meander lines or not meandered between the lines of ordinary high water thereof, of the state of Idaho, and all rivers, sloughs and streams flowing through any public lands of the state shall hereafter be public highways for the purpose of angling or fishing thereon and any right or title to such streams or lands between the high water flow lines or within the meander lines of navigable streams shall be subject to the right of any person owning a fish license of this state, who desires to fish therein or along the banks, to go upon the same for such purpose.
>
> "**36-907. Navigable streams for fishing.**—For the purpose of this act, the following streams or parts of streams are declared navigable streams: ... and every other stream or part of a stream on which logs or timber can be floated to market or the place of use during the high water season of the year. For the purpose of this act, logs and timber are defined as any cut timber having a diameter in excess of six (6) inches; high water is defined as the time of year when the stream normally carries its greatest volume."

The trial court found that under the provisions of I.C. § 36-907, Silver Creek is a navigable stream as it is a stream on which logs or timber having a diameter in excess of six (6) inches can be floated to market or other place of use, and that under the provisions of I.C. § 36-901, Silver Creek is a public highway for the purpose of angling or fishing thereon and therein along the bed, channels and banks thereof up to the high water flow line. We have examined the record in this case and find that, although conflicting, there is substantial, competent evidence to support the trial court's finding. Accordingly, the trial court's finding will not be set aside on appeal....

The trial court further found that the public's right to use Silver Creek extended not only to the incidents of fishing pursuant to I.C. § 36-901, but also boating, swimming, hunting and all recreational purposes. In so doing, the trial court found that Silver Creek was "navigable" under both the early and more modern tests of navigability. The court then found that as the title to all water in Silver Creek belongs to the State of Idaho under Article 15, section 1, Idaho Constitution, and I.C. § 42-101, subject to appropriative rights, that there is an easement in the state on behalf of the public for a right of way through the natural channels of Silver Creek for such waters upon and over the lands submerged by them. The trial court set forth the following as the test of navigability in Idaho: Any stream which, in its natural state, will float logs or any other commercial or floatable commodity, or is capable of being navigated by oar or motor propelled small craft, for pleasure or commercial purposes, is navigable. In so holding, the trial court reasoned that in accordance with modern authorities, the basic question of navigability is simply the suitability of a particular water for public use.

We affirm the trial court's statement of the test for navigability and its conclusion that Silver Creek, under the test as stated was navigable. We also affirm the trial court's findings concerning the right of the public to use Silver Creek for recreational purposes. In *People v. Mack,* 97 Cal.Rptr. 448 (1971), the California appellate court, in addressing itself to similar issues, stated:

> "The modern determinations of the California courts, as well as those of several of the states, as to the test of navigability can well be restated as follows: Members of the public have the right to navigate and to exercise the incidents of navigation in a lawful manner at any point below high water mark of the waters of this state which are capable of being navigated by oar or motor propelled small craft."

The court further stated:

> "It hardly needs citation of authorities that the rule is that a navigable stream may be used by the public for boating, swimming, fishing, hunting and all recreational purposes."

...

Appellant urges this Court to adhere to the test of navigability that is used in federal actions where title to stream beds is at issue. However, the question of title to the bed of Silver Creek is not at issue in this proceeding. This is not an action by the State of Idaho or respondent to quiet title to the bed of a navigable stream. It is an action to declare the rights of the public to use a navigable stream. The federal test of navigability involving as it does property title questions, does not preclude a less restrictive state test of navigability establishing a right of public passage wherever a stream is physically navigable by small craft....

Under the test of navigability adopted herein, there is substantial, competent evidence to support the trial court's finding that Silver Creek is navigable. Accordingly, such finding will not be disturbed on appeal....

Judgment affirmed.

Notes & Question

1. The Montana court considered the issue of boating and walking on the bed of a river to be one of both title and use. The Idaho court considered the same question to be merely an issue of use. Which is the better approach?

Public Rights: The Public Trust Doctrine and Water Allocation

In 1983, California was the first state to address whether the Public Trust Doctrine articulated in *Illinois Central* imposes an ongoing duty on a state to ensure that private use of water rights is not harming public values in trust assets. Following the California adoption of the application of the PTD to water rights in *National Audubon Society v. Superior Court of Alpine County* (*Mono Lake*) (Figure 15.2), you will learn about two other approaches taken by states. First, Nevada takes the view that the obligations of the state with respect to trust resources is embodied in its water use act. In contrast, Idaho

Figure 15.2 Mono Lake. Ron Reiring, *Mono Lake, CA* (2008).

disclaims by statute any application of the PTD to water rights. These three approaches represent the likely range of approaches of other states that might address this issue.

National Audubon Society v. Superior Court of Alpine County

Supreme Court of California
658 P.2d 709 (1983)

Opinion

BROUSSARD, Justice—Mono Lake, the second largest lake in California, sits at the base of the Sierra Nevada escarpment near the eastern entrance to Yosemite National Park. The lake is saline; it contains no fish but supports a large population of brine shrimp which feed vast numbers of nesting and migratory birds. Islands in the lake protect a large breeding colony of California gulls, and the lake itself serves as a haven on the migration route for thousands of Northern Phalarope, Wilson's Phalarope, and Eared Greve. Towers and spires of tufa on the north and south shores are matters of geological interest and a tourist attraction.

Although Mono Lake receives some water from rain and snow on the lake surface, historically most of its supply came from snowmelt in the Sierra Nevada. Five fresh-water streams—Mill, Lee Vining, Walker, Parker and Rush Creeks—arise near the crest of the range and carry the annual runoff to the west shore of the lake. In 1940, however, the Division of Water Resources, the predecessor to the present California Water Resources Board, granted the Department of Water and Power of the City of

Los Angeles (hereafter DWP) a permit to appropriate virtually the entire flow of four of the five streams flowing into the lake. DWP promptly constructed facilities to divert about half the flow of these streams into DWP's Owens Valley aqueduct. In 1970 DWP completed a second diversion tunnel, and since that time has taken virtually the entire flow of these streams.

As a result of these diversions, the level of the lake has dropped; the surface area has diminished by one-third; one of the two principal islands in the lake has become a peninsula, exposing the gull rookery there to coyotes and other predators and causing the gulls to abandon the former island. The ultimate effect of continued diversions is a matter of intense dispute, but there seems little doubt that both the scenic beauty and the ecological values of Mono Lake are imperiled.

Plaintiffs filed suit in superior court to enjoin the DWP diversions on the theory that the shores, bed and waters of Mono Lake are protected by a public trust. Plaintiffs' suit was transferred to the federal district court, which requested that the state courts determine the relationship between the public trust doctrine and the water rights system, and decide whether plaintiffs must exhaust administrative remedies before the Water Board prior to filing suit. The superior court then entered summary judgments against plaintiffs on both matters, ruling that the public trust doctrine offered no independent basis for challenging the DWP diversions, and that plaintiffs had failed to exhaust administrative remedies. Plaintiffs petitioned us directly for writ of mandate to review that decision; in view of the importance of the issues presented, we issued an alternative writ....

This case brings together for the first time two systems of legal thought: the appropriative water rights system which since the days of the gold rush has dominated California water law, and the public trust doctrine which, after evolving as a shield for the protection of tidelands, now extends its protective scope to navigable lakes. Ever since we first recognized that the public trust protects environmental and recreational values ... the two systems of legal thought have been on a collision course....

Attempting to integrate the teachings and values of both the public trust and the appropriative water rights system, we have arrived at certain conclusions which we briefly summarize here. In our opinion, the core of the public trust doctrine is the state's authority as sovereign to exercise a continuous supervision and control over the navigable waters of the state and the lands underlying those waters. This authority applies to the waters tributary to Mono Lake and bars DWP or any other party from claiming a vested right to divert waters once it becomes clear that such diversions harm the interests protected by the public trust. The corollary rule which evolved in tideland and lakeshore cases barring conveyance of rights free of the trust except to serve trust purposes cannot, however, apply without modification to flowing waters. The prosperity and habitability of much of this state requires the diversion of great quantities of water from its streams for purposes unconnected to any navigation, commerce, fishing, recreation, or ecological use relating to the source stream. The state must have the power to grant nonvested usufructuary rights to appropriate water even if diversions harm public trust uses. Approval of such diversion without considering public trust values, however, may result in needless destruction of those values. Accordingly, we believe that before state courts and agencies approve water diversions they should consider the effect of such diversions upon interests protected by the public trust, and attempt, so far as feasible, to avoid or minimize any harm to those interests.

The water rights enjoyed by DWP were granted, the diversion was commenced, and has continued to the present without any consideration of the impact upon the public trust. An objective study and reconsideration of the water rights in the Mono Basin is long overdue. The water law of California—which we conceive to be an integration including both the public trust doctrine and the board-administered appropriative rights system—permits such a reconsideration; the values underlying that integration require it.

...

2. *The Public Trust Doctrine in California.*

"By the law of nature these things are common to mankind—the air, running water, the sea and consequently the shores of the sea." (Institutes of Justinian 2.1.1.) From this origin in Roman law, the English common law evolved the concept of the public trust, under which the sovereign owns "all of its navigable waterways and the lands lying beneath them 'as trustee of a public trust for the benefit of the people.' "... The State of California acquired title as trustee to such lands and waterways upon its admission to the union...

Three aspects of the public trust doctrine require consideration in this opinion: the purpose of the trust; the scope of the trust, particularly as it applies to the nonnavigable tributaries of a navigable lake; and the powers and duties of the state as trustee of the public trust. We discuss these questions in the order listed.

(a) *The purpose of the public trust.*

The objective of the public trust has evolved in tandem with the changing public perception of the values and uses of waterways. As we observed in *Marks v. Whitney*, "[p]ublic trust easements [were] traditionally defined in terms of navigation, commerce and fisheries."... We went on, however, to hold that the traditional triad of uses—navigation, commerce and fishing—did not limit the public interest in the trust res. In language of special importance to the present setting, we stated that "[t]he public uses to which tidelands are subject are sufficiently flexible to encompass changing public needs.... There is a growing public recognition that one of the most important public uses of the tidelands—a use encompassed within the tidelands trust—is the preservation of those lands in their natural state, so that they may serve as ecological units for scientific study, as open space, and as environments which provide food and habitat for birds and marine life, and which favorably affect the scenery and climate of the area."...

Mono Lake is a navigable waterway.... It supports a small local industry which harvests brine shrimp for sale as fish food, which endeavor probably qualifies the lake as a "fishery" under the traditional public trust cases. The principal values plaintiffs seek to protect, however, are recreational and ecological—the scenic views of the lake and its shore, the purity of the air, and the use of the lake for nesting and feeding by birds ... it is clear that protection of these values is among the purposes of the public trust.

(b) *The scope of the public trust.*

Early English decisions generally assumed the public trust was limited to tidal waters and the lands exposed and covered by the daily tides.... It is, however, well settled in the United States generally and in California that the public trust is not limited by the reach of the tides, but encompasses all navigable lakes and streams....

Mono Lake is, as we have said, a navigable waterway.... The streams diverted by DWP, however, are not themselves navigable. Accordingly, we must address in this case a question not discussed in any recent public trust case—whether the public trust limits conduct affecting nonnavigable tributaries to navigable waterways.

This question was considered in two venerable California decisions. [One decision involves hydraulic mining on non-navigable tributaries that threatened the navigability of a downstream river. In the second the court found that dams on tributaries to a navigable river were not exempt from consideration of their impact on navigability simply due to their location on upstream, non-navigable tributaries.]

...

... the principles recognized by those decisions apply fully to a case in which diversions from a nonnavigable tributary impair the public trust in a downstream river or lake. "If the public trust doctrine applies to constrain *fills* which destroy navigation and other public trust uses in navigable waters, it should equally apply to constrain the *extraction* of water that destroys navigation and other public interests. Both actions result in the same damage to the public interest."...

We conclude that the public trust doctrine, as recognized and developed in California decisions, protects navigable waters from harm caused by diversion of nonnavigable tributaries.

(c) *Duties and powers of the state as trustee.*

In the following review of the authority and obligations of the state as administrator of the public trust, the dominant theme is the state's sovereign power and duty to exercise continued supervision over the trust. One consequence, of importance to this and many other cases, is that parties acquiring rights in trust property generally hold those rights subject to the trust, and can assert no vested right to use those rights in a manner harmful to the trust.

[The court relies on *Illinois Central* to assert the continuing duty of the state to maintain control over the trust.] ...

In summary, the foregoing cases amply demonstrate the continuing power of the state as administrator of the public trust, a power which extends to the revocation of previously granted rights or to the enforcement of the trust against lands long thought free of the trust....

Since the public trust doctrine does not prevent the state from choosing between trust uses ... the Attorney General of California, seeking to maximize state power under the trust, argues for a broad concept of trust uses. In his view, "trust uses" encompass all public uses, so that in practical effect the doctrine would impose no restrictions on the state's ability to allocate trust property. We know of no authority which supports this view of the public trust,.... Most decisions and commentators assume that "trust uses" relate to uses and activities in the vicinity of the lake, stream, or tidal reach at issue...

Thus, the public trust is more than an affirmation of state power to use public property for public purposes. It is an affirmation of the duty of the state to protect the people's common heritage of streams, lakes, marshlands and tidelands, surrendering that right of protection only in rare cases when the abandonment of that right is consistent with the purposes of the trust.

3. *The California Water Rights System.*

"It is laid down by our law writers, that the right of property in water is usufructuary, and consists not so much of the fluid itself as the advantage of its use." ... Accordingly, Water Code section 102 provides that "[a]ll water within the State is the property of the people of the State, but the right to the use of water may be acquired by appropriation in the manner provided by law."

... [The court describes the history of California water law including the ability of the California Water Board to deny diversions that affect instream values.]

4. *The relationship between the Public Trust Doctrine and the California Water Rights System.*

As we have seen, the public trust doctrine and the appropriative water rights system administered by the Water Board developed independently of each other. Each developed comprehensive rules and principles which, if applied to the full extent of their scope, would occupy the field of allocation of stream waters to the exclusion of any competing system of legal thought. Plaintiffs, for example, argues that the public trust is antecedent to and thus limits all appropriative water rights, an argument which implies that most appropriative water rights in California were acquired and are presently being used unlawfully.... Defendant DWP, on the other hand, argues that the public trust doctrine as to stream waters has been "subsumed" into the appropriative water rights system and, absorbed by that body of law, quietly disappeared; according to DWP, the recipient of a board license enjoys a vested right in perpetuity to take water without concern for the consequences to the trust.

We are unable to accept either position. In our opinion, both the public trust doctrine and the water rights system embody important precepts which make the law more responsive to the diverse needs and interests involved in the planning and allocation of water resources. To embrace one system of thought and reject the other would lead to an unbalanced structure, one which would either decry as a breach of trust appropriations essential to the economic development of this state, or deny any duty to protect or even consider the values promoted by the public trust. Therefore, seeking an accommodation which will make use of the pertinent principles of both the public trust doctrine and the appropriative water rights system, and drawing upon the history of the public trust and the water rights system, the body of judicial precedent, and the views of expert commentators, we reach the following conclusions:

a. The state as sovereign retains continuing supervisory control over its navigable waters and the lands beneath those waters....

b. As a matter of current and historical necessity, the Legislature, acting directly or through an authorized agency such as the Water Board, has the power to grant usufructuary licenses that will permit an appropriator to take water from flowing streams and use that water in a distant part of the state, even though this taking does not promote, and may unavoidably harm, the trust uses at the source stream. The population and economy of this state depend upon the appropriation of vast quantities of water for uses unrelated to in-stream trust values....

c. The state has an affirmative duty to take the public trust into account in the planning and allocation of water resources, and to protect public trust uses whenever feasible.... As a matter of practical necessity the state may have to approve appropriations despite foreseeable harm to public trust uses. In so doing, however, the state must bear in mind its duty ... to preserve, so far as consistent with the public interest, the uses protected by the trust.

Once the state has approved an appropriation, the public trust imposes a duty of continuing supervision over the taking and use of the appropriated water....

The state accordingly has the power to reconsider allocation decisions even though those decisions were made after due consideration of their effect on the public trust.... The case for reconsidering a particular decision, however, is even stronger when that decision failed to weigh and consider public trust uses. In the case before us, the salient fact is that no responsible body has ever determined the impact of diverting the entire flow of the Mono Lake tributaries into the Los Angeles Aqueduct....

It is clear that some responsible body ought to reconsider the allocation of the waters of the Mono Basin....

Notes & Questions

1. Why does the court reject the idea that the PTD merely represents the will of the people and thus water may be dedicated to whatever the State allows?
2. How does the court justify application of the PTD to water diversions from nonnavigable tributaries to Mono Lake?
3. What uses does the PTD extend to in California?
4. A very interesting study on the application of the PTD to water rights in California since the 1984 ruling showed less impact on the protection of public trust resources than expected.[8]

---

8. *See* Dave Owen, *The Mono Lake Case, the Public Trust Doctrine, and the Administrative State*, 45 U.C. Davis L. Rev. 1099 (2012).

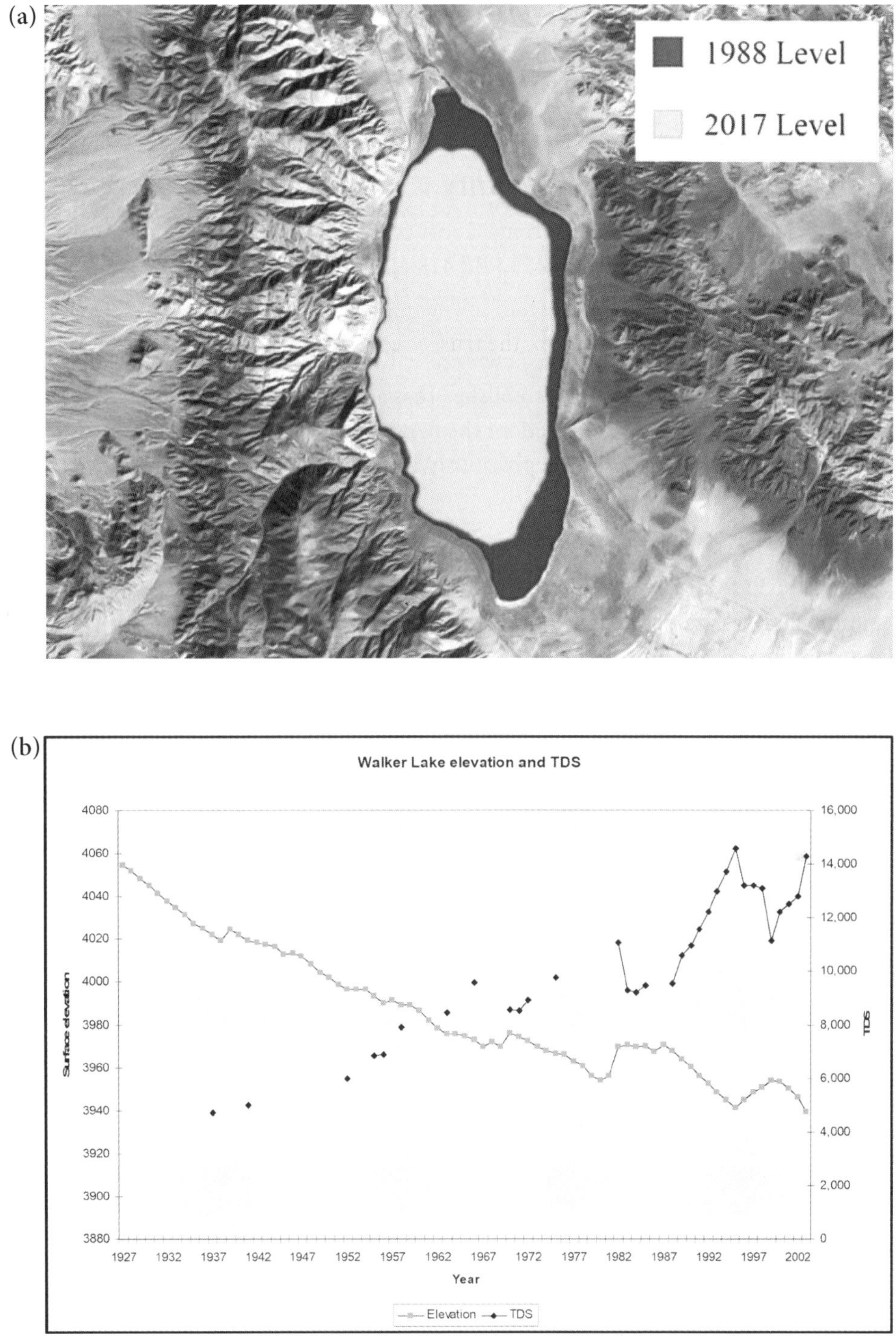

Figure 15.3 (a) Walker Lake showing the bathtub ring from former higher lake level 1988, and the lower level in 2017. (b) Graph showing the decline in lake level for Walker Lake and corresponding increase in salinity between 1927 and 2012. Source: Koami Soulemane Hayibo and Joshua M. Pearce, *Foam-Based Floatovoltaics: A Potential Solution to Disappearing Terminal Natural Lakes*, Renewable Energy 188, February 2022. DOI: 10.1016/j.renene.2022.02.085.

Nevada takes the view that the Public Trust Doctrine is subsumed in its water use act. They did so in a case involving Walker Lake, just one drainage north of Mono Lake and, like Mono Lake, a terminal lake created by inland drainage (Figure 15.3). Look for the court's reasoning and the language it finds relevant in the water use act.

Mineral County v. Lyon County

Supreme Court of Nevada
473 P.3d 418 (2020)

OPINION

By the Court, STIGLICH, J.—In *Lawrence v. Clark County*, we adopted the public trust doctrine, which generally establishes that a state holds its navigable waterways in trust for the public. We are asked for the first time to consider whether the doctrine permits reallocating water rights previously settled under Nevada's prior appropriation doctrine.

...

We conclude that the public trust doctrine as implemented through our state's comprehensive water statutes does not permit the reallocation of water rights already adjudicated and settled under the doctrine of prior appropriation. In doing so, we reaffirm that the public trust doctrine applies in Nevada and clarify that the doctrine applies to all waters within the state, including those previously allocated under prior appropriation. We further hold that the state's statutory water scheme is consistent with the public trust doctrine by requiring the State Engineer to consider the public interest when allocating and administering water rights. But in recognizing the significance of finality in water rights, our Legislature has expressly prohibited reallocating adjudicated water rights that have not been otherwise abandoned or forfeited in accordance with the state's water statutes....

...

While we note that the parties here do not dispute whether the public trust doctrine applies in Nevada, they dispute (1) whether such doctrine applies to rights already adjudicated and settled under the doctrine of prior appropriation, and (2) whether such doctrine applies to nonnavigable waters, navigable

[The court provides similar background on the public trust doctrine to that found in the Mono Lake case. The court uses similar reasoning to the Mono Lake case in finding that the public trust doctrine applies to vested water rights and to non-navigable tributaries to navigable waterways]

...

Nevada's water statutes are consistent with the public trust doctrine

Although we recognize that the public trust doctrine applies to prior appropriated rights and that the doctrine has always inhered in Nevada's water law, we hold that Nevada's comprehensive water statutes are already consistent with the public trust doctrine because they (1) constrain water allocations based on the public interest and (2) satisfy all of the elements of the dispensation of public trust property...

Nevada's statutes regulating water use require the State Engineer to consider the public interest in allocating water rights

The Legislature has established a comprehensive statutory scheme regulating the procedures for acquiring, changing, and losing water rights in Nevada. Much of Nevada's water laws were rewritten and codified in 1913, bringing all of the state's surface waters and artesian groundwater under state ownership and regulation by the State Engineer.... In bringing all of the state's water under comprehensive regulation, the Legislature declared that "[t]he water of all sources of water supply within the boundaries of the State whether above or beneath the surface of the ground, belongs to the public." NRS 533.025.

...

The ... fundamental principle that the water statutes embrace is beneficial use. Specifically, "[b]eneficial use shall be the basis, the measure and the limit of the right to the use of water." NRS 533.035;.... Beneficial use is declared "a public use," NRS 533.050, and by statute includes uses such as irrigation, power, municipal supply, domestic use, mining, livestock watering, and storage, NRS 533.340. In 1969, "any recreational purpose," which includes fishing and wildlife habitations, was additionally deemed a beneficial use.... NRS 533.023 was added in 1989 to define "[w]ildlife purposes" to include "the watering of wildlife and the establishment and maintenance of wetlands, fisheries and other wildlife habitats."...

To ensure that water is being used beneficially and for public use, Nevada's water law charges the State Engineer with approving and rejecting applications. *See* NRS 533.325.... In considering whether to approve or reject applications, the State Engineer must consider whether the proposed action is "environmentally sound" and "an appropriate long-term use which will not unduly limit the future growth and development in the basin" for groundwater applications, NRS 533.370(3)(c)–(d), and must reject any permit applications detrimental to the public interest, NRS 533.370(2).... These considerations are consistent with the public trust doctrine.

Appellants argue, however, that the statutory scheme does not ensure that the state is fulfilling its continuous public trust duties. They maintain that the statutory scheme does not place an affirmative fiduciary duty on the state to assure that public trust resources are available for future generations. We disagree.

First, the statutes constrain water usage to uses that are necessary and terminate water rights when water is not used beneficially, thereby ensuring against waste.... Second, the statute recognizes that water rights may be abandoned.... Finally, the State Engineer is permitted to declare preferred uses and regulate groundwater in the interest of public welfare, which includes curtailing groundwater rights during water supply shortages. NRS 534.120.... The statutory scheme therefore sufficiently places an affirmative duty on the State Engineer to maintain public trust resources.

...

The state's water statutes recognize the importance of finality in water rights and therefore do not permit reallocation of adjudicated water rights

As part of Nevada's comprehensive water statutes, which we conclude adhere to the public trust doctrine, the Legislature enacted NRS 533.185 to establish a judicial decree regarding a water right permit. Regarding those judicial decrees, NRS 533.210(1) provides that:

> The decree entered by the court, as provided by NRS 533.185, *shall be final and shall be conclusive* upon all persons and rights lawfully embraced within the adjudication....

(Emphasis added.) NRS 533.0245 then prohibits the State Engineer from carrying out his or her duty "in a manner that conflicts with any applicable provision of a decree or order issued by a state or federal court."

Respondents argue that the plain language of Nevada's water law statutes prohibit reallocating adjudicated water rights, and we agree. "When the language of a statute is plain and unambiguous, [this] court should give that language its ordinary meaning and not go beyond it."... NRS 533.210 expressly provides that decreed water rights "shall" be final and conclusive.... The statutes also provide an explicit exception wherein a decree could be modified only within three years, NRS 533.210, and the State Engineer is expressly prohibited from allocating water in a manner that conflicts with such finality, NRS 533.0245.

We note that such recognition of finality is vital in arid states like Nevada. In *Arizona v. California*, the United States Supreme Court recognized that "[c]ertainty of rights is particularly important with respect to water rights in the Western United States," and "[t]he doctrine of prior appropriation ... is itself largely a product of the compelling need for certainty in the holding and use of water rights."... To permit reallocation would create uncertainties for future development in Nevada and undermine the public interest in finality and thus also the management of these resources consistent with the public trust doctrine.

...

We recognize the tragic decline of Walker Lake.... But while we are sympathetic to the plight of Walker Lake and the resulting negative impacts on the wildlife, resources, and economy in Mineral County, we cannot use the public trust doctrine as a tool to uproot an entire water system, particularly where finality is firmly rooted in our statutes. We cannot read into the statutes any authority to permit reallocation when the Legislature has already declared that adjudicated water rights are final, nor can we substitute our own policy judgments for the Legislature's....

...

Notes & Questions

1. Nevada's statutes declare that "beneficial use is declared 'a public use.'" What is the importance of this declaration to the case?
2. What aspects of Nevada's water statutes does the court find to be consistent with the ongoing obligation to protect the public trust for future generations?
3. What options are left for Mineral Co. to save Walker Lake, or for other communities seeking to preserve a public trust asset?

The state of Idaho took a third approach in the following statute from the Idaho Code, Title 58 Public Lands, Chapter 12 Public Trust Doctrine:

58-1201. FINDINGS. The legislature hereby finds and declares:

(1) Upon admission of the state of Idaho into the union, the title to the beds of navigable waters became state property, and subject to its jurisdiction and disposal under the equal footing doctrine. According to the United States supreme court's decision in *Shively v. Bowlby*, the state has the right to dispose of the beds of navigable waters, "in such manner as [it] might deem proper, ... subject only to the paramount right of navigation and commerce." The state has the right to determine for itself "to what extent it will preserve its rights of ownership in them, or confer them on others," *Shively v. Bowlby*, 152 U.S. 1, 56 (1893); and

(2) Since the admission of the state of Idaho into the union, article XV of the constitution of the state of Idaho has governed the appropriation and use of the waters of Idaho. Pursuant to article XV of the constitution of the state of Idaho, the legislature of the state of Idaho has enacted a comprehensive system of laws for the appropriation, transfer and use of the waters of Idaho, which addresses the public interest therein; and

...

(4) The common law doctrine known as the public trust doctrine, adopted by inference in section 73-116, Idaho Code, has guided the alienation or encumbrance of the title to the beds of navigable waters held in trust by the state. The public trust doctrine has been cited in court decisions and pleadings in ways that have created confusion in the administration and management of the waters and endowment lands; and

(5) The public's interest in the environment is protected in other parts of Idaho's constitutional or statutory law; and

(6) The purpose of this act is to clarify the application of the public trust doctrine in the state of Idaho and to expressly declare the limits of this common law doctrine in accordance with the authority recognized in each state to define the extent of the common law.

58-1202. DEFINITIONS. For the purposes of this chapter, the following definitions apply: ... [The statute uses the federal definition for "navigable waters."]

58-1203. LIMITATIONS TO THE APPLICATION OF THE PUBLIC TRUST DOCTRINE.

(1) The public trust doctrine as it is applied in the state of Idaho is solely a limitation on the power of the state to alienate or encumber the title to the beds of navigable waters as defined in this chapter....

(2) The public trust doctrine shall not be applied to any purpose other than as provided in this chapter. Specifically, but without limitation, the public trust doctrine shall not apply to:

...

(b) The appropriation or use of water, or the granting, transfer, administration, or adjudication of water or water rights as provided for in article XV of the constitution of the state of Idaho and title 42, Idaho Code, or any other procedure or law applicable to water rights in the state of Idaho;

...

Notes & Questions

1. Consider that states hold the beds and banks of navigable rivers, as well as the overlying water, due to federal law. If the beds and banks of navigable rivers were transferred subject to the public trust, and the duties under the public trust are prescribed by federal law as in *Illinois Central*, is there an argument that federal law imposes the same duty on the transfer of authority over water from the federal to state governments? If so, which of the three approaches taken by western states might be vulnerable?

Chapter 16

The Commerce Clause: Federal Development

Introduction

The federal right to regulate and develop navigable waterways has its origins in the Navigational Servitude (discussed in the previous Chapter as the federal authority that remains on transfer of the beds and banks to a state on statehood) and federal authority to regulate interstate commerce. Both authorities have their source in the Commerce Clause, as discussed in Part I. Federal interest in using these authorities to spur settlement in the western United States arose in the late 1800s.

As the leader of one of four geologic surveys of the arid western lands,[1] John Wesley Powell recognized that the limited water supply would control western development. He reported to Congress in 1878 that collective development of water would be necessary to realize the economic potential of the West.[2] But it was not until 1894 that the first federal effort to spur collective development of western water infrastructure began with passage of the Carey Act.[3] The Carey Act would be referred to today as a "public-private" partnership. The Act resulted in land grants to western states, with states controlling sale and settlement as well as private contracting for development of water infrastructure. The economics did not pan out and only Idaho and Wyoming developed significant Carey Act projects.[4]

1. "On March 2, 1867, Congress for the first time authorized western explorations in which geology would be the principal objective: a study of the geology and natural resources along the fortieth parallel route of the transcontinental railroad, under the Corps of Engineers, and a geological survey of the natural resources of the new State of Nebraska, under the direction of the General Land Office." Two surveys were led under this authorization. One focused on the geology of the transcontinental railroad line led by Clarence King, then-director of the U.S. Geological Survey. Ferdinand Hayden led one focused on Nebraska. Separately, John Wesley Powell, a geology professor at Illinois State Normal University, led a survey through the Grand Canyon of the Colorado River, by boat, in 1869. The fourth survey was led by Lieutenant George Wheeler of the Army Corps of Engineers focused on sites for military posts and wagon routes in Arizona and Nevada. USGS, *The Four Great Surveys of the West*, CIRCULAR 1050 (2019), https://pubs.usgs.gov/circ/c1050/surveys.htm.

2. John Wesley Powell, *Report on the Lands of the Arid Region of the United States*, USGS UNNUMBERED MONOGRAPH, (1879).

3. Carey Act, 43 U.S.C. § 641 et seq.; *see also* Hugh T. Lovin, *The Carey Act in Idaho, 1895–1925: An Experiment in Free Enterprise Reclamation*, 78(4) PACIFIC NORTHWEST Q.122, 133 (1987).

4. *Id.*

A mere eight years later, Congress passed the 1902 Reclamation Act, which envisioned federal development of western water projects and has provided substantial federal subsidies to irrigate the West. The term "Reclamation" envisioned a reclaiming of arid western lands for human use.[5] The Act focused on the settlement of public lands for small family farms. Reclamation projects may also have flood control and hydropower production as secondary purposes to irrigation.

The Reclamation Act

As you read the following text of the Reclamation Act, pay attention to: which states are included as beneficiaries of the Act;[6] what is the acreage limitation for receipt of project water by any single landowner; what is necessary for water infrastructure to transfer from the federal government to the irrigators; and what aspects of a project will always remain with the federal government. You will see in Sections 1 and 5 that the Act establishes a "reclamation fund" to be financed initially by sale of public lands within the reclamation states, and to be replenished by repayment of construction and operation and maintenance costs by the irrigators who benefit from the projects. You will also see that it was originally contemplated that the Department of Interior would identify suitable projects. In reality, with the exception of the projects initially selected, most Reclamation projects required congressional authorization and appropriations. The "fund" was simply inadequate, and the economics of irrigated agriculture did not provide the level of profits necessary for repayment. As a result, repayment was often extended over long periods, and portions of project costs were charged to secondary uses of dams, including hydropower production and flood control. Finally, read Section 8 carefully. It will be the focus of the case that follows the Act.

1902 Reclamation Act

FIFTY-SEVENTH CONGRESS.
Sess. I. CH. 1093. 1902. 32 Stat. 388

—An Act Appropriating the receipts from the sale and disposal of public lands in certain States and Territories to the construction of irrigation works for the reclamation of arid lands.

Be it enacted by the Senate and House of Representatives of the United States of America in Congress assembled, That all moneys received from the sale and disposal of public lands in Arizona, California, Colorado, Idaho, Kansas, Montana, Nebraska, Nevada, New Mexico, North Dakota, Oklahoma, Oregon, South Dakota, Utah, Washington, and Wyoming, beginning in … nineteen hundred and one, … shall be and the same

---

5. United States Bureau of Reclamation, *The Bureau of Reclamation: A Very Brief History* (2022), https://www.usbr.gov/history/borhist.html.

6. Note that Texas was not included in the original Act because it had no federal public lands. It was added in 1906.

are hereby, reserved, set aside, and appropriated as a special fund in the treasury to be known as the "reclamation fund," to be used in the examination and survey for and construction and maintenance of irrigation works for the storage, diversion, and development of waters for the reclamation of arid and semiarid lands in the said States and Territories, and for the payment of all other expenditures provided for in this Act....

...

Sec. 2 That the Secretary of the Interior is hereby authorized and directed to make examinations and surveys for, and to locate and construct, as herein provided, irrigation works for the storage, diversion, and development of waters, including artisan wells....

Sec. 3, That the Secretary of the Interior shall, before giving the public notice provided for in section four of this Act, withdraw from public entry the lands required for any irrigation works contemplated under the provisions of this Act, and shall restore to public entry any of the lands so withdrawn when, in his judgment, such lands are not required for the purposes of this Act; and the Secretary of the Interior is hereby authorized, at or immediately prior to the time of beginning the surveys for any contemplated irrigation works, to withdraw from entry, except under the homestead laws, any public lands believed to be susceptible of irrigation from said works: *Provided*, ... that public lands which [the Department] is proposed to irrigate by means of any contemplated works shall be subject to entry only under the provisions of the homestead laws in tracts of not less than forty nor more than one hundred and sixty acres, and shall be subject to the limitations, charges, terms, and conditions herein....

Sec. 4. That upon the determination of the Secretary of the Interior that any irrigation project is practicable, he may cause to be let contracts for the construction of the same, in such portions or sections as it may be practicable to construct and complete as parts of the whole project, providing the necessary funds for such portions or sections are available in the reclamation fund, and thereupon be shall give public notice of the lands irrigable under such project, and limit of area per entry, which limit shall represent the acreage which, in the opinion of the Secretary, may be reasonably required for the support of a family upon the lands in question; also of the charges which shall be made per acre upon the said entries and upon lands in private ownership which may be irrigated by the waters of the said irrigation project, and the number of annual installments, not exceeding ten, in which such charges shall be paid and the time when such payments shall commence. The said charges shall be determined with a view of returning to the reclamation fund the estimated cost of construction of the project, and shall be apportioned equitably....

Sec. 5. That the entryman upon lands to be irrigated by such works shall, in addition to compliance with the homestead laws, reclaim at least one-half of the total irrigable area of his entry for agricultural purposes, and before receiving patent for the lands covered by his entry shall pay to the Government the charges apportioned against such tract, as provided in section four. No right to the use of water for land in private ownership shall be sold for a tract exceeding one hundred and sixty acres to any one landowner, and no such sale shall be made to any landowner unless he be an actual bona fide resident on such land, or occupant thereof residing in the neighborhood of said land, and no such right shall permanently attach until all payments therefore are made.... All moneys received from the above sources shall be paid in the reclamation fund....

SEC. 6. That the Secretary of the Interior is hereby authorized and directed to use the reclamation fund for the operation and maintenance of all reservoirs and irrigation works constructed under the provisions of this Act: *Provided*, That when the payments required by this Act are made for the major portion of the lands irrigated from the waters of any of the works herein provided for, then the management and operation of such irrigation works shall pass to the owners of the lands irrigated thereby, to be maintained at their expense under such form of organization and under such rules and regulations as may be acceptable to the Secretary of the Interior: *Provided*, That the title to and the management and operation of the reservoirs and the works necessary for their protection and operation shall remain in the Government until otherwise provided by Congress.

SEC. 7. That where in carrying out the provisions of this Act it becomes necessary to acquire any rights to property, the Secretary of the Interior is hereby authorized to acquire the same for the United States by purchase or by condemnation under the judicial process, and to pay from the reclamation fund the sums which may be needed for that purpose....

SEC. 8. That nothing in this Act shall be construed as affecting or intending to affect or to in any way interfere with the laws of any State or Territory relating to the control, appropriation, use, or distribution and the Secretary of the Interior, in carrying out the provisions of this Act, shall proceed in conformity with such laws, and nothing herein shall in any way affect any right of any State or of the Federal Government or of any landowner, appropriator, or user of water in to, or from any interstate stream or the waters thereof: *Provided*, That the right to the use of water acquired under the provisions of this Act shall be appurtenant to the land irrigated, and beneficial use shall be the basis, measure, and the limit of the right.

SEC. 9. That it is hereby declared to be the duty of the Secretary of the Interior in carrying out the provisions of this Act, so far as the same may be practicable and subject to the existence of feasible irrigation projects, to expend the major portion of the funds arising from the sale of public lands within each State and Territory hereinbefore named for the benefit of arid and semiarid lands within the limits of such State or Territory....

SEC. 10. That the Secretary of the Interior is hereby authorized to perform any and all acts and to make such rules and regulations as may be necessary and proper for the purpose of carrying the provisions of this Act into full force and effect.

Approved, June 17, 1902.

Notes & Questions

1. Which states are included as beneficiaries of the Act?
2. What is the acreage limitation for receipt of project water by any single landowner?
3. What is necessary for water infrastructure to transfer from the federal government to the irrigators?
4. What aspects of a project will always remain with the federal government?

Federalism and the Reclamation Act

Section 8 of the Reclamation Act, by providing that "the Secretary of the Interior, in carrying out the provisions of this Act, shall proceed in conformity with "the laws of any State or Territory relating to the control, appropriation, use, or distribution," sets up a tension between federal and state governments over the law controlling water use from federal projects. Over the years, several cases have reached the U.S. Supreme Court regarding areas of conflict between state law and the Reclamation Act. In 1978, the case of *California v. United States*, 438 U.S. 645, reviewed these prior cases and addressed the question of how far a state may go in conditioning the use of water from a Reclamation project.

It is useful to know some of the history leading to the case. The decision to dam the Stanislaus River, one of the last free-flowing rivers in California, came as the environmental movement was on the rise in the mid-twentieth century. Opposition to the dam centered on whether the storage was necessary given that few people had entered into contracts with the Bureau of Reclamation for use of the water that would result from the project. The opposition led to formation of Friends of the River, an environmental organization that would become a major player in the fight that signaled the end of the major twentieth-century dam-building era in the West.[7] The New Melones Dam was nevertheless built (Figure 16.1).

In addition to its relation to a major environmental policy battle, the case draws the line between the so-called "deference" to state water law and federal primacy. In doing so, it must address cases thought to have settled the issue. Pay attention to how the Court distinguishes the earlier cases interpreting Section 8 and how it handles what it refers to as "dictum" in those cases.

7. Friends of the River, *Past Work* (2022), https://www.friendsoftheriver.org/our-work/past-work/.

Figure 16.1 New Melones Dam on the Stanislaus River. Source: U.S. Bureau of Reclamation California-Great Basin Digital Library, *New Melones Unit*, Central Valley Project (2023), https://www.usbr.gov/mp/ccao/newmelones/planning-visit/gallery.html.

California v. United States

Supreme Court of the United States
438 U.S. 645 (1978)

Opinion

Mr. Justice REHNQUIST delivered the opinion of the Court.—The United States seeks to impound 2.4 million acre-feet of water from California's Stanislaus River as part of its Central Valley Project. The California State Water Resources Control Board ruled that the water could not be allocated to the Government under state law unless it agreed to and complied with various conditions dealing with the water's use. The Government then sought a declaratory judgment in the District Court for the Eastern District of California to the effect that the United States can impound whatever unappropriated water is necessary for a federal reclamation project without complying with state law. The District Court held that, as a matter of comity, the United States must apply to the State for an appropriation permit, but that the State must issue the permit without condition if there is sufficient unappropriated water. 403 F.Supp. 874 (1975). The Court of Appeals for the Ninth Circuit affirmed, but held that § 8 of the Reclamation Act of 1902, 32 Stat.

390, as codified, 43 U.S.C. §§ 372, 383, rather than comity, requires the United States to apply for the permit. 558 F.2d 1347 (1977). We granted certiorari to review the decision of the Court of Appeals insofar as it holds that California cannot condition its allocation of water to a federal reclamation project. 434 U.S. 984 (1977). We now reverse.

I

...

In order to correctly ascertain the meaning of the Reclamation Act of 1902, we must recognize the obvious truth that the history of irrigation and reclamation before that date was much fresher in the minds of those then in Congress than it is to us today. "[T]he afternoon of July 23, 1847, was the true date of the beginning of modern irrigation. It was on that afternoon that the first band of Mormon pioneers built a small dam across City Creek near the present site of the Mormon Temple and diverted sufficient water to saturate some 5 acres of exceedingly dry land.... During the subsequent half century, irrigation expanded throughout the arid States of the West, supported usually by private enterprise or the local community.... By the turn of the century, however, most of the land which could be profitably irrigated by such small-scale projects had been put to use. Pressure mounted on the Federal Government to provide the funding for the massive projects that would be needed to complete the reclamation, culminating in the Reclamation Act of 1902....

...

If the term "cooperative federalism" had been in vogue in 1902, the Reclamation Act of that year would surely have qualified as a leading example of it. In that Act, Congress set forth on a massive program to construct and operate dams, reservoirs, and canals for the reclamation of the arid lands in 17 Western States. Reflective of the "cooperative federalism" which the Act embodied is § 8, whose exact meaning and scope are the critical inquiries in this case:

> "*[N]othing in this Act shall be construed as affecting or intended to affect or to in any way interfere with the laws of any State or Territory relating to the control, appropriation, use, or distribution of water used in irrigation,* or any vested right acquired thereunder, *and the Secretary of the Interior, in carrying out the provisions of this Act, shall proceed in conformity with such laws,* and nothing herein shall in any way affect any right of any State or of the Federal Government or of any landowner, appropriator, or user of water in, to, or from any interstate stream or the waters thereof: *Provided,* That the right to use of water acquired under the provisions of this Act shall be appurtenant to the land irrigated, and beneficial use shall be the basis, the measure, and the limit of the right." 32 Stat. 390 (emphasis added).

...

The New Melones Dam, which this litigation concerns, is part of the California Central Valley Project, the largest reclamation project yet authorized under the 1902 Act.... The Dam, which will impound 2.4 million acre-feet of water of California's

Stanislaus River, has the multiple purposes of flood control, irrigation, municipal use, industrial use, power, recreation, water-quality control, and the protection of fish and wildlife. The waters of the Stanislaus River that will be impounded behind the New Melones Dam arise and flow solely in California.

The United States Bureau of Reclamation, as it has with every other federal reclamation project, applied for a permit from the appropriate state agency, here the California State Water Resources Control Board, to appropriate the water that would be impounded by the Dam and later used for reclamation.... After lengthy hearings, the State Board found that unappropriated water was available for the New Melones Dam during certain times of the year. Although it therefore approved the Bureau's applications, the State Board attached 25 conditions to the permit. California State Water Resources Control Board, Decision 1422 (Apr. 14, 1973). The most important conditions prohibit full impoundment until the Bureau is able to show firm commitments, or at least a specific plan, for the use of the water.... The State Board concluded that without such a specific plan of beneficial use the Bureau had failed to meet the California statutory requirements for appropriation.

> "The limited unappropriated water resources of the State should not be committed to an applicant in the absence of a showing of his actual need for the water within a reasonable time in the future. When the evidence indicates, as it does here, that an applicant already has a right to sufficient water to meet his needs for beneficial use within the foreseeable future, rights to additional water should be withheld and that water should be reserved for other beneficial uses." *Id.,* at 16.

II

The history of the relationship between the Federal Government and the States in the reclamation of the arid lands of the Western States is both long and involved, but through it runs the consistent thread of purposeful and continued deference to state water law by Congress. [The Court covers the history of the mining and homestead acts and federal acceptance of water allocation under local custom, and ultimate control by states learned in Parts I and II.]

...

... In *United States v. Rio Grande Dam & Irrig. Co.*, for example, New Mexico's authority to adopt a prior appropriation system of water rights for the Rio Grande River was challenged. The Court unhesitatingly held that "as to every stream within its dominion a State may change [the] common law rule and permit the appropriation of the flowing waters for such purposes as it deems wise." 174 U.S., at 702–703. The Court noted that there are two limitations to the States' exclusive control of its streams—reserved rights "so far at least as may be necessary for the beneficial uses of the government property," *Id.*, at 703, and the navigation servitude.... "Unquestionably the State ... has a right to appropriate its waters, and the United States may not question such appropriation, unless thereby the navigability of the [river] be disturbed." *Id.*, 690 U.S., at 709.

...

III

It is against this background that Congress passed the Reclamation Act of 1902.... In his first message to Congress after assuming the Presidency, Theodore Roosevelt continued the cry for national funding of reclamation and again recommended that state law control the distribution of water....

As a result of the public demand for federal reclamation funding, a bill was introduced into the 57th Congress to use the money from the sale of public lands in the Western States to build reclamation projects in those same States. The projects would be built on federal land and the actual construction and operation of the projects would be in the hands of the Secretary of the Interior. But the Act clearly provided that state water law would control in the appropriation and later distribution of the water. As originally introduced, § 8 of the Reclamation Act provided: ...

> "[N]othing in this act shall be construed as affecting or intended to affect or to in any way interfere with the laws of any State or Territory relating to the control, appropriation, use, or distribution of water used in irrigation; but State and Territorial laws shall govern and control in the appropriation, use, and distribution of the waters rendered available by the works constructed under the provisions of this act: *Provided,* That the right to the use of water acquired under the provisions of this act shall be appurtenant to the land irrigated, and beneficial use shall be the basis, the measure, and the limit of the right."

From the legislative history of the Reclamation Act of 1902, it is clear that state law was expected to control in two important respects. First, and of controlling importance to this case, the Secretary would have to appropriate, purchase, or condemn necessary water rights in strict conformity with state law....

Second, once the waters were released from the Dam, their distribution to individual landowners would again be controlled by state law. As explained by Senator Clark of Wyoming, [*Id.,* at 2222]:

"[I]t is right and proper that the various States and Territories should control in the distribution. The conditions in each and every State and Territory are different. What would be applicable in one locality is totally and absolutely inapplicable in another.... In each and every one of the States and Territories affected, after a long series of experiments, after a due consideration of conditions, there has arisen a set of men who are especially qualified to deal with local conditions...."

...

As Representative Sutherland, later to be a Justice of this Court, succinctly put it, "if the appropriation and use were not under the provisions of the State law the utmost confusion would prevail." *Id.,* at 6770. Different water rights in the same State would be governed by different laws and would frequently conflict....

...

IV

For almost half a century, this congressionally mandated division between federal and state authority worked smoothly. No project was constructed without the approval of the Secretary of the Interior,.... But state laws relating to water rights were observed in accordance with the congressional directive contained in § 8 of the Act of 1902. In 1958, however, the first of two cases was decided by this Court in which private landowners or municipal corporations contended that state water law had the effect of overriding specific congressional directives to the Secretary of the Interior as to the operation of federal reclamation projects. In *Ivanhoe Irrigation District v. McCracken* the Supreme Court of California decided that California law forbade the 160-acre limitation on irrigation water deliveries expressly written into § 5 of the Reclamation Act of 1902, and that therefore, under § 8 of the Reclamation Act, the Secretary was required to deliver reclamation water without regard to the acreage limitation. Both the State of California and the United States appealed from this judgment, and this Court reversed it, saying:

> "Section 5 is a specific and mandatory prerequisite laid down by the Congress as binding in the operation of reclamation projects, providing that '[n]o right to the use of water ... shall be sold for a tract exceeding one hundred and sixty acres to any one landowner.... Without passing generally on the coverage of § 8 in the delicate area of federal-state relations in the irrigation field, we do not believe that the Congress intended § 8 to override the repeatedly reaffirmed national policy of § 5." 357 U.S., at 291–292, 78 S.Ct., at 1184.

Five years later, in *City of Fresno v. California* this Court affirmed a decision of the United States Court of Appeals for the Ninth Circuit holding that § 8 did not require the Secretary of the Interior to ignore explicit congressional provisions preferring irrigation use over domestic and municipal use....

Petitioners do not ask us to overrule these holdings, nor are we presently inclined to do so. Petitioners instead ask us to hold that a State may impose any condition on the "control, appropriation, use, or distribution of water" through a federal reclamation project that is not inconsistent with clear congressional directives respecting the project. Petitioners concede, and the Government relies upon, dicta in our cases that may point to a contrary conclusion. Thus, in *Ivanhoe,* the Court went beyond the actual facts of that case and stated:

> "As we read § 8, it merely requires the United States to comply with state law when, in the construction and operation of a reclamation project, it becomes necessary for it to acquire water rights or vested interests therein.... We read nothing in § 8 that compels the United States to deliver water on conditions imposed by the State."

Like dictum was repeated in *City of Fresno,* and in this Court's opinion in *Arizona v. California* where the Court also said:

> "The argument that § 8 of the Reclamation Act requires the United States in the delivery of water to follow priorities laid down by state law has already been disposed of by this Court in *Ivanhoe Irr. Dist. v. McCracken,* ... and reaffirmed in *City of Fresno v. California....* Since § 8 of the Reclamation Act did not subject the Secretary to state law in disposing of water in [*Ivanhoe*], we cannot, consistently with *Ivanhoe,* hold that the Secretary must be bound by state law in disposing of water under the Project Act."

While we are not convinced that the above language is diametrically inconsistent with the position of petitioners, ... or that it squarely supports the United States, it undoubtedly goes further than was necessary to decide the cases presented to the Court. *Ivanhoe* and *City of Fresno* involved conflicts between § 8, requiring the Secretary to follow state law as to water rights, and other provisions of Reclamation Acts that placed specific limitations on how the water was to be distributed. Here the United States contends that it may ignore state law even if no explicit congressional directive conflicts with the conditions imposed by the California State Water Control Board....

In *Arizona v. California,* the States had asked the Court to rule that state law would control in the distribution of water from the Boulder Canyon Project, a massive multistate reclamation project on the Colorado River.... After reviewing the legislative history of the Boulder Canyon Project Act, 43 U.S.C. § 617 *et seq.,* the Court concluded that because of the unique size and multistate scope of the Project, Congress did not intend the States to interfere with the Secretary's power to determine with whom and on what terms water contracts would be made.... While the Court in rejecting the States' claim repeated the language from *Ivanhoe* and *City of Fresno* as to the scope of § 8, there was no need for it to reaffirm such language except as it related to the singular legislative history of the Boulder Canyon Project Act.

But because there is at least tension between the above-quoted dictum and what we conceive to be the correct reading of § 8 of the Reclamation Act of 1902, we disavow the dictum to the extent that it would prevent petitioners from imposing conditions on the permit granted to the United States which are not inconsistent with congressional provisions authorizing the project in question. Section 8 cannot be read to require the Secretary to comply with state law only when it becomes necessary to purchase or condemn vested water rights. That section does, of course, provide for the protection of vested water rights, but it also requires the Secretary to comply with state law in the "control, appropriation, use, or distribution of water." Nor, as the United States contends, does § 8 merely require the Secretary of the Interior to file a notice with the State of his intent to appropriate but to thereafter ignore the substantive provisions of state law. The legislative history of the Reclamation Act of 1902 makes it abundantly clear that Congress intended to defer to the substance, as well as the form, of state water law. The Government's interpretation would trivialize the broad language and purpose of § 8.

Indeed, until recently, it has been the consistent position of the Secretary of the Interior and the Bureau of Reclamation, who are together responsible for executing the provisions of the Reclamation Act of 1902, that in appropriating water for reclamation purposes the Bureau must comply with state law. The Bureau's operating instructions, for example, provide:

> "State and Federal law and policy establish the framework for project formulation. *Project plans must comply with State legal provisions or priorities for beneficial use of water....* In some cases, ... State laws ... have been modified to meet specific conditions in the authorization of particular projects." U.S. Department of Interior, Bureau of Reclamation, Reclamation Instructions § 116.3.1 (1959) (emphasis added).

...

V

Because the District Court and the Court of Appeals both held that California could not impose any conditions whatever on the United States' appropriation permit, those courts did not reach the United States' alternative contention that the conditions actually imposed are inconsistent with congressional directives as to the New Melones Dam. Nor did they reach California's contention that the United States is barred by principles of collateral estoppel from challenging the consistency of the permit conditions. Assuming, *arguendo,* that the United States is still free to challenge the consistency of the conditions, resolution of their consistency may well require additional factfinding. We therefore reverse the judgment of the Court of Appeals and remand for further proceedings consistent with this opinion.

Reversed and remanded.

Mr. Justice WHITE, with whom Mr. Justice BRENNAN and Mr. Justice MARSHALL join, dissenting.

Notes & Questions

1. On remand, the Ninth Circuit Court of Appeals found all 25 conditions on the permit issued by the California State Water Resources Control Board to pass the test of "consistency" with the Reclamation Act. *United States v. California*, 694 F.2d 1171 (9th Cir. 1981) The judge in the Ninth Circuit case on remand, Anthony Kennedy, was soon to become Justice Kennedy. Among the conditions were the following: Condition 1 states in part: "Until further notice of the State Water Resources Control Board, the water shall be used only for preservation and enhancement of fish and wildlife, recreation and water quality control purposes. Further order of the Board shall be preceded by a showing that the benefits that will accrue from a specific proposed use will outweigh any damage that would result to fish, wildlife and recreation in the watershed above New Melones Dam and that the permittee has firm commitments to deliver water for such other purposes."
2. The Court states: "From the legislative history of the Reclamation Act of 1902, it is clear that state law was expected to control in two important respects." What are the "two important respects" the Court refers to?

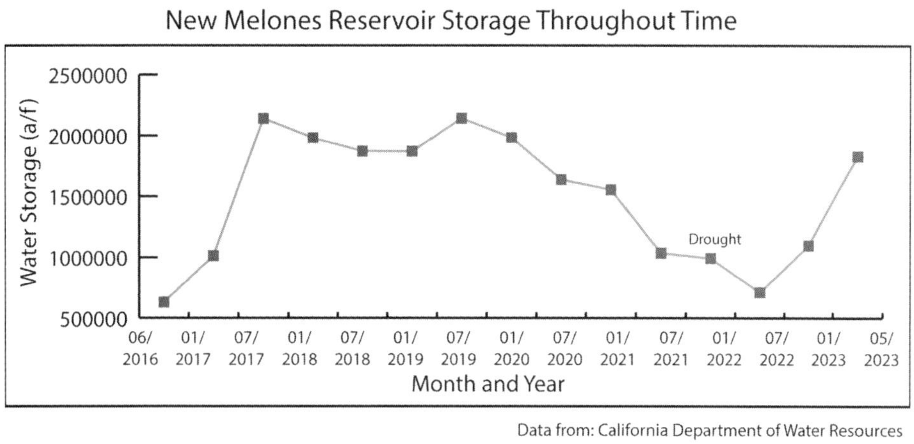

Figure 16.2 New Melones storage showing drought years. Source: California Department of Water Resources.

3. The Court states that "there is at least a tension" between statements made in *Ivanhoe* and *City of Fresno*, and the ruling here that a state may place conditions on a state water permit for a Bureau of Reclamation project as long as the conditions are not inconsistent with federal law. Both *Ivanhoe* and *City of Fresno* found state requirements to be inconsistent. What was the inconsistency found in each case?
4. The reservoir behind New Melones Dam was ultimately contracted and filled. It was nevertheless heralded as the end of the big dam-building era in the United States. No major dam has been built in the United States since.[8] Figure 16.2, above, gives you an idea of the ongoing controversy over its use today.

The goal of the Reclamation Act was to catalyze development of small family farms throughout the West. The Act's limit in Section 5 of 160 acres for recipients of Reclamation project water that was the subject of the dispute in *Ivanhoe*, "was designed to distribute the benefits of the public domain widely by favoring actual settlers against monopolists and speculators of that day."[9] The 160-acre limit was equal to the maximum size of parcels under the Homestead Act of 1862.

The Reclamation Act was successful in its goal of agricultural development in the West. From the Bureau of Reclamation's own history:

> Reclamation operates about 180 projects in the 17 Western States. The total Reclamation investment for completed project facilities in September of 1992 was about $11.0 billion. Reclamation projects provide agricultural, household, and industrial water to about one-third of the population of the American West. About 5 percent of the land area of the West is irrigated, and Reclamation provides water to about one-fifth of that acreage (in 1992, some 9,120,000

8. William Robert Lowry, Dam Politics: Restoring America's Rivers (2003).

9. Paul S. Taylor, *The 160-Acre Water Limitation and the Water Resources Commission*, 3(3) Pol. Rsch. Q. 435, 435 (1950), *available at*: https://journals.sagepub.com/doi/abs/10.1177/106591295000300307 .

acres). Reclamation is a major American generator of electricity. In1993 Reclamation had 56 power plants on-line and generated 34.7 billion kilowatt hours of electricity.[10]

The favorable economics of western irrigated agriculture were substantially enhanced by federal subsidy brought about by extensions on repayment timelines and pricing of water that in some cases was lower than even operation and maintenance costs.[11] "For example, the Central Valley Project, one of the Bureau's California projects, enjoys a subsidy estimated at $3.5 billion."[12] It was, however, less successful in developing a society of small family farmers. Instead, the Act ended up supporting large agricultural operations with much of the subsidy going to farms with acreage in excess of 160 acres. As a result, according to a 1981 Bureau report, 31% of reclamation land was held by the top 3% acreage holders,[13] and "only twenty-three percent of the land receiving subsidized water was farmed in operations of 160 acres or less."[14] The use of leasing, trusts, corporate entities, and holding of land by multiple family members were some of the means to circumvent the acreage limitation.[15]

A lawsuit filed against the Bureau of Reclamation in 1975 sought enforcement of the 160-acre limit and resulted in an order to the agency to commence rulemaking.[16] Given the implications of enforcement for western agriculture, the effort ultimately led to a political solution in the form of the Reclamation Reform Act of 1982 (RRA).[17] The following paragraphs summarize key aspects and rely both on the text of the RRA and the context provided by a law review article based on a report "presented to the Committee on Energy and Natural Resources, U.S. Senate, on Oct. 1, 1987."[18]

The compromise found in the RRA begins with an increase in the size of acreage that may receive subsidized water to 960 acres for individual recipients (defined to include spouse and dependents) and 640 acres for corporate entities of 25 or more persons. The limits apply to any "landholding" benefiting the recipient directly or indirectly whether owned, leased, or held in trust, as well as land held in multiple districts. The 960 and 640 acreage limits are to be calculated based on equivalency to class I land. Class 1 are the lands with the best soils and, therefore, the highest crop yield. Acreage allowed is increased for each class of land from class II and beyond.

---

10. U.S. Bureau of Reclamation, *Reclamation History*, March 5, 2022, https://www.usbr.gov/history/borhist.html#:~:text=Congress%20passed%20the%20Reclamation%20Act,arid%20lands%20for%20human%20use.

11. Hamilton Candee, *The Broken Promise of Reclamation Reform*, 40 Hastings L.J. 657 at 665 (1989).

12. *Id.* at 657, n 3.

13. *Id.* at 656, n 4.

14. *Id.* at 661.

15. *Id.* at 663.

16. *Id.* at 662.

17. Reclamation Reform Act, Title II of Public Law 97-293, 96 Stat. 1261 (1982). The text of the RRA can be found at the U.S. Bureau of Reclamation webpage at https://www.usbr.gov/rra/, and the agency regulations to implement it at 43 CFR Part 426, 428.

18. Candee, *supra* at 657.

The subsidized fees associated with these lands must at least cover annual operation and maintenance costs. Land in excess of the new acreage limits may receive project water, but only at full cost. Full cost must reflect construction repayment, operation and maintenance, and interest.

To achieve these reforms, existing contracts with the Bureau for water delivery would need to be amended. The so called "hammer clause"[19] of the RRA provides that subsidized project water must be limited to the original 160 acres (with the broader definition of landholding to include leased land and land held in trust) if the contract was not revised within a five-year timeline. Full cost would be applied to any additional landholding.

Initial implementation under rules promulgated by the Reagan administration were heavily criticized for containing multiple loopholes.[20] The rules cited above sought to close those loopholes and were promulgated in 1996 during the Clinton administration.

Ownership of Water Rights Serviced by Reclamation Projects

While Section 8 of the Reclamation Act and its interpretation in *California v. United States* requires the Bureau of Reclamation to seek water rights from the state for a Reclamation project, it does not indicate who holds that water right once obtained—the Bureau; the irrigation district; or the landholder who puts the water to beneficial use? The next three cases address that issue in part, but you will see in Part VI on adjudication that sufficient ambiguity remains (or arguably remains) to result in conflicting decisions by state courts.

The first case, *Ickes v. Fox*, 300 U.S. 82 (1937), turns on a highly technical issue. The U.S. Bureau of Reclamation sought reduction in delivery of water to irrigators who would not amend contracts to reflect the need for a new reservoir (and hence, to cover its cost). The case turned on *who* held the water rights for the project. If the irrigators (Fox et al.) held the water rights, then the suit for specific performance of delivery of water against the Secretary of the Interior (Ickes) may go forward. If the United States owned the water rights, it needed to be joined as an indispensable party. Without a waiver of immunity to join the United States, the suit would be dismissed. The following excerpt includes only the text of the case relevant to ownership of the water rights.

---

19. *Id*. at 666.
20. *Id*. at 668–82.

Ickes v. Fox

Supreme Court of the United States
300 U.S. 82 (1937)

Opinion

Mr. Justice SUTHERLAND delivered the opinion of the Court—The sole question in each of these three cases is whether the United States is an indispensable party defendant....

Petitioner, as Secretary of the Interior, has charge of the administration of the Reclamation Act of June 17, 1902 (32 Stat. 388), as amended. In 1906, the then Secretary of the Interior approved a reclamation project known as the 'Sunnyside Unit of the Yakima Project'; and purchased from the Washington Irrigation Company the Sunnyside Canal, together with the water appropriations and irrigation system connected therewith. At the time of the purchase, certain arid and unirrigated lands described in the bill, thereafter and now owned by respondents, were within the unit embraced by the project.

The then owners of the lands, predecessors of respondents in title, and other owners of similar lands, incorporated the Sunnyside Water Users Association under the lands within the reclamation project, and lands within the reclamation project, and agreed to take water from the project to irrigate such lands.

The association, on May 7, 1906, entered into a contract with the United States,...

...

... it was determined by representatives of the successive Secretaries that 4.84 acre feet of water per annum per acre was necessary to beneficially and successfully irrigate respondents' lands;...

Respondents and their predecessors, it is alleged, have fully complied with the terms of the Reclamation Act and all obligations in connection with their water rights, and have paid to the government all sums due on account of construction charges, and all operation and maintenance charges, and have acquired vested water rights sufficient to beneficially and successfully irrigate their lands—namely, 4.84 acre feet of water per acre per annum; and that such water rights are appurtenant to their lands.

The bill further alleges that in 1930 the Commissioner of Reclamation desired to construct the Cle Elum Reservoir ... and without consulting respondents or other water users in the Sunnyside Unit of the Yakima Project, the Commissioner charged the sum of $1,000,000 to that unit and district, and informed the Secretary to that effect....

The bill further alleges that the Secretary and other officials agreed with designated persons to attempt to force and coerce respondents, and other water users in the district, to induce the district to agree to pay the additional sum; otherwise, to force and coerce them to sign water-rental applications or be deprived of a portion of the water owned by them. In pursuance thereof, public notice was given and an order issued limiting their rights to 3 acre feet per acre, and exacting a specified rental charge for additional water....

It is further alleged that 3 acre feet of water per acre is not, never has been, and will not in the future be sufficient to beneficially irrigate respondents' lands; but would leave a large part thereof barren and nonproductive, thereby forcing about half of their lands to bear construction, maintenance charges, taxes, and assessments upon the whole thereof....

Respondents had made all stipulated payments and complied with all obligations by which they were bound to the government, and, long prior to the issue of the notices and orders here assailed, had acquired a vested right to the perpetual use of the waters as appurtenant to their lands. Under the Reclamation Act, *supra*, as well as under the law of Washington, 'beneficial use' was 'the basis, the measure, and the limit of the right.'... Although the government diverted, stored, and distributed the water, the contention of petitioner that thereby ownership of the water or water rights became vested in the United States is not well founded. Appropriation was made not for the use of the government, but, under the Reclamation Act, for the use of the landowners; and by the terms of the law and of the contract already referred to, the water rights became the property of the landowners, wholly distinct from the property right of the government in the irrigation works.... The government was and remained simply a carrier and distributor of the water (Id.), with the right to receive the sums stipulated in the contracts as reimbursement for the cost of construction and annual charges for operation and maintenance of the works. As security therefore, it was provided that the government should have a lien upon the lands and the water rights appurtenant thereto—a provision which in itself imports that the water rights belong to another than the lienor, that is to say, to the landowner.

The federal government, as owner of the public domain, had the power to dispose of the land and water composing it together or separately; and by the Desert Land Act of 1877 (c. 107, 19 Stat. 377), if not before, Congress had severed the land and waters constituting the public domain and established the rule that for the future the lands should be patented separately. Acquisition of the government title to a parcel of land was not to carry with it a water right; but all nonnavigable waters were reserved for the use of the public under the laws of the various arid-land states. *California Oregon Power Co. v. Cement Co.*, 295 U.S. 142. And in those states, generally, including the state of Washington, it long has been established law that the right to the use of water can be acquired only by prior appropriation for a beneficial use; and that such right when thus obtained is a property right, which, when acquired for irrigation, becomes, by state law and here by express provision of the Reclamation Act as well, part and parcel of the land upon which it is applied.

[The Court concludes that the United States is not an indispensable party]

The decree of the court below is affirmed.

Affirmed.

The second case, *Nebraska v. Wyoming*, 325 U.S. 589 (1945), was brought by Nebraska for an equitable apportionment of the waters of the North Platte River among itself, Wyoming, and Colorado. The river had been heavily developed for Reclamation projects. The case will be covered in more detail in the following Chapter on interstate apportionment. The section covered here addresses the assertion of the United States that it owns the water rights for Reclamation projects, and thus is entitled an apportionment of those waters free and clear of state control.

Nebraska v. Wyoming

Supreme Court of the United States
325 U.S. 589 (1945)

Opinion

Mr. Justice DOUGLAS delivered the opinion of the Court.

...

IV.

Claim of United States to Unappropriated Water. The United States claims that it owns all the unappropriated water in the river. It argues, that it owned the then unappropriated water at the time it acquired water rights by appropriation for the North Platte Project and the Kendrick Project. Its basic rights are therefore said to derive not from appropriation but from its underlying ownership which entitles it to an apportionment in this suit free from state control. The argument is that the United States acquired the original ownership of all rights in the water as well as the lands in the North Platte basin by cessions from France, Spain and Mexico in 1803, 1819, and 1848, and by agreement with Texas in 1850.... But we do not stop to determine what rights to unappropriated water of the river the United States may have. For the water rights on which the North Platte Project and the Kendrick Project rest have been obtained in compliance with state law. Whether they might have been obtained by federal reservation is not important. Nor, as we shall see, is it important to the decree to be entered in this case that there may be unappropriated water to which the United States may in the future assert rights through the machinery of state law or otherwise.

...

Sec. 8 of the Reclamation Act, 43 U.S.C.A. §§ 383, 372 provided:

> 'That nothing in this Act shall be construed as affecting or intended to affect or to in any way interfere with the laws of any State or Territory relating to the control, appropriation, use, or distribution of water used in irrigation, or any vested right acquired thereunder, and the Secretary of the Interior, in carrying out the provisions of this Act, shall proceed in conformity with such laws, and nothing herein shall in any way affect any right of any State or of the Federal

> Government or of any landowner, appropriator, or user of water in, to, or from any interstate stream or the waters thereof: Provided, That the right to the use of water acquired under the provisions of this Act shall be appurtenant to the land irrigated, and beneficial use shall be the basis, the measure, and the limit of the right.'...

The Secretary of the Interior pursuant to § 3 of the Reclamation Act, 43 U.S.C.A. § 416, withdrew from public entry certain public lands in Nebraska and Wyoming which were required for the North Platte Project and the Kendrick Project. Initiation of both projects was accompanied by filings made pursuant to § 8 in the name of the Secretary of the Interior for and on behalf of the United States. Those filings were accepted by the state officials as adequate under state law. They established the priority dates for the projects. There were also applications to the States for permits to construct canals and ditches. They described the land to be served. The orders granting the applications fixed the time for completion of the canal, for application of the water to the land, and for proof of appropriation. Individual water users contracted with the United States for the use of project water. These contracts were later assumed by the irrigation districts. Irrigation districts submitted proof of beneficial use to the state authorities on behalf of the project water users. The state authorities accepted that proof and issued decrees and certificates in favor of the individual water users. The certificates named as appropriators the individual landowners. They designated the number of acres included, the use for which the appropriation was made, the amount of the appropriation, and the priority date. The contracts between the United States and the irrigation districts provided that after the stored water was released from the reservoir it was under the control of the appropriate state officials.

All of these steps make plain that those projects were designed, constructed and completed according to the pattern of state law as provided in the Reclamation Act. We can say here what was said in *Ickes v. Fox*:

> 'Although the government diverted, stored, and distributed the water, the contention of petitioner that thereby ownership of the water or water rights became vested in the United States is not well founded. Appropriation was made not for the use of the government, but, under the Reclamation Act, for the use of the landowners; and by the terms of the law and of the contract already referred to, the water rights became the property of the landowners, wholly distinct from the property right of the government in the irrigation works.... The government was and remained simply a carrier and distributor of the water ..., with the right to receive the sums stipulated in the contracts as reimbursement for the cost of construction and annual charges for operation and maintenance of the works.'

The property right in the water right is separate and distinct from the property right in the reservoirs, ditches or canals. The water right is appurtenant to the land, the owner of which is the appropriator. The water right is acquired by perfecting an appropriation, i.e., by an actual diversion followed by an application within a reasonable time of the water to a beneficial use.... Indeed § 8 of the Reclamation Act provides as we have seen that 'the right to the use of water acquired under the provisions of this Act shall be appurtenant to the land irrigated, and beneficial use shall be the basis, the measure, and the limit of the right.'

We have then a direction by Congress to the Secretary of the Interior to proceed in conformity with state laws in appropriating water for irrigation purposes. We have a compliance with that direction. Pursuant to that procedure individual landowners have become the appropriators of the water rights, the United States being the storer and the carrier.... We intimate no opinion whether a different procedure might have been followed so as to appropriate and reserve to the United States all of these water rights. No such attempt was made. Though we assume arguendo that the United States did own all of the unappropriated water, the appropriations under state law were made to the individual landowners pursuant to the procedure which Congress provided in the Reclamation Act. The right so acquired are as definite and complete as if they were obtained by direct cession from the federal government. Thus even if we assume that the United States owned the unappropriated rights, they were acquired by the landowners in the precise manner contemplated by Congress.

...

It is so ordered.

The third and final case, *Nevada v. United States,* 463 U.S. 110 (1983) (a case you read an excerpt from in the context of Native American water rights in Part III), involves an effort by the United States to reallocate water from a Reclamation project to use for habitat improvement for a fishery of historical importance to the Pyramid Lake Paiute Tribe. The case turns on whether this is simply a reallocation of water owned by the federal government or whether the irrigators using project water own the water rights. If the former, then the United States could proceed, but if the latter then the irrigators held a property right that could not be reallocated without triggering a Taking of private property. The irrigators argued that the United States was precluded by a decree (known as the Orr Ditch decree), which had allocated the disputed water to project water users. To understand how the parties arrived at this point requires a bit more information on the steps that were necessary to establish a Reclamation project.

Locations chosen for Reclamation projects generally had a combination of good, arable soil, a water supply capable of development to irrigate that soil, a feasible dam site, and people interested in project development.[21] Public lands within the project area were withdrawn by the agency, then reopened for homestead. By the time these

21. Often those interested had considerable power—none more so than the Newlands project on the Truckee and Carson Rivers, which is the subject of *Nevada v. United States*. Senator Francis Newlands held land in the project area and was the lead sponsor of the Reclamation Act of 1902, also known as the Newlands Act.

projects were being developed in the early twentieth century, much water development had already taken place. Accordingly, as part of the process of designing a project, Reclamation had to determine if unappropriated water was available. This required adjudication of existing water rights to determine their priority and quantity. In some cases, irrigators with preexisting water rights entered contracts with Reclamation, turning over their water rights to the project in exchange for the more reliable project water. In other cases, irrigators retained their senior water rights with a source from natural flow rather than stored water that must be administered in priority with the junior project water rights.

Nevada v. United States involves irrigation of the Newlands Project from the Truckee and Carson Rivers that flow across the California/Nevada state line. Thus, the United States sought adjudication of existing water rights in federal district court in 1913. The resulting decree, issued in 1944, is overseen by the federal district court through appointment of a water master.

Complicating the adjudication is the fact that the Pyramid Lake Paiute Indian Reservation had water rights yet to be developed or adjudicated. The United States claimed water rights on their behalf, but only in the amount necessary for a small amount of irrigation. The Tribe had long relied on the cui-ui and Lahonton cutthroat trout fisheries at Pyramid Lake, but no water was decreed to ensure the habitat necessary for the fisheries.[22] In the early 1970s the United States sought to remedy that error. If the Reclamation water right belongs to the federal government, they may simply reallocate the water. The process for any reallocation is to file suit in the court with jurisdiction over the original decree—federal district court. Note also that we have included the portion of the case addressing whether it is even appropriate for the United States to have represented both the Tribe and the Project in the case adjudicating their water rights. This will provide you with some background for the next section on federal development of irrigation water for Indian reservations.

Nevada v. United States

Supreme Court of the United States
463 U.S. 110 (1983)

Opinion

REHNQUIST, Justice—In 1913 the United States sued to adjudicate water rights to the Truckee River for the benefit of the Pyramid Lake Indian Reservation and the planned Newlands Reclamation Project. Thirty-one years later, in 1944, the United States District Court for the District of Nevada entered a final decree in the case pursuant to a settlement agreement. In 1973 the United States filed the present action in

22. For details on the water rights of the Pyramid Lake Paiute Reservation and the historic disputes with the Newlands Project, see Barbara Cosens, *Farmers, Fish, Tribal Power, and Poker: Reallocating Water in the Truckee River Basin, Nevada and California,* 10 U.C. Hastings, West-Northwest: J. Envt'l L. & Pol'y 89 (2003).

the same court on behalf of the Pyramid Lake Indian Reservation seeking additional water rights to the Truckee River. The issue thus presented is whether the Government may partially undo the 1944 decree, or whether principles of *res judicata* prevent it, and the intervenor Pyramid Lake Paiute Tribe, from litigating this claim on the merits.

Nevada has, on the average, less precipitation than any other State in the Union. Except for drainage in the southeastern part of the State into the Colorado River, and drainage in the northern part of the State into the Columbia River, the rivers that flow in Nevada generally disappear into "sinks." Department of Agriculture Yearbook, Climate and Man (1941). The present litigation relates to water rights in the Truckee River, one of the three principal rivers flowing through west central Nevada. It rises in the High Sierra in Placer County, California, flows into and out of Lake Tahoe, and thence down the eastern slope of the Sierra Nevada mountains. It flows through Reno, Nevada, and after a course of some 120 miles debouches into Pyramid Lake, which has no outlet.

...

The origins of the cases before us are found in two historical events involving the Federal Government in this part of the country. First, in 1859 the Department of the Interior set aside nearly half a million acres in what is now western Nevada as a reservation for the area's Paiute Indians. In 1874 President Ulysses S. Grant by executive order confirmed the withdrawal as the Pyramid Lake Indian Reservation. The Reservation includes Pyramid Lake, the land surrounding it, the lower reaches of the Truckee River, and the bottom land alongside the lower Truckee.

Then, with the passage of the Reclamation Act of 1902, ... the Federal Government was designated to play a more prominent role in the development of the West. That Act directed the Secretary of the Interior to withdraw from public entry arid lands in specified western States, reclaim the lands through irrigation projects, and then to restore the lands to entry pursuant to the homestead laws and certain conditions imposed by the Act itself. Accordingly, the Secretary withdrew from the public domain approximately 200,000 acres in western Nevada, which ultimately became the Newlands Reclamation Project. The Project was designed to irrigate a substantial area in the vicinity of Fallon, Nevada, with waters from both the Truckee and the Carson Rivers.

The Carson River, like the Truckee, rises on the eastern slope of the High Sierra in Alpine County, California, and flows north and northeast over a course of about 170 miles, finally disappearing into Carson sink. The Newlands Project accomplished the diversion of water from the Truckee River to the Carson River....

Before the works contemplated by the Project went into operation, a number of private landowners had established rights to water in the Truckee River under Nevada law. The Government also asserted on behalf of the Indians of the Pyramid Lake Indian Reservation a reserved right under the so-called "implied-reservation-of-water" doctrine set forth in *Winters v. United States*.... The United States therefore filed a complaint in the United States District Court for the District of Nevada in March, 1913, commencing what became known as the *Orr Ditch* litigation. The Government, for the benefit of both the Project and the Pyramid Lake Reservation, asserted a claim to 10,000 cubic feet of water per second for the Project and a claim to 500 cubic feet per second for the Reservation. The complaint named as defendants all water users on the Truckee River in Nevada. The Government expressly sought a final decree quieting title to the rights of all parties.

Following several years of hearings, a Special Master issued a report and proposed decree in July of 1924....

... [A temporary decree was entered in 1926 and ultimately a settlement providing for irrigation of 5875 acres on the Reservation with a priority date of 1859 and irrigation of 232,800 acres within the Newlands Reclamation Project resulted in the District Court entering] ... a final decree adopting the agreement on September 8, 1944. No appeal was taken. Thus, 31 years after its inception the *Orr Ditch* litigation came to a close.

On December 21, 1973 the Government instituted the action below seeking additional rights to the Truckee River for the Pyramid Lake Indian Reservation; the Pyramid Lake Paiute Tribe was permitted to intervene in support of the United States....

In its complaint the Government purported not to dispute the rights decreed in the *Orr Ditch* case. Instead, it alleged that *Orr Ditch* determined only the Reservation's right to "water for irrigation," ... not the claim now being asserted for "sufficient waters from the Truckee River [for] the maintenance and preservation of Pyramid Lake, [and for] the maintenance of the lower reaches of the Truckee River as a natural spawning ground for fish," .... The complaint further averred that in establishing the Reservation the United States had intended that the Pyramid Lake fishery be maintained. Since the additional water now being claimed is allegedly necessary for that purpose, the Government alleged that the executive order creating the Reservation must have impliedly reserved a right to this water....

The defendants below asserted *res judicata* as an affirmative defense, saying that the United States and the Tribe were precluded by the *Orr Ditch* decree from litigating this claim. Following a separate trial on this issue, the District Court sustained the defense and dismissed the complaint in its entirety.

...

II

The Government opens the "Summary of Argument" portion of its brief by stating: "The court of appeals has simply permitted a reallocation of the water decreed in *Orr Ditch* to a single party—the United States—from reclamation uses to a Reservation use with an earlier priority. The doctrine of *res judicata* does not bar a single party from reallocating its water in this fashion...." ... We are bound to say that the Government's position, if accepted, would do away with half a century of decided case law relating to the Reclamation Act of 1902 and water rights in the public domain of the West.

It is undisputed that the primary purpose of the Government in bringing the *Orr Ditch* suit in 1913 was to secure water rights for the irrigation of land that would be contained in the Newlands Project, and that the Government was acting under the aegis of the Reclamation Act of 1902 in bringing that action.... Section 8 of that Act provides:

> "That nothing in this Act shall be construed as affecting or intended to affect or to in any way interfere with the laws of any State or Territory relating to the control, appropriation, use, or distribution of water used in irrigation, or any vested right acquired thereunder, and the Secretary of the Interior, in carrying out the provisions of this Act, shall proceed in conformity with such laws, and nothing herein shall in any way affect any right of any State or of the Federal Government or of any landowner, appropriator, or user of water in, to, or from any interstate stream or the waters thereof: *Provided,* That the right to the use of water acquired under the provisions of this Act shall be appurtenant to the land irrigated, and beneficial use shall be the basis, the measure, and the limit of the right."

In *California v. United States,* we described in greater detail the history and structure of the Reclamation Act of 1902, and stated:

> "The projects would be built on federal land and the actual construction and operation of the projects would be in the hands of the Secretary of the Interior. But *the Act clearly provided that state water law would control in the appropriation and later distribution of the water.*" *Id.,* at 664, 98 S.Ct., at 2995 (emphasis added).

In two leading cases, *Ickes v. Fox* and *Nebraska v. Wyoming* this Court has discussed the beneficial ownership of water rights in irrigation projects built pursuant to the Reclamation Act.... [The Court quotes the language covered earlier in this Chapter from the two cases]

The law of Nevada, in common with most other western States, requires for the perfection of a water right for agricultural purposes that the water must be beneficially used by actual application on the land. Such a right is appurtenant to the land on which it is used.

In the light of these cases, we conclude that the Government is completely mistaken if it believes that the water rights confirmed to it by the *Orr Ditch* decree in 1944 for use in irrigating lands within the Newlands Reclamation Project were like so many bushels of wheat, to be bartered, sold, or shifted about as the Government might see fit. Once these lands were acquired by settlers in the Project, the Government's "ownership" of the water rights was at most nominal; the beneficial interest in the rights confirmed to the Government resided in the owners of the land within the Project to which these water rights became appurtenant upon the application of Project water to the land. As in *Ickes v. Fox* and *Nebraska v. Wyoming,* the law of relevant State and the contracts entered into by the landowners and the United States make this point very clear....

The Government's brief is replete with references to its fiduciary obligation to the Pyramid Lake Paiute Tribe of Indians, as it properly should be. But the Government seems wholly to ignore in the same brief the obligations that necessarily devolve upon it from having mere title to water rights for the Newlands Project, when the beneficial ownership of these water rights resides elsewhere.

Both the briefs of the parties and the opinion of the Court of Appeals focus their analysis of *res judicata* on provisions relating to the relationship between private trustees and fiduciaries, especially those governing a breach of duty by the fiduciary to the beneficiary. While these undoubtedly provide useful analogies in a case such as this, they cannot be regarded as finally dispositive of the issues. This Court has long recognized "the distinctive obligation of trust incumbent by the Government" in its dealings with Indian tribes, see, *e.g., Seminole Nation v. United States*. These concerns have been traditionally focused on the Bureau of Indian Affairs within the Department of the Interior.

But Congress in its wisdom, when it enacted the Reclamation Act of 1902, required the Secretary of the Interior to assume substantial obligations with respect to the reclamation of arid lands in the western part of the United States. Additionally, in § 26 of the Act of April 21, 1904, ch. 1402, 33 Stat. 225, Congress provided for the inclusion of irrigable lands of the Pyramid Lake Indian Reservation within the Newlands Project, and further authorized the Secretary, after allotting five acres of such land to each Indian belonging to the Reservation, to reclaim and dispose of the remainder of the irrigable Reservation land to settlers under the Reclamation Act.

Today, particularly from our vantage point nearly half a century after the enactment the Indian Reorganization Act of 1934, ch. 576, 48 Stat. 984, 25 U.S.C. § 461 *et seq.*, it may well appear that Congress was requiring the Secretary of the Interior to carry water on at least two shoulders when it delegated to him both the responsibility for the supervision of the Indian tribes and the commencement of reclamation projects in areas adjacent to reservation lands. But Congress chose to do this, and it is simply unrealistic to suggest that the Government may not perform its obligation to represent Indian tribes in litigation when Congress has obliged it to represent other interests as well. In this regard, the Government cannot follow the fastidious standards of a private fiduciary, who would breach his duties to his single beneficiary solely by representing potentially conflicting interests without the beneficiary's consent. The Government does not "compromise" its obligation to one interest that Congress obliges it to represent by the mere fact that it simultaneously performs another task for another interest that Congress has obligated it by statute to do.

With these observations in mind, we turn to the principles of *res judicata* that we think are involved in this case.

... [The Court goes on to] "affirm the Court of Appeals' finding that the cause of action asserted below and the cause of action asserted in *Orr Ditch* are one and the same. We also affirm the Court of Appeals' finding that the *Orr Ditch* decree concluded the controversy on this cause of action between, on the one hand, the *Orr Ditch* defendants, their successors in interest, and subsequent appropriators of the Truckee River, and, on the other hand, the United States and the Tribe. We reverse the Court of Appeals, however, with respect to its finding concerning the Truckee-Carson Irrigation

District, and the Project farmers it represents, and hold instead that the *Orr Ditch* decree also ended the dispute raised between these parties and the plaintiffs below.

It is so ordered.

Notes & Questions

1. What prevents the United States from simply reallocating Reclamation Project water?
2. Note that the Court seems to equate the fiduciary obligation of the United States to recipients of Reclamation Project water to its fiduciary obligation to Tribes? For those of you who have studied federal Indian law, is this consistent with the law? For those who have not studied this area, go back to *Winters* and see if you can make an argument one way or the other.
3. Synergy between seasonal timing of the growing municipal water needs of Reno and Sparks, Nevada, and the needs for spawning flows upstream from Pyramid Lake led to a major settlement led by the late Senator from Nevada, Harry Reid, in 1990. The Truckee-Carson-Pyramid Lake Water Rights Settlement Act (Public Law 101-618, Title II), is an excellent model of reconciliation of divergent interests through negotiated settlement. For more information, see Barbara Cosens, *Farmers, Fish, Tribal Power, and Poker: Reallocating Water in the Truckee River Basin, Nevada and California*, 10 U.C. Hastings, West-Northwest: J. Envt'l L. & Pol'y 89 (2003).

Tribal Irrigation Projects and Congressional Funding

At nearly the same time that Congress passed the Reclamation Act, the United States also began to develop irrigation projects designed to support agricultural efforts on Indian reservations. An early example of this comes from the Fort Belknap Reservation, which was at the center of the controversy that gave rise to *Winters v. United States*.

Indian irrigation projects vastly differed from other federal irrigation projects. As documented by the National Water Commission in 1973, much of that difference can be attributed to congressional privileging of federal non-Indian irrigation projects, while federal officials simultaneously worked to limit tribal development of water resources, particularly those that competed with non-Indian needs.[23]

---

23. *See* Water Policies for the Future, *A Final Report of the National Water Comm'n*, at 474–475 (Jun. 14, 1973).

After the Supreme Court issued the *Winters* decision in 1908, tribes requested that the Bureau of Indian Affairs (BIA) issue guidance on whether the riparian doctrine or the prior appropriation doctrine would apply to allocation of the tribal water rights.[24] Because of uncertainty surrounding the *Winters* decision, the BIA implemented the prior appropriation doctrine on tribal reservations to ensure Indian water rights would be recognized by the western states.[25]

In 1913, prior to rulings on the water rights associated with allotted land discussed in Part III, the BIA formulated an official irrigation policy that narrowly applied the *Winters* Doctrine only on unallotted land.[26] The BIA assumed the implied reserved water right would dissolve once a tribal member owned a parcel.[27] The BIA's interpretation of the application of the *Winters* Doctrine caused detrimental legal problems for allottees with land near an Indian irrigation project, as you learned in Part III.[28]

The BIA continuously relied on a mixture of state law prior appropriation (applied to allotments) and the *Winters* Doctrine (applied to land held in trust for the tribe).[29] But out of "political necessity," it tended to defer to state law to secure protection for beneficial use.[30] To encourage development for beneficial use, tribes and the BIA began leasing farmland to non-Indians.[31] *Id.* at 120. However, problems resulted from leasing reservation land. According to studies by BIA, the non-Indian lessees failed to take care of the land, the best land was leased to non-Indians, the leases were at low rates, the non-Indians had better production than the Indians, and there was a loss of reservation land through sale.[32] As a result of leasing reservation land to obtain water rights under the prior appropriation doctrine, approximately 71% of all irrigated tribal land was farmed by non-Indians by 1974.[33]

Further, the BIA struggled to get funding from Congress for Indian irrigation projects.[34] Only seven percent of Indian reservation land was irrigated in 1975.[35] Instead, funds went to the Bureau of Reclamation for federal irrigation projects or to tribal social welfare programs rather than Indian irrigation projects.[36] The BIA remained ineffective in the development of Indian irrigation projects. McCool discusses three reasons for this failure. First, constant reorganization resulted in instability within the

---

24. Daniel McCool, Command of the Waters: Iron Triangles, Federal Water Development, and Indian Water 114 (2d ed. 1994).

25. *Id.*

26. *Id.* at 114–15.

27. *Id.* at 115.

28. *Id.* at 116–17.

29. *Id.* at 118.

30. *Id.* at 119.

31. *Id.*

32. *Id.* at 120 (citing the 1923 Annual Report of the Chief Engineer for BIA at 8).

33. *Id.* at 121.

34. *Id.* at 122.

35. *Id.* at 159.

36. *Id.* at 122, 134, 146.

agency.[37] Second, BIA lacked the data and expertise for effective project management and faced a hostile political environment in efforts to obtain funding.[38] Third, the BIA lacked clear political goals and program legitimacy, leading to a poor reputation.[39]

In 1973, the National Water Commission described the situation in the early twentieth century as thus:

> [f]ollowing *Winters*, more than 50 years elapsed before the Supreme Court again discussed significant aspects of Indian water rights. During most of this 50-year period, the United States was pursuing a policy of encouraging the settlement of the West and the creation of family-sized farms on its arid lands. In retrospect, it can be seen that this policy was pursued with little or no regard for Indian water rights and the *Winters* doctrine. With the encouragement, or at least the cooperation, of the Secretary of the Interior—the very office entrusted with protection of all Indian rights—many large irrigation projects were constructed on streams that flowed through or bordered Indian Reservations, sometimes above and more often below the Reservations. With few exceptions the projects were planned and built by the Federal Government without any attempt to define, let alone protect, prior rights that Indian tribes might have had in the waters used for the projects. Before *Arizona v California* ... actions involving Indian water rights generally concerned then existing uses by Indians and did not involve the full extent of rights under the *Winters* doctrine. In the history of the United States Government's treatment of Indian tribes, its failure to protect Indian water rights for use on the Reservations it set aside for them is one of the sorrier chapters.[40]

The BIA deference to prior appropriation also led non-Indians to believe that reserved water rights would not be asserted,[41] increasing tension when they ultimately were. Change in policy began in the mid-twentieth century, ultimately leading to the U.S. Supreme Court ruling in *Arizona v. California*, which you covered in Part III, but the hostility and perception that their predecessors were misled persists among non-Indians irrigating in Indian Country.

Today the BIA is involved in the management of approximately 16 irrigation projects (Figure 16.3) that serve approximately 25,000 water users who irrigate around 780,000 acres.[42] Most were developed between 1904 and 1920. Each project is managed slightly differently to address each reservation's unique mix of tribal trust, individual allotments, leased, and fee land being serviced by the project. Some are managed directly by the tribe. For example, Public Law 93-638 authorized the Shoshone-Paiute

37. *Id.* at 148.

38. *Id.* at 149.

39. *Id.* 153–156.

40. Water Policies for the Future, *supra* at 474–475.

41. *Id.* at 119.

42. United States Bureau of Indian Affairs, *Irrigation* (2022), https://www.bia.gov/service/irrigation/what-irrigation-services.

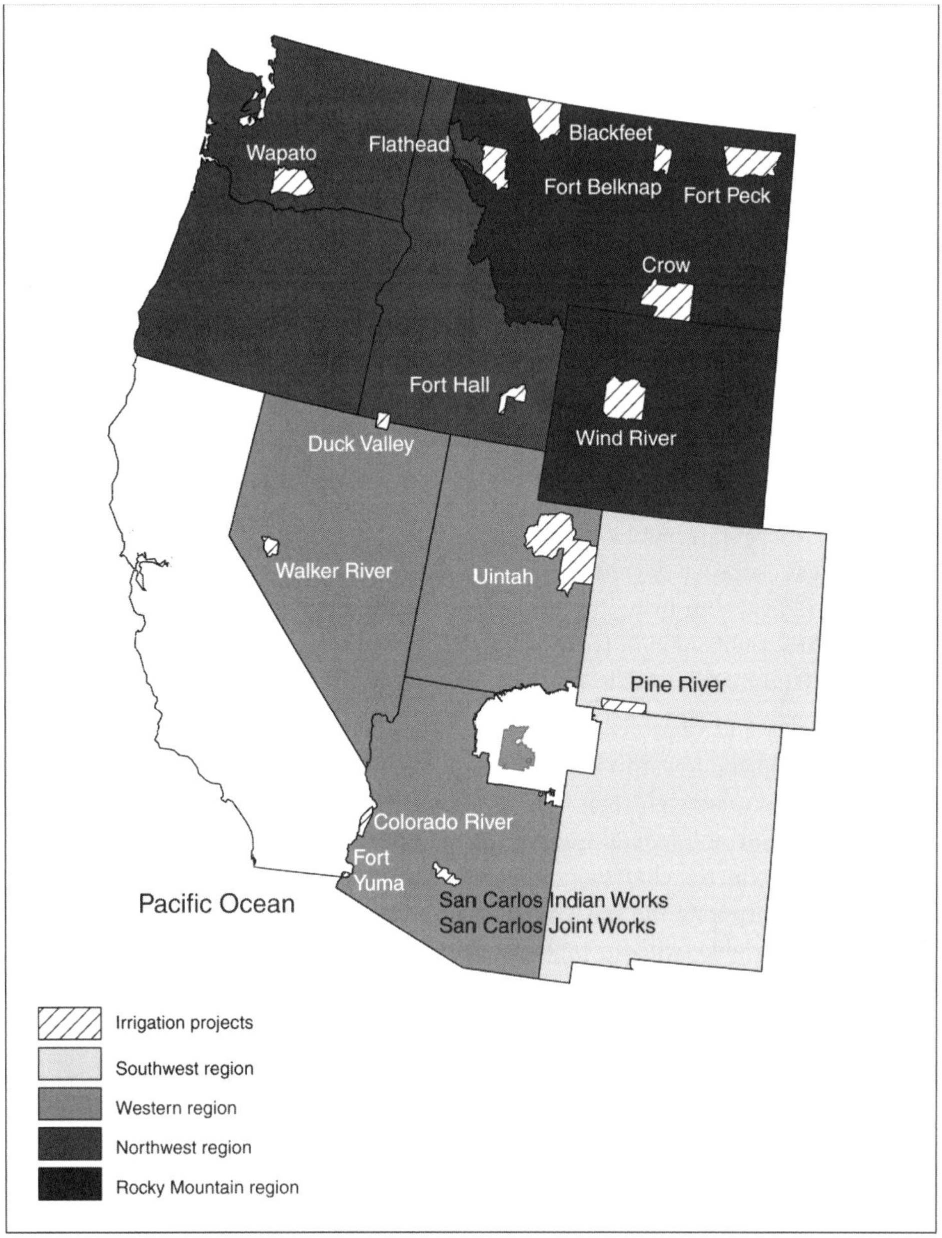

Figure 16.3 Map showing 16 current BIA Indian irrigation projects throughout the United States. Source: Bureau of Indian Affairs; U.S. General Accounting Office, *Indian Irrigation Projects: Deferred Maintenance and Financial Sustainability Issues Remain Unresolved* (2015), https://www.gao.gov/assets/gao-15-453t.pdf.

Tribe to manage the Duck Valley Indian Irrigation Project. Many, such as the Flathead Irrigation Project in northwestern Montana, primarily serve non-Indian irrigators that lease tribal lands or hold reserved water rights pursuant to *Confederated Colville Tribes v. Walton*, you learned about in Part III.

Each Indian irrigation project has its own origin story, and the details for how they were initially created and paid for differ. Unlike their non-Indian counterparts, it does not appear that tribes or tribal members were usually expected to pay back the initial construction costs for these projects. Instead, most projects were initiated and funded through congressional appropriations. However, end-users are responsible for paying some portion of the operation and maintenance of the irrigation project. How those costs are assessed, as well as other details regarding Indian irrigation project management, is covered by the administrative rules of the BIA.[43]

Because of the ad hoc nature of their creation, each Indian irrigation project obtains its water rights differently. Unfortunately, due to the history outlined above, most were initiated without any effort to expressly incorporate the *Winters* Doctrine or reserved water rights. Some reservations, such as the Wapato Irrigation Project on the Yakama Reservation, sourced their water rights from congressional acts that authorized direct river diversions. Others contracted with Reclamation and/or acquired water rights initiated pursuant to state law. However, once adjudicated, the water necessary to service Indian irrigation projects is invariably incorporated into the tribal reserved irrigation water rights claim using the PIA quantification methodology. For example, the reserved water rights held in trust for the Yakama Nation include water sufficient to irrigate the lands of the Wapato Irrigation Project.

The complex and variable history of how these projects were developed cautions against litigation and toward a negotiated settlement concerning the nature and scope of the associated water right. State, federal, and tribal negotiators avoided the complex patchwork of state and federal water rights appurtenant to the Fort Hall Indian Irrigation Project (which includes a portion that services non-Indians *off-reservation*) by agreeing to incorporate the water for the on-reservation portion of the project into the tribal water rights (with an 1868 priority date) while recognizing the water rights off-reservation pursuant to state law. In this way the parties were able to avoid the cost, time, uncertainty, and extreme complexity of litigating these water rights and instead developed a tailored, equitable solution through negotiations.

Navigation, Flood Control, and Hydropower

While beyond the scope of this text, this Chapter would be incomplete without mentioning the substantial federal development of rivers for navigation, flood control, and hydropower. Federal development of western rivers has been undertaken by the U.S. Army Corps of Engineers (USACE) for purposes of navigation and flood control under the Rivers and Harbors Act.[44] USACE dams may have both irrigation and hydropower production as secondary purposes. The Act also prohibits obstruction

43. 25 CFR 171.
44. 33 U.S.C. et seq.

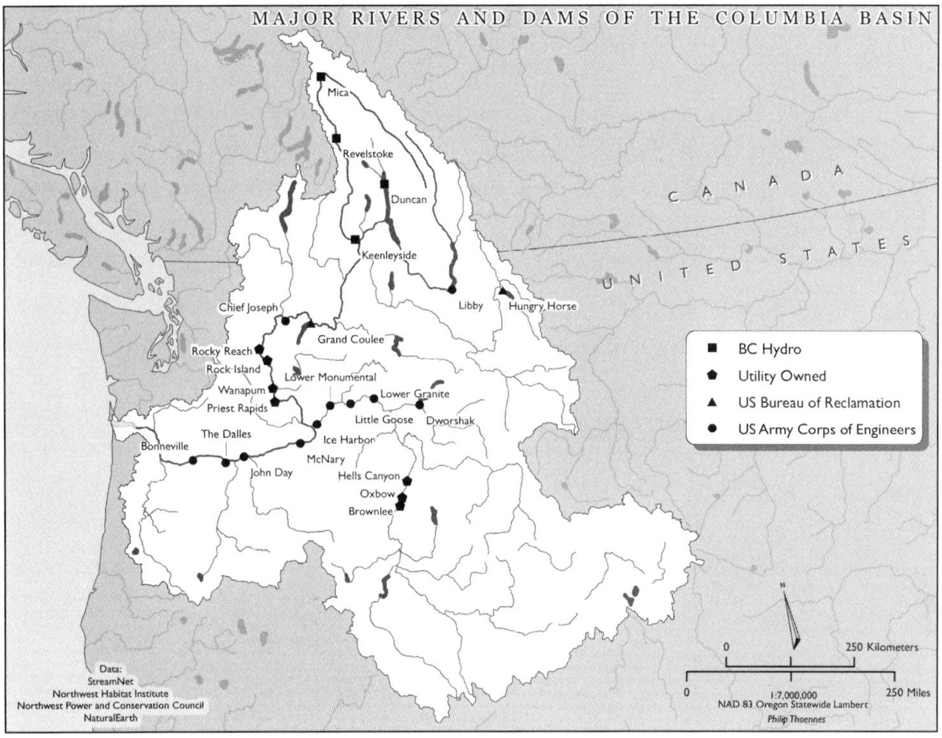

Figure 16.4 Map of the Columbia River Basin showing the major hydropower facilities. Source: Northwest Power and Conservation Council.

or alteration of navigable waterways without a permit from the USACE.[45] Thus, any private dam on a navigable waterway requires a permit.

The USACE has extensive development on the Columbia River (as well as the Missouri, which has its headwaters in Montana) for purposes of both navigation and flood control with hydropower as a secondary benefit (Figure 16.4). Public utility-owned dams on the mid-Columbia in Washington, and private utility owned dams on the Snake River in Idaho are permitted under the Act and also produce substantial hydropower. The combination of Reclamation dams, utility and private dams, and Canadian dams, has made the Columbia River the largest producer of hydropower in North America, with the region currently receiving approximately 60% of its energy needs from hydropower.

45. 33 U.S.C. 403.

Chapter 17

Interstate Water Allocation

Introduction

State boundaries often do not follow surface (Figure 17.1) or groundwater basin boundaries. As a result, disputes arise among states on shared water courses and aquifers. Five means are used to resolve these disputes.

First, states may invoke the original jurisdiction of the U.S. Supreme Court provided by Article III, Section 2 of the Constitution, extending the jurisdiction of the Court "to Controversies between two or more States." This Chapter will begin with the leading cases setting forth the doctrine of equitable apportionment—the federal common law developed by the U.S. Supreme Court to resolve these disputes.

Second, states may enter into a negotiated agreement allocating water on a shared water course or aquifer with the approval of Congress. This is interpreted from the negative statement in Article I, Section 10, Clause 3 of the Constitution, stating: "No state shall, without the Consent of Congress, ... enter into any Agreement or Compact with another State." Thus, with congressional approval, any state may enter a Compact.

Figure 17.1 Major river basins of the United States showing their relation to state lines. Source: U.S. Global Change Research Program, THIRD NATIONAL CLIMATE ASSESSMENT 77 (2017).

Congressional "consent" has been given both prior to negotiation of a compact and following its completion. This Chapter will provide an example from the Bear River shared by Idaho, Wyoming, and Utah. Compacts are not limited to apportionment of water. This Chapter also discusses the Compact among Washington, Oregon, Montana, and Idaho establishing the Northwest Power and Conservation Council. Once approved by Congress, a compact is considered federal law and conflict over interpretation and implementation may be resolved under the original jurisdiction of the U.S. Supreme Court. You will see an example of U.S. Supreme Court interpretation of a Compact in Part V in the case of *Montana v. Wyoming,* 563 U.S. 368 (2011), concerning the Yellowstone River Compact.

Third, in the case of *Arizona v. California*, 373 U.S. 546 (1963), which you have seen in the context of quantification of Native American reserved water rights (Part III) and extension of the doctrine of reserved water rights to federal reservations (Part IV, Chapter 14), the U.S. Supreme Court determined that Congress may apportion an interstate river by congressional act. While it came as a surprise to the parties in that case that Congress had that authority and had exercised it in the Boulder Canyon Act, congressional apportionment has only been exercised since with the agreement of the states involved and their participation in drafting the Act. Its advantage over a compact may be that it is more efficient to obtain the approval of Congress alone, rather than Congress and each state's legislature—the process followed for approval of a compact.

Fourth, governmental and private parties on water courses shared across state lines may seek a federal court adjudication under the diversity jurisdiction of the Constitution. Diversity jurisdiction arises out of Article III, Section 2, Clause 1 of the Constitution, extending federal court jurisdiction "to Controversies ... between Citizens of different States." This approach was used, for example, on water courses shared by California and Nevada, including on the Truckee, Carson, and Walker Rivers, as well as on the Raft River shared by Utah and Idaho. The adjudication results in administration of water allocation in priority through a court-appointed watermaster.[1]

Fifth, states always have the option of entering into a cooperative agreement. Although the compact clause of the Constitution expressly applies to "any Agreement," the U.S. Supreme Court has limited the application of "the terms 'compact' or 'agreement' ... to the formation of any combination tending to the increase of political power in the states, which may encroach upon or interfere with the just supremacy of the United States.[2] Thus, for example, the Pacific Northwest states of Idaho and Washington have a cooperative agreement seeking to stabilize the aquifer shared by the communities of Moscow, Idaho, and Pullman, Washington (and others including the University of Idaho and Washington State University). The committee was originally established in 1967 to address declining groundwater levels. In 1992, the cities and universities sharing the aquifer agreed to a management plan to take voluntary steps

1. *See, e.g.,* 1944 Orr Ditch Decree, United States v. Orr Water Ditch Co., Equity No. A3 (D. Nev. 1944) (Truckee River); 1936 Walker River Decree, United States v. Walker River Irrigation District, Equity No. C-125 (1936) (Walker River).

2. Virginia v. Tennessee, 148 U.S. 503, 519 (1893).

to stabilize the aquifer. The fact that all measures are voluntary and that the Palouse Basin Aquifer Committee established by the agreement exists solely for the purpose of obtaining studies, planning, and exchange of information, and lacks enforcement authority across state lines, avoids invoking the Compact Clause. The effort has been reported as highly successful.[3] This approach has also been used in combination with parallel state legislation in the states involved. While the legislation may be altered unilaterally by a state, the approach is considered more durable than a cooperative agreement alone because it presents an additional hurdle (a change in state law) before a breach of the agreement may occur.

The remainder of this Chapter will explore the first three of these approaches.

The Original Jurisdiction of the U.S. Supreme Court: Equitable Apportionment

This section provides the basis for understanding a suit invoking the original jurisdiction of the U.S. Supreme Court over disputes among states, under Article III, Section 2 of the Constitution. The U.S. Code, Title 22 § 1251(a), makes it clear that this jurisdiction is not only "original," but "exclusive."

Before turning to several foundational cases, it is important to understand that it is not the normal course of events for a case to begin in the Supreme Court. The Court is not accustomed to acting as a trial court. U.S. Supreme Court Rule 17 sets forth the procedure for seeking the Court's original jurisdiction. The Supreme Court has also developed what is now referred to as a "threshold" for asserting its original jurisdiction:

> Before this court can be moved to exercise its extraordinary power under the Constitution to control the conduct of one state at the suit of another, the threatened invasion of rights must be of serious magnitude and it must be established by clear and convincing evidence.[4]

Once this threshold is met, the Supreme Court rules do not provide details on how the Court must proceed. Rather than act as a trial court, it is the practice of the Court to appoint a Special Master to hear the case, make findings of fact, and conclusions of law. The Court then hears the parties' exceptions to the Report of the Special Master. While the Court provides deference to the Report on findings of fact, it considers the conclusions of law *de novo*.

You will read three cases. The first, *Kansas v. Colorado*, 206 U.S. 46 (1907), pronounces what will become the doctrine of equitable apportionment when it calls on the principle of equality of rights among states. The doctrine seeks to avoid giving

3. Palouse Basin Aquifer Committee (Jan. 1, 2022), http://palousebasin.org/about/.

4. New York v. New Jersey, 256 U.S. 296, 309 (1921) (citing Missouri v. Illinois, 200 U.S. 496, 521) (1906) (stating: "Before this court ought to intervene, the case should be of serious magnitude, clearly and fully proved, and the principle to be applied should be one which the court is prepared deliberately to maintain against all considerations on the other side.").

advantage to a state due to location on the watershed or the doctrine it uses to allocate water. The second, *Nebraska v. Wyoming,* 325 U.S. 589 (1945), sets forth the factors the Court will consider in arriving at an equitable apportionment. Finally, the recent case of *Mississippi v. Tennessee,* 142 S. Ct. 31 (2021), makes it clear that the doctrine extends to shared groundwater aquifers. These cases, similar to trial court orders, are extremely fact-intensive. Special Masters' reports may be over 500 pages, and prior to *Mississippi v. Tennessee*, the Court often incorporated some of that detail in its opinion. Despite the focus of this book on understanding the science underlying water rights cases, the excerpts will avoid that detail and present the Supreme Court's federal common law for equitable apportionment of interstate water bodies.

The first case, *Kansas v. Colorado*, involved the adjudication of the Arkansas River, which originates in Colorado and flows into Kansas. As you read the case, consider that this is the first time the Court must articulate a principle for allocation of water between two states. Matters were further complicated because the states applied different water rights doctrines. Colorado is a prior appropriation state and argued that priority of use should be the central consideration in the case. Kansas is primarily a riparian state and, as the downstream state, it argued that the Supreme Court should require Colorado to ensure the continuation of the Arkansas River's (pronounced "Our-Kansas" river by those representing Kansas) natural flow into Kansas. You'll see that the Court applied neither of these doctrines. Instead, it looks to the principle between states of equality of rights. Pay attention to the types of evidence the Court indicates it might look at in determining equality of rights.

Kansas v. Colorado

Supreme Court of the United States
206 U.S. 46 (1907)

Opinion

Mr. Justice Brewer delivered the opinion of the court:

...

Turning now to the controversy as here presented, it is whether Kansas has a right to the continuous flow of the waters of the Arkansas river, as that flow existed before any human interference therewith, or Colorado the right to appropriate the waters of that stream so as to prevent that continuous flow, or that the amount of the flow is subject to the superior authority and supervisory control of the United States.... Clearly this controversy is one of a justiciable nature. The right to the flow of a stream was one recognized at common law, for a trespass upon which a cause of action existed.

...

... Now the question arises between two states, one recognizing generally the common-law rule of riparian rights and the other prescribing the doctrine of the public ownership of flowing water. Neither state can legislate for, or impose its own policy upon the other.... It does not follow, however, ... that the controversy ceases to be one of a justiciable nature, or that there is no power which can take cognizance of the controversy and determine the relative rights of the two states. Indeed, the disagreement, coupled with its effect upon a stream passing through the two states, makes a matter for investigation and determination by this court.

. . .

. . . The clear language of the Constitution vests in this court the power to settle those disputes. . . .

One cardinal rule, underlying all the relations of the states to each other, is that of equality of right. Each state stands on the same level with all the rest. It can impose its own legislation on no one of the others, and is bound to yield its own views to none. Yet, whenever, as in the case of *Missouri v. Illinois*, supra, the action of one state reaches, through the agency of natural laws, into the territory of another state, the question of the extent and the limitations of the rights of the two states becomes a matter of justiciable dispute between them, and this court is called upon to settle that dispute in such a way as will recognize the equal rights of both and at the same time establish justice between them. In other words, through these successive disputes and decisions this court is practically building up what may not improperly be called interstate common law.

. . .

. . . [Our inquiry] is not limited to the simple matter of whether any portion of the waters of the Arkansas is withheld by Colorado. We must consider the effect of what has been done upon the conditions in the respective states, and so adjust the dispute upon the basis of equality of rights as to secure as far as possible to Colorado the benefits of irrigation without depriving Kansas of the like beneficial effects of a flowing stream. . . .

. . .

It cannot be denied, in view of all the testimony (for that which we have quoted is but a sample of much more bearing upon the question), that the diminution of the flow of water in the river by the irrigation of Colorado has worked some detriment to the southwestern part of Kansas, and yet, when we compare the amount of this detriment with the great benefit which has obviously resulted to the counties in Colorado, it would seem that equality of right and equity between the two states forbids any interference with the present withdrawal of water in Colorado for purposes of irrigation.

. . .

The decree which, therefore, will be entered, will be one dismissing the petition of the intervener, without prejudice to the rights of the United States to take such action as it shall deem necessary to preserve or improve the navigability of the Arkansas river. The decree will also dismiss the bill of the state of Kansas as against all the defendants, without prejudice to the right of the plaintiff to institute new proceedings whenever it shall appear that, through a material increase in the depletion of the waters of the Arkansas by Colorado, its corporations or citizens, the substantial interests of Kansas are being injured to the extent of destroying the equitable apportionment of benefits between the two states resulting from the flow of the river. . . .

Notes & Questions

1. In considering equality of rights among states, what does the Court balance between Colorado and Kansas?

2. The disputes over the Arkansas River did not end with the dismissal of this case. In *Colorado v. Kansas* 320 U.S. 383, 393–394 (1943) the Court uses the threshold concept to dismiss the case and states:

   > In such disputes as this, the court is conscious of the great and serious caution with which it is necessary to approach the inquiry whether a case is proved. Not every matter which would warrant resort to equity by one citizen against another would justify our interference with the action of a state, for the burden on the complaining state is much greater than that generally required to be borne by private parties. Before the court will intervene the case must be of serious magnitude and fully and clearly proved.... And in determining whether one state is using, or threatening to use, more than its equitable share of the benefits of a stream, all the factors which create equities in favor of one state or the other must be weighed as of the date when the controversy is mooted.

   The states then turned to negotiation. In 1949, Congress approved the Arkansas River Compact between Kansas and Colorado. Article IV-D of the Compact allows future development "*[p]rovided*, that the waters of the Arkansas river, ... shall not be materially depleted in usable quantity or availability for use to the water users in Colorado and Kansas under this Compact by such future developments or construction."

   Cases concerning the interpretation of an interstate compact may also seek the original jurisdiction of the U.S. Supreme Court. In *Kansas v. Colorado,* 514 U.S. 673, 694 (1995), Kansas finally found victory after Colorado allowed substantial increase in development of hydrologically connected groundwater in the basin. The Court states: "The Special Master concluded that 'regardless of which burden of proof applies,' he had "no difficulty in concluding that [post-Compact groundwater] pumping in Colorado ha[d] caused material depletions of the usable Stateline flows of the Arkansas River, in violation of the Arkansas River Compact." ... We agree with this determination, and thus overrule Colorado's exception."

In the following case of *Nebraska v. Wyoming,* 325 U.S. 589 (1945), the Court is dealing with three states (Colorado was added to the litigation) that employ the doctrine of prior appropriation in the area in question—the North Platte River (Figure 17.2). Nevertheless, the Court determines that priority is not the sole consideration among states. The Court lists a number of factors that have become important in the federal common law of equitable apportionment. Pay attention to those factors. More detail on the facts are provided in this case to help you understand the factors. This case is less known for its statement about how it will handle changing water supply. Since longer periods of drought may occur across the West with climate change, take note of what the Court says.

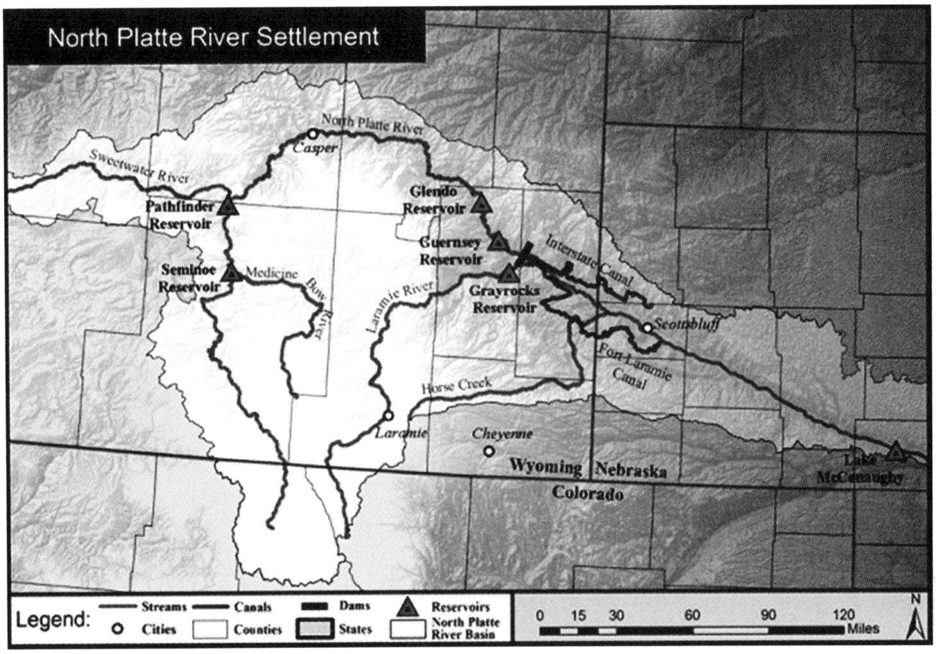

Figure 17.2 North Platte River Basin. Nebraska Dept. of Natural Resources, *Water Planning: North Platte River Settlement* (2023), https://dnr.nebraska.gov/file/np1jpg.

Nebraska v. Wyoming

Supreme Court of the United States
325 U.S. 589 (1945)

Opinion

Mr. Justice DOUGLAS delivered the opinion of the Court—Nebraska brought this suit in 1934 against Wyoming, invoking our original jurisdiction under Article III, Section 2 of the Constitution. Colorado was impleaded as a defendant. The United States was granted leave to intervene. Issues were joined. A Special Master, Honorable Michael J. Doherty, was appointed and hearings were held before him. The matter is before us on exceptions to his report.

I.

The controversy pertains to the use for irrigation purposes of the water of the North Platte River, a non-navigable stream. Nebraska alleged that Wyoming and Colorado by diversions of water from the river for irrigation purposes were violating the rule of priority of appropriation in force in the three States and depriving Nebraska of water to which she was equitably entitled. The prayer was for a determination of the equitable share of each State in the water and of the priorities of all appropriations in both States, and for an injunction restraining the alleged wrongful diversions....

The North Platte River rises in Northern Colorado ... enters Wyoming west of Cheyenne, ... turns east across the Great Plains and proceeds easterly and southerly into and across Nebraska.... In North Park it is a rapid mountain stream. In eastern Wyoming it gradually broadens out, losing velocity. In western and central Nebraska its channel ranges from 3000 to 6000 feet; it frequently divides into small channels; and in times of low water is lost in the deep sands of its bed....

...

The river basin in Colorado and Wyoming is arid, irrigation being generally indispensable to agriculture. Western Nebraska is partly arid and partly semi-arid. Irrigation is indispensable to the kind of agriculture established there. Middle Nebraska is sub-humid. Some crops can be raised without irrigation. But the lack of irrigation would seriously limit diversification. Eastern Nebraska, beginning at Grand Island, is sufficiently humid so as not to justify irrigation.

Irrigation in the river basin began about 1865,.... Prior to 1909 the development in Colorado and Wyoming was relatively more rapid than in Nebraska. Since 1910 the acreage under irrigation in Colorado increased about 14 per cent, that of Wyoming 31 per cent, and that of Nebraska about 100 per cent.... The large increase in Nebraska is mainly attributable to the use of storage water from the Pathfinder Reservoir....

The Pathfinder Reservoir is part of the 'North Platte Project' which followed the adoption by Congress in 1902 of the Reclamation Act.... Pathfinder was completed in 1913. It has a capacity of 1,045,000 acre feet, which is 79 per cent of the average annual run-off of the North Platte River at that point. This project includes an auxiliary channel reservoir called Guernsey, located above Whalen, Wyoming....

...

The North Platte Project has greatly increased the water resources of the river available for irrigation. Unused and wasted water are stored and held over from one season to another....

There is a second large federal irrigation project in Wyoming known as the Kendrick project,...

The combined storage capacity of the reservoirs of these two federal projects—Kendrick and North Platte—is 2,313,270 acre feet which, as the Special Master found, is 175 per cent of the long-time average annual run-off of the river at Pathfinder.

...

Since 1930 only one year equaled the mean of the 1904 to 1930 period. Previous droughts had not exceeded two or three years. The present cycle has persisted for 13 years.

The commencement of this dry cycle plus the initiation of the Kendrick project precipitated the present controversy. Nebraska rests her case essentially on evidence of shortage and of misappropriation of water by the upper States since 1930 and of threats of more serious shortage and diversions in the future.

II.

The equitable apportionment which Nebraska seeks is based on the principle of priority of appropriation applied interstate. Colorado and Wyoming have the rule of priority of appropriation as distinguished from the rule of riparian rights.... Nebraska on the other hand was originally a riparian doctrine State.... But when the more arid sections of the State were settled and the need for irrigation increased, legislation was enacted adopting the appropriation principle.... The adoption of the rule of appropriation did not extinguish riparian rights which had previously vested.... But riparian rights may be condemned in favor of appropriators; and violation of riparian rights by appropriators will not be enjoined, only compensation or damages being awarded....More important, the rights asserted by Nebraska in this suit are based wholly on appropriations which have been obtained and recognized under Nebraska law.... Hence we, like the Special Master, treat the case as one involving appropriation rights not only in Colorado and Wyoming but in Nebraska as well.

...

... The evidence supports the finding of the Special Master that the dependable natural flow of the river during the irrigation season has long been over-appropriated. A genuine controversy exists. The States have not been able to settle their differences by compact....

What we have then is a situation where three States assert against a river, whose dependable natural flow during the irrigation season has long been over appropriated, claims based not only on present uses but on projected additional uses as well.... If there were a surplus of unappropriated water, different considerations would be applicable. Cf. *State of Arizona v. California*, 298 U.S. 558. But where there is not enough water in the river to satisfy the claims asserted against it, the situation is not basically different from that where two or more persons claim the right to the same parcel of land. The present claimants being States we think the clash of interests to be of that character and dignity which makes the controversy a justiciable one under our original jurisdiction.

...

V.

There is some suggestion that if we undertake an apportionment of the waters of this interstate river, we embark upon an enterprise involving administrative functions beyond our province.... The gravity and importance of the case are apparent. The difficulties of drafting and enforcing a decree are no justification for us to refuse to perform the important function entrusted to us by the Constitution....

We recognize the difficulties of the problem. The matter is a delicate one and extremely complex. To begin with we are confronted with the problem of equitable apportionment. The Special Master recommended a decree based on that principle. That was indeed the principle adopted by the Court in *State of Wyoming v. Colorado*, supra, where an apportionment of the waters of an interstate stream was made between two States, each of which had the rule of appropriation. In speaking of that rule in application to a controversy between States the Court, through Mr. justice Van Devanter, said: "The cardinal rule of the doctrine is that priority of appropriation gives superiority of right. Each of these states applies and enforces this rule in her own territory, and it is the one to which intending appropriators naturally would turn for guidance. The principle on which it proceeds is not less applicable to interstate streams and controversies than to others. Both states pronounce the rule just and reasonable as applied to the natural conditions in that region, and to prevent any departure from it the people of both incorporated it into their Constitutions. It originated in the customs and usages of the people before either state came into existence, and the courts of both hold that their constitutional provisions are to be taken as recognizing the prior usage rather than as creating a new rule. These considerations persuade us that its application to such a controversy as is here presented cannot be other than eminently just and equitable to all concerned." ... Since Colorado, Wyoming, and Nebraska are appropriation States, that principle would seem to be equally applicable here.

That does not mean that there must be a literal application of the priority rule. We stated in *State of Colorado v. Kansas*, supra, that in determining whether one State is "using, or threatening to use, more than its equitable share of the benefits of a stream, all of the factors which create equities in favor of one state or the other must be weighed as of the date when the controversy is mooted." That case did not involve a controversy between two appropriation States. But if an allocation between appropriation States is to be just and equitable, strict adherence to the priority rule may not be possible. For example, the economy of a region may have been established on the basis of junior appropriations. So far as possible those established uses should be protected though strict application of the priority rule might jeopardize them. Apportionment calls for the exercise of an informed judgment on a consideration of many factors. Priority of appropriation is the guiding principle. But physical and climatic conditions, the consumptive use of water in the several sections of the river, the character and rate of return flows, the extent of established uses, the availability of storage water, the practical effect of wasteful uses on downstream areas, the damage to upstream areas as compared to the benefits to downstream areas if a limitation is imposed on the former—these are all relevant factors. They are merely an illustrative not an exhaustive catalogue. They indicate the nature of the problem of apportionment and the delicate adjustment of interests which must be made.

...

The decree recommended by the Special Master departs from the theory of allocation advanced by the parties. In recommending his apportionment the Special Master did not rest on the long-time average flow of the river. We have discussed the drought which has persisted in this river basin since 1930. No one knows whether it has run its course or whether it represents a new norm. There is no reliable basis for prediction. But a controversy exists; and the decree which is entered must deal with conditions as they obtain today. If they substantially change, the decree can be adjusted to meet the new conditions.

[The Court goes on to apply these principles to the objections to the Report of the Special Master on each stretch of the river.] ...

The parties may within ninety days submit the form of decree to carry this opinion into effect....

It is so ordered.

Notes & Questions

1. List the factors the Court will consider in addition to priority. What types of experts and data would be needed to address these factors in making the case for a state?
2. What language tells you the list in #1 is a nonexhaustive list? As attorney for a state you would want to think of other factors that weigh in favor of your client.
3. How does the Court handle the potential for future changes in water supply?
4. Note that the Reclamation storage is said to exceed the annual natural flow of the river by 175%. This is common to allow for carryover storage during a few years of drought but was insufficient for the 13-year drought of the Dust Bowl era experienced prior to this suit. Reclamation storage on the Colorado River is five times (or 500%) the average annual flow measured before climate change. In contrast, the Columbia River with its infrequent pre-climate-change drought, has storage for only 40% of the average annual flow. This nevertheless differs for tributaries in drier parts of the Columbia River basin.

You learned in the notes following *Kansas v. Colorado* that the Court has allowed a suit to go forward under a compact when upstream groundwater pumping adversely affects downstream surface water flow.[5] But until its recent ruling in *Mississippi v. Tennessee,* 142 S. Ct. 31 (2021), the Court had not had occasion to determine if equitable apportionment applies to a groundwater aquifer. This case gives you the opportunity to see the Roberts Court handle a water issue of first impression, and in doing so, to set the stage for development of federal common law on application of equitable apportionment to groundwater.

Unlike the first two cases in which you are presented with only a fraction of the opinion to focus your study on key aspects, this excerpt includes most of the opinion. In part, this reflects the brevity of the opinion, likely due to its sole focus on the legal issue of whether equitable apportionment applies to groundwater. However, you are also given both facts and rules to illustrate why you need to understand the terminology and physical aspects of hydrogeology/hydrology. In addition, more information on procedure is provided to illustrate how these issues arise and the various ways they may manifest in court (in this case it was not originally a suit for equitable apportionment); the process of appointment of a Special Master; and the status of the Report of the Special Master. Citations we have left out are to the Report or the hearing record—not your standard citations in a Supreme Court case—thus illustrating some of the differences under original jurisdiction. The extent of the aquifer in question is shown in Figure 17.3.

5. *See* Kansas v. Colorado, 514 U.S. 673, 694 (1995).

Mississippi v. Tennessee

Supreme Court of the United States
142 S. Ct. 31 (2021)

Opinion

Chief Justice ROBERTS delivered the opinion of the Court—The City of Memphis sits on the banks of the Mississippi River in the southwest corner of Tennessee. Arkansas marks the City's western border, and Mississippi its southern. Hundreds of feet beneath Memphis lies one of the City's most valuable resources: the Middle Claiborne Aquifer. Workers discovered the aquifer in 1886 while drilling a well for the Bohlen-Huse Ice Company. Ever since, water pumped from the aquifer has provided Memphis with an abundant supply of clean, affordable drinking water.

The Middle Claiborne Aquifer underlies other States too, including Mississippi. This case began in 2014 when Mississippi invoked our original jurisdiction and sought leave to file a bill of complaint against Tennessee. Mississippi alleges that Tennessee's pumping has taken hundreds of billions of gallons of water that were once located beneath Mississippi. It seeks at least $615 million in damages, as well as declaratory and injunctive relief. We granted Mississippi leave to file its complaint and appointed a Special Master to oversee proceedings. The Special Master has now issued his report, which recommends that this Court dismiss Mississippi's complaint with leave to amend. Both Mississippi and Tennessee have filed exceptions.

I. A.

... [The Middle Claiborne Aquifer] underlies portions of eight States in the Mississippi River Basin: Alabama, Arkansas, Illinois, Kentucky, Louisiana, Mississippi, Missouri, and Tennessee. See Report of Special Master.... Many of these States, including Mississippi and Tennessee, draw significant amounts of groundwater from the aquifer....

To extract water from an aquifer, people drill wells. Pumps then draw water to the surface, where it is processed and piped to customers. Pumping does not just bring water to the surface; it also lowers water pressure at the site of the well. Water is naturally drawn to this area of lower pressure. This, in turn, "causes a pattern of lower or depressed water levels around the wells." Report of Special Master.... Hydrogeologists call such areas "cones of depression." These cones of depression can be local—say, the size of a backyard. Or they can be regional, stretching out for many miles from a pumping site....

The City of Memphis, through its public utility, the Memphis Light, Gas and Water Division (MLGW), pumps approximately 120 million gallons of groundwater from the Middle Claiborne Aquifer each day.... It does so using more than 160 wells located in and around Memphis.... Some of these wells are located just a few miles from the Mississippi-Tennessee border, though all are drilled straight down such that none crosses the physical border between the States.... MLGW's pumping contributes to a cone of depression that underlies both the City of Memphis and DeSoto County, Mississippi. Report of Special Master....

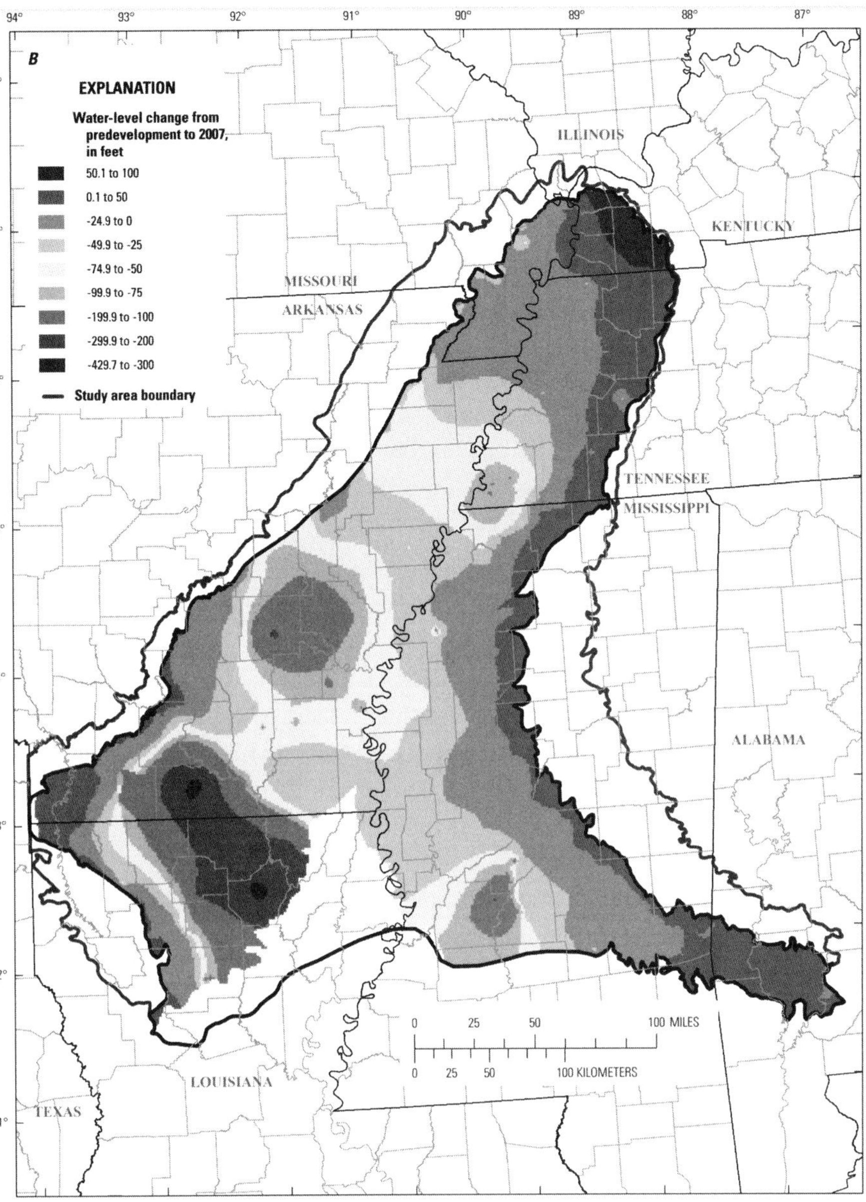

Figure 17.3 The Middle Claiborne Aquifer. Source: CLARK ET AL., GROUNDWATER AVAILABILITY OF THE MISSISSIPPI EMBAYMENT, USGS PROFESSIONAL PAPER 1785 24 (2011), https://pubs.usgs.gov/pp/1785/pdf/PP1785.pdf.

Mississippi argues that MLGW's pumping has altered the historic flow of groundwater within the Middle Claiborne Aquifer. Mississippi concedes that some water naturally flows from the part of the aquifer beneath Mississippi to the part beneath Tennessee. But only to the extent of some 30 to 60 feet per year.... Mississippi contends that MLGW's pumping has substantially hastened this existing flow, allowing Memphis to take billions of gallons of groundwater that otherwise would have remained under Mississippi for thousands of years.

B

In 2005, prior to the present litigation, the Attorney General of Mississippi sued the City of Memphis and MLGW in Federal District Court. The suit alleged that Memphis had wrongfully appropriated groundwater belonging to Mississippi through its pumping activities. Mississippi sought hundreds of millions of dollars in damages.

The District Court dismissed the suit for failure to join Tennessee, which it determined was an indispensable party. *Hood ex rel. Miss.* v. *Memphis*, 533 F.Supp.2d 646, 651 (N.D. Miss. 2008). The Fifth Circuit then affirmed. *Hood ex rel. Miss.* v. *Memphis*, 570 F.3d 625 (2009).

Both decisions turned in large part on what is known as "equitable apportionment." Under that doctrine, this Court allocates rights to a disputed interstate water resource after one State sues another under our original jurisdiction. See *Kansas* v. *Colorado*, 206 U.S. 46, 97–98 (1907). Traditionally, equitable apportionment has been the exclusive judicial remedy for interstate water disputes, unless a statute, compact, or prior apportionment controls. This Court has never before held that an interstate aquifer is subject to equitable apportionment, so Mississippi's suit implicated a question of first impression.

The Court of Appeals, affirming the District Court, held that interstate aquifers are comparable to interstate rivers and are thus subject to equitable apportionment. It reasoned that an aquifer "flows, if slowly." *Hood ex rel. Miss.*, 570 F.3d at 630. And it said the fact that an aquifer is "located underground, as opposed to resting above ground," was of "no analytical significance." *Ibid.* Because determining "Mississippi and Tennessee's relative rights to the Aquifer" brought the case within the equitable apportionment doctrine, the Court of Appeals affirmed the District Court's holding that Tennessee was an indispensable party. *Id.*, at 630–631; see also Fed. Rule Civ. Proc. 19(a). Joinder of Tennessee in the lower federal courts was not possible, however, because this Court has exclusive jurisdiction over suits between States. See U.S. Const., Art. III, § 2; 28 U.S.C. § 1251(a). So the Fifth Circuit held that the District Court had properly dismissed the suit. *Hood ex rel. Miss.*, 570 F.3d at 632–633; Fed. Rule Civ. Proc. 19(b).

Mississippi then petitioned for a writ of certiorari. It also sought leave to file a bill of complaint against Tennessee, Memphis, and MLGW under our original jurisdiction. The proposed complaint requested over $1 billion in damages for the alleged taking of Mississippi's water. In the alternative, it sought equitable apportionment of the aquifer, with a damages award for past diversions of groundwater. We declined to grant certiorari, 559 U.S. 904 (2010), and denied without prejudice Mississippi's request for leave to file a bill of complaint, 559 U.S. 901 (2010).

C

In 2014, Mississippi again sought leave from this Court to file a bill of complaint against Tennessee, Memphis, and MLGW. That is the basis of this suit. Mississippi's complaint alleges that MLGW "has forcibly siphoned into Tennessee hundreds of billions of gallons of high quality groundwater owned by Mississippi." ... It says that MLGW's "mechanical pumping" is to blame and that the "groundwater taken by Defendants from within Mississippi's borders would have never under normal, natural circumstances been drawn into Tennessee." ... This "wrongful taking," the State contends, "is evidenced by a substantial drop in pressure and corresponding drawdown of stored groundwater" in northwest Mississippi, and by a cone of depression extending miles into its territory.... As a result, Mississippi says, it has to drill its own wells deeper to access the aquifer, and use more electricity to pump water to the surface....

Mississippi claims an absolute "ownership" right to all groundwater beneath its surface—even after that water has crossed its borders.... It argues that Tennessee's pumping thus amounts to a tortious taking of property, and it seeks at least $615 million in damages.... Mississippi expressly disclaims equitable apportionment, arguing that the "fundamental premise of this Court's equitable apportionment jurisprudence—that each of the opposing States has an equality of right to use the waters at issue—does not apply to this dispute." ...

We granted Mississippi leave to file its complaint and appointed Judge Eugene E. Siler, Jr., of the Sixth Circuit to serve as Special Master. He has ably discharged his duties. Following motions practice, discovery, and a five-day evidentiary hearing, the Special Master issued a report recommending that we dismiss Mississippi's complaint, but with leave to amend. He first determined that the Middle Claiborne Aquifer is an interstate water resource. He found that the aquifer is a "single hydrogeological unit," that Tennessee's pumping affects groundwater beneath Mississippi, and that prior to such pumping, "groundwater flowed between Mississippi and Tennessee"—a fact Mississippi "does not dispute." Report of Special Master....

The Special Master then concluded that, because the aquifer is an interstate water resource, equitable apportionment is the appropriate remedy. He recognized that equitable apportionment "stands alone as the federal common-law principle for disputes over interstate water," ... and saw "no compelling reason to chart a new path for groundwater resources," .... Because Mississippi's complaint did not seek equitable apportionment, the Special Master recommends that we dismiss it. But he also recommends that we grant Mississippi leave to file an amended complaint seeking equitable apportionment, though the State has not yet sought such leave.

Mississippi and Tennessee both filed exceptions to the Special Master's report. Mississippi objects to the Special Master's recommendation that we dismiss the suit. It argues that the Special Master erred in finding the water in the Middle Claiborne Aquifer subject to equitable apportionment. Tennessee objects only to the Special Master's recommendation that we grant Mississippi leave to amend its complaint.

We "conduct an independent review of the record, and assume the ultimate responsibility for deciding all matters." *Kansas* v. *Nebraska*, 574 U.S. 445, 453 (2015) (internal quotation marks omitted). Based on that review, we dismiss Mississippi's complaint and decline to grant leave to amend.

II. A

Equitable apportionment aims to produce a fair allocation of a shared water resource between two or more States. See *Colorado* v. *New Mexico*, 459 U.S. 176, 183 (1982). The doctrine's "guiding principle" is that States "have an equal right to make a reasonable use" of a shared water resource. *Florida* v. *Georgia*, 141 S.Ct. 1175, 1180, (2021).

... We have also applied the doctrine ... in situations where the pumping of groundwater has affected the flow of interstate *surface* waters, see *Nebraska* v. *Wyoming*, 515 U.S. 1, 14 (1995). We have even applied the doctrine to anadromous fish—such as Chinook salmon and steelhead trout—that migrate between the Pacific Ocean and spawning grounds in the Columbia-Snake River system, "travel[ing] through several States during their lifetime." See *Idaho ex rel. Evans* v. *Oregon*, 462 U.S. 1017, 1018–1019 (1983).

Mississippi correctly observes that we have never considered whether equitable apportionment applies to interstate aquifers.... Confronted as we are with this matter of first impression, we resist general propositions and focus our analysis on whether equitable apportionment of the Middle Claiborne Aquifer would be "sufficiently similar" to past applications of the doctrine to warrant the same treatment. *Idaho ex rel. Evans*, 462 U.S., at 1024 (adopting such an approach in extending the doctrine to anadromous fish). We conclude that it would.

First, we have applied equitable apportionment only when transboundary resources were at issue.... The Middle Claiborne Aquifer's "multistate character" seems beyond dispute.... Mississippi concedes that the "geologic formation in which the groundwater is stored straddles two states." ... Indeed, a core premise of Mississippi's suit is that Tennessee is pumping water that was once in Mississippi. The evidence shows that wells in Memphis and wells in northwest Mississippi are "pumping from the same aquifer." ...

Also pertinent is that the Middle Claiborne Aquifer contains water that flows naturally between the States. All of our equitable apportionment cases have concerned such water, *Kansas v. Colorado*, 206 U.S., at 98, or fish that live in it, *Idaho ex rel. Evans*, 462 U.S., at 1024,. Mississippi suggests the Middle Claiborne Aquifer is distinguishable from interstate rivers and streams because its natural flow is "extremely slow." ... But we have long applied equitable apportionment even to streams that run dry from time to time. See *Kansas* v. *Colorado*, 206 U.S., at 115. And although the transboundary flow here may be a mere "one or two inches per day," ... that amounts to over 35 million gallons of water per day, and over ten billion gallons per year,.... So the speed of the flow, at least in the context of this case, does not place the aquifer beyond equitable apportionment.

Finally, it is clear that actions in Tennessee "reach ... through the agency of natural laws" to affect the portion of the aquifer that underlies Mississippi. Tennessee's pumping has contributed to a cone of depression that extends miles into northern Mississippi.... Mississippi itself contends that this cone of depression has reduced groundwater storage and pressure in northern Mississippi.... It also alleges that Tennessee's pumping is "siphoning" tens of millions of gallons of groundwater each day from Mississippi's portion of the aquifer.... Such interstate effects are a hallmark of our equitable apportionment cases....

For these reasons, we hold that the waters of the Middle Claiborne Aquifer are subject to the judicial remedy of equitable apportionment.

B

Mississippi contends that it has sovereign ownership of all groundwater beneath its surface, so equitable apportionment ought not apply. We see things differently. It is certainly true that "each State has full jurisdiction over the lands within its borders, including the beds of streams and other waters." But such jurisdiction does not confer unfettered "ownership or control" of flowing interstate waters themselves. Thus, we have "consistently denied" the proposition that a State may exercise exclusive ownership or control of interstate "waters flowing within her boundaries." Although our past cases have generally concerned streams and rivers, we see no basis for a different result in the context of the Middle Claiborne Aquifer. When a water resource is shared between several States, each one "has an interest which should be respected by the other." Mississippi's ownership approach would allow an upstream State to completely cut off flow to a downstream one, a result contrary to our equitable apportionment jurisprudence.

...

We conclude that the waters contained in the Middle Claiborne Aquifer are subject to equitable apportionment. We therefore overrule Mississippi's exceptions and adopt the Special Master's recommendation to dismiss the bill of complaint.

III

After recommending that this Court dismiss Mississippi's suit, the Special Master went on to recommend that we grant the State leave to file an amended complaint seeking equitable apportionment. We decline to decide whether Mississippi should be granted such leave, because the State has never sought it. As Mississippi itself emphasizes—literally—it has "*not yet requested equitable apportionment.*" ...

Nor can we assume Mississippi will do so. Mississippi's initial pleadings in this case disavowed equitable apportionment entirely.... ("This case does not fall within the Court's equitable apportionment jurisprudence."). The State instead sought relief under principles of tort law. And the proceedings below reflected this posture, focusing on the physical properties of the aquifer and Tennessee's pumping. An equitable apportionment case would require us to consider a broader range of evidence. Such evidence often includes not only the physical properties and flow of a water resource, but also existing uses, the availability of alternatives, practical effects, and the costs and benefits to the States involved. A just equitable apportionment might also require the joinder of additional parties, cf. Fed. Rule Civ. Proc. 19(a), as Mississippi and Tennessee are not the only States that rely on the Middle Claiborne Aquifer for groundwater,.... Finally, if Mississippi were to seek leave to amend, its complaint would be subject to our longstanding rule that a "State seeking equitable apportionment under our original jurisdiction must prove by clear and convincing evidence some real and substantial injury or damage."

As Mississippi has neither sought leave to amend nor tendered a proposed complaint seeking equitable apportionment, we have no occasion to determine how these and other pertinent principles might apply.

Mississippi has failed to show that it is entitled to relief. We therefore overrule Mississippi's exceptions to the Special Master's report, sustain Tennessee's, and dismiss the case.

It is so ordered.

Notes & Questions

1. Mississippi's argument is simply that it owns the water beneath the surface of its territory and that should be the basis for a remedy. How does the Court address this?
2. According to Mississippi, pumping in Memphis, Tennessee, is causing a cone of depression that extends into Mississippi. Explain how this happens. What is the harm to Mississippi?
3. The Special Master recommended that Mississippi be given leave to amend its complaint to seek an equitable apportionment. Why does the Court reject this? What must Mississippi do if it now wants an equitable apportionment?
4. What does the Court state that it has applied the doctrine of equitable apportionment to other than water?

Negotiated Agreement under the Compact Clause

Article I, Section 10, Clause 3 of the Constitution allows states to enter into a negotiated "agreement or compact with another state" with the consent of Congress. The Supreme Court has made it clear in both establishing a threshold requirement to a suit for equitable apportionment, and its comments in cases failing to meet the threshold, that its preference is for states to exercise this option. In applying the threshold requirement in *Colorado v. Kansas* 320 U.S. 383, 393–394 (1943), the Court states:

> The reason for judicial caution in adjudicating the relative rights of states in such cases is that, while we have jurisdiction of such disputes, ... they involve the interests of quasi-sovereigns, present complicated and delicate questions, and, due to the possibility of future change of conditions, necessitate expert administration rather than judicial imposition of a hard and fast rule. Such controversies may appropriately be composed by negotiation and agreement, pursuant to the compact clause of the Federal constitution. We say of this case, as the court has said of interstate differences of like nature, that such mutual accommodation and agreement should, if possible, be the medium of settlement, instead of invocation of our adjudicatory power. *Id.* at 392.

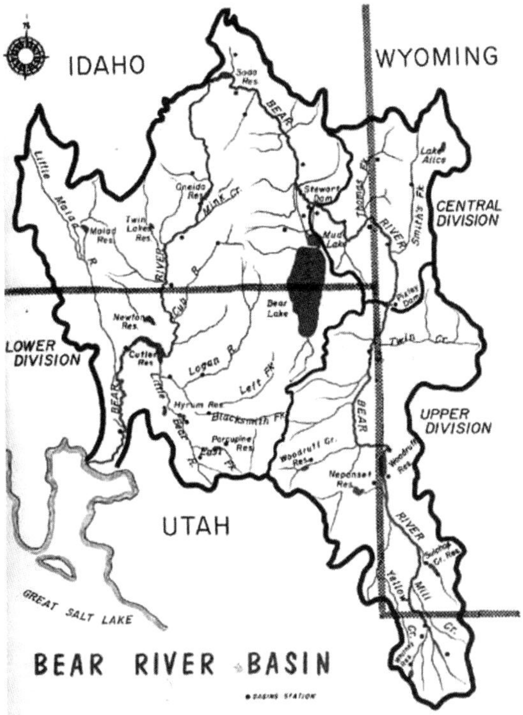

Figure 17.4 The Bear River Basin. Utah Division of Water Rights, *History of the Bear River Compact* (2023), https://waterrights.utah.gov/techinfo/bearrivc/history.html.

The Bear River Compact among Idaho, Utah, and Wyoming (Figure 17.4) gives you an idea of the components of a Compact. Generally, compacts are highly technical and are developed around physical solutions to the supply problem and provide a mechanism for enforcement and for ongoing dialogue as circumstances change. Excerpts will be used to inform these aspects.

Summary of the Bear River Compact

The Bear River Compact was entered into by Idaho, Utah, and Wyoming in 1958, and substantially amended in 1978, with ratification by the three states' legislatures in 1979, followed by congressional consent on February 8, 1980. *See* Public Law 96-189 (1980). From its table of contents, (Table 17.1) you can see the scope of issues it covers.

Table 17.1 illustrates that a compact is a highly technical document addressing allocation from direct flow and storage; the handling of conveyance structures as well as interstate infrastructure. The first three articles are of considerable importance.

Article I states:

A. The major purposes of this Compact are to remove the causes of present and future controversy over the distribution and use of the waters of the Bear River; to provide for efficient use of water for multiple purposes; to permit additional development of the water resources of Bear River; to pro-

Table 17.1 The list of articles in the Bear River Compact from the Table of Contents

Article I	Statement of Purpose
Article II	Definition of Terms
Article III	Bear River Commission
Article IV	Allocation of Direct Flow
Article V	Lower Division Allocation
Article VI	Allocation of Storage
Article VII	New Projects
Article VIII	Rights in Other Signatory States
Article IX	Conveyance of Stored Water between States
Article X	Rights in Interstate Canals
Article XI	Applications for Appropriation, Etc.
Article XII	Legal Actions and Proceedings
Article XIII	Existing Rights of United States
Article XIV	Review of Compact Provisions
Article XV	Termination
Article XVI	Severability
Article XVII	Ratification and Effective Date

mote interstate comity; and to accomplish an equitable apportionment of the waters of the Bear River among the compacting States.

B. The physical and all other conditions peculiar to the Bear River constitute the basis for this Compact. No general principle or precedent with respect to any other interstate stream is intended to be established.

This not only gives you an idea of the goals of the parties, but the types of issues that will be addressed. Consider that I(B) was likely thought necessary to disclaim any precedent for use in an equitable apportionment suit by use of the term "equitable apportionment" in section I(A). This should give you a hint of the mine field of potential secondary impacts that awaits anyone drafting an agreement of this type.

You should already be familiar with the notion that the definition section of a major statutory scheme (e.g., the Clean Water Act) is critical to understanding the statute itself. The same is generally true of compacts. The definition section, Article II, is primarily used in the Bear River Compact to define the various names of infrastructure components. Keep in mind, however, that definitions may also be used to define or even to redefine various terms used in water law.

Of significant importance in a compact are provisions that seek to reduce future conflict by creating a forum for ongoing dialogue. The creation of the Bear River Commission in Article III furthers this goal. Article III creates a nine-member Commission:

three from each state for purposes of enforcement of the compact. While the language is simple, the webpage of the Bear River Commission (https://www.bearrivercommission.org/) indicates that it provides a repository for hydrologic data, data on water use, new uses, changes etc., that is shared among the states. Regular meetings of the Commission provide a forum for dialogue. The Commission's webpage refers to the broad statement of purpose in Article I to capture its duty and, in doing so, makes the goal "to remove the causes of present and future controversy over the distribution and use of the waters of the Bear River; to provide for efficient use of water for multiple purposes; to permit additional development of the water resources of Bear River; to promote interstate comity; and to accomplish an equitable apportionment of the waters of the Bear River among the compacting States," an ongoing, rather than a one-time, effort.

Finally, the concluding articles in the compact include provisions aimed at finality and certainty. The requirement that all three states must agree before the compact may be terminated provides a degree of measured certainty by providing water users of each state a low risk of change in the rules moving forward.

Every compact is highly tailored to the circumstances, both physical and social, of its setting, and thus each compact captures that complexity. In fact, the need to account for that complexity if an allocation is truly to be equitable is what drives the Supreme Court to urge states to negotiate.

Despite all these efforts, disputes do arise under compacts that the parties are unable to settle. In Part V, you will read a case involving the interpretation of the Yellowstone River Compact among Montana, North Dakota, and Wyoming. The case involves a rising problem in western water basins. States, through recapture rules and the federal Bureau of Reclamation, through policy, have long encouraged efficiency improvements in irrigation infrastructure. Viewed from the perspective of a single farm, this makes sense. Unfortunately, viewed from the system, this reduces water for downstream interests. In the case of *Montana v. Wyoming*, that downstream area is across a state line.

In concluding our section on Compacts, remember that this is the favored process due to the complexity of the problem and the preference for placing control in the sovereigns that share the water course. Also keep in mind that a compact may have a significant effect on shared water without addressing water allocation. For example, the major interstate issues in the Columbia River Basin focus more on hydropower and flood control, with irrigation being an important but secondary issue. As a result, the major interstate compact in the Pacific Northwest created the Northwest Power and Conservation Council with congressional consent given in the Northwest Power Act.[6] According to the Council's website, the Council was formed among: "Idaho, Montana, Oregon, and Washington to develop a regional power plan and fish and wildlife program to balance the Northwest's environment and energy needs. Our mission is

6. 94 Stat. 2697; Pub. L. No. 96-501.

to ensure, with public participation, an affordable and reliable energy system while enhancing fish and wildlife in the Columbia River Basin."[7]

Congressional Allocation

The second method we will cover is the authority of Congress to allocate an interstate river among its states. As noted in the introduction to this Chapter, the announcement in *Arizona v. California*, 373 U.S. 546 (1963), that Congress had the power to apportion an interstate river and that it had done so for the Colorado River (Figure 17.5) when it passed the Boulder Canyon Act, came as a shock to western water interests. It continues to be held up as a reason to fear congressional involvement in western water, even in approving a compact. Consider this fear of Congress doing something against the interests of a water basin as one of the West's water myths. First, the Boulder Canyon Act was passed in the face of an inability of the lower Colorado River basin states to achieve a compact, despite the federal preference that disputes be resolved prior to expenditure of Reclamation funds. Second, the dam that would be built under the Act—the Boulder Canyon, now Hoover Dam—would have the capacity to store almost twice the average annual flow (at the time) of the river and would thus control the water supply for the lower basin. It would be entirely federally operated. Finally, and most importantly, congressional apportionment has only been used since 1963 with the consent and involvement of congressional members from the states involved. For example, California and Nevada thought it more efficient to go straight to Congress with their settlement on the Truckee and Carson Rivers (Truckee-Carson-Pyramid Lake Water Rights Settlement Act of 1990, Pub.L. No. 101-618, Title II), avoiding state legislative battlegrounds necessary for a Compact. Keep these thoughts in mind as well as the complex problem the Court faces as you read the following case. The following background should help you with the complexity of the case.

The states of the Colorado River Basin had long feuded over how its waters should be allocated. That history, which is set forth in the full opinion in detail, is summarized here. In 1922, the states negotiated a compact to divide the waters of the Colorado River. That compact would have split the Colorado River into two basins, arbitrarily selecting Lee's Ferry as the dividing point (Figure 17.5). It would have allocated 7.5 million acre-feet to the states upstream from that point, and 7.5 million acre-feet to the downstream states of Arizona, California, and Nevada. The upper basin states were able to come to an agreement among themselves about how to apportion their 7.5 million acre-feet, but the lower basin states could not reach agreement and Arizona refused to sign the Compact. Congress got involved in 1928 when it passed the Boulder Canyon Act. That Act authorized approval of the 1922 Compact, allocating water between the upper and lower basin if six of the seven states including California signed, and California passed legislation limiting their share to 4.4 million acre-feet/year plus half of any surplus. The California legislature complied and the lower basin

7. Northwest Power and Conservation Council, *About* (2023), https://www.nwcouncil.org/about/.

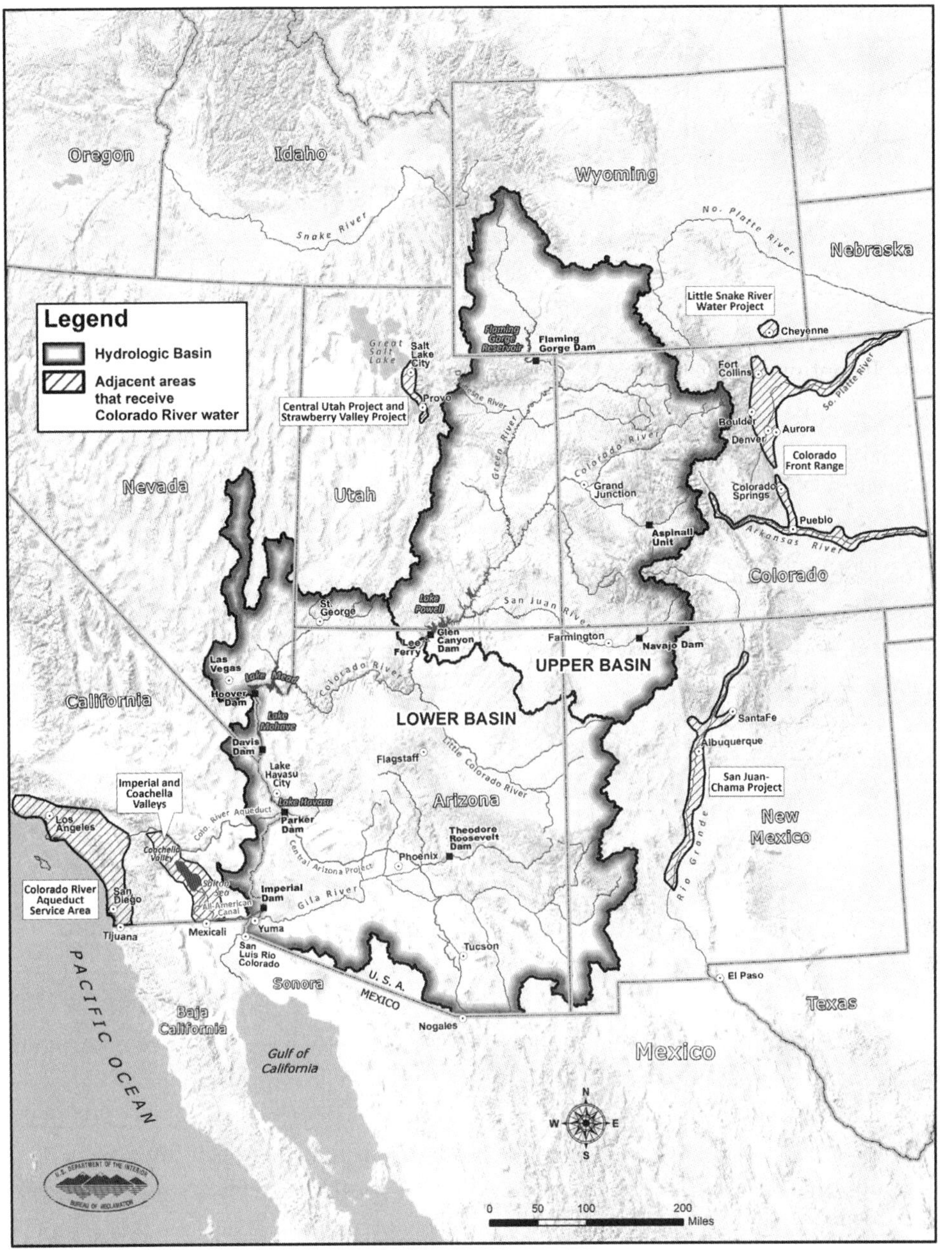

Figure 17.5 Colorado River Basin showing the upper and lower basin, the primary tributaries, and use of River water outside the basin in hatched. U.S. Bureau of Reclamation, Colorado River Basin Water Supply and Demand Study 2 (2012), https://www.usbr.gov/watersmart/bsp/docs/finalreport/ColoradoRiver/CRBS_Executive_Summary_FINAL.pdf.

states entered a Compact adopting the apportionment in the Act allocating 2.8 million acre-feet to Arizona, 4.4 million acre-feet to California, and 300,000 acre-feet to Nevada, with Arizona and California splitting half of any surplus. Unfortunately, the Boulder Canyon Act did not indicate whether the apportionment applied to the water at the point it is measured between the upper and lower basin (just below Glen Canyon Dam at Lee's Ferry), or whether it included downstream tributaries. This was of particular importance to Arizona since its Gila River contributes, on average, two million acre-feet to the Colorado River well below Lee's Ferry. Even though the apportionment adds up to the 7.5 million acre-feet measured at Lee's Ferry, California asserted that the water from the Gila was surplus water, entitling California to half. California continued to develop Colorado River water above the 4.4 million acre-feet it was allocated in the Boulder Canyon Act and Arizona sued California in the late 1950s. As you learned in Part III, because the suit would decide the allocation of the lower basin, the United States intervened and made claims on its own behalf and on behalf of the tribes that had reservations on the mainstem of the River within the lower Basin. The ultimate opinion of the Supreme Court following a hearing on exceptions to the Report of the Special Master settled many outstanding disputes related to the nature and scope of the *Winters* Doctrine.

To emphasize the complexity of this type of case, consider this from the opinion: "The Master conducted a trial lasting from June 14, 1956, to August 28, 1958, during which 340 witnesses were heard orally or by deposition, thousands of exhibits were received, and 25,000 pages of transcript were filled. Following many motions, arguments, and briefs, the Master in a 433-page volume reported his findings, conclusions, and recommended decree, received by the Court on January 16, 1961." *Arizona v. California*, 373 U.S. at 551.

Arizona v. California

Supreme Court of the United States
373 U.S. 546 (1963)

Opinion

Mr. Justice Black delivered the opinion of the Court—In 1952 the State of Arizona invoked the original jurisdiction of this Court by filing a complaint against the State of California and seven of its public agencies.... Later, Nevada, New Mexico, Utah, and the United States were added as parties either voluntarily or on motion.... The basic controversy in the case is over how much water each State has a legal right to use out of the waters of the Colorado River and its tributaries.... As we see this case, the question of each State's share of the waters of the Colorado and its tributaries turns on the meaning and the scope of the Boulder Canyon Project Act passed by Congress in 1928.... That meaning and scope can be better understood when the Act is set against its background—the gravity of the Southwest's water problems; the inability of local groups or individual States to deal with these enormous problems; the continued failure of the States to agree on how to conserve and divide the waters; and the ultimate action by Congress at the request of the States creating a great system of dams and public works nationally built, controlled, and operated for the purpose of conserving and distributing the water.

The Colorado River itself rises in the mountains of Colorado and flows generally in a southwesterly direction for about 1,300 miles through Colorado, Utah, and Arizona and along the Arizona-Nevada and Arizona-California boundaries, after which it passes into Mexico and empties into the Mexican waters of the Gulf of California....

... The natural flow of the Colorado was too erratic, the river at many places in canyons too deep, and the engineering and economic hurdles too great for small farmers, larger groups, or even States to build storage dams, construct canals, and install the expensive works necessary for a dependable year-round water supply....

It is not surprising that the pressing necessity to transform the erratic and often destructive flow of the Colorado River into a controlled and dependable water supply.... [On] May 18, 1920, Congress passed a bill offered by Congressman Kinkaid of Nebraska directing the Secretary of the Interior to make a study and report of diversions which might be made from the Colorado River for irrigation in the Imperial Valley.... The ... Report recommended that the United States construct as a government project not only an all-American canal from the Colorado River to the Imperial Valley but also a dam and reservoir at or near Boulder Canyon....

The prospect that the United States would undertake to build as a national project the necessary works to control floods and store river waters for irrigation was apparently a welcome one for the basin States. But it brought to life strong fears in the northern basin States that additional waters made available by the storage and canal projects might be gobbled up in perpetuity by faster growing lower basin areas, particularly California, before the upper States could appropriate what they believed to be their fair share.... [The Court covers the effort to enter a Compact in 1922, under a 1921 authorization from Congress.]

... [In discussing the Compact, the Court covers key articles of importance to this opinion.] This compromise divides the entire basin into two parts, the Upper Basin and the Lower Basin, separated at a point on the river in northern Arizona known as Lee Ferry.... Article III (a) of the Compact apportions to each basin in perpetuity 7,500,000 acre-feet of water ... a year from the Colorado River System, defined in Article II (a) as 'the Colorado River and its tributaries within the United States of America.' In addition, Article III (b) gives the Lower Basin 'the right to increase its beneficial consumptive use ... of such waters by one million acre-feet per annum.' Article III (c) provides that future Mexican water rights recognized by the United States shall be supplied first out of surplus over and above the aggregate of the quantities specified in (a) and (b), and if this surplus is not enough the deficiency shall be borne equally by the two basins. Article III (d) requires the Upper Basin not to deplete the Lee Ferry flow below an aggregate of 75,000,000 acre-feet for any 10 consecutive years. Article III (f) and (g) provide a way for further apportionment by a compact of 'Colorado River System' waters at any time after October 1, 1963. While these allocations quieted rivalries between the Upper and Lower Basins, major differences between the States in the Lower Basin continued. Failure of the Compact to determine each State's share of the water left Nevada and Arizona with their fears that the law of prior appropriation would be not a protection but a menace because California could use that law to get for herself the lion's share of the waters allotted to the Lower Basin. Moreover, Arizona, because of her particularly strong interest in the Gila, intensely resented the Compact's inclusion of the Colorado River tributaries in its allocation scheme and was bitterly hostile to having Arizona tributaries, again particularly the Gila, forced to contribute to the Mexican burden. Largely for these reasons, Arizona alone, of all the States in both basins, refused to ratify the Compact....

Seeking means which would permit ratification by all seven basin States, the Governors of those States met at Denver in 1925 and again in 1927. As a result of these meetings the Governors of the upper States suggested, as a fair apportionment of water among the Lower Basin States, that out of the average annual delivery of water at Lee Ferry required by the Compact—7,500,000 acre-feet—Nevada be given 300,000 acre-feet, Arizona 3,000,000, and California 4,200,000, and that unapportioned waters, subject to reapportionment after 1963, be shared equally by Arizona and California. Each Lower Basin State would have 'the exclusive beneficial consumptive use of such tributaries within its boundaries before the same empty into the main stream,' except that Arizona tributary waters in excess of 1,000,000 acre-feet could under some circumstances be subject to diminution by reason of a United States treaty with Mexico. This proposal foundered because California held out for 4,600,000 acre-feet instead of 4,200,000 ... and because Arizona held out for complete exemption of its tributaries from any part of the Mexican burden....

Between 1922 and 1927 Congressman Philip Swing and Senator Hiram Johnson, both of California, made three attempts to have Swing-Johnson bills enacted, authorizing construction of a dam in the canyon section of the Colorado River and an all-American canal....

Finally, the fourth Swing-Johnson bill passed both Houses and became the Boulder Canyon Project Act of December 21, 1928, 45 Stat. 1057.... The projects authorized by the Act were the same as those provided for in the prior defeated measures, but in other significant respects the Act was strikingly different. The earlier bills had offered no method whatever of apportioning the waters among the States of the Lower Basin. The Act as finally passed did provide such a method, and, as we view it, the method chosen was a complete statutory apportionment intended to put an end to the long-standing dispute over Colorado River waters. To protect the Upper Basin against California should Arizona still refuse to ratify the Compact, ... § 4(a) of the Act as finally passed provided that, if fewer than seven States ratified within six months, the Act should not take effect unless six States including California ratified and unless California, by its legislature, agreed 'irrevocably and unconditionally * * * as an express covenant' to a limit on its annual consumption of Colorado River water of 'four million four hundred thousand acre-feet of the waters apportioned to the lower basin States by paragraph (a) of Article III of the Colorado River compact, plus not more than one-half of any excess or surplus waters unapportioned by said compact.' Congress in the same section showed its continuing desire to have California, Arizona, and Nevada settle their own differences by authorizing them to make an agreement apportioning to Nevada 300,000 acre-feet, and to Arizona 2,800,000 acre-feet plus half of any surplus waters unapportioned by the Compact. The permitted agreement also was to allow Arizona exclusive use of the Gila River, wholly free from any Mexican obligation, a position Arizona had taken from the beginning. Sections 5 and 8(b) of the Project Act made provisions for the sale of the stored waters. The Secretary of the Interior was authorized by s 5 'under such general regulations as he may prescribe, to contract for the storage of water in said reservoir and for the delivery thereof at such points on the river and on said canal as may be agreed upon, for irrigation and domestic uses * * *.' Section 5 required these contracts to be 'for permanent service' and further provided, 'No person shall have or be entitled to have the use for any purpose of the water stored as aforesaid except by contract made as herein stated.' Section 8(b) provided that the Secretary's contracts would be subject to any compact dividing the benefits of the water between Arizona, California, and Nevada, or any two of them, approved by Congress on or before January 1, 1929, but that any such compact approved after that date should be 'subject to all contracts, if any, made by the Secretary of the Interior under section 5 hereof prior to the date of such approval and consent by Congress.'

The Project Act became effective on June 25, 1929, by Presidential Proclamation, ... after six States, including California, had ratified the Colorado River Compact and the California legislature had accepted the limitation of 4,400,000 acre-feet ... as required by the Act. Neither the three States nor any two of them ever entered into any apportionment compact as authorized by §§ 4(a) and 8(b). After the construction of Boulder Dam the Secretary of the Interior, purporting to act under the authority of the Project Act, made contracts with various water users in California for 5,362,000 acre-feet, with Nevada for 300,000 acre-feet, and with Arizona for 2,800,000 acre-feet of water from that stored at Lake Mead.

The Special Master appointed by this Court found that the Colorado River Compact, the law of prior appropriation, and the doctrine of equitable apportionment—by which doctrine this Court in the absence of statute resolves interstate claims according to the equities—do not control the issues in this case. The Master concluded that, since the Lower Basin States had failed to make a compact to allocate the waters among themselves as authorized by §§ 4(a) and 8(b), the Secretary's contracts with the States had within the statutory scheme of §§ 4(a), 5, and 8(b) effected an apportionment of the waters of the mainstream which, according to the Master, were the only waters to be apportioned under the Act. The Master further held that, in the event of a shortage of water making it impossible for the Secretary to supply all the water due California, Arizona, and Nevada under their contracts, the burden of the shortage must be borne by each State in proportion to her share of the first 7,500,000 acre-feet allocated to the Lower Basin, that is, 4. /7.5 by California, 2. 8/7.5 by Arizona, and . 3/7.5 by Nevada, without regard to the law of prior appropriation.

Arizona, Nevada, and the United States support with few exceptions the analysis, conclusions, and recommendations of the Special Master's report....

California is in basic disagreement with almost all of the Master's Report. She argues that the Project Act, like the Colorado River Compact, deals with the entire Colorado River System, not just the mainstream. This would mean that diversions within Arizona and Nevada of tributary waters flowing in those States would be charged against their apportionments and that, because tributary water would be added to the mainstream water in computing the first 7,500,000 acre-feet available to the States, there would be a greater likelihood of a surplus, of which California gets one-half. The result of California's argument would be much more water for California and much less for Arizona. California also argues that the Act neither allocates the Colorado River waters nor gives the Secretary authority to make an allocation. Rather she takes the position that the judicial doctrine of equitable apportionment giving full interstate effect to the traditional western water law of prior appropriation should determine the rights of the parties to the water. Finally, California claims that in any event the Act does not control in time of shortage. Under such circumstances, she says, this Court should divide the waters according to the doctrine of equitable apportionment or the law of prior appropriation, either of which, she argues, should result in protecting her prior uses.

... Resolution of this dispute requires a determination of what apportionment, if any, is made by the Project Act and what powers are conferred by the Act upon the Secretary of the Interior.... In this situation we should and do exercise our jurisdiction.

I. ALLOCATION OF WATER AMONG THE STATES AND DISTRIBUTION TO USERS.

We have concluded, for reasons to be stated, that Congress in passing the Project Act intended to and did create its own comprehensive scheme for the apportionment among California, Arizona, and Nevada of the Lower Basin's share of the mainstream waters of the Colorado River, leaving each State its tributaries. Congress decided that a fair division of the first 7,500,000 acre-feet of such mainstream waters would give 4,400,000 acre-feet to California, 2,800,000 to Arizona, and 300,000 to Nevada; Arizona and California would each get one-half of any surplus. Prior approval was therefore given in the Act for a tri-state compact to incorporate these terms. The States, subject to subsequent congressional approval, were also permitted to agree on a compact with different terms. Division of the water did not, however, depend on the States' agreeing to a compact, for Congress gave the Secretary of the Interior adequate authority to accomplish the division. Congress did this by giving the Secretary power to make contracts for the delivery of water and by providing that no person could have water without a contract.

A. Relevancy of Judicial Apportionment and Colorado River Compact.—... Where Congress has so exercised its constitutional power over waters courts have no power to substitute their own notions of an 'equitable apportionment' for the apportionment chosen by Congress....

...

... However, the Project Act by referring to the Compact in several places, does make the Compact relevant to a limited extent. To begin with, the Act explicitly approves the Compact and thereby fixes a division of the waters between the basins which must be respected. Further, in several places the Act refers to terms contained in the Compact. For example, § 12 of the Act adopts the Compact definition of 'domestic,' ... and § 6 requires satisfaction of 'present perfected rights' as used in the Compact.... Obviously, therefore, those particular terms, though originally formulated only for the Compact's allocation of water between basins, are incorporated into the Act and are made applicable to the Project Act's allocation among Lower Basin States. The Act also declares that the Secretary of the Interior and the United States in the construction, operation, and maintenance of the dam and other works and in the making of contracts shall be subject to and controlled by the Colorado River Compact.... These latter references to the Compact are quite different from the Act's adoption of Compact terms. Such references, unlike the explicit adoption of terms, were used only to show that the Act and its provisions were in no way to upset, alter, or affect the Compact's congressionally approved divisions of water between the basins. They were not intended to make the Compact and its provisions control or affect the Act's allocation among and distribution of water within the States of the Lower Basin. Therefore, we look to the Compact for terms specifically incorporated in the Act, and we would also look to it to resolve disputes between the Upper and Lower Basins, were any involved in this case. But no such questions are here. We must determine what apportionment and delivery scheme in the Lower Basin has been effected through the Secretary's contracts. For that determination, we look to the Project Act alone.

B. Mainstream Apportionment.—The congressional scheme of apportionment cannot be understood without knowing what water Congress wanted apportioned. Under California's view, which we reject, the first 7,500,000 acre-feet of Lower Basin water, of which California has agreed to use only 4,400,000, is made up of both mainstream and tributary water, not just mainstream water. Under the view of Arizona, Nevada, and the United States, with which we agree, the tributaries are not included in the waters to be divided but remain for the exclusive use of each State. Assuming 7,500,000 acre-feet or more in the mainstream and 2,000,000 in the tributaries, California would get 1,000,000 acre-feet more if the tributaries are included and Arizona 1,000,000 less....

California's argument that the Project Act, like the Colorado River Compact, deals with the main river and all its tributaries rests on ... Article III(a), referred to by § 4(a), apportioned in perpetuity to the Lower Basin the use of 7,500,000 acre-feet of water per annum 'from the Colorado River System,' which was defined in the Compact as 'that portion of the Colorado River and its tributaries within the United States of America.'

Arizona argues that the Compact apportions between basins only the waters of the mainstream, not the mainstream and the tributaries. We need not reach that question, however, for we have concluded that whatever waters the Compact apportioned the Project Act itself dealt only with water of the mainstream. In the first place, the Act, in § 4(a), states that the California limitation, which is in reality her share of the first 7,500,000 acre-feet of Lower Basin water, is on 'water of and from the Colorado River', not of and from the 'Colorado River System.' But more importantly, the negotiations among the States and the congressional debates leading to the passage of the Project Act clearly show that the language used by Congress in the Act was meant to refer to mainstream waters only. Inclusion of the tributaries in the Compact was natural in view of the upper States' strong feeling that the Lower Basin tributaries should be made to share the burden of any obligation to deliver water to Mexico which a future treaty might impose. But when it came to an apportionment among the Lower Basin States, the Gila, by far the most important Lower Basin tributary, would not logically be included, since Arizona alone of the States could effectively use that river. Therefore, with minor exceptions, the proposals and counter proposals over the years, culminating in the Project Act, consistently provided for division of the mainstream only, reserving the tributaries to each State's exclusive use.

The most important negotiations among the States, which in fact formed the basis of the debates leading to passage of the Act, took place in 1927 when the Governors of the seven basin States met at Denver in an effort to work out an allocation of the Lower Basin waters acceptable to Arizona, California, and Nevada....

...

Statements made throughout the debates make it quite clear that Congress intended the 7,500,000 acre-feet it was allocating, and out of which California was limited to 4,400,000, to be mainstream water only....

That the apportionment was from the mainstream only is also strongly indicated by an analysis of the second paragraph of § 4(a) of the Act. There Congress authorized Arizona, Nevada, and California to make a compact allocating to Nevada 300,000 acre-feet and to Arizona 2,800,000 plus one-half of the surplus, which, with California's 4,400,000 and half of the surplus, would under California's interpretation of the Act exhaust the Lower Basin waters, both mainstream and tributaries. But Utah and New Mexico, as Congress knew, had interests in Lower Basin tributaries which Congress surely would have protected in some way had it meant for the tributaries of those two States to be included in the water to be divided among Arizona, Nevada, and California....

Finally, in considering California's claim to share in the tributaries of other States, it is important that from the beginning of the discussions and negotiations which led to the Project Act, Arizona consistently claimed that she must have sole use of the Gila, upon which her existing economy depended....

C. The Project Act's Apportionment and Distribution Scheme.—The legislative history, the language of the Act, and the scheme established by the Act for the storage and delivery of water convince us also that Congress intended to provide its own method for a complete apportionment of the mainstream water among Arizona, California, and Nevada.

First, the legislative history. [The Court explains the frustration with the inability of the states to reach a compromise stating:] In hearings on the House bill that became the Project Act, Congressman Arentz of Nevada, [stated] 'there must be some power which will say to California.... When the bill first reached the Senate floor, it had a provision, added in committee, limiting California to 4,600,000 acre-feet, ... and Senator Hayden on December 6 proposed reducing that share to 4,200,000.... The next day, December 7, Mr. Pittman, senior Senator from Nevada, vigorously argued that Congress should settle the matter without delay. He said,

> 'What is the difficulty? We have only minor questions involved here. There is practically nothing involved except a dispute between the States of Arizona and California with regard to the division of the increased water that will be impounded behind the proposed dam; that is all. * * * Of the 7,500,000 acre-feet of water let down that river they have gotten together within 400,000 acre-feet. They have got to get together, and if they do not get together Congress should bring them together.'...

The day after that, December 8, New Mexico's Senator Bratton suggested an amendment splitting the difference between the demands of Arizona and California by limiting California to 4,400,000 acre-feet.... On the tenth, reflecting the prevailing sense of urgency for decisive action, Senator Bratton emphasized that this was not a dispute limited simply to two States:

> .... I still hold to the belief that somewhere between the two figures we must fix the amount, and that this difference of 400,000 acre-feet should not be allowed to bar and preclude the passage of this important measure dealing with the enormous quantity of 15,000,000 acre-feet of water and involving seven States as well as the Government.'

The very next day, December 11, this crucial amendment was adopted,...

...

Not only do the closing days of the debate show that Congress intended an apportionment among the States but also provisions of the Act create machinery plainly adequate to accomplish this purpose, whatever contingencies might occur.... Congress made sure, however, that if the States did not agree on any compact the objects of the Act would be carried out, for the Secretary would then proceed, by making contracts, to apportion water among the States and to allocate the water among users within each State.

... Having undertaken this beneficial project, Congress, in several provisions of the Act, made it clear that no one should use mainstream waters save in strict compliance with the scheme set up by the Act. Section 5 authorized the Secretary 'under such general regulations as he may prescribe, to contract for the storage of water in said reservoir and for the delivery thereof at such points on the river * * * as may be agreed upon, for irrigation and domestic uses * * *.' To emphasize that water could be obtained from the Secretary alone, § 5 further declared, 'No person shall have or be entitled to have the use for any purpose of the water stored as aforesaid except by contract made as herein stated.' The supremacy given the Secretary's contracts was made clear in § 8(b) of the Act, which provided that, while the Lower Basin States were free to negotiate a compact dividing the waters, such a compact if made and approved after January 1,

1929, was to be 'subject to all contracts, if any, made by the Secretary of the Interior under section 5' before Congress approved the compact.

...

The argument that Congress would not have delegated to the Secretary so much power to apportion and distribute the water overlooks the ways in which his power is limited and channeled by standards in the Project Act. In particular, the Secretary is bound to observe the Act's limitation of 4,400,000 acre-feet on California's consumptive uses out of the first 7,500,000 acre-feet of mainstream water.

...

In undertaking this ambitious and expensive project for the welfare of the people of the Lower Basin States and of the Nation, the United States assumed the responsibility for the construction, operation, and supervision of Boulder Dam and a great complex of other dams and works. Behind the dam were stored virtually all the waters of the main river, thus impounding not only the natural flow but also the great quantities of water previously allowed to run waste or to wreak destruction. The impounding of these waters, along with their regulated and systematic release to those with contracts, has promoted the spectacular development of the Lower Basin. Today, the United States operates a whole network of useful projects up and down the river,.... It was only natural that the United States, which was to make the benefits available and which had accepted the responsibility for the project's operation, would want to make certain that the waters were effectively used....

...

III. APPORTIONMENT AND CONTRACTS IN TIME OF SHORTAGE.

... There remains the question of what shall be done in time of shortage. The Master, while declining to make any findings as to what future supply might be expected, nevertheless decided that the Project Act and the Secretary's contracts require the Secretary in case of shortage to divide the burden among the three States in this proportion: California 4. 4/7.5; Arizona 2. 8/7.5; Nevada . 3/7. 5. While pro rata sharing of water shortages seems equitable on its face, ... more considered judgment may demonstrate quite the contrary. Certainly we should not bind the Secretary to this formula....

It must be remembered that the Secretary's decision may have an effect not only on irrigation uses but also on other important functions for which Congress brought this great project into being—flood control, improvement of navigation, regulation of flow, and generation and distribution of electric power. Requiring the Secretary to prorate shortages would strip him of the very power of choice which we think Congress, for reasons satisfactory to it, vested in him and which we should not impair or take away from him....

None of this is to say that in case of shortage, the Secretary cannot adopt a method of proration...

V. CLAIMS OF THE UNITED STATES

[These reserved water rights for Indian Reservations and federal reservations have been covered in Part III.]

VI. DECREE.

While we have in the main agreed with the Master, there are some places we have disagreed and some questions on which we have not ruled. Rather than adopt the Master's decree with amendments or append our own decree to this opinion, we will allow the parties, or any of them, if they wish, to submit before September 16, 1963, the form of decree to carry this opinion into effect, failing which the Court will prepare and enter an appropriate decree at the next Term of Court.

It is so ordered.

Notes & Questions

1. The Court quotes the attempted Compact for the division of water between the upper and lower basin as 7.5 million acre-feet to each. It then states: "Article III (d) requires the Upper Basin not to deplete the Lee Ferry flow below an aggregate of 75,000,000 acre-feet for any 10 consecutive years." Under this language, who bears the burden of a prolonged drought—the upper or lower basin?
2. Arizona held out for total control of the Gila River and prevailed. What were the consequences for California?
3. The Court rejects the pro-rata share of curtailment during drought, leaving the decision to the Secretary of the Interior. Seeking to avoid a unilateral decision, Secretaries in recent years have facilitated extensive negotiations leading to agreements on drought contingency plans. In 2019, Congress approved the plans. In 2021 the first shortage was declared on the Colorado River, thus requiring implementation of the contingency plan. Shortage was again declared in 2022 and for the first time in history the annual release from Glen Canyon Dam (immediately above Lee's Ferry) was reduced to 7.0 million acre-feet. For more information on the plans, see the Reclamation website: https://www.usbr.gov/dcp/.

Chapter 18

International Water Law

Introduction

International law governs the interaction of "states" (meaning nations). We will use the term "nation-states" to avoid confusion with U.S. states that are subnational governments and not considered actors in international law. You learn about international law in Part IV because the federal government is the level in the United States that engages in international law (although see the reference to UNDRIP below).

This Chapter will focus on international law related to allocation and use of freshwater river basins. Recognizing that many students of water law may not have studied international law, this Chapter will begin with a primer on international law, including domestic law governing federal engagement in international law. The Chapter will then turn to (1) the UN Convention on the Law of the Non-Navigational Uses of International Watercourses,[1] which is not ratified by the United States, but considered to reflect customary (defined below) international law; (2) the Human Right to Water and Sanitation,[2] addressing the collective desire to improve individual rights to *access* to safe drinking water and sanitation, rather than international *obligations*; and (3) the UN Declaration on the Rights of Indigenous Peoples (UNDRIP),[3] to discuss general principles influencing the status of indigenous people in international water law. The Chapter will conclude with a discussion of the Columbia River Treaty (CRT) and the current effort to modernize it as an example of an international water law treaty.

1. United Nations, *Convention on the Law of the Non-navigational Uses of International Watercourses*, G.A. Res. 51/229 (May 21, 1997).

2. United Nations, *The Human Right to Water and Sanitation*, G.A. Res. 64/292 (July 28, 2010).

3. United Nations, *Declaration on the Rights of Indigenous Peoples*, G.A. Res. 61/295 (Sept. 13 2007).

Primer on International Law[4]

International law recognizes the sovereign jurisdiction of a nation-state over its territory and citizens; thus, it is binding only by consent among nations. Unlike domestic law, there is no international legislature with the authority to pass binding law. The United Nations serves as a forum for international diplomacy. Its resolutions and conventions must be adopted by a nation-state to be binding on it. Only two areas have been recognized as exceptions to this limitation: nation-states must not participate in slavery or genocide regardless of failure to consent to any agreement prohibiting such actions.

Sources of international law of importance to shared water courses are custom and treaties. Customary international law is exactly what the name implies, law recognized out of "state practice" (meaning the general tendency of nation-states to abide by the unwritten law), and "opinio juris" (referring to documents and pronouncements that indicate the compliance of a nation-state with a particular practice is out of a sense of legal obligation as opposed to a political or moral obligation). Nation-states may opt out of a customary law through "persistent objection" (through diplomatic statements and writings indicating that the nation-state does not recognize the particular customary practice). Again, the prohibitions on genocide and slavery are considered "preemptory norms," which are practices that a nation-state may not opt out of through persistent objection. The UN Convention on the Law of the Non-Navigational Uses of International Watercourses (discussed below), while developed as a treaty and ratified by 37 nation-states (not including the United States, Mexico, or Canada), is considered to reflect, at least in its means for allocation of benefits, customary international law. It is discussed in this Chapter for the purpose of illustrating customary international law regarding shared watercourses.

The most important sources of law for water courses are treaties. The Vienna Convention of the Law of Treaties (VCLT),[5] while not ratified by the United States, is considered to reflect customary international law governing treaties. Both Canada and Mexico are parties to the treaty. The VCLT defines a "treaty" as:

> ... an international agreement concluded between [nation-] States in written form and governed by international law, whether embodied in a single instrument or in two or more related instruments and whatever its particular designation ...[6]

Thus, a written document concluded between nation-states need not be called a "treaty" to be interpreted as one governed by public international law. Importantly

4. Much of the information in this section, and in particular the discussion of U.S. domestic law in international law, was originally prepared for a white paper for the Munk School of Global Affairs, Program on Water, and for stakeholders in the Columbia River Basin. The white paper is: N. Bankes and B. Cosens, *The Future of the Columbia River Treaty* (June 11, 2012), https://transboundarywaters.science.oregonstate.edu/content/resources.

5. Vienna Convention on the Law of Treaties, Vienna, 23 May 1969 (hereinafter "VCLT").

6. VCLT, Art. 2(1)(a).

terms such as "convention," "protocol," "accord," and "exchange of notes" are common. Amendment, modification, or termination of a treaty may occur at any time by agreement of the parties to a treaty.[7] Treaties may also allow amendment, modification, or termination by less than all the parties by its own terms.[8]

The VCLT is silent on whether indigenous nations may be party to a treaty recognized in international law. The UN Declaration on the Rights of Indigenous Peoples was adopted by a majority of the United Nations General Assembly, with Australia, Canada, New Zealand, and the United States voting against (as well as 11 abstentions). The four countries voting against have since reversed their positions. Article 37 of UNDRIP recognizes indigenous peoples as actors in international law by stating:

> Indigenous peoples have the right to the recognition, observance and enforcement of treaties, agreements and other constructive arrangements concluded with [nation-] States or their successors and to have [nation-] States honour and respect such treaties, agreements and other constructive arrangements.

Because water sources are geographically bound, international water law gives rise to bi- and multi-lateral treaties among those sharing a water course. According to the Transboundary Freshwater Dispute Database at Oregon State University,[9] there are 310 river basins shared across international borders with over 600 transboundary agreements entered since 1820.[10] In the United States, rivers are shared with both Canada and Mexico. The United States has water treaties with Mexico on the Rio Grande/Rio Bravo, Colorado, and Tijuana Rivers, covering issues ranging from water infrastructure to water quantity and quality.[11] The United States has water treaties with Canada on the Great Lakes, the Niagara and St. Lawrence Rivers, the St. Mary and Milk Rivers, and the Columbia River, covering numerous issues including water infrastructure, water quantity and quality, navigation, flood control, fisheries, and hydropower development.[12] The Columbia River Treaty will be covered in more detail below.

International law is not sufficient (referred to as not "self-executing") to require specific actions by citizens without additional domestic action to implement international law. In the United States, Congress generally acts to pass legislation addressing implementation of an international treaty. Similarly, domestic law determines the authority and process for entry into an international agreement.

The U.S. Constitution vests the power to negotiate international agreements with the Executive branch, providing that "[the President] shall have Power, by and with the Advice and Consent of the Senate, to make Treaties, provided two thirds of the Senators

---

7. VCLT Article IV covers amendment and modification; Article V covers termination.

8. *Id.*

9. Oregon State University, *Program in Water Conflict Management and Transformation*, Transboundary Freshwater Dispute Database, https://tinyurl.com/3njkdfk3.

10. *Id.* at *Data and Datasets*, https://tinyurl.com/4fjyhmf5.

11. *Id.* at *International Freshwater Treaties (by River Basin)*, http://gis.nacse.org/tfdd/treaties.php.

12. *Id.*

present concur . . ."[13] The U.S. Supreme Court recognizes this exclusive power to negotiate.[14] The Senate may appoint observers to negotiations.[15] Within the Executive branch, the President generally delegates the task of negotiation to the Department of State.[16] U.S. states or their subdivisions do not have the authority to enter into a treaty,[17] nor is there any requirement for state representation in negotiations. Nevertheless, through the authority of the Executive to appoint the negotiators, state, community, or tribal representatives could be appointed to a negotiating team or invited as observers.[18]

It is important to understand the steps necessary to allow the President to ratify an agreement that has the force of a treaty in international law if you are advising clients with interests on an international waterbody. It turns out that the steps necessary for the President to ratify an international agreement is a gray area in domestic law despite the clear directive of the U.S. Constitution requiring the advice and consent of the Senate. In practice, agreements that have the force and validity of a treaty in international law have been ratified by the Executive (1) with the advice and consent of a two-thirds majority of the Senate; (2) with authorization by Congress; or (3) with unilateral executive action. [19] The term "treaty" is reserved in domestic law for those agreements ratified with the advice and consent of the Senate.[20] Nevertheless, under international law, all three forms of agreement would be referred to as a "treaty" with the force of international law.[21] The U.S. Senate website includes information on the

---

13. U.S. Const. Art. II, § 2. *See also* Congressional Research Service for the Library of Congress. *Treaties and Other International Agreements: The Role of the United States Senate*. A Study Prepared for the Committee on Foreign Relations, United States Senate, 106th Congress, 2d Sess., S. Prt. 106-71 at 16 (2001).

14. *United States v. Curtiss-Wright Export Corp.*, 299 U.S. 304, 319 (1936) ("In this vast external realm, with its important, complicated, delicate and manifold problems, the President alone has the power to speak or listen as a representative of the nation. He makes treaties with the advice and consent of the Senate; but he alone negotiates. Into the field of negotiation the Senate cannot intrude; and Congress itself is powerless to invade it. As Marshall said in his great argument of March 7, 1800, in the House of Representatives, 'The President is the sole organ of the nation in its external relations, and its sole representative with foreign nations.' Annals, 6th Cong., col. 613."); *see also* Congressional Research Service op. cit. note 104 (noting that the initial intent of the framers of the Constitution that the Senate play an advisory role throughout negotiations was quickly abandoned.)

15. Congressional Research Service, *supra* note 13 at 14.

16. U.S. Department of State, *Founding: The Department of State*, 1783, http://future.state.gov/when/timeline/1784_timeline/founding_dos.html.

17. U.S. Const. Art. I, § 10. "No State shall enter into any Treaty . . ." It should be noted that states do have authority to enter compacts with each other with the approval of Congress. U.S. Const., Art. I, § 10. In addition, states may enter informal arrangements such as the MOU between Montana and British Columbia, referred to in an earlier section.

18. United States Department of State, *Circular 175: Procedures on Treaties*, Revised Feb. 25, 1985, at 11 FAM 730.3; Congressional Research Service *supra* note 13 at 98.

19. United States Department of State, op. cit. note 111 at 11FAM 721.2(b).

20. U.S. Const. Art. II, § 2.

21. Vienna Convention on the Law of Treaties, Article 2, Section 1(a), defining "treaty" as "an international agreement concluded between States in written form and governed by international law, whether embodied in a single instrument or in two or more related instruments and whatever its particular designation." *See also* Congressional Research Service *supra* note 13 at 1 and 4.

growing use of means other than ratification on the advice and consent of the Senate to enter into international agreements, stating that "[a]ccording to a 1984 study by the Senate Committee on Foreign Relations, '88.3 percent of international agreements reached between 1946 and 1972 were based at least partly on statutory authority; 6.2 percent were treaties [with the advice and consent of the Senate], and 5.5 percent were based solely on executive authority.'"[22] In 1952 alone, "the United States signed 14 treaties and 291 executive agreements."[23]

The Department of State criteria for determining when the advice and consent of the Senate is required lists eight factors.[24] These factors (in italics) along with their potential application to a water treaty are:

(1) *The degree of commitment or risk for the entire Nation*: Water treaties are generally considered of regional concern. However, with increasing national focus on non-carbon-based electricity (e.g., hydropower), and the role of a particular river system in trade, this factor may be important in the future.

(2) *Whether the agreement is intended to affect state laws*: Because of the regional nature of a water basin and the fact that water allocation is of importance to state law, this is a key factor in the likelihood that a water treaty rises to the level of the advice and consent of Congress.

(3) *Whether the agreement requires enabling legislation*: This will depend on the agreement, but federal funding is often needed for changes in infrastructure.

(4) *Past U.S. practice*: U.S. practice has been to consider water agreements with both Canada and Mexico to be treaties requiring the advice and consent of the Senate.

(5) *The preference of Congress*: State Department rules call for consultation with the Senate when questions exist concerning the appropriate procedure to be followed when entering into an international agreement.[25] Because of the regional importance of a major water source, congressional representatives from the area are likely to seek the process of the advice and consent of the Senate.

(6) *The degree of formality desired*: Similar to the goal of certainty in state and tribal water allocation law, the need for certainty regarding a river on which a regional economy and culture depends tends to argue in favor of a formal, binding agreement.

---

22. United States Senate, *Art & History: Origins & Development: Powers and Procedures: Treaties: Executive Agreements*, https://tinyurl.com/33ac2t7v; *see also* Congressional Research Service op. cit. note 104 at 1 and 22.

23. *Id.* Note that the seeming discrepancy in counting the number of Executive Agreements is caused by the fact that most studies label both Executive Agreements and Congressional-Executive Agreements as Executive Agreements.

24. United States Department of State, op. cit. note 111 at 721.2(b); Congressional Research Service *supra* note 13 at 26.

25. United States Department of State. op. cit. note 111 at 721.4(b).

(7) *The proposed duration and the need for prompt conclusion*: This will depend on the particular agreement, but major water use and allocation treaties are generally expected to last a long time to provide certainty for water infrastructure investment.

(8) *General international practice on similar agreements*: A treaty with the advice and consent of the Senate has been the practice of the United States in its dealings with both Canada and Mexico.

Application of these criteria generally results in an international water agreement being determined to fall into the category of a "treaty" requiring the advice and consent of a two-thirds majority of the Senate. Nevertheless, certain amendments might be subject to unilateral executive action if considered within the scope of the original treaty, and minor agreements could conceivably be accomplished through one of the other means. The two-thirds Senate majority requirement means that no less than 67 Senators must consent for the treaty to be ratified. In addition, Senate informal customary practices allow one senator to place a hold on a bill, blocking it from reaching the Senate floor for a vote.[26] Voting can also be blocked by a filibuster on the Senate floor. Although recently subjected to greater transparency,[27] these practices remain a strong tool for any Basin state opposing a new or modified treaty that comes before Congress. As a result, the Congressional Research Service recommends "legislative-executive consultation prior to or during negotiations."[28]

General International Water Law

This section covers international agreements and customary law that are related to water.

United Nations Convention on the Law of the Non-Navigational Uses of International Watercourses

A global framework for international agreements on shared water courses was developed in 1997 and entered into force on August 17, 2014, 90 days after deposit of the instrument confirming the 35th ratification as required by the framework. The United States is not a party, possibly because treaties had already been entered on its major international water courses shared with Canada or Mexico. Nevertheless, certain aspects of the Convention, including its requirement of equitable and reasonable utilization of water, a duty to notify of impending harm, and a duty not to use the

26. Walter J. Olezek, *"Holds" in the Senate*, Congressional Research Service Report 98-712 (May 19, 2008).

27. *Id.*; Walter J. Olezek, *Senate Policy on "Holds": Action in the 110th Congress*. Congressional Research Service Report RL34255 (March 14, 2008).

28. Congressional Research Service. *supra* note 13 at 16.

watercourse in a way that harms other nation-states are considered to reflect customary international law. As you read the excerpt, consider how equitable and reasonable utilization compares to the U.S. Supreme Court common law of equitable apportionment applicable among U.S. states.

UN Convention on the Law of the Non-Navigational Uses of International Watercourses

The Parties to the present Convention,

...

Having in mind Article 13, paragraph 1 (a), of the Charter of the United Nations, which provides that the General Assembly shall initiate studies and make recommendations for the purpose of encouraging the progressive development of international law and its codification,

...

Have agreed as follows:

PART I. INTRODUCTION

Article 1 Scope of the present Convention

...

Article 2 Use of terms

For the purposes of the present Convention:

1. "Watercourse" means a system of surface waters and groundwaters constituting by virtue of their physical relationship a unitary whole and normally flowing into a common terminus;

...

Article 3 Watercourse agreements

1. In the absence of an agreement to the contrary, nothing in the present Convention shall affect the rights or obligations of a watercourse State arising from agreements in force for it on the date on which it became a party to the present Convention.
2. Notwithstanding the provisions of paragraph 1, parties to agreements referred to in paragraph 1 may, where necessary, consider harmonizing such agreements with the basic principles of the present Convention.
3. Watercourse States may enter into one or more agreements, hereinafter referred to as "watercourse agreements", which apply and adjust the provisions of the present Convention to the characteristics and uses of a particular international watercourse or part thereof.

...

Article 4 Parties to watercourse agreements

...

PART II. GENERAL PRINCIPLES

Article 5 Equitable and reasonable utilization and participation

1. Watercourse States shall in their respective territories utilize an international watercourse in an equitable and reasonable manner. In particular, an international watercourse shall be used and developed by watercourse States with a view to attaining optimal and sustainable utilization thereof and benefits therefrom, taking into account the interests of the watercourse States concerned, consistent with adequate protection of the watercourse.
2. Watercourse States shall participate in the use, development and protection of an international watercourse in an equitable and reasonable manner. Such participation includes both the right to utilize the watercourse and the duty to cooperate in the protection and development thereof, as provided in the present Convention.

Article 6 Factors relevant to equitable and reasonable utilization

1. Utilization of an international watercourse in an equitable and reasonable manner within the meaning of article 5 requires taking into account all relevant factors and circumstances, including:
   a. Geographic, hydrographic, hydrological, climatic, ecological and other factors of a natural character;
   b. The social and economic needs of the watercourse States concerned;
   c. The population dependent on the watercourse in each watercourse State;
   d. The effects of the use or uses of the watercourses in one watercourse State on other watercourse States;
   e. Existing and potential uses of the watercourse;
   f. Conservation, protection, development and economy of use of the water resources of the watercourse and the costs of measures taken to that effect;
   g. The availability of alternatives, of comparable value, to a particular planned or existing use.
2. In the application of article 5 or paragraph 1 of this article, watercourse States concerned shall, when the need arises, enter into consultations in a spirit of cooperation.
3. The weight to be given to each factor is to be determined by its importance in comparison with that of other relevant factors. In determining what is a reasonable and equitable use, all relevant factors are to be considered together and a conclusion reached on the basis of the whole.

Article 7 Obligation not to cause significant harm

1. Watercourse States shall, in utilizing an international watercourse in their territories, take all appropriate measures to prevent the causing of significant harm to other watercourse States.
2. Where significant harm nevertheless is caused to another watercourse State, the States whose use causes such harm shall, in the absence of agreement to such use,

take all appropriate measures, having due regard for the provisions of articles 5 and 6, in consultation with the affected State, to eliminate or mitigate such harm and, where appropriate, to discuss the question of compensation.

Article 8 General obligation to cooperate

...

Article 9 Regular exchange of data and information

...

Article 10 Relationship between different kinds of uses

1. In the absence of agreement or custom to the contrary, no use of an international watercourse enjoys inherent priority over other uses.

...

PART III. PLANNED MEASURES

... [Articles 11–19 address the duty to notify other nation-states on a shared watercourse of planned measures, provide data and information on any anticipated adverse effects, and provide a period for comment.]

PART IV. PROTECTION, PRESERVATION AND MANAGEMENT

Article 20 Protection and preservation of ecosystems

Watercourse States shall, individually and, where appropriate, jointly, protect and preserve the ecosystems of international watercourses.

Article 21 Prevention, reduction and control of pollution

...

Article 22 Introduction of alien or new species

Watercourse States shall take all measures necessary to prevent the introduction of species, alien or new, into an international watercourse which may have effects detrimental to the ecosystem of the watercourse resulting in significant harm to other watercourse States.

Article 23 Protection and preservation of the marine environment

...

Article 24 Management

1. Watercourse States shall, at the request of any of them, enter into consultations concerning the management of an international watercourse, which may include the establishment of a joint management mechanism.

...

Article 25 Regulation

[Covers cooperation on regulation of flow]

Article 26 Installations

[Covers the duty to maintain and ensure the safety of water infrastructure]

PART V. HARMFUL CONDITIONS AND EMERGENCY SITUATIONS

Article 27 Prevention and mitigation of harmful conditions

Watercourse States shall, individually and, where appropriate, jointly, take all appropriate measures to prevent or mitigate conditions related to an international watercourse that may be harmful to other watercourse States, whether resulting from natural causes or human conduct, such as flood or ice conditions, water-borne diseases, siltation, erosion, salt-water intrusion, drought or desertification.

Article 28 Emergency situations

1. For the purposes of this article, "emergency" means a situation that causes, or poses an imminent threat of causing, serious harm to watercourse States or other States and that results suddenly from natural causes, such as floods, the breaking up of ice, landslides or earthquakes, or from human conduct, such as industrial accidents.
2. A watercourse State shall, without delay and by the most expeditious means available, notify other potentially affected States and competent international organizations of any emergency originating within its territory.

...

PART VI. MISCELLANEOUS PROVISIONS

Article 29 International watercourses and installations in time of armed conflict

...

Article 30 Indirect procedures

...

Article 31 Data and information vital to national defense or security

...

Article 32 Non-discrimination

...

Article 33 Settlement of disputes

1. In the event of a dispute between two or more parties concerning the interpretation or application of the present Convention, the parties concerned shall, in the absence of an applicable agreement between them, seek a settlement of the dispute by peaceful means in accordance with the following provisions.
2. If the parties concerned cannot reach agreement by negotiation requested by one of them, they may jointly seek the good offices of, or request mediation or conciliation by, a third party, or make use, as appropriate, of any joint watercourse institutions that may have been established by them or agree to submit the dispute to arbitration or to the International Court of Justice.

... [Additional provisions address measures if the above fails]

PART VII. FINAL CLAUSES

Article 34 Signature

The present Convention shall be open for signature by all States and by regional economic integration organizations from 21 May 1997 until 20 May 2000 at United Nations Headquarters in New York.

Article 35 Ratification, acceptance, approval or accession

1. The present Convention is subject to ratification, acceptance, approval or accession by States and by regional economic integration organizations. The instruments of ratification, acceptance, approval or accession shall be deposited with the Secretary-General of the United Nations.

...

Article 36 Entry into force

1. The present Convention shall enter into force on the ninetieth day following the date of deposit of the thirty-fifth instrument of ratification, acceptance, approval or accession with the Secretary-General of the United Nations.

...

Article 37 Authentic texts

The original of the present Convention, of which the Arabic, Chinese, English, French, Russian and Spanish texts are equally authentic, shall be deposited with the Secretary-General of the United Nations.

IN WITNESS WHEREOF the undersigned Plenipotentiaries, being duly authorized thereto, have signed this Convention.

DONE at New York, this twenty-first day of May one thousand nine hundred and ninety-seven.

Notes & Questions

1. How do the factors that determine equitable and reasonable utilization compare with the factors for equitable apportionment articulated by the U.S. Supreme Court in *Nebraska v. Wyoming*?
2. The customary duty to notify of impending harm comes out of a case in 1949 between the UK and Albania after a series of shipping incidents involving mines placed by Albania in the Corfu Channel.[29] This duty extends beyond watercourses.
3. The customary duty on a nation-state not to allow its territory to be used in a manner that harms another nation-state comes out of a 1938 arbitration agreement between the United States and Canada to resolve the U.S. claim that sulfur dioxide emissions

29. *United Kingdom of Great Britain and Northern Ireland v. the People's Republic of Albania* (Int. Ct. Just. 1949), https://www.icj-cij.org/public/files/case-related/1/001-19490409-ORD-01-00-EN.pdf.

from the Trail Smelter at Trail, British Columbia, were causing extensive harm to livestock and land in the state of Washington.[30]

4. Consider this hypothetical: a cyanide heap leach pond at a private gold mine breaches and cyanide-laden water flows down a river into another nation-state and kills all aquatic life in the river in both countries. What, if any, duty applies to the upstream nation-state?

Human Right to Water and Sanitation

On July 28, 2010, the General Assembly of the United Nations adopted resolution 64/292 on the human right to water and sanitation. A resolution is not a treaty and you will see from the language below that resolution 64/292 expresses the desire to address the problem of access to safe drinking water and sanitation, but does not articulate enforceable measures or standards.

After stating, among other things, "that approximately 884 million people lack access to safe drinking water and that more than 2.6 billion do not have access to basic sanitation, and [the signing nation-states are] alarmed that approximately 1.5 million children under 5 years of age die and 443 million school days are lost each year as a result of water- and sanitation-related diseases," the resolution provides:

> *The General Assembly,*
>
> 1. *Recognizes* the right to safe and clean drinking water and sanitation as a human right that is essential for the full enjoyment of life and all human rights;
>
> 2. *Calls upon* States and international organizations to provide financial resources, capacity-building and technology transfer, through international assistance and cooperation, in particular to developing countries, in order to scale up efforts to provide safe, clean, accessible and affordable drinking water and sanitation for all;...

The UN defines the right as implying the following criteria.[31] The water is:

> *Sufficient.* Meaning each person has access to 50–100 litres/day (13–26 gallons/day). [Note that, according to EPA the average American household uses 300 gallons/day.]
>
> *Safe.* Meaning it meets drinking water quality standards under the guidelines of the World Health Organization.
>
> *Acceptable.* Meaning that sanitation provides culturally appropriate privacy.
>
> *Physically accessible.* Meaning water can be accessed within 1000 meters [.6 miles] of the home and take less than 30 minutes to collect.

30. United Nations, *Trail Smelter Arbitration* (16 April 1938), https://legal.un.org/riaa/cases/vol_III/1905-1982.pdf.

31. United Nations Department of Economic and Social Affairs, *Human Right to Water* (March 30, 2022), https://www.un.org/waterforlifedecade/human_right_to_water.shtml.

> *Affordable.* Meaning cost should not exceed 3% of household income. [Note that U.S. average annual household income in 2020 was $67,521. Three percent of this is $2025.]

While the UN resolution is not binding, nothing prevents a nation-state or even a subnational government from seeking to achieve its goals. In 2012 California adopted AB 685, recognizing that "every human being has the right to safe, clean, affordable, and accessible water adequate for human consumption, cooking, and sanitary purposes." The bill requires state agencies to consider "safety, affordability, and accessibility—that agencies must consider when revising, adopting, or establishing policies, regulations, and grant criteria related to domestic water use."[32] No other state has adopted this approach. The American Society of Civil Engineers (ASCE) 2021 Report Card for America's infrastructure gives drinking water a C+ because the system is aging and underfunded, and wastewater a D+ because wastewater facilities are reaching capacity at the same time they are approaching the end of their lifespans.[33]

Notes & Questions

1. If the human right to water were an enforceable right, what would that look like? Is a nation-state with far fewer resources than the United States obligated to provide its citizens with safe drinking water and sanitation?
2. Look at your water bill (recognizing that most landlords pay the water bill, if you rent, look at one for a family member). See if you can calculate the water use per person in the household per day and the annual cost per day. How does this compare to the criteria for the Human Right to Water?

United Nations Declaration on the Rights of Indigenous Peoples (UNDRIP)

UNDRIP is a declaration, not a treaty, and is considered aspirational by some, and a reflection of customary law by others. In 2007, 143 UN member states voted in favor of UNDRIP. This did not initially include the United States, Canada, Australia, or New Zealand.[34] However, Australia adopted UNDRIP in 2009, and the United States, Canada, and New Zealand in 2010. The press release announcing the support of the Obama Administration for the Declaration states:

> *The United States supports the Declaration, which—while not legally binding or a statement of current international law—has both moral and political force.*[35]

---

32. University of California, Berkeley, School of Law, *The Human Right to Water Bill in California: An Implementation Framework for State Agencies* (May 2013).

33. American Society of Civil Engineers, *Report Card for America's Infrastructure* (March 30, 2022), https://infrastructurereportcard.org/.

34. S. James Anaya, *The Human Rights of Indigenous Peoples: United Nations Developments*, 35 U. Haw. L. Rev. 983, 994 (2013).

35. Announcement of U.S. Support for the United Nations Declaration on the Rights of Indigenous Peoples (2010), https://tinyurl.com/mryn8tve. This language is an example of what a nation-state uses to opt out of something that could be considered customary law.

UNDRIP is not water-specific, but certain of its provisions are important in this context. At the core of UNDRIP is the right of Indigenous peoples to self-determination,[36] set forth in Article 3. While UNDRIP does not define "self-determination," you will read Articles 4, 18, 19, 23, 29, and 32 to gain insight on its embodiment in the declaration in ways that are of particular relevance to water. These articles set forth the rights of Indigenous peoples to self-government, establishment of their own institutions, authority to identify and prioritize development of their resources, participation in decision-making affecting them, and the right to free, prior, informed consent on any matter affecting their lands or resources.

UNDRIP

> *Article 3:* Indigenous peoples have the right to self-determination. By virtue of that right they freely determine their political status and freely pursue their economic, social and cultural development.
>
> *Article 4:* Indigenous peoples, in exercising their right to self-determination, have the right to autonomy or self-government in matters relating to their internal and local affairs, as well as ways and means for financing their autonomous functions.
>
> *Article 18:* Indigenous peoples have the right to participate in decision-making in matters which would affect their rights, through representatives chosen by themselves in accordance with their own procedures, as well as to maintain and develop their own indigenous decision-making institutions.
>
> *Article 19:* States shall consult and cooperate in good faith with the indigenous peoples concerned through their own representative institutions in order to obtain their free, prior and informed consent before adopting and implementing legislative or administrative measures that may affect them.
>
> *Article 23:* Indigenous peoples have the right to determine and develop priorities and strategies for exercising their right to development. In particular, indigenous peoples have the right to be actively involved in developing and determining health, housing and other economic and social programmes affecting them and, as far as possible, to administer such programmes through their own institutions.
>
> *Article 29*
>
> 1. Indigenous peoples have the right to the conservation and protection of the environment and the productive capacity of their lands or territories and resources. States shall establish and implement assistance programmes for indigenous peoples for such conservation and protection, without discrimination.
>
> 2. States shall take effective measures to ensure that no storage or disposal of hazardous materials shall take place in the lands or territories of indigenous peoples without their free, prior and informed consent.

36. Jason Robison et al., *Indigenous Water Justice*, 22 Lewis & Clark L. Rev. 841, 850 (2018).

3. States shall also take effective measures to ensure, as needed, that programmes for monitoring, maintaining and restoring the health of indigenous peoples, as developed and implemented by the peoples affected by such materials, are duly implemented.

Article 32

1. Indigenous peoples have the right to determine and develop priorities and strategies for the development or use of their lands or territories and other resources.

2. States shall consult and cooperate in good faith with the indigenous peoples concerned through their own representative institutions in order to obtain their free and informed consent prior to the approval of any project affecting their lands or territories and other resources, particularly in connection with the development, utilization or exploitation of mineral, water or other resources.

3. States shall provide effective mechanisms for just and fair redress for any such activities, and appropriate measures shall be taken to mitigate adverse environmental, economic, social, cultural or spiritual impact.

Notes & Questions

1. Is the *Winters* Doctrine consistent with self-determination?
2. Is the federal development of the Columbia River consistent with free, prior, informed consent?
3. For an article looking at what consistency with UNDRIP would require in the United States and Australia, see Robison et al., *Indigenous Water Justice*, 22 LEWIS & CLARK L. REV. 841, 850 (2018).

Treaties in International Law

The United States has bilateral water treaties with Mexico and with Canada. This section will use the Columbia River Treaty (CRT) with Canada as an example. At the time of development of this casebook, the United States and Canada are in the process of renegotiation of the CRT. This section concludes with the status of those negotiations.

The Columbia River's mainstem flows 2,000 kilometers (1,243 miles) from its headwaters in the Rocky Mountains of British Columbia, crossing the United States-Canada border before it empties into the Pacific Ocean along the border between Oregon and Washington (Figure 18.1(a)). The Columbia River Basin is roughly the size of France. Seventeen First Nations, 15 Native American Tribes, seven states, one province, and two countries have interests in the river basin (Figure 18.1(b)).[37] The average annual

---

37. RICHARD KYLE PAISLEY ET AL., UNIVERSITIES CONSORTIUM ON COLUMBIA RIVER GOVERNANCE, A SACRED RESPONSIBILITY: GOVERNING THE USE OF WATER AND RELATED RESOURCES IN

(a)

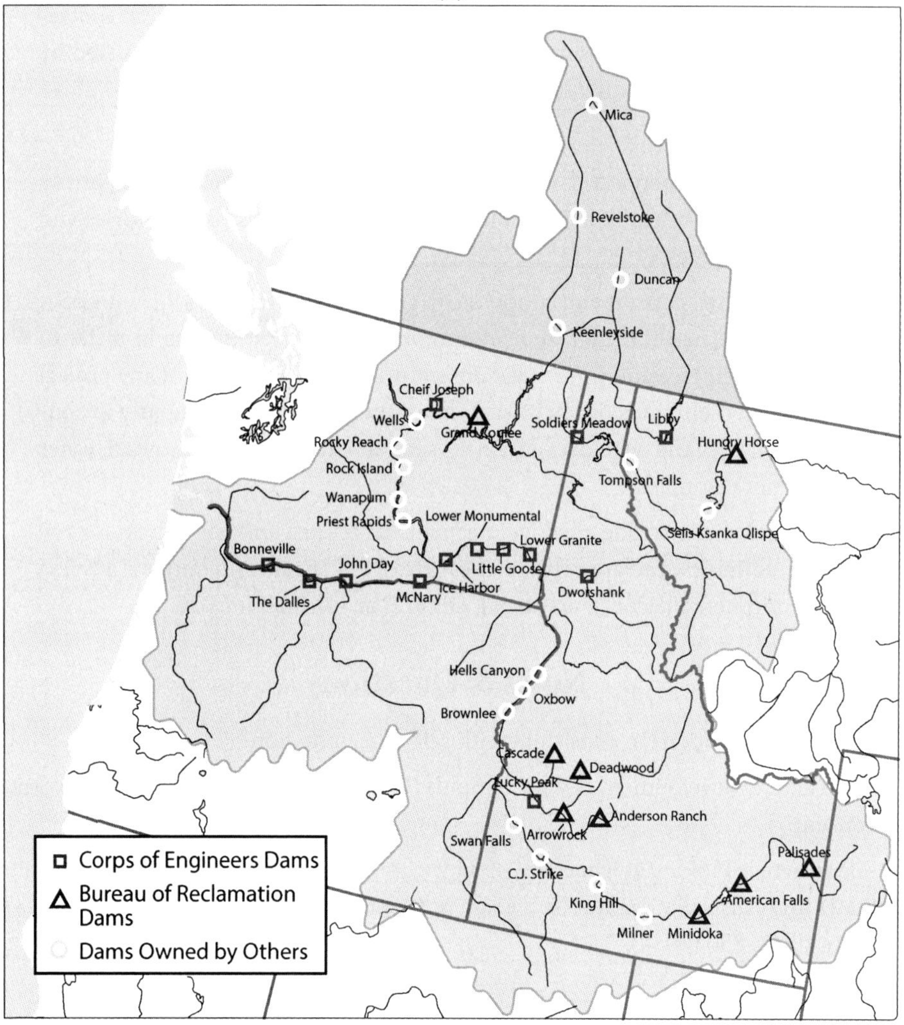

Figure 18.1 (a) The Columbia River Basin showing the major federal and private dams and the international border. Source: (a) USACE.

runoff for the Columbia River Basin is 200 million acre-feet.[38] Although 15% of the Basin lies within Canada,[39] almost 40% of the average annual flow and 50% of the peak flow originates in Canada.[40] However, the yearly flow of the Columbia fluctu-

---

THE INTERNATIONAL COLUMBIA BASIN THROUGH THE PRISM OF TRIBES AND FIRST NATIONS (2015), https://tinyurl.com/2v2w8tt5.

38. U.S. BUREAU OF RECLAMATION, U.S. ARMY CORPS OF ENGINEERS & BONNEVILLE POWER ADMIN., THE COLUMBIA RIVER SYSTEM INSIDE STORY 5 (2001), https://www.bpa.gov/power/pg/columbia_river_inside_story.pdf. The year-to-year variability of unregulated peak flow on the Columbia is 1:34, compared to a mere 1:2 on the Saint Lawrence River or 1:25 on the Mississippi River.

39. James Barton & Kelvin Ketchum, *Columbia River Treaty: Managing for Uncertainty, in* TRANSBOUNDARY RIVER GOVERNANCE IN THE FACE OF UNCERTAINTY: THE COLUMBIA RIVER TREATY 43 (Barbara Cosens ed., 2012).

40. *Id.* at 43.

(b)

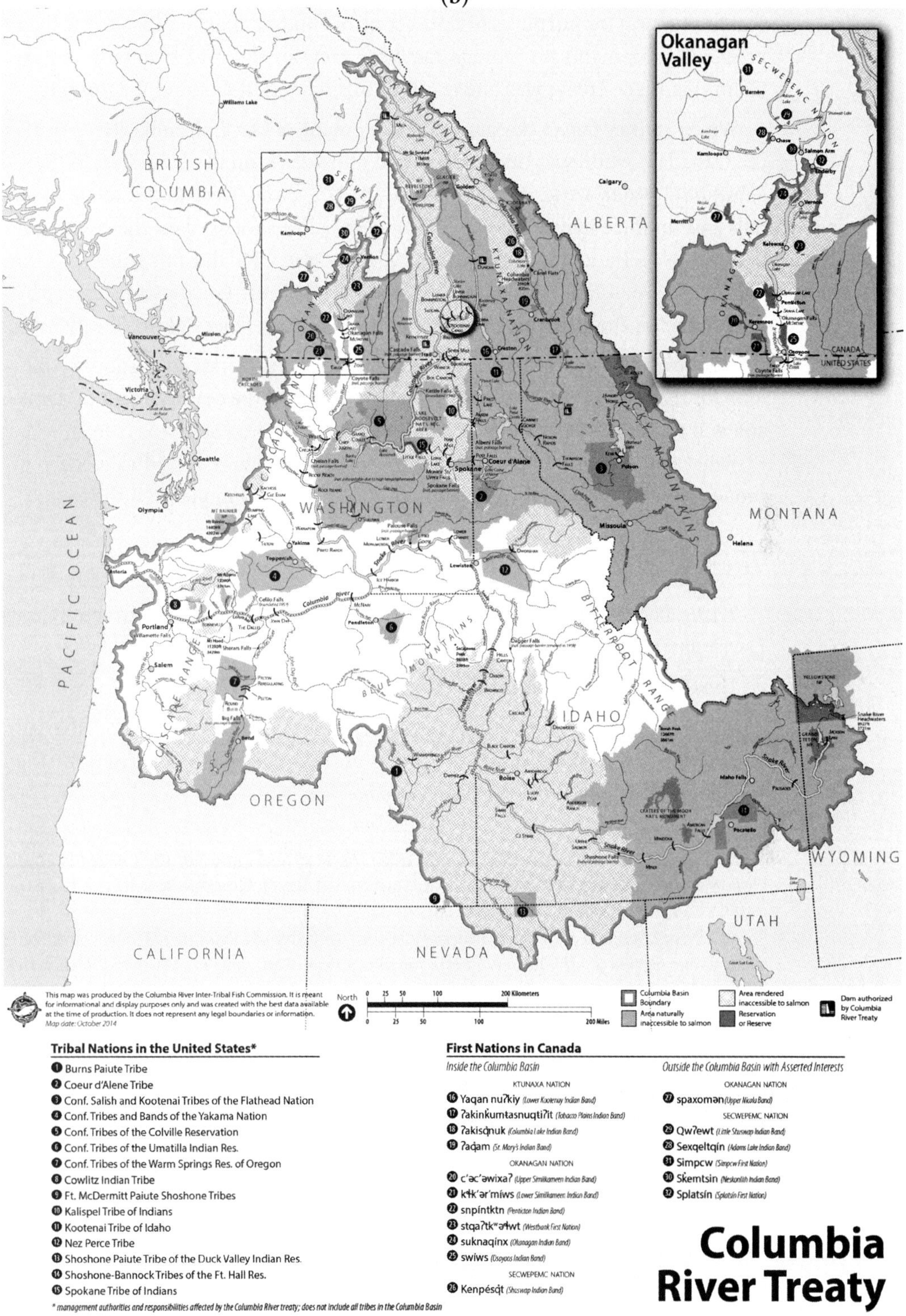

Figure 18.1 (b) Columbia River Basin showing Native American Reservations on the U.S. side and First Nations on the Canada side. Light-gray shaded areas are blocked from salmon migration by dams. Source (b): Columbia River InterTribal Fish Commission.

ates considerably around what might be considered "average" annual flow. To reduce that fluctuation for purposes of flood control and to enhance capacity for hydropower production, demand for storage facilities grew in the mid-twentieth century.[41] The Columbia River Treaty was one result of this increased demand for storage.[42]

When studies began on shared development of the Columbia River in the 1940s, the Canada portion was undammed and most dams on the U.S. portion did not store substantial water. Instead, the purposes of U.S. dams were to aid navigation around falls and produce hydropower.[43] Treaty negotiations focused on the concept of shared benefits. Negotiations concluded in 1961, but the CRT did not enter into force until September 16, 1964, following delays resulting from (successful) efforts by British Columbia (or, the "Province") to be the primary beneficiary of the Treaty in Canada.[44]

Treaties, like statutes, can be difficult to read and understand. To guide your reading, look for the following: (1) what are the two purposes the development of dams in Canada will serve? (2) what is the period of time the United States pays for flood control? (3) what is the "Canadian entitlement" and is it to be delivered as electric power or money? and (4) what is the expertise of those who will implement the treaty?

The Columbia River Treaty

Treaty between Canada and the United States of America relating to Cooperative Development of the Water Resources of The Columbia River Basin

The Governments of Canada and the United States of America

Recognizing that their peoples have, for many generations, lived together and cooperated with one another in many aspects of their national enterprises, for the greater wealth and happiness of their respective nations, and

---

41. *See* Paul W. Hirt & Adam M. Sowards, *The Past and Future of the Columbia River, in* THE COLUMBIA RIVER TREATY REVISITED: TRANSBOUNDARY RIVER GOVERNANCE IN THE FACE OF UNCERTAINTY 115, 121 (Barbara Cosens ed., 2012).

42. *Treaty Between the United States of America and Canada Relating to Cooperative Development of the Water Resources of The Columbia River Basin*, U.S.-Can., Jan. 17, 1961, 15.2 U.S.T. 1555 [hereinafter CRT].

43. John Shurts, *Rethinking the Columbia River Treaty, in* THE COLUMBIA RIVER TREATY REVISITED: TRANSBOUNDARY RIVER GOVERNANCE IN THE FACE OF UNCERTAINTY, *supra* note 14, at 193. Exceptions to this run-of-the-river approach were the Grand Coulee Dam, a federal facility, which was completed on the mainstem in 1942 for irrigation and permanently blocked salmon runs from reaching Canada; and the Hungry Horse Dam, completed on the tributary, the South Fork of the Flathead, in 1953. *Id.*

44. CRT, *supra* note 42; *See also* Hirt & Sowards, *The Past and Future of the Columbia River, in* THE COLUMBIA RIVER TREATY REVISITED: TRANSBOUNDARY RIVER GOVERNANCE IN THE FACE OF UNCERTAINTY, at 115–136; Mouat, *The Columbia Exchange: A Canadian Perspective on the Negotiation of the Columbia River Treaty 1944–1964, in* THE COLUMBIA RIVER TREATY REVISITED: TRANSBOUNDARY RIVER GOVERNANCE IN THE FACE OF UNCERTAINTY, *supra* note 14, at 14–42; John Shurts, *Rethinking the Columbia River Treaty, in* THE COLUMBIA RIVER TREATY REVISITED: TRANSBOUNDARY RIVER GOVERNANCE IN THE FACE OF UNCERTAINTY, at 192–248.

Recognizing that the Columbia River Basin, as a part of the territory of both countries, contains water resources that are capable of contributing greatly to the economic growth and strength and to the general welfare of the two nations, and

Being desirous of achieving the development of those resources in a manner that will make the largest contribution to the economic progress of both countries and to the welfare of their peoples of which those resources are capable, and

Recognizing that the greatest benefit to each country can be secured by cooperative measures for hydroelectric power generation and flood control, which will make possible other benefits as well.

Have agreed as follows:

ARTICLE I

Interpretation

...

ARTICLE II

Development by Canada

1. Canada shall provide in the Columbia River basin in Canada 15,500,000 acre-feet of storage usable for improving the flow of the Columbia River.
2. In order to provide this storage, which in the Treaty is referred to as the Canadian storage, Canada shall construct dams:
   (a) on the Columbia River near Mica Creek, British Columbia, with approximately 7,000,000 acre-feet of storage;
   (b) near the outlet of Arrow Lakes, British Columbia, with approximately 7,100,000 acre-feet of storage; and
   (c) on one or more tributaries of the Kootenay River in British Columbia downstream from the Canada-United States of America boundary with storage equivalent in effect to approximately 1,400,000 acre-feet of storage near Duncan Lake, British Columbia.
3. Canada shall commence construction of the dams as soon as possible after the ratification date.

ARTICLE III

Development by the United States of America Respecting Power

1. The United States of America shall maintain and operate the hydroelectric facilities included in the base system and any additional hydroelectric facilities constructed on the main stem of the Columbia River in the United States of America in a manner that makes the most effective use of the improvement in stream flow resulting from operation of the Canadian storage for hydro-electric power generation in the United States of America power system.

2. The obligation in paragraph (1) is discharged by reflecting in the determination of down-stream power benefits to which Canada is entitled the assumption that the facilities referred to in paragraph (1) were maintained and operated in accordance therewith.

ARTICLE IV

Operation by Canada

1. For the purpose of increasing hydroelectric power generation in Canada and in the United States of America, Canada shall operate the Canadian storage in accordance with Annex A and pursuant to hydroelectric operating plans made thereunder. For the purpose of this obligation an operating plan if it is either the first operating plan or if in the view of either Canada or the United States of America it departs substantially from the immediately preceding operating plan must, in order to be effective, be confirmed by an exchange of notes between Canada and the United States of America.
2. For the purpose of flood control until the expiration of sixty years from the ratification date, Canada shall
   (a) operate in accordance with Annex A and pursuant to flood control operating plans made thereunder
      (i) 80,000 acre-feet of the Canadian storage described in Article II(2)(a),
      (ii) 7,100,000 acre-feet of the Canadian storage described in Article II(2)(b),
      (iii) 1,270,000 acre-feet of the Canadian storage described in Article II(2)(c),

   provided that the Canadian entity may exchange flood control storage under subparagraph (ii) for flood control storage additional to that under subparagraph (I), at the location described in Article II(2)(a), if the entities agree that the exchange would provide the same effectiveness for control of floods on the Columbia River at the Dalles, Oregon;

   (b) operate any additional storage in the Columbia River basin in Canada, when called upon by an entity designated by the United States of America for that purpose, within the limits of existing facilities and as the entity requires to meet flood control needs for the duration of the flood period for which the call is made.
3. For the purpose of flood control after the expiration of sixty years from the ratification date, and for so long as the flows in the Columbia River in Canada continue to contribute to potential flood hazard in the United States of America, Canada shall, when called upon by an entity designated by the United States of America for that purpose, operate within the limits of existing facilities any storage in the Columbia River basin in Canada as the entity requires to meet flood control needs for the duration of the flood control period for which the call is made.

...

ARTICLE V

Entitlement to Downstream Power Benefits

1. Canada is entitled to one half the downstream power benefits determined under Article VII.
2. The United States of America shall deliver to Canada at a point on the Canada-United States of America boundary near Oliver, British Columbia, or such other place as the entities may agree upon, the downstream power benefits to which Canada is entitled, less
   (a) transmission loss,
   (b) the portion of the entitlement disposed of under Article VIII(1), and
   (c) the energy component described in Article VIII(4).
3. The entitlement of Canada to downstream power benefits begins for any portion of Canadian storage upon commencement of its operation in accordance with Annex A and pursuant to a hydroelectric operating plan made thereunder.

ARTICLE VI

Payment for Flood Control

1. For the flood control provided by Canada under Article IV(2)(a) the United States of America shall pay Canada in United States funds:
   (a) 1,200,000 dollars upon the commencement of operation of the storage referred to in subparagraph (a)(i) thereof,
   (b) 52,100,000 dollars upon the commencement of operation of the storage referred to in subparagraph (a)(ii) thereof, and
   (c) 11,100,000 dollars upon the commencement of operation of the storage referred to in subparagraph (a)(iii) thereof.

...

ARTICLE VII

Determination of Downstream Power Benefits

1. The downstream power benefits shall be the difference in the hydroelectric power capable of being generated in the United States of America with and without the use of Canadian storage, determined in advance, and is referred to in the Treaty as the downstream power benefits.

...

2. The downstream power benefits to which Canada is entitled shall be delivered as follows:
   (a) dependable hydroelectric capacity as scheduled by the Canadian entity, and
   (b) average annual usable hydroelectric energy in equal amounts each month, or in accordance with a modification agreed upon under paragraph (4).
3. Modification of the obligation in paragraph (3)(b) may be agreed upon by the entities.

ARTICLE VIII

Disposal of Entitlement to Downstream Power Benefits

...

ARTICLE IX

Variation of Entitlement to Downstream Power Benefits

...

ARTICLE X

East-West Standby Transmission

...

ARTICLE XI

Use of Improved Stream Flow

...

ARTICLE XII

Kootenai River Development

1. The United States of America for a period of five years from the ratification date, has the option to commence construction of a dam on the Kootenai River near Libby, Montana, to provide storage to meet flood control and other purposes in the United States of America. The storage reservoir of the dam shall not raise the level of the Kootenai River at the Canada-United States of America boundary above an elevation consistent with a normal full pool elevation at the dam of 2,459 feet, United States Coast and Geodetic Survey datum, 1929 General Adjustment, 1947 International Supplemental Adjustment.

...

ARTICLE XIII

Diversions

...

ARTICLE XIV

Arrangements for Implementation

1. Canada and the United States of America shall each, as soon as possible after the ratification date, designate entities and when so designated the entities are empowered and charged with the duty to formulate and carry out the operating arrangements necessary to implement the Treaty. Either Canada or the United States of America may designate one or more entities. If more than one is designated the powers and duties conferred upon the entities by the Treaty shall be allocated among them in the designation.
2. In addition to the powers and duties dealt with specifically elsewhere in the Treaty the powers and duties of the entities include:

(a) coordination of plans and exchange of information relating to facilities to be used in producing and obtaining the benefits contemplated by the Treaty,

(b) calculation of and arrangements for delivery of hydroelectric power to which Canada is entitled for providing flood control,

(c) calculation of the amounts payable to the United States of America for standby transmission services,

...

(h) preparation of the hydroelectric operating plans and the flood control operating plans for the Canadian storage together with determination of the downstream power benefits to which Canada is entitled,

...

(j) making appropriate arrangements for delivery to Canada of the downstream power benefits to which Canada is entitled including such matters as load factors for delivery, times and points of delivery, and calculation of transmission loss,

(k) preparation and implementation of detailed operating plans that may produce results more advantageous to both countries than those that would arise from operation under the plans referred to in Annexes A and B.

...

ARTICLE XV

Permanent Engineering Board

1. A permanent Engineering Board is established consisting of four members, two to be appointed by Canada and two by the United States of America. The initial appointments shall be made within three months of the ratification date.
2. The Permanent Engineering Board shall:
   (a) assemble records of the flows of the Columbia River and the Kootenay River at the Canada-United States of America boundary;
   (b) report to Canada and the United States of America whenever there is substantial deviation from the hydroelectric and flood control operating plans and if appropriate include in the report recommendations for remedial action and compensatory adjustments;
   (c) assist in reconciling differences concerning technical or operational matters that may arise between the entities;
   (d) make periodic inspections and require reports as necessary from the entities with a view to ensuring that the objectives of the Treaty are being met;
   (e) make reports to Canada and the United States of America at least once a year of the results being achieved under the Treaty and make special reports concerning any matter which it considers should be brought to their attention;
   (f) investigate and report with respect to any other matter coming within the scope of the Treaty at the request of either Canada or the United States of America.

3. Reports of the Permanent Engineering Board made in the course of the performance of its functions under this Article shall be prima facie evidence of the facts therein contained and shall be accepted unless rebutted by other evidence.
4. The Permanent Engineering Board shall comply with directions, relating to its administration and procedures, agreed upon by Canada and the United States of America as evidenced by an exchange of notes.

ARTICLE XVI

Settlement of Differences

1. Differences arising under the Treaty which Canada and the United States of America cannot resolve may be referred by either to the International Joint Commission for decision.
2. If the International Joint Commission does not render a decision within three months of the referral or within such other period as may be agreed upon by Canada and the United States of America, either may then submit the difference to arbitration by written notice to the other.
3. Arbitration shall be a tribunal composed of a member appointed by Canada, a member appointed by the United States of America and a member appointed jointly by Canada and the United States of America who shall be Chairman. If within six weeks of the delivery of a notice under paragraph (2) either Canada or the United States of America has failed to appoint its member, or they are unable to agree upon the member who is to be Chairman, either Canada or the United States of America may request the President of the International Court of Justice to appoint the member or members. The decision of a majority of the members of an arbitration tribunal shall be the decision of the tribunal.
4. Canada and the United States of America shall accept as definitive and binding and shall carry out any decision of the International Joint Commission or an arbitration tribunal.
5. Provision for the administrative support of a tribunal and for remuneration and expenses of its members shall be as agreed in an exchange of notes between Canada and the United States of America.
6. Canada and the United States of America may agree by an exchange of notes on alternative procedures for settling differences arising under the Treaty, including reference of any difference to the International Court of Justice for decision.

ARTICLE XVII

Restoration of Pre-Treaty Legal Status

...

ARTICLE XVIII

Liability for Damage

...

ARTICLE XIX

Period of Treaty

1. The Treaty shall come into force on the ratification date.
2. Either Canada or the United States of America may terminate the Treaty other than Article XIII (Except paragraph (1) thereof), Article XVII and this Article at any time after the Treaty has been in force for sixty years if it has delivered at least ten years written notice to the other of its intention to terminate the Treaty.
3. If the Treaty is terminated before the end of the useful life of a dam built under Article XII then, notwithstanding termination, Article XII remains in force until the end of the useful life of the dam.
4. If the Treaty is terminated before the end of the useful life of the facilities providing the storage described in Article IV(3) and if the conditions described therein exist then, notwithstanding termination, Articles IV(3) and VI(4) and (5) remain in force until either the end of the useful life of those facilities or until those conditions cease to exist, whichever is the first to occur.

****Registration with the United Nations*

In conformity with Article 102 of the Charter of the United Nations, the Treaty shall be registered by Canada with the Secretariat of the United Nations.

This Treaty has been done in duplicate copies in the English language.

IN WITNESS WHEREOF the undersigned, duly authorized by their respective Governments, have signed this Treaty at Washington, District of Columbia, United States of America, this seventeenth day of January, 1961.

For Canada

John G. Diefenbaker
Prime Minister of Canada

E.D. Fulton
Minister of Justice

A.D.P. Heeney
Ambassador Extraordinary and Plenipotentiary of Canada to the United States of America

For the United States of America

Dwight D. Eisenhower
President of the United States of America

Christian A. Herter
Secretary of State

Elmer F. Bennett
Under Secretary of the Interior

Notes & Questions

1. What are the two purposes the development of dams in Canada will serve?
2. What is the period of time the United States pays for flood control for?
3. What is the "Canadian entitlement" and is it to be delivered as electric power or money?
4. What is the expertise of those who will implement the treaty?
5. Note that British Columbia is the primary operator and beneficiary of the dams in Canada. Unlike U.S. states, provinces control dam building and hydropower licensing as well as water allocation in Canada. The Province of British Columbia held up entry into force of the CRT from 1961 to 1964 while it negotiated for greater control with the federal government of Canada.

Renegotiation of the Columbia River Treaty[45]

On September 16, 2024, the 60 years of a high level of flood control provided by the CRT will expire.[46] The CRT allows unilateral termination of certain portions of the CRT, including the shared benefits from joint hydropower operation, beginning in 2024 by providing notice at least 10 years in advance.[47] The process of review of the Columbia River Treaty began with joint modeling of the river by the U.S. Bonneville Power Administration, the U.S. Army Corps of Engineers, and B.C. Hydro in 2009. Following this effort, formal, separate, review processes were instituted in the United States and in Canada.

While the parties to the CRT could simply agree to extend the flood control provisions with additional payment from the United States, considerable changes have occurred since 1964.[48] These changes include energy markets, climate, the viability of anadromous fish species and their listing under U.S. law, values with respect to both the environment and public expectations of transparency and participation in governance, and the capacity of Native American and First Nations governments to participate and seek to influence major diplomatic efforts regarding the watercourses

---

45. For background on the Columbia River Treaty and the review process, *see* Barbara Cosens, *The Columbia River Treaty: An Opportunity for Modernization of Basin Governance*, 27(1) Colo. Nat. Res., Energy & Envt'l L. Rev. 1 (2016).

46. CRT Article XIX(2). To date, neither party has exercised this option.

47. CRT Article IV(2).

48. In 2009, the University of Idaho College of Law held a conference focused on what had changed since 1964, and an edited volume was published on the topic. *The Columbia River Treaty Revisited: Transboundary River Governance in the Face of Uncertainty, A Project of the Universities Consortium on Columbia River Governance* (Barbara Cosens ed., 2012). The Universities Consortium on Columbia River Governance (UCCRG), made up of representatives of public universities on both sides of the border, was formed at that conference and went on to organize four more annual conferences to inform the public on the review process, UCCRG, https://transboundarywaters.ceoas.oregonstate.edu/universities-consortium-columbia-river-governance.

they live on.[49] As this book goes to press, negotiators from the U.S. Department of State, with representatives of Native American Tribes participating as experts, British Columbia and Canada with First Nations observers, appear to be negotiating a treaty that will include ecosystem function as a treaty purpose. An initial agreement in principle is expected, or an interim agreement on flood risk management, is hoped for by September 2024. The latest press releases include:

> **March 29, 2023**
>
> **Canada and the United States meet for the 16th round of Columbia River Treaty negotiations**
>
> The Province of B.C. issued an update following the 16th round of negotiations to modernize the Columbia River Treaty, which took place March 22 and 23 in Washington, D.C. During this session, conversations between the Canadian and American delegations focused on strengthening co-operation to support aquatic life and biodiversity in the Columbia River Basin, ongoing studies regarding salmon reintroduction, flood-risk management, and the connection between hydropower operations and Canada's desire for greater flexibility in how its treaty dams are operated.
>
> Prime Minister Justin Trudeau and U.S. President Joe Biden jointly released a statement on March 24 expressing that both countries "will intensify their work over the coming months toward agreement on a modernized treaty regime that will support a healthy and prosperous Columbia River Basin." The two leaders stated that the focus will be on "flood-risk management, power generation, and environmental benefits that are shared equitably by both countries and the Indigenous Peoples and Tribal nations, communities, and stakeholders in this watershed."[50]
>
> On February 13, 2024, the U.S. Department of State released remarks from a meeting between Secretary Antony J. Blinken and Canadian Foreign Minister Mélanie Joly, in which the first item raised by Secretary Blinken was the Columbia River Treaty. He stated: "... when it comes to our bilateral issues, we have a shared responsibility to manage the Columbia River, and we've been working on an agreement to modernize the work that we do together, and hope very much that we can bring that to conclusion soon."[51]

---

49. Barbara Cosens, *The Columbia River Treaty: An Opportunity for Modernization of Basin Governance*, 27(1) Colo. Nat. Res., Energy & Envt'l L. Rev. 1 (2016).

50. British Columbia, *Columbia River Treaty News* (March 29, 2023), https://engage.gov.bc.ca/columbiarivertreaty/.

51. Secretary Antony J. Blinken and Canadian Foreign Minister Mélanie Joly before Their Meeting, Remarks of Antony J. Blinken, Secretary of State, February 13, 2024, URL: https://www.state.gov/secretary-antony-j-blinken-and-canadian-foreign-minister-melanie-joly-before-their-meeting-3/.

Part V

The Administrative and Statutory Overlay on the Common Law

The economic growth and population boom that followed World War II resulted in increasing stress on water allocation. This led western leaders to realize the need to manage water more carefully and most states began to establish science-based agencies to oversee the allocation, regulation, and management of water resources.[1] Although some of the need for a record of all water use was catalyzed by the passage of the Reclamation Act (covered in Part IV), under which project identification required that states develop an understanding of existing water rights and a means to allocate between existing uses and those associated with new storage development, the drive for science-based management did not occur until the latter half of the twentieth century. Most states began with establishment of an office of the state engineer during the early Reclamation era, then developed that office into major administrative agencies staffed with hydrologists, hydrogeologists, and agricultural engineers in the second half of the twentieth century (links to agency websites for the four states in the Columbia River Basin that are focused on in this casebook are provided in Table V.1). Some states established the state ownership of water and authority for its regulation in the state constitution (links and language provided in Table V.1). Most western states now have complex statutory schemes and administrative rules for the allocation, distribution, and

1. Colorado is a noted exception to this. While Colorado has an office of the State Engineer that has authority with respect to groundwater development, applications to obtain or alter a water right go to the relevant state district court designated as the water court. This casebook focuses on states with administrative systems because the states that rely on a science-based agency to permit, enforce, and manage water rights include: (1) all of the Pacific Northwest states; and (2) the majority of other western states. For information on the Office of the State Engineer in the Colorado Division of Water Resources, see https://dwr.colorado.gov/. For information on the Colorado Water Courts, see https://www.courts.state.co.us/Courts/Water/Index.cfm.

management of water (links to statutes and administrative rules for the four states in the Columbia River Basin that are focused on in this casebook are provided in Table V.2).

The establishment of agencies moved the allocation, enforcement, and management of water resources under the umbrella of Administrative Law. As a result, any proceeding with the agency (e.g., application for permit or change in use or a request by senior water users for a priority call on junior water users) that is appealed to the judiciary will generally receive deference for its scientific determinations and for interpretation of the law if within the scope of the legislative delegation to the agency.[2] Thus, the use of science-based agencies alters how the law is interpreted and applied both procedurally and substantively. Establishment of administrative water agencies alone would have altered interpretation of water law, but along with the agencies came legislative development of statutes addressing water. Increasingly in the twentieth century, states enacted comprehensive water use acts that would incorporate, alter, and go beyond the common law to address new issues in water management. Thus, understanding the language of a water statute for the modern practice of water law involves a deep understanding of both the common law and administrative law.

Part V focuses on this administrative overlay on the common law resulting from the establishment of agencies and also some of the common substantive changes to the common law due to the development of comprehensive water legislation. Idaho law will be used as the focus to allow a comprehensive overview of a single system. Chapter 19 provides a brief overview of Administrative Law. This should not be a substitute for taking a course specifically on the subject, but will allow you to understand some of the ways in which the establishment of an administrative agency changes the allocation, regulation, and management of water. Chapter 20 addresses the development of permit systems that allow pre-development investigation into the impacts of new uses of water. Chapter 21 looks at administrative means to provide flexibility for both water users and state management, as well as the statutory basis for continuing agency oversight of changes in use. In keeping with the systems approach to water law of this book, and the use of Idaho as an example of an administrative system, Chapter 22 explores some of the specific ways in which the statutory overlay has been used to alter the substance of the common law. Chapter 23 will describe the setting of the largest area of irrigated water use in Idaho, the Eastern Snake Plain. Much of the development of water law in Idaho hinges on the fact that this area has developed both its surface and ground water resources to their limit. Understanding this setting is essential to understand the disputes in the next chapter. Chapter 24 uses the example of conjunctive management of surface and ground water (i.e., management of the two sources as if they are a single connected source), in Idaho's Eastern Snake Plain to explore the role of an administrative agency in water rights enforcement as well as the change in the role of the judiciary when a water dispute begins with an administrative decision.

---

2. The leading cases in federal law on agency deference will be covered in Chapter 19. In federal law, this is currently in a state of flux; state agency decisions will fall under state administrative law, and it remains to be seen if it will follow any changes in federal law.

Table V.1

Excerpts from the relevant state constitutional provisions addressing water and links to the state water agency for each of the four states of focus in the Columbia River Basin.

State	Constitutional Provisions	Agency and Website
Idaho	Idaho Constitution; Adopted 1889; Article XV: Water Rights; Section 1 and 7: https://sos.idaho.gov/elect/stcon/article_XV.html Section 1: USE OF WATERS A PUBLIC USE. The use of all waters now appropriated, or that may hereafter be appropriated ... is hereby declared to be a public use, and subject to the regulations and control of the state in the manner prescribed by law. Section 7: STATE WATER RESOURCE AGENCY. There shall be constituted a Water Resource Agency, composed as the Legislature may now or hereafter prescribe ...	Idaho Department of Water Resources https://idwr.idaho.gov/
Montana	Montana Constitution; the revised constitution was adopted in 1972; Article IX: Environment and Natural Resources; Section 3: Water Rights https://leg.mt.gov/bills/mca/title_0000/article_0090/part_0010/section_0030/0000-0090-0010-0030.html (2) The use of all water that is now or may hereafter be appropriated ... shall be held to be a public use. (3) All surface, underground, flood, and atmospheric waters within the boundaries of the state are the property of the state for the use of its people and are subject to appropriation for beneficial uses as provided by law. (4) The legislature shall provide for the administration, control, and regulation of water rights and shall establish a system of centralized records, in addition to the present system of local records.	Montana Department of Natural Resources and Conservation, Division of Water Resources http://dnrc.mt.gov/divisions/water
Oregon	No constitutional provisions specific to water rights	Oregon Water Resources Department https://www.oregon.gov/owrd/pages/index.aspx
Washington	Washington Constitution; Adopted 1889; Article XXI; Section 1 https://tinyurl.com/Washconst. PUBLIC USE OF WATER. The use of the waters of this state for irrigation, mining and manufacturing purposes shall be deemed a public use.	Washington Department of Ecology, Water and Shorelines, Water Supply https://ecology.wa.gov/Water-Shorelines

Table V.2

The relevant statutes and administrative rules for each of the four states of focus in the Columbia River Basin.

State	Statutes	Administrative Rules
Idaho	Idaho Statutes, Title 42: Irrigation and Drainage—Water Rights and Reclamation https://legislature.idaho.gov/statutesrules/idstat/Title42/	Idaho Administrative Code 37: Department of Water Resources https://adminrules.idaho.gov/rules/current/37/index.html
Montana	Montana Code Annotated, Title 85: Water Use https://www.leg.mt.gov/bills/mca/title_0850/chapters_index.html	ARM (Administrative Rules of Montana) 36: Department of Natural Resources and Conservation https://rules.mt.gov/gateway/Department.asp?DeptNo=36
Oregon	Oregon Revised Statutes, Volume 15: Water Resources, Agriculture and Food, Title 45: Water resources: irrigation, drainage, flood control, reclamation https://www.oregonlegislature.gov/bills_laws/Pages/ORS.aspx	OAR (Oregon Administrative Rules) Chapter 690: Water Resources Department https://secure.sos.state.or.us/oard/displayChapterRules.action?selectedChapter=183
Washington	Revised Code of Washington Title 90: Water Rights—Environment https://apps.leg.wa.gov/rcw/default.aspx?Cite=90	WAC (Washington Administrative Code) Title 508: Department of Ecology, Water Resources https://apps.leg.wa.gov/wac/default.aspx?cite=508

Chapter 19

An Introduction to Administrative Law

Introduction

Administrative Law, enacted at both the federal level (applicable to federal agencies) and state level (applicable to state agencies), governs the decision-making process used by administrative agencies, including the review of agency process and decisions by the judiciary.[1] The term "Administrative Procedure Acts" or "APAs" will be used to refer to both federal and state acts in this Chapter. Legitimacy in a democracy is derived from direct elections of those who govern. While the leadership of an administrative agency is generally appointed by the Executive Branch, under the U.S. Constitution for federal agencies, or state constitution for state agencies, the vast majority of agency employees are civil servants. This creates a potential accountability gap that is thought to increase with the scale of government and as agencies become increasingly removed from those whom their decisions affect. The primary means of providing legitimacy for the decisions of agencies is their basis in expertise and their adherence to administrative law.

Five Means of Providing Legitimacy in Agency Decision-Making through Administrative Law

The following paragraphs, based on a 2006 article by Daniel Esty,[2] briefly describe the five ways in which administrative law promotes legitimacy and relates them specifically to water agency practice, which you will learn about in this Part. The five sources of legitimacy are: (1) systemic: legitimacy based on the existence of checks and balances among the three branches of government; (2) results-based: legitimacy derived from the fact that decisions are based on objective (i.e., scientific in the context of natural resources and environmental decisions) expertise; (3 and 4) order-based and deliberative: legitimacy based on the fact that rules provide for uniform implementation of the law and are clear, stable, and developed with public input; and (5) proce-

1. For an excellent and more thorough introduction to administrative law, see William F. Fox, *Introduction, Chapter 1*, in UNDERSTANDING ADMINISTRATIVE LAW (4th Ed. 2000).

2. D.C. Esty, *Good Governance at the Supranational Scale: Globalizing Administrative Law*, 115 YALE L.J. 1490 (2006).

dural: legitimacy based on decision-making that is open, transparent, and provides information to the public about the basis for the decision.

Systemic Legitimacy

Executive power exercised through agencies is balanced through the system of checks and balances established by the state and federal constitutions. As entities established to implement the law, agencies may not act outside their delegation of authority from Congress or the state legislature. This authority is found both in the agency's "organic act"—i.e., the legislation establishing the agency, and in any additional statutes the agency is delegated the authority to implement. Thus, the language of the statute delegating authority is critical to the validity of an agency action. Chapters 20, 21, 22, and 24 of this Part will engage you in reading and understanding examples of key areas of water legislation found in most western states. Of course, this raises the question of who interprets the delegation of authority. Judicial review is the other area in which the system of checks and balances plays a role. APAs authorize review of a final agency action. The federal scope of review of agency actions is generally similar to that found in state APAs and covers:

> To the extent necessary to decision and when presented, the reviewing court shall decide all relevant questions of law, interpret constitutional and statutory provisions, and determine the meaning or applicability of the terms of an agency action. The reviewing court shall—
>
> 1. compel agency action unlawfully withheld or unreasonably delayed; and
> 2. hold unlawful and set aside agency action, findings, and conclusions found to be
>   a. arbitrary, capricious, an abuse of discretion, or otherwise not in accordance with law;
>   b. contrary to constitutional right, power, privilege, or immunity;
>   c. in excess of statutory jurisdiction, authority, or limitations, or short of statutory right; without observance of procedure required by law;
>   d. unsupported by substantial evidence in a case ... reviewed on the record of an agency hearing provided by statute; or
>   e. unwarranted by the facts to the extent that the facts are subject to trial de novo by the reviewing court.
>
> In making the foregoing determinations, the court shall review the whole record or those parts of it cited by a party, and due account shall be taken of the rule of prejudicial error.[3]

3. 5 U.S.C. §706, Pub. L. 89-554, Sept. 6, 1966, 80 Stat. 393.

In Chapter 24 on conjunctive management, you will have occasion to read challenges to agency action involving 1.a–d., and some of the ways courts handle review of agency action.

Results through Science-Based Legitimacy

By employing science as the basis of decision-making, science-based agencies such as those that administer water rights obtain a degree of legitimacy. You will see this in Chapters 21, 22, and 24 in the delegation of authority to the water agency to make scientific determinations on water availability and impacts of a new water use on existing water rights. But as science in areas of high uncertainty such as climate change is increasingly contested, science plays a more limited role in at least the perception of legitimacy. In fact, in recent years the degree of uncertainty in complex problems has been used to undermine the legitimacy of agency decision making. You will see in Chapter 24 how the agency's use of a collaborative process to engage representatives of water users in developing a complex hydrologic model to predict the impact of groundwater pumping on surface water helped overcome this tendency to use uncertainty to challenge agency science.

Order-Based and Deliberative Legitimacy

To ensure transparency in decision-making, uniform application of the law, and public input to how the law will be implemented, agencies use rulemaking, authorized by administrative law. Administrative rules are promulgated to fill in both the substantive and procedural details on how specific legislation will be implemented. Administrative rules, however, may not go beyond the authorizing legislation. The term "promulgated" in this context means both "to make known or public the terms of (a proposed law)" and "to put (a law or rule) into action or force."[4] Thus, APAs require publication of notice and opportunity for public comment before an agency rule may go into effect. In recent years, federal and some state APAs have added the concept of negotiated rulemaking to facilitate public input to the rulemaking process.[5]

While a rule may be challenged as outside the statutory delegation of authority, or as unconstitutional, it does have the force of law. In fact, a challenge to an agency action may be based on the failure of an agency to follow its own rules. Links to Administrative Rules promulgated by water agencies in Idaho, Montana, Oregon, and Washington can be found in Table V.2 in the Introduction to this Part.

In Chapter 24 you will study the administrative rules promulgated by the Idaho Department of Water Resources to implement conjunctive management of surface and ground water. Faced with the problem of enforcing water rights from these two connected, yet physically different sources for the first time, the agency went to great

4. Merriam-Webster Online Dictionary, *Promulgate* (definition #2) (2023), https://www.merriam-webster.com/dictionary/promulgate.

5. *See* 5 U.S.C. §§ 561–570a.

lengths to provide details on how it would proceed. You will also learn about both the facial constitutional challenge to the rules, and the challenges as the rules are applied to specific circumstances. This provides the opportunity to study the process from rule development to implementation, including judicial challenges at every step.

Finally, it should be noted that federal agency actions that impact the environment (as do most water decisions) require compliance with the National Environmental Policy Act (NEPA). States, with their own so-called mini-NEPAs, may have similar requirements. The federal NEPA requires the agency to develop information on the environmental impact of a particular action, to provide that information to the public, and to take and respond to public comments. The details of NEPA or state NEPAs are beyond the scope of this textbook, but it is important to understand that it goes beyond the procedural requirement of open records (discussed next) and places an affirmative duty on agencies to develop and make public information on environmental impacts of a proposed project.

Procedural Legitimacy

Since the middle of the twentieth century, both state and federal APAs have included sunshine laws. These are laws that serve legitimacy through transparency in decision-making—i.e., shining light on government agency process. They require that agency records be open to the public and that meetings at which decisions are to be made be open to the public and notice of the meeting provided. The ultimate goal is that the public may understand the basis for a decision and the tradeoffs being made. Procedural legitimacy also applies to agencies in their adjudicative role in which an agency may hold a hearing, take evidence, and issue findings of fact and conclusions of law. While similar to a trial court hearing, the rules of evidence may be more relaxed and, rather than relying on a jury, the agency turns to its own expertise to sort through the facts. Nevertheless, the procedural protections of notice, hearing, and a record are all afforded, and the parties may seek review of the final decision in court. In Chapter 24 you will see an agency acting in its adjudicative role when it implements a call for water (i.e., curtailment order) against junior groundwater pumpers. The agency may be asked to hold a hearing on the factual basis for the call and/or the application of the law.

Judicial Deference to Agency Interpretation of the Law

One further area of administrative law relevant to the following Chapters is the degree to which the court should defer to agency interpretation of the law it is charged with implementing. The law governing this question is judicially constructed and goes to the balance of power between the executive and judicial branch when a court reviews an agency decision. This area of law has developed in the federal courts since 1944 and corresponds with the rise of science-based agencies. It has equivalents in state judicial opinions. This is also an area of law currently in a state of flux. As this volume goes to press, the U.S. Supreme Court has overturned 40 years of precedent that had established the basis for agency deference in interpretation of the law the agency is charged with implementing. It remains to be seen how this might alter administrative practice. In addition, state equivalents and modifications to what was federal law on deference currently remain in place. As this area of law evolves, the authors will post updates on the casebook website. The following paragraphs briefly review: (1) the prior federal approach under *Chevron v. NRDC*, 467 U.S. 837 (1984), and *United States v. Mead*, 533 U.S. 218 (2001), generally referred to as "*Chevron* deference"; (2) the recent U.S. Supreme Court ruling in *Loper Bright Enterprises v. Raimondo*, 603 U.S. ___ (Slip Op. June 28, 2024);[6] and conclude with the current State of Idaho's approach under *J.R. Simplot Co., Inc. v. Idaho State Tax Commission,* 820 P.2d 1206 (Idaho 1991).

Chevron *Deference: 1984–2024*

Science-based agencies are generally charged with implementing a vast body of law. When called upon to make factual determinations, whether in areas of natural resource management, enforcement, or rulemaking, courts will generally defer to the expertise of the agency in its scientific interpretations of the facts. The controversy arises when the agency must interpret or fill gaps in the law. As a student, you learn that the seminal case of *Marbury v. Madison*[7] holds that, under the U.S. Constitution, it is the judicial branch that has the final say on what the law is. But what happens when an agency is specifically delegated the authority to implement law that is ambiguous, leaves gaps, and may take a combination of scientific and legal knowledge to interpret? Did Congress intend the agency to do so? Or does the final say remain with the judiciary? In 1944, the U.S. Supreme Court articulated a concept of "respect" for the agency interpretation of the law.[8] This was followed by rulings in 1984[9] and 2001[10] that tailored the degree of deference to the type of procedure the agency was undertaking (e.g., rulemaking or enforcement). The result of this evolution in the law follows.

Prior to the 2024 ruling, a federal court considering the degree of deference to afford an agency interpretation of the law must first inquire into the nature of the agency procedure in which the law was interpreted. In an agency interpretation of a guidance or other document that was not developed through a formal rulemaking or adjudicative proceeding, the court should use its own interpretation of the law while affording the agency opinion "respect," if warranted.[11] In explaining the reasons for deference, the Court in *Skidmore* states: "the Administrator's policies are made in pursuance of

6. Decided together with *Relentless, Inc. v. Department of Commerce,* No. 22-1219.
7. 5 U.S. 137 (1803).
8. Skidmore v. Swift, 323 U.S. 134 (1944)
9. Chevron v. NRDC, 467 U.S. 837 (1984)
10. United States v. Mead, 533 U.S 218 (2001)
11. *Id.*

official duty, based upon more specialized experience and broader investigations and information than is likely to come to a judge in a particular case."[12]

In contrast, if the agency action did involve formal rulemaking or agency adjudication, the analysis from the cases of *Chevron v. NRDC*, 467 U.S. 837 (1984), and *United States v. Mead*, 533 U.S 218 (2001), generally referred to as "*Chevron* deference" applies. This involves three steps with the step later added by *Mead* referred to as "*Chevron* step zero."

> Step 0: "Congress delegated authority to the agency generally to make rules carrying the force of law, and that the agency interpretation claiming deference was promulgated in the exercise of that authority."[13]
>
> Step 1: Is the language of the statute ambiguous? If not, the plain language of the statute applies.
>
> Step 2: If the statute is ambiguous, is the agency interpretation reasonable?

An agency interpretation that failed Step 0 might still qualify for *Skidmore* "respect." Do not be fooled by the relative simplicity of the test once an action passes Step 0. Individual judges differed on whether the determination in Step 1 of whether the meaning of the statutory language is clear may be informed by reading the statute as a whole and considering the overarching intent of the statute or referring to the legislative history. In addition, what is plain language to one person may be ambiguous to another. Thus, the decision by a court to defer to an agency's interpretation of the law, or not, carries with it considerable room for judicial discretion. Nevertheless, where an agency is specifically delegated rule-making authority, must interpret the statute in the exercise of that authority, and must rely on expertise specific to the agency (such as hydrology in the case of a water agency), deference was likely. Finally, in an agency interpretation of its own administrative rule, the Court will defer to the agency interpretation if the agency rule is "genuinely ambiguous" unless the "court concludes that an interpretation does not reflect an agency's authoritative, expertise-based, 'fair[, or] considered judgment.'"[14]

---

12. *Id.* at 139.

13. United States v. Mead, 533 U.S 218, 218 (2001).

14. Kisor v. Wilkie, 139 S. Ct. 2400, 2414 (2019) (quoting *Auer*, 519 U.S. at 462). Since 1997, this has been covered by *Auer v. Robbins*, 519 U.S. 452 (1997), holding that in an agency interpretation of its own administrative rule, the Court will defer to the agency interpretation unless "clearly erroneous." In 2019, the U.S. Supreme Court revisited *Auer* in a case involving a Vietnam War veteran seeking disability benefits. The Court stated: "This Court has often deferred to agencies' reasonable readings of genuinely ambiguous regulations. We call that practice *Auer* deference, ... [citing *Auer*] The only question presented here is whether we should overrule those decisions, discarding the deference they give to agencies. We answer that question no. *Auer* deference retains an important role in construing agency regulations. But even as we uphold it, we reinforce its limits. *Auer* deference is sometimes appropriate and sometimes not. Whether to apply it depends on a range of considerations that we have noted now and again, but compile and further develop today. The deference doctrine we describe is potent in its place, but cabined in its scope." Kisor v. Wilkie, 139 S. Ct. 2400, 2408 (2019).

It is also important to note that there were signals that the Roberts Court might narrow or even eliminate *Chevron* deference long before it occurred. Former Justice Scalia began this process by finding the plain language of many statutes to be clear and lacking any ambiguity (thus failing Step 1 in the *Chevron* test). As law students, for whom language is the primary tool of your future profession, you likely know by now that most language can be interpreted in more than one way, and that most statutes are not a model of clarity. Justice Scalia was a brilliant man, and his resort to plain language was more likely an indication of his desire to narrow *Chevron* deference without overturning precedent, than his failure to grasp the pitfalls of communication. Justices Alito and Thomas signaled a greater willingness to overturn precedent, concerned that *Chevron* deference undermines the authority of the Court to be the final arbiter of the meaning of the law. In *King v. Burwell*,[15] Chief Justice Roberts carved out what could have become a very broad exception stating that *Chevron* "does not provide the appropriate framework ... [when the issue of concern] is a question of deep 'economic and political significance, ... [and the agency] has no expertise in [the area in question]...."[16] This approach, referred to as the "major questions doctrine" was further developed in *West Virginia v. EPA*,[17] in which the Court carved out an exception for "extraordinary cases" in which the Court will "presume that 'Congress intends to make major policy decisions itself, not leave those decisions to agencies.'[18] The Court goes on to state:

> Thus, in certain extraordinary cases, both separation of powers principles and a practical understanding of legislative intent make us "reluctant to read into ambiguous statutory text" the delegation claimed to be lurking there. To convince us otherwise, something more than a merely plausible textual basis for the agency action is necessary. The agency instead must point to "clear congressional authorization" for the power it claims. [citations omitted][19]

15. 576 U.S. 473 (2015).

16. *Id.* at 474. The issue in *King v. Burwell* concerned the availability of tax credits under the Affordable Care Act on Federal Exchanges. Thus, the basis for finding the issue of "deep economic and political significance" does not seem to go to the economic impact on the nation or its relevance to the nation's political foundations, but to the fact that the tax credits were a key reform within politically controversial legislation.

17. 142 S. Ct. 2587 (2022).

18. *Id.* at 2609, quoting the dissent in a denial of rehearing in *United States Telecom Assn. v. FCC*, 855 F.3d 381, 419 (D.C. Cir. 2017).

19. 142 S. Ct at 2609. The major question of policy in *West Virginia v. EPA* was a rule under the Clean Power Plan allowing shifting of energy generation from coal to clean sources as a means of emission reduction, as an alternative to the more traditional specific site emission controls.

Chevron *Overturned: June 28, 2024*

In its 2024 term the Court heard two cases: *Loper Bright Enterprises v. Raimondo* and *Relentless v. Department of Commerce,*[20] which provided it with the opportunity to overturn *Chevron*. It took that opportunity. It is much too early to understand the full implications of this ruling, thus, the following paragraphs will merely summarize the Court's opinion. Both cases involve challenges to an agency rule promulgated under the Magnuson-Stevens Fishery Conservation Act[21] by the National Marine Fisheries Service.

The Court begins by identifying the delegation of adjudicative power to the federal judiciary in Article III of the U.S. Constitution[22] and quotes *Marbury v. Madison* for the concept that "[i]t is emphatically the province and duty of the judicial department to say what the law is."[23] The Court reviews the history of affording "respect" to agency interpretations of the law, but concludes that "'[r]espect,' though, was just that. The views of the Executive Branch could inform the judgment of the Judiciary, but did not supersede it."[24] The Court also reviews changes during the expansion of administrative agencies under The New Deal, with corresponding deference to findings of fact by an agency while retaining judicial authority to interpret the law.[25] In doing so, the Court quotes *Skidmore* (among other cases) for the concept that:

> the "interpretations and opinions" of the relevant agency, "made in pursuance of official duty" and "based upon ... specialized experience," "constitute[d] a body of experience and informed judgment to which courts and litigants [could] properly resort for guidance," even on legal questions. [*Skidmore*], at 139–140. "The weight of such a judgment in a particular case," the Court observed, would "depend upon the thoroughness evident in its consideration, the validity of its reasoning, its consistency with earlier and later pronouncements, and all those factors which give it power to persuade, if lacking power to control." [*Skidmore v. Swift & Co.*, 323 U.S. 134] at 140.

The Court further notes that "[s]uch deferential review, though, was cabined to factbound determinations...." The Court goes on to note that "the Court was far from consistent in reviewing deferentially even such factbound [sic] statutory determinations."[26]

The Court draws the line at deference to interpretation of the law in any context. In doing so, it notes that the Federal Administrative Procedures Act (APA) was passed in 1946 specifically "'as a check upon administrators whose zeal might otherwise have

20. Loper Bright Enterprises v. Raimondo, 603 U.S. ___ (Slip Op. June 28, 2024), decided together with *Relentless, Inc. v. Department of Commerce,* No. 22-1219.

21. 16 U.S.C. §§ 1801 *et seq.*

22. Slip op. at 7.

23. Slip op. at 7 *quoting* 5 U.S. 137 (1803).

24. Slip op. at 9.

25. Slip op. at 9–10.

26. Slip op. at 12.

carried them to excesses not contemplated in legislation creating their offices.'"[27] The Court finds *Chevron* to be in violation of the federal Administrative Procedures Act, quoting from the following language:

> SCOPE OF REVIEW.—To the extent necessary to decision and when presented, *the reviewing court shall decide all relevant questions of law*, interpret constitutional and statutory provisions, and determine the meaning or applicability of the terms of an agency action. [emphasis added][28]

The Court states later in the opinion that:

> *Chevron* defies the command of the APA that "the reviewing court"—not the agency whose action it reviews—is to "decide *all* relevant questions of law" and "interpret ... statutory provisions." §706 (emphasis added). It requires a court to *ignore*, not follow, "the reading the court would have reached" had it exercised its independent judgment as required by the APA. *Chevron*, 467 U.S., at 843, n. 11. And although exercising independent judgment is consistent with the "respect" historically given to Executive Branch interpretations, see, *e.g.*, *Edwards' Lessee*, 12 Wheat., at 210; *Skidmore*, 323 U. S., at 140, *Chevron* insists on much more. It demands that courts mechanically afford *binding* deference to agency interpretations, including those that have been inconsistent over time.[29]

In addition to finding *Chevron* in violation of the APA, the Court also looks to the reasoning behind the ruling finding that implementation of *Chevron* has proven "unworkable" because the concept of ambiguity is ambiguous, and rather than represent an intended delegation of authority by Congress to the agency, is likely "unintentional" due to "the imperfection of the human faculties."[30]

The Court further concludes that:

> *Chevron*'s presumption is misguided because agencies have no special competence in resolving statutory ambiguities. Courts do. The Framers anticipated that courts would often confront statutory ambiguities and expected that courts would resolve them by exercising independent legal judgment.[31]

The Court does note that *Skidmore* remains good law, stating:

> The APA, in short, incorporates the traditional understanding of the judicial function, under which courts must exercise independent judgment in determining the meaning of statutory provisions. In exercising such judgment, though, courts may—as they have from the start—seek aid from the interpre-

---

27. Slip op. at 13 *quoting* United States v. Morton Salt Co., 338 U.S. 632, at 644 (1950).

28. 5 U.S.C. § 706. Note that the Court does not quote the first part of the sentence, stating "to the extent necessary" and goes on to find the sentence clear in its meaning, stating: "The text of the APA means what it says." Slip op. at 15.

29. Slip op. at 21.

30. Slip op. at 22 quoting *The Federalist* No. 37 at 236.

31. Slip op. at 23.

> tations of those responsible for implementing particular statutes. Such interpretations "constitute a body of experience and informed judgment to which courts and litigants may properly resort for guidance" consistent with the APA. *Skidmore*, 323 U. S., at 140. And interpretations issued contemporaneously with the statute at issue, and which have remained consistent over time, may be especially useful in determining the statute's meaning.[32]

State Approach to Deference: Idaho's Simplot *Test*

In Chapter 24, you will learn about the application of state tests for deference in the context of rulemaking, agency use of a hydrologic model, and agency adjudication of enforcement actions. It is quite possible that in the area of state water allocation, the complexity of the science necessary to solve disputes tends to weigh in favor of agency deference and avoids the controversies currently playing out in federal courts. In this highly technical area, even a test of mere "respect" for agency interpretation may result in rulings in favor of the agency. Nevertheless, it is likely that this controversy will find its way to state courts. This section provides a brief example of a state test for deference using Idaho's *Simplot* test as an example.

The Idaho Supreme Court begins by noting that:

> In carrying out this responsibility it is well established that "[i]t is the duty of courts in construing statutes to ascertain the legislative intent and to give effect thereto." … In determining legislative intent, this Court will examine "the reasonableness of the proposed interpretations, and the policy behind the statutes" so that "all sections of applicable statutes [can] be construed together." … However, the courts are not alone in their responsibility to interpret and apply the law. As the need for responsive government has increased, numerous executive agencies have been created to help administer the law. To carry out their responsibility, administrative agencies are generally "clothed with power to construe [the law] as a necessary precedent to administrative action." … As a result, this Court has long followed the rule that the construction given to a statute by the executive and administrative officers of the State is entitled to great weight and will be followed by the courts unless there are cogent reasons for holding otherwise. [citations omitted][33]

The court nevertheless points to its own questioning of this principle stating:

> "While myriad cases state that the construction given a statute by an administrative agency is entitled to great weight, *see Kopp v. State,* 100 Idaho 160, 163, 595 P.2d 309, 312 (1979) (*see* cases cited within); *Public Utilities Commission v. V-1 Oil Co.,* 90 Idaho 415, 420, 412 P.2d 581, 586 (1966) (*see* cases cited within), the proposition is commonly stated with the proviso that the administrative construction will not be followed if there are cogent reasons for hold-

32. Slip op. at 16–17.
33. 820 P.2d at 854.

> ing otherwise. *Id.* In addition, there are two unanimous decisions of this Court which establish the position that whether an administrative construction is correct is ultimately a question for judicial decision."[34]

The Court reviews the narrowing of the rule of agency deference in other western states, including Oregon, Nevada, Alaska, and Utah, as well as its own recent rulings.[35] It then states:

> Because the strength of the traditional rule of judicial deference is uncertain in Idaho as a result of our decision in *Idaho Fair Share,* as it is elsewhere, we deem it necessary to review our case history to determine the motivating rationale of this rule and thereby attempt to determine the continuing validity, if any, and proper application of the rule to the instant case.[36]

The court then reviews its prior basis for deference to agencies, finding that it is of particular importance when: (1) "the rule ensures repose when important interests have "grown up" in reliance on an interpretation in existence for a number of years";[37] (2) "an agency interpretation represents a 'practical' interpretation," defined to mean that the statute is "general and therefore cannot address all of the details necessary for its effective implementation";[38] (3) "the legislature is charged with knowledge of how its statutes are interpreted. By not altering the statutory text [following agency interpretation] the legislature is presumed to have sanctioned the agency interpretation";[39] (4) "an agency construction is entitled to additional weight when it is formulated *contemporaneously* with the passage of the statute in question,"[40] with the assumption being that the agency may have been involved in the enactment of the statute; and (5) "when an agency, 'as a coordinate branch of government,' construes a statute under its administrative area of responsibility courts should recognize and defer to the expertise developed by the agency.... Because the judiciary in Idaho is intended to apply a general background to the law, the expertise of an agency is often useful in technical areas of the law where the risk of failing to understand all of the implications of a decision are great."[41]

The court then reviews its own weakening of the rule of deference, while noting that in parallel, the U.S. Supreme Court had strengthened deference with its ruling in *Chevron.*[42] It then states:

---

34. *Id. quoting* Idaho Fair Share v. Public Utils. Comm'n, 113 Idaho 959, 751 P.2d 107 (1988).

35. 820 P.2d at 855–866.

36. 820 P.2d at 856. The case referred to *Idaho Fair Share v. Public Utils. Comm'n*, 751 P.2d 107 (Idaho 1988), introduced a concept of "free review" in which it entirely "ignore[d] the statutory construction of the [Public Utilities] Commission."

37. 820 P.2d at 858.

38. *Id.*

39. 820 P.2d at 859.

40. *Id.* (emphasis in original).

41. *Id.*

42. 820 P.2d at 861–862.

> After reviewing our extensive case history, as well as the holdings of the U.S. Supreme Court and various other state courts, we hold that the rule of deference to agency statutory constructions retains continuing validity. We hold that a standard of "free review" is not applicable to agency determinations. Accordingly, we hereby clarify and limit *Idaho Fair Share* to the extent that case implied that the standard of free review was appropriate for reviewing an agency's statutory interpretations.
>
> In determining the appropriate level of deference to be given to an agency construction of a statute, we are of the opinion that a court must follow a four-prong test. The court must first determine if the agency has been entrusted with the responsibility to administer the statute at issue. Only if the agency has received this authority will it be "impliedly clothed with power to construe" the law.[43]

The four prongs of the *Simplot* test articulated in *J.R. Simplot Co., Inc. v. Idaho State Tax Commission,* 820 P.2d 1206 (Idaho 1991), are:

> 1. "The court must first determine if the agency has been entrusted with the responsibility to administer the statute at issue. Only if the agency has received this authority will it be "impliedly clothed with power to construe" the law."[44]
>
> 2. "[T]he agency's statutory construction must be reasonable … deference would not be appropriate when an agency interpretation 'is so obscure and doubtful that it is entitled to no weight or consideration.'"[45]
>
> 3. "[A] court must determine that the statutory language at issue does not expressly treat the precise question at issue. An agency construction will not be followed if it contradicts the clear expressions of the legislature because 'the court, as well as the agency, must give effect to the unambiguously expressed intent of Congress.'"[46]
>
> 4. "If an agency, with authority to administer a statutory area of the law, has made a reasonable construction of a statute on a question without a precise statutory answer then, under the fourth prong of the test, a court must ask whether any of the rationales underlying the rule of deference are present. If the underlying rationales are absent then their absence may present "cogent reasons" justifying the court in adopting a statutory construction which differs from that of the agency."[47]

---

43. 820 P.2d at 862 (citations omitted).
44. *Id.*
45. *Id.* (citation omitted).
46. *Id.* citing *Chevron.*
47. 820 P.2d 862.

Chapter 20

State Permit Systems

Introduction

By the turn of the twentieth century, water supplies in some parts of the West were developed to the point that administration was necessary, particularly during the high-use irrigation season. Under the common law, water rights could be developed simply by the act of diversion and application to a beneficial use. Although this provides visual notice to anyone wanting to draw water from the same source, it provides no record of rights from a source or how those rights interact under conditions of variable supply. Accordingly, any effort to distribute water in a time of shortage had to begin with a determination of the relative rights of the water uses in question. The resulting lawsuits would take months or even years to complete, providing no relief during the period of water shortage. This was a highly inefficient means of managing water when the need for priority distribution became increasingly commonplace. This Chapter will use Idaho as an example of how states responded to this need. This requires an introduction to a bit of Idaho water law history.

Idaho began by addressing the need for notice and recording. An act passed in 1899 (Sess. Laws, 1899, p. 380, § 5) provided the option to post notice of intent to appropriate in the vicinity of the diversion point and record with the county. You learned in Part II that this provided a means for a developer of large water infrastructure to lock in a priority date of the date of posting provided the claim was perfected into a right by application to beneficial use.[1] You also learned that this method did not eliminate the ability to perfect a water right through the act of diversion and application to a beneficial use.

In 1903, the Idaho legislature attempted to create a centralized recording of water rights obtained exclusively through a permit application to the Office of the State Engineer, stating: "'all rights to divert and use the waters of this state for beneficial purposes shall hereafter be acquired and confirmed under the provisions of this chapter.' (§ 3252)."[2] In a dispute between a water user who sought a permit under the 1903 system and a water user who sought to obtain a water right by diversion and application to a beneficial use, the Idaho Supreme Court held in *Nielson v. Parker* that the legislature merely intended to centralize the process of posting and recording from the county to

1. Sand Point Water & Light Co. v. Panhandle Development Co., 83 P. 347 (Idaho 1905).
2. Nielson v. Parker, 115 P. 488 (Idaho 1911).

the state and, despite the language "all rights ... shall hereafter be acquired and confirmed under the provisions of this chapter," had no intent to eliminate the common law process of diversion and application to a beneficial use.[3] While this ruling based on legislative intent could have been cleared up by an act of the legislature clarifying its intent, the court had also stated that in considering this dispute "we should not lose sight of the provisions of § 3, art. 15 of the constitution, which prescribes that 'The right to divert and appropriate the unappropriated waters of any natural stream to beneficial uses, shall never be denied. Priority of appropriation shall give the better right as between those using the water'. . . ."[4] This led to the interpretation that the Idaho Constitution prevents establishment of a permit system as the exclusive means to obtain a water right and would be followed by a half century of continued acquisition of water rights in Idaho through diversion and application to a beneficial use. With scholars questioning this interpretation, the Legislature decided to test the issue and in 1963 passed an exclusive permit system for acquisition of a water right to groundwater.[5] In 1968, the Idaho Supreme Court upheld the exclusive groundwater permit system,[6] and in 1971 the Legislature adopted an exclusive permit system for surface water.[7] This Chapter will use the Idaho system for acquisition of a water right to discuss the criteria that provide for certain inquiries prior to issuance of a permit, the process for obtaining a permit, and the exemptions from the permit process.

Obtaining a Permit: Criteria

Administrative permit systems not only allow tracking of water rights, but also generally provide substantive requirements, including a process that allows determination of water availability and the adequacy of the applicant's plan prior to any development of water. This section will cover the substantive permit criteria process using Idaho as an example.

The criteria that must be met for the Idaho Department of Water Resources to issue a permit are found in Title 42, Section 203A(5) of the Idaho Statutes, stating:

> The director of the department of water resources shall find and determine from the evidence presented to what use or uses the water sought to be appropriated can be and are intended to be applied. In all applications whether protested or not protested, where the proposed use is such:
>
> (a) that it will reduce the quantity of water under existing water rights, or
>
> (b) that the water supply itself is insufficient for the purpose for which it is sought to be appropriated, or

3. *Id.*
4. *Id.*
5. Idaho Code § 42-229.
6. *State ex rel. Tappan v. Smith*, 444 P.2d 412 (Idaho 1968).
7. Idaho Code § 42-201.

> (c) where it appears to the satisfaction of the director that such application is not made in good faith, is made for delay or speculative purposes, or
>
> (d) that the applicant has not sufficient financial resources with which to complete the work involved therein, or
>
> (e) that it will conflict with the local public interest as defined in section 42-202B,[8] Idaho Code, [note that the definition in 42-203B was added in 1996, after the case of *Hardy v. Higginson* below] or
>
> (f) that it is contrary to conservation of water resources within the state of Idaho, or
>
> (g) that it will adversely affect the local economy of the watershed or local area within which the source of water for the proposed use originates, in the case where the place of use is outside of the watershed or local area where the source of water originates;
>
> the director of the department of water resources may reject such application and refuse issuance of a permit therefor, or may partially approve and grant a permit for a smaller quantity of water than applied for, or may grant a permit upon conditions.[9]

The following subsections address the criteria in greater detail. Criteria (a) and (b) will be addressed under the heading "water availability"; criteria (c) and (d) as "preventing speculation"; criterion (e) as "the public interest"; criterion (f) as "conservation of state resources"; and criterion (g) as "adverse effect on the local economy: area of origin protections."

Water Availability

Criteria (a) and (b) require inquiry into the availability of water in the source to ensure no injury to existing water rights. This requires review of both the demand on the source and the hydrology. Criterion (a), or the no-injury rule, also looks at aspects of the application beyond water supply, including the manner of diversion and conveyance, to determine if the proposed method of diversion might injure another water right.

Criterion (b) requires the agency to determine whether the water supply can meet demand. This determination is not a simple process of adding up the existing water rights and subtracting that from the average supply. This mistake is often made in commentaries noting that a water supply is over appropriated because there is, on average, less water in the system than the water rights on paper. The nuances of water supply and demand make this a more complex inquiry. First, a water right expresses

---

8. Idaho Code § 42-202B(3) provides: "Local public interest'" is defined as the interests that the people in the area directly affected by a proposed water use have in the effects of such use on the public water resource."

9. Idaho Code § 42-203A(5).

the maximum rate that can be diverted, but water is rarely used 24/7. Variation in timing of use may allow additional rights on a "fully appropriated" water source. Second, it can be said that it is rare indeed for a surface water source in the western United States to flow at its calculated average. Not only is there high seasonal variation, particularly in snow-fed watersheds, but even without climate change there was high year-to-year variability. If a junior water user can still develop an economic enterprise without use of water every year, or with use outside the irrigation season, the appropriation may be viable despite the appearance of "over appropriation." With climate change increasing the energy in the atmosphere, the range of variability is becoming greater (i.e., higher highs and lower lows). This may challenge current approaches to determining water availability prospectively.

To interpret a statute implemented by an administrative agency and to understand how the agency will apply it, the first place to look is the agency administrative rules. Administrative rules provide details on how the agency will implement the statute. By providing more complete information on both process and substance, administrative rules increase the likelihood that a legal requirement will be applied in a uniform manner and, if not followed, provide the astute attorney with a clear basis for a challenge. For Idaho, these can be found in the Idaho Administrative Procedure Act 37—the rules applicable to the Department of Water Resources.

IDAPA 37.03.08 covers water appropriations and provides the following for the implementation of the requirement of water availability:

> 045. EVALUATION CRITERIA. . . . The Director will use the following criteria in evaluating whether an application to appropriate unappropriated water . . . should be approved, denied, approved for a smaller amount of water or approved with conditions.
>
> a. . . . A proposed use will be determined to reduce the quantity of water under an existing water right (i.e., injure another water right) if:
>
>> i. The amount of water available . . . will be reduced below the amount recorded by permit, license, decree or valid claim or the historical amount beneficially used by the water right holder under such recorded rights, whichever is less.
>>
>> ii. The holder of an existing water right will be forced to an unreasonable effort or expense to divert his existing water right. Protection of existing groundwater rights are subject to reasonable pumping level provisions of Section 42-226, Idaho Code;
>>
>> iii. The quality of the water available to the holder of an existing water right is made unusable for the purposes of the existing user's right, and the water cannot be restored to usable quality without unreasonable effort or expense.
>>
>> iv. An application that would otherwise be denied because of injury to another water right may be approved upon conditions which will mitigate

> losses of water to the holder of an existing water right, as determined by the Director.
>
> ....
>
> b. ...water supply will be determined to be insufficient for the proposed use if water is not available for an adequate time interval in quantities sufficient to make the project economically feasible (direct benefits to applicant must exceed direct costs to applicant), unless there are noneconomic factors that justify application approval. In assessing such noneconomic factors, the Director will also consider the impact on other water rights if the project is abandoned during construction or after completion, the impact on public resource values, and the cost to local, state and federal governments of such an abandonment.[10]

In making the determination of water availability, the administrative rules on burden of proof are critical. Go back and look at Idaho Code § 42-203A(5) as you review the rule below.

> 04. Burden of Proof. a. Burden of proof is divided into two (2) parts: first, the burden of coming forward with evidence to present a prima facie case, and second, the ultimate burden of persuasion.
>
> b. The burden of coming forward with evidence is divided between the applicant and the protestant as follows:
>
> > i. The applicant shall bear the initial burden of coming forward with evidence for the evaluation of criteria (a) through (d) of Section 42-203A(5), Idaho Code;
> >
> > ii. The applicant shall bear the initial burden of coming forward with evidence for the evaluation of [the public interest] criterion ... of Section 42-203A(5)[(e)], Idaho Code,.... The protestant shall bear the initial burden of coming forward with evidence for those factors relevant to criterion (e) of Section 42-203A(5), Idaho Code, of which the protestant can reasonably be expected to be more cognizant than the applicant.
>
> ...
>
> c. The applicant has the ultimate burden of persuasion for the criteria of Section 42-203A, Idaho Code....
>
> d. For unprotested applications or permits to be reprocessed, the Director will evaluate the application, information submitted ... and information in the files and records of the department, and the results of any studies the department may conduct to determine compliance with the appropriate criteria.
>
> e. In protested matters the Director will ... circulate to the parties information from department studies and field examinations....[11]

---

10. IDAPA 37.03.08.45 (updated 3-18-2022).
11. IDAPA 37-03-08-04 (updated 3-18-2022).

It is also common for the state's water resource agency to place a moratorium or closure on new permits for all or a portion of a source based on a comprehensive study. This avoids denial of permits on an ad hoc, case-by-case basis. When you study the conjunctive management of surface and ground water in Chapter 24, you will learn about the context in which the Idaho Department of Water Resources (IDWR) placed a moratorium on new permits for groundwater wells in Idaho's Eastern Snake Plain.[12]

Notes & Questions

1. What is the difference between the "initial burden of coming forward with evidence for the evaluation of criteria" and the "ultimate burden of persuasion?"
2. Note two very interesting provisions of the administrative rules to implement the no-injury rule. First, the proposed diversion may not alter the water quality such that an existing use can no longer be used for its purpose. Second, the applicant may mitigate injury (whether to water quality, timing of flow, amount of flow, etc.) and it is up to the IDWR Director, not the person found injured, to determine if the mitigation is adequate. Neither of these inquiries would have been available at common law. The remedy for the first might have been through a common law nuisance suit. The second would only have been possible through a settlement between the applicant and the party who would be injured. If that party simply wanted to block the new water right, they could hold out. Discuss these provisions and the ways in which implementation by a scientific agency alters water management.

Preventing Speculation

One of the long-standing tenets of state ownership of water is that water is to be used to maximize the benefits to the public. As a result, states seek to prevent speculation or other reasons for delaying development of a water right once a permit is approved. Except in cases where the applicant does not have sufficient funding to develop the water, it is difficult to tell if the water right is being sought for speculative purposes at the time of application review. The next case, *Washington State Sugar Co. v. Goodrich,* illustrates the use of interim and final deadlines to ensure that the applicant is not sitting on the right. The case also explains at what point between application and final development of a water use that a property right to the continued use of the water

12. Amended Moratorium Order, *In the Matter of Applications for Permits for the Diversion and Use of Surface and Ground Water within the Eastern Snake River Plain Area and the Boise River Drainage*, April 30, 1993; Moratorium Order, *In the Matter of Applications for Permits for Diversion and Use of Surface and Ground Water within the Snake River Basin Upstream from Milner Dam*, January 6, 1993; Amended Moratorium Order, *In the Matter of Applications for Permits for the Diversion and Use of Surface and Ground Water within the Boise River Drainage Area*, May 3, 1995; Amended Snake River Basin Moratorium Order, *In the Matter of Applications for Permits for the Diversion and Use of Surface and Groundwater within the Snake River Basin* (October 21, 2022), Amended Snake River Basin Moratorium Order, SRB Moratorium, October 21, 2022 (idaho.gov).

arises. This is important because no issue of regulatory Taking exists prior to the point when the claim becomes a use right.

The following timeline of claims to water from Lewellyn Creek in Kootenai County, Idaho, will help you understand the sequence of events in the case. The area in question is the agricultural area of the Rathdrum Prairie in northern Idaho. It is also helpful to know that in the period following the Civil War, sugar cane was in short supply and efforts to use sugar beets increased. In 1899, the beet sugar factory built by the Washington State Sugar Company in Waverly, Washington (near the Idaho state line), opened. But the supply of sugar beets decreased due to a combination of blight, change to production of higher value crops, and an end to sugar beet subsidy in 1903 by the state of Washington.[13] The following sequence of events may reflect the desire of the sugar company to go into its own production of sugar beets.

Timeline:

- 1891: Goodrich and Hall settled on Lewellyn Creek. Goodrich constructed a ditch for domestic water use. Method: diversion and application to a beneficial use.
- No later than 1894: Hall enlarged and extended the ditch from Goodrich to his place and both Hall and Goodrich began using water for irrigation. Method: posting and filing with the county.
- Nov. 11, 1899: Roush claimed 100 cfs to run a sawmill. Note that a sawmill would have been an instream use with minor changes in the timing of flow if storage were needed to create sufficient head. Method: notice and posting. While not clear in the case, it is this right that is primarily at issue when Washington State Sugar Co. acquires it and seeks approval of a change in use to move the point of diversion and place of use out of the stream.

Recall that in 1903 the legislature established a permit system through the Office of the State Engineer (now IDWR) and that in 1911 the Idaho Supreme Court, in *Nielson v. Parker*, found it to supersede the posting and filing with the county but not to create an exclusive permit system. A water right could still be created by diversion and application to a beneficial use.

- June 4, 1906: McBee claimed 25 cfs. Method: permit application to State Engineer.
- May 17, 1907: McBee assigns his interests to water from Lewellyn Creek to Biggs.
- July 15, 1907: Biggs claimed 9.6 cfs. Method: permit application to State Engineer

13. Karen Trebitz, *Irrigation History in the Rathdrum Prairie and Spokane Valley: Thirty Years of Developing Water Delivery and Fifty Years of System Rehabilitations* (2015), https://idwr.idaho.gov/wp-content/uploads/sites/2/projects/spokane-valley-rathdrum-prairie/trebitz-irrigation-history-in-the-rathdrum-prairie-and-spokane-valley.pdf.

- September 14, 1908, Biggs transfers his permits, including that acquired from McBee, to Washington State Sugar Co. Method: recorded in the Office of the State Engineer.
- September 23, 1908: Roush transfers his interests in Lewellyn Creek to Washington State Sugar Co. via written conveyance.
- October 1908: Washington State Sugar Co. began work on the Corbin ditch and flume with intake located above the Hall-Goodrich ditch. Completed in 1910 or 1911, conveying water about five miles to the watershed of Sage Creek.

Washington State Sugar Co. v. Goodrich

Supreme Court of Idaho
27 Idaho 26 (1915)

[Petition for Rehearing, denied after minor modifications to the decree.]

Opinion

BUDGE, J.—... [Washington State Sugar Co.] bases its right to the use of waters of Lewellyn creek upon permits Nos. 2158 and 2978, also upon J. C. Roush's appropriation. Permit No. 2978, application of Beggs for 9.6 cubic feet per second of time of the waters of Lewellyn creek, contains necessary information required under the statutes, describing the lands to be irrigated, the quantity of water claimed, estimated cost of work, description of works for diversion, time required for the completion of the construction of the work and the approval of the state engineer, which permit, when approved, was subject to the following limitations and conditions, to wit:

> "Work to begin on or before October 9, 1907, and to continue diligently and uninterruptedly to completion. * * * One-fifth of the work above specified to be completed on or before February 10, 1909. The whole of said work to be completed on or before August 10, 1910. The time for proof of beneficial use of water appropriated in accordance herewith, to extend to August 10, 1913."

Permit No. 2158, which is McBee's application to appropriate 25 cubic feet per second of time of the waters of Lewellyn creek, contains the same conditions and limitations set out in permit No. 2978, and has indorsed thereon the approval of the state engineer on the 28th day of July, 1906, and provides that one-fifth of the work specified in the permit shall be completed on or before January 28, 1909; the whole of said work to be completed on or before July 28, 1911. The time for making proof of beneficial use of the water attempted to be appropriated was extended to July 28, 1915.

...

[Idaho law] provides:

> "Every holder of a permit which shall be issued under the terms and conditions of an application filed hereafter, appropriating 25 cubic feet or less per second, must, within 60 days from the date upon which said permit issues from the office of the state engineer, commence the excavation or construction

> of the works by which he intends to divert the water, and must prosecute the work diligently and uninterruptedly to completion, unless temporarily interrupted through no fault of the holder of such permit by circumstances over which he has no control. * * * The holder of any permit who shall fail to comply with the provisions of this section within the time or times specified, shall be deemed to have abandoned all right under his permit."

... There is no evidence in the record that work was commenced under the McBee or Beggs permits, within 60 days from the date, upon which the permits were issued from the office of the state engineer, or that one-fifth of the work specified in said permits and required to be done by the state engineer was done, or that the whole of said work was completed on or before July 28, 1911, and August 10, 1910, as provided in said permits. Neither was there any testimony offered as an excuse for any interruptions with said work under circumstances over which the holder of the permit had no control. Under the McBee permit, proof of the completion of the work should have been made practically two years prior to the commencement of this action, and under the Beggs permit, proof of the completion of the work should have been made approximately three years prior to the commencement of this suit.

The evidence is conclusive that neither McBee nor Beggs at any time subsequent to the date of the issuance of the permits, even attempted to comply with the conditions therein contained. If there was a compliance with any of the conditions of said permit, it was by appellant when it began the construction of the Corbin ditch and flume connecting the waters of Lewellyn creek with the waters of Sage creek in the month of October, 1908, and this alleged compliance was upon the theory that the statutes, at the time of the issuance of the permit, did not provide a forfeiture by operation of law, until the time fixed in said permit for the submission of proof of beneficial use of the waters appropriated, which time, under permit No. 2158, was extended to July 28, 1915, and under permit No. 2978 to August 10, 1913. A total failure, however, to commence the work within the time specified in the permit, or to complete one-fifth of the work within the time limited in the permit, would not be cured by extending the time within which to make proof of the beneficial use of the water so attempted to be appropriated.

The state is the sovereign owner of the right to appropriate and use all of the stream waters which are within the jurisdiction of the state. The state, by enactment of appropriate laws, permits private persons to use its right to appropriate and use the flow of stream water. A water right claim is not a water right. A water right claim is a declaration of intention, made in a written form prescribed by statute, to give public notice of intention to create water rights identical with descriptions stated in the writing, commonly referred to as a water right. Although they are not, water right claims have become commonly regarded as being the same thing as water rights. One is a mere declaration of intention to create a water right which may never be anything more than an intention. By a compliance with conditions of the permit, the water right claim then becomes a water right.... A failure to put the water to a beneficial use, or to comply with the conditions of the permit, is an abandonment of the use, and this would be true whether or not there was a statute containing such a provision.

...

The granting by the state engineer of a permit for the right to use the waters of this state, in and of itself secures to the applicant no right to the use of the waters applied for in said permit, unless there be a substantial compliance with each and every provision of the statute relating to or in any manner affecting the issuance of such permit and a fulfillment of the conditions and limitations therein, but a compliance with the conditions and limitations prescribed in such permit initiates a right to the use of the water in the applicant, and said right then becomes a vested one and dates back to the issuance of said permit.

...

[Idaho law] provides:

> "If the holder of a permit to appropriate the public waters shall fail to comply with the requirements of his permit as to the commencing of work * * * or the completion of one-fifth (1/5) of the construction work within one-half (1/2) the time allowed for the entire completion of such construction work, or shall fail to complete the entire construction work within the time specified in his permit, said permit may be canceled and voided by the state engineer as hereinafter provided at the instance of any person or persons holding any permit for the diversion of water from the same stream."

...

From the record in this case it is clear to our minds that no right was initiated under the McBee or Beggs permits; that the statutes governing the issuance of said permit, as well as the conditions and limitations therein prescribed, were not substantially complied with, either by the appellant or its predecessors, and that the order made by the state engineer on the 9th day of January, 1911, canceling permits Nos. 2158 and 2978, was a valid one....

...

We, therefore, conclude that the court did not err in finding that McBee and Beggs did not commence or complete, in whole or in part, the work necessary to convey the waters of Lewellyn creek to and upon the lands described in the permit, or upon the lands of the appellant, within the time or in the manner provided in said permits.

...

Notes & Questions

1. Why impose strict interim deadlines for water development that will take multiple years?
2. At what point does Washington State Sugar argue that they acquired a property right to the use of water? Does the Court agree? According to the Court, what type of right does Washington State Sugar have after it acquires a permit but before it puts the water to beneficial use?

3. What is the priority date of a water right, which a permit was applied for and obtained on January 1, 1905, and with the application of due diligence, the water diversion was completed, and water applied to a beneficial use on June 1, 1906? In this hypothetical, no interim deadlines were imposed.

The Public Interest

The public interest criterion was added to Idaho's permit criteria statute in 1978, at a time of growing recognition of the public nature of water resources and the ecosystem services they provide.[14] The next case addresses when in the process of permit application the public interest can be raised and reviewed by IDWR. The case has also been chosen for this text to help you understand who can raise the statutory requirement of "public interest" in an objection to a permit, and how "public interest" is defined. The setting of the case is a natural pool in Box Canyon in southern Idaho. The natural pool is home to a rare species of fish.

Hardy v. Higginson

Supreme Court of Idaho
123 Idaho 485 (1993)

Opinion

REINHARDT, J. PRO TEM.—Earl Hardy (Hardy) appeals the appellate decision of the district court which affirmed in part the decision of the Director of the Idaho Department of Water Resources (IDWR) allowing Hardy to amend his two existing water permits. Affirmed in part and remanded for further findings.

The facts of this case are not in dispute. Hardy holds two water permits to divert water from Box Canyon Creek to Blind Canyon for the purpose of fish propagation. The first permit, NO. 36-7091, was granted in 1971 and established a single point of diversion for 300 c.f.s. The second permit, NO. 36-7334, was granted in 1975 and established six points of diversion for 600 c.f.s. Five of Hardy's points of diversion are located at or below a natural sculpin pool in Box Canyon Creek, and the other two are located above the sculpin pool. In 1988, Hardy applied for an application to amend his water permits to secure an additional point of diversion which would coincide with a right-of-way granted by the Bureau of Land Management (BLM) over BLM land adjacent to Box Canyon Creek. This proposed point of diversion is located downstream from the sculpin pool.

Upon receipt of Hardy's application, the Director of the Idaho Department of Water Resources (Director) published statewide notice seeking protests against approval of the proposed amendments.

---

14. Note that Idaho's statute specifically limits the public interest criteria to "local" public interest. Idaho Code § 42-203A(5)(e).

Twelve protests were filed on the basis that the proposed amendments were against the public interest. Hardy filed a motion to dismiss the protests on the grounds that the public interest was not a proper basis for protest. The Director denied the motion.

A hearing was held on September 28, 1988. Hardy renewed his motion to dismiss the protestants, which was again denied. At the hearing, Hardy testified that the proposed amendments would not result in an increased use of water, nor would they adversely affect the water rights of others. Hardy also submitted the testimony of Robert Cordell, the BLM Resource Area Manager for the Box Canyon area, who testified that in BLM's estimation, the proposed point of diversion was preferable over the existing points of diversion as far as environmental considerations were concerned, and that there would be no adverse environmental impacts other than those already identified and addressed by BLM. The "Right-of-Way/Temporary Use Permit" issued by BLM, and an environmental assessment prepared by BLM, were placed in the record to establish which environmental factors the BLM took into consideration in granting Hardy's right-of-way. The only other significant testimony came from the protestants which generally stressed that the new diversion would be contrary to the local public interest because of the adverse impacts on aesthetics, recreation and fishing. None of the protestants lived or owned property in Box Canyon.

In an order and amended order issued November 29, 1988, and February 17, 1989, respectively, the Director approved the proposed amendments. However, based on the local public interest, the Director imposed various conditions on the amended permits. The Director stated that Hardy must abandon his approved points of diversion located at and below the sculpin pool once all the required approvals for use of the new point of diversion were given. As to the two points of diversion located above the sculpin pool, the Director ruled that the local public interest required Hardy to divert water from these points only "to the extent that such diversion can occur without increasing or decreasing the water levels, temperature, quality, and/or flow velocity within the natural sculpin pool located downstream." The Director also ordered Hardy to construct a measuring device at the new point of diversion to measure the amount of water entering the new diversion. This condition was in addition to a similar condition imposed by the BLM in granting Hardy's right-of-way which required Hardy to construct a measuring device at the proposed diversion to assure a minimum stream flow of 75 c.f.s.

Hardy appealed the Director's decision to the district court which affirmed the authority of the IDWR to consider the local public interest in proceedings to amend a water permit under I.C. § 42-211....

Hardy appeals the district court's decision and order of remand, raising the following issues:

1. Whether the Director may consider the local public interest in amending a water permit under I.C. § 42-211.

....

II. LOCAL PUBLIC INTEREST UNDER I.C. § 42-211

The Director placed conditions upon Hardy's water permits to protect the local public interest. The director determined that he could consider the local public interest under I.C. § 42-211 because: (1) he was required to give notice and address protests under the provisions of the third paragraph of I.C. § 42-211, which refers to I.C. § 42-203A, which in turn refers to the local public interest; and (2) he could consider the local public interest when considering whether the "rights of others would be adversely affected" by the proposed amendment as directed in the first paragraph of I.C. § 42-211. The Director also concluded that persons filing a protest based on local public interest grounds do not have to own property or have a water right in Box Canyon.

Hardy argues that because he was amending a permit and not applying for a new permit, the Director was confined to the language of I.C. § 42-211, which does not include the phrase "local public interest." Hardy maintains that the deletion of the phrase "local public interest" from I.C. § 42-211 indicates that the legislature only intended the director to consider the effect of the amendment on the water rights of others and to determine whether the change would result in the diversion and use of more water than originally permitted. Hardy also argues that the Director's determination that the protestants could file protests based on the local public interest, even though they do not own property or water rights in Box Canyon, is contrary to the definition of "local public interest" set forth in I.C. § 42-203A as "the affairs of the people in the area directly affected by the proposed use."

The IDWR, on the other hand, maintains that if the Director, in his discretion under paragraph one of I.C. § 42-211, deems it appropriate to publish notice, then such notice shall be published in the manner provided in paragraph three of I.C. § 42-211. The third paragraph of I.C. § 42-211 states that protests may be filed against the application for amendment and heard by the Director in the same manner as provided in I.C. § 42-203A, which allows for consideration of the local public interest. The IDWR argues that this is the most reasonable construction of I.C. § 42-211 because this construction is consistent with the statutory scheme announced by the legislature.

We find the IDWR's position to be the most persuasive. Under I.C. § 42-203A, any application to appropriate water in Idaho is subject to the local public interest standard. Likewise, any change to a water right under I.C. § 42-222 is also subject to a determination that the change is in the local public interest as stated in I.C. § 42-203A. To say that an amendment to a water permit under I.C. § 42-211 is not subject to a local public interest investigation would allow a prospective water user to circumvent this criterion. It is clear from the legislative scheme that this result was not intended.

Regarding the Director's conclusion that the protestants in this case were proper parties despite the fact that they do not have water rights in Box Canyon, we find the case of *Shokal v. Dunn,* 109 Idaho 330, 707 P.2d 441 (1985), to be instructional. In *Shokal,* this Court found that the legislature intended the public interest on the local scale to include the public interest elements listed in I.C. § 42-1501 which includes the protection of fish and wildlife habitat. The Court further stated:

> By using the general term "the local public interest," the legislature intended to include any locally important factor impacted by proposed appropriations.
>
> ***
>
> For example, in an area heavily dependent on recreation and tourism *or specifically devoted to preservation in its natural state,* [IDWR] may give great consideration to the aesthetic and *environmental ramifications* of granting [or amending] a permit which calls for substantial modification of the landscape or stream.

109 Idaho at 338–39, 707 P.2d 449–50 (emphasis added).

In this case, the Box Canyon area is designated by the BLM as an Area of Critical Environmental Concern (ACEC). The values justifying the ACEC designation include the identification of four candidate threatened and endangered aquatic species, one of which is the Shoshone sculpin, and the scenic and unique natural qualities of the area. Clearly, the protection of this habitat falls within the local public interest as defined in *Shokal.* The protestants, although having no water rights within Box Canyon, sought to protect these locally important factors and thus their interests were properly considered by the Director.

III. CONDITIONS IMPOSED ON POINTS OF DIVERSION ABOVE THE SCULPIN POOL

The Director conditioned the amount of water Hardy could divert from his points of diversion above the sculpin pool "to the extent that such diversion can occur without increasing or decreasing the water levels, temperature, quality, and/or flow velocity within the natural sculpin pool located downstream." Hardy argues that it was error for the Director to place a condition on these points of diversion because they are a part of a previously approved water permit which constitutes a vested right or a contractual right to divert water which cannot be interfered with by a retroactive application of the local public interest standard.[15] As support for his argument, Hardy cites to I.C. § 42-204 which reads in part as follows:

> The department of water resources shall issue a permit for any approved application, make a record of the approval and provide a copy of the permit to the applicant, who shall be authorized, on receipt thereof, to proceed with the construction of the necessary works for the diversion of such water, and to take all steps required to apply the water to a beneficial use and perfect the proposed appropriation.

The district court disagreed with Hardy, finding that "any application to amend a permit offers the entire permit to the IDWR for review, and since the rights are inchoate at this time, the entire permit is subject to scrutiny under the public interest

---

15. Hardy's original permits were issued in 1971 and 1975. The local public interest standard was included in I.C. § 42-203A in 1978.

considerations added to the statutes after the original permits were issued." We agree with the rationale of the district court.

In *Big Wood Canal Co. v. Chapman* the Court held that there was no retroactive application of a statute which extended the time for making proof of application of water to a beneficial use because the affected permittee in that case had only an inchoate or contingent right which was vulnerable to being abridged or modified by law. In describing the type of right a water permittee has, the Court stated:

> "By application for permit ... the permittee secures an inchoate right which will ripen into a legal and complete appropriation by compliance with the statutory steps. Such right is merely a contingent right, which may ripen into a complete appropriation, or may be defeated by a failure of the holder to meet the statutory requirements. The permit, therefore, is not an appropriation of the public waters of the state. It is not real property. It is merely a consent given by the state to construct and acquire real property."

Likewise, in *Hidden Springs Trout Ranch, Inc. v. Allred* the Court held that an applicant for a water permit did not possess the type of vested rights which were immune to subsequent legislation. Although the Court specifically noted that it was not addressing the situation where a water permit is involved, the Court defined an applicant's rights as inchoate rights "which may ripen into a vested interest following proper statutory adherence.

Because Hardy's water permits only give him an inchoate or contingent right to put the water to a beneficial use, it was not improper for the Director to impose conditions upon his whole permit based on the local public interest. However, this is not to say that a permittee requesting an amendment to a water permit must accept the conditions imposed by the Director at the risk of losing any previously approved points of diversion. If a permittee finds the conditions to be unsatisfactory, the permittee should be allowed to withdraw the application for amendment and be left with what the permittee had before submitting the application to the IDWR. Similarly, a permittee should be allowed to appeal any conditions imposed by a Director, to ensure that such conditions were not imposed unreasonably or arbitrarily, without fear of losing the State's consent to put the water to a beneficial use under the terms of the original permit.

....

Notes & Questions

1. Take note of the administrative process that took place in *Hardy v. Higginson*. That process was initiated by protests, which triggered an evidentiary hearing. Appeals to the decision of the hearing officer, called "exceptions," are made to the director, who issues a final decision. At that point, the parties have exhausted their administrative remedies and are free to appeal the director's decision to the district court.
2. How does the court define "the local public interest" in the permit criteria of Idaho Code § 42-203A(5)? Note that definitions were added to the permit statute in 1996.

The "local public interest" is now defined as: "the interests that the people in the area directly affected by a proposed water use have in the effects of such use on the public water resource." Idaho Code § 42-203B(3).

3. Must the person raising an objection to the permit or permit amendment have a water right that might be affected? Does the court consider the issue of who can object as an issue of constitutional or statutory standing?
4. What problem is the court concerned with if it rules that the criteria that apply on initial application for a permit do not apply to an amendment to the permit application?
5. Note that the court finds the IDWR interpretation of the statute "persuasive" and does not discuss deference. Idaho law has a case equivalent to *Chevron*, *J.R. Simplot Co. v. Idaho State Tax Commission,* 120 Idaho 849, 820 P.2d 1206 (1991), but it is not discussed in this case.
6. Note that the public interest criteria were added to the statute between the original permit and the application to amend. Just as in the 1915 case of *Washington State Sugar Co. v. Goodrich*, the court holds that IDWR may apply new criteria because the applicant has no vested property right until the diversion is completed and water is applied to a beneficial use.
7. The pool and surrounding 350-acre area were purchased by the Nature Conservancy in 1999 and transferred to the State of Idaho in 2016. The Earl M. Hardy Box Canyon Natural Preserve is now part of the Thousand Springs State Park administered by the Idaho Department of Parks and Recreation.

Conservation of State Resources

The final two criteria for denial of a permit by IDWR are that the water use: (1) will be "contrary to conservation of water resources within the state;" or (2) "will adversely affect the local economy of the watershed or local area." Both address the transfer of water. The first is intended to address a transfer out of state. The second explicitly addresses "the case where the place of use is outside of the watershed or local area where the source of water originates." This section addresses the transfer of water out of the state and the U.S. Supreme Court ruling that water is an "article of commerce" in *Sporhase v. Nebraska*. This will be followed by a discussion of source protection laws developed to comply with *Sporhase* and the types of impacts that may result.

The U.S. Supreme Court ruling in the following case of *Sporhase v. Nebraska*—that water is an article of commerce—is important for two reasons. First, it means that state regulation of out-of-state water transfer must be limited to prevent undue burden on interstate commerce. Pay attention to the types of regulation the Court discusses as appropriate and its relation to how the state regulates its own citizens. Second, it means that Congress may regulate water despite its tendency to defer to the states. Following this case, the United States entered an era in which the Rehnquist Court sought to limit federal interference with state control of water. Rehnquist wrote the dissent in

Sporhase. The scope of federal authority to regulate water use has not been tested since *Sporhase*, but the scope of its authority to regulate water quality under the Clean Water Act has led to numerous cases, with clear guidance remaining elusive. You may study this in a course on Environmental Law.

Sporhase v. Nebraska

Supreme Court of the United States
458 U.S. 941(1982)

Opinion

Justice STEVENS delivered the opinion of the Court—Appellants challenge the constitutionality of a Nebraska statutory restriction on the withdrawal of ground water from any well within Nebraska intended for use in an adjoining State. The challenge presents three questions under the Commerce Clause: (1) whether ground water is an article of commerce and therefore subject to congressional regulation; (2) whether the Nebraska restriction on the interstate transfer of ground water imposes an impermissible burden on commerce; and (3) whether Congress has granted the States permission to engage in ground water regulation that otherwise would be impermissible.

Appellants jointly own contiguous tracts of land in Chase County, Nebraska, and Phillips County, Colorado. A well physically located on the Nebraska tract pumps ground water for irrigation of both the Nebraska tract and the Colorado tract. Previous owners of the land registered the well with the State of Nebraska in 1971, but neither they nor the present owners applied for the permit required by Neb.Rev.Stat. § 46-613.01 (1978). That section provides:

> "Any person, firm, city, village, municipal corporation or any other entity intending to withdraw ground water from any well or pit located in the State of Nebraska and transport it for use in an adjoining state shall apply to the Department of Water Resources for a permit to do so. If the Director of Water Resources finds that the withdrawal of the ground water requested is reasonable, is not contrary to the conservation and use of ground water, and is not otherwise detrimental to the public welfare, he shall grant the permit if the state in which the water is to be used grants reciprocal rights to withdraw and transport ground water from that state for use in the State of Nebraska."

Appellee brought this action to enjoin appellants from transferring the water across the border without a permit. The trial court rejected the defense that the statute imposed an undue burden on interstate commerce and granted the injunction. The Nebraska Supreme Court affirmed. 208 Neb. 703, 305 N.W.2d 614 (1981). It held that, under Nebraska law, ground water is not "a market item freely transferable for value among private parties, and therefore [is] not an article of commerce." *Id.*, at 705, 305 N.W.2d, at 616.

…

The second asserted distinction is that water, unlike other natural resources, is essential for human survival. Appellee, and the *amici curiae* that are vitally interested in conserving and preserving scarce water resources in the arid Western States, have convincingly demonstrated the desirability of state and local management of ground water. But the States' interests clearly have an interstate dimension. Although water is indeed essential for human survival, studies indicate that over 80% of our water supplies is used for agricultural purposes. The agricultural markets supplied by irrigated farms are worldwide. They provide the archetypical example of commerce among the several States for which the Framers of our Constitution intended to authorize federal regulation. The multistate character of the Ogallala aquifer—underlying appellants' tracts of land in Colorado and Nebraska, as well as parts of Texas, New Mexico, Oklahoma, and Kansas—confirms the view that there is a significant federal interest in conservation as well as in fair allocation of this diminishing resource. Cf. *Arizona v. California*, 373 U.S. 546, 83 S.Ct. 1468, 10 L.Ed.2d 542 (1963).

The Western States' interests, and their asserted superior competence, in conserving and preserving scarce water resources are not irrelevant in the Commerce Clause inquiry. Nor is [Nebraska's] claim to public ownership without significance. Like Congress' deference to state water law, see *infra*, at 3465–3467, these factors inform the determination whether the burdens on commerce imposed by state ground water regulation are reasonable or unreasonable. But appellee's claim that Nebraska ground water is not an article of commerce goes too far: it would not only exempt Nebraska ground water regulation from burden-on-commerce analysis, it would also curtail the affirmative power of Congress to implement its own policies concerning such regulation. See *Philadelphia v. New Jersey*, 437 U.S. 617, 621–623 (1978). If Congress chooses to legislate in this area under its commerce power, its regulation need not be more limited in Nebraska than in Texas and States with similar property laws. Ground water overdraft is a national problem and Congress has the power to deal with it on that scale.

II

Our conclusion that water is an article of commerce raises, but does not answer, the question whether the Nebraska statute is unconstitutional. For the existence of unexercised federal regulatory power does not foreclose state regulation of its water resources, of the uses of water within the State, or indeed, of interstate commerce in water. Determining the validity of state statutes affecting interstate commerce requires a more careful inquiry:

> "Where the statute regulates evenhandedly to effectuate a legitimate local public interest, and its effects on interstate commerce are only incidental, it will be upheld unless the burden imposed on such commerce is clearly excessive in relation to the putative local benefits. If a legitimate local purpose is found, then the question becomes one of degree. And the extent of the burden that will be tolerated will of course depend on the nature of the local interest involved, and on whether it could be promoted as well with a lesser impact on interstate activities."

The only purpose that appellee advances for § 46-613.01 is to conserve and preserve diminishing sources of ground water. The purpose is unquestionably legitimate and highly important,16 and the other aspects of Nebraska's ground water regulation demonstrate that it is genuine. Appellants' land in Nebraska is located within the boundaries of the Upper Republican Ground Water Control Area, which was designated as such by the Director of the Nebraska Department of Water Resources based upon a determination that there is "[a]n inadequate ground water supply to meet present or reasonably foreseeable needs for beneficial use of such water supply." Neb. Rev. Stat. § 46-658(1) (Supp. 1981); see App. 56–60. Pursuant to § 46-666(1), the Upper Republican Natural Resources District has promulgated special rules and regulations governing ground water withdrawal and use. See App. 61–82. The rules and regulations define as "critical" those townships in the control area in which the annual decline of the ground water table exceeds a fixed percentage; appellants' Nebraska tract is located within a critical township. The rules and regulations require the installation of flow meters on every well within the control area, specify the amount of water per acre that may be used for irrigation, and set the spacing that is required between wells. They also strictly limit the intrastate transfer of ground water: transfers are only permitted between lands controlled by the same groundwater user, and all transfers must be approved by the District Board of Directors. *Id.*, at 68–69.

The State's interest in conservation and preservation of ground water is advanced by the first three conditions in § 46-613.01 for the withdrawal of water for an interstate transfer. Those requirements are "that the withdrawal of the ground water requested is reasonable, is not contrary to the conservation and use of ground water, and is not otherwise detrimental to the public welfare." Although Commerce Clause concerns are implicated by the fact that § 46-613.01 applies to interstate transfers but not to intrastate transfers, there are legitimate reasons for the special treatment accorded requests to transport ground water across state lines. Obviously, a State that imposes severe withdrawal and use restrictions on its own citizens is not discriminating against interstate commerce when it seeks to prevent the uncontrolled transfer of water out of the State. An exemption for interstate transfers would be inconsistent with the ideal of evenhandedness in regulation. At least in the area in which appellants' Nebraska tract is located, the first three standards of § 46-613.01 may well be no more strict in application than the limitations upon intrastate transfers imposed by the Upper Republican Natural Resources District.

Moreover, in the absence of a contrary view expressed by Congress, we are reluctant to condemn as unreasonable, measures taken by a State to conserve and preserve for its own citizens this vital resource in times of severe shortage. Our reluctance stems from the "confluence of [several] realities." *Hicklin v. Orbeck*, 437 U.S. 518, 534 (1978). First, a State's power to regulate the use of water in times and places of shortage for the purpose of protecting the health of its citizens—and not simply the health of its economy—is at the core of its police power. For Commerce Clause purposes, we have long recognized a difference between economic protectionism, on the one hand, and health and safety regulation, on the other. See *H. P. Hood & Sons v. Du Mond*, 336 U.S. 525, 533 (1949). Second, the legal expectation that under certain circumstances each State may restrict water within its borders has been fostered over the years not only by our equitable apportionment decrees, see, *e.g., Wyoming v. Colorado*, 353 U.S. 953 (1957), but also by the negotiation and enforcement of interstate compacts. Our law therefore has recognized the relevance of state boundaries in the allocation of scarce water resources. Third, although appellee's claim to public ownership of Nebraska ground water cannot justify a total denial of federal regulatory power, it may support a limited preference for its own citizens in the utilization of the resource. See *Hicklin v. Orbeck, supra*, 437 U.S., at 533–534, 98 S.Ct., at 2491. In this regard, it is relevant that appellee's claim is logically more substantial than claims to public ownership of other natural resources. See *supra*, at 3462–3461. Finally, given appellee's conservation efforts, the continuing availability of ground water in Nebraska is not simply happenstance; the natural resource has some indicia of a good publicly produced and owned in which a State may favor its own citizens in times of shortage. A facial examination of the first three conditions set forth in § 46-613.01 does not, therefore, indicate that they impermissibly burden interstate commerce. Appellants, indeed, seem to concede their reasonableness.

Appellants, however, do challenge the requirement that "the state in which the water is to be used grants reciprocal rights to withdraw and transport ground water from that state for use in the State of Nebraska"—the reciprocity provision that troubled the Chief Justice of the Nebraska Supreme Court. Because Colorado forbids the exportation of its ground water, the reciprocity provision operates as an explicit barrier to commerce between the two States. The State therefore bears the initial burden of demonstrating a close fit between the reciprocity requirement and its asserted local purpose.

The reciprocity requirement fails to clear this initial hurdle. For there is no evidence that this restriction is narrowly tailored to the conservation and preservation rationale. Even though the supply of water in a particular well may be abundant, or perhaps even excessive, and even though the most beneficial use of that water might be in another State, such water may not be shipped into a neighboring State that does not permit its water to be used in Nebraska. If it could be shown that the State as a whole suffers a water shortage, that the intrastate transportation of water from areas of abundance to areas of shortage is feasible regardless of distance, and that the importation of water from adjoining States would roughly compensate for any exportation to those States, then the conservation and preservation purpose might be credibly advanced for the reciprocity provision. A demonstrably arid State conceivably might be able to marshal evidence to establish a close means-end relationship between even a total ban on the exportation of water and a purpose to conserve and preserve water. Appellee, however, does not claim that such evidence exists. We therefore are not persuaded that the reciprocity requirement—when superimposed on the first three restrictions in the statute—significantly advances the State's legitimate conservation and preservation interest; it surely is not narrowly tailored to serve that purpose. The reciprocity requirement does not survive the "strictest scrutiny" reserved for facially discriminatory legislation. *Hughes v. Oklahoma, supra*, 441 U.S., at 337.

...

The reciprocity requirement of Neb.Rev.Stat. § 46-613.01 (1978) violates the Commerce Clause. We leave to the state courts the question whether the invalid portion is severable. The judgment of the Nebraska Supreme Court is reversed, and the case is remanded for proceedings not inconsistent with this opinion.

It is so ordered.

Notes & Questions

1. The Court notes that there is elevated reason for state concern with out-of-state water transfers. The Nebraska statute stated:

   > Any person, firm, city, village, municipal corporation or any other entity intending to withdraw ground water from any well or pit located in the State of Nebraska and transport it for use in an adjoining state shall apply to the Department of Water Resources for a permit to do so. If the Director of Water Resources finds that the withdrawal of the ground water requested is reasonable, is not contrary to the conservation and use of ground water, and is not otherwise detrimental to the public welfare, he shall grant the permit if the state in which the water is to be used grants reciprocal rights to withdraw and transport ground water from that state for use in the State of Nebraska.

   What language does the Court find in the statute that violates the Commerce Clause?
2. In reference to your answer to question 1: Does the Court say this requirement would never be allowed? If not, what would the circumstances be?
3. What type of science would you want to be able to present if defending the denial of an out-of-state transfer based on the Idaho statute that requires the permit to be denied if "it is contrary to conservation of water resources within the state of Idaho"?
4. In 1990, the Idaho legislature added Chapter 4 to its water use act to require additional criteria for out-of-state transfers. Consider whether any of the added criteria violate *Sporhase*.
   a. The supply of water available to the state of Idaho;
   b. The current and reasonably anticipated water demands of the state of Idaho;
   c. Whether there are current or reasonably anticipated water shortages within the state of Idaho;
   d. Whether the water that is the subject of the application could feasibly be used to alleviate current or reasonably anticipated water shortages within the state of Idaho;
   e. The supply and sources of water available to the applicant in the state where the applicant intends to use the water; and

f. The demands placed on the applicant's supply in the state where the applicant intends to use the water.[16]

5. Following *Sporhase*, many states modified or enacted statutes to address out-of-state transfers within the bounds of the ruling. For example, detailed requirements are set forth in Mont. Stat. §85-2-311(4):

> (a) The state of Montana has long recognized the importance of conserving its public waters and the necessity to maintain adequate water supplies for the state's water requirements, including requirements for federal non-Indian and Indian reserved water rights.... Although the state of Montana also recognizes that, under appropriate conditions, the out-of-state transportation and use of its public waters are not in conflict with the public welfare of its citizens or the conservation of its waters, the criteria in this subsection (4) must be met before out-of-state use may occur.
>
> (b) The department may not issue a permit for the appropriation of water for withdrawal and transportation for use outside the state unless the applicant proves by clear and convincing evidence that:
>
> > (i) ...
> >
> > (ii) the proposed out-of-state use of water is not contrary to water conservation in Montana; and
> >
> > (iii) the proposed out-of-state use of water is not otherwise detrimental to the public welfare of the citizens of Montana.
>
> (c) In determining whether the applicant has proved by clear and convincing evidence that the requirements of subsections (4)(b)(ii) and (4)(b)(iii) are met, the department shall consider the following factors:
>
> > (i) whether there are present or projected water shortages within the state of Montana;
> >
> > (ii) whether the water that is the subject of the application could feasibly be transported to alleviate water shortages within the state of Montana;
> >
> > (iii) the supply and sources of water available to the applicant in the state where the applicant intends to use the water; and
> >
> > (iv) the existing legal demands of water rights placed on the applicant's supply in the state where the applicant intends to use the water.
>
> (d) When applying for a permit or a lease to withdraw and transport water for use outside the state, the applicant shall submit to and comply with the laws of the state of Montana governing the appropriation, lease, and use of water.

16. Idaho Code § 42-401(3).

Adverse Effect on the Local Economy: Area of Origin Protections

The physical transfer of water from one watershed to another has long been controversial, with one of the more colorful disputes being the conveyance of water from California's Owens Valley to Los Angeles (made famous in the 1974 Roman Polanski film *Chinatown*). Without such transfers, much of the urban development in the U.S. southwest and the agricultural development in areas like the Imperial Valley of California (made possible by transfer from the Colorado River) would not have been possible. What drives area of origin protection statutes is the desire to ensure that the economic growth in the region benefiting from the water transfer does not come at the expense of the future of the area of the water source.

Important to the understanding of the impact of an out-of-watershed transfer is that the use is 100% consumptive from the perspective of the watershed of origin. In other words, there is no return flow—all the water transferred leaves the watershed permanently. In modern times, in which most water sources in the arid west are substantially developed for both in- and out-of-stream uses, major out-of-watershed proposals usually take place in the context of a purchase of existing water rights that are transferred to a new location and use. Those types of transfers, referred to as a "change of use of an existing water right" will be discussed in the next Chapter.

Because agriculture represents approximately 80% of water diversion in the West, it is often the source for purchase of an existing water right. For purposes of understanding the effect of transfers on the local economy, it is useful to know that taking land out of agricultural production can have secondary effects in the rest of the local economy, particularly if that local economy thrives on commerce that supports the agricultural activities. For additional depth on area of origin protections, Lawrence MacDonnell's excellent report to the State of Washington legislature in 2008 compiles the approaches used by different states and the types of impact out-of-watershed transfers may have.[17]

Exemptions from the Permit Process

In a report to the Western States Water Council (WSWC is the organization of all state water management agencies in the western states), published in *Environmental Law* in 2010, Nathan Bracken stated that:

> Every WSWC member state with the exception of Utah and California, which do not have a statewide groundwater permitting process, exempts certain

17. Lawrence J. MacDonnell, *Protecting Local Economies: Legislative Options to Protect Rural Communities in Northeast Washington from Disproportionate Economic, Agricultural, and Environmental Impacts when Upstream Water Rights Are Purchased and Transferred for Use, or Idled and Used as Mitigation, in a Downstream Watershed or County,* Report to the Legislature, State of Washington (November 30, 2008).

> groundwater uses from its permitting procedures, its adjudication procedures, or both.[18]

In general, these exemptions apply to domestic and stock watering wells up to a certain size. Bracken's report covers the specific exemption in each state. These exemptions stem from a time when states sought to encourage homesteading, and the amount of water drawn from a hand-dug well for domestic use, including a subsistence garden, and for livestock watering was considered *de minimis*. Today the rate of domestic well development would overload the state administrative system if permits were required, but these exemptions provide a loophole for water provision for subdivisions in arid land. If each lot has a private domestic well, each is exempt from the permitting process. Thus, while the cumulative impact of water development (as multiple exempt wells) may cause harm to other water users, there will be no investigation of injury or water availability. In Idaho, you will learn that the size of the well given the exemption is sufficient to allow a water duty on landscaping that exceeds the presumed water duty for crops in Idaho. As Bracken noted in 2010: "[t]here are over a million exempt domestic and livestock wells located throughout the West."[19] In response, states have attempted to address the cumulative impact of exempt wells through their water use statutes and/or their subdivision statutes, without overwhelming the capacity of their permit systems.

This section will begin with Idaho's exempt well statute as an example and how Idaho has addressed the question of administration of exempt wells. It will then look to other states for some of the emerging issues associated with the cumulative impact of exempt well development. You will learn how Washington has handled the division of duties between its water management agency and the counties' process of planning, zoning, and subdivision approval in *Whatcom County v. Hirst*. Finally, you will learn about a constitutional challenge to the exemption in New Mexico in a basin closed to new permits for non-exempt water use. The case of *Bounds v. New Mexico* rests on the difference between issuance of a water right and administration of that right and differs from the approach taken by Washington.

Water Use Act Permit Exemptions: Idaho

Idaho law provides:

> The excavation and opening of wells and the withdrawal of water therefrom for domestic purposes shall not be subject to the permit requirement under section 42-229, Idaho Code; providing such wells and withdrawal devices are subject to inspection by the department of water resources and the department of environmental quality and providing further that the drilling of such wells shall be subject to the licensing provisions of section 42-238, Idaho Code.

---

18. Nathan Bracken, *Exempt Well Issues in the West*, 40 Envt'l L. 141, 146 (2010).
19. *Id.* at 145.

> Rights to ground water for such domestic purposes may be acquired by withdrawal and use.[20]

Domestic purpose is defined by Idaho law as:

> (a) The use of water for homes, organization camps, public campgrounds, livestock and for any other purpose in connection therewith, including irrigation of up to one-half (1/2) acre of land, if the total use is not in excess of thirteen thousand (13,000) gallons per day, or
>
> (b) Any other uses, if the total use does not exceed a diversion rate of four one-hundredths (0.04) cubic feet per second and a diversion volume of twenty-five hundred (2,500) gallons per day.[21]

To address the problem of the cumulative impact of subdivisions reliant on individual lot wells, the domestic purpose definition goes on to state:

> (2) For purposes of the sections listed in subsection (1) of this section, domestic purposes or domestic uses shall not include water for multiple ownership subdivisions, mobile home parks, or commercial or business establishments, unless the use meets the diversion rate and volume limitations set forth in subsection (1)(b) of this section.
>
> (3) Multiple water rights for domestic uses or domestic purposes, as defined in this section, shall not be established or exercised in a manner to satisfy a single combined water use or purpose that would not itself come within the definition of a domestic use or purpose under this section.[22]

While this is a similar approach to other states, the 13,000 gallon per day ("gpd") cap is much higher than in neighboring states. Washington, for example, applies a limit of 5,000 gpd.[23] You learned in Part I that agricultural land in Idaho has a presumptive water duty of five acre-feet per acre. Consider that 13,000 gpd applied to one-half acre of landscaping year around results in a water duty of 29 acre-feet per acre, highlighting the concern with the cumulative impact of exempt wells on residential land when converted from farmland.

Idaho does not separately address water availability in laws related to the development of housing subdivisions but does require developers to file information with the county that identifies the type of water supply their subdivisions will use. Thus, Idaho requires developers to submit to the county a recorded plat to certify if it will be served by individual wells, an existing water system, or that sufficient capital is available to develop a new water system.[24] In the *Whatcom County* case you will learn that Washington places additional duties on counties to ensure water availability.

---

20. Idaho Code § 42-227.
21. Idaho Code § 42-111(1).
22. Idaho Code §42-111 (2); (3).
23. Wash. Rev. Code §90.44.050.
24. Idaho Code § 50-1334.

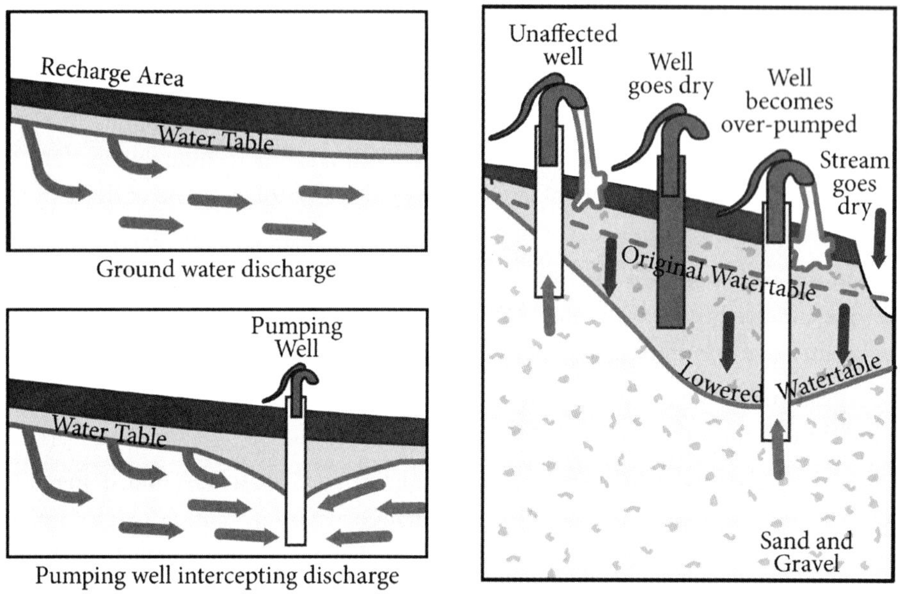

Figure 20.1 The impact of well pumping on stream flow and on other wells. Source: Designed by Leilanee Taylor.

Regulation of Domestic Wells through Subdivision Laws: Washington

Washington State provides an example of a state that relies on its land use laws to address the cumulative impact of exempt wells. The State's Growth Management Act, enacted in 1990, required counties to determine whether there is an adequate water supply before approving a subdivision application or new building permit. As you'll see in *Whatcom County v. Hurst*, Whatcom County relied on the State Department of Ecology to make that determination by concluding that as long as the water agency had not closed the area to exempt wells, water for that method of appropriation was still available.

Hirst also provides a glimpse at the interaction between wells and environmental flows. Chapter 22 will cover the statutory introduction of water rights for environmental or "instream" flows to western water law, but the following case will expose you to their enforcement. In this case, it is the minimum instream flows that are not being satisfied. Figure 20.1 illustrates how pumping from a well may cause loss of base flow from a stream by turning a stretch that gains water from groundwater to a losing stretch in which water is lost to groundwater from the stream. Understanding the case requires background on the water resource planning process in Washington, which relies on a watershed-based process rather than a state process as done in Idaho.

The 1971 Washington Water Resources Act[25] authorized the development of a comprehensive water planning process within regional boundaries established through

25. Wash. Rev. Code 90.54.

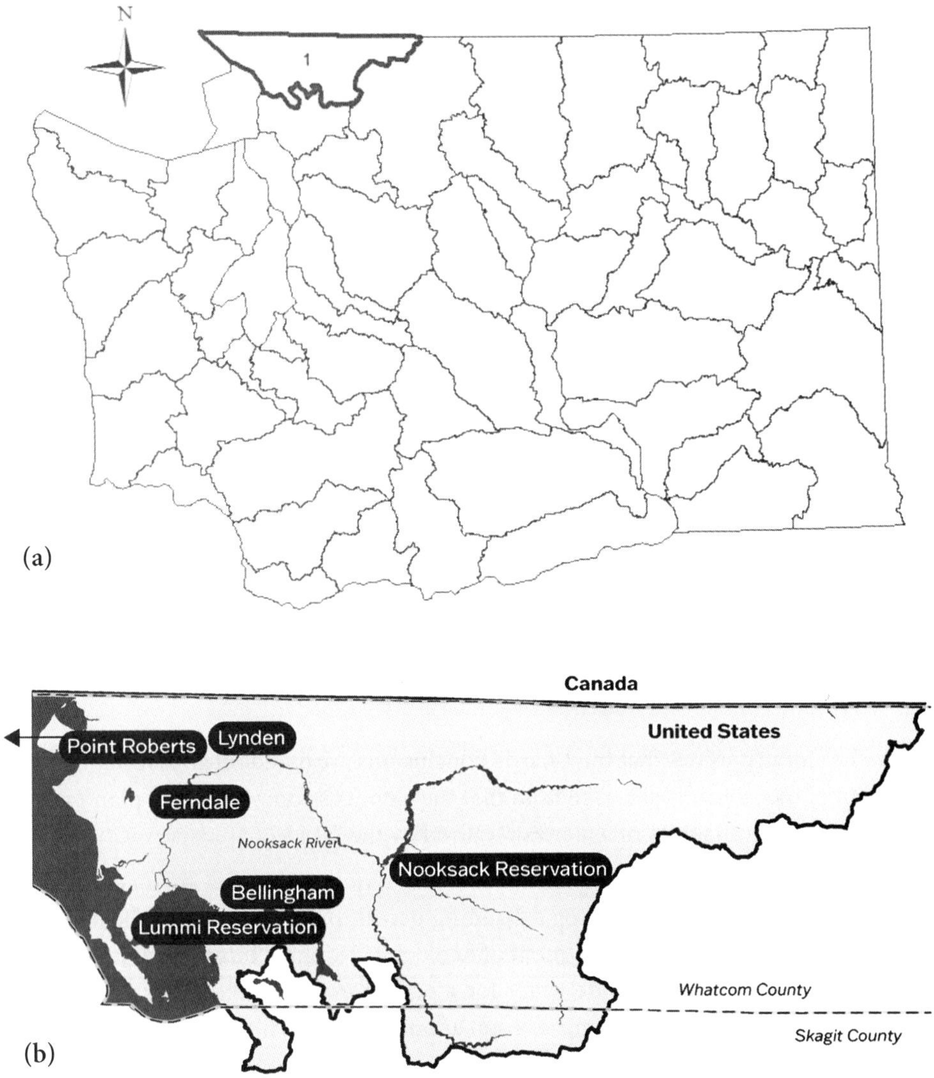

Figure 20.2 (a) This shows the 62 WRIAs in Washington State. (b) WRIA 1 is the Nooksack WRIA referred to in *Whatcom Co. v. Hirst*. It includes Whatcom County and part of Skagit County. Source: Designed by Leilanee Taylor.

input from "state agencies, Indian tribes, local government, and interested parties,"[26] and authorized the Department of Ecology to promulgate rules and modify existing rules to develop the process.[27] Ecology established 62 Water Resource Inventory Areas (WRIA), based on watershed boundaries to implement the process.[28] The instream flow rules established for WRIA 1 (the Nooksack WRIA at issue in *Whatcom Co. v. Hirst*, Figure 20.2) can be found in the Washington Administrative Code at WAC 173-501.

26. Wash. Rev. Code 90.54.045 (2).
27. Wash. Rev. Code 90.54.040; 045.
28. WAC 173.500.040; 990.

As you read the case, consider why, despite the WRIA process, Washington may have chosen to place the burden on the counties to determine the availability of water rather than the agency with expertise in water resources. Note that it is a long-standing debate in western development as to whether the arid nature of the land should be a factor in limiting growth.

Whatcom County v. Hirst

Supreme Court of Washington
381 P.3d 1, 186 Wash.2d 648 (2016)

Opinion

WIGGINS, J.—[Whatcom County amended its comprehensive plan and zoning code to comply with the Growth Management Act (GMA or Act) by allowing subdivision and building permits that rely on private exempt wells if the proposed well sites are not within an area determined by Ecology to lack water for development. Hirst challenged the validity of the County's implementation of the GMA before the Western Washington Growth Management Hearings Board (Board). The Board found the County's approach did not meet the requirements of the GMA, and remanded to the County rather than invalidate the plan. Both Hirst and the County sought review of this decision.]

... The County argues that the Board's conclusions are based on an erroneous interpretation of the law and asks us to hold that the County's comprehensive plan protects the quality and availability of water as required by the GMA.

We reject the County's arguments. The GMA requires counties to ensure an adequate water supply before granting a building permit or subdivision application. The County merely follows the Department of Ecology's "Nooksack Rule"; it assumes there is an adequate supply to provide water for a permit-exempt well unless Ecology has expressly closed that area to permit-exempt appropriations. This results in the County's granting building permits for houses and subdivisions to be supplied by a permit-exempt well even if the cumulative effect of exempt wells in a watershed reduces the flow in a water course below the minimum instream flow. We therefore hold that the County's comprehensive plan does not satisfy the GMA requirement to protect water availability and that its remaining arguments are unavailing. We reverse the Court of Appeals in part and remand to the Board for further proceedings.

...

II. Procedural History

...

A. Board's discussion of applicable law

The Board held a hearing and issued a final decision and order (FDO). The Board began its decision by citing to the "Applicable Law" as provided by the GMA. As the Board observed, the GMA imposes several requirements on a local government's planning. Relevant here, the GMA requires counties to consider and address water resource issues in land use planning. *Kittitas County v. E. Wash. Growth Mgmt. Hr'gs Bd.*, 256 P.3d 1193 (Wash. 2011) (counties must regulate to ensure land use is not inconsistent with available water resources). Accordingly, a county's comprehensive plan must "'provide for protection of the quality and quantity of groundwater used for public water supplies.'" The GMA also requires counties to plan for a rural element that "'include[s] measures that ... protect ... surface water and groundwater resources.'"

...

In addition to these planning requirements, the Board noted that the GMA provides 13 goals to guide the development of a county's comprehensive plan. These include a goal to "'[p]rotect the environment and enhance the state's high quality of life, including air and water quality, and the availability of water.'" Read collectively, these goals convey some conceptual guidance for growth management.

The Board interpreted these planning requirements and goals to indicate that:

> patterns of land use and development in rural areas must be consistent with protection of instream flows, groundwater recharge, and fish and wildlife habitat. A County's Comprehensive Plan rural lands provision must include measures governing rural development to protect water resources.

FDO at 21.

The GMA does not define the requirements to plan for the protection of water resources found in [the Washington code]. The Act also fails to define how the requirements are to be met. Thus, Hirst argued that the County's comprehensive plan must itself protect the availability of water resources, placing the burden on local governments to protect the availability of water protect groundwater resources and ensure an adequate water supply when it approves a building permit. The County countered that it complied with the GMA by drafting a comprehensive plan that incorporates and is consistent with Ecology's regulations in water resource inventory area (WRIA). [From footnote 4: "WRIAs establish instream flows affecting the approval of water rights permits and appropriations for most of the state ..."] In evaluating this relationship between Ecology's responsibility to protect water pursuant to the Water Resources Act of 1971 (WRA), chapter 90.54 RCW, and the responsibility of local governments to protect water availability and quality pursuant to the GMA, the Board stated that "it is the local government—and not Ecology—that is responsible to make the decision on water adequacy as part of its land use decision, and in particular, with respect to exempt wells." FDO at 23.

B. Board's findings and conclusions on water quality and availability

Hirst presented considerable evidence and the Board found substantial evidence of limits on water availability in rural Whatcom County. These water availability limitations were reflected in findings that a large portion of the County is in year-round or seasonally closed watersheds and that most of the water in the Nooksack watershed was already legally appropriated. The Board also found that average minimum instream flows in portions of the Nooksack River "are not met an average of 100 days a year." Despite the limited water availability, 1,652 permit-exempt well applications have been drilled in otherwise closed basins since 1997 and an additional 637 applications were pending in March 2011. Further, the Board noted that the County recognized as early as 1999 that this proliferation of rural, permit-exempt wells was creating "'difficulties for effective water resource management.'"

The Board concluded that the County failed to comply with the GMA, specifically with the requirement to protect surface water and groundwater resources pursuant to RCW 36.70A.070(5)(c).... finding that

> the water supply provisions referenced [by the amended policies] do not require the County to make a determination of the legal availability of groundwater in a basin where instream flows are not being met.

FDO at 40. Implicit in this conclusion is the Board's determination that water is not presumptively available for permit-exempt withdrawals in WRIA 1 ... the Board denied Hirst's request for a declaration of invalidity and instead remanded the ordinance to the County to take corrective action.

Both parties appealed separately.... The cases were consolidated....

The Court of Appeals reversed the Board, holding that the Board erroneously interpreted and applied the law in holding that the ordinance failed to comply with the GMA.... The Court of Appeals affirmed the Board's decision not to declare the ordinance invalid, holding that the decision was a proper exercise of the Board's discretion.

We granted review and now reverse the Court of Appeals in part.

ANALYSIS

...

Consistent with the Board's determination, Hirst asserts that the GMA requires local governments to determine ... that water is legally available before issuing building permits or approving subdivisions that rely on permit-exempt appropriations. Thus, Hirst asserts that the comprehensive plan results in water withdrawals that impact minimum instream flows.

The County responds that its comprehensive plan protects the availability of water ... [by relying] on a permit-exempt well for its water supply only when the proposed well "does not fall within the boundaries of an area where [Ecology] has determined by rule that water for development does not exist." ... In effect, the County's position is that water is presumptively available—i.e., that "not unavailable" is synonymous with "available."

In effect, the County delegates the decision on water availability to Ecology's Nooksack Rule, chapter 173-501 WAC. The Nooksack Rule establishes minimum instream flows for WRIA 1, covering most of the County. However, the County argues—and Ecology agrees—that the closures and minimum flow requirements established by the rule are not applicable to permit-exempt wells in the County.... The County asserts that under the GMA, the proper inquiry is whether its comprehensive plan is consistent with Ecology's regulations designed to protect water and to ensure that water is legally available.

We reject these arguments in the context of the GMA challenge before us. The GMA places an independent responsibility to ensure water availability on counties, not on Ecology. To the extent that there is a conflict between the GMA and the Nooksack Rule, the later-enacted GMA controls.

Ecology adopted the Nooksack Rule in 1985 ... [recognizing] that groundwater withdrawals can have significant impacts on surface water flows, and Ecology must consider this effect when issuing permits for groundwater appropriation. [citation omitted]

We hold that the same standard applies to counties when issuing building permits and subdivision approvals. We have been protective of minimum instream flow rules and have rejected appropriations that interfere with senior instream flows. *E.g., Swinomish Indian Tribal Cmty. v. Dep't of Ecology,* 311 P.3d 6 (Wash. 2013); *Foster v. Dep't of Ecology,* 362 P.3d 959 (Wash. 2015). Our jurisprudence and well-established principles of statutory interpretation lead us to affirm the Board's decision that the County's comprehensive plan does not satisfy the GMA requirement to protect water availability.

...

II. The Board Correctly Ruled That the County's Rural Element Fails to Comply with the Requirement to Protect Water Availability

We reverse the Court of Appeals and hold that the Board properly interpreted and applied the law in concluding that the County's comprehensive plan fails to provide for the protection of water resources. The Board's decision properly placed the burden on the County to ensure the availability of water under the GMA pursuant to the legislative intent, relevant statutory schemes when read in context and as a whole, and this court's jurisprudence considering groundwater appropriations that impact minimum flows.

A. Washington's history of water regulation

... In 1945, the legislature passed the groundwater code to subject the withdrawal of groundwater to the permitting process then applicable to surface water rights in order to protect senior water rights and the public welfare. Specified withdrawals were exempt from these permit requirements:

> [A]ny withdrawal ... for single or group domestic uses in an amount not exceeding five thousand gallons a day ... is and shall be exempt from the provisions of this section, but, to the extent that it is regularly used beneficially, shall be entitled to a right equal to that established by a permit issued under the provisions of this chapter.

RCW 90.44.050. These permit-exempt withdrawals are appropriations. Recognizing that any withdrawal of water impacts the total availability of water, we have held that an appropriator's right to use water from a permit-exempt withdrawal is subject to senior water rights, including the minimum flows established by Ecology. These exemptions existed in part because the legislature's goal in 1945 was to encourage the development and settlement of rural family farms drawing between 200 and 1,500 gallons of water per day.

These legislative priorities continued to change as Washington's population increased and the limitations on its natural resources became more apparent.... "In 1955, the legislature declared the policy of the State to be that sufficient water flow be maintained in streams to support fish populations and authorized rejection of water right applications if these flows would be impaired." ...

... Once established, minimum flows are like any other appropriative water right in that they are subject to the rule of "first in time is the first in right."

The WRA was intended to ensure adequate water to "meet the needs of the state's growing population" while concurrently maintaining "instream resources and values." RCW 90.54.010(1)(a). To balance growth and stream maintenance, the WRA directed Ecology to allocate waters in a way that maximizes the net benefits to the people of the state and to retain "base flows necessary to provide for preservation of wildlife, fish, scenic, aesthetic and other environmental values, and navigational values." Included in this mandate is the authority to establish minimum water flows and water levels, base flows, and WRIAs. At this time, the legislature also made Ecology the primary administrator of chapter 90.03 RCW, concerning surface waters, and of chapter 90.44 RCW, concerning groundwater.

...

In 1990 and 1991, the legislature addressed issues related to water use when it enacted the GMA "'in response to public concerns about rapid population growth and increasing development pressures in the state.'" [citations omitted] This legislation followed "decades of lax and optional land use regulations." [citation omitted] Through the GMA, the legislature sought to minimize "uncoordinated and unplanned growth," ....

...

D. The County's plan fails to protect the availability of water resources

...

The County argues that placing responsibility for protecting water resources on local governments transfers Ecology's statutory responsibility to administer chapter 90.44 RCW to the counties. They are wrong under our description of the proper division of authority set forth in *Kittitas County:* "Ecology is responsible for appropriation of groundwater by permit ..., the County is responsible for land use decisions that affect groundwater resources."

...

The County specifically contrasts its cooperative efforts with the actions at issue in *Kittitas County*, where we affirmed the Board's finding of noncompliance in part because the policies in that case effectively evaded compliance with Ecology's water permitting requirements. Asserting that its plan is entirely consistent with Ecology's regulations, the County urges us to find that its comprehensive plan is GMA compliant.

This argument is incongruous: the fact that the County's provisions are wholly consistent with Ecology's regulations does not, by itself, render them consistent with the GMA's requirements. We require counties "to plan for land use in a manner that is consistent with the laws regarding protection of water resources and establishing a permitting process." However, nothing in *Kittitas County* or in the GMA suggests that consistency with Ecology's regulations is sufficient for GMA compliance.... The Board correctly found that the County's plan does not satisfy these requirements.

....

E. The County plan is inconsistent with our minimum flows jurisprudence

In addition to the deficiencies in the County's comprehensive plan under the GMA, the Board properly ruled that the plan is inconsistent with our decisions protecting closed basins and minimum flows from groundwater appropriations. There is no question that a permit-exempt well may not infringe on an earlier-established right to water under the doctrine of prior appropriation.... The GMA protects these senior water rights by requiring local governments to determine that applicants for building permits or subdivision developments have demonstrated that an adequate water supply is legally available before authorizing approval.

Here, the Board specifically found that the "water supply provisions referenced ... do not require the County to make a determination of the legal availability of groundwater," with the result that the County's ordinance directly conflicts with the standard announced in *Postema.* FDO at 40. In *Postema,* we held that a minimum flow, once established by Ecology, is an existing water right that may not be impaired by subsequent groundwater withdrawals.

Though *Postema* was specifically decided in the context of Ecology's requirements prior to issuing permits, the rule in Washington is that groundwater appropriations cannot impede minimum flows. It would be incongruous to limit *Postema* to the holding that Ecology must consider the effect of groundwater appropriations on minimum flows when issuing permits but that the County does not need to consider these same impacts when issuing building permits. The County emphasizes that Ecology expressly does not engage in the usual review of a permit application when considering permit-exempt wells and exempt-use applications are not reviewed for impairment of existing rights. This argument misses the mark—the GMA explicitly assigns that task to local governments.

...

CONCLUSION

We reverse the Court of Appeals and hold that the County's comprehensive plan does not satisfy the GMA requirements to protect water availability or water quality. However, we affirm the Court of Appeals' holding that the Board did not abuse its discretion in declining to make a finding of invalidity. We therefore reverse the Court of Appeals in part and remand to the Board for further proceedings consistent with this opinion.

Notes & Questions

1. What is the basis for the court's determination that it is the county, under the Growth Management Act, and not the Department of Ecology, under the WRIA planning process of the Water Resources Act, that must determine if water is available for a subdivision reliant on exempt wells?
2. Should land use policies consider limits on water supply?
3. In 2018, in response to *Whatcom County v. Hirst*, the Washington legislature passed Senate Bill 6091 to ensure: "that water is available to support development." The legislation puts the burden back on Ecology while requiring coordination with counties. For WRIAs with a watershed plan, a cap on exempt wells of 3000 gpd is imposed, and for those without a plan, a cap of 950 gpd is imposed. To ensure coordination, all building permits and subdivision approvals must be tracked by the counties and provided to Ecology annually.
4. An alternative approach that is nevertheless at the city level rather than the State water agency, is taken by the City of Santa Fe. The City is frequently held up as one of the most progressive programs to assure water supply and growth are in sync in the country. Among its measures are: (1) its own domestic well permitting program, which only allows a new domestic well if the property is not near a city water line; (2) offset requirements for new development that includes a program for credits based on retrofitting of existing systems and a water bank that can facilitate water transfers for new development.[29] In Chapter 21 you will learn about water banks as an efficient means of transferring an existing water right to a new use.

The Constitutional Challenge to Domestic Well Exemptions: New Mexico

Bounds v. New Mexico is the first constitutional challenge to the cumulative impact of domestic well exemption. The suit arose in the upper Rio Mimbres watershed, which is located in the southwestern corner of New Mexico. The basin is over-appropriated, meaning that water demand already outstrips supply. As a result, the State of New Mexico had closed the basin to new water permits. Domestic water uses are exempt from the permit process and from that moratorium.

In response, senior water users asserted that continued development of exempt wells within an area determined to be closed to new permits due to lack of water availability

---

29. City of Santa Fe, *Development Water Budgets Ordinance* 14-8.13 (2013), https://tinyurl.com/ykrhnbhh; City of Santa Fe, *Water Rights Transfer Ordinance* 25-12 (2012), https://tinyurl.com/47sya375.

constitutes a Taking of senior water rights. Pay close attention to the court's distinction between issuance of a permit and administration of a right. This is a distinction you will see again in the conjunctive management cases introduced in Chapter 24. Under the court's ruling, consider what evidence Horace Bounds will need to show harm and what the consequences of a call on domestic wells might look like if he is successful.

Bounds v. New Mexico

Supreme Court of New Mexico
306 P.3d 457 (2013)

BOSSON, Justice—Horace Bounds is a rancher and farmer in the Mimbres basin in southwestern New Mexico, a fully appropriated and adjudicated basin. Bounds, joined by the New Mexico Farm and Livestock Bureau (collectively Petitioners), brought a facial constitutional challenge against the New Mexico Domestic Well Statute (DWS), NMSA 1978, Section 72-12-1.1 (2003), which requires the State Engineer to issue domestic well permits without determining the availability of unappropriated water. Petitioners contend that the DWS violates the New Mexico constitutional doctrine of prior appropriation as well as due process of law. Petitioners' arguments persuaded the district court but not the Court of Appeals, which reversed in a published opinion. Agreeing with the substance of that opinion, we affirm the Court of Appeals. For the reasons that follow, we hold that the DWS does not violate either the doctrine of prior appropriation set forth in the New Mexico Constitution or the guarantees of due process of law.

BACKGROUND

Bounds has the adjudicated right to irrigate 157.63 acres of farm and ranchland with some of the most senior surface water rights along the Upper Mimbres....

This case began on June 15, 2006, when Bounds filed an action for declaratory judgment in the Sixth Judicial District Court. The first count of his complaint asked the district court to declare the DWS unconstitutional because it requires the State Engineer to issue domestic well permits without regard to the availability of unappropriated water, to the detriment of senior water users and in violation of the doctrine of prior appropriation. The second count sought a declaration that the issuance of domestic well permits under the DWS constitutes a taking of vested property rights without compensation, in violation of the United States Constitution, the New Mexico Constitution, and 42 U.S.C. § 1983 (2006). Finally, Bounds sought an injunction preventing the State Engineer from issuing new domestic well permits without first determining that unappropriated water is available.

Before he filed this suit asking the district court to enjoin the State Engineer from issuing further permits under the DWS, Bounds took full advantage of the statute's simple permitting procedures. According to the record, he currently has five domestic and livestock wells, most recently drilled in 2005 and all acquired under the same permitting process that Bounds now challenges. Bounds also enjoyed the benefit of this statute when he subdivided and sold a portion of his farm in 1998. According to the State Engineer, the twelve-lot "subdivision was approved by Grant County, New Mexico, for the sale of individual lots to be served by domestic wells." Jo Bounds, Horace's wife, testified that four of the twelve lots have been developed, leaving five to eight lots yet to drill domestic wells.

... the State Engineer filed a motion for summary judgment. The State Engineer argued that the DWS "is a clear expression of legislative intent to treat certain necessary water uses differently," and that "[i]n creating this distinction, the Legislature has articulated a class of uses of public water that is reasonably subject to treatment outside the scope of the general scheme of appropriations." Thereafter, the parties stipulated to allowing the court to decide the legal issues presented on the pleadings, record, and evidence submitted.

The district court ultimately concluded that the DWS is unconstitutional as a matter of law "because it creates an impermissible exception to the priority administration system."... In addition, the court found a lack of evidence to support Bounds' claim of impairment of existing rights or his claim to related monetary damages. The court dismissed Bounds' takings claim. The State Engineer appealed the district court's constitutional ruling to the Court of Appeals.

Reversing the district court, the Court of Appeals ... concluded that

> the priority doctrine [in the New Mexico Constitution] is not a system of administration.... That the Legislature determines that domestic well permits are to be issued upon application without prior evaluation of water availability or impairment is not, in and of itself, a per se violation of the priority doctrine or of the Legislature's constitutional duty to assure that senior water rights are protected under the priority doctrine. Although a basin is considered fully appropriated with no unappropriated water available, we do not see how the Legislature is forbidden under a facial constitutional attack from nevertheless enacting an exception to its existing statutory regime permitting additional appropriation for domestic purposes as long as senior water rights are not in fact impaired or subject to impending impairment....

Id. ¶ 45.

... For the reasons that follow, we affirm the facial constitutionality of the DWS.

DISCUSSION

A. Standard of Review

... "'It is well settled that there is a presumption of the validity and regularity of legislative enactments.'" [citations omitted] We will uphold a statute "unless we are satisfied beyond all reasonable doubt that the Legislature went outside the bounds fixed by the Constitution in enacting the challenged legislation." *Id.* We do not "inquire into the wisdom or policy of an act of the Legislature." *Id.*...

B. Preliminary Matters

Petitioners' first argument is relatively straightforward. As NMFLB explains,

> [i]n 1972, the State Engineer declared the Mimbres Basin to be closed and as such, no additional water was available for appropriation. Thus, when the State Engineer made the determination that no additional water was available for appropriation, he became bound by the constitutional provisions of N.M. Const. art. XVI, §§ 1, 2, and 3, and NMSA 1978, § 72-12-4. No further permits could be issued for the appropriation of groundwater in the Mimbres Basin.

Accordingly, the argument goes, if the DWS requires the State Engineer to issue domestic well permits when there is no additional water available for appropriation, the statute must necessarily impact senior water users whose rights are secured by the New Mexico Constitution. As an initial matter, we address certain basic flaws in this and other arguments advanced by Petitioners.

First and foremost, Petitioners have brought a facial challenge. In the district court, Bounds was unable to show any actual injury, any impairment of his existing senior rights as a result of the DWS. Accordingly, Bounds was unable to pursue an as-applied challenge in which specific facts would be relevant and was left with only a facial challenge.

... Generally, "[i]n a facial challenge to [a statute], we consider only the text of the [statute] itself, not its application; whereas, in an as-applied challenge, we consider the facts of the case to determine whether application of the [statute] even if facially valid deprived the challenger of a protected right." [citations omitted]. Looking at the specific situation in the Mimbres basin—a fully appropriated and fully adjudicated basin—would require us to review the DWS as applied to Bounds, or at least as applied to the basin, and Bounds was unable to prove that the DWS caused any specific injury to himself or others.

Second, a separate argument advanced by Bounds—that the issuance of further permits in the Mimbres basin necessarily impairs senior water users—would require this Court, in order to rule for Petitioners, to hold that a new domestic well permit for taking water in a fully appropriated basin, even for only one well, constitutes impairment as a matter of law. Yet, under our well-established case law, this Court has repeatedly rejected the notion of impairment as a matter of law, or per se impairment as it has been called in the past.

...

Accordingly, there can be no constitutional challenge to the statute without at least a specific probability of impairment in a given case.

Under our precedent, we could decline to reach the merits of this case. That said, however, we exercise our discretion to decide these important issues. As we stated in *City of Albuquerque v. Campos*, "*[i]f*, as in the present case, the questions of public importance are likely to recur, ... reason exists for the exercise by this court of its inherent discretion to resolve those questions." [citations omitted]

...

[History of the statute granting domestic wells and other small wells exemption from aspects of the permitting statute is discussed by the court. It then goes on to provide the current law.]

The portion dealing with domestic wells was recodified to NMSA 1978, Section 72-12-1.1 (2003). It states that

> A person, firm or corporation desiring to use public underground waters described in this section for irrigation of not to exceed one acre of noncommercial trees, lawn or garden or for household or other domestic use shall make application to the state engineer for a well on a form to be prescribed by the state engineer. Upon the filing of each application describing the use applied for, the state engineer *shall* issue a permit to the applicant to use the underground waters applied for; provided that permits for domestic water use within municipalities shall be conditioned to require the permittee to comply with all applicable municipal ordinances enacted pursuant to Chapter 3, Article 53 NMSA 1978.

Section 72-12-1.1 (emphasis added).

By contrast, NMSA 1978, Section 72-12-3 (2001), sets out the permitting process prescribed for most other ground water appropriations, such as those for agricultural and industrial use, but which does not apply to permits for domestic wells. According to Section 72-12-3(D), the State Engineer is required, upon the filing of an application, to cause notice to be published in a newspaper. Thereafter, any person claiming that the new appropriation will impair existing water rights must be allowed to protest the application. *Id.* Even if no one objects,

> the state engineer shall, if he finds that there are in the underground stream, channel, artesian basin, reservoir or lake unappropriated waters or that the proposed appropriation would not impair existing water rights from the source, is not contrary to conservation of water within the state and is not detrimental to the public welfare of the state, grant the application and issue a permit to the applicant to appropriate all or a part of the waters applied for, subject to the rights of all prior appropriators from the source.

Section 72-12-3(E)....

In 2006, the State Engineer promulgated regulations specifically for domestic wells. *See* 19.27.5 NMAC (8/15/2006, as amended through 10/31/2011). These regulations allow the State Engineer to manage domestic wells in various ways. For example, 19.27.5.13 NMAC subjects domestic wells to certain conditions of approval, the most important of which is curtailment to protect existing water rights in times of shortage: "The right to divert water under [a domestic well] permit is subject to curtailment by priority administration as implemented by the state engineer or a court." 19.27.5.13(B)(11) NMAC.

In addition to imposing conditions upon domestic well permits, the regulations also provide for the State Engineer to "declare all or part of a stream connected aquifer as a domestic well management area *to prevent impairment to valid existing surface water rights.*" 19.27.5.14 NMAC (emphasis added). This and other regulations allow the State Engineer to declare a management area and create specific administrative guidelines for that particular basin to ensure that senior surface water users are not harmed by junior domestic wells. *See* 19.27.5.14(A). In addition, the regulations significantly reduce the maximum diversion from new domestic wells in the management area to 0.25 acre-feet per year or even less, as required by the State Engineer. *See* 19.27.5.14(C).

. . .

D. The DWS Is Not Facially Unconstitutional

Looking at the language in Article XVI, Section 2 of the New Mexico Constitution upon which Petitioners rely—"[p]riority of appropriation shall give the better right"—it is clear that priority administration, including curtailment when justified, is what this Section mandates. "Shall give the *better* right" is a phrase meant to apply to two existing, yet competing, water rights. This phrase implies that two rights are at issue, since if there were only one right, that right could not be *better,* as there would be nothing to be better than. "Priority of appropriation" tells us *how* to determine which right is better. Thus, the entire phrase "priority of appropriation shall give the better right" is meant to dictate how conflicts between water users can be resolved—by priority administration—in which junior users are diminished or cut off when necessary in favor of senior users. In short, this language means that priority administration—exactly what Petitioners desire to protect their senior water rights—may be used to determine how water is allocated in times of shortage. This language deals with how rights, already acquired, will be administered.

This portion of the New Mexico Constitution does not mandate any particular *permitting* procedure. In fact, this language does not appear to pertain to how one *acquires* a water right, as opposed to how that right is *used* and *administered.*

The DWS, on the other hand, is a permitting statute. It dictates the procedure for how one acquires a permit to drill a domestic well.... The statute does not, however, dictate how the permit is administered. In fact, the DWS is entirely silent as to how permits issued under that statute are administered. Nothing in the language of the DWS prevents domestic well permits from being administered in the same way as all other water rights, including priority administration—exactly what Article XVI, Section 2 of the New Mexico Constitution requires.

Theoretically, the State Engineer could issue a domestic well permit and immediately administer priority to curtail diversion under that permit. While this might seem absurd at first glance, further examination suggests otherwise. In such an instance, a permit—even if temporarily inoperative—would give the applicant a priority date. Should conditions in the particular basin change, curtailment by priority administration could be lifted, and the permit holder could then divert water under that permit with a priority date set at the original date when the permit issued. In this regard, the permit would serve as a placeholder should more water become available in the future. The State Engineer has essentially done this in the Gila basin, issuing permits that do not allow for an actual diversion. Depending on the circumstances, the State Engineer could apply a similar procedure elsewhere to meet a growing shortage of water and imminent threat to senior water users.

This discussion reveals the basic flaw in Petitioners' argument. Petitioners are mistakenly equating the issuance of a permit under the DWS with an absolute right to take and use water pursuant to that permit. It would only be in the case of such an absolute water right that the mere issuance of a permit in a fully appropriated basin would necessarily take water from senior users and impair senior water rights. However, the DWS does not create such an unconditional right—at least not on its face.

All water rights, including those of Petitioners as well as those created by the DWS, are inherently conditional.... They are conditioned on the *availability* of water to satisfy that right....

...

Despite these legal provisions for priority administration of domestic wells, Petitioners argue that for practical and political reasons the State Engineer will never really curtail domestic wells. Petitioners rely on the deposition of former State Engineer John D'Antonio, in which he stated that he would not curtail *indoor use* of a domestic well. The district court incorrectly took this deposition testimony to mean that Mr. D'Antonio would *never* curtail domestic wells in any manner. We understand the concern. This Court has previously noted the practical challenges facing the state in curtailing the use of domestic wells. *See Herrington v. State of N.M. ex rel. Office of State Eng'r*, 2006-NMSC-014, ¶ 50, 139 N.M. 368, 133 P.3d 258.

But such speculation about what the State Engineer may or may not do in the future cannot form the basis of a facial challenge in the present.

...

Though Petitioners' facial challenge proves unpersuasive, we emphasize that senior water users do have other recourse under the law. A water user who is able to show actual or impending impairment can make a priority call against junior users and, if that fails, the water user could then file an as-applied challenge against the DWS....

Accordingly, we hold that the DWS does not on its face violate the New Mexico Constitution, and we affirm the decision of the Court of Appeals ...

CONCLUSION

For the above reasons, we hereby affirm the Court of Appeals.

Notes & Questions

1. How does the court use the difference between obtaining a water right and the administration of that right to find the domestic well exemption facially constitutional even in a closed basin?
2. What scientific evidence will Horace Bounds need to present to show harm from domestic well pumping?
3. The court leaves open the possibility of a call on junior domestic wells if a senior water user shows harm. Consider the differences between New Mexico's use of priority administration after development occurs to Washington's approach to determining water availability prior to development. Which is the better approach?
4. In considering the size of domestic well exemptions, recall from Part IV that the internationally recognized Human Right to Water requires that a person has access to water that is: (1) sufficient, meaning 13–26 gallons/person/day; (2) safe, meaning it meets drinking water standards; (3) accessible, meaning within .6 miles of the household; (4) affordable, meaning costs no more than three percent of household income. Places in the world that do not meet this standard include parts of the Navajo Reservation in the western United States. From the Introduction to Part I:

   Clean water supplies and sanitation remain major problems in many parts of the world, with 20% of the global population lacking access to safe drinking water. Around 1.1 billion people globally do not have access to improved water supply sources, while 2.4 billion people do not have access to any type of improved sanitation facility. About two million people die every year due to water-borne diseases from fecal pollution of surface waters; most of them are children less than five years of age.

Chapter 21

State Regulation of Changes in an Existing Water Right

Introduction

Along with the growing need to track water rights and provide a prospective analysis of whether water is both physically and legally available (which led to permit systems), full development of water resources led to the need for ongoing management. This ongoing management required increased flexibility and tighter control to force efficiency—both designed to maximize beneficial use.

Flexibility was introduced through processes for change in various aspects of the water rights, including point of diversion, place of use, type of use, and period of use. This allowed the same water user to alter crop mix and location in response to changes in commodity prices and irrigation technology. Since water rights could be transferred to a new user both with and without a sale of land, it also provided a means of tracking transfers.

The statutory effort to tighten control to ensure greater beneficial use of water focused on the difficulty of proving abandonment at common law. Recall from Part II that abandonment, or loss through nonuse, generally requires a showing of intent. Simple nonuse was insufficient to show intent. Statutory forfeiture removes the requirement of intent by providing a presumption of forfeiture after a specified period of nonuse.

Coincident with the rise of administrative systems governed by statute, arid states realized that the long history of development through diversion and application to a beneficial use left them with an incomplete database. To remedy this, some western states commenced basin-wide or state-wide general adjudications. A general water adjudication is a judicial process to determine the attributes of all water rights and to create a central database as the foundation for future management. Adjudication will be the topic of Part VI; but an area of overlap occurs in the context of change in use and will be covered here. Change in water rights statutes apply retroactively, meaning that even pre-permit rights must comply with the change process. However, many changes occurred prior to the statutory system, and even with the statutory system, changes occurred beneath the radar and without compliance with the statutory system. With improving irrigation technology, some changes improved efficiency and it was a common practice to "spread" saved water to additional acreage. Studies indicated that this was a major problem within Reclamation projects where people sought to avoid the federal assessment and soils analysis required to move water to another location. Problems involved in handling these past changes and associated enlargements in use are covered here (even though they were often discovered during adjudication) because they introduce some of the complexities that arise in evaluation of proposed changes. This also sets the stage for the final sections in this Chapter—the emerging problem of the impact of individual efforts to increase efficiency on system-wide water supply—highlighted in the U.S. Supreme Court case of *Montana v. Wyoming*.

Process for Change in an Existing Water Right

The following excerpt from Idaho's change in water right statutes is provided as an example of how states with administrative agencies handle change in use. Note that the language makes clear that compliance with the process applies not just to permitted water rights, but to all existing water rights. Note the bulleted list of criteria. The first, no injury, differs from the permit statutes as discussed below. The second, no enlargement, is specific to the change water rights statute and will also be discussed below. You will recognize the rest from the permit statute. Recall that you learned in the previous Chapter in *Hardy v. Higginson*, that to avoid circumvention of permit requirements, the same requirements apply to the permit application, amendment, and change in water right.

Idaho's Change in Water Right Statute[1]

> Idaho Code 42-222. CHANGE IN POINT OF DIVERSION, PLACE OF USE, PERIOD OF USE, OR NATURE OF USE OF WATER UNDER ESTABLISHED RIGHTS.... (1) Any person, entitled to the use of water whether represented by license issued by the department of water resources, by claims to water rights by reason of diversion and application to a beneficial use as filed under the provisions of this chapter, or by decree of the court, who shall desire to change the point of diversion, place of use, period of use or nature of use of all or part of the water, under the right shall first make application to the department of water resources for approval of such change ... [forms, filing fees, notice, opportunity to protest] Upon the receipt of any protest, ... it shall be the duty of the director of the department of water resources to investigate the same and to conduct a hearing thereon....
>
> ... [provisions covering municipal water rights or change to municipal use discussed below]

1. Note that change in water rights statutes are also referred to as "water transfer" statutes, identifying the largest volume of types of "change."

The director of the department of water resources shall examine all the evidence and available information and shall approve the change in whole, or in part, or upon conditions, provided [The following is reorganized from the statute for ease of reading and understanding. No language has been altered.]

- no other water rights are injured thereby,
- the change does not constitute an enlargement in use of the original right,
  - The director may consider consumptive use, as defined in section 42-202B, Idaho Code, as a factor in determining whether a proposed change would constitute an enlargement in use of the original water right.
  - The transfer of the right to the use of stored water for irrigation purposes shall not constitute an enlargement in use of the original right even though more acres may be irrigated, if no other water rights are injured thereby.
- the change is consistent with the conservation of water resources within the state of Idaho and is in the local public interest as defined in section 42-202B, Idaho Code,
- the change will not adversely affect the local economy of the watershed or local area within which the source of water for the proposed use originates,
- in the case where the place of use is outside of the watershed or local area where the source of water originates, and the new use is a beneficial use, which in the case of a municipal provider shall be satisfied if the water right is necessary to serve reasonably anticipated future needs as provided in this Chapter.
- The director shall not approve a change in the nature of use from agricultural use where such change would significantly affect the agricultural base of the local area.

A copy of the approved application for change shall be returned to the applicant and he shall be authorized upon receipt thereof to make the change and the original water right shall be presumed to have been amended by reason of such authorized change. In the event the director of the department of water resources determines that a proposed change shall not be approved as provided in this section, he shall deny the same and forward notice of such action to the applicant by certified mail, which decision shall be subject to judicial review as hereafter set forth. Provided however, minimum stream flow water rights may not be established under the local public interest criterion, and may only be established pursuant to chapter 15, title 42, Idaho Code.

No-Injury Rule

While the requirement of no injury sounds similar to the permit requirement that a proposed water use will not "reduce the quantity of water under existing water rights," its timing renders it different. Pursuant to the concept that a water user has the right to take the water source as they find it, the no-injury rule found in the change in water rights statute applies to both senior and junior water users in existence at the time of the change application. For example, a change that moves the point of diversion upstream from a junior water use and, as a result, lowers the water level below the junior's diversion, would cause injury to the junior water right in violation of the statute.

No Enlargement Rule

The change in water right statute prohibits enlargement of a water right. You will learn in *Fremont-Madison Irrigation District and Mitigation Group v. Idaho Ground Water Appropriators, Inc.*, 926 P.2d 1301 (Idaho 1996), that Idaho defines an enlargement to "include such events as an increase in the number of acres irrigated, an increase in the rate of diversion or duration of diversion." Thus, a water user seeking to expand acreage, increase diversion rate or volume must obtain a new water right with a new priority date. You will learn below that a major loophole in this prohibition on enlargement allows a water user to increase the volume of water consumed (not the volume applied) on the same acreage through efficiency improvements and recapture of wastewater. While this loophole was allowed to incentivize efficiency improvements, it has resulted in systemic problems on a number of western rivers (discussed below in the case between Montana and Wyoming).

Notes & Questions

1. If no one objects to the proposed change in a water right, must the application be approved?
2. Does the change statute allow a change in type of use from, for example, irrigation to municipal use? If so, what might be the challenges to this type of change?

Temporary Change in a Water Right

Periodic fallowing of land, changes in cropping, or changes in industrial operations may lead to surplus water on a short-term basis, with the water right holder seeking to maintain the water right in the long run. Similarly, other water users may have a short-term need for additional water. This situation is particularly prevalent during drought. The transaction costs of multiple transfer processes are a disincentive to short-term transfers. The threat of a finding of forfeiture or common law abandonment is a disincentive to temporary nonuse of all or a portion of a water right. To address these issues, many states have established water banks to reduce transaction costs by protecting banked water against loss for nonuse and avoiding the problem of needing an exact match between transferor and transferee. Some states also provide expedited procedures for temporary transfers during drought. The Idaho water bank statutes and process provide an example of how this works.

Water Supply Bank

Idaho's water supply bank statutes can be found at §§ 42-1761–1766 of the Idaho Code and administrative rules are found at IDAPA 37.02.03. The statutes establish both a statewide water market administered by the Idaho Water Resource Board (IWRB)[2] and storage water rental pools associated with watershed reservoir systems, which are administered by local rental committees appointed by the IWRB.[3] In addition, the Shoshone-Bannock Tribes administer a Tribal water supply bank in the upper Snake River reservoir storage system.[4] While rental pools rely on reservoir storage of banked water, the Lemhi River has a natural flow rental pool established in an effort to move water to environmental flows.[5]

The metaphor of a financial bank is useful in understanding how a water bank works. While individuals may be willing to loan money to others, the chances of an exact match between funds available and funds needed is rare. Banks serve as intermediaries. People with surplus cash may place it in a savings account. Someone needing funds—for example, for a home mortgage—may seek a loan. Not only is an exact match between lender and recipient unnecessary, but the volume of transactions provides a certain level of protection against risk of individual default (even in the absence of federal insurance). Similarly, water "deposited" in a water bank merges with all other deposits, allowing a broader range of potential withdrawals and providing a centralized screening process on both deposit and withdrawal. Tables 21.1 and 21.2 below illustrate how successful this strategy is in Idaho. To understand the process, it is useful to view water banking first from the perspective of the person banking water and second from the perspective of the person seeking to withdraw water.

People seeking to bank water must apply to the Idaho Water Resource Board (IWRB) or the local committee appointed by the IWRB. The Department of Water Resources (the agency that provides staff for the independent IWRB) administrative rules address the criteria for approval as follows.

> The Board will consider the following in determining whether to accept an offered water right into the Board's water supply bank:
>
> a. Whether the applicant is the current owner, title holder or contract water user of the water right proposed to be transferred to the Board's water supply bank or has authority to act on behalf of the owner;
>
> b. Whether all necessary consents have been filed with the Board;
>
> c. Whether the information available to the Board indicates that the water right has been abandoned or forfeited;
>
> d. Whether the offering price or requested rental rate is reasonable;

2. Idaho Code § 42-1761.
3. Idaho Code § 42-1765.
4. IDAPA 37.02.04.
5. Idaho Code § 42-1765A.

e. Whether acquisition of the water right will be contrary to the State Water Plan;

f. Whether the application is in the local public interest as defined in Idaho Code § 42-1763;

g. The probability of selling or renting the water right from the Board's water supply bank;

h. Whether there are sufficient funds on hand to acquire the water right for the Board's water supply bank, provided that, if there are insufficient funds, or if in the opinion of the Board, existing funds should not immediately be expended for such acquisition, the Board may find that the water right should be acquired on a contingency basis, with payment to be made to the seller or lessor only after water is subsequently sold or rented from the Board's water supply bank; and

i. Such other factors as determined to be appropriate by the Board.[6]

Banked water is "not subject to forfeiture for nonuse ... while retained in or rented from the water supply bank."[7]

From the viewpoint of those seeking water, the Idaho Department of Water Resources (IDWR) must approve withdrawals (lease or rental) from the water supply bank or rental pool.[8] Withdrawal may be for up to five years, or longer with IWRB approval.[9] IDWR must provide notice and follow the process for a change if the withdrawal is for more than five years, but may waive that process if it is for five or fewer years.[10] IDWR must deny the withdrawal if:

> it will reduce the quantity of water available under other existing water rights, the water supply involved is insufficient for the purpose for which it is sought, the rental would cause the use of water to be enlarged beyond that authorized under the water right to be rented, the rental will conflict with the local public interest ..., or the rental will adversely affect the local economy of the watershed or local area within which the source of water for the proposed use originates, in the case where the place of use is outside of the watershed or local area where the source of water originates."[11]

With the exception of water released from the water bank for anadromous fish species,[12] banked water may not be withdrawn for use out of state. Title 42, Chapter 4, discussed in the previous Chapter, provides the only means for out-of-state transfers.[13]

---

6. IDAPA 37.02.03.025.06.
7. Idaho Code § 42-1764(2).
8. Idaho Code § 42-1763.
9. IDAPA 37.02.03.30.05.
10. DAPA 37.02.03.30.02.
11. Idaho Code § 42-1763.
12. Idaho Code § 42-1763A.
13. Idaho Code § 42-1763.

Table 21.1 shows the various sources of requests for rental water from the IWRB bank in one year, 2016. While the majority of water moves between irrigators, it is interesting to note that one quarter of the requests come from non-irrigation uses, including minimum stream flows, wildlife, and aesthetics. Table 21.2 shows that rental volumes are in the tens of thousands of acre-feet per year.

Water Bank Rental

Irrigation	72%
Ground Water Recharge	3%
Commercial	3%
Wildlife/Aesthetic/Recreation	3%
Stockwater, Commercial	3%
Stockwater	3%
Mitigation by Nonuse	3%
Minimum Stream Flow	3%
Irrigation Storage	3%

Table 21.1 Sources of state water bank rental requests in 2016. Source of data: Idaho Department of Water Resources.

Rented Volume by Year (Acre-Feet)

2013	75000
2014	84000
2015	85000
2016	76000
2017	70000
2018	70000
2019	63000

Table 21.2 Yearly rental volume illustrates that the role of the water supply bank in moving water to more urgent needs is not insignificant. Source of data: Idaho Department of Water Resources.

Expedited Change Process During Drought Conditions

As you learned in Part I, climate change is a manifestation of increased energy in the atmosphere due to an increase in greenhouse gases. The result is not only a general warming trend but increases in extreme weather events. Longer and deeper droughts are of concern to people and communities reliant on irrigated agriculture. With Idaho's Snake River basin being third in irrigated agriculture productivity in the nation (with California's Central Valley and Imperial Irrigation District being first and second), the concern rises to the state level. In response, the Idaho legislature enacted an expedited, temporary (generally the transfer expires at the end of the calendar year) change process for use during a period of declared drought emergency.[14]

Published notice and an objection period is not required for a temporary change and IDWR need only examine the change to ensure no injury.[15] The temporary change may only be done to provide replacement water for a use that would receive a full supply absent drought.[16] To protect other interests, the statute provides that:

> [t]he recipient of an approved temporary change issued pursuant to this section shall assume all risk that the diversion and use of the water may cause injury to other water rights, that the change constitutes an enlargement in use of the original right, that the use is not consistent with the conservation of water resources within the state of Idaho and that such use is not in the local public interest.[17]

Notes & Questions

1. How does a water bank reduce transaction costs?
2. What benefits does the person banking water receive?
3. Does the applicant for water from a water bank avoid the criteria applied to a change in use process?
4. How does shifting the risk of harm for a temporary transfer to the recipient expedite the transfer process?

Statutory Forfeiture

Changes in a water right may also occur through operation of law. In Part II you learned about the common law concept of abandonment—also referred to as "use it or lose it." Abandonment was very difficult to prove due to the requirement of intent. With the need to more carefully manage water as demand grew, state legislatures passed forfeiture statutes that eliminated a requirement of intent and provided for a presumption of forfeiture after a statutory period of non-use. Idaho Code § 42-222(2) provides an example of a forfeiture statute:

> All rights to the use of water acquired under this chapter or otherwise shall be lost and forfeited by a failure for the term of five (5) years to apply it to the

---

14. Idaho Code § 42-222A (enacted in 1993 and amended in 2001). Note that drought emergency is done for specific areas by IDWR on approval by the Governor and occurs when water supply is below "average." *See* Idaho Department of Water Resources, *Drought Declarations* (June 6, 2022), https://idwr.idaho.gov/water-data/drought-declarations/.

15. Idaho Code § 42-222A(3).

16. Idaho Code § 42-222A(6).

17. Idaho Code § 42-222A(5).

> beneficial use for which it was appropriated and when any right to the use of water shall be lost through nonuse or forfeiture such rights to such water shall revert to the state and be again subject to appropriation under this chapter; except that any right to the use of water shall not be lost through forfeiture by the failure to apply the water to beneficial use under certain circumstances as specified in section 42-223, Idaho Code. The party asserting that a water right has been forfeited has the burden of proving the forfeiture by clear and convincing evidence.

The period may be extended for up to an additional five years on a showing of "good and sufficient reason for nonapplication to beneficial use." 42-222(3). The exceptions to forfeiture, listed in 42-223, are extensive and are paraphrased here:

> (1) The water right is associated with "land contracted in a federal cropland set-aside program" ...;
>
> (2) The water right is held by a municipal provider for "future needs." ...;
>
> (3) The water right "is not needed to maintain full beneficial use ... because of land application of waste for disposal purposes" ...;
>
> (4) The non-use "is to comply with the provisions of a ground water management plan" ...;
>
> (5) The water right has been "placed in the water supply bank or is retained in or rented from the water supply bank" ...;
>
> (6) The "nonuse results from circumstances over which the water right owner has no control." ...;
>
> (7) The right is "held by an ... entity which holds water rights for distribution to its landowners, shareholders or members" ... and the nonuse is "by such landowners, shareholders or members, unless the nonuse is subject to the control of such entity";
>
> (8) The "water right held by an irrigation district ..." and the land it is appurtenant to has been excluded "from the district" provided ... "the exclusion does not result from circumstances over which the district has control."
>
> (9) "... the nonuse results from a water conservation practice, which maintains the full beneficial use authorized by the water right,"
>
> (10) "... the nonuse results from the water right being used for mitigation purposes approved by the director of the department of water resources including as a condition of approval for a new water right appropriation ... a water right transfer ... a water exchange ... or a mitigation plan...."
>
> (11) "... a beneficial use related to mining, mineral processing or milling ... so long as the nonuse results from a closure, suspension or reduced production of the mine, processing facility or mill due in whole or in part to mineral prices, ... and the water right owner has maintained the property and mineral rights for potential future mineral production."

(12) "... if, after the five (5) year period of nonuse, use of the water is resumed prior to a claim of right by a third party. A third party has made a claim of right if the party has:

(a) Instituted proceedings to declare a forfeiture;

(b) Obtained a valid water right authorizing the use of such water with a priority date prior to the resumption of use; or

(c) Used the water made available by nonuse pursuant to an existing water right.

Water resource agencies do not have the time or resources to enforce statutes like the forfeiture one against every water right in the state. Instead, issues of forfeiture generally come up in two situations: (1) an adjudication of water rights (you will see this in the next section on enlargement in use); and (2) a water right change process. The following case (with the location of water diversions shown in Figure 21.1) arises in a change process and illustrates not only the application of the law, but the difference between forfeiture and abandonment and the defenses that remain under the forfeiture statute.

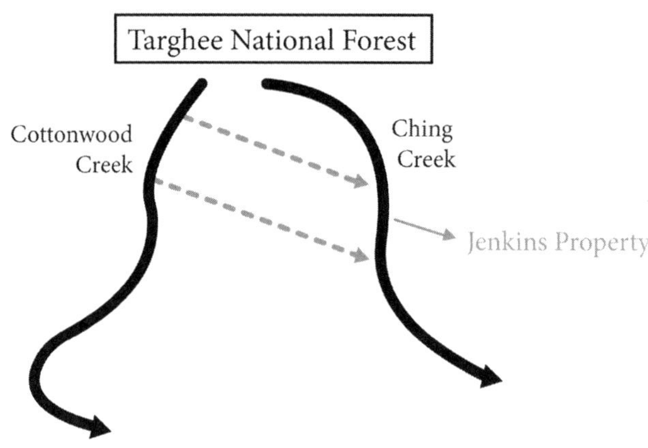

Figure 21.1 Showing the configuration of the two creeks, the intermittent connection between the two creeks and the diversion to Jenkins' property for the next principal case. Source: Design by Leilanee Taylor.

Jenkins v. Department of Water Resources

Supreme Court of Idaho
103 Idaho 384, 647 P.2d 1256 (1982)

SHEPARD, J.—This is an appeal from an order of the district court which affirmed the director of the Department of Water Resources denial of appellant Jenkins' application to transfer the point of diversion of his decreed water right. We affirm.

... [Figure 21.1 illustrates the facts. Jenkins claims two water rights, one from Ching Creek and one from Cottonwood Creek, but diverts both from Ching Creek downstream from where two intermittent streams connect the two creeks bringing water from Cottonwood Creek to Ching Creek. Both water rights were the subject of a 1930 federal court decree. The issue of forfeiture comes up when Jenkins seeks to change the diversion point for both rights.]

Several water users on both Ching and Cottonwood Creeks protested these proposed transfers, and the district water master recommended that the Department deny the transfer of the Cottonwood right. A hearing was held thereon at which all parties were represented by counsel. Thereafter the director of the Department issued an order granting the transfer of the point of diversion of the Ching Creek right but denying the transfer of the point of diversion of the Cottonwood Creek right. The director found that no water had been diverted from Cottonwood Creek for use on Jenkin's land for the previous 18 years. He also found that waters of both Ching and Cottonwood Creeks were overappropriated. He concluded that to allow a resumption of use of the Cottonwood right would represent an enlargement of the use over the prior 18 years, that the water users would be injured thereby, and that I.C. Idaho Sess. Laws § 42-222 authorized denial of an application in such circumstances. The director relied upon that portion of I.C. § 42-222 which provides for the forfeiture of a water right not used for five years.

From that decision of the director, Jenkins appealed to the district court. At the outset Jenkins contended that the Department lacked jurisdiction to determine an abandonment or forfeiture and objected to the district court making such a determination on appeal from a decision of the Department. The district court reserved judgment on that issue and held a trial de novo.

...

The trial court found that water from Cottonwood Creek only flowed to Ching Creek irregularly during the spring run off and that any such contribution was not the result of a physical diversion. The court also found that Jenkins took only 3.2 cfs of water from Ching Creek which was the amount he was entitled to under his Ching Creek right, and therefore he received no water in excess of his Ching Creek right, which could be construed as Cottonwood right water. The court also found that there was insufficient water in the two creeks to meet the then present demand. The court held that the director of the Department had jurisdiction to determine the issues of abandonment or forfeiture as a part of his determination of injury to other water rights, and that even if the director was without that jurisdiction, the district court hearing the case de novo did have the necessary jurisdiction to make that determination. The court affirmed the decision of the director of the Department in all respects.

....

Jenkins next asserts that the findings of the district court are insufficient upon which to base a conclusion that his Cottonwood Creek water right was lost through abandonment or forfeiture. We note initially that care must be taken in this type of proceeding to distinguish between abandonment and forfeiture....

.... The record shows only non-use, disclosing no intent to abandon, and hence Jenkins did not lose his water right by common law abandonment.

We then proceed to a determination of whether the findings are sufficient to support a determination of a statutory forfeiture. Jenkins argues that the court below found no point of diversion on Cottonwood Creek for the 2.4 cfs of decreed water, and such was erroneous in view of the decree of the federal court. That decree was an unreported decision of the federal district court in *Suave v. Abbot,* decided in 1930. That decree establishes that there had been a diversion on Cottonwood Creek and that the water was beneficially used upon the land to which it is appurtenant up to the time of the decree. *Morgan v. Udy,* 79 P.2d 295 (Idaho 1938). Hence, it is established that until the time of that decree, Jenkins' predecessor in interest was using the 2.4 cfs of Cottonwood water. The decree does not establish that the 2.4 cfs of water has continued to flow from one creek to the other, nor does it establish that Jenkins or his predecessors continued to apply that water to a beneficial use on the land following the 1930 decree.

Statutory forfeiture is based upon the legislative declaration in I.C. § 42-222(2) that water rights may be lost if they are not applied to a beneficial use for a period of five continuous years. Certain defenses to forfeiture have been recognized. Extension of the five year period may be made upon a showing of good cause, providing the application for extension is made within the first five-year period. I.C. § 42-222(2). Also wrongful interference with a water right or failure to use the water because of circumstances over which the water right holder has no control have been recognized as defenses. Further, if use of the water right is resumed after the five year period, but before any third parties make a claim in the water, then the courts will decline to declare a forfeiture. Here Jenkins has raised none of these defenses, and the record is devoid of any evidence to indicate that any of the established defenses would be applicable even if argued. The entire case was tried and appealed on Jenkins' theory that he had used the Cottonwood water the entire time.

Forfeitures are not favored, and clear and convincing proof is required to support a forfeiture. Here it was found that Jenkins had not used his Cottonwood water right for 18 years *i.e.,* 1961–1979. It is clear that the director of the Department of Water Resources relied on the forfeiture statute in his decision, and that decision was affirmed by the trial court "in all respects". While the record could have been made more clear by a specific conclusion of the trial court as to forfeiture, we do not deem such absence to be fatal here.

In abandonment and forfeiture cases, this Court has applied the rule that when there is substantial but conflicting evidence to support the findings of the trial court, those findings will not be disturbed on appeal. Here the evidence before the trial court was conflicting in numerous issues, *i.e.,* there was dispute over how much water Jenkins used, how many acres it was applied to, the amount and frequency of water flow in the channels between Cottonwood and Ching Creeks, and the soil porosity of those channels. The court found against Jenkins on all of those issues. There is substantial, albeit conflicting, evidence indicating that Jenkins failed to use Cottonwood Creek water for a beneficial use between 1961 and 1979, a period of 18 years. The water master testified that he had delivered water from the two creeks for those 18 years, but has not delivered nor been requested to deliver to Jenkins the 2.4 cfs water out of Cottonwood Creek. The trial court found that the channels from Cottonwood Creek to Ching Creek do not carry a regular flow of water except during the spring runoff. Those facts are supported by clear and convincing evidence, and support the conclusion of statutory forfeiture.

We have examined Jenkins remaining assignments of error and find them to be without merit.

Accordingly, we affirm the order of the district court, which in turn affirmed the decision of the Director of the Department of Water Resources which denied the application for the transfer of the point of diversion of Jenkins' Cottonwood water right.

MCFADDEN, BISTLINE AND DONALDSON, JJ., CONCUR.

Notes & Questions

1. What are the primary differences between abandonment and forfeiture?
2. Think back to the chapter in Part 1 on hydrology. Why is it unlikely that an irrigation water right that relies on the natural flow of the stream (as opposed to storage) is able to divert water that only comes from another stream during high spring runoff?

Enlargement and Change in Use in the Adjudication Context

You will study adjudication in Part VI. Adjudication is the judicial process of determining the relative rights among those participating—basically, who gets what water, when, and for what. A general adjudication requires all those claiming water on the source to be adjudicated to file claims. You will learn in Part VI that a number of western states have undergone general adjudication on either a state-wide or basin-by-basin approach since the 1970s in response to the need to more closely manage water. In the process of doing so, they discovered that substantial change in use had occurred without compliance with any state-required process, or federal process for those within a Reclamation project. In some cases, after implementing efficiency improvements, irrigators "spread" water to additional acreage. Figure 21.2 shows the various ways water has been transferred (i.e., "spread") without compliance with state process.

Judicial enforcement of state water law as written would result in loss of these water rights that have failed to use the change process. In an effort to protect these uses, states like Idaho and Montana attempted to pass legislative fixes. The first attempt by Idaho was found unconstitutional due to the harm to other water users who would have been protected by the no-injury rule had the change in water right process been complied with—thus the government's implementation of the statute would be a Taking. While

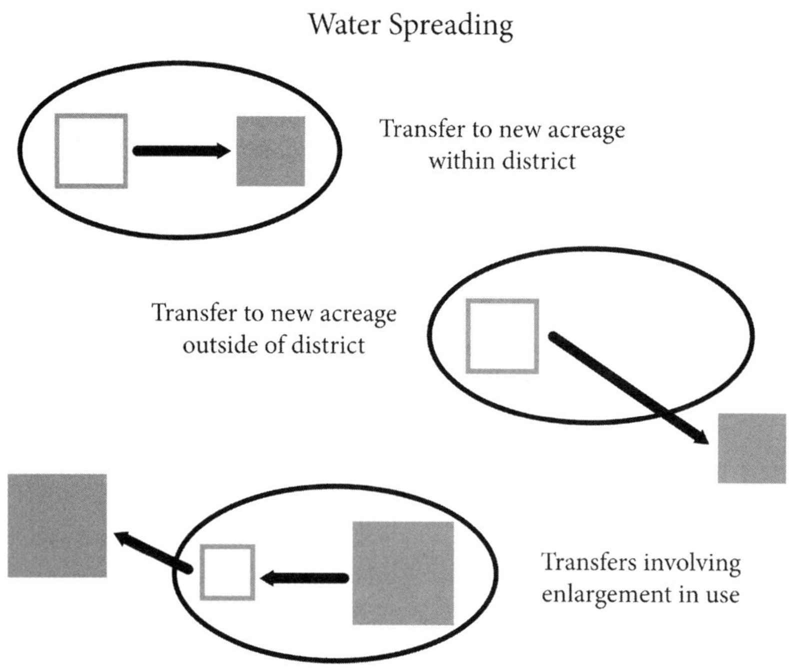

Figure 21.2 Water spreading is the movement of water within and outside of an irrigation district without following state change in use procedures (and often Reclamation procedures if within a Reclamation project).[18] Water spreading occurs with and without an increase in acreage irrigated. Note that, unfortunately, the term "water spreading" is also used to describe the method of flood irrigation and there is no relation between the two uses of the term. Source: Design by Leilanee Taylor.

addressing the problem of water spreading may appear to be an issue specific to these adjudications, water spreading is a much larger, West-wide problem. Understanding the mix of executive, legislative, and judicial forums necessary to resolve this type of issue is important to serving your client. Not every issue begins (or ends) in the courtroom.

Relevant parts of the two statutes passed in the legislature's second, successful, attempt to provide amnesty follow.

Idaho Code § 42-1425: Accomplished Transfer [see Figure 21.3]

> (2) Any change of place of use, point of diversion, nature or purpose of use or period of use of a water right by any person entitled to use of water … may be claimed in the applicable general adjudication even though the person has not complied with sections 42-108 and 42-222, Idaho Code, provided no other water rights existing on the date of the change were injured and the change did not result in an enlargement of the original right.

---

18. Note that Reclamation requires soils assessment and a fee for movement of water to new land outside the district boundaries and state law requires an additional process to change the district boundaries. These additional avoided processes and costs are beyond the scope of this textbook, but nevertheless of importance to any client in this position.

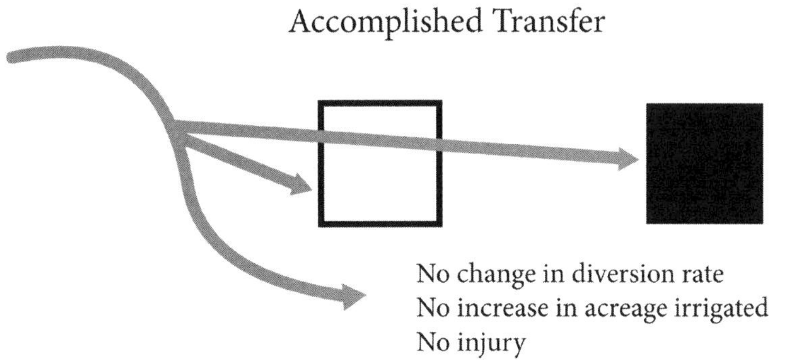

Figure 21.3 Amnesty Statute, Idaho Code § 42-1425, allows an accomplished transfer to the same number of acres if there is no change in diversion rate and no injury to other water rights in existence on the date of the change. Source: Design by Leilanee Taylor.

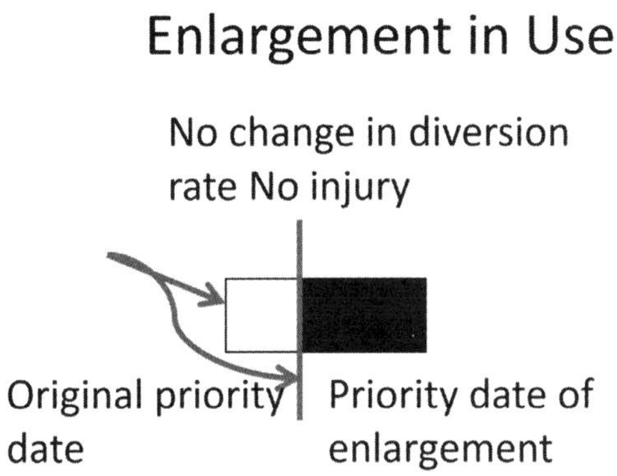

Figure 21.4 Amnesty Statute, Idaho Code 42-1426, allows an enlargement in use if there is no change in diversion rate and no injury to other water rights in existence on the date of the change. The increased acreage receives the priority date of enlargement. Source: Design by Leilanee Taylor.

Idaho Code § 42-1426: Enlargement in Use [see Figure 21.4]

> (2) The mandatory permit requirements of sections 42-201 and 42-229, Idaho Code, are waived, and a new water right may be decreed for the enlarged use of the original water right . . . , with a priority date as of the date of completion of the enlargement . . . provided however, that the rate of diversion of the original water right and the separate water right for the enlarged use, combined, shall not exceed the rate of diversion authorized for the original water right; and . . . the enlargement in use did not injure water rights existing on the date of the enlargement of use. An enlargement may be decreed if conditions directly related to the injury can be imposed on the original water right and the new water right that mitigate any injury to a water right existing on the date of enactment of this act. If injury to a water right later in time cannot be mitigated, then the new right for the enlarged use shall be advanced to a date one (1) day later than the priority date for the junior water right injured by the enlargement. . . .

The following case involves the challenges to this second attempt by the Idaho legislature to pass the so-called "amnesty" statutes. Pay attention to how "enlargement" in use is defined, and why this allows the Idaho Supreme Court to uphold the statutes in *Fremont-Madison Irrigation District v. Idaho Ground Water Appropriators*. Make a list of the requirements for amnesty for an enlargement in use under 42-1426 before reading the case and the consequences and options for those failing to meet the requirements.

In re SRBA Case No. 39576 Fremont-Madison Irrigation District and Mitigation Group v. Idaho Ground Water Appropriators, Inc.

Supreme Court of Idaho
926 P.2d 1301 (1996)

SCHROEDER, Justice

I. BACKGROUND AND PRIOR PROCEEDINGS

This case addresses the constitutionality of statutes relating to the Snake River basin adjudication (SRBA), which are collectively referred to as the "amnesty statutes." I.C. §§ 42-1425, 42-1426, & 42-1427. The facts are not in dispute. Some background concerning the methods of perfecting water rights and the elements of those water rights is helpful in understanding the present ...

Until 1971 Idaho recognized two methods of appropriating water of the state both of which were equally valid: the statutory method of appropriation and the constitutional method of appropriation. "A person desiring to appropriate the waters of a stream may do so, either by actually diverting the water and applying it to beneficial use, or he may pursue the statutory method by posting and recording his notice, and commencing and prosecuting his work within the statutory time."

Section 42-201 of the Idaho Code was changed in 1971 to require a mandatory permit system. *See* 1971 Idaho Session Laws, ch. 177 at 843. An appropriator whose right was based upon a valid, although unadjudicated, constitutional method of appropriation retained a senior claim in relation to a person holding a later issued permit. Nevertheless, those rights acquired by the constitutional method through diversion and appropriation to beneficial use prior to 1971 remain valid, I.C. §§ 42-103, -201, so long as any alleged water right has been duly registered with the Idaho Department of Water Resources consistent with I.C. § 42-243 (1990). Failure to have registered a constitutional use waived any entitlement to the use of water unless a claim for that right was filed in the SRBA as required by I.C. § 42-245 (Supp.1994).

The Idaho Legislature enacted statutes requiring the adjudication of the entire Snake River and all of its tributaries, commencing the SRBA on November 19, 1987. The historical development and procedural framework of the SRBA has been thoroughly set forth in *In re SRBA Case No. 39576.*

In 1985 the legislature provided presumptions relevant to the SRBA adjudication. Section 42-1416 of the Idaho Code (1985), provided in pertinent part, "Expansion of the use after acquisition of a valid unadjudicated water right in violation of the mandatory permit requirements shall be presumed to be valid and to have created a water right with a priority date as of the completion of the expansion, in the absence of injury to other appropriators." I.C. § 42-1416(2) (repealed 1994). Section 42-1416 of the Idaho Code was an attempt to provide "amnesty" for illegal expansions. Four years later the legislature enacted an accomplished transfer statute, I.C. § 42-1416A, which permitted users who had undertaken transfers of water rights without compliance with the statutory provisions of I.C. § 42-222 to have the transfer confirmed in the course of the general SRBA adjudication. I.C. § 42-1416A (repealed 1994).

On February 4, 1994, the district court declared the "presumption" statute, I.C. § 42-1416, and the "accomplished transfer" statute, I.C. § 42-1416A, unconstitutional. In response the legislature repealed I.C. §§ 42-1416 and 42-1416A and enacted the "amnesty statutes" at issue in this case. According to the Statement of Purpose, the new legislation was tailored to protect the "status quo water use by some water users who had failed to follow the statutory procedure for development of some of their water uses." The new legislation was designed to protect "the water uses originally intended to be protected by the 'presumption' and 'accomplished transfer' statute" and "significant investments by water users and tax base for local governments by helping to maintain status quo water uses."

...

II. IDAHO CODE SECTION 42-1425 IS CONSTITUTIONAL AS WRITTEN

Section 42-1425 of the Idaho Code is entitled "Accomplished transfers" and addresses a change in the place of use, purpose of use, point of diversion, nature of use or period of use of an existing water right. I.C. § 42-1425(2) (Supp.1995). The purpose of I.C. § 42-1425 is to streamline the adjudication process by providing a substitute for the transfer process required by I.C. § 42-222 and to protect existing water uses which were the result of past transfers, regardless of compliance with statutory mandates.

Section 42-1425(2) of the Idaho Code provides for a transfer of an existing water right for any change made prior to the date of commencement of the SRBA, regardless of compliance with sections 42-108 and 42-222, "provided no other water rights existing on the date of the change were injured and the change did not result in an enlargement of the original right." I.C. § 42-1425(2). Therefore, two limitations exist for an accomplished transfer: (1) there must be no injury to other water rights existing on the date of the change, and (2) the transfer cannot constitute an "enlargement" of the original right. I.C. § 42-1425(2).

Section 42-1425 of the Idaho Code does not define enlargement. The district court viewed the absence of such a definition as raising an issue as to whether the statute was constitutionally void for vagueness on its face. In resolving this issue, the district court applied a "core meaning" analysis to determine whether a person of reasonable intelligence can discern the meaning of the term "enlargement" as used in the amnesty statutes. A non-criminal statute is not unconstitutionally vague where its terms are such that an ordinary person exercising common sense can sufficiently understand and fulfill its proscriptions.

In an effort to discern the meaning of enlargement, the district court referred to the definition of "expanded use" found in section 42-1416B for guidance. That statute defines "expanded use" as follows:

> "Expanded use" means an increase in the number of acres irrigated, or other additional use, under a valid ground water right without any increase in the rate of diversion or volume of water diverted.

I.C. §42-1416B(5)(a) (1990). The district court's reference to I.C. §42-1416B(5)(a)'s definition of "expanded use" was misplaced. Section 42-1416B of the Idaho Code addresses "critical ground water areas," and the definition section states that the following definitions apply, "[f]or the purposes of this section". I.C. §42-1416B(5).

The term "enlargement" has been used to refer to any increase in the beneficial use to which an existing water right has been applied, through water conservation and other means. *See* I.C. §42-1426(1)(a). An enlargement may include such events as an increase in the number of acres irrigated, an increase in the rate of diversion or duration of diversion. Section 42-1425 of the Idaho Code allows the various transfers of use of a water right to be claimed in the general adjudication "even though the person has not complied with sections 42-108 and 42-222, Idaho Code, provided no other water rights existing on the date of the change were injured and the change did not result in an enlargement of the original right." I.C. §42-1425(2). An increase in the volume of water diverted is an enlargement and is not allowed under I.C. §42-1425. However, a water user may seek an enlargement under I.C. §42-1426, subject to the limitations set forth in I.C. §1426.

The limitations in section 42-1425 protect other water users from injury to their rights resulting from a recognition of the transfers that are memorialized in the adjudication. Proceeding under section 42-1425 a water user cannot obtain a transfer that constitutes either an enlargement of the water right or otherwise injures water rights existing on the date of the change. Section 42-1425 of the Idaho Code is constitutional as written.

III. IDAHO CODE SECTION 42-1426 ALLOWS AN ENLARGEMENT THAT INCREASES THE VOLUME OF WATER DIVERTED

If a water user seeks an enlargement in the adjudication the request must be pursuant to Section 42-1426 of the Idaho Code which allows the "enlargement" of existing water rights under certain conditions, unlike proceedings under section 42-1425 which do not allow an enlargement. The parties disagree as to the legal definition of "enlargement."

...

The district court interpreted I.C. § 42-1426(2) to mean that a permitted enlargement cannot increase in the rate of diversion *or* annual volume of water diverted. The district court found that decreeing a priority date as of the date of completion of the enlargement will not violate Article XV, § 3 of the Idaho Constitution if the claimant has met the burden of proving "an absence of any injury and if the enlargement does not include any increase in the rate of diversion or annual volume of water diverted."

"Where a statute or constitutional provision is clear we must follow the law as written." The statute imposes only two limitations on obtaining such a waiver for an enlargement with a priority date as of the date of enlargement: (1) "that the rate of diversion of the original water right and the separate water right for the enlarged use, combined, shall not exceed the rate of diversion authorized for the original water right;" and (2) "that the enlargement in use did not injure water rights existing on the date of the enlargement of use." *Id.* Section 42-1426 of the Idaho Code does not proscribe enlargements that include an increase in the volume of water diverted, so long as the enlargement does not exceed the rate of diversion originally authorized or injure water rights existing on the date of the enlarged use. The Court cannot engraft a condition that does not exist in the legislation. The question is whether that legislation as written is constitutional. As explained in the following section, the provision for enlargements in section 42-1426 is constitutional because of the mitigation provisions.

V. THE ENLARGEMENT PROVISION IN SECTION 42-1426 IS CONSTITUTIONAL AS A CONSEQUENCE OF THE MITIGATION PROVISION

Section 42-1426(2) of the Idaho Code provides that an enlargement shall only be allowed if it does not injure water rights existing on the date of enlargement of use. Further, "[i]f injury to a water right later in time cannot be mitigated, then a new right for the enlarged use shall be advanced to a date one (1) day later than the priority date for the junior water right injured by the enlargement." I.C. § 42-1426(2).

Section 42-1426 of the Idaho Code would violate Article XV, § 3 of the Idaho Constitution if it allowed a party with a claim for an enlargement to unconditionally receive a priority date as of the date of enlargement regardless of injury to junior appropriators. However, that is not the case. The clear and unambiguous language of the statute provides that only those enlargements which do not increase the rate of diversion, do not injure other water rights existing on the date of enlargement, and which fully mitigate any potential injury to junior water rights existing as of the date of enactment of the amnesty statutes are permitted. I.C. § 42-1426(2). Section 42-1426 of the Idaho Code is constitutional as written because it provides that an enlargement cannot be allowed that would injure a junior appropriator....

The issue of mitigation cannot be decided in a vacuum. But it is clear that if there are no mitigation provisions that will assure that there will be no injury to the junior appropriator, the new right for the enlarged use must be advanced to a date one day later than the priority date for the junior water right injured by the enlargement. The provision for advancement of the priority date is adequate protection to junior appropriators. The enlargement provision of section 42-1426 is constitutional.

...

IX. CONCLUSION

In the most recent SRBA decision, this Court stated that "to the extent that the 1994 legislation is a constitutional exercise of the Legislature's power to enact substantive law, that legislation is to be given due deference and respect." The "amnesty" statutes, I.C. §§ 42-1425, 42-1425, and 42-1427, are constitutional as written and must be "given due deference and respect." *Id.* No costs are awarded on appeal. No attorney fees are awarded on appeal.

Notes & Questions

1. List the requirements for amnesty for an accomplished transfer. List the requirements for amnesty for an enlargement in use, the consequences of meeting the requirements, and options for failure to meet the requirements. What from the lists allowed the court to find the amnesty statutes constitutional?
2. How do the statutes define "enlargement in use"? The court? What type of enlargement is allowed by each amnesty statute according to the Idaho Supreme Court? According to the district court?

Water Recapture and Reuse: Efficiency Improvements

While the *no-injury rule* is a cornerstone of western water law in application to both new water rights and changes in existing rights, it does not apply if the injured party was relying on wastewater due to inefficient conveyance or application of water to a beneficial use. To avoid creating a disincentive to efficiency improvements as technology and economics change, a water user is allowed to recapture and reuse water that would otherwise be "wasted" through seepage or runoff. The case of *Hidden Springs Trout Ranch v. Hagerman Water Users* illustrates the principle and the consequences for someone who has come to rely on wastewater. Consider the importance of the policy in favor of efficiency improvements as well as the type of science that would be necessary to distinguish "waste" water from a new source of water.

Hidden Springs Trout Ranch, Inc. v. Hagerman Water Users Inc.

Supreme Court of Idaho
619 P.2d 1130 (1980)

BISTLINE, J.—Involved here are competing rights to the waters arising from springs located on land owned by plaintiff-appellant Hidden Springs Trout Ranch, Inc. (hereinafter "Hidden Springs"). Defendant-respondent Hagerman Water Users, Inc. (hereinafter "Hagerman") has a decree to the water dating back to 1906, and owns and operates diversion works which conduct the water to the lands of its shareholders.... [Hagerman, the senior water user, developed water from two springs conveying it through a combination of pipes and ditches. Sufficient water seeped from the lower ditch that a spring, referred to as Spring A, formed. Hidden Springs developed Spring A.] Hagerman repaired its diversion works in 1976, causing a spring located on Hidden Springs' land (known as "Spring A") to dry up.... Hidden Springs ... brought suit in the court below to enjoin Hagerman from interfering with ... Spring A.... Following trial, the district court dismissed Hidden Springs' complaint, finding Hagerman within its rights as senior appropriator of the water. Finding no error, we affirm.

....

... Hagerman throughout the years attempted to reduce the seepage from the lower ditch by various means. In July of 1976, when Hagerman installed 20-inch steel pipe in the 238 foot section, the seepage loss was eliminated and Spring A dried up.

...

Hidden Springs also contends that Hagerman never put the water which seeped from the lower ditch to a beneficial use. It argues that the seepage was waste water, and that since the water has been allowed simply to escape back to the creek, it could not be said to have been put to a beneficial use. However, it has long been settled law in Idaho that a senior appropriator of water retains his right to surface waste and seepage water, and may reclaim it, even though such water has been used by a junior appropriator, even for as long as forty years. *Colthorp v. Mountain Home Irrigation District*, 157 P.2d 1005 (1945). In *Colthorp* the senior appropriator used his water to irrigate very porous soil. Approximately 75% of the water returned by seepage to Canyon Creek, from which point it was used by the junior appropriator. After the senior appropriator changed his point of diversion, the seepage ceased. The junior appropriator sued to enforce his claimed right to the seepage water. The trial court's denial of relief to the junior appropriator was affirmed on appeal:

> It is true, as contended by appellant, and as will have been observed, the right to appropriate seepage water is recognized, still and nevertheless, in construing these sections in *Sebern v. Moore* this court held "surface waste and seepage water may be appropriated ... *subject to the right of the owner to cease wasting it, or in good faith to change the place or manner of wasting it, or to recapture it, so long as he applies it to a beneficial use.*"

Hidden Springs acknowledges this general proposition—that a senior appropriator may reclaim "waste water" which until that point had been used by a junior appropriator—but attempts to draw a distinction between different kinds of waste water. According to Hidden Springs, the waste water in *Colthorp* was runoff or seepage which resulted from irrigation. In the present case, however, the water was lost *en transit* before reaching the point of use. As noted by the trial court, this is an ingenious distinction, but no support is found for it in the case law. In fact, case law indicates that the opposite is true; that no distinction is to be drawn between waste water appropriated after it has been put to irrigation use and waste water seeping from irrigation canals. *See Bower v. Big Horn Canal Association*, 307 P.2d 593 (Wyo. 1957). Moreover, it would be difficult to establish such a precedent on the basis of public policy. No appropriator of waste water should be able to compel any other appropriator to continue the waste of water which benefits the former. *Crawford v. Inglin*, 44 Idaho 663, 258 P. 541 (1927). While the waste of the original appropriator is not to be encouraged, the recognition of a right in a third person to enforce the continuation of waste will not result in more efficient uses of water.

The rule instead has been that some loss of water through seepage or evaporation is considered a prerogative of the appropriator, so long as the loss is reasonable. The senior appropriator retains his right to all of the water, including that which is lost through reasonable seepage, and thus may reclaim it, for instance, by improving his transmission system. It is clear from the trial court's memorandum opinion, which also served as its findings of fact and conclusions of law, that the amount of waste occurring prior to Hagerman's installation of the pipe was found to be reasonable....

Hidden Springs argues in the alternative that the waters forming Spring A were abandoned or forfeited by Hagerman. This Court has frequently stated that "(f)orfeitures are abhorrent and all intendments are to be indulged against a forfeiture." This Court also stated in *Thompson v. Bingham* that "as against the original appropriator and owner, an adjoining land owner cannot acquire a prescriptive right to waste or seepage water." *Id.* at 308, 302 P.2d at 949–50.

There is a distinction in Idaho law between abandonment and forfeiture. Abandonment requires the proof of intent to abandon along with a showing of actual relinquishment or surrender of water rights. Forfeiture, on the other hand, is based on the statutory provision that water which is not put to a beneficial use for five years reverts to public ownership, and may be appropriated. I.C. § 42-222(2).

The parties stipulated to the fact that over the years Hagerman had tried repeatedly to reduce the seepage loss from the open ditch. These efforts culminated in the placement of the steel pipe referred to above. It is clear from the stipulated facts that Hagerman never intended to abandon the water forming Spring A. Absent such intent, no abandonment can be found.

In order to establish forfeiture, Hidden Springs had to show that the water was not put to a beneficial use for a period of at least five years prior to this suit. Here, the evidence convinced the trial court that the water as a whole was put to a beneficial use. While in a sense it might be said that the seepage water was not being beneficially used by Hagerman, we do not look exclusively to that part which seeped, but to the use made of the water as a whole. So long as that water which arrived at its destination was put to a beneficial use, and so long as the amount of water lost through seepage during the transportation of that water from its place of origin to its place of use was reasonable, it cannot be said that the mere fact of seepage transformed it into water not beneficially used.

In short, the trial court's conclusion that Hagerman retained its senior title to the water which through seepage formed Spring A must be affirmed.

....

The judgment is affirmed.

DONALDSON, C.J., AND SHEPARD, BAKES AND MCFADDEN, JJ., CONCUR.

Notes & Questions

1. Is there an argument that water users have no choice but to pursue economic efficiency improvements?
2. Why is the water seeping from the ditch not considered forfeited?
3. Will all efficiency improvements improve water supply?

The Yellowstone River Basin (Figure 21.5) is the location of your next case. The case of *Montana v. Wyoming* arose under the original jurisdiction of the U.S. Supreme Court. Recall the methods for interstate water allocation discussed in Part IV. Montana, Wyoming, and North Dakota entered a Compact for the allocation of the Yellowstone River. Suits among states for interpretation of a Compact, like this one, qualify for the Supreme Court's original jurisdiction.

The case involves a rising problem in western water basins. States and the federal Bureau of Reclamation have long encouraged efficiency improvements in irrigation infrastructure. Measures such as lining canals, switching from flood to sprinkler irrigation, leveling fields, and monitoring soil moisture could greatly improve the ratio between the amount of water consumed and the amount diverted for the crop—i.e., the efficiency. Many farms in the upper tributaries to the Yellowstone River acquired irrigation water rights in the early twentieth century. At that time, the primary method for irrigation was flood irrigation, whereby large quantities of water were diverted directly onto the field with some consumed by the crop, but a high percentage of that diverted being lost to runoff or percolation. Today, the most common irrigation method in this region is sprinkler irrigation using center pivots, which is more efficient in water delivery to the crops with far less excess runoff or percolation.

Viewed from the perspective of a single farm, efficiency improvements make sense. Unfortunately, increasing efficiency may not make sense if viewed from the perspective of the system. Inefficient systems become efficient on a system-wide basis by reusing return flows repeatedly as water moves down the system. On-farm measures

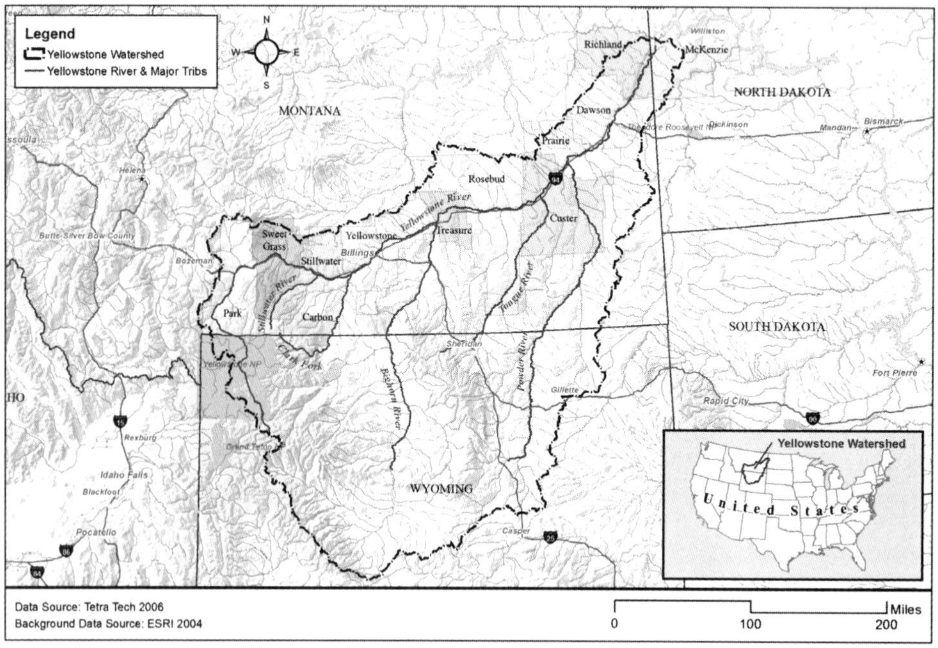

Figure 21.5 Yellowstone River Basin showing Wyoming in the headwaters with tributaries such as the Bighorn River, and Montana located downstream. Montana State Library, *Watershed Reference Maps, Reference Maps* (2006), https://msl.mt.gov/geoinfo/data/yellowstone_river/ReferenceMaps.

to increase efficiency may reduce the amount of water diverted, but up to a point they generally also increase crop yield which means the crop consumes more water.[19] The result, as you will see in *Montana v. Wyoming,* is that downstream water users see less and less flow. Pay attention to the sources of law the Court turns to in determining if the increased use in Wyoming through efficiency improvements violates the Compact. Also consider the arguments associated with the Compact definition of "beneficial use," and whether the compact altered the definition from its common law understanding.

Montana v. Wyoming

Supreme Court of the United States
563 U.S. 368 (2011)

Opinion

Justice THOMAS delivered the opinion of the Court.

This case arises out of a dispute between Montana and Wyoming over the Yellowstone River Compact (or Compact). Montana alleges that Wyoming has breached Article V(A) of the Compact by allowing its pre-1950 water appropriators to increase their net water consumption by improving the efficiency of their irrigation systems. The new

19. R.G. Huffaker and N.K. Whittlesey, *Agricultural Water Conservation Legislation: Will It Save Water?* Choices Fourth Quarter 24–28 (1995).

systems, Montana alleges, employ sprinklers that reduce the amount of wastewater returned to the river, thus depriving Montana's downstream pre-1950 appropriators of water to which they are entitled. The Special Master has filed a First Interim Report determining, as relevant here, that Montana's allegation fails to state a claim because more efficient irrigation systems are permissible under the Compact so long as the conserved water is used to irrigate the same acreage watered in 1950. We agree with the Special Master and overrule Montana's exception to that conclusion.

I

From its headwaters in Wyoming, the Yellowstone River flows nearly 700 miles northeast into Montana and then North Dakota, where it joins the Missouri River. Several of its tributaries, including the Clarks Fork, Tongue, Powder, and Bighorn Rivers, also begin in Wyoming and cross into Montana before joining the main stem of the Yellowstone River. This river system's monthly and annual flows, which are dictated largely by snow melt, vary widely. In 1964, for example, the flow in the Tongue and Powder Rivers was nearly 10 times the 1961 flow.... As the rivers came into heavy use for irrigation, it became expedient to build water storage facilities for preserving the heaviest flows....

Before funding new water storage facilities, Congress sought agreement as to the allocation of the Yellowstone River system among Wyoming, Montana, and North Dakota. In 1932, Congress granted the States permission to negotiate a compact.... Finally, in 1951 Montana, Wyoming, and North Dakota ratified the Yellowstone River Compact, and Congress consented to it. Act of Oct. 30, 1951, 65 Stat. 663.

The Yellowstone River Compact divides water into three tiers of priority. First, Article V(A) provides: "Appropriative rights to the beneficial uses of the water of the Yellowstone River System existing in each signatory State as of January 1, 1950, shall continue to be enjoyed in accordance with the laws governing the acquisition and use of water under the doctrine of appropriation."

In February 2008, we granted Montana leave to file a bill of complaint against Wyoming for breach of the Compact. Montana alleged that Wyoming had breached the Compact by consuming more than its share of the Tongue and Powder Rivers.... Specifically, Montana claimed that Wyoming was appropriating water for a number of new, post-1950 uses: irrigating new acreage; building new storage facilities; conducting new groundwater pumping; and increasing consumption on existing agricultural acreage.... According to Montana's complaint, the Compact did not permit Wyoming to use water for any of these practices as long as Montana's pre-1950 users' rights remained unfulfilled....

In response, Wyoming filed a motion to dismiss the complaint. We appointed a Special Master and referred the motion to him. After briefing and argument, the Special Master recommended that we deny Wyoming's motion, because at least some of Montana's allegations state a claim for relief. The Special Master found that "Article V of the Compact protects pre-1950 appropriations in Montana from new surface and groundwater diversions in Wyoming, whether for direct use or for storage, that prevent adequate water from reaching Montana to satisfy those pre-1950 appropriations." ... But the Special Master agreed with Wyoming that Montana's allegations regarding "efficiency improvements by pre-1950 appropriators in Wyoming" do not state a claim for relief.... The States did not object to most of the Special Master's findings, and we have issued orders accordingly.... Montana has filed an exception to the Special Master's rejection of its increased-efficiency allegation. It is this exception that is before us....

II

Article V(A) of the Compact states that "[a]ppropriative rights to the beneficial uses of [water] ... existing in each signatory State as of January 1, 1950, shall continue to be enjoyed in accordance with the laws governing the acquisition and use of water under the doctrine of appropriation." Montana claims that its pre-1950 appropriators' rights are not "continu[ing] to be enjoyed" because upstream pre-1950 appropriators in Wyoming have increased their consumption by switching from flood to sprinkler irrigation. Montana alleges that sprinkler systems increase crop consumption of water and decrease the volume of runoff and seepage that returns to the Tongue and Powder rivers by 25% or more.... As a result, even if Wyoming's pre-1950 water users divert the same quantity of water as before, less water reaches Montana. According to Montana, Article V(A) prohibits Wyoming from allowing this practice when it deprives Montana's pre-1950 users of their full water rights.

The question, therefore, is whether Article V(A) allows Wyoming's pre-1950 water users—diverting the same quantity of water for the same irrigation purpose and acreage as before 1950—to increase their consumption of water by improving their irrigation systems even if it reduces the flow of water to Montana's pre-1950 users. Montana makes two basic arguments: that background principles of appropriation law, to the extent they are incorporated into the Compact, do not allow such an increase in consumption; and that even if they do, the terms of the Compact amended those principles in Montana's favor. The Special Master rejected these arguments, and so do we.

A

Because Article V(A) of the Compact protects "[a]ppropriative rights to the beneficial uses of [water]" as of 1950 "in accordance with the laws governing the acquisition and use of water under the doctrine of appropriation," we begin with an overview of appropriation doctrine....

...

For our purposes, Montana's pre-1950 water users are similar to junior appropriators. As between the States, the Compact assigned the same seniority level to all pre-1950 water users in Montana and Wyoming.... But as Montana concedes, precisely because of this equal seniority, its downstream pre-1950 users cannot stop Wyoming's upstream pre-1950 users from fully exercising their water rights. Thus, when the rivers are low, Montana's downstream pre-1950 users might get no water at all because the equally senior users upstream in Wyoming may lawfully consume all of the water....

… subject to the fulfillment of all senior users' existing rights, under the no-injury rule junior users can prevent senior users from enlarging their rights to the junior users' detriment….

Montana's pre-1950 users can therefore "insist that [Wyoming's pre-1950 users] confine themselves strictly within the rights which the law gives them, that is, to the amount of water within the extent of their appropriation which they actually apply to some beneficial use." 2 Kinney § 784, at 1366. That general proposition is undisputed; the dispute here is in its application. Is a switch to more efficient irrigation with less return flow within the extent of Wyoming's pre-1950 users' existing appropriative rights, or is it an improper enlargement of that right to the detriment of Montana's pre-1950 water users?

As the Special Master observed, the law of return flows is an unclear area of appropriation doctrine…. The States have not directed us to any case on all fours with this one. Indeed, "[n]o western state court appears to have conclusively answered the question."…

Despite the lack of clarity, the Special Master found several reasons to conclude that Wyoming's pre-1950 users may switch to sprinkler irrigation. He found that the scope of the original appropriative right includes such a change so long as no additional water is diverted from the stream and the conserved water is used on the same acreage for the same agricultural purpose as before. We agree with the Special Master.

1

First, although the no-injury rule prevents appropriators from making certain water-right changes that would harm other appropriators, a change in irrigation methods does not appear to run afoul of that rule in Montana and Wyoming….

But the no-injury rule is not absolute; it generally concerns changes in the location of the diversion and the place or purpose of use…. Accordingly, certain types of changes can occur even though they may harm downstream appropriators…. For instance, an appropriator may increase his consumption by changing to a more water-intensive crop so long as he makes no change in acreage irrigated or amount of water diverted…. Ordinary, day-to-day operational changes or repairs also do not violate the no-injury rule. See, *e.g.*, 1 Wiel § 56, at 51 ("Would the fact that my pump has for years dripped water onto a neighbor's ground give him a right to say that my pump must go on leaking?")….

Improvements to irrigation systems seem to be the sort of changes that fall outside the no-injury rule as it exists in Montana and Wyoming. Those changes are not to the "place of diversion, or place or purpose of use," … and thus seem to be excluded, much like crop changes or day-to-day irrigation adjustments or repairs. This is also consistent with the fact that by 1950 both States had statutes regulating certain changes to water rights, but neither required farmers to take official action before adjusting irrigation methods…. Like the Special Master, we find this to be persuasive evidence that the States considered such changes permissible.

...

2

The doctrine of recapture also supports treating improvements in irrigation efficiency as within the original appropriative right. Under this doctrine, an appropriator who has diverted water for irrigation purposes has the right to recapture and reuse his own runoff and seepage water before it escapes his control or his property. An appropriator is entitled to the "exclusive control [of his appropriated water] so long as he is able and willing to apply it to beneficial uses, and such right extends to what is commonly known as wastage from surface run-off and deep percolation, necessarily incident to practical irrigation." ... See also *Arizona Pub. Serv. Co. v. Long* ("No appropriator can compel any other appropriator to continue the waste of water which benefits the former. If the senior appropriator, through scientific and technical advances, can utilize his water so that none is wasted, no other appropriator can complain").

Montana contends that this rule does not apply when the runoff or seepage water would, if not recaptured, return to the same stream from which it was originally drawn. There is some support for Montana's position—that a beneficial user may not reuse water at all, even while it is still on his property, if it otherwise would flow back to the same stream—especially in Utah and Colorado cases.... But other authorities draw no such exception based on where the runoff or seepage is heading.... And Montana cites no case from either State here in which a court has recognized, much less found controlling, the idea that a water user may not reuse his own wastewater while it is still on his property simply because it otherwise would return to the original stream.

In fact, Montana and Wyoming appear to apply, without qualification, the basic doctrine that the original appropriator may freely recapture his used water while it remains on his property and reuse it for the same purpose on the same land. For example, in *Binning v. Miller,* 55 Wyo. 451, 102 P.2d 54 (1940), a man was diverting water from a creek fed largely by irrigation runoff and seepage from Binning's property. Although the court found that the man had a right to that water once Binning's runoff and seepage had become a natural stream, it noted that his right remained subject to Binning's right "to use the water above mentioned for beneficial purposes upon the land for which the seepage water was [originally] appropriated." *Id.*, at 477, 102 P.2d, at 63. In a later case, the court explained that the man could not "secure a permanent right to continue to receive the water" because Binning "might find better ways of utilizing the water on the same land so that less waste and seepage would occur."

Similarly, in *Bower v. Big Horn Canal Assn.*, the court held that Bower could appropriate water as it seeped across his property from the Big Horn Canal toward a nearby river. The court added, however, that Bower's right was subject always to the Big Horn Canal's right: "No appropriator can compel any other appropriator to continue the waste of water which benefits the former." Importantly, the court noted that "[i]f the senior appropriator by a different method of irrigation can so utilize his water that it is all consumed in transpiration and consumptive use and no waste water returns by seepage or percolation to the river, no other appropriator can complain."

...

The law in Montana is similar. The Montana Supreme Court has explained that "the general rule ... is that the owner of the right to use the water—his private property while in his possession,—may collect it, recapture it, before it leaves his possession." *Rock Creek Ditch & Flume Co. v. Miller,* 17 P.2d 1074, 1080 (Mont. 1933); see also A. Stone, Montana Water Law 66 (1994) (noting that, according to the "early cases," while "the water is still seeping and running off one's own land, the landowner is free to recapture and further use it").

...

The Wyoming and Montana doctrine of recapture strongly suggests that improvements in irrigation efficiency are within the original appropriative right of Wyoming's pre-1950 water users. By using sprinklers rather than flood irrigation, those water users effectively recapture water. The sprinklers, by reducing loss due to seepage and runoff, operate much like, if more efficiently than, cruder recapture systems involving ditches or pits. They are simply different mechanisms for increasing the volume of water available to the crops without changing the amount of diversion....

3

...

For all of these reasons, we hold that the doctrine of appropriation in Wyoming and Montana allows appropriators to improve their irrigation systems, even to the detriment of downstream appropriators.... Accordingly, if Article V(A) simply incorporates background principles of appropriation law, it allows Wyoming's pre-1950 water users to improve their irrigation efficiency, even to the detriment of Montana's pre-1950 users.

B

Montana, however, takes another tack. It argues that even if background principles of appropriation law do not support its position, Article V(A) of the Compact does not protect the full scope of ordinary appropriative rights. Montana claims that the Compact's definition of "beneficial use" restricts the scope of protected pre-1950 appropriative rights to the net volume of water that was actually being consumed in 1950. We agree with the Special Master that this argument also fails.

1

Article V(A) protects "[a]ppropriative rights to the beneficial uses of ... water." "Beneficial use," in turn, is defined in Article II(H) as "that use by which the water supply of a drainage basin is depleted when usefully employed by the activities of man." 65 Stat. 665. Montana contends that "beneficial use" is thus defined as the *amount of* depletion. According to Montana, any activity that increases pre-1950 water users' depletions in Wyoming beyond pre-1950 levels exceeds the scope of the appropriative rights that Article V(A) protects.... On this basis, Montana asserts that the Compact requires (subject to river conditions) that the same quantity of water that was reaching Montana as of January 1, 1950, continue to do so.

2

We acknowledge that "beneficial use" refers to a type of use that involves some depletion, as all irrigation does. See Report 61. The part of the Compact's definition of "beneficial use" that refers to depletion—"that use by which the water supply ... is depleted"—is fairly clear. It begins with "that use," and the words that follow merely explain that "that use" must be a use that "deplete[s]" the "water supply." Nothing in the language suggests that "beneficial use" means a measure of the *amount* of water depleted. A "beneficial use" within the meaning of the Compact, therefore, is a *type* of use that depletes the water supply.

This plain reading makes sense in light of the circumstances existing in the signatory States when the Compact was drafted. At that time, Wyoming had a statutory preference for irrigation, a type of depletive use, over power generation, a nondepletive use. Wyo. Comp. Stat. Ann. §71-402 (1945). It makes sense that the Compact would have been written to protect the irrigation uses that were legislatively favored and represented the predominant use of the Yellowstone River system. See Tr. of Oral Arg. 45–47; 65 Stat. 663 (Compact Preamble) (noting that the Compact recognizes "the great importance of water for irrigation in the signatory States").

Montana's reading of the Compact, by contrast, does not follow from the text and would drastically redefine the term "beneficial use" from its longstanding meaning. The amount of water put to "beneficial use" has never been defined by net water consumption. The quantity of water "beneficially used" in irrigation, for example, has always included some measure of necessary loss such as runoff, evaporation, deep percolation, leakage, and seepage (regardless of whether any of it returns to the stream). So, water put to "[b]eneficial use is not what is actually consumed but what is actually necessary in good faith."...

If the Compact's definition of "beneficial use" were meant to drastically redefine the term into shorthand for net water consumption, we would expect far more clarity....

We agree with the Special Master that the definition of beneficial use in the Compact is unremarkable. Article V(A) does not change the scope of the pre-1950 appropriative rights that it protects in both States.

3

Finally, if Article V(A) were intended to guarantee Montana a set quantity of water, it could have done so as plainly as other compacts that do just that. By 1950, Wyoming itself had entered into at least one compact that defined water rights in terms of depletion....

* * *

We conclude that the plain terms of the Compact protect ordinary "[a]ppropriative rights to the beneficial uses of [water] ... existing in each signatory State as of January 1, 1950." Art. V(A), *ibid.* And the best evidence we have shows that the doctrine of appropriation in Wyoming and Montana allows appropriators to improve the efficiency of their irrigation systems, even to the detriment of downstream appropriators. Montana's allegation that Wyoming has breached Article V(A) of the Compact by allowing its pre-1950 water users to increase their irrigation efficiency thus fails to state a claim. Accordingly, Montana's first exception to the Special Master's First Interim Report is overruled.

It is so ordered.

Notes & Questions

1. The Court looks to how Montana and Wyoming treat efficiency improvements that do not include expansion of irrigated acreage. What is the rule in each state?
2. Interestingly, Montana's "salvage" water statute goes farther than most states to incentivize efficiency improvements. Under Montana law, "'Salvage' means to make water available for beneficial use from an existing valid appropriation through application of water-saving methods." MONT. CODE ANN. 85-2-102(23). The Code then states:

   > It is the declared policy of the state in 85-1-101 to encourage the conservation and full use of water. Consistent with this policy, holders of appropriation rights who salvage water may retain the right to the salvaged water for beneficial use. Except for a short-term lease pursuant to 85-2-410, any use of the right to salvaged water for any purpose or in any place other than that associated with the original appropriation right must be approved by the department as a change in appropriation right ... MCA 85-2-419

   What is the protection against the problem in *Montana v. Wyoming* in the quoted statute?
3. The Yellowstone River Compact includes a definition of "beneficial use." What is the key language in the definition that leads to the argument that the term "beneficial use" means only the amount of water consumed? How does the Court address this argument? Note that Justice Scalia, in his dissenting opinion, says that "depleted" means "depleted," stating:

   > [T]he Compact's focus on whether a use depletes a river's water supply—not whether it diverts the river's flow—significantly limits the volume of water to which Wyoming is entitled. For purposes of the Compact, Wyoming may lay claim only to its beneficial users' net consumption of water, that is, the volume of water diverted from the river minus the volume that flows (or seeps) back into the river's channel.
   >
   > This interpretation, and only this interpretation, gives meaning to the definition's use of the word "depleted." I cannot write off as an accident the choice of this word rather than the word consistently used elsewhere in the Compact: "diverted."
4. A 1995 article by agricultural economists from Washington State University provides a good overview of the problems that can arise from certain efficiency improvements and calls for legislation that limits incentives for efficiency improvements to those

that reduce water consumption.[20] The authors point to The California Agricultural Water Conservation and Management Act of 1992 for model language that encourages only those efficiency improvements that reduce consumption by using the following definition:

> (a) "Water conservation" means the reduction of the amount of water consumed or irretrievably lost in the process of satisfying beneficial uses which can be achieved either by improving the technology or the method for diverting, transporting, applying, reusing, salvaging, or recovering water, or by implementing other conservation methods.[21]

5. Note that no mention has been made of Native American water rights in discussion of the Yellowstone River Compact, although there are certainly reservations in the Yellowstone Basin. Article VI of the Compact states: "Nothing contained in this Compact shall be so construed or interpreted as to affect adversely any rights to the use of the waters of Yellowstone River and its tributaries owned by or for Indians, Indian tribes, and their reservations." Given that the lawsuit suggests full to over appropriation, this disclaimer offered few answers when the rights of the Wind River Reservation were litigated and those of the Northern Cheyenne and the Crow were negotiated. These types of challenges will be addressed in Part VI.

---

20. R.G. Huffaker and N. K. Whittlesey, *Agricultural Water Conservation Legislation: Will it Save Water?* Choices Fourth Quarter 24–28 (1995).

21. California Water Code, Division 6, Part 2.1 §10521.

Chapter 22

State Statutory Changes to the Common Law

Introduction

In most western states, the common law of water allocation developed for over 100 years prior to the passage of comprehensive water use acts. Statutes may incorporate the common law, use terms of art with a common law meaning, or change the common law. Rarely does a statute explicitly state the intent to do so. Even if the legislature intended to change the common law, if the result will be an uncompensated taking of any of the sticks in the bundle of a use right, courts will attempt to find an interpretation that does not render the statute unconstitutional. As a result, it is not sufficient to simply read a statute. Water law practitioners must read the common law relevant to the issue in question, the statute, any related administrative rules, and any administrative or judicial opinions interpreting the statute. All of this must be done in light of any state constitutional provisions pertaining to water. It is also important to investigate the administrative practice in implementing the statute, because in areas requiring agency implementation (e.g., an area delegated to an agency and, in particular, one that requires scientific knowledge to interpret the statute), the agency interpretation, reflected in its practice, may be given deference.

This Chapter provides three examples of changes to the common law via statute. The first example covers an area in which the change from the common law is clear: the elimination of the diversion requirement to allow water rights for instream flow. This is a modern deviation from the common law in most states. You will learn about two very different approaches by studying Idaho and Oregon's statutes. The second example also covers an area in which the change is clear: the establishment of a means to identify future municipal needs and avoid the risk of abandonment of some of the water held without use. This exposes you to the interaction of various areas of government—i.e., planning and water provision—and the type of information needed to develop a major water right. What is also unusual about this area is the lack of use municipalities in Idaho have made of the opportunity for certainty. Only when you look back to the interaction between law and the technology used to develop municipal water, which comes primarily from groundwater in Idaho, is it clear why. This emphasizes the need to understand the law, science, and technology of water use if you are to appropriately advise your client. The third example involves the common law problem of means of diversion of groundwater—i.e., well depth. In this case, reading both the Idaho common law and the statute will identify the clear statutory change on the well depth that receives protection. The statute, however, contains additional language that is ambiguous in its application. This example also presents you with a statutory approach to groundwater mining—i.e., the drawdown of a groundwater resource resulting in long-term decline in storage and the scientific difficulty of determining if mining is occurring and, if so, how much. Prior to statutory systems, groundwater mining was only addressed by common law governing well interference and well depth, allowing aquifer depletion to continue in many places throughout the West.

The Diversion Requirement: Instream Flows

Recall from Part II that the common law requirement of diversion and application to a beneficial use meant that a non-diversionary use could not acquire a water right. Thus, instream flow for navigation, fisheries, preservation of water quality, recreation, or aesthetics could not be protected through the system of water rights. Note that, internationally, instream rights are referred to as "environmental flows." Most statutory systems in the western United States use the term "minimum stream flow" or "instream flow," recognizing the broader range of purposes, including commercial purposes. Running water through a turbine by use of a dam was considered a diversion, thus hydropower facilities were within the common law system of water rights. As water development continued to levels of full appropriation, negative impacts on uses reliant on instream flows began to be felt. In states like Idaho with recreation (including white water rafting and sport fishing) currently its fastest-growing industry, this began to affect multiple interests. While the diversion requirement provided notice to new developers of the demand on a water source under the common law system, this need became irrelevant with a permit system, formal notice, determination of water availability, and an opportunity to object prior to development. State legislatures began to pass statutes providing for instream flows and recognizing the broad range of instream water use as beneficial use.

The following section looks at the question of whether a state constitution requires diversion for appropriation, or whether legislation may change that requirement. The case also illustrates the tension between the language of a state constitution and the evolving concept of beneficial use in legislation as social values change.

Idaho Department of Parks v. Idaho Department of Water Administration

Supreme Court of Idaho
530 P.2d 924 (1974)

Opinion

SHEPARD, Chief Justice—This is an appeal and a cross-appeal from a judgment of the district court in an action wherein the Idaho Department of Parks, pursuant to statute, sought to appropriate in trust for the people of Idaho certain unappropriated waters of the Malad Canyon. The case presents for consideration three primary questions:

1. May an agency of the State of Idaho, without express constitutional authority, appropriate waters and obtain a priority water right;
2. Does the appropriation of water for the purposes of recreation and the preservation of scenic views constitute a 'beneficial use';
3. In Idaho may there be created a valid appropriative water right in the absence of an actual physical diversion of the water from its natural locus or condition.

In 1971 the Idaho Legislature enacted I. C. § 67-4307. In essence the statute directs the Department of Parks of the State of Idaho to appropriate in trust for the people of Idaho certain unappropriated natural waters of the Malad Canyon in Gooding County, Idaho. Additionally, it declares (1) that the preservation of the waters for scenic beauty and recreation uses is a beneficial use of water; (2) that the public use of those waters is of greater priority than any other use save domestic consumption, and (3) that the unappropriated state land located between the highwater marks on either bank of these waters is to be used and preserved in its present condition as a recreational site for the people of Idaho.

Pursuant to the statute the Idaho Department of Parks filed an application for a permit to appropriate the waters specified by the statute. The waters in question arise in part at least from springs in the canyon and are natural waters. There appears no argument but that there is unappropriated water available for appropriation.

That application was protested by the Idaho Water Users Association, Twin Falls Canal Company, and North Side Canal Company under the provisions of I.C. § 42-203. Those parties are cross-appellants herein and are hereafter designated 'Water Users.'

...

The Department of Water Administration issued a decision July 6, 1972 holding that a state agency can lawfully appropriate waters of a natural stream and that recreation and aesthetic uses are beneficial uses of water, but found that in Idaho there can be no valid appropriation of water without at least a proposed physical diversion or reduction of water to possession. Finding that there was no proposed physical diversion or reduction to possession intended on the part of the Department of Parks, the Department of Water Administration refused to issue the permit.

[This appeal is based on the district court's denying summary judgment on questions 1 and 2 and upholding the Department's determination on issue 3 that legislation allowing appropriation of a water right without a diversion is unconstitutional.]

...

I.

The Water Users are the only parties which assert that the district court erred when it held that a state agency can constitutionally appropriate unappropriated waters of natural streams. The Water Users argue that to allow such an appropriation would eliminate the availability of that water for appropriation by private parties, thus violating article 15, section 3 of the Idaho Constitution. In pertinent part it is stated therein:

> 'The right to divert and appropriate the unappropriated waters of any natural stream to beneficial uses, shall never be denied * * *.'

Authority for the assertion of the Water Users is not found in the plain language of that constitutional provision since there is no limitation therein to 'private parties' as distinguished from the state or a state agency. We deem it common knowledge and it is pointed out in the decision of the Department of Water Administration that in Idaho and throughout the western states, state agencies frequently appropriate water, i.e., the Fish and Game Department appropriates water for pisciculture, state universities appropriate and consume water, the Department of Parks utilizes water to maintain state parks....

...

II.

The Water Users also assert error in the trial court's determination that the preservation of aesthetic values and recreational opportunities for the citizens of this state is a beneficial use in the sense that they will support an appropriative water right under the Idaho Constitution.

The foundation of the Water Users' argument is that the five uses specified in article 15, section 3 of the Constitution, i.e., domestic, agriculture, mining, manufacturing and power are exclusive and thus are the only uses that are cognizable beneficial uses under our Constitution. We reject that argument.

We find no support for the position of the Water Users in the discussions reported in II Idaho Constitutional Convention, Proceedings and Debate 1889 (1912), as pertaining to article 15, section 3. It appears that insofar as particular uses were mentioned in the debates, discussion was confined to the establishment of preferences for certain uses over others under certain circumstances. Such establishment of preferences appears to be a common feature of water law in the west. See 1 W. A. Hutchins, Water Rights Laws in the Nineteen Western States, supra. While it is well established in western water law that an appropriation of water must be made for a 'beneficial use,' nevertheless in Idaho at least the generic term 'beneficial use' has never been judicially or statutorily defined. Our research does not disclose any case in which any court has attempted to define the term 'beneficial use.' Comment, Water Appropriation for Recreation, I Land and Water Law Review 209, 210 (1966).

Consideration of the statute in question herein indicates clearly that the legislature has declared that '(t)he preservation of water in the area described for its scenic beauty and recreational purposes necessary and desirable for all citizens of the state ... is hereby declared to be a beneficial use of such water.' We note that numerous other western states have recognized through legislation that utilization of water for scenic or recreational purposes is a beneficial use. 1 W. A. Hutchins, Water Rights Laws in the Nineteen Western States, ch. 8, pp. 542 (1971). Such legislation in other states carries no binding effect on this court but, in the absence of persuasive case law to the contrary, it would appear to indicate that the use of water for providing recreational and aesthetic pleasure represents an emerging recognition in this and other states of social values and benefits from the use of water. See Final Report to the President and to the Congress of the United States by the National Water Commission, Ch. 7, sec. E, p. 271 et seq. (1973). The statute in question herein recognizes aesthetic and recreational values and benefits which will accrue to the people of the state in respect to the waters of Malad Canyon. We find no basis upon which to disturb that declaration of the legislature that in this instance those values and benefits constitute 'beneficial uses.' The decision of the district court upon this issue is affirmed.

III.

We now reach the final issue as to whether there must be an actual physical diversion of the water in order to support an appropriation. This issue was raised upon appeal by both the Department of Water Administration and the Water Users, both of whom assert error in the trial court's determination that such physical diversion was not necessary.

The precise language of article, 15, section 3, does not bear on this question but merely declares '(t)he right to divert and appropriate the unappropriated waters of any natural stream to beneficial use, shall never be denied....' Certain language in the late case of *Glenn Dale Ranches, Inc. v. Shaub*, 94 Idaho 585, 494 P.2d 1029 (1972) and the earlier cases of *Sandpoint Water and Light Company v. Panhandle Development Company*, 11 Idaho 405, 83 P. 347 (1905), and *Hutchinson v. Watson Slough Ditch Co.*, 16 Idaho 484, 101 P. 1059 (1909) can be read as suggesting that our constitution requires an actual physical diversion of water in order to claim an appropriative right. However, a close reading of those cases indicates that the actual holdings of the cases insofar as they relate to the necessity of an actual physical diversion are based on statutory requirements.

We hold that our Constitution does not require actual physical diversion. We deem it clear that until the time of the enactment of the statute in question herein Idaho's statutory scheme regulating the appropriation of water has contemplated an actual physical diversion.

...

... As a general proposition [Idaho law requires that] one must set forth the location and description of a proposed physical diversion of water in an application for a permit to appropriate water. I.C. s 42-202. The Idaho legislature in 1971 made compliance with the statutory permit procedure mandatory. Idaho Session Laws, Ch. 177 (1971); See I.C. § 42-103, 42-201.

In the statute before us, I.C. § 67-4307, the Idaho legislature has clearly stated a policy at odds with its previous general statutory scheme of water appropriation. I.C. § 67-4307 directs parks 'to appropriate (not 'divert and appropriate') the unappropriated natural spring flow' of the Malad Canyon and declares the 'preservation of water in the area described for its scenic beauty and recreational purposes' is a beneficial use. Furthermore, the statute states that 'license shall issue at any time upon proof of beneficial use to which said waters are now dedicated.' We deem it clear that the legislature intended no physical diversion of water be required in the appropriation of the subject waters.

It is axiomatic that where a general statute and a specific statute deal with the same subject matter and are in conflict, the provisions of the specific statute must control. It is also clear that where two statutes conflict the latest expression of the legislative will must prevail.

We deem it to be the intent of the Idaho Legislature to dispense with any physical diversion requirement in the case of the appropriation directed in I.C. § 67-4307. Any other construction would nullify the obvious purpose of I.C. § 67-4307. Courts should if possible in construing a statute give it an interpretation which does not in effect nullify the statute.

The judgment of the district court is affirmed and the case is remanded to the Department of Water Administration for further proceedings consistent with the views contained herein. Costs to respondent.

Notes & Questions

1. May the list of beneficial uses grow beyond domestic, agriculture, mining, manufacturing, and power? If so, why did the framers of the Idaho Constitution specifically list them as beneficial uses?
2. According to the court, how do changes in the economy and society's values play into the analysis of whether a use is "beneficial?"
3. How does the court measure the "benefit" of a use?
   a. The economic value of the use;
   b. The social value of the use to the public good;
   c. The number of people directly benefiting from the use;
   d. All of the above.

Most states now have comprehensive statutes for the recognition of instream flow water rights as a beneficial use. Idaho and Oregon will serve as examples of different approaches. The two states are particularly different in how they address the fact that the late recognition of instream flow rights means a very junior priority date, which might provide limited results on over appropriated streams. Pay attention to the different approaches to this problem, and consider which approach(es) may provide the flexibility needed as climate change reduces summer flow in the region.

Idaho 1978 Minimum Instream Flow Act

Idaho's 1978 Minimum Stream Flow Act begins by declaring "that minimum stream flow is a beneficial use of water." Note the various justifications used in the following language:

> 42-1501. LEGISLATIVE PURPOSE—MINIMUM STREAM FLOW DECLARED BENEFICIAL USE. The legislature of the state of Idaho hereby declares that the public health, safety and welfare require that the streams of this state and their environments be protected against loss of water supply to preserve the minimum stream flows required for the protection of fish and wildlife habitat, aquatic life, recreation, aesthetic beauty, transportation and navigation values, and water quality. The preservation of the water of the streams of this state for such purposes when made pursuant to this act is necessary and desirable for all the inhabitants of this state, is in the public interest and is hereby declared to be a beneficial use of such water. The legislature further declares that minimum stream flow is a beneficial use of water of the streams of this state for the purpose of protecting such waters from interstate diversion to other states or by the federal government for use outside the boundaries of the state of Idaho....

The Idaho Water Resources Board is the only entity that may hold minimum stream flow rights in Idaho. The following statute provides the process to establish such rights, which includes review by the Idaho Department of Water Resources:

> 42-1503. APPLICATION TO APPROPRIATE—PROCESS—JUDICIAL REVIEW. Whenever the board [IRWB by definition] desires to appropriate a minimum stream flow of the unappropriated waters of any stream, it shall submit an application to the director [of IDWR by definition]....
>
> Approval of any such application must be based upon a finding that such appropriation of minimum stream flow:
>
> (a) will not interfere with any vested water right, permit, or water right application with priority of right date earlier than the date of receipt in the office of the director of a complete application for appropriation of minimum stream flow filed under the provisions of this act;
>
> (b) is in the public, as opposed to private, interest;
>
> (c) is necessary for the preservation of fish and wildlife habitat, aquatic life, recreation, aesthetic beauty, navigation, transportation, or water quality of the stream;

> (d) is the minimum flow or lake level and not the ideal or most desirable flow or lake level; and
>
> (e) is capable of being maintained as evidenced by records of stream flows and water levels and the existing or future establishment of necessary gauging stations and bench marks.

Despite the limitation allowing only the IWRB to hold a minimum stream flow right, the statutes allow "Any person, association, municipality, county, state or federal agency may, in writing, request that the board consider the appropriation of a minimum stream flow of the unappropriated waters of any stream...." Idaho Code § 42-1504. The IWRB must consider, but may refuse, the request.

For purposes of enforcement "the director shall consider any approved application for appropriation of minimum stream flow filed under the provisions of this act as a water right with priority date as of the date of receipt in the office of the director of a complete application."[1]

While this late priority date is essential to the constitutionality of the statutes, it provides little protection for instream interests on watersheds that are already dewatered during certain times of the year. To address this problem, Idaho responds on a case-by-case basis to watersheds in which those with interests are seeking improved instream flows. Idaho's approach has been to establish a watershed-specific water supply bank (you learned about water banks earlier in this Part) to allow existing water rights to be voluntarily moved to instream flow. Establishment of this approach on the Lemhi River uses the following language:

> 42-1506. LEMHI RIVER—MINIMUM STREAM FLOW APPROPRIATION. (1) The water resource board is hereby authorized and directed to appropriate and hold in trust for the people of the state of Idaho a minimum stream flow water right in a designated reach of the Lemhi river...
>
> (2) The water resource board shall appropriate the minimum stream flow water right authorized under this section in accordance with the provisions of section 42-1503, Idaho Code. In acting upon the application for permit, the director of the department of water resources need not determine that the appropriation is capable of being maintained based upon records of existing stream flows because it is anticipated that the water right will be maintained through operation of the water supply bank within the Lemhi river basin consistent with the provisions of section 42-1765A, Idaho Code....

The Nez Perce Tribe Water Rights Settlement, in which numerous minimum stream flows were established, used a similar process. It provides for the development of water banks for select dewatered streams in the Salmon and Clearwater basins (watersheds tributary to the Snake River). This aspect of the agreement is implemented by Idaho Code § 42-1507. In addition, that settlement provided federal funding to purchase

---

1. Idaho Code § 42-1505.

instream flow waters for anadromous fish on the Snake River (a tributary to the Columbia River). This aspect of the agreement is implemented by Idaho Code § 42-1763B.

Oregon 1987 In-Stream Water Rights Act

Similar to Idaho, Oregon law expressly states that "[a]n in-stream water right does not require a diversion or any other means of physical control over the water." ORS 537.332 (3). Under the 1987 Act, in-stream water rights are, by definition, "held in trust by the [Oregon] Water Resources Department for the benefit of the people of the State of Oregon." Oregon Revised Statutes (ORS) Title 45: 537.348. The 1987 Act provides four means to create an in-stream water right.[2]

First: conversion of minimum perennial stream flow. Prior to its 1987 In-stream Water Rights Act, Oregon had a process of establishing minimum perennial stream flows since 1955. The 1987 Act converted these to in-stream water rights with a priority date of their establishment. Oregon Revised Statutes, Title 45: 537.346.

Second, state agencies could seek establishment of new in-stream water rights by the regional Water Resources Commission (Oregon Water Resources Commission Districts are regionally based and issue certificates for water rights) for the following specific needs:

> State Department of Fish and Wildlife for "public uses relating to the conservation, maintenance and enhancement of aquatic and fish life, wildlife and fish and wildlife habitat. . . ."[3]
>
> Department of Environmental Quality to "protect and maintain water quality standards. . ."[4]
>
> State Parks and Recreation Department for "public uses relating to recreation and scenic attraction. . . .[5]

Third, in contrast to the Idaho approach of using watershed specific water banks, anyone may convert an existing water right to an in-stream right:

> Purchase, lease or gift of water right for conversion to in-stream water right; priority dates. (1) Any person may purchase or lease all or a portion of an existing water right or accept a gift of all or a portion of an existing water right for conversion to an in-stream water right. Any water right converted to an in-stream water right under this section shall retain the priority date of the water right purchased, leased or received as a gift. At the request of the person the Water Resources Commission shall issue a new certificate for the in-stream

2. Adell Amos, *Freshwater Conservation in the Context of Energy and Climate Policy: Assessing Progress and Identifying Challenges in Oregon and the Western United States,* 12 U. Denver L. Rev. 1, 67–99.

3. Or. Rev. Stat. Title 45: 537.336 (1).

4. Or. Rev. Stat. Title 45: 537.336 (2).

5. Or. Rev. Stat. Title 45: 537.336 (3).

> water right showing the original priority date of the purchased, gifted or leased water right.[6]

Once a water right is converted to an in-stream right, it is held by the Oregon WRD.

Fourth, up to 75% of water "conserved" through efficiency improvements may be converted to an in-stream water right.

> (3) After determining the quantity of conserved water, if any, required to mitigate the effects on other water rights, the commission shall allocate 25 percent of the remaining conserved water to the state and 75 percent to the applicant, [with certain qualifications based on financing of conservation measures] ... If the commission determines that the water allocated to the state is necessary to support in-stream flow purposes in accordance with ORS 537.332 ... to 537.360 ..., the water shall be converted to an in-stream water right....[7]

Oregon law defines "conservation" as "the reduction of the amount of water diverted to satisfy an existing beneficial use achieved either by improving the technology or method for diverting, transporting, applying or recovering the water or by implementing other approved conservation measures."[8] It defines "conserved water" as the amount of the reduction in diversion needed after conservation measures are implemented.[9] Note that this approach has been criticized for the reasons you learned about in the previous Chapter covering efficiency improvements.[10] Remember that not all efficiency improvements reduce the amount of water actually consumed even though the amount diverted may be less.

Notes & Questions

1. You are legal counsel for a nonprofit that seeks to improve water flows in Idaho and Oregon for sport fishing. Your client has asked you what its options are under the Idaho and Oregon systems of water rights. Make a list of options in each state and the information you would want to prepare to pursue each option.

Municipal Water Rights

In Part II, you learned that municipalities may hold water for probable future demands without the risk of abandonment at common law. While this is a considerable help to planning, it also carries some risk. A municipality must rely heavily on the opinion of the city attorney concerning whether they may be able to prove that the water rights they are holding for future demand are not excessive in the event of a lawsuit alleging abandonment or forfeiture. Importantly, the water rights the municipality

---

6. OR. REV. STAT. Title 45: 537.348.

7. OR. REV. STAT. Title 45: 537.470.

8. OR. REV. STAT. Title 45: 537.455(1).

9. OR. REV. STAT. Title 45: 537:455(2).

10. R.G. Huffaker & N.K. Whittlesey, *Agricultural Water Conservation Legislation: Will it Save Water?* CHOICES FOURTH QUARTER 24, 28 (1995).

is holding probably cost taxpayer dollars. Fortunately for that poor, underappreciated city attorney, water use acts have included processes for municipalities to seek approval of future needs prospectively. In reading the Idaho statutes passed for this purpose, consider what types of information would need to be developed to seek approval of water rights for future municipal needs.

Idaho's 1996 Municipal Water Rights Act was passed for the following stated purpose:

> ... The legislation seeks to define and limit the authority of municipal water providers to develop and hold water rights for reasonably anticipated future needs and to allow water to be applied to expanding service areas.... Municipalities would be required to provide information to describe their service area, to establish a reasonable planning horizon, and to show that the water rights are needed for reasonably anticipated future needs.[11]

Under the Act, those who may benefit from establishing future needs are termed a "municipal provider." The term includes municipalities, but also a private corporation providing a public water supply (e.g., the city of Boise, Idaho, is served by a private water corporation) and a subdivision of the state authorized to provide water for municipal purposes (e.g., this applies to the University of Idaho, which has its own wells and infrastructure to serve its facilities, including residence halls).[12] It also includes public or private entities providing a public water supply (this might apply to a subdivision developer).[13] Municipal purposes include "water for residential, commercial, industrial, irrigation of parks and open space, and related purposes."[14] "Public water supply" is defined as:

> "a system for the provision to the public of water for human consumption through pipes or other constructed conveyances, if such system has at least fifteen (15) service connections, regardless of the number of water sources or configuration of the distribution system, or regularly serves an average of at least twenty-five (25) individuals daily at least sixty (60) days out of the year. Such term includes any collection, treatment, storage and distribution facilities that are under the control of the operator of such system and used primarily in connection with such system, and any collection or pretreatment storage facilities not under such control that are used primarily in connection with such system. Such term does not include any special irrigation district."[15]

Water that may be held for what is referred to as "reasonably anticipated future needs" (RAFN) is defined as:

> "... future uses of water by a municipal provider for municipal purposes within a service area which, on the basis of population and other planning data, are reasonably expected to be required within the planning horizon of each

11. Idaho S.B. 1535.
12. Idaho Code § 42-202B(5).
13. Idaho Code § 42-202B(5)(c) referencing 39-103(12).
14. Idaho Code § 42-202B(6).
15. Idaho Code § 39-103(12).

> municipality within the service area not inconsistent with comprehensive land use plans approved by each municipality. Reasonably anticipated future needs shall not include uses of water within areas overlapped by conflicting comprehensive land use plans."[16]

Pay attention to the tie between RAFN and comprehensive planning. In areas of rapid growth (such as Idaho's Treasure Valley), municipalities may compete for territory, resulting in overlap in the land they are planning for future annexation. The provision preventing application of RAFN to areas of overlap in land use plans provides an incentive to collaborate to eliminate the conflict. The Act defines the terms "planning horizon" and "service area" used in this provision. The planning horizon is deferred to IDWR, suggesting it will be a context-based determination:

> "the length of time that the department determines is reasonable for a municipal provider to hold water rights to meet reasonably anticipated future needs."[17]

The service area is:

> that area within which a municipal provider is or becomes entitled or obligated to provide water for municipal purposes....[18]

Application to establish RAFN, like any proposed water right, is made to IDWR with the following guidelines:

> An application proposing an appropriation of water by a municipal provider for reasonably anticipated future needs shall be accompanied by sufficient information and documentation to establish that the applicant qualifies as a municipal provider and that the reasonably anticipated future needs, the service area and the planning horizon are consistent with the definitions and requirements specified in this chapter. The service area need not be described by legal description nor by description of every intended use in detail, but the area must be described with sufficient information to identify the general location where the water under the water right is to be used and the types and quantity of uses that generally will be made.[19]

Once the application is approved, the municipality has an ongoing duty to report application of the water to beneficial use on or before the time the use was anticipated, including providing "a description of the current service area."[20] Idaho law allows incremental recognition of a license to use the water as the water right is developed and the right is adjusted down if less is used than anticipated.[21] Nevertheless, the water held for future needs is considered a water right, not a mere claim:

> A water right held by a municipal provider to meet reasonably anticipated future needs shall be deemed to constitute beneficial use, and such rights shall

---

16. Idaho Code § 42-202B(8).
17. Idaho Code § 42-202B(7).
18. Idaho Code § 42-202B(9).
19. Idaho Code § 42-202(2).
20. Idaho Code § 42-217(1)(d).
21. Idaho Code § 42-219(1).

not be lost or forfeited for nonuse unless the planning horizon specified in the license has expired and the quantity of water authorized for use under the license is no longer needed to meet reasonably anticipated future needs.[22]

Municipalities may also seek to acquire existing water rights and transfer them to municipal purposes under the change in water right statute 42-222, studied in the previous Chapter. Additional information is required if the transferred right is to be held as part of the municipality's reasonable anticipated future needs.[23]

Notes & Questions

1. Make a list of the information you, as city attorney working with your water department, will need to compile to apply for your city's reasonably anticipated future needs. Your city does not contract out its provision of municipal water.
2. It turns out that as of the writing of this casebook, the Idaho Municipal Water Rights Act of 1996 has not been heavily used. This is not because it is a bad or burdensome approach. It turns out that municipal water rights for groundwater wells have been permitted at the maximum capacity of the well (i.e., the installed capacity), under the common law concept that municipal water can be held for future needs. Generally, well fields are not developed with the plan to pump every well at maximum capacity 24/7. Wells must be serviced and maintained. With the obligation to serve its citizens, a municipality is likely to seek a margin of safety to reduce risk in the event of a problem within the system. Also, to reduce risk, municipal providers seek greater redundancy in supply than is required for economic uses. Thus, installed capacity is likely to be substantially more than initial needs. This has left a substantial margin for future growth for many municipalities. Adding to this is that in some areas housing growth is served by conversion of farm acreage with water rights. There may, however, come a time when the Municipal Water Rights Act begins to play a greater role.

Groundwater

As you learned in Parts I and II, groundwater development was limited until the post-WWII intersection of pumping technology and cheap rural electricity made it economic to develop groundwater for large-scale uses such as irrigation and municipal use. The common law had addressed local well interference through state-by-state decisions on whether to protect well depth of senior water users and possibly hinder groundwater development, or not to protect well depth and possibly catalyze a race to the bottom. In the next subsection you will see that Idaho took a third approach to regulating means of diversion in its statutory scheme by letting engineering and economics determine the appropriate well depth in a particular area.

Large-scale groundwater development also led to a new issue that most states had not had occasion to address as the common law developed—groundwater mining. As

22. Idaho Code § 42-223(2).
23. Idaho Code § 42-222(1).

major aquifers in the California Central Valley,[24] and the Ogallala aquifer, which crosses eight states in the Great Plains of the United States, saw major declines due to irrigation pumping, states began to address this issue by statute. In the following subsections you will first read the statutes addressing means of diversion and groundwater mining, then see their application in a case that must rely on the science to determine whether well depletion is caused by a local drawdown (i.e., a cone of depression), or by actual long-term depletion ("mining") of the aquifer. Pay attention to the science involved.

Means of Diversion

Recall from Part II that "means of diversion," which translates to well depth in the case of groundwater wells, is not considered part of the bundle of sticks in the property rights for a water use right. Recall also that states take two approaches to the relative rights of water users when a deep junior well interferes with a shallow senior well: (1) the race to the bottom caused by no protection for shallow, senior wells that results in the shallow well owner bearing the burden of deepening the well; and (2) absolute protection for well depth that generally results in the deep well owner paying to deepen the shallow well. Idaho, in the case of *Noh v. Stoner,* 53 Idaho 651 (1933), chose absolute protection under common law.

The Idaho Ground Water Act includes the following provision:

> ... Prior appropriators of underground water shall be protected in the maintenance of reasonable ground water pumping levels as may be established by the director of the department of water resources as herein provided....[25]

This provision clearly alters the absolute pump level protection of *Noh v. Stoner*. It does so by authorizing the director of IDWR to set a "reasonable" pump level. In doing so, they may consider the technology and economics of well drilling and pumping, as well as the characteristics of the specific aquifer. But what happens when the economics of irrigation are used to set the pump level, and an irrigation well interferes with a shallow domestic well? Until 1978, the Idaho Ground Water Act exempted domestic wells from all of its provisions. The Idaho Supreme Court ruled in *Parker v. Wallentine*, 650 P.2d 648 (1982), that the blanket exemption meant that I.C. § 42-226 did not apply to domestic wells and issued a temporary injunction against pumping from the irrigation well (owned by Wallentine) to be removed if Wallentine paid for the cost of deepening the domestic well. In 1978, the Idaho legislature amended the Ground Water Act to exempt domestic wells only from the permit provisions of I.C. § 42-229. It remains to be seen if courts will develop equitable solutions to address future interference between large wells and domestic wells.

---

24. In the 1960s and 1970s, before the recent reliance on groundwater during drought, the USGS estimated that the approximately 800 million acre-feet in storage in California's Central Valley aquifers was being depleted at a rate of about 800,000 acre-feet per year. Gilbert L. Bertoldi, Richard H. Johnston & K.D. Evenson, *Ground Water in the Central Valley, California*—A Summary Report, U.S. Geological Survey Professional Paper 1401-A (1991).

25. Idaho Code § 42-226.

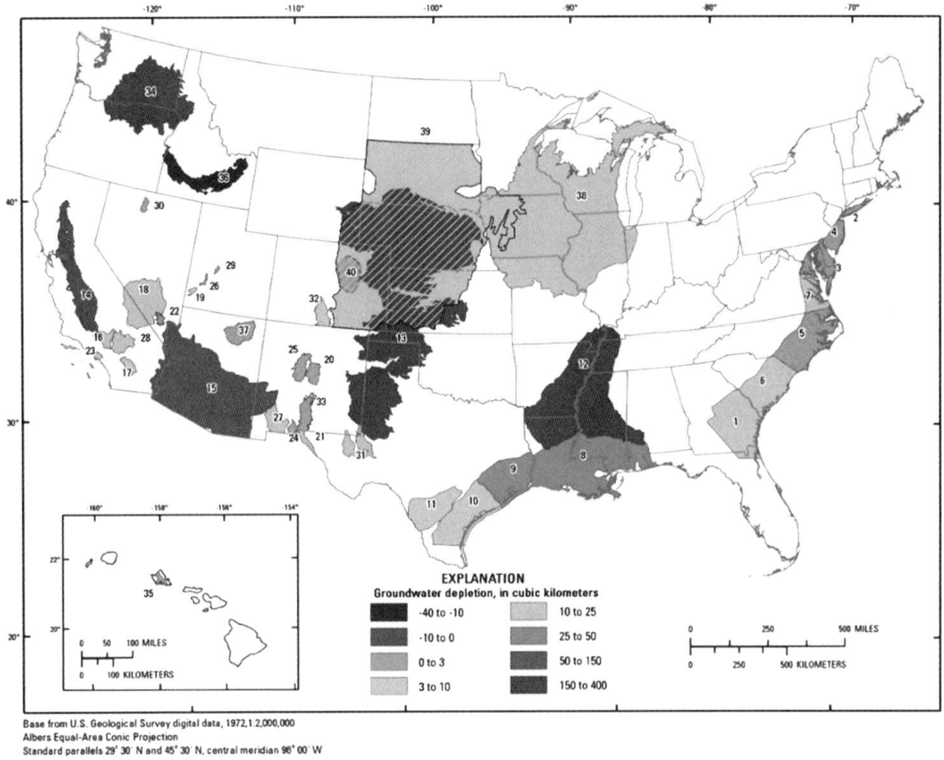

Figure 22.1 USGS map showing cumulative groundwater depletion in aquifer systems in the United States. Source: USGS Water Science School, *Map of U.S. Showing Groundwater Levels Trends, 1900 to 2008* (2008), https://www.usgs.gov/media/images/map-us-showing-groundwater-levels-trends-1900-2008.

Groundwater Mining

Recall that groundwater aquifers are like a reservoir in that they provide storage. Aquifers may or may not also have a flow component created by the influx of natural recharge and discharge to surface water sources. Groundwater mining is the reduction in storage in a groundwater aquifer (although you will see that the exact language of statutory definitions vary). Depletion of groundwater aquifers is an increasing problem in the United States as shown in Figure 22.1.

Figure 22.2 illustrates the major depletions of the Central Valley aquifers in California when farmers switched from surface to ground water during drought. It also illustrates the technology now available to detect these changes through satellite imaging. Depending on the competence of the aquifer, depletion may lead to land subsidence, leading to permanent collapse of pore space—i.e., irreversible loss of storage. Studies show that the San Joaquin aquifer shrank "permanently by as much as 5.25 percent" during the first two decades of the twenty-first century.[26]

---

26. Joshua Rapp Learn, *Western Droughts Caused Permanent Loss to Major California Groundwater Source*, American Geophysical Union Blog Phys.Org (March 19, 2019), https://phys.org/news/2019-03-western-droughts-permanent-loss-major.html#google_vignette. *See also* Chandrakanta Ojha et al., *Groundwater Loss and Aquifer-System Compaction in San Joaquin Valley During 2012–2015 Drought*, 124(3) J. Geophysical Rsch: Solid Earth 3127 (2019).

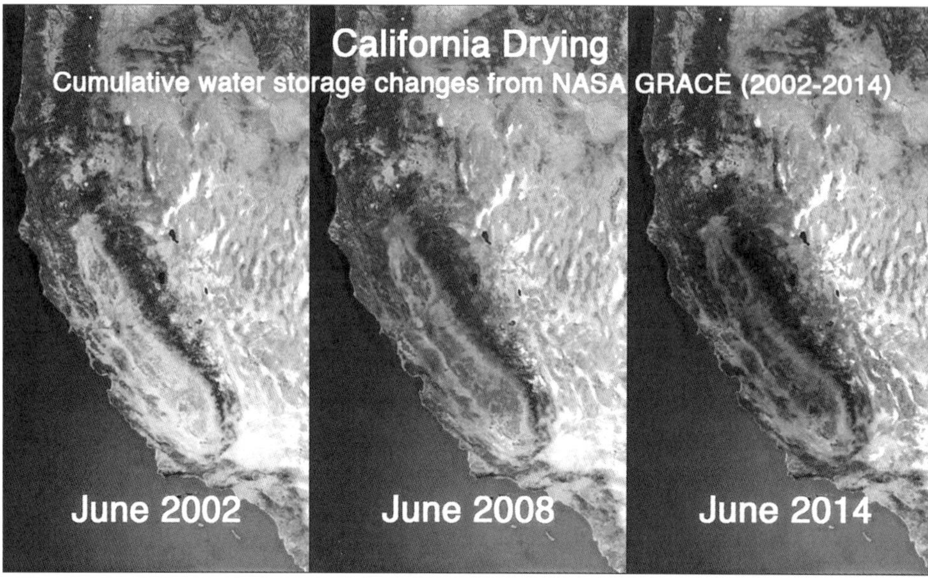

Figure 22.2 Twelve-Year Change in California Groundwater Storage. Sebastian Macias, *Groundwater Depletion in California's Central Valley* (Dec. 7, 2020), https://storymaps.arcgis.com/stories/0c1fce0700c4465180b3258c4751ecbb. The study relies on data from GRACE: NASA's Gravity Recovery and Climate Experiment Satellite.[27]

The fourth National Climate Assessment found that depletions from the Ogallala Aquifer in the Plains states, shown in Figure 22.3, cut across a wide interstate swath of irrigated agriculture. In a region that suffered severely from the 1930s' Dust Bowl, "well outputs in the central and southern parts of the aquifer are declining due to excessive pumping, and prolonged droughts have parched the area, bringing back Dust Bowl-style storms..."[28]

See Part I and Chapters 23 and 24 for the interesting situation in the Eastern Snake Plain Aquifer (ESPA), in which surface water irrigation initially increased aquifer storage until the 1950s, then the storage declined as increased groundwater pumping and efficiency improvements in surface water irrigation reduced recharge.

States have taken a variety of approaches to managing groundwater depletion. The following paragraphs look at the approaches of Idaho, Washington, and Montana.

The Idaho Ground Water Act provides:

> "... Water in a well shall not be deemed available to fill a water right therein if withdrawal therefrom of the amount called for by such right would affect, contrary to the declared policy of this act, the present or future use of any prior

27. For a peer-reviewed publication on the study, *see* J.S. Famiglietti, *Satellites Measure Recent Rates of Groundwater Depletion in California's Central Valley*, AGU Journals (2011).

28. Michon Scott, *National Climate Assessment: Great Plains' Ogallala Aquifer Drying Out*, February 19, 2019, https://www.drought.gov/documents/national-climate-assessment-great-plains-ogallala-aquifer-drying-out.

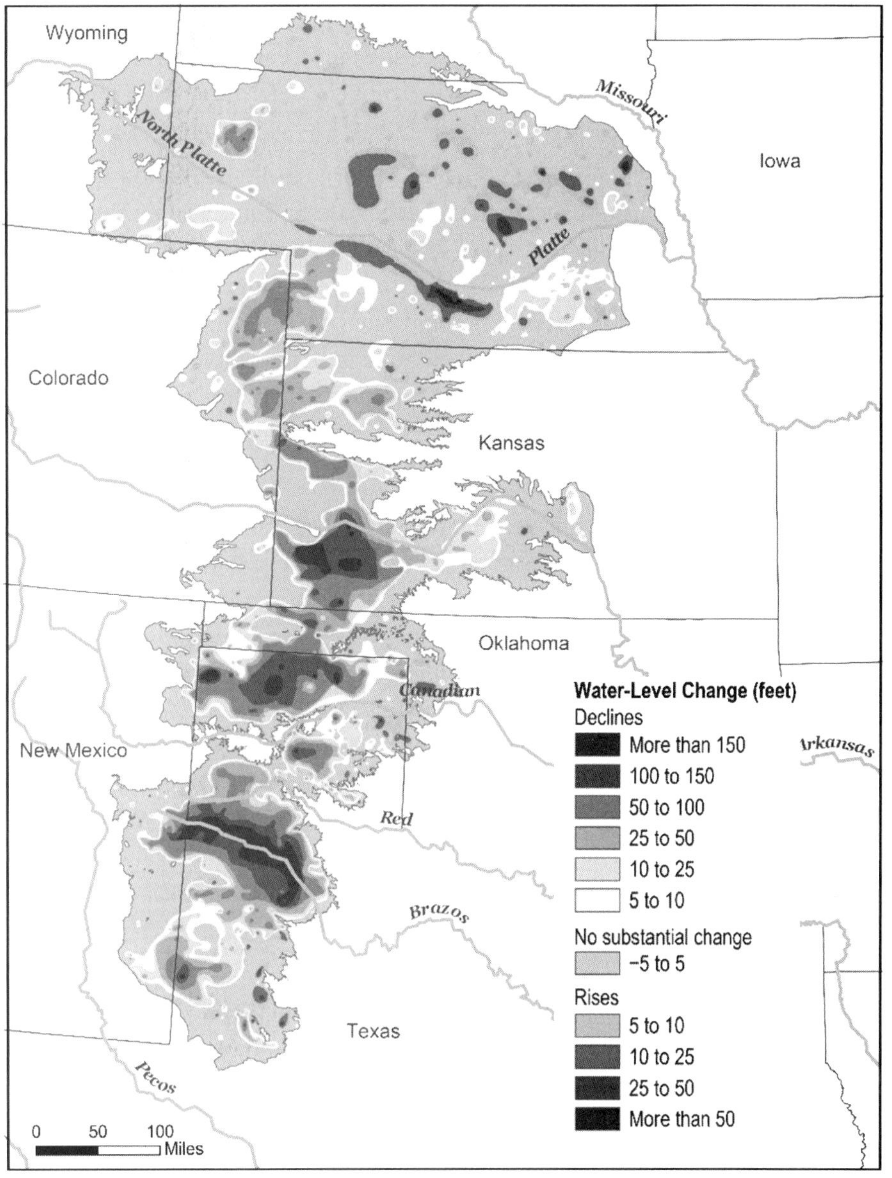

Figure 22.3 Depletion of the Ogallala Aquifer. Source: Scott, Michon, *National Climate Assessment: Great Plains' Ogallala Aquifer drying out* (Feb. 19, 2019), https://www.climate.gov/news-features/featured-images/national-climate-assessment-great-plains%E2%80%99-ogallala-aquifer-drying-out.

> surface or ground water right or result in the withdrawing of the ground water supply at a rate beyond the reasonably anticipated average rate of future natural recharge."[29]

The first part of this language articulates the no-injury rule. The second part is Idaho's approach to prohibiting mining. This approach of equating maximum pumping to natural recharge allows calculation of a precise cap on pumping. The calculation of

29. Idaho Code § 42-237A(g).

recharge is a complex puzzle of water balance that requires information on size and decline of the aquifer, pumping, precipitation, and surface water outflow from springs and streams. Static test wells may need to be drilled to determine water level without the impact of pumping.

Under Idaho's approach, if natural discharge is occurring in addition to pumping, water levels may still fall until the aquifer reaches a new equilibrium. You will learn from the conjunctive management cases in Chapter 24 that this approach may not address those who rely on natural discharge, leaving them to rely on priority administration to address harm. In addition, this approach does not address development of an aquifer that has limited recharge. This became an issue when the Palouse aquifer that serves the University of Idaho and Washington State University declined approximately 100 feet from 1935 to 2007. In recent years, regional cooperative efforts focused on conservation appear to have stabilized the aquifer.

Similar to Idaho, Washington statutes apply the doctrine of prior appropriation to groundwater development.[30] The Department of Ecology must administer groundwater wells in priority and:

> ... [t]he department ... shall have the jurisdiction to limit withdrawals by appropriators of groundwater so as *to enforce the maintenance of a safe sustaining yield* from the groundwater body. For this purpose, the department shall have authority and it shall be its duty from time to time, as adequate factual data become available, to designate groundwater areas or subareas, to designate separate depth zones within any such area or subarea, or to modify the boundaries of such existing area, or subarea, or zones to the end that the withdrawals therefrom may be administratively controlled ... *in order that overdraft of public groundwaters may be prevented so far as is feasible....* (*emphasis added*)[31]

From the language of the statute, it appears that "safe sustaining yield" means a rate of pumping that does not result in "overdraft" of the groundwater. The Groundwater Act, passed by the Washington Legislature in 1945, contained the provision protecting senior groundwater rights by requiring a "safe sustaining yield."[32] In 2015, the Washington Supreme Court clarified that curtailment to achieve safe sustaining yield applies in priority, stating:

> Generally, RCW 90.44.130 protects "prior appropriator[s]," i.e., senior water users, from subsequent appropriators overdrafting public groundwater. The statute protects senior users by giving Ecology the power to limit subsequent appropriators' withdrawals to an amount that will "maintain and provide a safe sustaining yield in the amount of the prior appropriation." RCW 90.44.130.[33]

30. Wash. Rev. Code 90.44.040.
31. Wash. Rev. Code 90.44.130.
32. H.B. 536, Chapter 263, *Regulation of Ground Waters*, Section 12, Session Laws, 1945.
33. Cornelius v. Washington Department of Ecology, 344 P.3d 199, 211 (Wash. 2015).

The case involved municipal water wells at Washington State University. The court also held that the requirement of safe sustaining yield does not apply to applications for change in water right.[34]

Montana statutes allow response to overdraft on a case-by-case basis by addressing groundwater depletion through designation of a Controlled Groundwater Area. The Department of Natural Resources and Conservation may designate a controlled groundwater area if it finds:

> ... that any of the following criteria have been met and cannot be appropriately mitigated:
>
> (a) current or projected reductions of recharge to the aquifer or aquifers in the proposed controlled ground water area will cause ground water levels to decline to the extent that water right holders cannot reasonably exercise their water rights;
>
> (b) current or projected ground water withdrawals from the aquifer or aquifers in the proposed controlled ground water area have reduced or will reduce ground water levels or surface water availability necessary for water right holders to reasonably exercise their water rights;
>
> (c) current or projected ground water withdrawals from the aquifer or aquifers in the proposed controlled ground water area have induced or altered or will induce or alter contaminant migration exceeding relevant water quality standards;
>
> (d) current or projected ground water withdrawals from the aquifer or aquifers in the proposed controlled ground water area have impaired or will impair ground water quality necessary for water right holders to reasonably exercise their water rights based on relevant water quality standards;
>
> (e) ground water within the proposed controlled ground water area is not suited for beneficial use; or
>
> (f) public health, safety, or welfare is or will become at risk.[35]

Once designated, a controlled ground water area:

> ... may include but is not limited to the following control provisions:
>
> (a) a provision closing the controlled ground water area to further appropriation of ground water;
>
> (b) a provision restricting the development of future ground water appropriations in the controlled ground water area by flow, volume, purpose, aquifer, depth, water temperature, water quality, density, or other criteria that the department determines necessary;

---

34. *Id.*
35. Mont. Code Ann. 85-2-506(5).

(c) a provision requiring measurement of future ground water or surface water appropriations;

(d) a provision requiring the filing of notice on land records within the boundary of a permanent controlled ground water area to inform prospective holders of an interest in the property of the existence of a permanent controlled ground water area....

(e) a provision for well spacing requirements, well construction constraints, and prior department approval before well drilling, ...

(f) a provision for mitigation of ground water withdrawals;

(g) a provision for water quality testing;

(h) a provision for data reporting to the department; and

(i) other control provisions that the department determines are appropriate and adopts through rulemaking.

In settlement of federal reserved water rights for Yellowstone National Park, the United States and Montana agreed to use these statutes to establish a controlled groundwater area adjacent to the Park to protect the hydrothermal system within the Park and the recharge to that system.[36] An inventory of all wells in the area and metering (paid for by the federal government) of all wells is required. The size of a domestic well that is exempt from permit requirements is reduced within the area. An adaptive management approach is used in which the boundaries and restrictions may be changed based on review of data every five years by a joint federal/state scientific team. In addition to collecting data on pumping, temperature, and TDS (total dissolved solids), wells were inventoried to identify any contribution from the hydrothermal system. Boundaries were established based on hydrographic boundaries to capture mountain front recharge.[37] This novel approach and the list of reasons for designation and nonexclusive list of provisions illustrates that the case-specific approach of Montana may have greater versatility to address a variety of future groundwater issues.

The Hydrologic Interaction of Mining and Means of Diversion

Well interference can be the result of one of two problems: a shallow well is within the cone of depression from pumping of a nearby, deeper well; or pumping of the aquifer is causing depletion of storage—i.e., mining. Determining which situation is causing the problem is a question that requires substantial scientific investigation. The first problem is managed by the state's approach to well depth. The second requires curtailment of junior wells. Both problems manifest as well interference, with the water level dropping below the pump level of shallow wells as shown in Figure 22.4.

36. Mont. Code Ann. 85-20-401, Article IV, Yellowstone Controlled Groundwater Area.

37. Mont. Code Ann. 85-20-401, Article IV. For details on the negotiations, see D. Amman, B. Cosens & J. Specking, *Negotiation of the Montana-National Park Service Compact*, 5 Rivers 35 (1995).

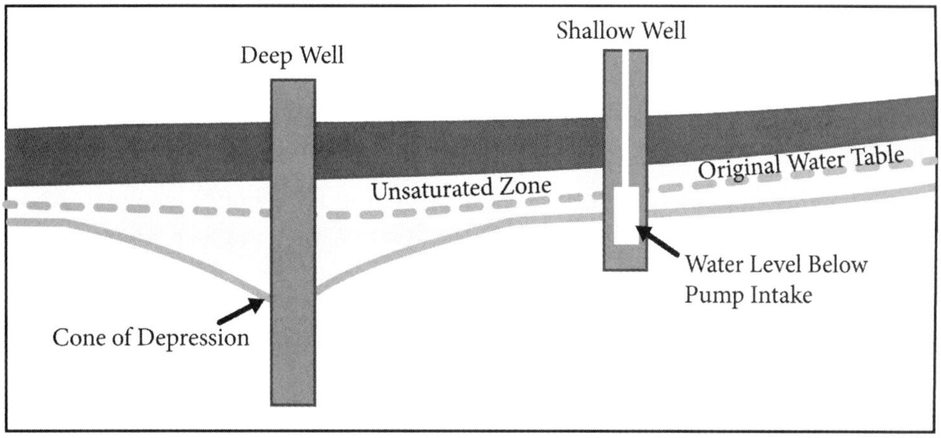

Figure 22.4 Drawdown of aquifer water level with pumping may cause the level to drop below pump levels in shallow wells. This may be a temporary feature of pumping with full rebound to original levels if pumping stops, or it may be indicative of aquifer mining—i.e., pumping in excess of recharge. Wayne Woldt et al., *Water Wise: Managing Low-Capacity Private Drinking Water Wells During Drought* (2013), University of Nebraska, Lincoln Extension, https://extensionpubs.unl.edu/publication/g2188/pdf/view/g2188-2013.pdf. Source: Design by Leilanee Taylor.

Under the first scenario, the water level will rebound to its original level if pumping stops. Under the second scenario, permanent depletion is occurring and, without additional recharge, the water level will not rebound to the original level and may remain below the pump levels of shallow wells.

The next case began with a battle of the experts in trial court over which scenario was occurring—pump interference or mining. The trial court determined that the problem was caused by aquifer mining. Note the precision of the number attributed to the amount of aquifer recharge. Consider that "precision" and "accuracy" are not the same thing. How does the court handle the fact that there is likely to be uncertainty in this determination? With deference to the trial court's determination of the cause in the face of conflicting evidence, the case becomes a question of interpretation of Idaho's Ground Water Act. The court must determine the meaning of the language in the Act:

> ... while the doctrine of 'first in time is first in right' is recognized, a reasonable exercise of this right *shall not block full economic development of underground water resources*, but early appropriators of underground water shall be protected in the maintenance of reasonable ground water pumping levels as may be established by the state reclamation engineer (director of the department of water administration) as herein provided (emphasis added).[38]

Does the goal of "full economic development of underground water resources" modify "first in time is first in right," or does it pertain to the language that follows it, suggesting a modification of the common law of ground water pumping levels under *Noh v. Stoner* that you read in Part II? See if you can unpack what the court decides.

38. Idaho Code § 42-226.

Baker v. Ore-Idaho Foods, Inc.

Supreme Court of Idaho
513 P.2d 627 (1973)

Opinion

SHEPARD, Justice—This is an appeal from a judgment for plaintiffs enjoining defendants from operating their irrigation wells. Defendants' wells pumped from a ground water aquifer underlying both plaintiffs' and defendants' land. This Court must for the first time, interpret our Ground Water Act (I.C. s 42-226 et seq.) as it relates to withdrawals of water from an underground aquifer in excess of the annual recharge rate. We are also called upon to construe our Ground Water Act's policies of promoting 'full economic development' of ground water resources and maintaining 'reasonable pumping levels.'

This case focuses on approximately 20 irrigation wells developed during the late 1950's and early 1960' in the Cottonwood Creek-Buckhorn Creek area of Cassia County in southern Idaho. The parties to this suit were engaged in farming operations in that area. Underlying this area is a limestone aquifer of unknown depth. This aquifer is recharged primarily by means of precipitation. There is not enough annual recharge water to satisfy the needs of all the well owners during the summer irrigation season.

Plaintiffs-respondents Baker, et al., originally brought this action in July 1965 seeking to enjoin defendants-appellants Ore-Ida Foods, et al. from pumping irrigation water from their wells until such time as plaintiffs' wells resumed normal production. In February, 1969 the case was tried to the district court sitting without a jury. The trial was essentially a battle between three hydrology experts presented respectively by the plaintiffs-respondents, defendants-respondents and defendants-appellants. The record in the case in voluminous including prolix water records extending back more than 20 years. The district court entered its amended decree October 5, 1971.

The district court found that the parties and their predecessors in interest had developed irrigation wells having a certain order of priority. The district court also found that all of the wells drew water from a common aquifer underlying the area.... The court further found that the aquifer is recharged primarily by precipitation, at an average rate of 5,500 acre ft. per year. The court concluded that during the period 1961 though 1968 the parties had withdrawn water from the aquifer far in excess of the annual recharge rate causing a 20 ft. per year drop in the aquifer's water level. In other words the parties were apparently 'mining' the aquifer, i.e., perennially withdrawing ground water at rates beyond the recharge rate.

The court calculated that one cubic foot per second of water flowing for 24 hours would produce 1.983 acre ft. and held that the average annual natural recharge could be pumped entirely by the four senior wells [owned by a mixture of Plaintiffs and Defendants]. The court enjoined pumping from all other wells and assigned further administration of its decree to the Idaho Department of Water Administration (IDWA), (formerly the Department of Reclamation, see I.C. § 42-1801a) [now IDWR].

The decree granted the IDWA full power to expand or limit the amounts of available water for pumping so long as the pumping never exceeded the annual rate of recharge. The amended decree also granted the IDWA the authority to modify its determination of the annual recharge rate.

Defendants-appellants have assigned as error the following factual findings of the trial court:

> That there is a single aquifer capable of metes and bounds description; that the aquifer is primarily recharged by precipitation; that the average annual recharge rate was 5,500 acre ft. per year; that all the wells involved in the case were on the same aquifer; that the water levels in these wells had declined in a similar manner from year to year.

We have examined the record at length and note that there is conflicting testimony as among the experts on all of these points. We conclude that the trial court's findings are supported by substantial, competent, although conflicting evidence and they will not be altered. Factual findings will not be disturbed on appeal when they are supported by substantial though conflicting evidence and they will not be set aside unless clearly erroneous.

Appellants assert that Idaho's Ground Water Act, I.C. § 42-226 et seq., has superseded Idaho's common law rules relating to ground water. Appellants argue that, although they are junior, they are nevertheless entitled, under the doctrine of correlative rights, to a mutual pro rata share of the water in the aquifer. Appellants further assert that pursuant to the Ground Water Act senior appropriators may only enjoin junior appropriators from pumping by showing that the juniors' pumping has exceeded reasonable pumping levels.

We must examine the evolution and development of water law to place these important ground water issues in their proper perspective. [The court's review begins with the Code of Hammurabi to more recent common law which you learned in Part II.]...

In summary, American courts apply one of the following doctrines to ground water:

1. Absolute ownership;
2. Absolute ownership as modified by reasonable use;
3. Correlative rights;
4. Prior appropriation.

The courts and legislatures have drawn further distinctions in applying these doctrines depending on whether the ground water lies in a rechargeable or a non-rechargeable aquifer. In a non-rechargeable aquifer the water is simply a stock resource and it can reasonably be determined when it will be totally exhausted. Decisions must be made as to whether to use it, when to use it and how to use it. New Mexico pioneered this area by imposing strict controls on withdrawals from its numerous non-rechargeable aquifers.

A rechargeable aquifer, however, is a flow resource and the real problem is how best to utilize the annual supply without overdrafting the stock which maintains the aquifer's water level. In the years since World War II, most western states have enacted legislation establishing administrative controls over ground water withdrawals.

The instant case requires construction of the Ground Water Act against the backdrop of the uneven development of our common law concerning ground water....

In *Hinton v. Little*, 296 P. 582 (Idaho 1931) the court eradicated the questionable historical distinction between underground streams and percolating waters and stated that all underground waters are percolating waters. Hinton again rejected the absolute ownership doctrine and held that the litigants could appropriate a common body of artesian water under their land.

Silkey v. Tiegs further expanded Hinton and ruled that percolating waters may be appropriated by diversion and application to a beneficial use. Silkey suggested that percolating waters may be appropriated by either the constitutional method or the statutory permit method.

In 1963 amendments to the Ground Water Act, I.C. § 42-229 altered the traditional assumption that ground water in Idaho could be appropriated by either the constitutional method or the permit method. We construed that amendment in *State ex rel. Tappan v. Smith*, 92 Idaho 451, 456, 444 P.2d 412, 417 (1968) ... Smith says the state may regulate appropriations of ground water without violating our constitutionally mandated prior appropriation system....

We turn now to problems concerning the maintenance of water table levels....

In a subsequent water table case, *Noh v. Stoner* the Court upheld an injunction forbidding a junior well owner from interfering with a senior's appropriation of ground water.... Noh suggests that a senior appropriator of ground water is forever protected from any interference with his method of diversion. Under Noh the only way that a junior can draw on the same aquifer is to hold the senior harmless for any loss incurred as a result of the junior's pumping. If the costs of reimbursing the senior became excessive, junior appropriators could not afford to pump from the aquifer.... Noh was inconsistent with the full economic development of our ground water resources.

Apparently our Ground Water Act was intended to eliminate the harsh doctrine of Noh:

> 'It is hereby declared that the traditional policy of the state of Idaho, requiring the water resources of this state to be devoted to beneficial use in reasonable amounts through appropriation, is affirmed with respect to the ground water resources of this state as said term is hereinafter defined*: and, while the doctrine of 'first in time is first in right' is recognized, a reasonable exercise of this right shall not block full economic development of underground water resources, but early appropriators of underground water shall be protected in the maintenance of reasonable ground water pumping levels as may be established by the state reclamation engineer (director of the department of water

administration) as herein provided. All ground waters in this state are declared to be the property of the state, whose duty it shall be to supervise their appropriation and allotment to those diverting the same for beneficial use. All rights to the use of ground water in this state however acquired before the effective date of this act are hereby in all respects validated and confirmed.' (Emphasis in original) I.C. § 42-226.

'In the administration and enforcement of this act and in the effectuation of the policy of this state to conserve its ground water resources, the state reclamation (director of the department of water administration) is empowered: (Emphasis in original) I.C. § 42-237a.

> 'g. To supervise and control the exercise and administration of all rights hereafter acquired to the use of ground waters and in the exercise of this power he may by summary order, prohibit or limit the withdrawal of water from any well during any period that he determines that water to fill any water right in said well is not there available. To assist the state reclamation engineer (director of the department of water administration) in the administration and enforcement of this act, and in making determinations upon which said orders shall be based, he may establish a ground water pumping level or levels in an area or areas having a common ground water supply as determined by him as hereinafter provided. Water in a well shall not be deemed available to fill a water right therein if withdrawal therefrom of the amount called for by such right would affect, contrary to the declared policy of this act, the present or future use of any prior surface or ground water right or result in the withdrawing the ground water supply at a rate beyond the reasonably anticipated average rate of future natural recharge.' (Emphasis supplied) I.C. § 42-237a, sub § g.

This portion of our Ground Water Act has been analyzed as follows:

> 'Ten of the thirteen states that have passed remedial ground water legislation have evidenced dissatisfaction with the law of appropriation as developed by the courts. By far the majority of these legislatures intended that full development should be the goal of subsurface water development. Yet, with the exception of Oklahoma's statute, none of the statutes unequivocally implements that intention. The Idaho statute, for example, recognizes the doctrine of priority but states that this doctrine 'shall not block full economic development of underground water resources....' The same sentence goes on to guarantee that 'early appropriators ... shall be protected in the maintenance of reasonable ... pumping levels....' It is evident that the goal of full development has been compromised by a recognition of some right in the appropriator to his means of diversion. If 'reasonable pumping levels' were interpreted by the court as requiring each appropriator to alter his means of diversion a little each year, or a little with each subsequent appropriator until full development was achieved, the statute would accomplish its purpose.'

Where the clear implication of a legislative act is to change the common law rule we recognize the modification because the legislature has the power to abrogate the common law. We hold Noh to be inconsistent with the constitutionally enunciated policy of optimum development of water resources in the public interest. Noh is further inconsistent with the Ground Water Act.

Although the trial court in the instant case said the Ground Water Act did not mitigate common law ruling of Noh this statement is merely dicta because the trial court did in fact apply the fundamental principles of the Ground Water Act.

Appellant argues in essence that mutual pro rata rights in the aquifer should be established. This argument is based upon the doctrine of correlative rights. The correlative rights doctrine is based upon the riparian principle of land ownership. The doctrine of correlative rights is repugnant to our constitutionally mandated prior appropriation doctrine. The court in *Hinton v. Little* expressly rejected the theory upon which the doctrine of correlative rights is based.

The Idaho Ground Water Act, I.C. § 42-237a(g) provides in pertinent part:

> '* * * Water in a well shall not be deemed available to fill a water right therein if withdrawal therefrom of the amount called for by such right would affect, contrary to the declared policy of this act, the present or future use of any prior surface or ground water right or result in the withdrawing the ground water supply at a rate beyond the reasonably anticipated average rate of future natural recharge.' (Emphasis supplied)

We now hold that Idaho's Ground Water Act forbids 'mining' of an aquifer. The evidence herein clearly shows that the pumping by all parties was steadily drawing down the water in the aquifer at the rate of 20 ft. per year. Since our statute explicitly forbids such pumping, the district court did not err in enjoining pumping beyond the 'reasonably anticipated average rate of future natural recharge.'

Perhaps dispositive of this case is the Act's prohibition of ground water 'mining.' The trial court found that the four senior appropriators would exhaust the aquifer's entire annual recharge. If the junior appropriators were permitted to continue pumping in the amount of their asserted rights they would mine the aquifer. Even so, appellants argue that 'under the facts presented, the court of equity should have decreed that each of the parties had a proportional interest in the water resource.' Appellants argue that our Act's phrases 'reasonable pumping levels' and 'full economic development' command a decree granting each of the appropriators, regardless of seniority, a proportionate amount of the aquifer's water.

We reiterate our holding that Idaho's Ground Water Act clearly prohibits the withdrawal of ground water beyond the average rate of future recharge. I.C. § 42-237a(g). In this regard Idaho differs from those of other less fortunate states because we have not yet had to develop legislation regarding withdrawals from non-rechargeable aquifers.

Idaho's Ground Water Act seeks to promote 'full economic development' of our ground water resources. I.C. § 42-226. Other western states have enacted analogous ground water legislation enunciating the same policy. Sax, J. L. Water Law, Planning & Policy 469 (1968). We hold that the Ground Water Act is consistent with the constitutionally enunciated policy of promoting optimum development of water resources in the public interest. Idaho Const. art. 15, § 7. Full economic development of Idaho's ground water resources can and will benefit all of our citizens.

Appellants contend that our Act's use of the phrase 'reasonable pumping levels' means that senior appropriators are not necessarily entitled to maintenance of historic pumping levels. We agree with appellants in this regard. However, our agreement avails appellants nothing because the trial court found the aquifer's water supply inadequate to meet the needs of all appropriators.

A senior appropriator is only entitled to be protected to the extent of the 'reasonable ground water pumping levels' as established by the IDWA. I.C. § 42-226. A senior appropriator is not absolutely protected in either his historic water level or his historic means of diversion. Our Ground Water Act contemplates that in some situations senior appropriators may have to accept some modification of their rights in order to achieve the goal of full economic development....

...

Because of the need for highly technical expertise to accurately measure complex ground water data the legislature has delegated to the IDWA the function of ascertaining reasonable pumping levels.... Implicit in this delegation is the recognition that reasonable pumping levels can be modified to conform to changing circumstances.... We note that the findings of the IDWA are vested with a presumption of correctness. *Keller v. Magic Water Co.*, 92 Idaho 276, 441 P.2d 725 (1968). Idaho's Administrative Procedure Act, I.C. § 67-5215 sets out standards for judicial review of such agency action.

In the case at bar it is apparent under our Ground Water Act that the senior appropriators may enjoin pumping by the junior appropriators to the extent that the additional pumping of the juniors' wells will exceed the 'reasonably anticipated average rate of future recharge.' The seniors may also enjoin such pumping to the extent that pumping by the juniors may force seniors to go below the 'reasonable pumping levels' set by the IDWA.

A necessary concomitant of this statutory matrix is that the senior appropriators are not entitled to relief if the junior appropriators, by pumping from their wells, force seniors to lower their pumps from historic levels to reasonable pumping levels. It should also be noted that those reasonable pumping levels are subject to later modification by the IDWA.

...

Appellants next claim that the district court erred in failing to defer primary jurisdiction to the IDWA. We applied the doctrine of primary jurisdiction in *Grever v. Idaho Telephone Co.*, 94 Idaho 900, 499 P.2d 1256 (1972). The doctrine is set forth in 3 Davis, Administrative Law Treatise, s 19.01 at 1.3 (1958) as follows:

> 'The doctrine of primary jurisdiction or exclusive primary jurisdiction or primary decision or preliminary resort or prior resort is not a doctrine that governs judicial review of administrative action. In this important respect, it is altogether different from the doctrines of exhaustion and of ripeness, which govern the timing of judicial review of administrative action. The doctrine of primary jurisdiction determines whether the court or agency should make the initial decision.
>
> 'The precise function of the doctrine of primary jurisdiction is to guide a court in determining whether the court should refrain from exercising its jurisdiction until after an administrative agency has determined some question or some aspect of some question arising in the proceeding before the court.'

I.C. § 42-1401 suggests that primary jurisdiction in water disputes may often rest with the IDWA. In the instant case the district court could have found primary jurisdiction in the IDWA because of the need to resolve the complex factual issues presented herein. This point need not be considered further because the trial court effectively mooted the primary jurisdiction question by relinquishing the entire matter to the...

The judgment of the district court is affirmed. Costs to Respondents.

Notes & Questions

1. According to the court, does the goal of "full economic development of underground water resources" modify "first in time is first in right," or does it pertain to the language that follows it, suggesting a modification of the common law of ground water pumping levels under *Noh v. Stoner* that you read in Part II?
2. If the court had ruled the other way—i.e., that the provision on full economic development was intended to allow out-of-priority administration, would the statute be constitutional?
3. Note that the issue of the language on "full economic development" comes up again in Idaho's efforts at conjunctive management of surface and ground water that you will study in Chapter 24. Considerable economic studies and court time were devoted to the argument that the language modified the priority system. The Idaho Supreme Court again rejects that argument, stating:The reference to "full economic development of underground water resources" does not mean that the ground water appropriator who is producing the greater economic benefit or would suffer the greater economic loss is entitled to the use of the ground water when there is insufficient water for both the senior and junior appropriators. If that were the basis for allocating water in times of shortage, then water would be allocated among farmers based upon the market prices of their respective crops and their expected yields. Rather, the purpose of the 1953 amendment was to change the holding in *Noh v. Stoner* that a prior appropriator of ground water was protected in his historic pumping level.[39]

---

39. Clear Springs Foods, Inc. v. IDWR, 252 P.3d 71, 83 (Idaho 2011).

Chapter 23

A Systems Approach to Western Water: The Setting

Idaho's Eastern Snake Plain serves as an excellent classroom for a systems approach to the study of modern water law and management by allowing application of the principles of hydrology within a single system where surface and ground water are highly connected, where there has been extensive human water development and use, and where there has been a mixture of tribal water rights, federal development, and state allocation. The Snake River is the largest tributary to the Columbia River (Figure 23.1 and the Eastern Snake Plain is underlain by an aquifer that is hydrologically connected to the river and is approximately the volume of Lake Erie. In addition to its value for illustrating the connected surface and groundwater system and its human development, the systems approach of this casebook requires that we focus on subsets of the Columbia River Basin when we look at the modern overlay of science-based administration and adjudication in this Part V and in Part VI.

As shown in Figure 23.1, the Snake River arises in Wyoming's Teton Mountains in the vicinity of Yellowstone and Grand Teton National Parks, at an elevation of over 8,000 feet. The Snake River is a snow-dominated watershed that relies on snowmelt to modulate flows throughout the summer months. By the time it reaches the western boundary of the Eastern Snake Plain near Bliss, Idaho, the Snake will have fallen to

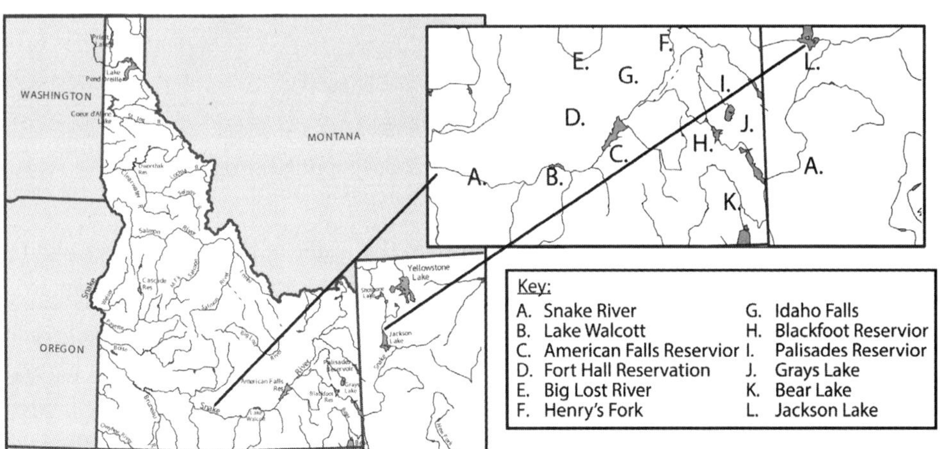

Map courtesy of the U.S. Geological Survey

Figure 23.1 Maps showing the Eastern Snake Plain. Source: Design by Leilanee Taylor.

Figure 23.2 Jackson Lake with the Reclamation dam that controls lake level and the outflow to the Snake River. Source: Bureau of Reclamation, *Jackson Lake Dam* (2023), https://www.usbr.gov/projects/index.php?id=162.

(a) (b)

Figure 23.3 (a) Flood (or furrow) irrigation vs (b) center-pivot sprinkler irrigation.

an elevation of just over 3,000 feet. In that span, the water of the Snake River will be diverted, stored, used, and reused for a variety of purposes throughout the Basin.

The only reach of the Snake River that continues to flow naturally is the small reach between its headwaters and Jackson Lake in Wyoming. Although originally a natural lake, the water level of Jackson Lake is now controlled by a dam operated by the United States Bureau of Reclamation at the Lake's outlet (Figure 23.2). Each spring, the lake is managed for flood control purposes until the spring highwaters have subsided. At that point, dam operators regulate outflows to (1) deliver irrigation water downstream consistent with water delivery contracts between the Bureau of Reclamation and water users; and (2) maintain a lake volume of approximately 800,000 acre-feet throughout the summer tourist months in Grand Teton National Park.

Although some irrigation takes place in this portion of the Basin, the primary driver of water use in this region is recreation and tourism in the regions of Yellowstone and Grand Teton National Parks. Whitewater rafting, hunting, fishing, animal-watching, and sightseeing, as well as other recreational activities, necessitate that water remain in the river (referred to as *in situ* use). Recreation as the driver of water use dominates until the river reaches the Palisades Reservoir, located on the Idaho side of the Wyoming-Idaho border (Figure 23.1). Palisades is the second of three Bureau of Reclamation reservoirs; like Jackson Lake upstream, it is managed for flood control and irrigation purposes. As a result, once the spring floods have passed through the system, the Bureau of Reclamation manages the reservoir during the summer months to maintain the maximum volume of water in storage possible while also servicing contracts to release water to irrigators.

Much of the water released from Palisades Reservoir is diverted into canals owned by irrigation districts and private canal companies. Irrigation districts are formed pursuant to state law for the purpose of allowing landowners to pool resources to raise funds to develop, maintain, and manage irrigation infrastructure. Irrigation districts are authorized to collect fees from landowners located within the district for these purposes. Canal companies are incorporated under state law for similar purposes and are a holdover from the time of the federal Carey Act that you learned about in Part IV. Both irrigation districts and canal companies hold water rights on behalf of their members and then deliver water to their members pursuant to their corporate bylaws. There are just under 50 such organizations in this portion of Idaho alone. Each has its own service area where it has developed canals to deliver water to each member's land. Members typically divert water from the canals and irrigate in one of two ways. Much of the land remains in the original irrigation method in this region of flood (or furrow) irrigation. Irrigators that flood irrigate divert water from canals through siphon tubes and allow the water to flow through furrows from one end of their field to the other (Figure 23.3(a)). This method of irrigation is inefficient, meaning that much of the water diverted is not actually consumed by the crops irrigated. Instead, it runs off the fields and back into other irrigation ditches or streams. Some returns to the Snake River (return flow) or infiltrates into the ground (groundwater recharge). Generally, flood irrigation requires approximately twice as much water to be diverted as is consumed, an efficiency of 50%.

To conserve water resources by improving efficiency (the ratio of the amount consumed to the amount diverted), many irrigators now use sprinkler irrigation. This method diverts water from the canal into piping that runs to either wheel line sprinklers that are moved manually by the irrigator or center-pivots that are motorized and move through a field according to an irrigation schedule (Figure 23.3(b)). Unlike flood irrigation, which requires a diversion sufficient for the water to run over the

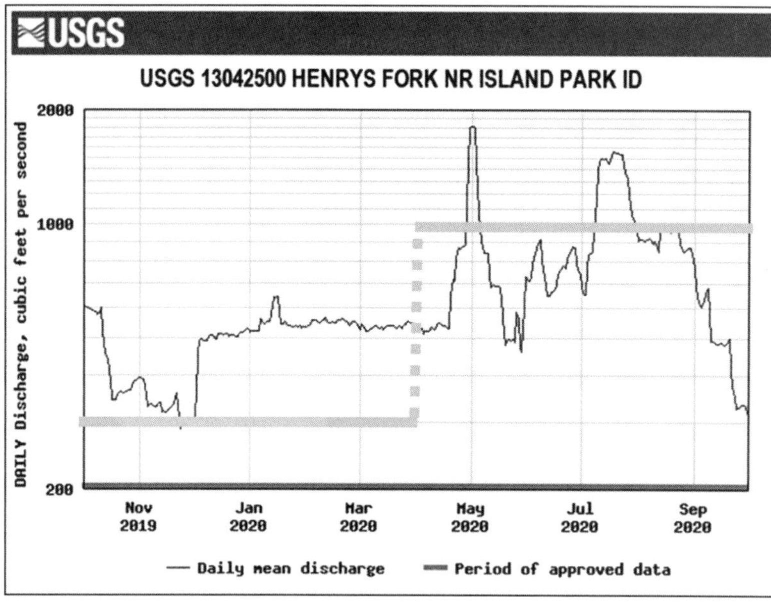

Figure 23.4 The daily flow for the Henry's Fork River, ID, with the State of Idaho minimum instream flow requirement superimposed as the horizontal lines.

entire field, sprinklers are pressurized, and the water diverted runs into piping and hoses. Sprinkler irrigation has an approximate efficiency of 75% (meaning that 75% of the water diverted is consumed by crops and 25% is runoff or seeps into the ground). You learned about some of the nuances and unintended consequences of efficiency improvements in Chapter 21.

Although agriculture is the primary economic driver in this region, water is used for many purposes and values. For example, the Henry's Fork of the Snake River flows into the mainstem downstream from Palisades Reservoir (Figure 23.1. Although much irrigation takes place along this stream, it is also a world-class trout stream. You will learn in Part V that the state of Idaho now recognizes instream flow water rights. Figure 23.4 depicts the minimum flow (the horizontal lines) superimposed over a hydrograph showing the streamflow in the Henry's Fork for water year 2020. As you can see, the minimum flow requirement is 300 cfs from October through April and then jumps to 1,000 cfs for the summer months. Those minimum flows were developed by technical experts working for the state of Idaho using methods that estimate the amount of water necessary to maintain the fishery and to ensure navigability for fishing and rafting purposes. Figure 23.4 shows that the minimum flow was not often attained in water year 2020. However, the picture would be worse if not for a locally driven collaborative of effort anglers, and irrigation interests started in 1984 (Henry's Fork Foundation). Efforts to improve instream flows include voluntary irrigator-to-irrigator water leases, crop changes, and agreements to forbear irrigation.[1] You learned more about *why*, as

1. Henry's Fork Foundation, https://www.henrysfork.org/.

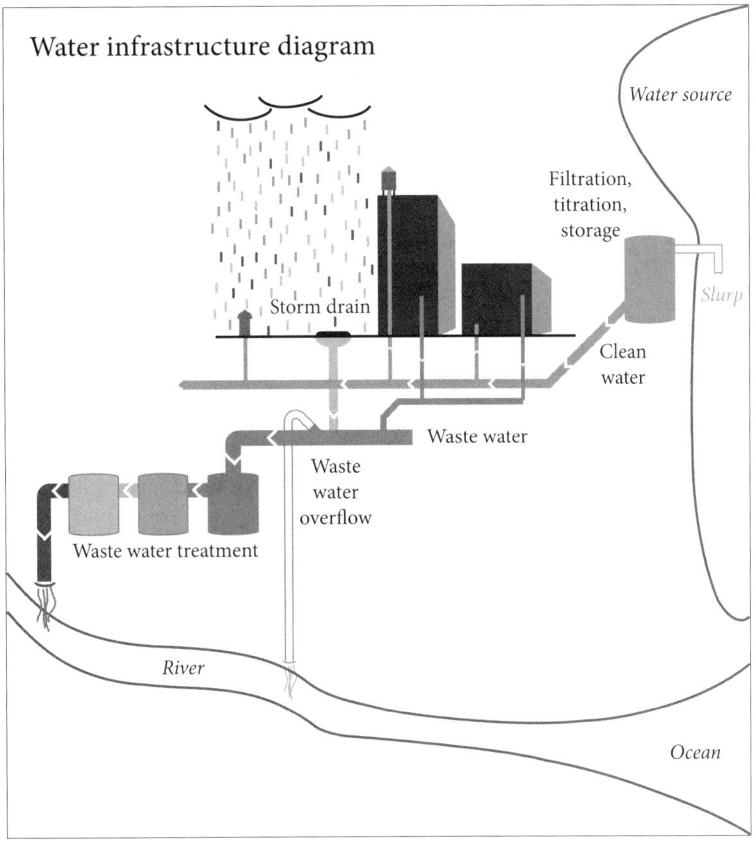

Figure 23.5 Typical municipal water infrastructure.

well as how, instream flow water rights are interrelated with other out-of-stream uses of water in Chapter 22.

Downstream from the Henry's Fork are the municipalities of Idaho Falls, Pocatello, and Blackfoot. These cities each divert both surface and groundwater necessary for their citizens' domestic, commercial, municipal, and industrial water uses. Figure 23.5 depicts a simple surface water municipal system. Water is diverted upstream from the community and is subject to treatment to ensure it meets drinking water quality standards. Treated water is then conveyed through a system of pipes to homes and businesses where it is used for domestic, commercial, and industrial purposes. It is also conveyed to and used at recreation facilities, parks, and other public areas. Once used, the water is conveyed through a separate sewer system to a different water treatment facility that is usually located downstream from the municipality. Some (but not all) storm water drains into this same conveyance system. That water is then treated to attain a certain level of quality before being discharged, either into the same surface water body where it was initially diverted or another water source.

Adjacent to Pocatello and Idaho Falls is the Fort Hall Indian Reservation. Fort Hall is the homeland of the Shoshone and Bannock peoples, who have lived in the region now known as the Great Basin since time immemorial. In 1868 they entered into the

(a) (b)

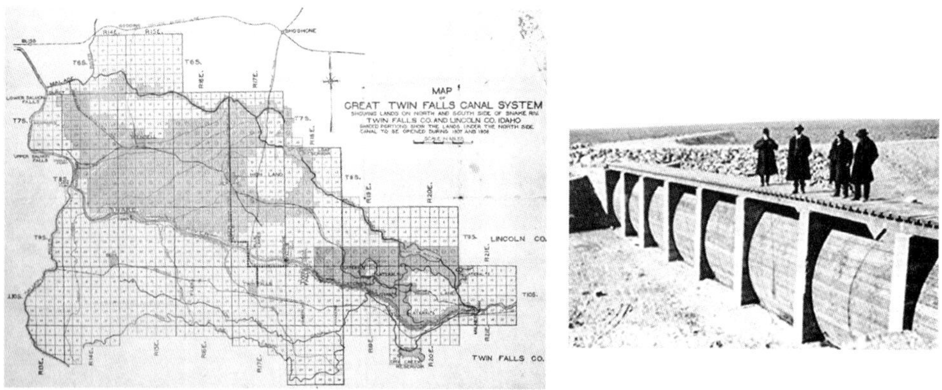

Figure 23.6 (a) Map showing the geographic extent of the Twin Falls and North Side Canal Companies in the Magic Valley, Idaho; and (b) a picture of the original headgates for the Twin Falls Canal.

Treaty of Fort Bridger with the United States, which set aside Fort Hall as their permanent home. The Shoshone-Bannock Tribes, like all federally recognized tribes in the United States, are sovereigns. As a result, the Tribes and the United States, not the State of Idaho, control management of their own water resources. The Tribes have water rights pursuant to a settlement of their rights under the reserved rights doctrine to use up to 581,000 acre-feet of water per year. That water is allocated to its membership, non-Indian water users, and to non-consumptive uses, including instream flows pursuant to a Tribal water code. You will learn more about tribal water management in Part VI.

Just downstream from the Fort Hall Indian Reservation is American Falls Reservoir. This is the last of the large Bureau of Reclamation reservoirs in the upper Snake River basin and serves to store water for much of the Magic Valley in south central Idaho. Like its sister reservoirs upstream, once the spring floods have passed through the system, the Bureau of Reclamation manages the reservoir during the summer months to maintain the maximum volume of water in storage possible while also servicing contracts to release water to irrigators. The Magic Valley is home to numerous canal companies and irrigation districts. These canal systems can be large and extensive (Figure 23.6). The State of Idaho manages this portion of the Snake River so that as close to 100% of the flow of the river as possible is diverted and used for agricultural purposes in this region. The State can employ this management strategy because an extensive spring network called Thousand Springs replenishes the Snake River just a few miles downstream from Milner Dam, the last point of diversion in this section (located near Burly, Idaho, Figure 23.1. Diminishment in this outflow from the Eastern Snake Plain Aquifer is one of the driving factors in the conjunctive management lawsuits you will read about in Chapter 24.

Scattered throughout the Snake River region, the United States has set aside a series of wildlife refuges, wild and scenic river corridors, recreation areas, national monu-

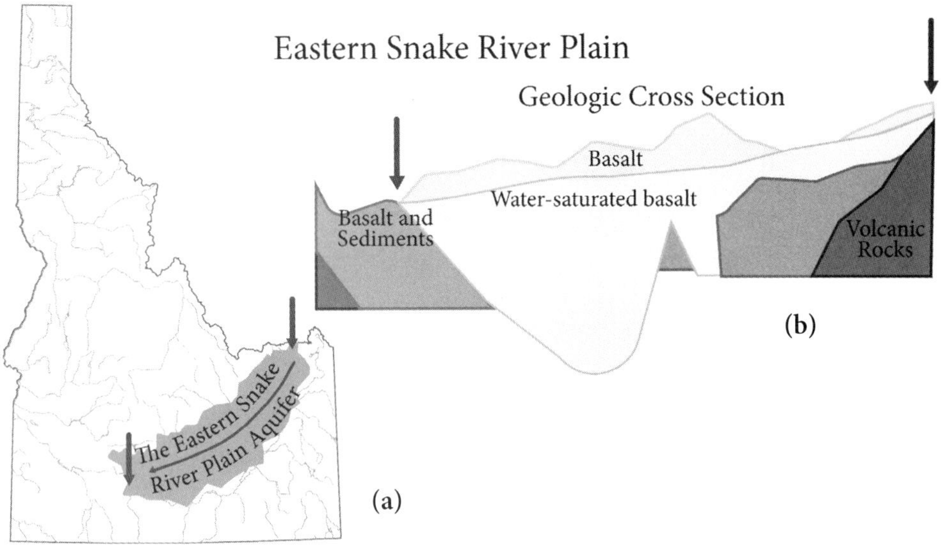

Map courtesy of the U.S. Geological Survey

Figure 23.7 (a) Map depicting the physical extent of the Eastern Snake Plain Aquifer and the general direction of groundwater flow in the Eastern Snake Plain Aquifer; and (b) Cross-section of the Eastern Snake Plain Aquifer. Source: Design by Leilanee Taylor.

ments, and other federal reservations. The wildlife refuges rely on the abundant water in the Snake River, and the resulting food and forage, to serve one of the major flyways for waterfowl that migrate long distances each year. Federal law protects the United States' right to manage these areas—along with the water within them—for the federal purposes for which the land was set aside. Those federal management goals can often be in tension with state water management priorities.

The Thousand Springs area near Bliss, Idaho, makes up the western edge of the Eastern Snake Plain. These springs are the result of the natural discharge of the Eastern Snake Plain Aquifer and play a prominent role in water resource management within Idaho, which you will learn about in Chapter 24.

Thousand Springs also demonstrates the close interrelationship between ground and surface water. Underlying most of the upper Snake River basin is the Eastern Snake Plain Aquifer, a massive, fractured, basalt aquifer that spans from Henry's Lake in Eastern Idaho to the Thousand Springs area near Bliss, Idaho. Figure 23.7(a) shows the physical extent of the Eastern Snake Plain Aquifer, and its cross-section (a vertical slice of the earth showing the rock formations beneath the ground—much like the layers of earth revealed in a tall road cut or the Grand Canyon) is shown in Figure 23.7(b). The Eastern Snake Plain Aquifer behaves much like the simple conceptual model of storage as similar to a bathtub introduced in Part I, Chapter 1, Figure 1.7. The aquifer is largely recharged in the mountainous area that makes up the border between Idaho, Montana, and Wyoming. From there, the groundwater largely flows in a southwest direction, with some water discharging into American Falls Reservoir, but most discharging back

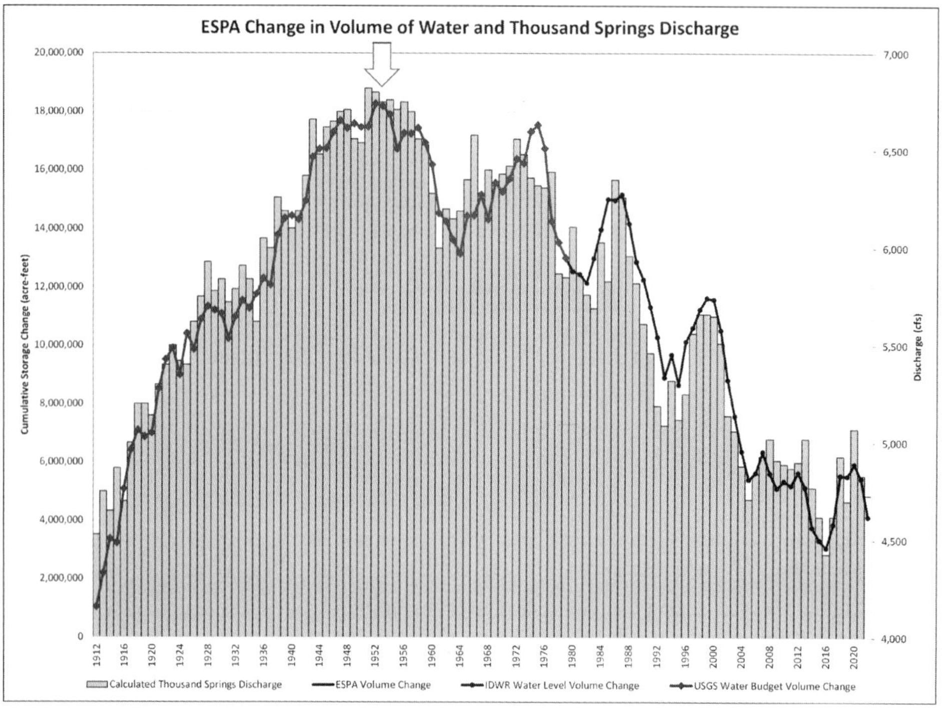

Figure 23.8 Volume Change of Water Stored within the Eastern Snake Plain Aquifer and Thousand Springs Total Discharge. Between the years 1912 and 1952 aquifer storage increased by over 17 million acre-feet. Between 1952 and 2015 storage had decreased by 13 million acre-feet. Source: Michael McVay and Kara Ferguson, Idaho Department of Water Resources (2023).

to the surface at Thousand Springs, where it contributes a large amount of flow to the Snake River.

Recall the water balance means that change in aquifer storage is equal to inflow minus outflow. For thousands of years the Eastern Snake Plain Aquifer had been in dynamic equilibrium. Thus, the discharge at Thousand Springs was roughly equal (albeit lagged) to the amount of water naturally recharging into the aquifer. Increased recharge would increase aquifer levels, which would result in a higher hydraulic gradient that would eventually cause increased outflows at Thousand Springs. Those increased discharges would remain until aquifer levels subsided, thereby reducing the hydraulic gradient and decreasing groundwater outflow.

Non-Indian settlers disrupted that balance in the late nineteenth century by introducing large-scale surface irrigation to the landscape. For 50 years (1912–1960), irrigators diverted surface water, conveyed it through a network of leaky canals and then used flood irrigation to spread it over a large swath of the landscape throughout the Eastern Snake Plain. As a result, a large quantity of surface water artificially recharged the aquifer, which caused aquifer levels to artificially rise—resulting in an artificial increase in discharge at Thousand Springs. Figure 23.8 illustrates the rise in the aquifer volume (left axis) and spring discharge (right axis) from 1912 through 1960.

Downstream water users took advantage of the increased discharge at Thousand Springs. Water rights were issued based on this artificially high discharge. In particular, use of the cold, clean spring discharge for aquaculture began in the first two decades of the 1900s. Today Idaho is the largest producer of farmed trout in the United States, providing 75% of the commercial supply. The flow-through system allows trout to be raised on cold, clear spring water with most of the water (albeit with, well, trout poop) returned to the Snake River.

The water balance in the Eastern Snake Plain Aquifer shifted once again starting in the 1950s when the combination of improved pumping technology adopted from the oil fields and the production of cheap rural electricity caused a rapid increase in large-scale groundwater development for irrigation. By the late 1970s, the number of acres irrigated in the Eastern Snake Plain by groundwater was nearly equal to the number irrigated by surface water. At the same time, many surface water irrigators switched from flood irrigation to more efficient sprinkler irrigation. As a result, more water was removed from the aquifer and less recharged the aquifer. Eventually, total outflow (the combination of pumping and natural discharge) began to exceed inflow, causing a precipitous decline in aquifer levels. With the decline in aquifer levels came a decrease in discharge at Thousand Springs. The legal result—a decades-long conflict between the people that have been using the water from Thousand Springs for the better part of a century and the relatively junior groundwater users. This systems view of the hydrologic and engineered system of the Eastern Snake Plain and its aquifer provides an excellent case study in water law, policy, science, and management within a single, highly connected system. It provides the setting for a systems approach to understanding the modern problem of conjunctive management of ground and surface water in Chapter 24, and adjudication in Chapter 25.

Chapter 24

State Agency Process and the Role of the Judiciary in Priority Administration

Introduction

Administration of water rights refers to all aspects of state agency implementation of a water rights act. This Chapter will focus on the process that water agencies engage in when a senior user seeks priority administration in times of shortage. A water call is a request by the senior user for curtailment of junior water rights in times of shortage. That process, which privileges water rights based upon the date they originated (i.e., "first in time is first in right"), is a fundamental part of the prior appropriation doctrine. The concept of "first in time is first in right" is an easy one to articulate but becomes infinitely more complex to implement. That complexity compounds once again in jurisdictions that conjunctively administer surface and ground water. Historically, ground and surface water were administered separately. However, as water demand continued to increase and scientific understanding of the interrelationship between ground and surface water developed, the separate administration of these resources became increasingly untenable. Thus, although some jurisdictions continue to administer ground and surface water separately, most states are transitioning to conjunctive administration. This Chapter begins by working through the basics of a priority water call so that you can begin to understand the conditions under which a call may be initiated, its process, and the defenses available to junior water users. From there, the bulk of the chapter centers on the development of conjunctive administration, focusing largely on its development in Idaho, which is currently the state on the forefront of the development of the legal and scientific bases for conjunctive administration.

Introduction to a Priority Call

This section will use Oregon as an example of the process of a priority call and Montana to understand one of the defenses a junior might raise—i.e., that the call is futile. This defense will be of particular importance in conjunctive management.

Oregon law is typical of states throughout the West, where "[w]atermasters [appointed by the Oregon Water Resources Department (OWRD)] enforce the priority dates of water rights. The request to cut off a junior user can originate from a watermaster's own investigation or a complaint from another appropriator, generally a senior right holder."[1] OWRD administrative rules guide the process of implementing a call. The watermaster is responsible for "investigat[ing] and respond[ing] to all complaints of water shortages or unlawful use based on a review of appropriate records and performance of field inspection. . . ."[2] That investigation may include expertise from OWRD's staff, which, as the science-based water agency for Oregon, includes hydrologists, water right specialists, hydrogeologists, well inspectors, and hydrographic technicians. The watermaster's task is to use stream flow and water use data along with field investigation to determine: (1) whether water supply is adequate to satisfy all of the water users' water rights; and if not, (2) the schedule of junior users who will need to curtail their use. OWRD then notifies those junior users that they must curtail or cease their water use. As Professor Amos notes:

> Most junior users comply with watermasters enforcement actions immediately—in 2005, the Commission reported a 96 percent compliance rate. Yet, if a junior user does not initially comply, the watermaster will issue a notice of violation. The notice specifies the nature of the violation, the request for compliance, a timeframe to comply, and the consequences for failure to comply. If the right holder does not comply even after the notice, the watermaster will then seek the aid of the Department through the region's enforcement manager for a formal enforcement. The enforcement manager is a part of the Department and after the formal enforcement, the Department can determine if there is sufficient evidence to pursue the matter or enforce civil penalties.[3]

Junior users are entitled to protest the water call and have a hearing wherein they can raise various defenses to the call. You have already learned about many of these defenses. In Part II we discussed the rule against waste. In the context of a water call, a junior user could argue that the amount of water the senior is seeking is beyond what is reasonably necessary for their beneficial use. If OWRD agrees, it may not require the junior to curtail their use. Likewise, the junior users may argue that the senior has forfeited and/or abandoned their senior water right (covered in Part II), and therefore should not be entitled to put out a water call. One additional defense that is common in these proceedings is the futile call doctrine. The following Montana case will help you understand that defense to a priority call. The case takes place in Montana's Teton River basin on the eastern Rocky Mountain front (Figure 24.1).

---

1. Adell Louise Amos, *Freshwater Conservation: A Review of Oregon Water Law and Policy*, Phase 1 Report prepared for The Nature Conservancy 50 (2009), https://tinyurl.com/5w4x87ms.

2. OAR 690-250-0100.

3. Amos, *Freshwater Conservation*, *supra*, at 50.

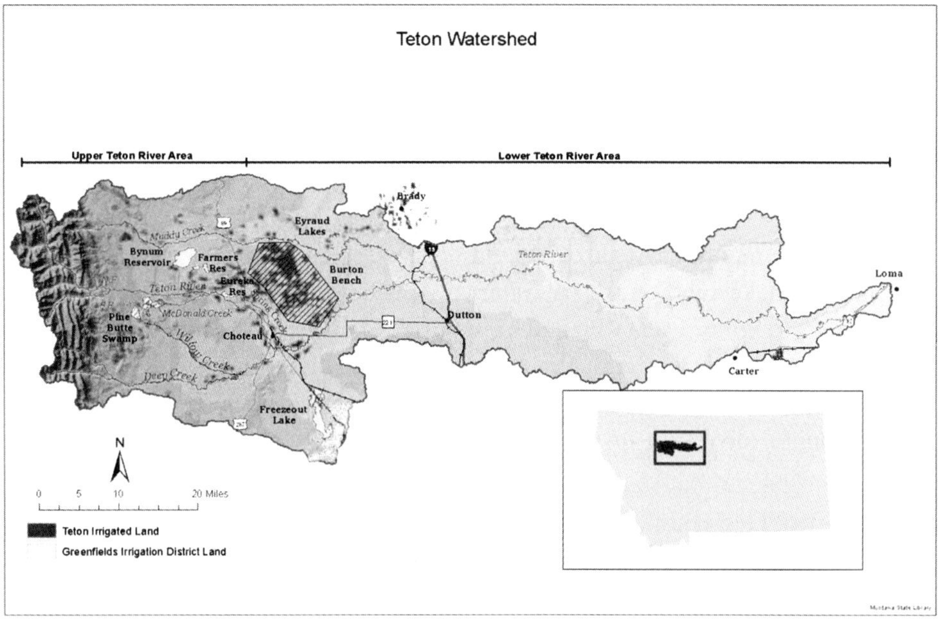

Figure 24.1 Teton River watershed, Montana, showing irrigated land. Source: Water Resources Division, Montana Department of Natural Resources and Conservation, TETON WATERSHED: WATER SUPPLY AND WATER USE STUDY REPORT, 2008–2012 DNRC REPORT: WR 2.D.7b (August 2016), https://dnrc.mt.gov/_docs/water/Hydro_science_data/Teton_Report_Final.pdf.

Kelly v. Teton Prairie, LLC

Supreme Court of Montana
376 P.3d 143 (2016)

WHEAT, J.—

FACTUAL AND PROCEDURAL BACKGROUND

The present dispute involves multiple water right holders on the mainstream of the Teton River, in Teton and Chouteau Counties, Montana. The headwaters of the Teton River are located in west-central Montana, northwest of the town of Choteau, along the Rocky Mountain Front. After leaving the mountains, the river flows east, making southeast and northeast turns through Teton and Chouteau Counties, to its confluence with the Marias River. The river has two main tributaries: Muddy Creek in the north, located near Collins; and Deep Creek in the south, located near the town of Choteau. The United States Geological Survey (USGS) maintains river gauges near the towns of Dutton and Loma.

The river's source of early season high flows is spring runoff, and the late season low flows are sustained by melting snowpack. It is common for stretches of the river to be completely dry by late summer. The Teton River does not have an onstream reservoir to stabilize late season flows....

... Each of the Appellees own property in Chouteau County and conduct farming and ranching operations. Teton Prairie owns property in Teton County, upstream from

Appellees' properties. Appellees hold water rights mainly for stockwater purposes, but also for domestic use. Teton Prairie's water rights are for irrigation, and Teton Prairie's rights are junior to all of Appellees' rights.

In July 2013, Appellees ascertained, through their own observations and through data available from the USGS-maintained river gauges, that flows had diminished such that they were not receiving the full extent of their water rights....

Later, in the month of August 2013, flows decreased again to the point to warrant Appellees to make another call for water.... Appellees' attorney sent another round of call letters to junior users who had been observed diverting water, including Teton Prairie. Despite the call, Teton Prairie continued to divert water, and in response Appellees filed suit in District Court. They claimed wrongful interference of a water right, wrongful diversion of water by a junior water right holder, and requested injunctive relief.

The parties filed counter-motions for summary judgment. In its motion, Teton Prairie requested the court determine Appellees' August call for water was futile,.... On June 22, 2015, the District Court issued an amended order granting Appellees' motion for summary judgment and denying Teton Prairie's counter-motion for summary judgment....

...

DISCUSSION

...

2. *Whether the District Court correctly found that Teton Prairie failed to establish the necessary elements to raise the defense of Futile Call Doctrine.*

The Futile Call Doctrine is an affirmative defense that a junior water right holder may invoke when the junior elects not to honor a call for water made by a senior appropriator. Under the doctrine, a call for water is deemed futile if the amount of water necessary to meet an appropriation will not reach a senior appropriator's point of diversion because of carriage losses. The underlying idea behind the Futile Call Doctrine is that the primary purpose of water appropriation is to put water to beneficial use. If a junior is required to respond to a call for water and the outcome will result in no beneficial use by the senior but only in the waste of water, then the junior is excused from responding to the call, and the waste, which is factually and legally undesirable, will be avoided.

While the defense of futile call has not explicitly been adopted in Montana, we have long recognized that the burden is placed on the junior user to show his actions are not injurious to the senior. Therefore, in this case, Teton Prairie, in seeking to excuse its disregard of Appellees' call, was required to show no useable water would reach Appellees' points of diversion. Here, testimony revealed Appellees were not receiving the full extent of their water rights. Expert testimony revealed usable water could have traveled to the Appellees' points of diversion between five to ten days after Teton Prairie ceased diverting. Therefore, the District Court correctly found that Teton Prairie failed to establish the necessary elements to successfully invoke the defense of futile call to defend its failure to respond to Appellees' call for water.

...

Notes & Questions

1. Notice the water call process in Montana is somewhat different from what was described in Oregon. Here, the attorney for the plaintiff sent letters to junior users seeking their voluntary curtailment. When they refused, the plaintiff filed suit in district court. According to the Montana Department of Natural Resources and Conservation:

   > If a water user feels that a water right is being adversely affected by the actions of another water user, the parties should talk to each other to see if the matter can be settled. If the matter cannot be settled, there are various options under Montana law for resolution.
   >
   > These options include petitioning the District Court to appoint a water commissioner or filing a temporary restraining order or preliminary INJUNCTION in District Court. If water is not reaching an appropriator's point of diversion, the appropriator can make a "call" on junior appropriators, which means contacting junior appropriators and documenting the request for water. Complaints may be filed with the DNRC. A water rights holder who is successful in going to court to stop someone without a water right from using water will be awarded attorney fees by the District Court.
   >
   > A District Judge may also appoint Water Masters to handle some disputes. County attorneys or the Attorney General may bring suit to stop illegal water use (section 3-7-311, MCA). County attorneys may also request assistance from the Attorney General in water right cases.
   >
   > Which option is best depends on the particular circumstance, how fast the matter needs to be settled, and the cost of the action.

   Montana Department of Natural Resources and Conservation, WATER RIGHTS IN MONTANA 42 (2014).

2. Who has the burden of establishing that a water call would be futile? Notice that the court found that it would take upwards of 10 days for the water Teton Prairie was using to reach Kelly's headgate. How should this factor into the court's futile call analysis?

3. In a part of the opinion not included in the excerpt, the Montana Supreme Court noted that senior appropriators are "entitled to insist that ... water remain, in order to carry the flow down to his point of diversion, although a large portion of it would be lost by evaporation and percolation." *Kelly*, 376 P.3d at 147 (quoting *Raymond v. Wimsette*, 31 P. 537, 540 (Mont. 1892)). This seems to indicate that the Court would refuse to find a call futile if even a small portion of the junior's water right would be

available for the downstream user. Does this seem like the more economically efficient way to use a scarce resource like water?

Conjunctive Management

In parallel with the vast increase in groundwater pumping for large irrigation and municipal uses that you learned about in Part II, the interrelationship between ground and surface water has led to impacts from what is generally junior groundwater pumping on senior surface water rights. States and Tribes must decide whether to enforce ground and surface water rights conjunctively or separately.

Before reading this section, go back to the portions of Part I on the scientific underpinnings of groundwater hydrology, paying particular attention to the interrelationship between surface water and groundwater. Despite that strong interrelationship, western states long administered groundwater and surface water separately.[4] With increasing development, many states are starting to rethink this approach.

Idaho's Conjunctive Management of Ground and Surface Water: Is It Mandated?

While some states like New Mexico and Colorado have long had some form of conjunctive management, the degree of interconnection of the surface and ground water on the Eastern Snake Plain (described in Chapter 23), and the interdependence of the irrigation economy in that area on both ground and surface water, has placed Idaho on the leading edge of both the science and law of conjunctive management. By the 1970s groundwater development in the Eastern Snake Plain was causing groundwater levels to decline, which was in turn causing reductions in spring flows in the Thousand Springs area near Bliss, Idaho. Alvin and Tim Musser held water rights to use some of those springs and initiated the following case, seeking to force the Idaho Department of Water Resources (IDWR) to implement a priority call after their springs began to dry up.

Musser v. Higginson

Supreme Court of Idaho
871 P.2d 809 (1994)

This case is a water distribution case. The primary issue presented is whether the trial court properly issued a writ of mandate ordering the director (the director) of the Idaho department of water resources (the department) immediately to comply with I.C. § 42-602 and distribute water in accordance with the doctrine of prior appropriation.

---

4. Tarlock and Robison, Law of Water Rights and Resources § 6:26 (2021).

...

I. THE BACKGROUND AND PRIOR PROCEEDINGS.

...

The Mussers' property is located within water district 36A (the district). The district is served by a watermaster (the watermaster) appointed by the director. The springs which supply the Mussers' water [via the Martin—Curran Tunnel] are tributary to the Snake River and are hydrologically interconnected to the Snake plain aquifer (the aquifer).

In the spring of 1993, the Mussers found that the tunnel did not supply them with sufficient water to fulfill their adjudicated water rights. As a result, they contend they planted less acreage than they had previously and that many of their crops were lost and damaged.

On May 25, 1993, other owners of water rights from the tunnel demanded that the watermaster deliver water to them. The watermaster relayed the demand to the director who rejected the demand. On June 16, 1993, the Mussers made a similar demand on the director for the "full and immediate delivery of their decreed water rights from the Curran Tunnel." The director denied the demand on the grounds that "the director is not authorized to direct the watermaster to conjunctively administer ground and surface water within Water District 36A short of a formal hydrologic determination that such conjunctive management is appropriate."

The Mussers sought a writ of mandate to compel the director: (1) to deliver their full decreed water rights, and (2) to control the distribution of water from the aquifer according to the priority date of the decreed water rights.

...

The trial court ... concluded that the director owes the Mussers "a clear legal duty to distribute water under the prior appropriation doctrine." The trial court determined that the director's failure to adopt rules and regulations enabling him to respond to the Mussers' demand for delivery of their water was a breach of his "mandatory, ministerial duty." The trial court also said the director's refusal to honor the Mussers' demand was "arbitrary and capricious" and that the Mussers had no "adequate, plain or speedy remedy at law."

The trial court issued a writ of mandate commanding the director "to immediately comply with I.C. § 42-602 and distribute water in accordance with the Constitution of the State of Idaho and the laws of this state commonly referred to as the Doctrine of Prior Appropriation...." The director and the department appealed ...

II. THE TRIAL COURT PROPERLY ISSUED A WRIT OF MANDATE COMMANDING THE DIRECTOR IMMEDIATELY TO COMPLY WITH I.C. § 42-602.

The director and the department assert that the trial court should not have issued the writ of mandate. We disagree.

In *Idaho Falls Redev. Agency v. Countryman,* 118 Idaho 43, 794 P.2d 632 (1990), the Court recapitulated the requirements for the issuance of a writ of mandate:

> In *Utah Power & Light Co. v. Campbell,* this Court stated that "[m]andamus will lie if the officer against whom the writ is brought has a 'clear legal duty' to perform the desired act, and if the act sought to be compelled is ministerial or executive in nature."...

I.C. § 42-602 provides:

> It shall be the duty of the director of the department of water resources to have *immediate direction and control* of the *distribution of water* from all of the streams, rivers, lakes, ground water and other natural water sources in this state to the canals, ditches, pumps and other facilities diverting therefrom. Distribution of water shall be accomplished either (1) *by watermasters* appointed as provided in this chapter and supervised by the director; *or* (2) *directly by employees of the department* of water resources under authority of the director in those areas of the state not constituted into water districts as provided in this chapter. *The director must execute the laws relative to the distribution of water in accordance with rights of prior appropriation as provided in section 42-106, Idaho Code.*
>
> The director of the department of water resources shall, in the distribution of water from the streams, rivers, lakes, ground water and other natural water sources, be governed by this title.

We conclude that the director's duty to distribute water pursuant to this statute is a clear legal duty. The director himself testified that he was aware that his duty to deliver water under I.C. § 42-602 is mandatory.

The director contends, however, that although his duty under I.C. § 42-602 is mandatory, the statute leaves to the director›s discretion the means that will be used to respond to calls for water. For more than three-quarters of a century, the Court has adhered to the following principle: "The fact that certain details are left to the discretion of the authorities does not prevent relief by *mandamus.*" *See also Moerder v. City of Moscow,* 263 P.2d 993, 998 (1953) ("Public officials may, under some circumstances, be compelled by writ of mandate to perform their official duties, although the details of such performance are left to their discretion.")

This principle applies to this case. The director's duty pursuant to I.C. § 42-602 is clear and executive. Although the details of the performance of the duty are left to the director›s discretion, the director has the duty to distribute water.

...

We affirm the trial court's issuance of the writ of mandate....

Notes & Questions

1. Does the Court find that surface and groundwater need to be conjunctively administered? On what basis? Is it a constitutional requirement? A statutory requirement? Does the Court interpret its own common law? Given the answer to this question, is the legislature and/or the Court empowered to change this rule?
2. Western states take a variety of approaches to conjunctive administration, ranging from fully separate administration to the fully integrated system that the Idaho Supreme Court mandated in *Musser*.

Idaho's Conjunctive Management of Ground and Surface Water: Constitutionality of Administrative Rules

Despite the clear recognition that connected ground and surface water should be managed as a single resource, implementation is not so simple. As you learned in Part I, groundwater behaves differently from surface water, including moving at a slower rate, having impacts from pumping propagate out in all directions, and having cumulative impacts over multiple years. To provide a fair, transparent, and systematic approach requires new rules on implementation that take into account groundwater hydrology.

While *Musser* was being litigated, the Idaho Department of Water Resources ("IDWR") began the process of promulgating new administrative rules to conjunctively manage water within the State. The rules are referred to as the Conjunctive Management Rules or CMRs.[5] In times of water shortage, those rules require a senior water right holder to petition IDWR to curtail junior users.[6] These petitions often occur as early as December or January, well in advance of the irrigation season. Water users are able to make these calls because of the availability of high-quality snowpack and reservoir data, which, at least historically, enabled water managers to predict hydrologic conditions well in advance of the summer irrigation season. Armed with those data, as well as other information related to the senior users' water needs, the Department will determine whether shortages are reasonably likely for the coming season and, if so, whether the senior user will likely experience "material injury" before determining whether to proceed with a call. The Department uses the following list of factors to determine if there is material injury to senior water use:

a. The amount of water available in the source from which the water right is diverted.
b. The effort or expense of the holder of the water right to divert water from the source.
c. Whether the exercise of junior-priority ground water rights individually or collectively affects the quantity and timing of when water is available to, and the cost of exercising, a senior-priority surface or ground water right. This may include

5. The CMRs may be found at IDAPA 37.03.11: Rules for Conjunctive Management of Surface and Ground Water Resources.
6. IDAPA 37.03.11.040.

the seasonal as well as the multiyear and cumulative impacts of all ground water withdrawals from the area having a common ground water supply.

d. If for irrigation, the rate of diversion compared to the acreage of land served, the annual volume of water diverted, the system diversion and conveyance efficiency, and the method of irrigation water application.

e. The amount of water being diverted and used compared to the water rights.

f. The existence of water measuring and recording devices.

g. The extent to which the requirements of the holder of a senior-priority water right could be met with the user's existing facilities and water supplies by employing reasonable diversion and conveyance efficiency and conservation practices; provided, however, the holder of a surface water storage right shall be entitled to maintain a reasonable amount of carry-over storage to assure water supplies for future dry years....

h. The extent to which the requirements of the senior-priority surface water right could be met using alternate reasonable means of diversion or alternate points of diversion, including the construction of wells or the use of existing wells to divert and use water from the area having a common ground water supply under the petitioner's surface water right priority.[7]

If the Department is reasonably certain that the senior will experience material injury, then it will issue a curtailment order. The order is site-specific and may: (1) "[r]egulate the diversion and use of water in accordance with the priorities of rights of the various surface or ground water users," and/or (2) "[a]llow out-of-priority diversion of water by junior-priority ground water users pursuant to a mitigation plan that has been approved by the Director."[8] Once that order has been issued, the parties are entitled to request a hearing wherein the junior users may raise factual and legal challenges to the Director's decision.[9] Curtailment may also be avoided if the junior water users develop a mitigation plan that meets the approval of the Director.[10]

Following promulgation of the CMRs, the American Falls Reservoir District became concerned that a shortage was going to occur during the 2005 irrigation season. American Falls Reservoir is the last of the major Bureau of Reclamation reservoirs in the Upper Snake River Basin. This massive reservoir stores a maximum volume of around 1.7 million acre-feet of water. Groundwater from the Eastern Snake Plain Aquifer flows directly into the reservoir, which gains water as a result. The region through which this groundwater flows has experienced extensive groundwater development.

The District petitioned IDWR for a curtailment order in early 2005. The Director issued an Initial Order for information in February 2005, and a Relief Order requiring curtailment in April 2005. Rather than seek a hearing on the Orders, the parties on

---

7. IDAPA 37.03.11.042.
8. IDAPA 37.03.11.040(a)–(b).
9. Idaho Code § 42-1701A.
10. IDAPA 37.03.11.043.

both sides petitioned the court on the grounds that the CMRs are unconstitutional. The result is the following case.

American Falls Reservoir Dist. No. 2 v. Idaho Dept. of Water Resources

Supreme Court of Idaho
154 P.3d 433 (2007)

TROUT, Justice

I. NATURE OF THE CASE

This appeal is in response to a district court decision finding the Rules for Conjunctive Management of Surface and Ground Water Resources (CM Rules or Rules) facially unconstitutional based on the court's determination that the Rules lacked certain "procedural components" necessary to the proper administration of water rights under Idaho's prior appropriation doctrine....

II. FACTUAL AND PROCEDURAL BACKGROUND

... It is ... [the] CM Rules, their application and their relationship to the provisions in Article XV of the Idaho Constitution which are at the center of the dispute presently before the Court.

... (Respondents and Intervenors [are] collectively referred to as American Falls).... In their January, 2005 Delivery Call, American Falls asked the Director to curtail junior ground water use during the 2005 irrigation season in order to meet the water needs of American Falls. On February 14, 2005, the Director issued an initial order (Initial Order) which, among other things, requested additional information from American Falls for the prior fifteen irrigation seasons relating to: diversions of natural flow, storage water, and ground water; number of water rights holders and their average monthly headgate deliveries; total amount of reservoir storage; amounts of water leased or made available to other users; and number of acres flood or sprinkler irrigated and types of crops planted. American Falls responded with information but also objected to the scope of the information requested. In the Initial Order, the Director indicated he would make a determination of likely injury after receiving inflow forecasts for the Upper Snake River Basin for the period April 1 through July 1, 2005. Within two weeks of receiving the joint inflow forecast on April 7, 2005, the Director issued a Relief Order, which determined that water shortages were reasonably likely in 2005 and would materially injure American Falls. In the Relief Order, after making extensive findings of fact, the Director made the following conclusions of law which are pertinent to the issues presently before this Court:

***

20. Resolution of the conjunctive administration issue lies in the application of two well established principles of the prior appropriation doctrine: (1) the principle of "first in time is first in right" and (2) the principle of optimum use of Idaho's water. Both of these principles are subject to the requirement of reasonable use.

21. "Priority of appropriations shall give the better right as between those using the water" of the state. Art. XV, § 3, Idaho Const. "As between appropriators, the first in time is first in right." Idaho Code § 42-106.

22. "[W]hile the doctrine of 'first in time is first in right' [applies to ground water rights] a reasonable exercise of this right shall not block full economic development of underground water resources." Idaho Code § 42-226.

***

36. There currently is no approved and effectively operating mitigation in place to mitigate for injury, if any, to the water rights held by or for the benefit of the members of [American Falls].

***

45. Based upon the Idaho Constitution, Idaho Code, the Conjunctive Management Rules, and decisions by Idaho courts, ... it is clear that injury to senior priority surface water rights by diversion and use of junior priority ground water rights occurs when diversion under the junior rights intercept a sufficient quantity of water to interfere with the exercise of the senior primary and supplemental water rights for the authorized beneficial use. Because the amount of water necessary for beneficial use can be less than decreed or licensed quantities, it is possible for a senior to receive less than the decreed or licensed amount, but not suffer injury. Thus, senior surface water right holders cannot demand that junior ground water right holders diverting water from a hydraulically-connected aquifer be required to make water available for diversion unless that water is necessary to accomplish an authorized beneficial use.

***

45[sic]. Contrary to the assertion of [American Falls], depletion does not equate to material injury. Material injury is a highly fact specific inquiry that must be determined in accordance with IDAPA conjunctive management rule 42. [American Falls] has no legal basis to seek the future curtailment of junior priority ground water rights based on injury alleged by [American Falls] to have occurred in prior years.

***

The Director identified and ordered the junior ground water rights holders subject to administration pursuant to the American Falls' Delivery Call, to provide "replacement" water sufficient to offset the depletions in American Falls' water supply or face immediate curtailment. Pursuant to I.C. § 42-1701A(3), the Relief Order provided that aggrieved parties were entitled to an administrative hearing on the Relief Order if requested within fifteen days, but that otherwise the Relief Order would become final. Both American Falls and IGWA requested an administrative hearing, which was set by the Director. However, before the hearing could be held, American Falls filed this declaratory judgment action in district court on August 15, 2005. Later, American Falls requested stays and continuances in the hearing schedule and to date, the administrative challenges to the Relief Order remain pending.

. . .

III. ISSUES ON APPEAL

1. Did the district court properly exercise jurisdiction before all administrative remedies were exhausted?

2. Did the district court err in holding that the CM Rules are facially unconstitutional based on a lack of certain "procedural components"?

. . .

V. DISCUSSION

. . .

It was the failure of the CM Rules to ". . . integrate the concomitant tenets and procedures related to a delivery call, which have historically been held to be necessary to give effect to the constitutional protections pertaining to senior water rights" with which the district court found fault, and it is that conclusion this opinion will analyze. The district court held:

> Specifically, the [CM Rules] fail: 1) to establish a procedural framework properly allocating the well established burdens of proof; 2) to define the evidentiary standards that the Director is [to] apply in responding to a call; 3) to give the proper legal effect to a partial decree: 4) to establish objective criteria necessary to evaluate the aforementioned factors; and 5) to establish a workable, procedural framework for processing a call in a time frame commensurate with the need for water—especially irrigation water.

With that background, we proceed with an analysis of the issues raised on appeal by the IDWR.

A. Did the district court properly exercise jurisdiction before all administrative remedies were exhausted?

. . . Although the district court found the CM Rules were unconstitutional on their face, the district court discussed the constitutionality of the Rules "as applied" to the facts of this case. The question is whether the court wrongfully exercised its authority in declaring the Rules invalid in reference to the particulars of this case before a factual record could be developed in an administrative hearing.

A party may challenge a statute as unconstitutional "on its face" or "as applied" to the party's conduct. A facial challenge to a statute or rule is "purely a question of law." Generally, a facial challenge is mutually exclusive from an as applied challenge. For a facial constitutional challenge to succeed, the party must demonstrate that the law is unconstitutional in *all* of its applications. In other words, "the challenger must establish that no set of circumstances exists under which the [law] would be valid." In contrast, to prove a statute is unconstitutional "as applied", the party must only show that, as applied to the defendant's conduct, the statute is unconstitutional. A district court should not rule that a statute is unconstitutional "as applied" to a particular case until administrative proceedings have concluded and a complete record has been developed....

...

... While it appears the district court attempted to conduct an analysis based on a facial challenge only, the court also ... stated that it would apply both a facial and an as applied analysis to the extent the facts were already established and to illustrate how the court believed the Director would be applying the CM Rules.

***

... Additionally, a district court cannot properly engage in an "as applied" constitutional analysis until a complete factual record has been developed. The district court should not blur the lines between a facial and as applied analysis by engaging in a hybrid analysis.

...

Therefore, this Court's review will be in terms of the CM Rules' constitutionality on their face and not in terms of the Rules' "threatened application" or "as applied." The issue is whether the challenged provisions are void in all possible applications, or whether there are a set of circumstances in which they may be constitutionally applied.

B. Did the district court err in holding that the CM Rules are facially unconstitutional based on a lack of certain "procedural components"?

As indicated above, the district court found that because the CM Rules failed to articulate certain procedural components of the prior appropriation doctrine according to Idaho law, the CM Rules are facially unconstitutional ... the district court observed:

> ... there are two additional primary and essential principles of Idaho's version of the prior appropriation doctrine which are at issue in the administration of established rights but which are absent from the [CM Rules]. They are that in times of shortage there is the presumption of injury to a senior by the diversion of a junior, and the well engrained burdens of proof.

Again, later in the opinion, ... the CM Rules fail:

> 1) to establish a procedural framework properly allocating the well established burdens of proof; 2) to define the evidentiary standards that the Director is [to] apply in responding to a call; 3) to give the proper legal effect to a partial decree: 4) to establish objective criteria necessary to evaluate the aforementioned factors; and 5) to establish a workable, procedural framework for processing a call in a time frame commensurate with the need for water—especially irrigation water.

However, as the IDWR points out, CM Rule 20.02 provides that: "[T]hese rules acknowledge all elements of the prior appropriation doctrine as established by Idaho law." "Idaho law," as defined by CM Rule 10.12, means "[T]he constitution, statutes, administrative rules and case law of Idaho." Thus, the Rules incorporate Idaho law by reference and to the extent the Constitution, statutes and case law have identified the proper presumptions, burdens of proof, evidentiary standards and time parameters, those are a part of the CM Rules. Due to the changing nature of the law and rules, it is unnecessary to incorporate extant law unless specifically necessary to a clear understanding of the particular Rule. This is a facial challenge to these Rules and if it is clear there are circumstances under which these Rules may be constitutionally applied to provide adequate procedural safeguards, then the Rules withstand a facial challenge. To the extent one can bring a constitutional claim based on a particular fact scenario that occurred and was permitted within the Rules, an "as applied" challenge is appropriate.

1. Burdens of proof and evidentiary standards

...

American Falls asserts on appeal that specific provisions of the Rules squarely contradict Idaho case law by placing the burden on the senior rather than the junior water user. American Falls argues that the seniors "are left to initiate a series of 'contested cases' and prove they are suffering 'material injury' before the Director and the watermasters will take any action.... Much emphasis is placed on CM Rule 30.01, which provides:

> **01. Delivery Call (Petition).** When a delivery call is made by the holder of a surface or ground water right (petitioner) alleging that by reason of diversion of water by the holders of one (1) or more junior-priority ground water rights (respondents) the petitioner is suffering material injury, the petitioner shall file with the Director a petition in writing containing, at least, the following...
>
> ...
>
> c. All information, measurements, data or study results available to the petitioner to support the claim of material injury.

IDAPA 37.03.11.30.01. American Falls also cites Rule 40.01, which states that responses to calls are made when a senior files a delivery call "alleging" he is suffering "material injury" and upon a finding by the Director that material injury is occurring. This, American Falls argues, places the burden on the senior to prove material injury. A plain reading of the CM Rules does not support that interpretation, particularly in the context of a facial challenge to the Rules. The Rules simply require that a senior who is suffering injury file a delivery call with the Director and allege that the senior is suffering material injury. This is presumably to make the Director aware that such injury is occurring and to give substance to the complaint. Additionally, the Rules ask that the petitioner include all available information to support the call in order to assist the Director in his fact-finding. Nowhere do the Rules state that the senior must prove material injury before the Director will make such a finding. To the contrary, this Court must presume that the Director will act in accordance with Idaho law, as he is directed to do under CM Rule 20.02. While it is possible the Director could apply the CM Rules in an unconstitutional manner, that would be an opportune time for an "as applied" challenge; however now, in the absence of such facts indicating the Director has misapplied the Rules in violation of Idaho law, our analysis is limited to the Rules as written, or "on their face," and the Rules do not permit or direct the shifting of the burden of proof. Therefore, this Court does not find that the failure to explicitly recite certain procedural components such as the burdens of proof makes the CM Rules unconstitutional on their face.

...

3. Lack of objective standards

The district court ... was concerned by "the absence of any objective standards from which to evaluate the criteria." Rule 42 lists factors the Director may consider in determining material injury.... Those factors, of necessity, require some determination of "reasonableness" and it is the lack of an objective standard—something other than "reasonableness"—which caused the district court to conclude the Rules were facially defective. Given the nature of the decisions which must be made in determining how to respond to a delivery call, there must be some exercise of discretion by the Director. While it may be that the Director could apply these factors in an unreasonable way, the Rules are not facially deficient ...

4. Failure to give legal effect to a partial decree

... These water rights have already been determined by the Snake River Basin Adjudication court, which, at the time of the adjudication of these rights, considered the Director's recommendations, which identified issues pertaining to quantity, purpose of use, point of diversion, etc. The CM Rules, the district court concluded, allow the Director to, in essence, re-adjudicate water rights by conducting a complete re-evaluation of the scope and efficiencies of a decreed water right in conjunction with a delivery call. In effect, the court stated, a senior who has an adjudicated water right through a partial decree must re-defend the elements of his adjudicated right each time he makes a delivery call.

...

CM Rule 42 lists factors "the Director may consider in determining whether the holders of water rights are suffering material injury and using water efficiently and without waste...." IDAPA 37.03.11.42.01. Such factors include the system, diversion, and conveyance efficiency, the method of irrigation water application and alternate reasonable means of diversion. *Id.* American Falls argues the Director is not authorized to consider such factors before administering water rights; rather, the Director is "required to deliver the *full quantity* of decreed senior water rights according to their priority" rather than partake in this re-evaluation (emphasis in original brief). American Falls asserts the Rules are defective in giving the Director, in essence, the authority to negotiate with the senior water right holder regarding the quantity of water he will enforce under a delivery call—a quantity that in some instances, has already been adjudicated.

Clearly, even as acknowledged by the district court, the Director may consider factors such as those listed above in water rights administration. Specifically, the Director "has the duty and authority" to consider circumstances when the water user is not irrigating the full number of acres decreed under the water right. If this Court were to rule the Director lacks the power in a delivery call to evaluate whether the senior is putting the water to beneficial use, we would be ignoring the constitutional requirement that priority over water be extended only to those using the water. Additionally, the water rights adjudications neither address, nor answer, the questions presented in delivery calls; thus, responding to delivery calls, as conducted pursuant to the CM Rules, do not constitute a re-adjudication. For example, the SRBA court determines the water sources, quantity, priority date, point of diversion, place, period and purpose of use. I.C. §§ 42-1411(2)(a)–(j). However, reasonableness is not an element of a water right; thus, evaluation of whether a diversion is reasonable in the administration context should not be deemed a re-adjudication. Moreover, a partial decree need not contain information on how each water right on a source physically interacts or affects other rights on that same source.

...

American Falls argues, though, that Rule 30.01 improperly shifts the burden to the senior appropriator who has already obtained a decreed right and forces the senior right holder to re-adjudicate or re-prove his decreed right whenever he makes a delivery call. The district court agreed and held that the Rules were fatally defective in not containing a presumption that "when a junior diverts or withdraws water in times of a water shortage, it is presumed that there is injury to a senior." The court cited *Moe v. Harger,* 77 P. 645, 647 (1904), as support for that holding. *Moe,* however, was a case dealing with competing surface water rights and this case involves interconnected ground and surface water rights. The issues presented are simply not the same.

When water is diverted from a surface stream, the flow is directly reduced, and the reduction is soon felt by downstream users unless the distances involved are great. When water is withdrawn from an aquifer, however, the impact elsewhere in the basin or on a hydrologically connected stream is typically much slower.

...

While perhaps the Rules can be read in different ways, they can be read consistently with constitutional and statutory principles....

The Rules should not be read as containing a burden-shifting provision to make the petitioner re-prove or re-adjudicate the right which he already has. We note that in the Initial Order entered in this case, the Director requested extensive information from American Falls for the prior fifteen irrigation seasons, to which American Falls objected in part. While there is no question that some information is relevant and necessary to the Director's determination of how best to respond to a delivery call, the burden is not on the senior water rights holder to re-prove an adjudicated right. The presumption under Idaho law is that the senior is entitled to his decreed water right, but there certainly may be some post-adjudication factors which are relevant to the determination of how much water is actually needed. The Rules may not be applied in such a way as to force the senior to demonstrate an entitlement to the water in the first place; that is presumed by the filing of a petition containing information about the decreed right. The Rules do give the Director the tools by which to determine "how the various ground and surface water sources are interconnected, and how, when, where and to what extent the diversion and use of water from one source impacts [others]." Once the initial determination is made that material injury is occurring or will occur, the junior then bears the burden of proving that the call would be futile or to challenge, in some other constitutionally permissible way, the senior's call.

For the purposes of the facial challenge with which we are faced in this appeal, the CM Rules do not unconstitutionally force a senior water rights holder to re-adjudicate a right, nor do the Rules fail to give adequate consideration to a partial decree. In an "as applied" challenge, it would be possible to analyze on a fully developed factual record whether the Director has improperly applied the Rules to place too great a burden on the senior water rights holder. Facially, however, the Rules do not do so.

...

Notes & Questions

1. What's the difference between a "facial" constitutional challenge versus an "applied" constitutional challenge? What must you do to bring an applied constitutional challenge? Why? How does the fact that American Falls may only bring a facial challenge affect the outcome of this case?
2. What is the court referring to when it discusses whether the CM rules "lack certain 'procedural components?'" Does the court find that the CM rules lack these procedural components? How did it come to its conclusion?
3. Where does the director look to determine material injury? What is the evaluation criteria the director must employ? What happens after a determination of material injury is made by the department?
4. Under Idaho law, who enjoys the presumption of entitlement to their water rights when water supplies are short? Are they automatically entitled to their full decreed amount? What information must a person submit along with their petition for a water call? Does the court agree that this constitutes impermissible burden shifting?
5. What is the interrelationship between the parties' adjudicated water rights and this administrative proceeding? Do the CM rules allow the director to "re-adjudicate" water rights? Ultimately, what becomes the limitation on the senior water holders' water rights in any given year?

Idaho's Conjunctive Management of Ground and Surface Water: Administrative Rules in Application

American Falls settled the overall constitutionality of the Conjunctive Management Rules. However, many questions about *how* those rules would be implemented remained unresolved. The gaps were particularly pressing in the Eastern Snake Plain, where conjunctive management required understanding the water use of tens of thousands of water users, many of whom were taking their water from the geologically complex Eastern Snake Plain Aquifer. Professor Cosens describes the scientific complexity of determining which groundwater wells to curtail when a senior water user seeks a call:

> Interaction between surface and ground water is often highly complex. Some of the water spread over the surface of the land by precipitation and irrigation will seep into the groundwater. Seepage will vary with the permeability of surface soils and geologic units, with rate of precipitation or application of water, and with the existing soil moisture content. Surface streams may lose water to, or gain water from groundwater. Flow rates vary within an aquifer. Many streams lose in some stretches while gaining in others. As a result of these and other variables, the impact of ground water use on surface water is not direct, immediate or one-to-one.[11] [citations omitted]

IDWR turned to hydrologic modeling as the way to manage uncertainty in determining which senior water rights are affected by pumping from which groundwater wells and by how much. Like it sounds, models provide a simplified representation of reality. In this case, IDWR worked with the University of Idaho's Water Resources Research Institute and used a collaborative process with water users to develop a model,[12] known as the Eastern Snake Plain Aquifer Model (ESPAM),[13] that provides mathematical representations of ground water flow and interaction with surface water in the Eastern Snake Plain. The modelers break the aquifer into a series of cells that are assumed to contain relatively homogenous hydrogeology. The model returns information on the probability that each cell is contributing water to a particular reach of the Snake River and the degree to which groundwater pumping from that cell reduces the contribution. Typical model output will show the impact of pumping decreasing from 90–100% to 0–10% as distance from the particular stream reach increases.

Models do not provide 100% accuracy of the natural system. Uncertainty is particularly prevalent in groundwater systems that we cannot actually see. As illustrated by the next case, not only does the ESPAM output only provide a probable range of impact for wells within a certain cell, it is not capable of being used to make a more specific determination that this specific well affects this specific surface water diversion. As a result, the wisdom of using groundwater models to decide something as important

---

11. Barbara Cosens, *The Role of Hydrology in the Resolution of Water Disputes,* 133 J. Contemp. Water Rsch. & Educ.: River Adjudications 17 (2006).

12. The collaborative modeling group was developed in 1998 and is referred to as the Eastern Snake Hydrologic Modeling Committee (ESHMC). Idaho Department of Water Resources, *Eastern Snake Plain Aquifer Model,* https://idwr.idaho.gov/water-data/projects/ESPAM/. For an overview of the process and the role of the model in conjunctive management, see Barbara Cosens, *The Role of Hydrology in the Resolution of Water Disputes,* 133 J. Contemp. Water Rsch. & Educ.: River Adjudications 17 (2006).

13. Idaho Department of Water Resources, *Eastern Snake Plain Aquifer Model,* https://idwr.idaho.gov/water-data/projects/ESPAM/.

is the curtailment of property rights was one for the courts to decide. It is a complex question of law and science and the issue of who bears the burden of proof is critical in that context. These issues came to the fore shortly after IDWR began using the ESPAM to make conjunctive curtailment decisions in the Eastern Snake Plain.

Clear Springs Foods, Inc. v. Idaho Dept. of Water Resources

Supreme Court of Idaho
252 P.3d 71 (2011)

Eismann, Chief Justice

This is an appeal from a decision on judicial review upholding curtailment orders issued against junior groundwater users because their withdrawals of water from the aquifer were causing material injury to senior appropriators' surface water rights. The senior appropriators also cross-appeal the failure to curtail additional groundwater pumping. We affirm the judgment of the district court.

I. FACTS AND PROCEDURAL HISTORY

The Snake River rises in western Wyoming, flows westward across the entire breadth of Idaho, turns northward forming Idaho's western boundary, and ultimately empties into the Columbia River. It is the largest and longest tributary of the Columbia River. As it crosses southern Idaho, it courses through the Snake River plain, a prominent depression extending about 400 miles in an east-west direction and ranging from 50 to 125 miles in width. Underlying the eastern portion of the plain is the Eastern Snake River Plain Aquifer (Aquifer), which is about 170 miles long and 60 miles wide. It is estimated that it contains up to a billion acre feet of water, which would be roughly the amount of water contained in Lake Erie.

Clear Springs Foods, Inc., (Clear Springs) and Blue Lakes Trout Farm, Inc., (Blue Lakes) (collectively called "Spring Users") are both engaged in fish farming. They each have water rights in certain springs emanating from the canyon wall along a section of the Snake River below Milner Dam in south central Idaho. Those springs are fed by the Aquifer. Members of the Idaho Ground Water Appropriators, Inc., the North Snake Ground Water District, and the Magic Valley Ground Water District (collectively called "Groundwater Users") have ground water rights entitling them to pump water from wells drilled into the Aquifer.

The Aquifer is predominately fractured Quaternary basalt having an aggregate thickness that, in some locations, may exceed several thousand feet. It decreases to shallow depths in the area where the springs emanate. The fractured basalt is characterized by high hydraulic conductivities that are typically 1,000 feet per day, but they range from 0.1 to 100,000 feet per day.

The ground water in the Aquifer is hydraulically connected to the Snake River and tributary surface waters at various places and in varying degrees. As a result, ground water can become surface water, and surface water can become ground water. The amount that becomes one or the other is largely dependent upon ground water elevations. When water is pumped from a well, it causes a cone-shaped lowering of the ground water elevation near the well. Surrounding ground water then flows into the cone from all sides, depleting ground water away from the well. When that occurs in an area hydraulically connected to a reach of the river or its tributaries, it results in a loss of water from the river or a loss of gain to the river.

Beginning in the 1950's, groundwater appropriations from the Aquifer increased dramatically. It now receives about 7.5 million acre-feet of recharge on an average annual basis and discharges about the same amount of water, with nearly 2.0 million acre-feet annually of that discharge in the form of depletions from ground water withdrawals. About 95% of the ground water diverted from the Aquifer is used for irrigation. The remainder is used for public, domestic, industrial, and livestock purposes.

...

In 1994, the Department adopted rules concerning conjunctive management of ground water and surface water for the entire state. The Department has also developed a calibrated ground water model to determine the effects on the Aquifer and hydraulically-connected reaches of the Snake River and its tributaries from pumping a single well in the Aquifer, from pumping selected groups of wells, and from surface water uses on lands above the Aquifer. In 2004, the Department, working in collaboration with other entities, completed reformulation of that model.

On March 22, 2005, Blue Lakes delivered a letter to the Department demanding that then-Director Karl J. Dreher require the local watermaster to administer water rights as required by Idaho Code § 42-607 in order to supply Blue Lakes with water under its senior rights. On May 2, 2005, Clear Springs delivered letters to the Director making a similar demand....

On August 1, 2007, then-Director David R. Tuthill, Jr., appointed a hearing officer to preside over an evidentiary hearing regarding the Spring Users' delivery calls. The hearing began on November 28, 2007, and continued for about twelve days. On January 11, 2008, the hearing officer issued his findings of fact, conclusions of law, and recommendation. After considering objections submitted by the parties, the Director issued a final order on July 11, 2008. Except as modified in the final order, he adopted the former Director's findings of fact and conclusions of law, the hearing officer's recommendations, and the curtailment orders.

Clear Springs filed a petition for judicial review, and Blue Lakes and the Groundwater Users filed cross petitions for judicial review. The district court affirmed most of the final order. *** The Groundwater Users appealed, and the Spring Users cross appealed.

II. ISSUES ON APPEAL

Issues Raised by Groundwater Users

...

C. Did the district court err in upholding the Director's determination that the ground water depletions caused material injury to the Spring Users' water rights?

D. Did the district court err in upholding the Director's determination that the Spring Users' delivery calls were not futile?

E. Did the district court err in upholding the Director's findings based upon the ground water model?

...

III. ANALYSIS

When reviewing agency action on a petition for judicial review, the district court must affirm the agency unless it finds that the agency's findings, inferences, conclusions, or decisions are: "(a) in violation of constitutional or statutory provisions; (b) in excess of the statutory authority of the agency; (c) made upon unlawful procedure; (d) not supported by substantial evidence on the record as a whole; or (e) arbitrary, capricious, or an abuse of discretion."... The district court cannot substitute its judgment for that of the agency as to the weight of the evidence on questions of fact....

...

C. Did the District Court Err in Upholding the Director's Determination that the Ground Water Depletions Caused Material Injury to the Spring Users' Water Rights?

...

The Groundwater Users contend that a decreased water supply is not sufficient to show material injury. Rather, they argue that there must be evidence showing that with more water the Spring Users could produce more fish and profitably sell them.

"The first appropriator of water for useful or beneficial purposes has the prior right thereto, and the right, once vested, will be protected and upheld, unless abandoned." *Bower v. Moorman*. The right to appropriate water is for "beneficial uses," Idaho Const. Art. XV, § 3, not merely for profitable businesses. Beneficial use is not defined in the Constitution, nor has it been comprehensively defined by statute or by this Court. However, a beneficial use is not limited to a use that generates a profit, or even income. For example, the Constitution lists using water for "domestic purposes" as a beneficial use. Idaho Const. Art. XV, § 3. We have held that "firefighting" is a beneficial use of water. Likewise, the legislature has declared as beneficial uses "drinking water," Idaho Code § 39-102(2), "the watering of domestic livestock," Idaho Code § 42-114, using low temperature geothermal resources "primarily for heat value," Idaho Code § 42-233, using instream water "for the protection of fish and wildlife habitat, aquatic life, recreation, aesthetic beauty, transportation and navigation values, and water quality," Idaho Code § 42-1501, and using water in lakes and water discharging from springs for "scenic beauty."

"Material injury" is defined by the Conjunctive Management Rules as "[h]indrance to or impact upon *the exercise of a water right* caused by the use of water by another person as determined in accordance with Idaho Law, as set forth in Rule 42." IDAPA 37.03.11.010.14 (emphasis added). The Rule requires impact upon the exercise of a water right. It does not require showing an impact on the profitability of the senior appropriator›s business. Such a holding would conflict with Article XV, § 3, of the Idaho Constitution, which states that "[p]riority of appropriation shall give the better right as between those using the water." It would also require the Director or watermaster to examine the businesses of the senior and junior appropriators to determine which one could make the greater profit from the use of the water when there is a shortage. If business profitability was the basis for appropriation, decreed water rights would become meaningless. The issue would be which appropriator at the time could make the greater profit by using the water.

... The district court did not err in holding that there was substantial evidence supporting the finding of material injury to the Spring Users' water rights.

D. Did the District Court Err in Upholding the Director's Determination that the Spring Users' Delivery Calls Were Not Futile...?

The Groundwater Users asserted prior to the agency hearing that the Spring Users' delivery calls were futile because the evidence "will show that there is little to no expectation that the shortages suffered by the spring users in this case will ever be restored." In his proposed findings of fact and conclusions of law, the hearing officer noted the challenge of applying the futile call rule when the junior appropriator is withdrawing ground water.

> [C]urtailing ground water pumping does not provide the immediacy of delivery to the senior user that would be present in the curtailment of surface water. Surface water travels in a channel from one source that may be seen to a destination that can be seen. It can be routed to a particular point. Ground water does not fall into this model. Its route is determined by the contours of fractured basalt interspersed at times with soil of a different composition. Part of the water curtailed may travel one direction, part another. The effects of curtailment may be years to be realized. The parameters of a futile call in surface to surface delivery do not fit in the administration of ground water. If the time for the delivery of water to avoid a futile call defense that is applicable in surface to surface water delivery were applied in calls for the curtailment of ground water, most calls would be futile. In effect ground water pumping could continue uncurtailed despite deleterious effects upon surface water use because curtailment would not have the immediate effect traditionally anticipated.

The hearing officer concluded that "the fact that curtailment will not produce sufficient water immediately to satisfy the senior rights does not render the calls futile.

A reasonable time for the results of curtailment to be fully realized may require years, not days or weeks."

...

... The district court upheld the Director's decision, noting that the conjunctive management rules acknowledge that relief from curtailment will not be immediate.

[The groundwater users did not raise this issue on appeal, instead they asserted that the spring users would need to show that the additional water would allow them to grow larger fish. The court held that an issue cannot be raised for the first time on appeal.]

...

E. Did the District Court Err in Upholding the Director›s Findings Based Upon the Ground Water Model?

Former-Director Dreher relied upon the Department's ground water model in issuing the curtailment orders. However, he found that the model had an uncertainty of up to ten percent due to the margin of error in stream gauges used in developing the model. Based upon that level of possible uncertainty, he limited the junior water rights curtailed.

The hearing officer also relied upon the model when making his recommended findings. He reasoned: "There is no better science available. Decisions had to be made and will have to be made. The limitations of the model are identifiable and important but they do not preclude reliance upon it. It has an acceptable level of reliability based on peer reviewed science."

In their objections submitted to the Director, the Groundwater Users urged the Director to consider other uncertainties in the model. They argued that the Director should "assign a more accurate level of predictive uncertainty between 20 and 30%, and to constrict the trim line accordingly." The Director declined to do so. He held that the "ground water model represents the best available science for determining the effects of ground water diversions and surface water uses on the [Aquifer] and hydraulically-connected reaches of the Snake River and its tributaries" and that there "is no other technical basis as reliable as the simulations from the ESPA ground water model that can be used to determine the effects of ground water diversions and surface water uses on the ESPA and hydraulically-connected reaches of the Snake River and its tributaries." The Director also found that "the degree of uncertainty associated with application of the [Aquifer] ground water model is 10 percent."

The Groundwater Users asserted to the district court that the Director erred by failing to take into account known uncertainties in the model....

On appeal, the Groundwater Users contend that the district court erred because "[t]he curtailment orders should be set aside because the Director failed to account for all known limitations of the [Aquifer] Model, resulting in a broader zone of curtailment than should have occurred." They argue that in addition to possible error from the stream gauges, "Model uncertainty also derives from non-uniform geology of the [Aquifer], variations within the Model cells, the assumption that well impacts are isotropic [the same in every direction], the assumption that all data was accurate and reliable, and the unaccounted for impacts of surface water diversions, precipitation recharge, and tributary underflow." They conclude by "ask[ing] the Court to set aside the curtailment orders and remand them to the Director with instructions to exercise his judgment in accounting for all contributing factors of Model uncertainty, and to re-define the area of curtailment accordingly."

...

There have been numerous studies of the geology of the Aquifer and ground water resources of the eastern Snake River Plain dating from 1902 to 1982, but none of them provide an adequate basis for the conjunctive management of water rights from surface and ground water sources. As a result, the Department contracted with the University of Idaho Water Resources Research Institute to develop a model. The model was calibrated to a twenty-two-year set of data from 1980 through 2002.

The hearing officer found that "[t]he limitations of the model are identifiable and important but they do not preclude reliance upon it. It has an acceptable level of reliability based on peer reviewed science." The Director adopted those findings, and found that the model " represents the best available science for determining the effects of ground water diversions and surface water uses on the [Aquifer] and hydraulically-connected reaches of the Snake River and its tributaries." He also found, "There currently is no other technical basis as reliable as the simulations from the [Aquifer] ground water model that can be used to determine the effects of ground water diversions and surface water uses on the [Aquifer] and hydraulically connected reaches of the Snake River and its tributaries." Those findings are not challenged on appeal. In fact, the Groundwater Users state, "The Model is the best science available for administering hydraulically connected surface and groundwater rights on the [Aquifer], but the Model is not perfect." They have failed to show that the Director abused his discretion in relying upon the model. He perceived the issue of utilizing the model as discretionary, he acted within the outer limits of his discretion and consistently with the legal standards applicable to the available choices, and he reached his decision through an exercise of reason. The district court did not err in upholding the Director's reliance upon the model.

...

IV. CONCLUSION

We affirm the judgment of the district court.

Notes & Questions

1. Unlike American Falls Reservoir District, IGWA properly exhausted its administrative remedies before going to the district court. As a result, the Idaho Supreme Court had a full record from which it could make its decisions. The case is instructive on the administrative process that should be followed to protest an agency decision. Like

American Falls, that process began with a petition to IDWR to curtail junior groundwater users. IDWR engaged in an investigation of the petition to satisfy itself that the spring users were in fact experiencing material injury under the conjunctive management rules. Then, without holding a hearing or providing opportunity for IGWA to respond, IDWR issued a curtailment order, which triggered the protest process.

Once a protest had been filed, the director of IDWR appointed a hearing officer to take evidence, make findings of fact, and conclusions of law. In this case, the evidentiary hearing spanned 12 days. Based on the evidence received, the hearing officer submitted a report to the Director of IDWR and the parties had an opportunity to object to that report. After considering the report and objections, the Director had the opportunity to adopt or reject (in full or part) the hearing officer's recommendation. The publishing of the Director's decision marks the point at which administrative remedies have been exhausted and the parties may seek judicial review.

2. IGWA argued that there was no material injury in this case because the spring users failed to establish that more water would result in more or larger fish. How does the Idaho Supreme Court address this question?
3. How does the futile call doctrine differ in the conjunctive management and/or groundwater situation when compared to a situation only involving surface water uses? Do those differences result in the inapplicability of the doctrine? How does the doctrine differ when groundwater is involved?
4. IGWA challenged the use of the model before the administrative hearing officer due to the high level of uncertainty and the inability to identify all the sources of uncertainty. The hearing officer and Director nevertheless accepted the model and the challenge is not raised on appeal. What is the reasoning of the hearing officer and the phrase used by Director in justifying the use of an imperfect tool for implementing the call? IGWA does challenge IDWR's use of what is referred to in the case as the "trim line" as a geographic line beyond which groundwater would not be curtailed because the model predicted wells beyond the line have an impact of 10% or less on the relevant stream reach. On what basis does IGWA argue for use of a larger margin of error? Does the court ultimately endorse IDWR's approach? Why? Note that IDWR has continued to refine ESPAM to reduce uncertainty and is currently on ESPAM version 2.2.[14]
5. Following considerable state funding for development of a Comprehensive Aquifer Management Plan, the water users of the Eastern Snake Plain focused on a physical solution. The water users reached a settlement[15] to avoid the yearly process of a call. The settlement was adopted as a mitigation plan by the Director of IDWR with

---

14. Idaho Department of Water Resources, *Eastern Snake Plain Aquifer Model* Documents, https://idwr.idaho.gov/water-data/projects/espam/documents/.

15. Settlement Agreement Entered Into June 30, 2015 Between Participating Members of the Surface Water Coalition and Participating Members of the Idaho Ground Water Appropriators, Inc., available at: https://idwr.idaho.gov/wp-content/uploads/sites/2/legal/swan-falls-settlement/20150630-Settlement-Agreement.pdf.

short-term mitigation measures and long-term measures to stabilize the aquifer, including:[16]

- Reduction in groundwater diversion of 240,000 acre-feet annually.
- Storage purchase of 50,000 acre-feet by IGWA for delivery to surface water users (using Idaho's water supply bank you learned about in Chapter 21.
- Reduced irrigation season for groundwater users.
- Mandatory metering.
- Support for the state recharge program.
- Safe harbor from a call for all groundwater users participating in the settlement.

16. *Id.*, Provision 3, Long Term Practices, Commencing 2016.

Part VI

Adjudication

A water rights adjudication is the judicial determination of the existence, nature, extent, and priority of water rights. Water rights adjudications are necessary because of the historical development of water resources in the West. Recall from Parts II and V that for much of the nineteenth and twentieth centuries no recording of a water right was necessary. Instead, all one had to do to appropriate a legally valid water right was divert water and put it to a beneficial use. Although that process was responsive to the practical realities of the era, it made enforcing the water rights difficult because no one conclusively knew the order of priorities, how much water each individual legally appropriated, and other important elements for enforcing water rights. The solution was adjudication; litigation wherein a court could take evidence on these issues and develop a comprehensive decree that listed—in order of priority—each water right holder in the lawsuit (or claiming water from the source in the case of a general adjudication), their quantity, point of diversion, place of use, period of use, and type of use. In times of shortage, the water master could then use the decree to curtail the judicially determined junior water users until the seniors received their water entitlement.

Originally, these adjudications were conducted on an ad hoc basis when one person's water use began to interfere with another. These were known as private adjudications, which included the determination of water rights for some—but not necessarily all—water users of a particular source. The ad hoc nature of private adjudications proved sufficient during early water resource management. Water use controversies were largely local affairs, which meant that private adjudications were sufficient to bind all the necessary parties. Water resource controversies increased as the population in the West continued to grow and water use became increasingly sophisticated toward the middle of the twentieth century. As a result, water managers needed a more comprehensive inventory that included all hydrologically connected water rights.

From this, the general stream adjudication was born. Unlike private adjudications, general stream adjudications are litigation that involves every claimant to water from a particular source (or at least all those within the state commencing the adjudication). These types of adjudications can be massive, incredibly complex, expensive, and time-consuming. Idaho's Snake River Basin Adjudication ("SRBA"), for example, had 158,591 claims, 43,822 contested cases, went to the Idaho Supreme Court on 36 occasions and the U.S. Supreme Court once.[1] The final unified decree for the SRBA is approximately 275,000 pages long, and it took 27 years to complete, which likely makes it the fastest general stream adjudication of its kind. In comparison, the Montana statewide general stream adjudication, which commenced in 1979, is anticipated to include approximately 219,000 water rights claims and is not expected to conclude until 2028.[2] Similarly, in Arizona, approximately 82,000 claims have been filed in the Gila River Adjudication, which commenced in 1974 and is currently about 33% completed.[3] Likewise, Arizona's Little Colorado River Adjudication commenced in 1978 in Arizona state court, contains around 14,000 claims, and is approximately 55% complete.[4]

Despite their size and complexity, general stream adjudications have come to be a major factor in establishing the database necessary to administer water in the West as watersheds have reached full appropriation. For states that now have exclusive permit systems and required processes for change in use allowing for continual updating of the database on water rights, a general stream adjudication need not be repeated. Nonetheless, many watersheds in the West have yet to be adjudicated and private adjudications continue to take place. Chapter 25 will provide general coverage of private and general adjudication.

States have a variety of reasons for undertaking general stream adjudications. In Idaho, the need arose for a database for enforcement following a lawsuit recognizing the seniority of a hydropower plant downstream from most of the state's major irrigation districts. In Montana, the decision to adjudicate the entire state was influenced by the desire to have a clear accounting of water rights in the event of an interstate dispute. Recall from Part IV that one of the factors in a suit for equitable apportionment is the extent of existing water use. A state unable to document that extent will be at a disadvantage.

In both Montana and Arizona, part of the impetus was the desire to quantify federal and tribal water rights. As you learned in Parts III and IV, reserved water rights must be quantified as the amount necessary for the purpose of the reservation and will carry the priority date of reservation establishment. The rights are not lost by nonuse; thus the absence of a clear quantification placed a cloud over state-based rights in a shared watershed. In Chapter 26 you will learn how the states gained jurisdiction over federal and tribal water rights through a congressional waiver of sovereign immunity, referred to as the McCarran Amendment. You will also learn about some of the conflicting rulings that have come from various state courts as a result.

Chapter 27 will cover the use of settlement processes to resolve federal and tribal water rights. You will learn about some of the innovative solutions that have resulted

---

1. Clive J. Strong, *SRBA Retrospective: A 27-Year Effort*, 57 Advocate 28 (Nov./Dec. 2014).

2. *Id.*

3. *Id.*

4. *Id.*

in development of water for tribes, protection of instream flows in national parks, and certainty for state-based water users on water courses shared with tribes and with federal land management agencies.

As noted above, providing a database to administer water rights in priority in times of shortage is one of the major aims of a general adjudication. With federal and tribal water rights included in the decrees from a general adjudication, the question arose regarding who administers tribal and federal water rights. Chapter 28 will cover this controversy and the variety of ways it has been approached, including some innovative solutions arrived at through settlement.

Chapter 25

Water Rights Adjudication

Introduction

The legal determination of the relative rights to water use on a shared watercourse is referred to as "adjudication." Private adjudication has long been available to resolve localized disputes among neighbors and will be covered in the initial section of this Chapter. In the mid-twentieth century it became increasingly necessary to determine the relative rights of all water users on a shared source as shortages appeared with the combination of optimized development and periods of drought. Joining all water users requires a general adjudication. This Chapter will review the process of a general adjudication using multiple states as examples. It will then turn to some of the complexities of case management using Idaho's Snake River Basin Adjudication (SRBA) as an example. Among our Columbia River Basin states, Idaho has the largest acreage in irrigated agriculture, particularly in its Snake River Plain. Idaho's Snake River Basin Adjudication (SRBA) began in 1987, and the final decree was entered on August 25, 2014. Thus, the SRBA provides an excellent example of general stream adjudication from beginning to end. The remaining sections in this Chapter will use the SRBA to discuss the steps in a general adjudication and the handling of a complex case to help you understand how a court navigates a case with over 100,000 claims and what that means for representation of clients.

Private Adjudication

The common law method for acquiring a water right through diversion and application to a beneficial use makes it difficult for a court to know with certainty whether the person claiming the right: (1) has legally appropriated a water right; and (2) if so, what the scope of the water right ought to be. As a result, many states have statutes that declare unadjudicated water rights to be the most junior on a stream. Idaho law, for example, provides that:

> any person or corporation claiming the right to the use of the waters of the stream or water supply comprising a water district, but not owning or having the use of an adjudicated or decreed right therein, or right therein evidenced by permit or license issued by the department of water resources, shall, for the purposes of distribution during times of water scarcity, be held to have a right subsequent to any adjudicated, decreed, permit, or licensed right from such

> stream or water supply, and the watermaster shall close all headgates or controlling works of diversions having no adjudicated, decreed, permit or licensed right if necessary to supply adjudicated, decreed, permit or licensed right in such stream or water supply.[1]

However, the Idaho Constitution states:

> The right to divert and appropriate the unappropriated waters of any natural stream to beneficial uses, shall never be denied, except that the state may regulate and limit the use thereof for power purposes....[2]

As you learned in Part V, this language was initially interpreted to allow continued acquisition of a water right by diversion and application to a beneficial use (under the misnomer of "constitutional" water rights), despite legislative attempts to develop an exclusive permit system. Ultimately this language was interpreted not to prevent legislative establishment of an exclusive permit system. Nevertheless, prior to this ruling, many water rights had been developed simply through diversion and application to beneficial use.

With the development of state water agencies, the initial act of enforcement goes through the agency with a request by a senior water user to place a "call" on (i.e., curtail) a junior water right.[3] The problem: the agency has no record of the water right developed through diversion and application to a beneficial use and thus has no basis to determine if the party seeking a "call" is indeed senior and entitled to the amount of water claimed. The Idaho Supreme Court addressed the scope of that property right for an unrecorded right and the dilemma faced by the agency in the following case. Note that, although Idaho is unique in its misnomer for "constitutional" water rights, it is not unique in having many rights developed without any recording. Thus, the concepts are relevant in other states. Note also that the defendant in this suit against the agency is the agency Director, Higginson. Should a new director be appointed during the proceeding, their name would be substituted for that of Higginson.

Nettleton v. Higginson

Supreme Court of Idaho
98 Idaho 87, 558 P.2d 1048 (1977)

DONALDSON, J.—This controversy involves a dispute between plaintiff-appellant J.H. Nettleton, a water user located in the Upper Reynolds Creek Water District, and defendant-respondent Department of Water Resources, which assumes distribution of waters of Reynolds Creek. Reynolds Creek is a natural stream located in Owyhee County, Idaho, and the Department of Water Resources, formerly the Department of Water Administration, divided the stream into two water districts. District 57-A which

1. Idaho Code § 42-607.
2. Idaho Const., art. XV, § 3.
3. Note that Colorado, with its water courts, is an exception to the use of science-based agencies. This difference was discussed in Part V.

is known as Upper Reynolds Creek District wherein the appellant owns property, and District 57-J which comprises Lower Reynolds Creek. [Nettleton's] lands are located in Upper Reynolds Creek, and it is stipulated he has three types of water rights, adjudicated rights, licensed rights, and unadjudicated "constitutional" rights.

[IDWR] claims direction and control of the distribution of all of the waters of Reynolds Creek within the boundaries of Upper Reynolds and Lower Reynolds, and has ordered the watermaster for Upper Reynolds to distribute the waters in Upper Reynolds as if both Upper and Lower Reynolds were one water district. Consistent with that policy, [IDWR's] position is that the decree of September 14, 1973, which adjudicated the rights of ten water users in Lower Reynolds, requires that the watermaster of Upper Reynolds recognize the priorities of those in Lower Reynolds in allocating the waters in his district.

The matter was submitted to the trial court upon stipulation of facts with [Nettleton] seeking to enjoin the [IDWR] from administering the distribution of waters from Reynolds Creek. The trial court granted [IDWR's] motion for summary judgment, from which [Nettleton] now appeals.

[Nettleton] assigns error to the lower court's failure to find the provisions of I.C. § 42-607 in violation of his constitutional rights. His challenge is threefold: first, that the statutory preference for "adjudicated, decreed, permit, or licensed right[s]" over the so-called unadjudicated "constitutional use" water rights in times of water scarcity is a deprivation of property without due process, IDAHO CONST. Art. I, § 13; U.S. CONST. Amend. XIV, § 1; second, that said statute is a denial of equal protection under the laws, U.S. CONST. Amend. XIV, § 1; and finally, I.C. § 42-607 authorizes a taking of property for a public use without payment of just compensation, IDAHO CONST. Art. 1, § 14.

We first consider [Nettleton's] contention that the statute amounts to a deprivation of property without due process of law. We agree that individual water rights are real property rights which must be afforded the protection of due process of law before they may be taken by the state.

The constitutional guarantee of procedural due process applies to governmental taking of legitimate property interests within the meaning of the Fifth or Fourteenth Amendments. It demands that if such a deprivation takes place, it must be accompanied by some type of notice and hearing. The United States Supreme Court, in *Fuentes v. Shevin,* 407 U.S. 67 (1972), held that except in "extraordinary circumstances" where some valid governmental interest justifies the postponement of notice and hearing, due process requires an adversary proceeding before a person can be deprived of his property interest.

[Nettleton], however, in order to invoke the protection of the Due Process Clause, must have a "significant property interest" which is being deprived by the state's actions pursuant to I.C. § 42-607. The difficulty appellant has in this case is apparent. His claimed property interest is that of a "constitutional use" water right, such right being created simply by diverting unappropriated waters and putting those waters to beneficial use. I.C. § 42-103 *et seq.* Such a right, unless adjudicated, is an unproven right, *i.e.,* no formal proceeding, neither judicial nor administrative, has established said right. Until such a water right is adjudicated, the only evidence that the right exists are the declarations of the claimant himself. Even if upon investigation by the Water Resources Board or some interested person a means of diversion, as claimed by appellant, is discovered, there still remains the unanswered questions concerning the date such diversion of water was put into operation; the amount of water being diverted; the use for which the water is being diverted; and the continuity in time of appellant's diversion of water. Thus, this Court, in considering appellant's due process argument, faces the same problem that the watermaster faces when attempting to distribute the waters in times of scarcity—*i.e.,* determining which claimed "constitutional use" rights are valid and which are unwarranted and unjustified claims for water under the guise of a "constitutional use right."

But even if [Nettleton] has sufficiently substantiated the existence of this claimed property interest so as to invoke the protections of the Due Process Clause, there are other reasons for rejection of this constitutional challenge.

Justice Powell, in a concurring opinion in *Mitchell v. W.T. Grant Company,* 416 U.S. 600 (1974), notes that the determination of what due process is required in a given context requires a balancing of both the nature of the governmental function involved and the private interests affected. 416 U.S. at 624–25. It is well-settled that the water itself is the property of the state, which has the duty to supervise the allotment of those waters with minimal waste to the private appropriators. In addition, the state's authority to regulate the distribution of the water is constitutionally based:

> The use of all waters now appropriated, or that may hereafter be appropriated for sale, rental or distribution; also of all water originally appropriated for private use, but which after such appropriation has heretofore been, or may hereafter be sold, rented, or distributed, is hereby declared to be a public use, and subject to the regulation and control of the state in the manner prescribed by law. IDAHO CONST. Art. 15, § 1.

The governmental function in enacting not only I.C. § 43-607, but the entire water distribution system under Title 42 of the Idaho Code is to further the state policy of securing the maximum use and benefit of its water resources. As to the private interests affected, it is obvious that in times of water shortage someone is not going to receive water. Under the appropriation system the right of priority is based on the date of one's appropriation, *i.e.,* first in time is first in right. However, as stated earlier, it is the state's duty to supervise the distribution of the waters through the Water Resource Board and its watermasters. In *DeRousse v. Higginson,* 505 P.2d 321 (Idaho 1973), the dissent aptly considered the practical difficulties facing the watermaster:

> It is to be kept in mind that the authority of the watermaster in his district is to control the delivery to the water from the source of supply *** into the respective ditches or canals leading from the main stream. The watermaster is

> confronted by two significant problems when delivering water within his water district: first, he must maintain the constitutional requirement of priority of water rights among the various users; second, he is confronted with the practical problem of delivering water to the correct point of diversion. When one considers the magnitude of the watermaster's problem of water delivery in his water district, it is evident that a proper delivery can only be effected when the watermaster is guided by some specific schedule or list of water users and their priorities, amounts, and points of diversion.***
>
> Only by having a specific list reciting the names of the water users, with their dates of priority, amounts, and points of diversion can such a system be administered. Since the so-called "constitutional use right" is unrecorded in respect to priority, amount and point of diversion, the whole system of delivery in a water district would be endangered if such a right were recognized.***
>
> *** All those individuals that enjoy the use of water by reason of having their rights adjudicated, or that have the use of water by reason of permits or licenses issued from the department of (water resources), are entitled to expect the state, which has granted them the right to the use of water, to protect them in their established rights.
>
> If [appellant's] interpretation [of the constitutionality] of I.C. § 42-607 is [followed], the validity of any decreed right or water permit or license would be placed in jeopardy. If anyone claimed a constitutional "use right," and took the water from the stream, the watermaster charged with the responsibility of administering the stream would be powerless to act. Consequently, a person enjoying a prior right established by a decree, permit or license, would be subject to losing his use of the water by anyone claiming a "constitutional use right" without regard to its priority.

The requirement of procedural due process is satisfied by the statutory scheme of Title 42 of the Idaho Code. Our holding is supported by a comparison of the state's duty as mandated by Article 15, § 1 of the Idaho Constitution with the appellant's ability, under I.C. § 42-1405, to at any time verify his "constitutional use right," thereby reaping the protective benefit of I.C. § 42-607 himself. Granted that when action is taken pursuant to I.C. § 42-607 there is no notice or hearing prior to the shutting off of the unadjudicated water rights, but as the United States Supreme Court noted in *Fuentes v. Shevin,* there are extraordinary situations when postponement of notice and a hearing is justified. It is justified when:

> First *** the seizure has been directly necessary to secure an important governmental or general public interest. Second, there has been a special need for very prompt action. Third, the State has kept strict control over its monopoly of legitimate force; the person initiating the seizure has been a government official responsible for determining, under the standards of a narrowly drawn statute, that it was necessary and justified in the particular instance. 407 U.S. at 91.

We find the above three requirements to be met in the present case and find no procedural due process violation in the actions of the watermaster pursuant to I.C. § 42-607.

[Nettleton] further contends that I.C. § 42-607 denies him equal protection of the laws as guaranteed by the Fourteenth Amendment to the United States Constitution. He claims that the statute discriminates against constitutional use appropriators in an arbitrary and capricious manner.

The state has a legitimate purpose in enacting I.C. § 42-607, that purpose being to protect all private water rights in times of water shortage. Since the classes involved in I.C. § 42-607 are non-suspect, *i.e.*, those with recorded water rights and those without, we need only find a rational relationship between the state's purpose and the enactment of the statute to uphold its constitutionality. Considering the problems of a "constitutional use" appropriation discussed earlier, the legislature and this Court recognize that we cannot adequately protect these rights unless the state's agent, the watermaster, has a specific record of the users' priority dates, use and points of diversion. We find that the legislative classification is rationally related to the state's purpose; and as it operates equally, uniformly and impartially on all persons within the same class, we find no denial of equal protection.

[Nettleton's] final constitutional challenge is that I.C. § 42-607 would constitute a taking of private property for public use without just compensation contrary to Idaho Constitution, Article 1, § 14. We do not agree with this argument. The right of appropriation does not carry with it an unconditional guarantee of water regardless of the supply of water available. In times of shortage one holding an unadjudicated water right stands in a position similar to he who holds the "recorded" water right of the lowest priority date. The fact that his diversion must be shut off to allow those with an earlier priority to receive water cannot be complained of as being a violation of Article 1, § 14 of the Idaho Constitution.

. . .

The judgment is reversed and remanded to the district court to order such a hearing before the Department of Water Resources in accordance with this opinion.

Notes & Questions

1. How did the Idaho Supreme Court address Nettleton's due process argument? Before you can be deprived of a property right without due process of law, you must first have a property interest. How did the court characterize Nettleton's property right in his water use?
2. How did the court address Nettleton's equal protection argument? What level of scrutiny did the court apply and why? How did that drive the outcome of the court's decision on this issue?
3. According to the court, what was the government's interest in I.C. § 42-607? What practical problems do unadjudicated water rights present to the water master? Do you think I.C. § 42-607 is a good solution to those problems?

4. Many private adjudications attempt to include all water users on a stream segment. Washington state alone has adjudicated roughly 80 stream segments. But the adjudication is not considered a "general adjudication" unless it binds all water users on a water source.

General Stream Adjudication

A general stream adjudication is a judicial or administrative proceeding that seeks a comprehensive determination of the existence, nature, extent, and priority of the water rights held by all water users relying on a particular water source. For example, Figure 25.1 shows the physical extent of Washington's Yakima River Basin Adjudication. That adjudication included not only the mainstem of the Yakima River, but also the adjudication of all water rights from tributary streams that flow into the Yakima River. From the viewpoint of water law as an area heavily informed by hydrology, you can think of this basin or watershed approach as aligning the legal process of adjudication with the nature of a hydrologically connected resource (with the caveat that a state adjudication must stop at the state border). Many older adjudications, including the Yakima River Adjudication, left out groundwater. In recognition of the strong interconnection between surface and groundwater, many modern adjudications include the determination of water rights for both surface and groundwater.

General stream adjudications in which the hydrologically connected water source crosses state lines can be commenced in federal court (you have seen examples in Part IV of the Truckee and Carson Rivers shared among California, Nevada, and the Pyramid Lake Paiute). Nevertheless, the majority of the general adjudications are commenced by states. Oregon statutes set up a process in which adjudication is an administrative action undertaken by the Water Resources Department.[4] Other states generally follow a process of adjudication in state court.

There are two primary reasons why states invest the substantial time and resources necessary to conduct a general stream adjudication.[5] First, general stream adjudications are necessary to develop a comprehensive inventory of all the water use within a basin. This need may arise when shortage becomes more frequent, yet without a determination of the priority and scope of a water right, enforcement is impossible. Senior water users may seek state adjudication to allow enforcement of their rights. For example, in Idaho, a state supreme court ruling determined that a small, old (i.e., senior), downstream hydropower plant on the Snake River owned by Idaho Power had not subordinated its water rights (meaning agreed to them being treated as junior) to

---

4. Or. Rev. Stat. §§ 539.021 et seq. OAR 690-028.

5. For differing views on the value of general adjudications, see MacDonnell, *Rethinking the Use of General Stream Adjudications*, 15(2) Wyo. L. Rev. 313 (2015); John Thorson, *Reflections on Western General Stream Adjudications upon the Signing of Wyoming's Big Horn River Adjudication Final Decree*, 15(2) Wyo. L. Rev. 383 (2015); and Michelle Bryan, *At the End of the Day: Are the West's General Stream Adjudications Relevant to Modern Water Rights Administration?* 15(2) Wyo. L. Rev. 461 (2015).

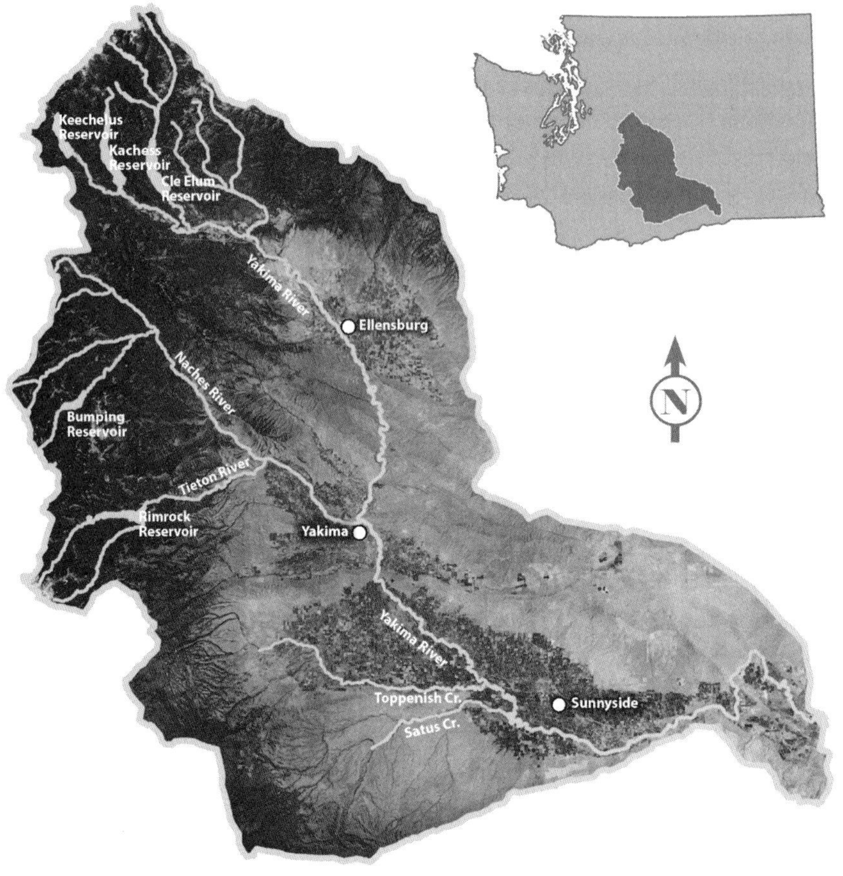

Figure 25.1 The Geographic Scope of the Yakima River Basin Adjudication in Washington. Source: Yakima River Basin Integrated Water Resource Management Plan Implementation Status Report 2017. Https://apps.ecology.wa.gov/publications/documents/1812005.pdf.

upstream water rights.[6] With the realization that this little dam[7] could force a frequent "call" on all of Idaho's major upstream agricultural interests, Idaho and Idaho Power reached a settlement that reduced the likelihood of a call, but also provided for legislation that would require a general stream adjudication to prepare for the possibility of a call. The need for a comprehensive inventory may also arise when the possibility of a suit for interstate allocation of water looms. As you learned in Part V, states must be able to show the extent of existing use if they are to protect their water-dependent economy in a suit for equitable apportionment.

Second, general stream adjudications are the sole mechanism through which states can involuntarily join the United States in a state court adjudication. This joinder is

6. Idaho Power Co. v. State, 661 P.2d 741 (Idaho 1983). *See also* Ann Y. Vonde et al., *Understanding the Snake River Basin Adjudication*, 52 IDAHO L. REV. 53 (2016).

7. For a wonderful read and account of this fiasco, see (Justice) JIM JONES, A LITTLE DAM PROBLEM (2016).

necessary if the adjudication is to include reserved water rights. This has been a driving factor in a number of states, including Montana, Washington, Wyoming, and Arizona, due to the cloud of uncertainty surrounding the scope of what, in the case of Native American reserved rights, are often the senior water rights on a connected resource.

The recent assessment done by the Washington Department of Ecology at the request of the legislature to determine which watersheds require adjudication, provides a statement of the difficulties faced by the agency tasked with management and enforcement of water rights in the absence of a general adjudication:

> Where we lack a defined court-decreed inventory of legal water use, Ecology's enforcement and compliance work to protect senior rights is time-intensive. This process leads to scattered appeals and litigation of individual decisions. Parties engaged in managing water, and planning for future water uses, encounter a number of problems when the oldest water rights (pre-code claims) remain unexamined for validity.
>
> Furthermore, federally-recognized Indian Tribes claim significant quantities of water, including water for reservation land and for fish habitat. Reservations may have their own water systems and irrigation uses that are unregulated by the state. If tribes claim that state users impair their legal water, Ecology cannot on its own determine how much water should be protected, and how much is available for other uses. Adjudication reconciles state and tribal water in a single process.[8]

General adjudication is a complex and time-consuming process. Idaho completed its Snake River Basin adjudication of 158,591 claims in 2014 after 27 years and has begun adjudication of the North Idaho Adjudication. Figure 25.2 shows the Idaho adjudication basins. Note that a state court has no jurisdiction to adjudicate water rights in neighboring states, thus despite the continuation of the rivers, the adjudication ends at the state boundary. Interstate disputes are left to the various processes described in Part V. The numbered areas within the SRBA in Figure 25.2 are subbasins and illustrate a method used to break a basin into smaller, bite-sized pieces consistent with basin hydrology.

Wyoming focused on a single basin in which both irrigation and tribal water rights were important. It completed its 37-year Big Horn watershed adjudication in 2014.[9]

Montana began its statewide adjudication in 1973 with major revisions in 1979. It is currently in the process of re-examining claims that did not go through the process the water court ultimately chose (claims examination will be discussed below under the

8. Robin McPherson and the Adjudication Staff, Water Resources Program, Washington Department of Ecology, *Water Resources Adjudication Assessment Legislative Report: Watersheds Proposed for Urgent Adjudication and Future Assessment Publication 20-22-084* at 4 (September 2020), https://apps.ecology.wa.gov/publications/documents/2011084.pdf.

9. *See* Jason A. Robison, *Wyoming's Big Horn General Stream Adjudication*, 15(2) Wyo. L. Rev. 243.

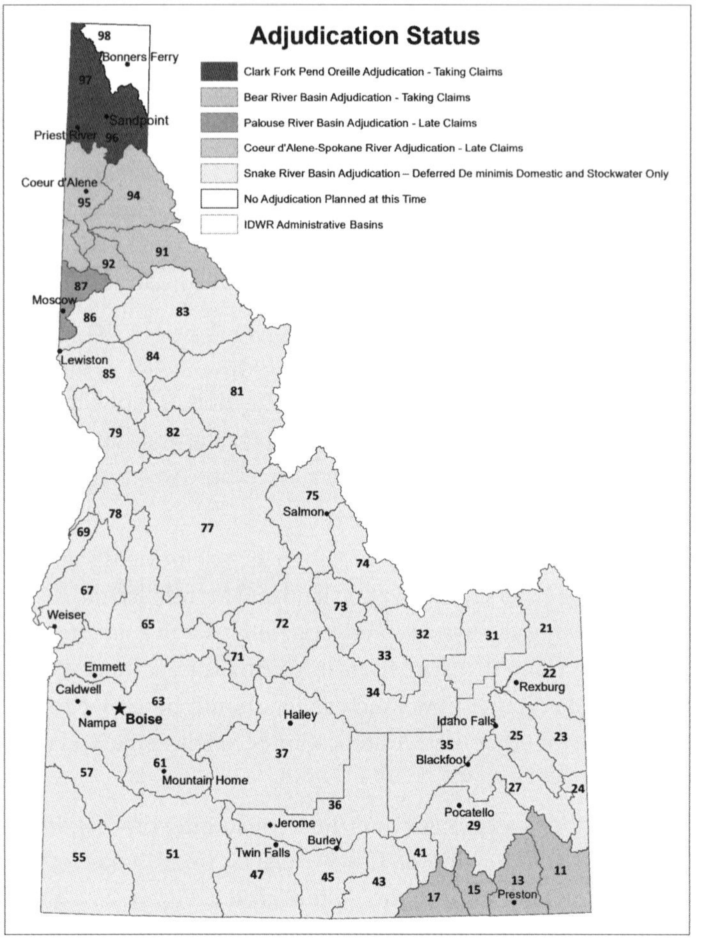

Figure 25.2 Map showing adjudication basins in Idaho. Two-thirds of the state lies within the completed Snake River Basin in light gray, covering most of the State. The Coeur d'Alene-Spokane River, and the Clark Fork-Pend Oreille River, in the Idaho panhandle are currently in the process of adjudication. Source: Idaho Department of Water Resources, Adjudication, https://idwr.idaho.gov/water-rights/adjudication/.

role of the state water agency). Figure 25.3 shows the subbasins for the Montana statewide adjudication. The shades represent the stage in adjudication of each subbasin.

Oregon has completed adjudication of some watersheds,[10] and is in the final review stage of the Klamath basin adjudication, begun in 1975,[11] and has not initiated any other adjudications. Figure 25.4 shows the Klamath basin, which is shared with California and several Native American tribes.

10. State of Oregon, Map of Adjudicated Areas Within Oregon (Surface Water), https://www.oregon.gov/owrd/programs/WaterRights/Adjudications/Documents/Adjudicated_Areas.pdf.

11. Oregon Water Resources Department, *Adjudications and Registrations* (2023), https://tinyurl.com/5n8efp9a.

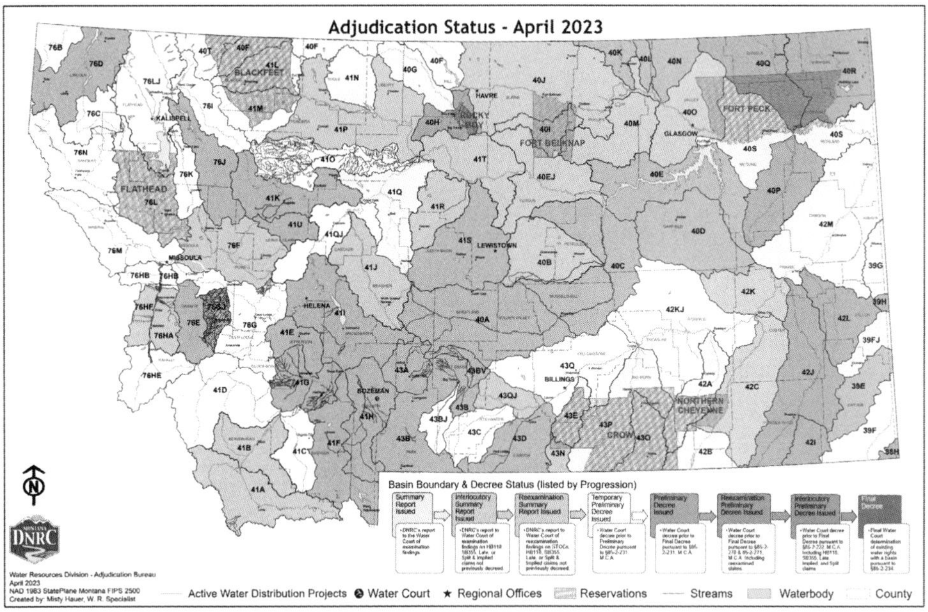

Figure 25.3 Montana adjudication subbasins showing their status in the statewide adjudication. Source: Montana Department of Natural Resources and Conservation, Water Adjudication, https://dnrc.mt.gov/Water-Resources/Water-Rights/Adjudication.

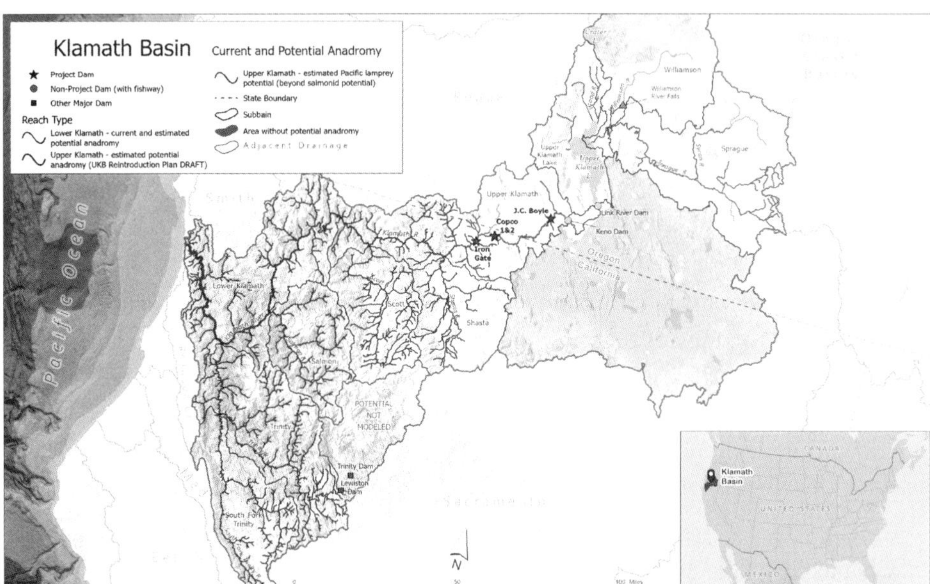

Figure 25.4 Map of the Klamath River Basin shared by Oregon and California. The Oregon Adjudication stops at the state line. The upper basin is where most of the irrigated agriculture is located. Source: California Fish Passage Forum, Klamath River Renewal Corporation & their Partners, Preparing the Klamath Basin for Dam Removal: A StoryMap Spotlighting Collaborative Efforts to Enhance Fish Passage in the Klamath River Basin in Honor of World Fish Migration Day 2020, https://storymaps.arcgis.com/stories/8d96c0764ed44643bad392cb73ef4c54.

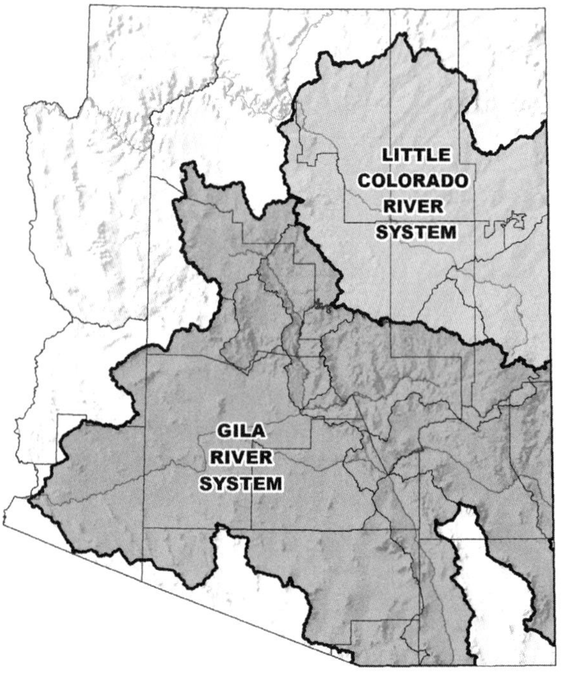

Figure 25.5 Map showing the locations of the Gila and Little Colorado River Basins. Both watersheds are tributary to the Colorado River. Both watersheds are currently under adjudication in Arizona. Source: Arizona Department of Water Resources, Arizona Adjudication Watersheds, https://new.azwater.gov/news/articles/2022-03-08.

Washington's Yakima Basin Adjudication took 42 years to adjudicate 2,300 claims,[12] and the state is in the pre-adjudication stages for the Nooksack and Upper Columbia basins. Figure 25.1 shows the Yakima Basin. Figure 20.2 in Chapter 20 shows the Nooksack and Upper Columbia Basins recommended by the Department of Ecology for adjudication.

Arizona, while outside the Columbia River Basin, is important to include because it has been key to many of the rulings and case management innovations adopted by other courts. Figure 25.5 shows the area of the Gila River[13] and Little Colorado River[14] adjudications in Arizona. The Gila River is the largest tributary to the Colorado River in Arizona and its importance to the state was emphasized when you read the case of *Arizona v. California* in the context of interstate disputes in Part IV.

The complex process of adjudication will be the focus of the remainder of this Chapter. Chapter 26 will focus on how states have obtained the authority to force the participation of the United States in an adjudication (whether in state court or an administrative adjudication as done by Oregon) and why that is only possible if the adjudication is

12. Washington Department of Ecology, *Ecology v. Aquavella* (2023), https://ecology.wa.gov/water-shorelines/water-supply/water-rights/adjudications/ecology-v-acquavella.

13. The Judicial Branch of Arizona, Maricopa County, *Gila River Adjudication* (2023), https://www.superiorcourt.maricopa.gov/SuperiorCourt/GeneralStreamAdjudication/gila.asp.

14. *Id.*

a comprehensive determination of all rights in a particular river basin—i.e., a "general" adjudication.

Case Management

With the goal of including and binding all water users in a general adjudication, ordinary procedure and case management are insufficient. State courts had to turn to lessons from complex case management and tailor them to the specific complexities of a water adjudication. This section will use Idaho to illustrate one approach in greater depth, while providing resources to understand the differences in Montana, Washington, Wyoming, and Oregon. These states pioneered the modern process of adjudication, and because of what they learned, future adjudications should be more efficient. Of note in the learning stages of the process is the formation of a nonprofit called Dividing the Waters by a group of adjudication judges and special masters, to provide a forum for education and dialogue among those tasked with these complex cases. The organization is now part of The National Judicial College,[15] and is a valuable resource to any court undertaking a water adjudication.

The following overview of the means states have developed to manage these complex cases will cover initiation of the adjudication, notice, defining manageable units, reliance on the expertise of the state water agency to examine claims, and the use of novel court procedures and special masters for dispute resolution.

Initiating the Adjudication

The adjudication process in each state is governed by statute, which provides the basic framework for how and when adjudications will proceed. Table 25.1 provides the relevant code sections of Idaho, Washington, Montana, Wyoming, Oregon, and Arizona. The Table also provides the special rules of procedure that some of these states have adopted to supplement their rules of civil procedure and grapple with the sheer size and complexity of a general adjudication. The special rules are generally by order of the court, but in Oregon, with its agency adjudication, they may be found in the agency's administrative rules.

---

15. The National Judicial College, *Dividing the Waters* (2023), https://www.judges.org/dividing_the_waters/about-dtw/. From the website:

> *Dividing the Waters* prepares the judges of today and tomorrow—across the nation—to apply the law, science, good judgment and wisdom in efficiently and effectively adjudicating water-related cases, to meet human and environmental needs.
>
> Dividing the Waters connects judges, special masters and referees who preside over complex water litigation to the information and training resources they need to resolve some of the most difficult disputes about how to allocate and share this most precious and communal resource.
>
> Dividing the Waters offers judicial officers with water cases an opportunity to collaborate as a network with a vast array of knowledge of water resources, law and management. The program relies on judges helping judges. Some participants specialize in water litigation and others have a long history with a complex water case.

Table 25.1

STATE	CODE PROVISIONS	SPECIAL RULES
Arizona	Arizona Revised Statutes §§ 45-251–264	Rules for Proceedings before the Special Master, *In re Gila River*, No. W1-11-10 (Nov. 1, 1991) (hereinafter "Gila River Rules of Procedure")
Idaho	Idaho Code § 42-1401 *et sec.*	Amended CSRBA Administrative Order 1: Rules of Procedure, *In re CSRBA*, No. 49576 (Mar. 4, 2015) (hereinafter "CSRBA A01")
Montana	Montana Code Annotated § 85-2-212, *et sec.*	WATER RIGHT ADJUDICATION RULES AMENDED BY THE MONTANA SUPREME COURT 2006 and 2008 Available at: https://courts.mt.gov/courts/water/LegalResources
Oregon	Oregon Revised Statutes § 539.005 *et sec.*	Oregon Administrative Rules 690-028
Washington	Washington Code Revised §§ 90.03.110–245	Special rules may be found in the initial orders of the superior court
Wyoming	Wyoming Code Annotated 1-37-106	Special rules may be found in the initial orders of the Special Master appointed by the district court

Table 25.1 Statutory provisions covering water adjudications and special rules of civil procedure for water adjudications for the primary Columbia River Basin states and Arizona.[16]

Adjudications may be commenced in several ways. First, a state legislature may direct the state water agency to petition the court to commence an adjudication.[17] Second, water users are often authorized to petition a water agency to seek commencement of an adjudication.[18] Finally, a water agency will identify a particular water basin that requires adjudication and is authorized to petition to commence an adjudication.[19]

Although different entities may lobby for the initiation of an adjudication, it is usually the state water agency or office of the attorney general that is vested with the legal authority to file a commencement petition with the judiciary.[20] Idaho law provides an illustrative list of the typical information that is required to be included in a commencement petition by the Idaho Department of Water Resources:

(a) a description of the proposed boundaries of the water system to be adjudicated and administered;

16. Note that Wyoming is a Columbia River Basin state, but its adjudication of the Big Horn Basin is within the Missouri River Basin.

17. *See, e.g.*, Idaho Code § 42-1406B (directing the Idaho Department of Water Resources to Commence the North Idaho Adjudication); WCA § 1-37-106 (directing the State Attorney General of Wyoming to file for commencement of an adjudication.

18. *See, e.g.*, Wash. Rev. Code 90.03.110.

19. *Id.*

20. *See, e.g.*, Wash. Rev. Code 90.03.110(1); Idaho Code § 42-1406B.

(b) a statement of why the public interest and necessity would be served by a general adjudication;

...

(d) a description of the general method proposed to ascertain and to serve claimants not disclosed following completion of the service required ...; and

(e) a prayer for relief requesting the district court to enter an order that commences the general adjudication.[21]

Petitions also usually include a statement of which court will take responsibility for the adjudication. Idaho statutes require the adjudication to be commenced in a district court within the watershed to be adjudicated and authorize the state supreme court to appoint the specific judge within that district to preside.[22] The SRBA took place in the district court for the Fifth Judicial District. However, once the Fifth Judicial District had gained 27 years of experience with the SRBA, including a roster of trained special masters (see below for their role in the process), the legislature chose to continue with the same court as a "court of special jurisdiction" for adjudication of the water basins in North Idaho.[23]

Excerpts from the Idaho Supreme Court provisional order appointing the Fifth Judicial District, and the district court commencement order for the North Idaho adjudication follow.

Provisional Order Re: Appointment of District Judge, Confirmation of Special Jurisdiction and Determination of Venue for the General Adjudications of the Coeur D'Alene-Spokane River Basin, the Palouse River Basin and the Clark Fork-Pend Oreille River Basins

September 29, 2006

WHEREAS pursuant to I.C. 5 42-1406B, upon the filing of petitions by the Director of the Idaho Department of Water Resources, the district court is authorized to commence separate general adjudications of the water rights for the Coeur d'Alene-Spokane River Basin, the Palouse River Basin and the Clark Fork-Pend Oreille River Basins, and

WHEREAS pursuant to I.C. 5 42-1406B, unless otherwise ordered by this Court, special jurisdiction for these general adjudications resides in the Snake River Basin Adjudication District Court of the Fifth Judicial District of the State of Idaho, and

21. Idaho Code § 42-1406.

22. Idaho Code § 42-1407(1).

23. Idaho Code § 42-1406B(2).

WHEREAS this Court is authorized and directed by I.C. 5 42-1406B to assign by order a district judge to preside over the general adjudications and to determine venue of such general adjudications, and

WHEREAS prior to the filing of petitions, in conjunction with the planning stages for the three general adjudications, the district court anticipated to be assigned to preside over the adjudications in conjunction with the Idaho Department of Water Resources, will be required to begin various logistical administrative matters including the incurring of related expenditures, and which in order to proceed with accordingly, require from this Court a provisional order confirming special jurisdiction, determining venue and assigning a district judge.

NOW THEREFORE, UNTIL FURTHER ORDER OF THIS COURT, THE FOLLOWING ARE

HEREBY ORDERED

..., that the presiding judge of the Snake River Basin Adjudication District Court, an office held at present by District Judge John M. Melanson, be and is hereby, assigned as the presiding judge over these actions as general adjudications of the water rights in the Coeur d'Alene-Spokane River Basin, the Palouse River Basin and the Clark Fork-Pend Oreille River Basins.

IT IS FURTHER ORDERED, that pursuant to I.C. 5 42-1406B special jurisdiction for these general adjudications is confirmed and shall reside in the Snake River Basin Adjudication District Court of the Fifth Judicial District of the State of Idaho, in and for the County of Twin Falls.

IT IS FURTHER ORDERED, that pursuant to I.C. 5 42-1406B and I.C. 5 42-1407 the Court does hereby designate the Snake River Basin Adjudication District Court of the Fifth Judicial District of the State of Idaho, in and for the County of Twin Falls, as the county and court of venue for these general adjudication proceedings and that all pleadings and documents with regard to these general adjudications shall be filed with the clerk of that court. Notwithstanding this designation of venue, hearings may be held by masters and the presiding district judge at such places within the State of Idaho as are designated by the masters or presiding judge for the convenience of the parties and witnesses....

On November 12, 2008, following the completion of notice (see below), Judge Melanson of the Fifth Judicial District issued the commencement order, stating, among other things, that:

> The Coeur d'Alene-Spokane River Basin Adjudication is commenced as authorized by I.C. § 42-1406B (Supp. 2008) as a general adjudication *inter se* of all rights arising under state or federal law to the use of surface and ground waters from the Coeur d'Alene-Spokane River Basin water system within the state of Idaho.

Following an assessment in 2020, the Washington Department of Ecology entered into a pre-adjudication process for the Nooksack and Upper Columbia watersheds.[24] The following statement is from the Washington Department of Ecology webpage on its process of developing the 2020 Assessment triggered by legislative request and funding in 2019:

> During the 2019 legislative session, the Legislature provided us funding to assess the needs and benefits of future adjudications. We looked statewide to assess watersheds that might benefit from adjudication, considering basins with senior tribal water rights, streamflow needs, and challenges caused by water user uncertainty and conflict. We conducted extensive outreach, met with tribes and local governments, and compiled water right, history, and habitat information.[25]

Washington law provides for similar requirements for a commencement petition to that of Idaho, but also requires the petition to clarify whether the adjudication will be of surface water, groundwater, or both.[26]

Arizona statutes require assignment of the adjudication to the superior court in the district in which the most claimants reside.[27] Similar to Idaho, the Arizona Supreme Court appoints the specific judge as well as a special master who, similar to a special master in a case of original jurisdiction in the U.S. Supreme Court (which you learned about in Part IV), presides over the case, takes evidence, and prepares a report for the presiding judge.[28]

Montana began its adjudication process in 1973, with an administrative process assigned to the Department of Natural Resources and Conservation. After the legislature ordered a study of the process, new legislation in 1979 set up the statewide Montana adjudication and established a Water Court with a chief water judge appointed by the chief justice of the Montana Supreme Court.[29] The task of the Water Court is to work itself out of a job by completing the adjudication, leaving administration to the agency (Department of Natural Resources and Conservation) and the water judge for each water division appointed from within the district courts.[30]

Defining Manageable Units

Once the adjudication is commenced, the first task of the adjudication court is to develop a sensible approach to efficient processing of water rights claims and litigation. On the recommendation of IDWR, and after some back and forth, the district court

24. Washington Department of Ecology, *Water Right Adjudications* (2023), https://ecology.wa.gov/water-shorelines/water-supply/water-rights/adjudications.

25. *Id.*

26. Wash. Rev. Code 90.03.110(1).

27. Ariz. Rev. Stat. §42-252.

28. *Id.*

29. Mont. Code Ann. § 3-7-221. *See also* Montana Legislative Environmental Policy Office, *A Short History of the Montana Water Court* (2015), https://tinyurl.com/2xhkckuu.

30. Mont. Code Ann. § 3-7-201.

entered an order dividing the Snake River Basin into 24 subbasins based on hydrologic units and began the adjudication with three "test basins" to allow experimentation with major procedural issues, including notice and the role of IDWR.[31]

Like Idaho, Montana's state-wide adjudication requires state claims to be adjudicated on a subbasin-by-subbasin basis. Litigation was stayed for federal reserved water rights, however, which were negotiated by tribes, the United States, and a Montana state commission.[32] This will be covered in Chapter 27.

In contrast to Idaho, Wyoming defined manageable units by issue. The Big Horn adjudication was split into three phases: (1) Indian reserved water rights and water rights for Indian allottees; (2) other federal reserved water rights; and (3) state law water rights.[33]

Washington's *Acquavella* adjudication followed the Wyoming approach of managing by issue. Washington used four tracks, each with different litigation schedules: (1) "Federal reserved right for Indian claims," (2) "Federal reserved rights for non-Indian claims," (3) "State-based rights of the major claimants," and (4) "State-based rights for other claimants by subbasin."[34]

Oregon statutes and administrative rules do not address this issue; however, two aspects of the Klamath Adjudication define the scope. First, the choice of a single watershed for adjudication. Second, limitation of the adjudication to claims to water rights that predate its mandatory permitting process, which passed into law in 1909.[35] O.R.S. § 539.005, *et sec.*

Notice

General stream adjudications are true *in rem* proceedings, which means that anyone who fails to file a claim to a water right will be precluded from doing so after the final decree has been entered.[36] As a result, there is a significant risk that individuals may lose valuable property rights if they do not know to engage in these adjudications. The constitutional right to procedural due process requires notice and the opportunity to be heard in any action that may affect a property interest. This seems like a simple requirement; however, general adjudications may have thousands of parties, most of whom are, by definition, unknown (hence the need for the adjudication in the first

31. Order Denying the Director's Plan for Filing Director's Reports in the Snake River Basin Adjudication, *In re SRBA,* Case No. 39576 (Jan. 30, 1992). *See also* Ann Y. Vonde et al., *Understanding the Snake River Basin Adjudication*, 52 Idaho L. Rev. 53, 67–68 (2016).

32. Mont. Code Ann. 85-2-702.

33. Jason A. Robison, *Wyoming's Big Horn General Stream Adjudication*, 15 Wyo. L. Rev. 243 (2015).

34. *See* Final Decree at 1–2, *In re the Matter of the Determination of the Rights to Use the Surface Waters of the Yakima River Drainage Basin*, No. 77-2-01484-5 (May 9, 2019) (hereinafter "*Acquavella* Final Decree").

35. Or. Rev. Stat. § 539.005 *et seq.*

36. *See, e.g.*, Final Unified Decree at 9, *In re SRBA*, No. 39576 (Aug. 26, 2014) (hereinafter "SRBA Final Unified Decree") ("All other water rights with a priority date before November 19, 1987, not expressly set forth in this Final Unified Decree are hereby decreed as disallowed.").

place). As a result, a fundamental early question in every water rights adjudication relates to how to provide sufficient notice to comply with the United States and state constitutions, without spending years seeking out potential claimants.

The United States Constitution requires the state's chosen method for providing notice to be "reasonably calculated, under all the circumstances, to apprise interested parties of the pendency of the action and afford them an opportunity to present their objections."[37] This requires the state to provide actual notice to known water rights users—those with permits, licenses, or other documented claims to water rights.[38] States vary in their approach to providing notice to the water users whose rights are undocumented. In Idaho, this would be the so-called "constitutional" rights acquired by diversion and application to a beneficial use. Most western states allow for notice for these individuals to be conducted through publication.[39] States often supplement notice by publication by requiring notice to be posted in county offices and by sending notice to anyone owning real property within the adjudication boundaries.

In addition to service to anyone with a recorded water right, Idaho requires:

> (2) The director shall serve copies of the notice of order as follows:
>
> (a) the director shall serve the notice of order on the state of Idaho and the United States;
>
> (b) the director shall serve the notice of order ... by publication once a week for three (3) consecutive weeks in a newspaper of general circulation published in each county in which any part of the water system, which is the subject of the general adjudication, is located. If there is no newspaper published within a county, then the copies shall be published in a newspaper having general circulation in that county;
>
> (c) the director shall post the notice of order in each county courthouse, county recorder's office, and county assessor's office in which any part of the water system is located....;
>
> (d) the director shall serve the notice of order by ordinary mail on each person listed as owning real property on the real property assessment roll within the boundaries of the water system to be adjudicated at the address listed on the real property assessment roll; and
>
> (e) the director shall file a copy of the notice of order commencing a general adjudication in the office of the county recorder in each county in which any part of the water system is located; ... from the time it is filed with the recorder for record, is constructive notice of the contents thereof within the county in which

37. Mullane v. Central Hanover Bank & Trust Co., 339 U.S. 306, (1950).

38. *See, e.g.*, Idaho Code § 42-1408; Wash. Rev. Code 90.03.130.

39. Tarlock and Robison, Law of Water Rights and Resources § 7:12 (2022).

State laws also specify the information necessary in the notice be sent out to potential water rights claimants. Once again, Idaho law provides a typical example:

> (1) Upon entry of a district court's order commencing a general adjudication, the director shall prepare a notice of order, using plain and concise language, that contains the following information or enclosures:
>
> (a) an order commencing a general adjudication has been entered, the date of entry of the order, and the district court that entered the order;
>
> (b) an illustration of the boundaries of the water system to be adjudicated and administered;
>
> (c) that [Idaho law] requires ... all claimants, except as specifically excluded by law, to file ... a notice of claim on a form furnished by the director; failure to file a required notice of claim will result in a court determination that no water right exists ...;
>
> ...
>
> (h) the date set by the director for filing a timely notice of claim, which shall not be less than ninety (90) days after service;
>
> ...[40]

Role of the State Water Agency in a State Court Adjudication—Claims Examination

State courts are not designed or staffed to manage voluminous amounts of data on the location and use of a water right. Thus, state water agencies are often called upon to play a role in receiving, ensuring completeness, cataloging, and examination of claims. In the initial stages of both the Idaho and Montana adjudications, the role of the agency as "objector" to claims not supported by the evidence was extremely controversial. Idaho addressed this with legislation clarifying that the Director of the Department of Water Resources is neither a party[41] to the adjudication nor an objector,[42] and defining the role as one of an "independent expert and technical assistant" to the court.[43]

States require claimants to state law water rights to provide specific information in their claims to the court. Using Idaho requirements as an example:

> (1) The director shall prepare and furnish on request a standard notice of claim form. The notice of claim form shall include the following:
>
> (a) The name and address of the claimant;
>
> (b) The source of water;

---

40. Idaho Code § 42-1408(1). *See also* Wash. Rev. Code 90.03.120.

41. Idaho Code § 42-1401B(3).

42. Idaho Code § 42-1401B(2).

43. Idaho Code § 42-1401B(1). For an excellent review of the role of IDWR in the Snake River Basin Adjudication, *see* Phillip J. Rassier, *The Role of the Idaho Department of Water Resources in the Snake River Basin Adjudication*, 52 Idaho L. Rev. 289 (2016).

> (c) The quantity of water claimed:
>
> > (i) The quantity of water claimed to be used for water rights acquired under state law shall describe the rate of diversion or, for an instream flow claim, a rate of water flow in cubic feet per second or the annual volume of diversion of water for use or storage in acre-feet per year, or both;
> >
> > . . .
>
> (d) The date of priority claimed:
>
> > (i) The date of priority claimed for water rights acquired under state law shall be from any license, permit, or decree; or if the right is not based upon a license, permit, or decree, then the date when the water was first applied to beneficial use . . . ;
> >
> > . . .
>
> (f) The legal description of the existing point(s) of diversion; if the claim is for an instream flow, then a legal description of the beginning and ending points of the claimed instream flow;
>
> (g) The purpose(s) of use and the period of use:
>
> > . . .
>
> (h) A legal description of the place of use:
>
> > . . .
>
> (i) The dates of any changes or enlargements in use . . . ;
>
> (j) Conditions on the exercise of any water right included in any decree, license, approved transfer application or other document; and
>
> (k) Such remarks and other matters as are necessary for definition of the right, ...[44]

As an "independent expert and technical assistant," the agency develops and compiles the database that will provide the basis for a decree and the post-adjudication administration of water. The Idaho Code provides that "the director shall commence an examination of the water system, the canals and ditches and other works, and the uses being made of water diverted from the water system for water rights acquired under state law."[45] In doing so,

> [t]he director and other employees of the department shall have authority to go upon all lands, both public and private, for the purpose of investigating the uses of water from any water source and may require the cooperation of the claimant in investigating the claimant's water use. The employee investigating the claimant's use shall make a reasonable effort to contact the claimant to schedule a date and approximate time for the examination. If the well or diversion works are located in a building other than an unlocked structure used

44. Idaho Code § 42-1409(1); *See also* Wash. Rev. Code 90.03.140; Mont. Code Ann. 85-2-224.

45. Idaho Code § 42-1410(1).

CLAIMANT NAME:	**United States of America Bureau of Indian Affairs as trustee for Yakama Nation and water users within the Wapato-Satus Unit of the Wapato Irrigation Project with the Yakama Indian Reservation**	COURT CLAIM NO. 02276 (A)03074 (A)05548 (A)07253
Certificate Number:	S4-84753-J	
Subbasin:	FI Federal Reserved (Indian)	
Source:	Yakima River	
Use:	Stock water and wildlife purposes	
Period of Use:	November 1 to March 1	
Quantity:	94 Cubic feet per second and 9,490 acre-feet per year	
Priority Date:	**June 30, 1859**	
Point of Diversion:	NE/NE/SW/ of Section 28, T. 12 N., R. 19 E.W.M (Old Reservation Canal)	
Place of Use:	Yakama Indian Reservation	
Limitations of Use:	This wate right is a federally reserved right and is not subject to state regulation, law or oversight.	

Figure 25.6 Entry in the Acquavella Final Decree for the Yakima Basin of the Abstract for one Water Right Held by the United States on Behalf of the Yakama Nation. State of Washington, Dept. of Ecology v. James J. Acquavella et al., No. 99373 (Sup. Ct. Yakima Nov. 18, 2021).

> solely for housing the well or other diversion works in which there is no reasonable expectation of privacy, the employee shall only enter the building in the absence of a court order after requesting and receiving the permission of the claimant or other occupant. The director may request the district court to issue an order compelling inspection and subpoenas requiring the attendance of any witness or the production of documents in accordance with the Idaho rules of civil procedure.[46]

Idaho's adjudication commenced just as the use of Geographic Information Systems (GIS) was becoming widespread. GIS allows digitized spatial data (data that is referenced to a geographic location) to be shown as layers on a base map. This technology allowed IDWR to develop an interactive database that you may use to access the location of any water right in map form.[47] Consider the difference between the pre-GIS abstract of water right (Figure 25.6) and a visual map depicting the place of use and point of diversion linked to a spreadsheet with similar information to the abstract. Since this is likely the future direction of any water rights database, consider taking a basic GIS course during law school or when you enter your practice. Irrigation water users will recognize their fields in map form, and use of GIS will result in a much more

46. Idaho Code § 42-1410(2).

47. Idaho Department of Water Resources, Maps and Spatial Data (2023), https://idwr.idaho.gov/gis/.

productive conversation than one in which you and your client stare at an abstract of a water right.

Once a claim has been examined, the agency will send its recommendations on any changes to the filed claim to the claimant. This is an opportunity to correct errors, but not to dispute the agency's determination. In Idaho, the agency files the results of its examination as the "Directors Report," by subbasin, with the SRBA court.[48]

Court Process Including Use of Special Masters for Dispute Resolution

The filing of the agency's report with the court provides notice to all claimants of the agency's findings related to the water rights in the subbasin. In many states, this is the point at which claimants may object, either to the agency's findings related to the claimant's own water right or to the agency's findings related to the existence and attributes of other water rights in the basin.[49] However, some states have slight variations on this practice. In Washington, for example, the Department of Ecology files a report that contains two motions to the court: one to decree the water right claims Ecology found to be substantiated by factual evidence and a second motion informing the court of the claims Ecology contests and asking the Court to make a determination on those claims.[50] The motion for determination of contested claims triggers the litigation process for those claims. Also, other claimants have the right to object to claims that are part of either of Ecology's motions. Objections will likewise trigger litigation on those claims where an objection has been filed.[51] The subbasin report carries considerable weight in court in Idaho:

> Each claimant of a water right acquired under state law has the ultimate burden of persuasion for each element of a water right. Since the director's report is prima facie evidence of the nature and extent of the water rights acquired under state law, a claimant of a water right acquired under state law has the burden of going forward with the evidence to establish any element of a water right that is in addition to or inconsistent with the description in a director's report. Any party filing an objection to any portion of the director's report shall have the burden of going forward with the evidence to rebut the director's report as to all issues raised by the objection.[52]

---

48. Idaho Code § 42-1411.
49. Idaho Code § 42-1412; Ariz. Rev. Stat. § 45-256(B); Or. Rev. Stat. § 539.100.
50. Wash. Rev. Code 90.03.640.
51. Wash. Rev. Code 90.03.160.
52. Idaho Code § 42-1411(5).

In contrast to Idaho, claimants in Washington adjudications retain the burden to establish the water right elements of any contested claims, notwithstanding the findings by Ecology.[53] Somewhere between Idaho and Washington is Arizona, which has a complex set of rules that assigns differing burdens of proof depending on whether the objector is objecting to their own water right or the water right of another.[54] If their own, they retain the burden of proof throughout the process while an objector to another's water right merely has the burden "to establish a prima facie case that the objectionable portions of the report are invalid or inadmissible. If a prima facie case is made, the burden then shifts to the land owner...."[55] The Arizona rules define "prima facie" as "evidence sufficient to allow the Master to reach a reasonable decision in favor of the objector unless the landowner offers evidence in rebuttal."[56] Unlike Idaho, Washington, and Arizona, Montana law gives deference to the claims themselves, finding "a claim of an existing right ... constitutes prima facie proof of its content until the issuance of a final decree."[57] As a result, any objector, "including claimants objecting to their own claims," must prove "by a preponderance of the evidence ... that the elements of the claim [as recommended] do not accurately reflect the ... water right...."[58]

Each court has a system for managing the volume of litigation these objections create and may issue rules that differ from those you would normally encounter in a state's rules of civil procedure. The SRBA court issued an initial administrative order, stating:

> ... The litigation of the SRBA will be governed by the Idaho Rules of Civil Procedure (I.R.C.P.), Idaho Rules of Evidence (I.R.E.) and the Idaho Appellate Rules (I.A.R.).
>
> b. These procedures supplement the I.R.C.P., I.R.E., I.A.R. and any other applicable laws or orders of this court only to the extent necessary to allow for the fair and expeditious resolution of all claims or issues in the SRBA....[59]

Idaho creates a subcase to the main adjudication for each contested case where an objection has been filed. In contrast to the main adjudication, where every claimant across the adjudication boundary is a party, the parties to these subcases are limited to the claimant, the objectors, and anyone who filed a "response" to an objection.[60] From that point forward, the only parties entitled to participate in litigation or settlement

---

53. Wash. Rev. Code 90.03.635.

54. *See* Gila River Rules of Procedure at § 13.05 *et seq.*

55. *Id.* at § 13.05[3].

56. *Id.* at § 13.05[3], n. 73.

57. Mont. Code Ann. 85-2-227.

58. Mont. Water Court Rules § 19 (2008).

59. *See, e.g.,* SRBA Administrative Order 1, Rules of Procedure, In re SRBA Case No. 39576 at Section 4; Attachments 1–7 (1997) [hereinafter CSRBA AO1] These rules were supplemented and modified as necessary as the adjudication proceeded. Ann Y. Vonde et al., *Understanding the Snake River Basin Adjudication*, 52 Idaho L. Rev. 53, 72 (2016).

60. CSRBA AO1 at § 11 *et seq.*

of these particular water rights are the parties to the subcase. Parties are encouraged to settle,[61] but if settlement is not possible, the subcase is referred to a special master.[62]

The use of special masters with specific expertise in water use and water law is common in a large adjudication to reduce the load on the presiding judge. The Idaho Code provides:

> ... (1) The district court may appoint one (1) or more special masters in any general adjudication.
>
> (2) The district court shall specify the powers and duties of a special master in the order of reference. The compensation and disqualification of a special master shall be governed by order or rule of the supreme court.[63]

The Idaho water court rules authorize both the presiding judge and special masters to order settlement conferences.[64] Those rules authorize the use of special masters not involved in the sub-proceeding to act as mediators free of charge.[65] The special master is also authorized to hold a hearing. In Idaho, a party may seek permissive review of any decision of the special master that "involves a controlling question of law as to which there are substantial grounds for difference of opinion and on which immediate consideration of the determination may advance the orderly resolution of the litigation...."[66] Likewise, once all issues of law and fact are resolved in the subcase, the master is directed to provide the district court with a report that provides the recommended elements of the water right at issue. Parties may file an exception to that report, triggering review by the district court.[67] The presiding judge will uphold the master's findings of fact, unless clearly erroneous, but exercises free review over questions of law.[68]

On completion of hearings for a subbasin, the SRBA court enters a "partial decree."[69] The partial decree and its predecessor, the subbasin report of the agency, provide a

---

61. For example, the Washington Legislature has a statement of policy finding that early settlement of contested claims is needed for a fair and efficient adjudication of water rights. Therefore, the department and other parties should identify opportunities for settlement following the date set by the court for filing evidence for all parties. To the extent consistent with court rules, the court ... is encouraged to urge as many parties to the adjudication as possible to reach timely agreement on claimed water rights.... Further, at appropriate times throughout the process the court ... is encouraged to direct parties to utilize alternative methods of dispute resolution, including informal meetings, negotiation, mediation, or other methods to reach agreement on disputed claims." WASH. REV. CODE 90.03.645. *See also* Montana Water Court Rules at § 16(a) (the court "promotes and will facilitate resolution of objections ... through settlement or mediation.").

62. *Id.; See also* Mont. Water Court Rules at § 11(a).

63. IDAHO CODE § 42-1422.

64. CSRBA AO1 at § 17.

65. CSRBA AO1 at § 17.

66. CSRBA AO1 at § 10(d).

67. CSRBA AO1 at § 18.

68. Higley v. Woodward, 861 P.2d 101, 104 (Idaho Ct. App. 1993).

69. IDAHO CODE § 42-1411(6); CSRBA AO1 at § 19.

basis for water right administration and enforcement pending a final decree incorporating all subbasins in the Snake River Basin.[70]

Use of hydrologic basins as the organizing principle in the SRBA left one other problem: how to handle an issue that comes up in one subbasin that is likely to repeat in numerous other subbasins. The limitation on parties to a subbasin proceeding would exclude others with interest in the outcome. The SRBA used a process of certification of an "issue of basin-wide concern" to allow a hearing on a specific issue that is open to any interest in the SRBA.[71] Any party may seek certification of an issue.[72] Once decided by the SRBA court, the issue could go directly to the Idaho Supreme Court on interlocutory appeal, allowing finalization of the issue and providing a uniform decision for all subbasins. Issues that were certified during the SRBA included some of the initial procedural orders, the cases on water spreading you read in Part V, and issues concerning federal and tribal water rights.

Notes & Questions

1. How does a general adjudication differ from a private adjudication?
2. List the types of things a judge newly assigned a general adjudication should consider to facilitate case management. How do these measures help case management?
3. The state water agency examines your client's water claim for a general adjudication and finds that while your client claimed a priority date of June 1, 1935, they did not put water to a beneficial use until June 1, 1991, and that the quantity put to a beneficial use was 0.5 cfs instead of the claimed 1.5 cfs. Does your client bear the burden of proving the agency wrong in Idaho? In Montana?

The Final Decree

The ultimate goal of the adjudication process is to develop a final decree, which constitutes a comprehensive inventory of the elements of every water right in the basin. The decree is relatively simple, containing only the basic elements of the water right along with any remarks the court found necessary for the future administration of the water right. These decrees become the primary document used by state water agencies to administer water rights in times of shortage.

In Idaho, the court enters a final unified decree only after *every* subcase has been fully resolved and partial decrees have been entered for *every* water right claimed in the adjudication. At that point, the final unified decree is simply a collection of the thousands of partial decrees entered over the years. Washington's process was similar in the *Acquavella* adjudication, wherein "conditional final orders" served the same role

70. Idaho Code § 42-1413; CSRBA AO1 at § 19.
71. CSRBA AO1 at § 16a(1).
72. *Id.*

as Idaho's "partial decrees," and were entered for uncontested claims or as water rights claims were litigated or settled. In 2019 those conditional final orders were combined into a final decree.[73]

Arizona's practice is slightly different. As mentioned above, the presiding judge in Arizona does not review water rights on an individual basis but instead receives a Catalog of Proposed Water Rights from the Special Master. After litigation has run its course and interlocutory appeals have been exhausted for a particular catalog, it is then integrated into a comprehensive report prepared by the Arizona Department of Water Resources ("DWR").[74] Once the catalogs for every subbasin in the adjudication have been reviewed and fully litigated, the DWR submits its comprehensive report to the Court, which holds one final objection period on the proposed decree before finalizing it into a final unified decree.[75]

Once the final decree is entered and all appeals have been exhausted, it serves as a final determination of all water rights that exist with a priority date predating the commencement of the adjudication.[76] Because these are true *in rem* proceedings, every person is thereafter "restrained, estopped and enjoined from asserting or claiming any rights, title or interest existing at the time [of commencement] in or to the water of [the adjudication]."[77]

73. *Acquavella* Final Decree at 3–6.

74. Gila River Rules of Procedure at § 17.00.

75. *Id.* at § 17.00(1).

76. *See, e.g.*, SRBA Final Unified Decree at 9, ("This Final Unified Decree is conclusive as to the nature and extent of all water rights with the Snake River Basin within the State of Idaho with a priority date prior to November 19, 1987. . . .").

77. *Acquavella* Final Decree at 6. *See also* SRBA Final Unified Decree at 10 ("All other water rights with a priority date before November 19, 1987, not expressly set forth in this Final Unified Decree are hereby decreed as disallowed.").

Chapter 26

Reserved Water Rights in State Court Adjudication

Introduction

As sovereign governments, both the United States and American Indian tribes have sovereign immunity from suit. As a result, neither can be drawn into litigation unless it has consented to suit in a "clear" waiver of sovereign immunity.[1] Although Congress may abrogate the sovereign immunity of tribes, such a waiver will "not be implied but must be unequivocally expressed."[2] Immunity from suit historically allowed the United States and/or tribes to control when they would initiate litigation regarding reserved water rights. Perhaps more importantly, it allowed for those water rights to be determined, quantified, and enforced by federal rather than state courts. This Chapter will cover the waiver of sovereign immunity by Congress to allow the United States to be joined in a general adjudication in state court, and the interpretation of that waiver to extend to federal and Native American reserved water rights.

Waiver of Sovereign Immunity: The McCarran Amendment of 1952

In 1952 Congress enacted a waiver of sovereign immunity to join the United States in a state adjudication. The waiver, known as the McCarran Amendment after its sponsor, Senator Patrick McCarran from Nevada, was enacted as a rider on an appropriation bill for the Department of Justice (the entity that tries to protect the sovereign immunity of the federal government). The Amendment states:

> Consent is given to join the United States as a defendant in any suit (1) for the adjudication of rights to the use of water of a river system or other source, or (2) for the administration of such rights, where it appears that the United

1. Thus, the U.S. Supreme Court in *United States v. Mitchell*, 445 U.S. 535, 538 (1980), stated that: [I]t is elementary that '[t]he United States, as sovereign, is immune from suit save as it consents to be sued . . . , and the terms of its consent to be sued in any court define that court's jurisdiction to entertain suit.' *United States v. Sherwood,* 312 U.S. 584, 586 (1941). A waiver of sovereign immunity 'cannot be implied but must be unequivocally expressed.' United States v. King, 395 U.S. 1, 4 (1969). *See* C & L Enters., Inc. v. Citizen Band Potawatomi Indian Tribe of Okla., 532 U.S. 411, 418 (2001).

2. Santa Clara Pueblo v. Martinez, 436 U.S. 49, 58–59 (1978) (also quoting *United States v. King*).

> States is the owner of or is in the process of acquiring water rights by appropriation under State law, by purchase, by exchange, or otherwise, and the United States is a necessary party to such suit.[3]

Research on the legislative history suggests that the McCarran Amendment was intended to address the narrow problem of increasing acquisition of state-based water rights by the federal government, while refusing to participate in state adjudications.[4] Professor Hedden-Nicely states:

> The proponents of the McCarran Amendment argued that the federal government's claim of sovereign immunity precluded state courts from either initiating an adjudication or administering previously decreed water rights that were subsequently acquired by the United States. This, according to the proponents of the bill, effectively paralyzed the states' ability to enforce their water laws because "all the supposedly settled water rights [were] subject to review and reexamination," whenever "the United States appear[ed] in a watershed." The upheaval caused by the federal government's actions created considerable anxiety that "the long years of travail through which the water laws of our Western States have pased [sic] ... have been in vain."
>
> The sponsors of the McCarran Amendment believed the federal claim of sovereign immunity unfair because, in those circumstances where it had acquired water rights pursuant to state law, the United States was acting in a proprietary rather than sovereign capacity but nonetheless claiming a "privilege of immunity that the original owner wouldn't have." It was this issue, which had nothing to do with Indian tribes whose rights are reserved by the United States in its sovereign capacity and who have sovereign immunity independent of the United States that was front and[5] center as the McCarran Amendment was considered and passed into law.[6]

It is the Reclamation Act that requires acquisition of water rights pursuant to state law as you learned in Part IV. In addition, under the Migratory Bird Conservation Act of 1929[7] (enacted in conjunction with the Migratory Bird Treaty Act of 1918 with Canada and Mexico[8]), certain national wildlife refuges were created through acquisition of private land and water rights. The United States maintains the existing state-based rights if relevant to the refuge, while also asserting any additional reserved water rights for the purpose of the refuge arising at the time of its establishment.

---

3. Act of July 10, 1952, Pub. L. No. 495, § 208, 66 Stat. 549, 560 (codified at 43 U.S.C. § 666 (2012)).

4. Dylan Hedden-Nicely, *The Legislative History of the McCarran Amendment: An Effort to Determine Whether Congress Intended for State Court Jurisdiction to Extend to Indian Reserved Water Rights*, 46 Envtl. L. 845 (2016)

5. Dugan v. Rank, 372 U.S. 609, 614 (1963).

6. Dylan Hedden-Nicely, *The Legislative History of the McCarran Amendment: An Effort to Determine Whether Congress Intended for State Court Jurisdiction to Extend to Indian Reserved Water Rights*, 46 Envtl. L. 845 (2016) (internal citations omitted).

7. 45 Stat. 1222.

8. *See* The Migratory Bird Treaty Act of 1918 (16 U.S.C. 703–712).

Requirements for State Jurisdiction under the McCarran Amendment

The first question to reach the U.S. Supreme Court was the issue of what type of adjudication to which the McCarran Amendment extends—any private or general adjudication? The case of *Dugan v. Rank*[9] involved a suit by irrigators downstream from a storage project that was part of the Bureau of Reclamation's Central Valley Project and diverted water from the Sacramento to the San Joaquin River, diminishing flow downstream on the Sacramento River. Recall from Part IV that Reclamation is required to follow state law in the acquisition of water rights, and that initial steps in a proposed project involved determination of existing uses and availability of water for the project. In this process, the practice of Reclamation was generally to enter agreements with existing water users whose rights might be affected by the project. These agreements often provided for relinquishment of the prior natural flow right in exchange for stored water from the project. The suit was brought by water users who refused to enter agreements and "sought to enjoin [the BOR] from storing or diverting water to the San Joaquin at Friant Dam or, in the alternative, to obtain a decree of a physical solution of water rights."[10] The Supreme Court spent little time on the issue, stating:

> We go directly to the question of joinder of the United States as a party. We agree with the Court of Appeals on this issue and therefore do not consider the contention at length. It is sufficient to say that the provision of the McCarran amendment, ... relied upon by respondents and providing that the United States may be joined in suits 'for the adjudication of rights to the use of water of a river system or other source,' is not applicable here. Rather than a case involving a general adjudication of 'all of the rights of various owners on a given stream,' S.Rep.No. 755, 82d Cong., 1st Sess. 9 (1951), it is a private suit to determine water rights solely between the respondents and the United States and the local Reclamation Bureau officials. In addition to the fact that all of the claimants to water rights along the river are not made parties, no relief is either asked or granted as between claimants, nor are priorities sought to be established as to the appropriative and prescriptive rights asserted.[11]

In contrast, the Ninth Circuit provided more analysis of the basis for its decision, which the Supreme Court agreed to and adopted in *Dugan v. Rank,* including legislative history of the McCarran Amendment.

9. 372 U.S. 609 (1963)
10. Dugan v. Rank, 372 U.S. 609, 614 (1963).
11. *Id.* at 618–619 (1963).

California v. Rank

Ninth Circuit Court of Appeals
293 F.2d 340 (1961)

...

II. The Jurisdictional Issues.

We proceed to the jurisdictional questions presented by this appeal. The first question is presented by the contention of the United States that it has not consented to suit and has improperly been joined as a party defendant.

If consent to suit is to be found, it must be through the provisions of the waiver of immunity statute passed by Congress in 1952, which has come to be known as the 'McCarran Amendment.' 66 Stat. 560, 43 U.S.C. § 666....

The question presented by the contention of the United States requires us to determine whether this suit can be regarded as one 'for the adjudication of rights to the use of water of a river system' within the meaning of § 666.

There can be little doubt as to the type of suit Congress had in mind. It was not a private dispute between certain water users as to their conflicting rights to the use of waters of a stream system; rather, it was the quasi-public proceeding which in the law of western waters is known as a 'general adjudication' of a stream system: one in which the rights of all claimants on a stream system, as between themselves, are ascertained and officially stated.

With reference to this type of suit, the Senate Report upon the bill which became § 666 quoted as follows from Pacific Live Stock Co. v. Lewis:

> 'All claimants are required to appear and prove their claims; no one can refuse without forfeiting his claim, and all have the same relation to the proceeding. It is intended to be universal and to result in a complete ascertainment of all existing rights, to the end, first, that the waters may be distributed, under public supervision, among the lawful claimants according to their respective rights without needless waste or controversy; second, that the rights of all may be evidenced by appropriate certificates and public records, always readily accessible, and may not be dependent upon the testimony of witnesses with its recognized infirmities and uncertainties; and, third, that the amount of surplus or unclaimed water, if any, may be ascertained and rendered available to intending appropriators.' S.Rep. No. 755, 82d Congress, 1st Session 5 (1951).

The senate report also incorporated correspondence between Senators Magnuson and McCarran. The former was disturbed by the thought that private water disputes could, under the bill, interfere with reclamation projects in which he was interested. Senator McCarran wrote (S.Rep. No. 755, 82d Congress, 1st Session 9 (1951)):

> 'You indicate that you visualize the possibility of an individual or group, having water rights on that stream, bringing suit to adjudicate their respective

> rights thereby preventing the Bureau of Reclamation from going ahead with the Hells Canyon project while litigation is in process or pending.
>
> 'S.18 is not intended to be used * * * for any other purpose than to allow the United States to be joined in a suit wherein it is necessary to adjudicate all of the rights of various owners on a given stream.'

In Miller v. Jennings, discussing the nature of the suit to which § 666 referred, the court stated:

> 'The United States has not given its consent to be joined as a defendant in every suit involving water rights. It may be made a party only in suits 'for the adjudication of rights to the use of water of a river system or other source.' There can be an adjudication of rights with respect to the upper Rio Grande only in a proceeding where all persons who have rights are before the tribunal.'

That opinion then quoted this court:

> 'The Ninth Circuit Court of Appeals has most succinctly stated the doctrine in this manner: 'The only proper method of adjudicating the rights on a stream, whether riparian or appropriative or mixed, is to have all owners of lands on the watershed and all appropriators who use water from the streams involved in another watershed in court at the same time.' *People of State of California v. United States*, 235 F.2d 647, 663 (9th Cir. 1956).

The question remains whether the suit at bar was for such a general adjudication of a river system as was contemplated by Congress.

In two respects we feel that [this suit] has failed to measure up. First, all claimants have not been joined. Second, neither the relief prayed for nor the decree includes the establishment of the rights of the claimants as between themselves. The controversy thus is limited to a private one between the claimants on the one hand and the officers of the Bureau of Reclamation on the other.

...

With respect to the private nature of the controversy, the district court recognized that this was not a suit in which the water users sought to enforce their rights as among themselves or to have given amounts of water declared and adjudicated as their rights. Nevertheless, since the suit required a judicial determination of rights to the use of waters of the San Joaquin, since such asserted rights were of the very essence of the suit and since their determination constituted the basic problem, the court ruled that the suit was such a one as to fall within the provisions of § 666....

It may well be that a general adjudication would require no more specific adjudication as to riparian and overlying rights than that which was here entered. As to the appropriative and prescriptive rights, however, the decree only purports to establish the rights of these plaintiffs as against the defendants. No priority is established save only that the rights are prior to those claimed by the defendant officials on behalf of the United States. As between the claimants themselves, their respective priorities are not established.

For these reasons, the suit at bar falls short of being one for a general adjudication. It is not such a suit as is contemplated by § 666. Consent to suit has not been conferred by the United States under that statute. The district court was without jurisdiction to join the United States and the United States must be dismissed from this proceeding.

...

Notes & Questions

1. *The Rule.* The rule outlined by the Ninth Circuit and affirmed by the United States Supreme Court is that in order for an adjudication to be considered comprehensive under the terms of the McCarran Amendment, it must: (1) determine the priority, quantity, and location of "all" water rights claims; (2) within the geographic extent of an entire watershed or river basin.
2. *Geographic Scope.* What constitutes an entire watershed or river basin? The Snake River Basin, for example, spans six states, drains approximately 100,000 square miles, has thousands of tributaries, and is home to hundreds of thousands of people. Must an adjudication of the Snake River include its entire area?
3. *All users.* The Ninth Circuit defined a "general" adjudication for purposes of the McCarran Amendment to be one where "the rights of all claimants on a stream system, as between themselves, are ascertained and officially stated."[12] But are some uses so small as to be considered *de minimis* in the context of an entire basin?

These questions set the stage for the following sections.

Geographic Scope of an Adjudication that Meets the Requirements of the McCarran Amendment

The question of the geographic scope required by McCarran comes up against the reality that general stream adjudications in state court are intrastate affairs. Thus, Idaho's Snake River Basin Adjudication included only those water rights that were from the Snake River and its tributaries within the State of Idaho. Although the Supreme Court has not addressed this directly, it has indicated that it too defines general stream adjudications to extend only to the portion of a river watershed that is within one state.[13] That definition is unlikely to change given that nearly all of the dozens of adjudications that have taken place so far have been limited to a single state.

But does an adjudication have to include an entire river basin within a particular state? According to a leading water law treatise, "[a] single river or tributary qualifies as a general adjudication, but the inclusion of tributaries may be necessary to obtain

12. California v. Rank, 293 F.2d 340, 347 (9th Cir. 1961).
13. *See Eagle County*, 401 U.S. at 520.

jurisdiction over the United States."[14] Meaning that a "general" adjudication under state law is not necessarily the same as a "general" adjudication for purposes of the McCarran Amendment Thus, for example, the Idaho Supreme Court concluded that:

> Th[e] history of the McCarran Amendment and the interpretations that the federal courts have given to it convince us that in order for the United States to be subject to the jurisdiction of the trial court in the Snake River basin adjudication, the rights of all claimants on the Snake River and all of its tributaries within the state of Idaho must be included in the adjudication.[15]

Comprehensiveness of an Adjudication that Meets the Requirements of the McCarran Amendment

The next question to be considered was: does "all" water users apply only to those with state-based rights? The McCarran Amendment and its legislative history are silent on reserved water rights. The Supreme Court's 1963 decision in *Arizona v. California* (postdating passage of the McCarran Amendment) awoke western water users to a new problem: the potentially massive amount of water reserved to the United States for federal and tribal lands. Rather than go back to Congress to seek a waiver of sovereign immunity to adjudicate reserved water rights, state governments pursued an interpretation of the McCarran Amendment that would extend the waiver of sovereign immunity to all federal water rights, including reserved water rights. By 1971, that argument had made its way to the United States Supreme Court in the context of reserved water rights for a national forest in Colorado. Although the issue began in state court, the question of the scope of the McCarran Amendment is a question of federal law, and thus may be taken to the U.S. Supreme Court following, in this case, a decision of the Colorado Supreme Court.

Prior to reading this case, it is important to understand why Colorado's unique system of ongoing judicial determination of water rights constitutes a "general adjudication." While the last paragraph of the case notes that it is a general adjudication, it is difficult to understand without a brief introduction to the Colorado system, which does not use a science-based administrative agency to manage the allocation of new water rights. Instead:

> [u]nder the Colorado Act, the State is divided into seven Water Divisions [Figure 26.1], each Division encompassing one or more entire drainage basins for the larger rivers in Colorado. Adjudication of water claims within each Division occurs on a continuous basis. Each month, Water Referees in each Division rule on applications for water rights filed within the preceding five months or refer those applications to the Water Judge of their Division. Every six months, the Water Judge passes on referred applications and contested decisions by Referees. A State Engineer and engineers for each Division are

14. Tarlock & Robison, Law of Water Rights and Resources § 7:4 (2021).

15. In re Snake River Basin Water System, 764 P.2d 78, 85 (Idaho 1988).

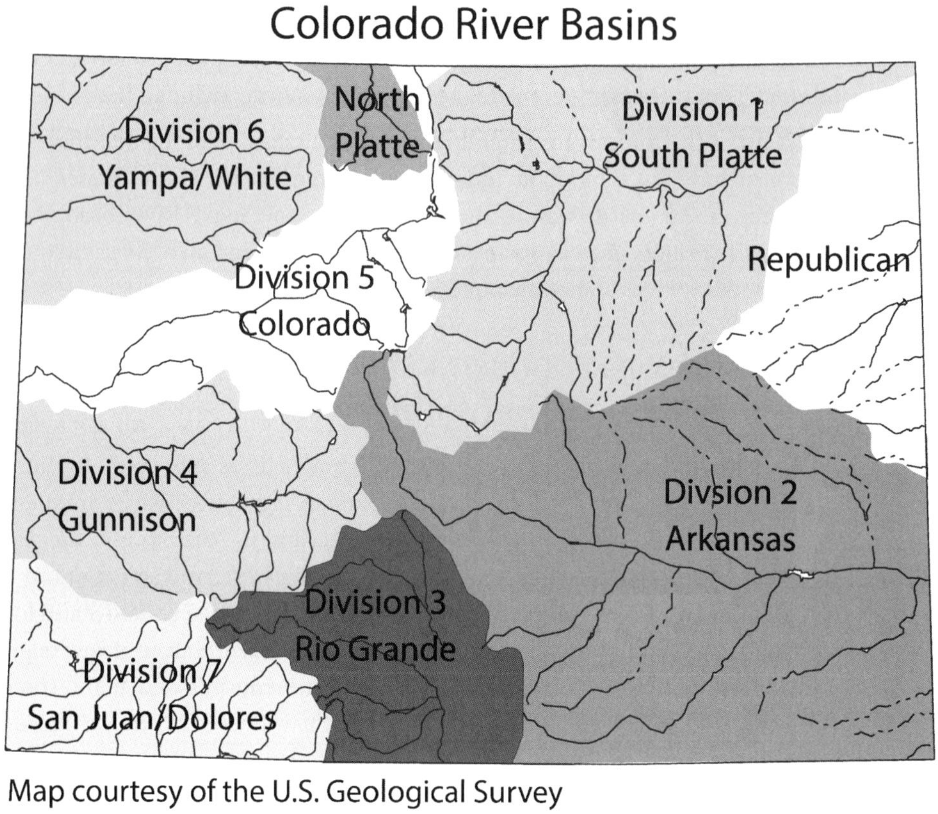

Figure 26.1 Map of Colorado water court divisions. Source: Colorado State University, Colorado Water Knowledge, Administration of Water Rights, https://waterknowledge.colostate.edu/water-management-administration/water-rights/administration-of-water-rights/.

> responsible for the administration and distribution of the waters of the State according to the determinations in each Division.[16]

Thus, the Colorado system of obtaining new water rights requires application to the water court instead of to a state water agency. The decision to award a water right takes place in what is basically an ongoing adjudication. Decrees remain open to the addition of new water rights.

United States v. District Court in and for Eagle County

Supreme Court of the United States
401 U.S. 520 (1971)

MR. JUSTICE DOUGLAS—Eagle River is a tributary of the Colorado River; and Water District 37 is a Colorado entity encompassing all Colorado lands irrigated by water of the Eagle and its tributaries. The present case started in the Colorado courts and is called a supplemental water adjudication [Colorado state law]. The Colorado court issued a notice which, inter alia, asked all owners and claimants of water rights

16. Colorado River Water Conservation Dist. v. United States, 425 U.S. 800, 804–05 (1976).

in those streams 'to file a statement of claim and to appear * * * in regard to all water rights owned or claimed by them.' The United States was served with this notice pursuant to [the McCarran Amendment]. The United States moved to be dismissed as a party, asserting that [the McCarran Amendment] does not constitute consent to have federal reserved water rights adjudicated in a state court the reserved water rights of the United States.

The objections of the United States were overruled by the state District Court and on a motion for a writ of prohibition the Colorado Supreme Court took the same view....

We affirm the Colorado decree.

It is clear from our cases that the United States often has reserved water rights based on withdrawals from the public domain. As we said in *Arizona v. California*, the Federal Government had the authority both before and after a State is admitted into the Union 'to reserve waters for the use and benefit of federally reserved lands.' The federally reserved lands include any federal enclave. In *Arizona v. California* we were primarily concerned with Indian reservations. The reservation of waters may be only implied and the amount will reflect the nature of the federal enclave. Here the United States is primarily concerned with reserved waters for the White River National Forest, withdrawn in 1905, Colorado having been admitted into the Union in 1876.

...

The consent to join the United States 'in any suit (1) for the adjudication of rights to the use of water of a river system or other source' would seem to be all-inclusive. We deem almost frivolous the suggestion that the Eagle and its tributaries are not a 'river system' within the meaning of the Act. No suit by any State could possibly encompass all of the water rights in the entire Colorado River which runs through or touches many States. The 'river system' must be read as embracing one within the particular State's jurisdiction. With that to one side, the first clause of s 666(a)(1), read literally, would seem to cover this case for 'rights to the use of water of a river system' is broad enough to embrace 'reserved' waters.

The main reliance of the United States appears to be on Clause 2 of s 666(a) which reads:

> '* * * for the administration of such rights, where it appears that the United States is the owner of or is in the process of acquiring water rights by appropriation under State law, by purchase, by exchange, or otherwise.'

This provision does not qualify s 666(a)(1), for (1) and (2) are separated by an 'or.' Yet even if 'or' be read as 'and', we see no difficulty with Colorado's position. Section 666(a)(2) obviously includes water rights previously acquired by the United States through appropriation or presently in the process of being so acquired. But we do not read s 666(a)(2) as being restricted to appropriative rights acquired under state law. In the first place 'the administration of such rights' in s 666(a)(2) must refer to the rights described in (1) for they are the only ones which in this context 'such' could mean; and as we have seen they are all-inclusive, in terms at least. Moreover, (2) covers rights acquired by appropriation under state law and rights acquired 'by purchase' or 'by exchange,' which we assume would normally be appropriative rights. But it also includes water rights which the United States has 'otherwise' acquired. The doctrine of ejusdem generis is invoked to maintain that 'or otherwise' does not encompass the adjudication of reserved water rights, which are in no way dependent for their creation or existence on state law. We reject that conclusion for we deal with an all-inclusive statute concerning 'the adjudication of rights to the use of water of a river system' which in s 666(a)(1) has no exceptions and which, as we read it, includes appropriate [sic] rights, riparian rights, and reserved rights.

It is said that this adjudication is not a 'general' one as required by *Dugan v. Rank*. This proceeding, unlike the one in *Dugan*, is not a private one to determine whether named claimants have priority over the United States. The whole community of claims is involved and as Senator McCarran, Chairman of the Committee reporting on the bill, said in reply to Senator Magnuson: 'S. 18 is not intended * * * to be used for any other purpose than to allow the United States to be joined in a suit wherein it is necessary to adjudicate all of the rights of various owners on a given stream. This is so because unless all of the parties owning or in the process of acquiring water rights on a particular stream can be joined as parties defendant, any subsequent decree would be of little value.'

...

Affirmed.

Notes & Questions

1. A close reading of the McCarran Amendment reveals at least two ways to construe its language. First, it could be read like this:

    > Consent is given to join the United States as a defendant in any suit (1) for the adjudication of rights to the use of water of a river system or other source, or (2) for the administration of such rights, ...
    >
    > where it appears that the United States is the owner of ... water rights by appropriation under State law, by purchase, by exchange, or otherwise and the United States is a necessary party to such suit.

    However, an equally plausible reading of the Amendment could be:

    > Consent is given to join the United States as a defendant in any suit (1) for the adjudication of rights to the use of water of a river system or other source, or ...
    >
    > (2) for the administration of such rights, where it appears that the United States is the owner of ... water rights by appropriation under State law, by purchase, by exchange, or otherwise and the United States is a necessary party to such suit.

    How would construction one differ from construction two? Would it lead to a different result? Which construction does the Court ultimately adopt?

2. The United States sought to invoke the rule of construction known as *ejusdem generis*. That rule applies "when specific words are followed by a general term such as 'or otherwise' and works to limit the objects encompassed by the general term to the same class as those specifically enumerated."[17] How does the Supreme Court interpret the "or otherwise" language in the McCarran Amendment?
3. Ultimately, what policy is the Supreme Court trying to effectuate by including reserved rights within the scope of the McCarran Amendment?

Eagle County provided some answers to the question of: what is a "general" adjudication for purposes of the McCarran Amendment? Questions remained on issues such as whether some uses are so small as to be considered *de minimis* in the context of an entire basin. Must groundwater be included? The following paragraphs describe how states have handled these questions in the absence of U.S. Supreme Court guidance.

You learned in Part V that domestic and stockwater uses are generally excluded from western permit systems. The inclusion of these numerous small uses in a general adjudication would involve substantial time and cost in the process of verification of a large number of claims, each involving a very small amount of water. Nevertheless, as you learned in Part V, their cumulative impact may be locally significant. To avoid those costs and to streamline these adjudications, some states have found creative ways to get around McCarran's comprehensive requirement for these rights.

For example, Idaho and the United States reached the following stipulation regarding *de minimis* uses in adjudication of the Coeur d'Alene-Spokane River Basin:

> The State of Idaho ... and the United States, ... stipulate that the following procedures for the adjudication of de minimis domestic and stock water claims as defined by Idaho Code § 42-1401A(4) and (11) shall be used in the [adjudication]:
>
> 1. All claimants of de minimis domestic and stock water uses as defined in Idaho as parties in this proceeding and will be bound by all decrees entered in this case, including the final decree....
> 2. De minimis claimants may elect to have their claims fully adjudicated now or to postpone the adjudication of their claims by following the alternative procedure ...
> 3. De minimis claimants may elect to defer adjudication of their claims to a later time in this proceeding ... [and] each de minimis claimant must agree to have any domestic or stock water claim decreed prior to seeking authorization from the Director to change the point of diversion, place of use, purpose of use, or period of use;[18]

---

17. Singer and Singer, 2A Sutherland Statutes and Statutory Construction § 47.17 (7th ed. 2015).

18. Stipulation for Establishment of Procedure for the Adjudication of Domestic and Stock Water Claims, In the District Court of the Fifth Judicial District of the State of Idaho in and for the County of Twin Falls, Case No. 49576 (2008).

The stipulation would result in deferral of an estimated 11,000 domestic and stock water uses, amounting to half of the water uses in the basin.[19] The adjudication court identified three factors in finding the proposed Coeur d'Alene-Spokane River Basin adjudication consistent with the McCarran Amendment. First, the United States (but not the Coeur d'Alene Tribe) stipulated that the procedure was consistent with the McCarran Amendment.[20] Second, the water users were technically joined to the adjudication, despite their claims being indefinitely deferred.[21] Finally, the court found persuasive the State's evidence that collectively, the *de minimis* claims consumed less than one percent of the Basin's annual water supply.[22] The court concluded that:

> [a]s a result of the sheer number of small domestic and stockwater claims typically present and the relatively small quantity of water these claims represent, it is not uncommon for small domestic and stockwater to be processed differently....[23]

In its objection to the commencement of the adjudication, the Coeur d'Alene Tribe criticized the State's analysis as ignoring the spatial and temporal complexity of the Basin. First, by focusing on the entire watershed, the State ignored the fact that domestic claims may have an outsized local effect on smaller streams within the Basin. Second, by focusing on the annual water supply, the State ignored how these water uses might affect water supply during the water-short summer months.

Although Idaho's approach of deferring *de minimis* uses is unique, the Idaho court was correct that these uses are often adjudicated on a more streamlined basis than their larger counterparts. For example, the Arizona adjudications require all users to file claims, but have developed a streamlined process for adjudicating some domestic and stockwater rights.[24] That process requires the special master to take evidence and find facts that demonstrate that these uses are in fact *de minimis*.[25] If so, the Master then quantifies these rights as a group. For example, all *de minimis* domestic rights in the San Pedro River Basin were adjudicated with a quantity "not to exceed 1 ac-ft/yr," while stockponds were capped at four acre-feet per year.

Should a "comprehensive" adjudication under the McCarran Amendment also include claims to water rights for groundwater? The Idaho Supreme Court interpreted the language of the McCarran Amendment that authorizes joinder of the United States "for the adjudication of rights to the use of water of a river system *or other source*" to

---

19. Memorandum Decision on Petition to Commence Coeur d'Alene-Spokane River Basin General Adjudication at 20, *In re CSRBA*, No. 49576 (Nov. 12, 2008).

20. *Id.* at 10.

21. *Id.* at 19.

22. *Id.* at 20.

23. *Id.* at 21–22.

24. *See, e.g.*, Memorandum Decision, Findings of Fact, and Conclusions of Law for Group 1 Cases Involving Stockwatering, Stockponds, and Domestic Uses at 6–7, *In re Gila River*, No. W1-11-10 (Nov. 14, 1994).

25. *Id.* at 11–34.

include "sources other than a river system, such as lakes or ground waters."[26] The Court went on to opine that "[i]t would destroy the intent of the McCarran Amendment to allow a river system to be fragmented into separate sources in order to obtain jurisdiction over the United States."[27] *Id.*

Other courts have come to contrary conclusions. The Ninth Circuit concluded that despite its exclusion of groundwater rights, Oregon's Klamath River Adjudication was consistent with the McCarran Amendment because "the use of 'or' [i.e., "river system *or* other source"] strongly suggests that the adjudication may be limited to *either* a river system *or* some other source of water, like groundwater, but need not cover both."[28] The Court buttressed this textual analysis with the fact that conjunctive management of ground and surface water is "too recent and too incomplete to infer that Congress intended to require comprehensive stream adjudications under the McCarran Amendment to include the adjudication of groundwater rights as well as rights to surface water."[29] The Arizona Supreme Court struck a middle ground between these two approaches, concluding that courts may "adopt a rationally based exclusion for wells having a de minimis effect on the river system.... A properly crafted de minimis exclusion will not cause piecemeal adjudication of water rights or in any way run afoul of the McCarran Amendment."[30] However, where the Arizona Department of Water Resources (DWR) concludes there is an interconnection between a well and adjacent surface water, that determination "constitutes clear and convincing evidence ... requir[ing] the well owner to come forward with evidence that DWR is wrong."[31]

Extension of McCarran to the United States as Trustee of Native American Reserved Water Rights

Eagle County concerned the adjudication of federal reserved water rights appurtenant to the White River National Forest. Whether the scope of the McCarran Amendment included reserved water rights held by the United States in trust for American Indian tribes remained an open question. The Supreme Court answered that question in the affirmative in *Colorado River Water Conservation District v. United States*.[32] This case also considers whether state court jurisdiction is exclusive—i.e., must a federal court dismiss the claims of the United States to reserved rights for the Tribes in favor of state court jurisdiction.

---

26. In re Snake River Basin Water System, 764 P.2d 78 at 86 (1988).

27. *Id.*

28. United States v. Oregon, 44 F.3d 758, 768 (9th Cir. 1994). Keep in mind that the relative importance of groundwater irrigation to the Snake River Basin in Idaho as compared to its importance in the Klamath Basin may also have influenced these decisions.

29. *Id.* at 770.

30. In re Gila River, 857 P.2d 1236, 1248 (Ariz. 1993).

31. *Id.* at 1246.

32. 424 U.S. 800 (1976).

The United States sought to initiate an adjudication for the determination of the water rights held in the San Juan and Dolores River Basins of Colorado for the benefit of the Southern Ute and Ute Mountain Ute Tribes. Rather than file claims in Division 7 of Colorado state water court, the United States filed its claims in federal district court in Denver.[33] The federal district court dismissed. The Tenth Circuit reversed, "holding that the suit of the United States was within district-court jurisdiction under 28 U.S.C. § 1345, and that abstention was inappropriate."[34] The U.S. Supreme Court granted certiorari.

Colorado River Water Conservation District v. United States

Supreme Court of the United States
424 U.S. 800 (1976)

Justice BRENNAN....

III

...

A

First, we consider whether the McCarran Amendment provided consent to determine federal reserved rights held on behalf of Indians in state court. This is a question not previously squarely addressed by this Court, and given the claims for Indian water rights in this case, dismissal clearly would have been inappropriate if the state court had no jurisdiction to decide those claims. We conclude that the state court had jurisdiction over Indian water rights under the Amendment.

[*Eagle County*] held that the provisions of the McCarran Amendment, whereby "consent is ... given to join the United States as a defendant in any suit (1) for the adjudication ... or (2) for the administration of (water) rights, where it appears that the United States is the owner ... by appropriation under State law, by purchase, by exchange, or otherwise ...," subject federal reserved rights to general adjudication in state proceedings for the determination of water rights. More specifically, the Court held that reserved rights were included in those rights where the United States was "otherwise" the owner.... Though *Eagle County* ... did not involve reserved rights on Indian reservations, viewing the Government's trusteeship of Indian rights as ownership, the logic of those cases clearly extends to such rights. Indeed, *Eagle County* spoke of non-Indian rights and Indian rights without any suggestion that there was a distinction between them for purposes of the Amendment.

Not only the Amendment's language, but also its underlying policy, dictates a construction including Indian rights in its provisions. *Eagle County* rejected the conclu-

33. Colorado River Water Conservation District. v. United States, 424 U.S. 800, 806 (citing *United States v. Akin*, 504 F.2d 115, 116 (10th Cir. 1974)).

34. *Id.*

sion that federal reserved rights in general were not reached by the Amendment for the reason that the Amendment "(deals) with an all-inclusive statute concerning 'the adjudication of rights to the use of water of a river system.'" ... This consideration applies as well to federal water rights reserved for Indian reservations. And cogently, the Senate report on the Amendment observed:

> "In the administration of and the adjudication of water rights under State laws the State courts are vested with the jurisdiction necessary for the proper and efficient disposition thereof, and by reason of the interlocking of adjudicated rights on any stream system, any order or action affecting one right affects all such rights. Accordingly all water users on a stream, in practically every case, are interested and necessary parties to any court proceedings. It is apparent that if any water user claiming to hold such right by reason of the ownership thereof by the United States or any of its departments is permitted to claim immunity from suit in, or orders of, a State court, such claims could materially interfere with the lawful and equitable use of water for beneficial use by the other water users who are amenable to and bound by the decrees and orders of the State courts....

Thus, bearing in mind the ubiquitous nature of Indian water rights in the Southwest, it is clear that a construction of the Amendment excluding those rights from its coverage would enervate the Amendment's objective.

Finally, legislative history demonstrates that the McCarran Amendment is to be construed as reaching federal water rights reserved on behalf of Indians. It was unmistakably the understanding of proponents and opponents of the legislation that it comprehended water rights reserved for Indians. In the Senate hearings on the Amendment, participants for the Department of Justice and the Department of the Interior made clear that the proposal would include water rights reserved on behalf of Indians. In addition, the Senate report on the amendment took note of a recommendation in a Department of the Interior report that no consent to suit be given as to Indian rights and rejected the recommendation.

The Government argues that because of its fiduciary responsibility to protect Indian rights, any state-court jurisdiction over Indian property should not be recognized unless expressly conferred by Congress.... [T]he Government's argument rests on the incorrect assumption that consent to state jurisdiction for the purpose of determining water rights imperils those rights or in some way breaches the special obligation of the Federal Government to protect Indians. Mere subjection of Indian rights to legal challenge in state court, however, would no more imperil those rights than would a suit brought by the Government in district court for their declaration, a suit which, absent the consent of the Amendment, would eventually be necessitated to resolve conflicting claims to a scarce resource. The Government has not abdicated any responsibility fully to defend Indian rights in state court, and Indian interests may be satisfactorily protected under regimes of state law. The Amendment in no way abridges any substantive claim on behalf of Indians under the doctrine of reserved rights. Moreover, as Eagle

County said, "questions (arising from the collision of private rights and reserved rights of the United States), including the volume and scope of particular reserved rights, are federal questions which, if preserved, can be reviewed (by the Supreme Court) after final judgment by the Colorado court." . . .

. . . .

B

Next, we consider whether the District Court's dismissal was appropriate under the doctrine of abstention. We hold that the dismissal cannot be supported under that doctrine in any of its forms.

. . .

C

Although this case falls within none of the abstention categories, there are principles unrelated to considerations of proper constitutional adjudication and regard for federal-state relations which govern in situations involving the contemporaneous exercise of concurrent jurisdictions [sic], either by federal courts or by state and federal courts. These principles rest on considerations of "(w)ise judicial administration, giving regard to conservation of judicial resources and comprehensive disposition of litigation." Generally, as between state and federal courts, the rule is that "the pendency of an action in the state court is no bar to proceedings concerning the same matter in the Federal court having jurisdiction. . . ." As between federal district courts, however, though no precise rule has evolved, the general principle is to avoid duplicative litigation. This difference in general approach between state-federal concurrent jurisdiction and wholly federal concurrent jurisdiction stems from the virtually unflagging obligation of the federal courts to exercise the jurisdiction given them. Given this obligation, and the absence of weightier considerations of constitutional adjudication and state-federal relations, the circumstances permitting the dismissal of a federal suit due to the presence of a concurrent state proceeding for reasons of wise judicial administration are considerably more limited than the circumstances appropriate for abstention. The former circumstances, though exceptional, do nevertheless exist.

It has been held, for example, that the court first assuming jurisdiction over property may exercise that jurisdiction to the exclusion of other courts. . . . In assessing the appropriateness of dismissal in the event of an exercise of concurrent jurisdiction, a federal court may also consider such factors as the inconvenience of the federal forum; the desirability of avoiding piecemeal litigation; and the order in which jurisdiction was obtained by the concurrent forums. No one factor is necessarily determinative; a carefully considered judgment taking into account both the obligation to exercise jurisdiction and the combination of factors counselling against that exercise is required. Only the clearest of justifications will warrant dismissal.

Turning to the present case, a number of factors clearly counsel against concurrent federal proceedings. The most important of these is the McCarran Amendment itself. The clear federal policy evinced by that legislation is the avoidance of piecemeal adjudication of water rights in a river system. This policy is akin to that underlying the rule requiring that jurisdiction be yielded to the court first acquiring control of property, for the concern in such instances is with avoiding the generation of additional litigation through permitting inconsistent dispositions of property. This concern is heightened with respect to water rights, the relationships among which are highly interdependent. Indeed, we have recognized that actions seeking the allocation of water essentially involve the disposition of property and are best conducted in unified proceedings. The consent to jurisdiction given by the McCarran Amendment bespeaks a policy that recognizes the availability of comprehensive state systems for adjudication of water rights as the means for achieving these goals.

As has already been observed, the Colorado Water Rights Determination and Administration Act established such a system for the adjudication and management of rights to the use of the State's waters. As the Government concedes and as this Court recognized in Eagle County and Water Div. 5, the Act established a single continuous proceeding for water rights adjudication which antedated the suit in [the federal court]. That proceeding "reaches all claims, perhaps month by month but inclusively in the totality." Additionally, the responsibility of managing the State's waters, to the end that they be allocated in accordance with adjudicated water rights, is given to the State Engineer.

Beyond the congressional policy expressed by the McCarran Amendment and consistent with furtherance of that policy, we also find significant (a) the apparent absence of any proceedings in the District Court, other than the filing of the complaint, prior to the motion to dismiss, (b) the extensive involvement of state water rights occasioned by this suit naming 1,000 defendants, (c) the 300-mile distance between the District Court in Denver and the court in Division 7, and (d) the existing participation by the Government in Division 4, 5, and 6 proceedings. We emphasize, however, that we do not overlook the heavy obligation to exercise jurisdiction. We need not decide, for example, whether, despite the McCarran Amendment, dismissal would be warranted if more extensive proceedings had occurred in the District Court prior to dismissal, if the involvement of state water rights were less extensive than it is here, or if the state proceeding were in some respect inadequate to resolve the federal claims. But the opposing factors here, particularly the policy underlying the McCarran Amendment, justify the District Court's dismissal in this particular case.

It is so ordered.

Notes & Questions

1. What underlying purpose of the McCarran Amendment does the Court ultimately rely on in making its determination? Given that both Washington and Wyoming placed reserved water rights in a separate phase of adjudication and Montana set up a separate process for such rights, is the Court's concern with "piecemeal" adjudication if reserved rights were addressed in federal court warranted?

2. What factors does the Court find important for determining that the federal court should dismiss the federal lawsuit in favor of the state court general stream adjudication? What factors suggest that this ruling may be unique to the Colorado system of water allocation?
3. Note that a tribe has only once exercised the right of review of a state court decision by the United States Supreme Court referred to in the case.[35] The result in the Wyoming adjudication, in which—prior to the recusal of Justice O'Connor—the Court would have diminished the PIA quantification out of "sensitivity" to existing state-based water rights (discussed in Part IV), shook Indian Country. With the Tribal Supreme Court Project developed in 2001,[36] tribes seek to coordinate appeals to reduce the chances of an unfavorable ruling.
4. Note also that the McCarran Amendment waiver of sovereign immunity covers only the United States, not tribal governments. Thus, a tribal government wishing to represent itself in a state adjudication must move to intervene. Tribes can choose whether they want to intervene in that suit to either: (1) make claims the United States fails to make; and/or (2) independently support the claims filed by the United States; and/or (3) otherwise participate in the adjudication process. What should a tribe consider in deciding whether to intervene?

Exclusivity of State Court Jurisdiction under the McCarran Amendment

The question left open in *Colorado River Water Conservation District v. United States* as to whether the state case must be filed first and, if so, how far into the adjudication the state must be, led to a rush to the courthouse. Legal scholar Jason Robison describes the rush in Wyoming:

> Slightly less than a year passed after the Supreme Court decided *Colorado River* in 1976 before the *Big Horn* adjudication arose.... On January 14, 1977, House Bill 188 was introduced in the Wyoming Legislature [authorizing a general adjudication].... Passing the House and Senate during the following week—without amendment and with literal or virtual unanimity in both chambers—Governor Ed Herschler signed the bill into law as W.S. § 1-37-106 on January 22, 1977. [fn 154: *See also* [Geoffrey O'Gara, What You See in Clear Water: Indians, Whites, and a Battle over Water in the American West (2000).] at 175 (quoting former Wyoming legislator Walt Urbigkit's description of the statute as "the fastest law ever enacted in history.")] ...
>
> Two days after passage of the adjudication statute, Wyoming Attorney General Frank Mendicino filed a complaint pursuant to it on January 24, 1977, in the District Court of the Fifth Judicial District in Washakie County....

35. Wyoming v. United States, 492 U.S. 406 (1989) (Big Horn I).
36. Native American Rights Fund, Tribal Supreme Court Project, https://sct.narf.org/.

... January 24, 1977—Fifth District Judge Harold Joffe issued an order initiating the *Big Horn* adjudication.[37]

The next case answers the question of whether the upholding of the federal court dismissal in *Colorado River Water Conservation District v. United States* is unique to Colorado. Its holding would set the stage for the major adjudications in the western United States in the twentieth century and those ongoing today.

Arizona v. San Carlos Apache Tribe of Arizona

Supreme Court of the United States
463 U.S. 545 (1983)

Justice BRENNAN delivered the opinion of the Court.

These consolidated cases form a sequel to our decision in *Colorado River Conservation District v. United States,* 424 U.S. 800, 96 S.Ct. 1236, 47 L.Ed.2d 483 (1976). That case held that (1) the McCarran Amendment, 43 U.S.C. § 666, which ... waived the sovereign immunity of the United States as to comprehensive state water rights adjudications, provides state courts with jurisdiction to adjudicate Indian water rights held in trust by the United States, and (2) in light of the clear federal policies underlying the McCarran Amendment, a water rights suit brought by the United States in federal court was properly dismissed in favor of a concurrent comprehensive adjudication reaching the same issues in Colorado state court. The [question]s this case are parallel ... (2) If the courts of such States do have jurisdiction to adjudicate Indian water rights, should concurrent federal suits brought by Indian tribes, rather than by the United States, and raising only Indian claims, also be subject to dismissal under the doctrine of *Colorado River?*

...

II

The two petitions considered here arise out of three separate consolidated appeals that were decided within three days of each other by the same panel of the Court of Appeals for the Ninth Circuit. In each of the underlying cases, either the United States as trustee or certain Indian tribes on their own behalf, or both, asserted the right to have certain Indian water rights in Arizona or Montana adjudicated in federal court.

The Montana Cases (No. 81-2188)

In January 1975, the Northern Cheyenne Tribe brought an action in the United States District Court for the District of Montana seeking an adjudication of its rights in certain streams in that State. Shortly thereafter, the United States brought two suits in the same Court, seeking a determination of water rights both on its own behalf and on behalf of a number of Indian Tribes, including the Northern Cheyenne, in the same streams. Each of the federal actions was a general adjudication which sought to

37. Jason A. Robison, *Wyoming's Big Horn General Stream Adjudication,* 15(2) Wyo. L. Rev. 244 at 267–269 (2015).

determine the rights *inter sese* of *all* users of the stream, and not merely the rights of the plaintiffs. On motion of the Northern Cheyenne, its action was consolidated with one of the Government actions. The other concerned Tribes intervened as appropriate.

At about the time that all this activity was taking place in federal court, the State of Montana was preparing to begin a process of comprehensive water adjudication under a recently passed state statute. In July 1975, the Montana Department of Natural Resources and Conservation filed petitions in state court commencing comprehensive proceedings to adjudicate water rights in the same streams at issue in the federal cases.

...

... In reaching this conclusion, the court relied in part on the infancy of both the federal and state proceedings in the Montana litigation, the possible inadequacy of the state proceedings (which it did not discuss in great detail), and the fact that the Indians (who could not be joined involuntarily in the state proceedings) might not be adequately represented by the United States in state court in light of conflicts of interest between the Federal Government's responsibilities as trustee and its own claims to water.

The Arizona Cases (No. 81-2147)

In the mid-1970s, various water rights claimants in Arizona filed petitions in state court to initiate general adjudications to determine conflicting rights in a number of river systems. In early 1979, process was served in one of the proceedings on approximately 12,000 known potential water claimants, including the United States. In July 1981, process was served in another proceeding on approximately 58,000 known water claimants, again including the United States. In each case, the United States was joined both in its independent capacity and as trustee for various Indian tribes.

In March and April of 1979, a number of Indian tribes whose rights were implicated by the state water proceedings filed a series of suits in the United States District Court for the District of Arizona, asking variously for removal of the state adjudications to federal court, declaratory and injunctive relief preventing any further adjudication of their rights in state court, and independent federal determinations of their water rights. A number of defendants in the federal proceedings filed motions seeking remand or dismissal....

...

We granted certiorari ...

III

A

At the outset of our analysis, a number of propositions are clear. First, the federal courts had jurisdiction here to hear the suits brought both by the United States and the Indian tribes. Second, it is also clear in this case, as it was in *Colorado River,* that a dismissal or stay of the federal suits would have been improper if there was no jurisdiction in the concurrent state actions to adjudicate the claims at issue in the federal suits....

...

IV

The second crucial issue in these cases is whether our analysis in *Colorado River* applies with full force to federal suits brought by Indian tribes, rather than by the United States, and seeking adjudication only of Indian water rights....

The United States and the various Indian respondents raise a series of arguments why dismissal or stay of the federal suit is not appropriate when it is brought by an Indian tribe and only seeks to adjudicate Indian rights. (1) Indian rights have traditionally been left free of interference from the States. (2) State courts may be inhospitable to Indian rights. (3) The McCarran Amendment, although it waived United States sovereign immunity in state comprehensive water adjudications, did not waive *Indian* sovereign immunity. It is therefore unfair to force Indian claimants to choose between waiving their sovereign immunity by intervening in the state proceedings and relying on the United States to represent their interests in state court, particularly in light of the frequent conflict of interest between Indian claims and other federal interests and the right of the Indians under 28 U.S.C. § 1362 to bring suit on their own behalf in federal court. (4) Indian water rights claims are generally based on federal rather than state law. (5) Because Indian water claims are based on the doctrine of "reserved rights," and take priority over most water rights created by state law, they need not as a practical matter be adjudicated *inter sese* with other water rights, and could simply be incorporated into the comprehensive state decree at the conclusion of the state proceedings.

Each of these arguments has a good deal of force. We note, though, that very similar arguments were raised and rejected in *Eagle County* and *Colorado River.* More important, all of these arguments founder on one crucial fact: If the state proceedings have jurisdiction over the Indian water rights at issue here, as appears to be the case, then concurrent federal proceedings are likely to be duplicative and wasteful, generating "additional litigation through permitting inconsistent dispositions of property." *Colorado River,* 424 U.S., at 819. Moreover, since a judgment by either court would ordinarily be res judicata in the other, the existence of such concurrent proceedings creates the serious potential for spawning an unseemly and destructive race to see which forum can resolve the same issues first—a race contrary to the entire spirit of the McCarran Amendment and prejudicial, to say the least, to the possibility of reasoned decision making by either forum. The United States and many of the Indian tribes recognize these concerns, but in responding to them they cast aside the sort of sound argument generally apparent in the rest of their submissions and rely instead on vague statements of faith and hope. The United States, for example, states that adjudicating Indian water right rights in federal court, despite the existence of a comprehensive state proceeding, would not

> "entail any duplication or potential for inconsistent judgments. The federal court will quantify the Indian rights only if it is asked to do so before the State court has embarked on the task. And, of course, once the United States district court has indicated its determination to perform that limited role, *we assume*

> the State tribunal will turn its attention to the typically more complex business of adjudicating all other claims on the stream. *In the usual case,* the federal court will have completed its function earlier and its quantification will simply be incorporated in the comprehensive State court decree." Brief for the United States 30 (emphasis added).

Similarly, the Navajo Nation states:

> "There is no reasonably foreseeable danger that [the federal action brought by the Navajo] will duplicate or delay state proceedings or waste judicial resources. While the Navajo claim proceeds in federal court, the state court *can* move forward to assess, quantify, and rank the 58,000 state claims. The Navajo federal action will be concluded long before the state court has finished its task." Brief for the Navajo Nation 22 (emphasis added; footnote omitted).

The problem with these scenarios, however, is that they assume a cooperative attitude on the part of state courts, state legislatures, and state parties which is neither legally required nor realistically always to be expected. The state courts need not "turn their attention" to other matters if they are prompted by state parties to adjudicate the Indian claims first. Moreover, considering the specialized resources and experience of the state courts, it is not at all obvious that the federal actions "will be concluded long before" the state courts have issued at least preliminary judgments on the question of Indian water rights.

...

The McCarran Amendment, as interpreted in *Colorado River,* allows and encourages state courts to undertake the task of quantifying Indian water rights in the course of comprehensive water adjudications. Although adjudication of those rights in federal court instead might in the abstract be practical, and even wise, it will be neither practical nor wise as long as it creates the possibility of duplicative litigation, tension and controversy between the federal and state forums, hurried and pressured decision making, and confusion over the disposition of property rights.

Colorado River, of course, does not require that a federal water suit must always be dismissed or stayed in deference to a concurrent and adequate comprehensive state adjudication. Certainly, the federal courts need not defer to the state proceedings if the state courts expressly agree to stay their own consideration of the issues raised in the federal action pending disposition of that action. Moreover, it may be in a particular case that, at the time a motion to dismiss is filed, the federal suit at issue is well enough along that its dismissal would itself constitute a waste of judicial resources and an invitation to duplicative effort.... Finally, we do not deny that, in a case in which the arguments for and against deference to the state adjudication were otherwise closely matched, the fact that a federal suit was brought by Indians on their own behalf and sought only to adjudicate Indian rights should be figured into the balance. But the most important consideration in *Colorado River,* and the most important consideration in any federal water suit concurrent to a comprehensive state proceeding, must be the "policy underlying the McCarran Amendment," ... and, despite the strong arguments raised by the respondents, we cannot conclude that water rights suits brought by Indians and seeking adjudication only of Indian rights should be excepted from the application of that policy or from the general principles set out in *Colorado River.* In the cases before us, assuming that the state adjudications are adequate to quantify the rights at issue in the federal suits, and taking into account the McCarran Amendment policies we have just discussed, the expertise and administrative machinery available to the state courts, the infancy of the federal suits, the general judicial bias against piecemeal litigation, and the convenience to the parties, we must conclude that the District Courts were correct in deferring to the state proceedings.

V

Nothing we say today should be understood to represent even the slightest retreat from the general proposition we expressed so recently in *New Mexico v. Mescalero Apache Tribe*: "Because of their sovereign status, [Indian] tribes and their reservation lands are insulated in some respects by an 'historic immunity from state and local control,' ...

We also emphasize, as we did in *Colorado River,* that our decision in no way changes the substantive law by which Indian rights in state water adjudications must be judged. State courts, as much as federal courts, have a solemn obligation to follow federal law. Moreover, any state court decision alleged to abridge Indian water rights protected by federal law can expect to receive, if brought for review before this Court, a particularized and exacting scrutiny commensurate with the powerful federal interest in safeguarding those rights from state encroachment.

The judgments of the Court of Appeals in each of these cases is reversed and the cases are remanded for further proceedings consistent with this opinion.

So ordered.

Justice MARSHALL, dissenting.

In *Colorado River Water Conservation District v. United States,* 424 U.S. 800, 96 S.Ct. 1236, 47 L.Ed.2d 483 (1976), this Court recognized a narrow rule of abstention governing controversies involving federal water rights. We stated that in light of "the virtually unflagging obligation of the federal courts to exercise the jurisdiction given them," *id.,* at 817, 96 S.Ct., at 1246, "[o]nly the clearest of justifications," *id.,* at 819, 96 S.Ct., at 1247, will warrant abstention in favor of a concurrent state proceeding. Substantially for the reasons set forth in Justice STEVENS' dissenting opinion, I believe that abstention is not appropriate in these cases. Unlike the federal suit in *Colorado River,* the suits here are brought by Indian tribes on their own behalf. These cases thus implicate the strong congressional policy, embodied in 28 U.S.C. § 1362, of affording Indian tribes a federal forum....

Justice STEVENS, with whom Justice BLACKMUN joins, dissenting.

"Nothing in the McCarran Amendment or in its legislative history can be read as limiting the jurisdiction of the federal courts." *Colorado River Water Conservation Dis-*

trict v. United States, 424 U.S. 800, 821, n. 2, 96 S.Ct. 1236, 1248, n. 2, 47 L.Ed.2d 483 (1976) (Stewart, J., dissenting)....

...

Federal adjudication of Indian water rights would not fragment an otherwise unified state court proceeding. Since Indian reserved claims are wholly dissimilar to state-law water claims, and since their amount does not depend on the total volume of water available in the water source or on the quantity of competing claims, it will be necessary to conduct separate proceedings to determine these claims even if the adjudication takes place in state court....

To justify virtual abandonment of Indian water rights claims to the state courts, the majority relies heavily on *Colorado River Water Conservation District, supra,* which in turn discovered an affirmative policy of federal judicial abdication in the McCarran Amendment. I continue to believe that *Colorado River* read more into that amendment than Congress intended, and cannot acquiesce in an extension of its reasoning....

Although in some respects Indian tribes' water claims are similar to other reserved federal water rights, different treatment is justified. States and their citizens may well be more antagonistic toward Indian reserved rights than other federal reserved rights, both because the former are potentially greater in quantity and because they provide few direct or indirect benefits to non-Indian residents. Indians have historically enjoyed a unique relationship with the federal government, reflecting the tribes' traditional sovereign status, their treaty-based right to federal protection, and their special economic problems....

One important aspect of the special relationship is 28 U.S.C. § 1362, which embodies a federal promise that Indian tribes will be able to invoke the jurisdiction of federal courts to resolve matters in controversy arising under federal law. Congress thereby assured Indians a neutral federal forum—a guarantee whose importance should not be underestimated. The Senate report noted,

> "There is great hesitancy on the part of tribes to use State courts. This reluctance is founded partially on the traditional fear that tribes have had of the States in which their reservations are situated. Additionally, the Federal courts have more expertise in deciding questions involving treaties with the Federal Government, as well as interpreting the relevant body of Federal law that has developed over the years." S.Rep. No. 1507, 89th Cong., 2d Sess. 2 (1966).
>
> Section 1362 also assured the tribes that they need not rely on the federal government to protect their interests, an important safeguard in light of the undeniable potential for conflicts of interest between Indian claims and other federal Government claims.

...

In my view, a federal court whose jurisdiction is invoked in a timely manner by an Indian tribe has a duty to determine the existence and extent of the tribe's reserved water rights under federal law. It is inappropriate to stay or dismiss such federal court proceedings in order to allow determinations by state courts.

. . .

Notes & Questions

1. What are the primary reasons given by the Court to extend *Colorado River* to situations in which the state adjudication and the federal court case are filed at roughly the same time? How do the dissenters view this differently?
2. What remedy does the Court point to for any problems with the outcome of the state adjudication?

The Federal Duty to Protect Tribal Water Rights

In the next Chapter you will learn about both the litigation and settlement that has taken place since the ruling in *San Carlos*. But first, we turn to a recent ruling on the nature of the federal duty to protect tribal water rights, *Arizona v. Navajo Nation*.[38] We include it here because it is so patently inconsistent with the ruling that the United States may be joined in a state adjudication for the purposes of representing tribal water rights despite the fact that the McCarran Amendment does not waive the immunity of the tribes.

Recall from *Colorado River Conservation District* in this Chapter and from Part III, that tribal reserved water rights, like tribal lands and other appurtenant natural resources, are owned by the United States in trust for the benefit of Indian tribes. This is the basis for allowing the federal government to speak for the tribal water rights in an adjudication. Also recall from *Nevada v. United States*, Chapter 11, that while the Court in that case did not find the fiduciary duty of the federal government to assert the water rights of the Tribe to outweigh the principles in favor of a final decree, it nevertheless found that duty to exists and to differ from that of a private fiduciary only in the area of conflict of interest (in that case the United States had been called on to represent the conflicting interests of the Pyramid Lake Paiute, and the water users drawing water from a Reclamation project.) A full explanation of the source of the federal trust responsibility is beyond the scope of this text. It is also a responsibility that the United States undertook in consideration of the billions of acres of land that were given up by tribes across the United States, a factor of importance in the case. In a recent report detailing the obligations of the federal government with respect to the fishing rights of Tribes on the Columbia River, the Department of the Interior states:

> The United States, "as a trustee for the Tribes, has a responsibility to protect their rights and resources." This means that each agency must "respect Indian

38. 599 U.S. 555 (2023)

> [T]ribal self-government and sovereignty, honor [T]ribal treaty and other rights, and strive to meet the responsibilities that arise from the unique legal relationship between the Federal Government and Indian [T]ribal governments." These responsibilities adhere to express and implied rights and "extend to any federal government action." [citations omitted][39]

The recent case of *Arizona v. Navajo Nation* demonstrates the United States' difficulty in properly balancing its duty to Indian tribes with its other responsibilities. It also demonstrates how the Supreme Court has struggled to hold the United States to its word. The history of the Navajo Treaty is long and complex, but best summed up by Justice Gorsuch in his dissent from the case:

> For centuries, the Navajo inhabited a stretch of land in "present-day northwestern New Mexico, northeastern Arizona, and the San Juan drainage beyond." J. Kessell, General Sherman and the Navajo Treaty of 1868: A Basic and Expedient Misunderstanding, 12 W. Hist. Q. 251, 253 (1981) (Kessell). This ancestral home was framed by "four mountains and four rivers" the Tribe considered sacred. Treaty Between the United States of America and the Navajo Tribe of Indians, With a Record of the Discussions That Led to Its Signing 2 (1968) (Treaty Record); see also E. Rosser, Ahistorical Indians and Reservation Resources, 40 Env. L. 437, 445 (2010). There, tribal members "planted their subsistence crops," "hunted and gathered," and "r[an] their livestock" over the plains.
>
> In the 1860s, that way of life changed forever. In the aftermath of the Mexican-American War—and following a period of rapid westward expansion—the United States found itself embroiled in a series of bitter conflicts with the Navajo. *** Before all was said and done, "the Navajo had to be literally starved into surrender." "[T]housands of U. S. troops roamed the Navajo [Country] destroying everything the Navajo could use; every field, storehouse, and hut was burned." Ibid. The campaign was "brief, blunt, and, when combined with a particularly difficult winter," effective. By the winter of 1863–1864, most of the Navajo had surrendered.
>
> That period of violence led to "the Long Walk." In truth, it was not one walk but many—over 53 separate incidents, according to some. Id., at 52. In each case, federal officers rounded up tribal members, "[h]erded [them] into columns," and marched them hundreds of miles from their home. "Many died en route, some shot by the souldiers." As one Navajo later recounted, people were killed "'on the spot if they sa[id] they [were] tired or sick or if they stop[ped] to help someone.'" Still "[o]thers fell victim to slavers with the full complicity of the U. S. officials."

39. Department of the Interior, *Historic and Ongoing Impacts of Federal Dams on the Columbia River Basin Tribes* (June 2024) at 19, https://www.doi.gov/libraries/pdf.js/web/viewer.html?file=https%3A%2F%2Fwww.doi.gov%2Fsites%2Fdefault%2Ffiles%2Fdocuments%2F2024-06%2Ftribal-circumstances-analysis.pdf.

Those who survived wound up at "a destination that surpassed their fears." Bosque Redondo was just what the officers had warned: a "semiarid, alkaline, fuel-stingy, insect-infested environment." And, just as they predicted, water proved a serious issue. The Tribe was forced to rely on a "'little stream winding through an immense plain.'" But its "water was bad." No surprise, then, that "[o]nly half the land under cultivation at the Bosque was productive." Ibid. No surprise either that even the productive land yielded "one disastrous crop failure after another." Further feeding the crisis, [the United States] "badly underestimated the number of Navajos who would end up at the Bosque Redondo." All told, the relocation proved a "catastrophe for the Navajo; 2,000 died there in four years."

"By 1868 even the U.S. government could see" that the present conditions could not persist. So it set out to relocate the Navajo once more. To that end, the United States sent members of the Indian Peace Commission to negotiate a new treaty with the Tribe. Led by General William Tecumseh Sherman, the Commission disfavored allowing the Navajo to return to their homeland. Doing that, the Commission feared, risked rekindling old hostilities. So Sherman tried to persuade the Navajo to relocate someplace else. Understanding the importance of water to the Navajo, he offered them assurances that other locations would have "plenty of water." Treaty Record 5.

The Navajo would have none of it. Their lead negotiator, Barboncito, refused to "go to any other country except [his] own." Any place else, he said, could "turn out another Bosque Redondo." "[O]utside [our] own country," Barboncito told Sherman, "we cannot raise a crop, but in it we can raise a crop almost anywhere." "[W]e know this land does not like us," he said of Bosque Redondo, and "neither does the water." Along the way, he spoke of "the heart of Navajo country," which he described as including a place where "the water flows in abundance." In the end, "[t]he will of the Navajos—personified in the intense resolve of Barboncito," won out. Sherman came to realize that, if he left the Navajo at Bosque Redondo, the dire conditions—including "'the foul character of [the] water'"—would eventually induce them to drift away from the encampment. And the Navajo flatly refused to move to some other unfamiliar place.

***

In the end, the Treaty of 1868 provided the Navajo less land per capita—two-thirds less—than the other Tribes the Indian Peace Commission would go on to negotiate with. It seems that owed, in no small part, to the negotiators' understanding that the Navajo had "already experienced irrigation agriculture" and could plausibly get by with less. Indeed, when providing instructions to the Indian Peace Commission about how they should negotiate with the Navajo, the Secretary of the Interior discussed the possibility of agriculture as bearing on the appropriate size of the Tribe's reservation. Unlike the

Navajo, he thought, "'[w]ild Indians cannot at once be transformed into farmers. They must pass through the intermediate stage of herdsmen. They must first become pastoral, then agricultural.'"

***

Fast forward to the present. Today, the Navajo Reservation has become "the largest Indian reservation in the United States," with over "17 million acres," and over "300,000 members." Its western boundary runs alongside a vast stretch of the Colorado River. Yet even today, water remains a precious resource. "Members of the Navajo Nation use around 7 gallons of water per day for all of their household needs"—less than one-tenth the amount the average American household uses. In some parts of the reservation, as much as 91% of Navajo households "lack access to water."

That deficit owes in part to the fact that no one has ever assessed what water rights the Navajo possess. For instance, "[a]lthough the Navajo Reservation is adjacent to the Colorado River, the Navajo Nation's rights to use water from the Colorado River" have never been adjudicated. The United States acknowledges that it holds certain water rights "in trust" for the Navajo. It does not dispute that it exercises considerable control over the disposition of water from the Colorado River. And it concedes that the Navajo's water rights "may ... include some portion of the mainstream of the Colorado." But instead of resolving what the Navajo's water rights might be, the United States has sometimes resisted efforts to answer that question.

The current legal regime governing the Colorado River began with a 1922 interstate compact between seven States. That agreement split the Colorado into two basins—an Upper Basin and a Lower Basin. The compact answered some high-level questions about which States could lay claim to which sections of the river. But it did not purport to "affec[t] the obligations of the United States of America to Indian [T]ribes." In that way, it left the Navajo with no insight into what water they could claim as their own.

Six years later, Congress entered the picture by passing the Boulder Canyon Project Act. That Act had a profound impact on the Lower Basin. It authorized the construction of the Hoover Dam and the creation of Lake Mead. More than that, it gave the Secretary of the Interior substantial power to divvy up the resulting impounded water. Failing agreement among the States in the region, the law authorized the Secretary to enter into contracts for the delivery of water and provided that "[n]o person" may have water from the mainstream of the Colorado in the Lower Basin "except by contract." In adopting this law, Congress hoped "to put an end to the long-standing dispute over Colorado River waters."

Reality never quite caught up to the law's ambitions. After an agreement among the States failed to emerge and the Secretary began issuing contracts to various users, Arizona in 1952 brought an original action in this Court against California seeking a declaration of its water rights in the Lower Basin. Several other States intervened. So did the United States. In doing so, the federal government claimed the need to "protect federal interests, including the rights of the Navajo Nation and twenty-four other Indian [T]ribes in the Lower Basin." As the litigation unfolded, however, the Navajo began to worry that the United States did not have their best interests in mind. In 1956, the Navajo Nation sought leave to file (along with six other Tribes) a motion seeking "to define the scope of the representation of the [T]ribes by the United States" and objecting to what they considered a "lack of effective representation and [a] conflict of interest." That motion was denied.

Proceeding without the Navajo, this Court referred the litigation to a Special Master. In time, the Special Master prepared a report and recommendation that omitted any mention of the Tribe. In response, the Navajo wrote to the Attorney General. They asked the United States to object to the Special Master's report on their behalf. The Navajo say they never received a response. For its part, the United States eventually did object—but not on the grounds the Navajo sought.

Having seen enough, the Navajo in 1961 moved to intervene. They "argued that the United States had failed to vigorously assert" their interests. More than that, the Tribe contended, the United States had "'abandoned the case so far as the adjudication of the rights of the Navajo Indians [was] concerned.'" The United States opposed the Tribe's motion. On its view, it had already "'undertaken representation of the interests of several Indian [T]ribes,'" so there was no need for the Court to hear from the Navajo. In any event, the United States assured the Court, it would continue to apply "'considerations of justice'" in its dealings with the Tribe. The government conceded, however, "no evidence had been submitted on behalf of the Navajo Nation for uses from the mainstream." And it conceded that "such evidence would have had to be submitted in order for the Court to consider the issue of the Navajo Nation's rights to the mainstream." As with their previous attempts to make their voices heard in the litigation, the Navajo's motion to intervene was denied.

In 1964, the litigation Arizona initiated more than a decade earlier culminated in a decree. See Arizona v. California, 376 U. S. 340. It allocated the Lower Basin Colorado River mainstream among various parties—including five other Tribes whose interests the United States did assert. The decree also permitted the federal government to release water pursuant to certain "valid contracts" and applicable federal laws. But the Tribe's rights remained in limbo. The United States never asserted any rights on the Navajo's behalf; the Navajo never received an opportunity to assert them for themselves. Since 1964, the decree governing the Lower Basin has been modified at various points. But it has never been modified to address the Navajo.

In the intervening years, the Navajo have asked the federal government—repeatedly—to assess their rights in the mainstream of the Colorado. In response to those inquiries, the Tribe received a letter from the Department of the Interior indicating that the Department still had not made "any decisions" about what water rights, if any, the Navajo may have in the river. The Department posited that figuring that out would be a "somewhat lengthy process," one that had "yet to be initiated."

Unwilling to wait indefinitely, the Navajo eventually filed this suit. In it, the Navajo sought "injunctive and declaratory relief to compel the Federal Defendants to determine the water required to meet the needs of the Nation's lands in Arizona and devise a plan to meet those needs to fulfill the promise of the United States to make the Nation's Reservation lands a permanent homeland for the Navajo people." In other words, the Tribe asked the United States to assess what water rights it holds in trust on the Tribe's behalf pursuant to the Treaty of 1868. And if it turns out the United States has misappropriated those water rights, the Tribe wants the federal government to come up with a plan to set things right.

Arizona v. Navajo Nation

United States Supreme Court
599 U.S. 555 (2023)

Justice Kavanaugh delivered the opinion of the Court.

[The facts are described in the dissenting opinion and excerpted above.]

....

The question in this suit concerns "reserved water rights"—a shorthand for the water rights implicitly reserved to accomplish the purpose of the reservation. The Navajos' claim is not that the United States has interfered with their water access. Instead, the Navajos contend that the treaty requires the United States to take affirmative steps to secure water for the Navajos—for example, by assessing the Tribe's water needs, developing a plan to secure the needed water, and potentially building pipelines, pumps, wells, or other water infrastructure—either to facilitate better access to water on the reservation or to transport off-reservation water onto the reservation. In light of the treaty's text and history, we conclude that the treaty does not require the United States to take those affirmative steps. And it is not the Judiciary's role to rewrite and update this 155-year-old treaty. Rather, Congress and the President may enact—and often have enacted—laws to assist the citizens of the western United States, including the Navajos, with their water needs.

I

....

Under the 1868 treaty, the Navajo Reservation includes not only the land within the boundaries of the reservation, but also water rights. Under this Court's longstanding reserved water rights doctrine, sometimes referred to as the *Winters* doctrine, the Federal Government's reservation of land for an Indian tribe also implicitly reserves the right to use needed water from various sources—such as groundwater, rivers, streams, lakes, and springs—that arise on, border, cross, underlie, or are encompassed within the reservation. Under the *Winters* doctrine, the Federal Government reserves water only "to the extent needed to accomplish the purpose of the reservation."

The Navajo Reservation lies almost entirely within the Colorado River Basin, and three vital rivers—the Colorado, the Little Colorado, and the San Juan—border the reservation. To meet their water needs for household, agricultural, industrial, and commercial purposes, the Navajos obtain water from rivers, tributaries, springs, lakes, and aquifers on the reservation.

Much of the western United States is arid. Water has long been scarce, and the problem is getting worse. From 2000 through 2022, the region faced the driest 23-year period in more than a century and one of the driest periods in the last 1,200 years. And the situation is expected to grow more severe in future years. So even though the Navajo Reservation encompasses numerous water sources and the Tribe has the right to use needed water from those sources, the Navajos face the same water scarcity problem that many in the western United States face.

Over the decades, the Federal Government has taken various steps to assist the people in the western States with their water needs. The Solicitor General explains that, for the Navajo Tribe in particular, the Federal Government has secured hundreds of thousands of acre-feet of water and authorized billions of dollars for water infrastructure on the Navajo Reservation.

In the Navajos' view, however, those efforts did not fully satisfy the United States's obligations under the 1868 treaty. The Navajos therefore sued the U. S. Department of the Interior, the Bureau of Indian Affairs, and other federal parties. As relevant here, the Navajos asserted a breach-of-trust claim arising out of the 1868 treaty and sought to "compel the Federal Defendants to determine the water required to meet the needs" of the Navajos in Arizona and to "devise a plan to meet those needs." The States of Arizona, Nevada, and Colorado intervened against the Tribe to protect those States' interests in water from the Colorado River.

According to the Navajos, the United States must do more than simply not interfere with the reserved water rights. The Tribe argues that the United States also must take affirmative steps to secure water for the Tribe—including by assessing the Tribe's water needs, developing a plan to secure the needed water, and potentially building pipelines, pumps, wells, or other water infrastructure.

The U. S. District Court for the District of Arizona dismissed the Navajo Tribe's complaint. In relevant part, the District Court determined that the 1868 treaty did not impose a duty on the United States to take affirmative steps to secure water for the

Tribe. The U. S. Court of Appeals for the Ninth Circuit reversed, holding in relevant part that the United States has a duty under the 1868 treaty to take affirmative steps to secure water for the Navajos. This Court granted certiorari.

II

When the United States establishes a tribal reservation, the reservation generally includes (among other things) the land, the minerals below the land's surface, the timber on the land, and the right to use needed water on the reservation, referred to as reserved water rights. Each of those rights is a stick in the bundle of property rights that makes up a reservation.

This suit involves water. To help meet their water needs, the Navajos obtain water from, among other sources, rivers, tributaries, springs, lakes, and aquifers on the reservation. As relevant here, the Navajos do not contend that the United States has interfered with their access to water. Rather, the Navajos argue that the United States must take affirmative steps to secure water for the Tribe—for example, by assessing the Tribe's water needs, developing a plan to secure the needed water, and potentially building pipelines, pumps, wells, or other water infrastructure.

The Tribe asserts a breach-of-trust claim. To maintain such a claim here, the Tribe must establish, among other things, that the text of a treaty, statute, or regulation imposed certain duties on the United States. The Federal Government owes judicially enforceable duties to a tribe "only to the extent it expressly accepts those responsibilities." Jicarilla, 564 U. S., at 177. Whether the Government has expressly accepted such obligations "must train on specific rights-creating or duty-imposing" language in a treaty, statute, or regulation. Navajo Nation, 537 U. S., at 506. That requirement follows from separation of powers principles. As this Court recognized in Jicarilla, Congress and the President exercise the "sovereign function" of organizing and managing "the Indian trust relationship." 564 U. S., at 175. So the federal courts in turn must adhere to the text of the relevant law—here, the treaty.[40]

In the Tribe's view, the 1868 treaty imposed a duty on the United States to take affirmative steps to secure water for the Navajos. With respect, the Tribe is incorrect. The 1868 treaty "set apart" a reservation for the "use and occupation of the Navajo tribe." 15 Stat. 668. But it contained no "rights-creating or duty-imposing" language that imposed a duty on the United States to take affirmative steps to secure water for the Tribe.

---

40. [1] The Navajos have suggested that the Jicarilla line of cases might apply only in the context of claims seeking damages from the United States pursuant to the Tucker Act and Indian Tucker Act. See 28 U. S. C. §§ 1491, 1505; see also Brief for Navajo Nation 29. But Jicarilla's framework for determining the trust obligations of the United States applies to any claim seeking to impose trust duties on the United States, including claims seeking equitable relief. That is because Jicarilla's reasoning rests upon separation of powers principles—not on the particulars of the Tucker Acts. As Jicarilla explains, the United States is a sovereign, not a private trustee, and therefore the trust obligations of the United States to the Indian tribes are established and governed by treaty, statute, or regulation, rather than by the common law of trusts. See 564 U. S., at 165, 177. Stated otherwise, the trust obligations of the United States to the Indian tribes are established by Congress and the Executive, not created by the Judiciary.

Notably, the 1868 treaty did impose a number of specific duties on the United States. *** But the treaty said nothing about any affirmative duty for the United States to secure water. And as this Court has stated, "Indian treaties cannot be rewritten or expanded beyond their clear terms." So it is here.

***

To be sure, this Court's precedents have stated that the United States maintains a general trust relationship with Indian tribes, including the Navajos. But as the Solicitor General explains, the United States is a sovereign, not a private trustee, meaning that "Congress may style its relations with the Indians a trust without assuming all the fiduciary duties of a private trustee, creating a trust relationship that is limited or bare compared to a trust relationship between private parties at common law." Therefore, unless Congress has created a conventional trust relationship with a tribe as to a particular trust asset, this Court will not "apply common-law trust principles" to infer duties not found in the text of a treaty, statute, or regulation. Here, nothing in the 1868 treaty establishes a conventional trust relationship with respect to water.

In short, the 1868 treaty did not impose a duty on the United States to take affirmative steps to secure water for the Tribe—including the steps requested by the Navajos here, such as determining the water needs of the Tribe, providing an accounting, or developing a plan to secure the needed water.

....

III

The Navajo Tribe advances several other arguments in support of its claim that the 1868 treaty requires the United States to take affirmative steps to secure water for the Navajos. None is persuasive.

First, the Navajos note that the text of the 1868 treaty established the Navajo Reservation as a "permanent home." 15 Stat. 671. In the Tribe's view, that language means that the United States agreed to take affirmative steps to secure water. But that assertion finds no support in the treaty's text or history, or in any of this Court's precedents. The 1868 treaty granted a reservation to the Navajos and imposed a variety of specific obligations on the United States—for example, building schools and a chapel, providing teachers, and supplying seeds and agricultural implements. The reservation contains a number of water sources that the Navajos have used and continue to rely on. But as explained above, the 1868 treaty imposed no duty on the United States to take affirmative steps to secure water for the Tribe. The 1868 treaty, as demonstrated by its text and history, helped to ensure that the Navajos could return to their original land.

***

[T]he Navajos [also] refer to the lengthy Colorado River water rights litigation that unfolded in a series of cases decided by this Court from the 1960s to the early 2000s, and they note that the United States once opposed the intervention of the Navajos in that litigation. The Navajos point to the United States's opposition as evidence that the United States has control over the reserved water rights. According to the Navajos, the United States's purported control supports their view that the United States owes trust duties to the Navajos. But the "Federal Government's liability" on a breach-of-trust claim "cannot be premised on control alone." United States v. Navajo Nation, 556 U. S. 287, 301 (2009). Again, the Federal Government must "expressly accep[t]" trust responsibilities in a treaty, statute, or regulation that contains "rights-creating or duty-imposing" language. The Navajos have not identified anything of the sort. In addition, the Navajos may be able to assert the interests they claim in water rights litigation, including by seeking to intervene in cases that affect their claimed interests, and courts will then assess the Navajos' claims and motions as appropriate.

[T]he Tribe argues that, in 1868, the Navajos would have understood the treaty to mean that the United States must take affirmative steps to secure water for the Tribe. But the text of the treaty says nothing to that effect. And the historical record does not suggest that the United States agreed to undertake affirmative efforts to secure water for the Navajos—any more than the United States agreed to farm land, mine minerals, harvest timber, build roads, or construct bridges on the reservation. The record of the treaty negotiations makes no mention of any water-related obligations of the United States at all.[41]

* * *

The 1868 treaty reserved necessary water to accomplish the purpose of the Navajo Reservation. See *Winters v. United States*, 207 U. S. 564, 576–577 (1908). But the treaty did not require the United States to take affirmative steps to secure water for the Tribe. We reverse the judgment of the U. S. Court of Appeals for the Ninth Circuit.

It is so ordered.

Justice Gorsuch, with whom Justice Sotomayor, Justice Kagan, and Justice Jackson join, dissenting.

Today, the Court rejects a request the Navajo Nation never made. This case is not about compelling the federal government to take "affirmative steps to secure water for the Navajos." Respectfully, the relief the Tribe seeks is far more modest. Everyone agrees the Navajo received enforceable water rights by treaty. Everyone agrees the United States holds some of those water rights in trust on the Tribe's behalf. And everyone agrees the extent of those rights has never been assessed. Adding those pieces together, the Navajo have a simple ask: They want the United States to identify the water rights it holds for them. And if the United States has misappropriated the Navajo's water rights, the Tribe asks it to formulate a plan to stop doing so prospectively. Because there is

41. [4] The intervenor States separately argue that the Navajo Tribe's claimed remedies with respect to the Lower Colorado River would interfere with this Court's decree in Arizona v. California, 547 U. S. 150 (2006). The question of whether certain remedies would violate the substance of this Court's 2006 decree is a merits question, not a question of subject-matter jurisdiction. Because we conclude that the treaty imposes no duty on the United States to take affirmative steps to secure water in the first place, we need not reach the question of whether particular remedies would conflict with this Court's 2006 decree.

nothing remarkable about any of this, I would affirm the Ninth Circuit's judgment and allow the Navajo's case to proceed.

***

...

For our purposes today, that leaves just one question: Can the Tribe state a legally cognizable claim for relief asking the United States to assess what water rights they have? Not even the federal government seriously disputes that it acts "as a fiduciary" of the Tribes with respect to tribal waters it manages. *Arizona II*, 460 U.S., at 627–628. Indeed, when it comes to the Navajo, the United States freely admits that it holds certain water rights for the Tribe "in trust." And of course, that must be so given that the United States exercises pervasive control over much water in the area, including in the adjacent Colorado River.

Those observations suffice to resolve today's dispute. As we have seen, that exact coupling—a fiduciary relationship to a specific group and complete managerial control over the property of that group—gives rise to a duty to account. The United States, we know, must act in a "legally [a]dequate" way when it comes to the Navajo's water it holds in trust. It follows, as the United States concedes, that the federal government could not "legally" dam off the water flowing to their Reservation, as doing so would "interfere with [the Tribe's] exercise of their" water rights. Implicit in that concession is another. Because *Winters* rights belong to the Navajo themselves, the United States cannot lawfully divert them elsewhere—just as a lawyer cannot dispose of a client's property entrusted to him without permission. And the only way to ensure compliance with that obligation is to give the Tribe just what they request—an assessment of the water rights the federal government holds on the Tribe's behalf.

III

The Court does not dispute most of this. It agrees that the Navajo enjoy "water rights implicitly reserved to accomplish the purpose of the reservation." It agrees that the United States cannot lawfully interfere with those water rights. And it leaves open the possibility that the Navajo "may be able to assert the interests they claim in water rights litigation." Really, the Court gets off the train just one stop short. It insists (and then repeats—again and again) that the United States owes no "affirmative duty" to the Navajo with respect to water, and therefore does not need to take any "affirmative steps" to help the Tribe on that score. This reasoning reflects three errors.

***

...

IV

Where do the Navajo go from here? To date, their efforts to find out what water rights the United States holds for them have produced an experience familiar to any American who has spent time at the Department of Motor Vehicles. The Navajo have waited patiently for someone, anyone, to help them, only to be told (repeatedly) that they have been standing in the wrong line and must try another. To this day, the United States has never denied that the Navajo may have water rights in the mainstream of the Colorado River (and perhaps elsewhere) that it holds in trust for the Tribe. Instead, the government's constant refrain is that the Navajo can have all they ask for; they just need to go somewhere else and do something else first.

The Navajo have tried it all. They have written federal officials. They have moved this Court to clarify the United States' responsibilities when representing them. They have sought to intervene directly in water-related litigation. And when all of those efforts were rebuffed, they brought a claim seeking to compel the United States to make good on its treaty obligations by providing an accounting of what water rights it holds on their behalf. At each turn, they have received the same answer: "Try again." When this routine first began in earnest, Elvis was still making his rounds on The Ed Sullivan Show.

If there is any silver lining here it may be this. While the Court finds the present complaint lacking because it understands it as seeking "affirmative steps," the Court does not pass on other potential pleadings the Tribe might offer, such as those alleging direct interference with their water rights. Importantly, too, the Court recognizes that the Navajo "may be able to assert the interests they claim in water rights litigation, including by seeking to intervene in cases that affect their claimed interests." After today, it is hard to see how this Court (or any court) could ever again fairly deny a request from the Navajo to intervene in litigation over the Colorado River or other water sources to which they might have a claim. Principles of estoppel, if nothing else, may have something to say about the United States' ability to oppose requests like that moving forward. All of which leaves the Navajo in a familiar spot. As they did at Bosque Redondo, they must again fight for themselves to secure their homeland and all that must necessarily come with it. Perhaps here, as there, some measure of justice will prevail in the end.

Notes & Questions

1. According to the Court, what must a tribe show to demonstrate that the United States has breached its trust responsibility to a tribe? Is that consistent with the *Winters* Doctrine? How does the majority articulate the Navajo Nation's prayer for relief? How does that drive the outcome of the case? What is the scope of the United States' responsibility to protect tribal water rights after *Navajo Nation*?
2. The Navajo Nation argued that both its 1848 and 1868 treaties included sufficiently affirmative statements by the United State so as to establish a judicially enforceable trust responsibility. In addressing this argument, did the majority apply the Indian canons of construction? Should it have? If it had, would the outcome of the case have been different?
3. Recall from *Colorado River Conservation District* that the Court's justification for including tribal reserved water rights in state court general stream adjudications is the United States' ownership of those water rights. Thus, the Court concluded that

the McCarran Amendment allows the United States to be joined those cases and make any claims it may have on behalf of tribes, despite no waiver of the immunity of tribes. Does *Navajo Nation* change that duty?

4. You will learn in the next chapter, that Indian water rights settlements often include congressional funding necessary to effectuate the terms of the settlement. Historically, one of the rationales for this funding is that it is necessary to compensate tribes for mismanagement of tribal water rights. Consequently, funding is conditioned on tribes agreeing to waive any liability the United States may have to the tribes. Does *Navajo Nation* change this arrangement? Will *Navajo Nation* make it more difficult for tribes to receive funding from Congress necessary to develop reservation water resources?

Chapter 27

Reserved Water Rights: Litigation and Settlement

Introduction

Following the interpretation that the McCarran Amendment led to deference to state court jurisdiction over reserved water rights, the general adjudications in many western states moved forward. Efforts to apply federal common law of reserved water rights on issues where there is no federal common law have resulted in numerous conflicting rulings from state court adjudications. This Chapter begins with examples of those conflicts.

States, the federal government, and tribes began to realize that litigation is costly, resulting in water rights that are often senior to most state-based water rights, yet exist only on paper. Tribes remain underfunded in water development relative to their non-Indian neighbors as you learned in Part IV. This Chapter will conclude by providing an overview of what is often referred to as the "settlement era" for reserved water rights.

State Adjudication: Conflicting Results

In Part III, you learned that states have differed on whether reserved water rights apply to groundwater. In Chapter 28 you will learn that the state court interpretation of whether the McCarran Amendment provides for state administration of reserved water rights differs among states. Chapter 28 will fill in the gap—beginning with the conflicting views on whether the purpose of a Native American reservation in the context of application of the *Winters* Doctrine is to establish a homeland.

Recall from Part III that in 1981 the Ninth Circuit recognized a homeland purpose in *Colville Confederated Tribes v. Walton* yet quantified it using the practically irrigable acreage method. The court then recognized a second purpose of fisheries. The court stated:

> These factors demonstrate that one purpose for creating this reservation was to provide a homeland for the Indians to maintain their agrarian society. In a similar setting, the Supreme Court agreed with a Master's finding that water was reserved to meet future as well as present needs, and concluded "that the only feasible and fair way by which reserved water for the reservation can be

> measured is irrigable acreage." *Arizona v. California*, 373 U.S. at 600–01. We conclude that, when the Colville reservation was created, sufficient appurtenant water was reserved to permit irrigation of all practicably irrigable acreage on the reservation.
>
> Providing for a land-based agrarian society, however, was not the only purpose for creating the reservation. The Colvilles traditionally fished for both salmon and trout. Like other Pacific Northwest Indians, fishing was of economic and religious importance to them. See *Washington v. Washington State Commercial Passenger Fishing Vessel Association*, 443 U.S. 658, 665, 99 S. Ct. 3055, 3064, 61 L.Ed.2d 823 (1978); *United States v. Winans,* supra; (1871) Report of the Commissioner of Indian Affairs 277.
>
> The Tribe's principal historic fishing grounds on the Columbia River have been destroyed by dams. The Indians have established replacement fishing grounds in Omak Lake by planting a non-indigenous trout.
>
> We agree with the district court that preservation of the tribe's access to fishing grounds was one purpose for the creation of the Colville Reservation. Under the circumstances, we find an implied reservation of water from No Name Creek for the development and maintenance of replacement fishing grounds.[1]

Colville did not put the issue of purpose to rest. You learned in the previous Chapter that Wyoming managed the scope of its Big Horn adjudication by dividing it by issue. Phase 1 focused on Indian reserved water rights and water rights for Indian allottees. The Shoshone and Northern Arapahoe Tribes of the Wind River Reservation asserted a homeland purpose for quantification of their reserved water rights. See Chapter 25 for a map of the Big Horn adjudication. In the following excerpt the Wyoming Supreme Court, by a 3–2 split, rejects the homeland purpose.

In re General Adjudication of All Rights to Use of Water in the Big Horn River System

(Big Horn I)

Wyoming Supreme Court

753 P.2d 76 (1988), *aff'd mem. sub. nom.*, 492 U.S. 406 (1989)[2]

...

IV PURPOSES OF THE WIND RIVER INDIAN RESERVATION

The special master's finding that the principal purpose for the creation of the reservation was to provide a permanent homeland for the Indians is not a factual determination. The master determined the purpose of the Indian reservation from the face

1. Colville Confederated Tribes v. Walton, 647 F.2d 42, 47–48 (9th Cir. 1981).

2. Recall that this is the case that was taken to the U.S. Supreme Court resulting in a brief affirmation by a 4–4 vote after Justice O'Connor recused herself. Later discovery of her draft majority opinion would have reduced the PIA quantification out of sensitivity to existing state-based water rights.

of the treaty as a matter of law.... The purposes of a treaty are ascertained by utilizing rules for determining the intent of parties to a contract.... The special master found as a matter of law that the treaty was unambiguous and ascertained the purpose for creation of the reservation from the four corners of the treaty, stating:

> "Analyzing the Treaty in its entirety, with specific reference to the above cited provisions, it is not at all unreasonable to conclude that the principal purpose for entering into this Treaty was to provide the Indians with a homeland where they could establish a permanent place to live and to develop their civilization just as any other nation throughout history has been able to develop its civilization."

The district court ascertained the purpose of the reservation from the treaty itself, stating: "On the very face of the Treaty, it is clear that its purpose was purely agricultural." This legal determination is fully reviewable by this court.

...

The court in *Colville Confederated Tribes v. Walton,* supra 647 F.2d 42, did not mandate that a single purpose for the reservation be found. Rather, the court applied the specific purpose test outlined in *United States v. New Mexico,* supra 438 U.S. at 702, 98 S.Ct. at 3015, in an Indian reserved water case and found two primary purposes: "to provide a homeland for the Indians to maintain their agrarian society,".... The validity of the ninth circuit's application of the New Mexico test has been drawn into question because the standards governing non-Indian federal reserved water rights differ from those governing Indian reserved water rights. F. Cohen, Handbook of Federal Indian Law, ch. 10 § 133, at 583–584 (1982 ed.); *State ex rel. Greely v. Confederated Salish and Kootenai Tribes of Flathead Reservation,* Mont., 712 P.2d 754, 766–767 (1985). See also *Montana v. Blackfeet Tribe of Indians,* 471 U.S. 759, 105 S.Ct. 2399, 2404, 85 L.Ed.2d 753 (1985). In *United States v. Adair,* supra 723 F.2d at 1408, the ninth circuit agreed that non-Indian federal reservation reserved water rights cases only provide useful guidelines to Indian reserved water rights.

...

It is well established that the judgment of the district court will be upheld for any proper reason appearing of record.... Considering the well-established principles of treaty interpretation, the treaty itself, the ample evidence and testimony addressed, and the findings of the district court, we have no difficulty affirming the finding that it was the intent at the time to create a reservation with a sole agricultural purpose. Indian treaties should be interpreted generously, ... and liberally in favor of the Indians, ... Nor should treaties be improperly construed in favor of Indians, for "'[W]e cannot remake history,'" ... and courts should not distort the words of a treaty to find rights inconsistent with its language....

Article 7 of the treaty refers to "said agricultural reservations." Article 6 authorizes allotments for farming purposes; Article 8 provides seeds and implements for farmers; in Article 9 "the United States agreed to pay each Indian farming a $20 annual stipend, but only $10 to 'roaming' Indians"; and Article 12 establishes a $50 prize to the ten best Indian farmers. The treaty does not encourage any other occupation or pursuit. The district court correctly found that the reference in Article 4 to "permanent homeland" does nothing more than permanently set aside lands for the Indians; it does not define the purpose of the reservation. Rather, the purpose of the permanent-home reservation is found in Articles 6, 8, 9, and 12 of the treaty.

The emphasis on education for Indians settled on "said agricultural reservations," in Article 7 also helps to define the purpose of the reservation....

...

The Court, while recognizing that the Tribes were the beneficial owners of the reservation's timber and mineral resources, ... and that it was known to all before the treaty was signed that the Wind River Indian Reservation contained valuable minerals, nonetheless concluded that the purpose of the reservation was agricultural. The fact that the Indians fully intended to continue to hunt and fish does not alter that conclusion.

... The district court, however, finding neither a dependency upon fishing for a livelihood nor a traditional lifestyle involving fishing, deleted the award. The district court did not err. The evidence is not sufficient to imply a fishery flow right absent a treaty provision.

... Neither the Tribes nor the United States has cited this court to any provision of the treaty or other evidence indicating that the parties contemplated in 1868 that a purpose of the reservation would be for the Indians to develop the minerals. The fact that the Tribes have since used water for mineral and industrial purposes does not establish that water was impliedly reserved in 1868 for such uses. The district court did not err in denying a reserved water right for mineral and industrial uses.

... A reserved water right for municipal, domestic and commercial uses was included within the agricultural reserved water award.... The court properly allowed a reserved water right for municipal, domestic, and commercial use.

... For the reasons stated above, the district court did not err in finding a sole agricultural purpose for the reservation or in subsuming livestock use within that purpose.

... The special master awarded 60% of historic flows for wildlife and aesthetic uses, consistent with his determination that the purpose of the reservation was to be a permanent homeland.... The district court did not err in holding that the Tribes and the United States did not introduce sufficient evidence of a tradition of wildlife and aesthetic preservation which would justify finding this to be a purpose for which the reservation was created and for which water was impliedly reserved.

The district court did not err in finding a sole agricultural purpose in the creation of the Wind River Indian Reservation. The Treaty itself evidences no other purpose, and none of the extraneous evidence cited is sufficient to attribute a broader purpose.

Notes & Questions

1. In *Big Horn I*, the Wyoming Supreme Court found the determination of the purpose of the reservation to be a question of law. Recall from the canons of treaty construction that a treaty is to be interpreted as the tribe(s) would have understood the language. Thus, on the issue of treaty interpretation, courts will allow testimony on oral history. Does testimony on oral history go to fact or law? If the court had viewed purpose as a question of fact, would it have made a difference?
2. What does the court mean when it says that water for purposes of livestock watering is "subsumed" in the award of water for agricultural purposes, and that municipal, domestic, and commercial uses are also "included" in that award?
3. What, if any, difference is there between the Ninth Circuit finding of a homeland purpose for an agrarian life quantified using PIA, and *Big Horn I*, rejecting the homeland purpose for an agrarian purpose quantified using PIA?

In 2001, the Arizona Supreme Court upheld the finding of the Special Master in the Gila River Adjudication that Indian reservations are established for the purpose of creating a homeland. Pay particular attention to the reasons, and to the method the court suggests for quantification. See Figure 25.5 in Chapter 25 for a map of the Gila River basin in Arizona.

In re the General adjudication of All Rights to Use Water in the Gila River System

Supreme Court of Arizona En Banc
201 Ariz. 307, 35 P.3d 68 (2001)

ZLAKET, Chief Justice—We are presented with another issue in the Gila River general stream adjudication. The facts and procedural history of this matter are well documented.... Today the court addresses issue 3: "What is the appropriate standard to be applied in determining the amount of water reserved for federal lands?"

...

B. Purpose

Generally, the "purpose of a federal reservation of land defines the scope and nature of impliedly reserved water rights." *United States v. Adair,* 723 F.2d 1394, 1419 (9th Cir.1983). However, when applying the *Winters* doctrine, it is necessary to distinguish between Indian and non-Indian reservations.

The government may exercise total dominion over water rights on federal non-Indian lands.... But unlike those attached to Indian lands, which have reserved water rights for "future needs and changes in use," *id.,* non-Indian reserved rights are narrowly quantified to meet the original, primary purpose of the reservation; water for secondary purposes must be acquired under state law. *See New Mexico,* 438 U.S. at 702, 98 S.Ct. at 3015....

Indian reservations, however, are different. In its role as trustee of such lands, the government must act for the Indians' benefit.... This fiduciary relationship is referred to as "one of the primary cornerstones of Indian law." ... Thus, treaties, statutes, and executive orders are construed liberally in the Indians' favor.... Such an approach is equally applicable to the federal government's actions with regard to water for Indian reservations. "The purposes of Indian reserved rights ... are given broader interpretation in order to further the federal goal of Indian self sufficiency." ...

The parties dispute the purposes of the several Indian reservations involved in this case. The United States and the tribal litigants argue that federal case law has preemptively determined that every Indian reservation was established as a permanent tribal homeland. The state litigants disagree, contending instead that the trial court must analyze each tribe's treaty or enabling documentation to determine that reservation's individual purpose. We need not decide whether federal case law has preemptively determined the issue. We agree with the Supreme Court that the essential purpose of Indian reservations is to provide Native American people with a "permanent home and abiding place," *Winters*, 207 U.S. at 565, that is, a "livable" environment. *Arizona I*, 373 U.S. at 599.

While courts may choose to examine historical documents in determining the purpose and reason for creating a federal reservation on non-Indian lands, the utility of such an exercise with respect to Indian reservations is highly questionable. This is so for a variety of reasons.

First, as pointed out by the state litigants, many Indian reservations were pieced together over time....

A second problem lies in the fact that congressional intent to reserve water for tribal land is not express, but implied....

Courts construe Indian treaties according to the way in which the Indians themselves would have understood them.... But the historical search for a reservation's purpose tends to focus only on the motives of Congress—tribal intent is easily and often left out of the equation. It is doubtful that any tribe would have agreed to surrender its freedom and be confined on a reservation without some assurance that sufficient water would be provided for its well-being.

The most recognizable difficulty with the historical approach is that many documents do not accurately represent the true reasons for which Indian reservations were created. It is well known that in the nineteenth century, the federal government made conflicting promises....

Despite what may be set forth in official documents, the fact is that Indians were forced onto reservations so that white settlement of the West could occur unimpeded....

...

Limiting an Indian reservation's purpose to agriculture, as the PIA standard implicitly does,

> assumes that the Indian peoples will not enjoy the same style of evolution as other people, nor are they to have the benefits of modern civilization. I would understand that the homeland concept assumes that the homeland will not be a static place frozen in an instant of time but that the homeland will evolve and will be used in different ways as the Indian society develops.

In re General Adjudication of All Rights to Use Water in the Big Horn River System, 753 P.2d 76, 119 (Wyo.1988) (Thomas, J., dissenting) [*Big Horn I*]; *see also Walton,* 647 F.2d at 47 (stating that courts consider Indians' "need to maintain themselves under changed circumstances" when determining a reservation's purpose).

Other right holders are not constrained in this, the twenty-first century, to use water in the same manner as their ancestors in the 1800s....

...

E. The PIA Standard

The trial court in this matter held that each Indian reservation was entitled to "the amount of water necessary to irrigate all of the *practicably irrigable acreage* (P.I.A.) on that reservation."...

...

The United States and tribal litigants argue that federal case law has preemptively established PIA as the standard by which to quantify reserved water rights on Indian reservations. We disagree. As observed by Special Master Tuttle in his *Arizona II* report, "the Court did not necessarily adopt this standard as the universal measure of Indian reserved water rights...." *Id.* at 556 n. 40 (quoting Special Master's Report at 90 (Feb. 22, 1981)). Indeed, nothing in *Arizona I* or *II* suggests otherwise.

On its face, PIA appears to be an objective method of determining water rights. But while there may be some "value of the certainty inherent in the practicably irrigable acreage standard," *Big Horn I,* 753 P.2d at 101, its flaws become apparent on closer examination.

The first objection to an across-the-board application of PIA lies in its potential for inequitable treatment of tribes based solely on geographical location. Arizona's topography is such that some tribes inhabit flat alluvial plains while others dwell in steep, mountainous areas.... Tribes who fail to show either the engineering or economic feasibility of proposed irrigation projects run the risk of not receiving any reserved water under PIA. *See, e.g., State ex rel. Martinez v. Lewis,* 116 N.M. 194, 861 P.2d 235, 246–51 (Ct.App.1993) (denying water rights to the Mescalero Apache Tribe, situated in a mountainous region of southern New Mexico, for failure to prove irrigation projects were economically feasible). This inequity is unacceptable and inconsistent with the idea of a permanent homeland.

Another concern with PIA is that it forces tribes to pretend to be farmers in an era when "large agricultural projects ... are risky, marginal enterprises....

Limiting the applicable inquiry to a PIA analysis not only creates a temptation for tribes to concoct inflated, unrealistic irrigation projects, but deters consideration of actual water needs based on realistic economic choices....

The PIA standard also potentially frustrates the requirement that federally reserved water rights be tailored to minimal need. Rather than focusing on what is necessary to fulfill a reservation's overall design, PIA awards what may be an overabundance of water by including every irrigable acre of land in the equation.

For the foregoing reasons, we decline to approve the use of PIA as the exclusive quantification measure for determining water rights on Indian lands.

F. Proper Factors for Consideration

Recognizing that the most likely reason for PIA's endurance is that "no satisfactory substitute has emerged," Dan A. Tarlock, *One River, Three Sovereigns: Indian and Interstate Water Rights,* 22 Land & Water L.Rev. 631, 659 (1987), we now enter essentially uncharted territory. In *Gila III,* this court stated that determining the amount of water necessary to accomplish a reservation's purpose is a "fact-intensive inquir[y] that must be made on a reservation-by-reservation basis." 195 Ariz. at 420, 989 P.2d at 748, We still adhere to the belief that this is the only way federally reserved rights can be tailored to meet each reservation's minimal need.

When *Big Horn I* went before the Supreme Court, one of the present state litigants, in an amicus brief, argued that there should be a "balancing of a myriad of factors" in quantifying reserved water rights. Rusinek, *supra,* at 397 (quoting Brief of Amicus Curiae Salt River Project Agric. Improvement & Power Dist. at 19, *Wyoming v. United States,* 492 U.S. 406, 109 S.Ct. 2994, 106 L.Ed.2d 342 (1989)). During oral argument in the present case, counsel for the Apache tribes made a similar argument. Considering the objective that tribal reservations be allocated water necessary to achieve their purpose as permanent homelands, such a multi-faceted approach appears best-suited to produce a proper outcome.

Tribes have already used this methodology in settling water rights claims with the federal government. One feature of such settlements has been the development of master land use plans specifying the quantity of water necessary for different purposes on the reservation....

While we commend the creation of master land use plans as an effective means of demonstrating water requirements, tribes may choose to present evidence to the trial court in a different manner. The important thing is that the lower court should have before it actual and proposed uses, accompanied by the parties' recommendations regarding feasibility and the amount of water necessary to accomplish the homeland purpose. In viewing this evidence, the lower court should consider the following factors, which are not intended to be exclusive.

A tribe's history will likely be significant. Deference should be given to practices requiring water use that are embedded in Native American traditions....

In addition to history, the court should consider tribal culture when quantifying federally reserved rights....

The court should also consider the tribal land's geography, topography, and natural resources, including groundwater availability....

In conjunction with natural resources, the court should look to a tribe's economic base in determining its water rights....

Past water use on a reservation should also be considered when quantifying a tribe's rights....

While it should never be the only factor, a tribe's present and projected future population may be considered in determining water rights. We recognize that the Supreme Court has rejected any quantification standard based solely on the "number of Indians." *Arizona II*, 460 U.S. at 617, 103 S.Ct. at 1390. However, if a federally reserved water right is to be tailored to a reservation's "minimal need," ...

Again, the foregoing list of factors is not exclusive. The lower court must be given the latitude to consider other information it deems relevant to determining tribal water rights. We require only that proposed uses be reasonably feasible. As with PIA, this entails a two-part analysis. First, development projects need to be achievable from a practical standpoint—they must not be pie-in-the-sky ideas that will likely never reach fruition. Second, projects must be economically sound. When water, a scarce resource, is put to efficient uses on the reservation, tribal economies and members are the beneficiaries.

...

Notes & Questions

1. What reasons does the court in *Gila V* give for finding that the purpose of an Indian reservation is to establish a homeland?
2. What problems does the court see with universal application of the PIA method of quantification? What alternative method to PIA does the court suggest for quantification of PIA? What are the difficulties in implementing this approach?
3. Is the court's analysis consistent with PIA as a quantification method only; or with PIA as both a quantification method and a limit on use?
4. In 2019, the Idaho Supreme Court adopted the homeland purpose in a case involving the reserved water rights of the Coeur d'Alene Tribe that went up on interlocutory appeal in the North Idaho Adjudication.[3] The court rejected application of the narrowing of the *Winters* Doctrine in *New Mexico* to Indian reservations, stating:

   > Given the substantive differences between Indian and non-Indian reservations, the broad interpretation of Indian reservation rights by the United States

---

3. In re CSRBA, Case No. 49576 Subcase No. 91-7755, United States v. Idaho, 448 P.3d 322 (Idaho 2019).

> Supreme Court, the persuasive reasoning given by the Montana and Arizona courts, the logic supporting the homeland purpose theory, as well as our own precedent, we hold the district court erred in utilizing the primary-secondary analysis set out in *New Mexico*. Therefore, purposes behind the creation of an Indian reservation should be more broadly construed and not limited solely to what may be considered a "primary" purpose.[4]

The court also rejected the approach in *Gila V* of dispensing with an analysis of the formative documents for the reservation, both because that analysis will determine if a homeland was intended for the specific reservation and will place bounds on the method(s) of quantification to apply.[5] The court then found the formative documents and historical context of the Coeur d'Alene Reservation to "demonstrate a homeland purpose consisting of the following uses: domestic, agriculture, hunting and fishing, plant gathering, and cultural."[6]

5. For analysis of the opinion in *Gila V* and the suggested method of quantification, see Barbara Cosens, *The Measure of Indian Water Rights: The Arizona Homeland Standard, Gila River Adjudication.* 42 Natural Resources J. 835 (2002).

The Settlement Era

Beginning in the late 1970s, some water users, tribes, and states began to realize that settlement might be a preferred option to litigation. The basis for a preference for settlement is generally characterized under two themes: (1) wet water—litigation of reserved water rights results in a paper water right, but as you will learn, settlement has become a means to obtain federal funds for development and protection of water for numerous needs on Indian reservations, including irrigation, domestic, commercial, industrial, and wildlife; and (2) tailored solutions—the ability to negotiate context-specific settlements has led to novel physical solutions that meet the needs determined by a specific tribe(s) while also avoiding major economic disruption of neighboring water use.[7] Federal funding for tribal participation in the settlement process supports tribal sovereignty and self-determination in these processes and presents a striking contrast to a litigation outcome imposed by a (often state) judge. Nevertheless, because settlement generally occurs against the backdrop and with a stay of adjudication, the judicial forum remains available to narrow issues when settlement discussions reach an impasse. This section will cover the process of Indian water right settlement, how it differs by state, and some of the novel solutions that have been reached.

---

4. *Id.* at 346.
5. *Id.* at 348.
6. *Id.* at 348–350.
7. Barabara Cosens, *2005 Indian Water Rights Settlement Conference Keynote Address*, 9 Denver Water L. Rev. 2 (2006).

Settlement Process

Settlement occurs in stages that often take years, and generally includes the following steps:

- Negotiation, including substantial data collection, hydrologic modeling, and joint technical evaluation of proposals. Depending on the state process, this stage may also include substantial public involvement and may take up to a decade.
- State approval, generally through legislation. The state goes first because the federal government wants state commitment before going to Congress.
- Federal ratification. This is done by Congress if funding or authorization for federal action is involved, otherwise by either the Secretary of Interior or Department of Justice. The federal government goes next because the tribe wants to know that the funding has been authorized and the agreement ratified before commitment.
- Tribal referendum, generally a vote of all eligible tribal members.
- Entry of the settlement in the adjudication, opportunity for objection, and entry in a final decree.
- Implementation—including appropriation of funding and any agreed-upon infrastructure construction.

The following paragraphs briefly describe the federal process in settlement, and some of the variations in state processes.

Almost a dozen settlements had been entered between tribal and state governments when President George H.W. Bush signed the 1989 Puyallup Tribe of Indians Settlement Act,[8] and expressed a preference for resolution of Indian water right disputes through settlement.[9] This led to development of the "Criteria and Procedures for the Participation of the Federal Government in Negotiations for the Settlement of Indian Water Rights Claims"[10] by the United States Department of the Interior; the establishment of the Working Group on Indian Water Rights Settlements, made up of Interior Assistant Secretaries and Solicitor, and the Indian Water Rights Office under the Secretary of the Interior.[11] The Working Group establishes settlement policies and makes

8. H.R. 932, The 1989 Puyallup Tribe of Indians Settlement Act.

9. In his statements on signing the "Puyallup Tribe of Indians Settlement Act of 1989," President Bush stated: "The Administration expects to continue to work toward settlement of legitimate Indian land and water rights claims to which the Federal Government is a party." George Bush, 1 Pub. Papers 771, 772 (June 21, 1989).

10. 55 Federal Register 9223-01(March 12, 1990). *See also* Congressional Research Service, Indian Water Rights Settlements, R44148, Updated October 13, 2023. Available at: https://crsreports.congress.gov/product/pdf/R/R44148; Barbara Cosens, *The 1997 Water Rights Settlement between the State of Montana and the Chippewa Cree Tribe of the Rocky Boy's Reservation—The Role of Community and of the Trustee*. 16 UCLA J. Envt'l L. & Pol'y 255 (1998).

11. Congressional Research Service, Indian Water Rights Settlements, R44148, at 3, Updated January 18, 2022. Available at: https://crsreports.congress.gov/product/pdf/R/R44148.

recommendations on settlement positions.[12] The Indian Water Rights Office is responsible for negotiation, coordination, and implementation of settlements, and reports to the Working Group.[13]

The Criteria and Procedures guide the process of federal participation in negotiations and their development of a position on the level of federal funding that Interior will support in Congress. The Criteria and Procedures require an evaluation of the positions of all parties, assessment of the value of the claim for the specific reservation, and allocation of any contributions by the state or non-Indian water interests, before the Working Group is to make any recommendations to the Secretary.[14] In reality, negotiations are a long process of technical, historical, and legal studies, explorations of ideas for settlement, and considerable back-and-forth to find a path that all parties can live with. The linear process contemplated by the Criteria and Procedures has been criticized as preventing any significant federal input until a settlement is completed,[15] the result being that some settlements end up going to Congress without the support of Interior.

Settlement resulting in "wet water" for a tribe is generally made possible through a combination of federal, state, and local (i.e., water interests) funding. In general, the federal funding is the largest. The Criteria and Procedures set forth the criteria for federal funding:

> 5. Federal contributions to a settlement should not exceed the sum of the following two elements:
>
> a. First, calculable legal exposure—litigation cost and judgment obligations if the case is lost; Federal and non-Federal exposure should be calculated on a present value basis taking into account the size of the claim, value of the water, timing of the award, likelihood of loss.
>
> b. Second, additional costs related to Federal trust or programmatic responsibilities (assuming the U.S. obligation as trustee can be compared to existing precedence.)—Federal contributions relating to programmatic responsibilities should be justified as to why such contributions cannot be funded through the normal budget process.[16]

Congressionally authorized federal contribution to Indian water rights settlement has ranged from no federal funding to over $1 billion.[17] The federal government does not have a systematic process identified for resolution of non-Indian federal reserved water rights, but nevertheless tends to have a preference for settlement of these as well.

---

12. *Id.*

13. *Id.*

14. 55 Federal Register 9223-01(March 12, 1990).

15. Barbara Cosens, *The 1997 Water Rights Settlement Between the State of Montana and the Chippewa Cree Tribe of the Rocky Boy's Reservation—The Role of Community and of the Trustee*, 16 UCLA J. Envt'l L. & Pol'y 255 (1998).

16. 55 Federal Register 9223-01 (March 12, 1990).

17. Congressional Research Service, Indian Water Rights Settlements, R44148, at 7–9 (January 18, 2022), https://crsreports.congress.gov/product/pdf/R/R44148

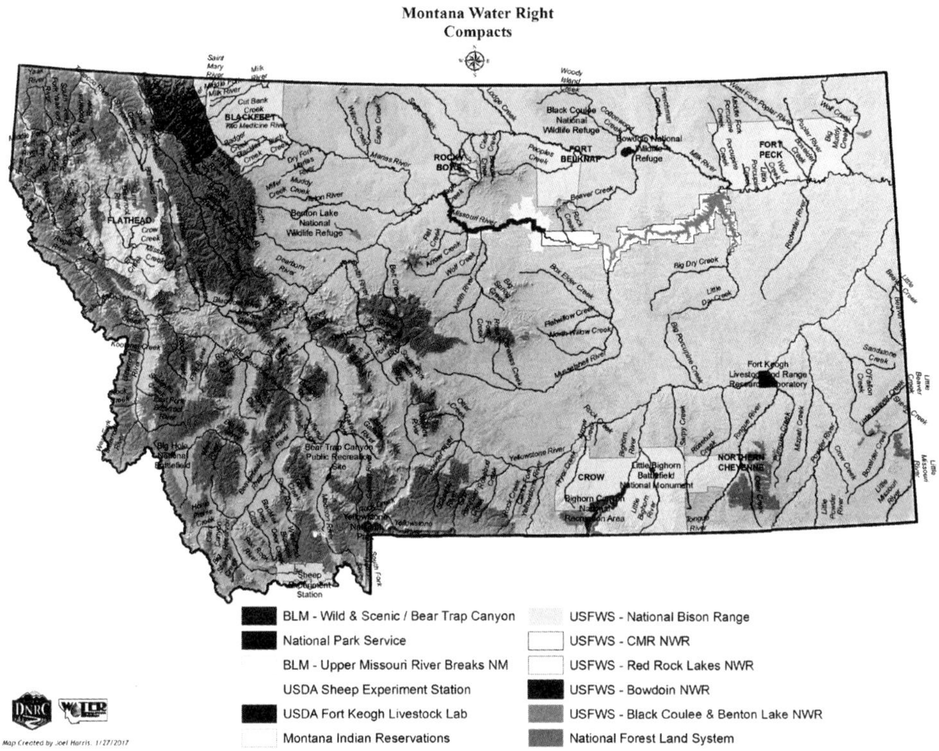

Figure 27.1 Map of the federal lands and Indian reservations in Montana with Compacts. Source: Montana Department of Natural Resources and Conservation, Compact Implementation Program, https://dnrc.mt.gov/_docs/water/2017-01-27_Compacts_State_Map.jpg.

Like state process for adjudication, state settlement process differs among states. Montana has the most unique and structured process. Figure 27.1 shows the federal and Indian lands with settlements, referred to as "Compacts" in Montana. In 1979, the Montana Legislature established the Reserved Water Rights Compact Commission (RWRCC), composed as follows:

> (1) There is created a reserved water rights compact commission. In negotiations, the commission is acting on behalf of the governor.
>
> (2) . . . , commissioners are appointed as follows:
>
> > (a) two members of the house of representatives appointed by the speaker, one from the majority party and one from the minority party;
> >
> > (b) two members of the senate appointed by the president, one from the majority party and one from the minority party;
> >
> > (c) four members designated by the governor; and
> >
> > (d) one member designated by the attorney general.[18]

18. Mont. Code Ann. 2-15-212.

The 1979 amendments to the Montana Water Use Act, which set forth the process of the state-wide general adjudication, included the following:

> Because the water and water rights within each water division are interrelated, it is the intent of the legislature to conduct unified proceedings for the general adjudication of existing water rights ... it is further intended that the state of Montana proceed under the provisions of this part in an effort to conclude compacts for the equitable division and apportionment of waters between the state and its people and the several Indian tribes claiming reserved water rights within the state....[19]
>
> The compact commission may also enter into separate negotiations with the federal government for the conclusion of compacts concerning the equitable division and apportionment of water between the state and its people and the federal government claiming non-Indian reserved waters within the state. The terms and conditions of such negotiations shall be the same as provided in this section for negotiations with Indian tribes.[20]

Adjudication of reserved water rights were suspended by the following provision:

> While negotiations for the conclusion of a compact under part 7 are being pursued, all proceedings to generally adjudicate reserved Indian water rights and federal reserved water rights of those tribes and federal agencies that are negotiating are suspended. The obligation to file water rights claims for those federal non-Indian and Indian reserved rights is also suspended.

The staff of the RWRCC includes people with expertise in law, policy, history, hydrology, agricultural engineering, fisheries, and Geographic Information Systems.[21]

State Executive policy throughout negotiations by the RWRCC required that negotiations with Indian Tribes be entered on a government-to-government basis. The combination of a politically appointed Commission, the statutory requirement of an equitable distribution of water, and the requirement of government-to-government negotiations placed the Commission in the position of mediator between water users and the Tribe or federal government. As a result, the Commission staff employ a robust process of public involvement throughout negotiations and often incorporate local knowledge and ideas in settlements.[22]

Arizona and Idaho do not have a statutory process for settlement, thus it takes place, if at all, in the normal course of an adjudication. In contrast to Montana's approach, the State is generally represented in settlement by the Office of the Attorney General.

---

19. Mont. Code Ann. 85-2-701(1).

20. Mont. Code Ann. 85-2-703.

21. Professor Cosens served as an attorney for the RWRCC from 1991–2000.

22. Barbara Cosens, *The 1997 Water Rights Settlement Between the State of Montana and the Chippewa Cree Tribe of the Rocky Boy's Reservation—The Role of Community and of the Trustee*. 16 UCLA J. Envt'l L. & Pol'y 255 (1998); D. Amman et al., *Negotiation of the Montana-National Park Service Compact*, 5 Rivers 35 (1995).

Major water interests in the adjudication generally have a seat at the table. Without the direction of an equitable solution, both Idaho and Arizona often undertake initial or periodic litigation to resolve intractable issues and narrow the legal uncertainty. The opinions earlier in this Chapter from each of these states on the homeland standard were the results of attempts to narrow issues.

Notes & Questions

1. Discuss the Criteria for federal contribution to settlement. What is meant by "calculable legal exposure" of the federal government? Do you see any problems with this method of calculation?
2. Discuss the differences among Wyoming (pure litigation), Idaho and Arizona (mixed litigation and settlement), and Montana (pure settlement). What are the advantages and disadvantages of each?

Settlements: Novel Solutions

According to the Congressional Research Service:

> As of 2021, 38 Indian water rights settlements had been federally approved, with total estimated costs in excess of $8.0 billion. Of these, 34 settlements were approved and enacted by Congress (4 were administratively approved by the U.S. Departments of Justice and the Interior).[23]

Congressional approval results in a Public Law containing authorization for any aspects of the settlement that require federal action or funding, but generally does not contain the settlement itself. Among the states, Montana is the only one that publishes the actual settlements.[24] Due to the difficulty of finding settlement documents, particularly those drafted prior to the digital age, Professor Cosens worked with Darcy Bushnell of the University of New Mexico Utton Center to develop a digital repository of settlements.[25]

Settlements have also been entered for National Parks and Monuments, National Forests, Wilderness Areas, Wild and Scenic Rivers, Wildlife Refuges, and other federal reservations. These settlements generally do not require funding, thus rarely require congressional action. The settlements are generally signed by the secretary of the appropriate agency and the Department of Justice and become finalized once entered in a court decree.

---

23. Congressional Research Service, Indian Water Rights Settlements, R44148, at Summary October 13, 2023), https://crsreports.congress.gov/product/pdf/R/R44148.

24. Montana's settlements can be found in Title 85, Chapter 20 of the Montana Code Annotated.

25. The repository can be found at: Native American Water Rights Settlement Project, UNM Digital Repository: https://digitalrepository.unm.edu/nawrs_comm/.

To provide sampling of the range of novel solutions in both Native American and federal settlements of reserved water rights, the remainder of this Chapter will look at: (1) the Northern Cheyenne/Montana Compact for a novel physical solution to water supply; (2) the Nez Perce/Idaho Settlement for an approach to protecting off-reservation instream flows; and (3) the Yellowstone National Park/Montana Compact for a novel approach to quantifying instream flow to preserve the natural hydrograph and an administrative approach to protecting the hydrothermal system of the Park. In the next Chapter you will look at the Confederated Salish and Kootenai/Montana Compact for a novel approach to administration.

One guiding principle in negotiations involving natural resources is that the legal and scientific uncertainty provides the room within which a successful negotiation takes place. If the legal uncertainty is high, it may be necessary to narrow the room for negotiation in court. If the scientific uncertainty is high, a novel approach may be necessary. Look for the role of legal and scientific uncertainty in each of the settlements described.

Northern Cheyenne-Montana Compact:[26] The 1991 Northern Cheyenne Compact with the State of Montana and the United States resolved the problem of insufficient water supply on the Tongue River to serve both the irrigation claims of the Tribe and the existing non-Indian water uses by looking to another problem in the watershed—an unsafe state dam upstream of the reservation (Figure 27.2). The physical solution required implementation of the Tongue River Dam Project to repair and enlarge the existing dam This provided an additional pool of 20,000 acre-feet that would go to the Tribe.[27] The congressional bill was passed without the support of Interior, when the State and Tribe reached a funding agreement that would provide federal funding to the Tribe, who would in turn loan it to the State to undertake the Project. The State's overhead cost at the time was roughly one-third that of the federal agencies, thus the agreement achieved a lower cost settlement with a larger portion of the funding ultimately ending up with the Tribe on repayment. This approach was found acceptable by Congress.[28]

Nez Perce-Idaho Settlement: The Nez Perce Tribe settlement with the State of Idaho and the United States was memorialized in 2004 in what is referred to as The Mediator's Term Sheet.[29] The Nez Perce Tribe is among those Tribes in the Columbia River Basin with off-reservation fishing rights protected by the treaty language recognizing the

---

26. The Compact can be found in the Montana Code Annotated at 85-20-301, and the state consent to modification after Congress altered some of the terms at 85-20-302. Other related documents, including the congressional act, can be found at: Native American Water Rights Settlement Project, UNM Digital Repository URL: https://digitalrepository.unm.edu/nawrs_comm/.

27. Mont. Code Ann. 85-20-301, Article II.A.2.b. and Public Law 102-374, Section 10. Note that the Tongue River is a tributary to the Yellowstone River and thus part of the Yellowstone River Compact you learned about in Part V. Recall that the Compact disclaimed any effect on Indian water rights without any reference to their quantification.

28. Public Law 102-374, Section 7.

29. Mediator's Term Sheet, April 20, 2004, available at: Native American Water Rights Settlement Project, UNM Digital Repository: https://digitalrepository.unm.edu/nawrs/94/.

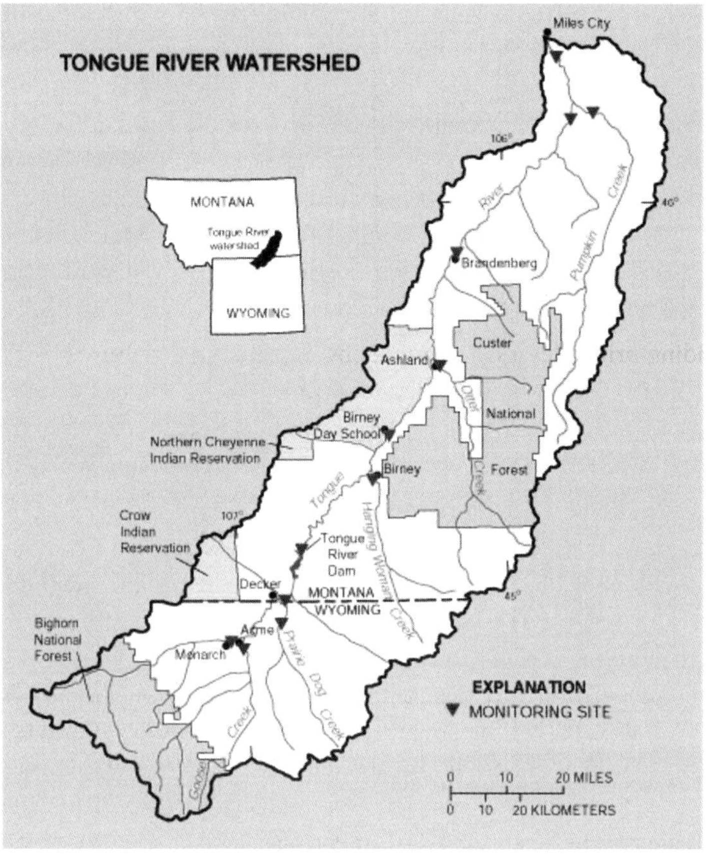

Figure 27.2 Tongue River Basin showing the location of the Tongue River Dam and the Northern Cheyenne Indian Reservation. Source: https://en.wikipedia.org/wiki/Tongue_River_(Montana).

"right of taking fish at all usual and accustomed places in common with citizens of the Territory."[30] While it is clear that fish need water to survive, claims to off-reservation instream flows have not fared well in state courts. In initial efforts to narrow issues related to the Nez Perce claims, the SRBA court found no off-reservation water rights, reasoning that reserved water rights must be appurtenant to reserved land.[31] The ruling was rendered moot by settlement, but is likely one of the factors that brought the Tribe to the table. Bringing the State and its water users to the table required a more innovative approach.

The Columbia River basin, which includes the Snake River as its largest tributary, includes the listing of one resident trout, four steelhead, and eight salmon populations

30. Treaty with the Nez Perces, 12 Stat. 957, Article 3 (1855).

31. In re SRBA, No 39576, Subcase No. 03-10022 (Idaho Dist. Ct. Judge Wood presiding, Nov. 10, 1999).

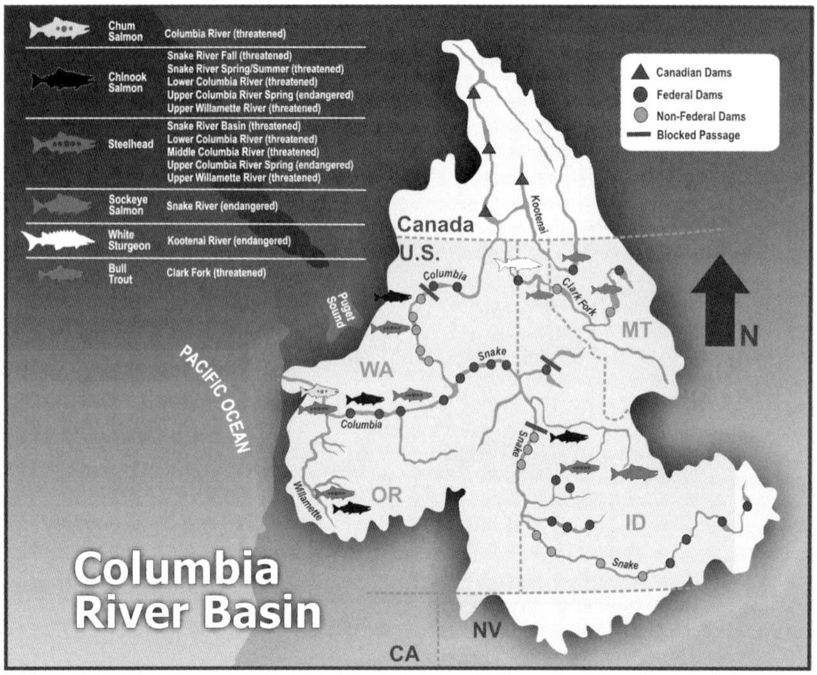

Figure 27.3 Listed species in the Columbia River Basin showing where they migrate, major hydropower dams. Source: Federal Caucus, the federal agencies working for endangered salmon and steelhead in the Columbia River Basin, Columbia Basin ESA Map, https://www.salmonrecovery.gov/AboutUs/ColumbiaRiverBasin/ColumbiaBasinMap.aspx.

on the endangered species list (Figure 27.3).[32] Under the Endangered Species Act, the federal dams on the Snake River (Reclamation dams in the Upper Snake, and USACE navigation and hydropower dams on the lower Snake River) are subject to the Biological Opinions prepared for the Federal Columbia River Power System. These BiOps result in flow requirements that may require spill during the spring out-migration of salmon and steelhead smolts.[33] In addition, timber harvest is subject to requirements on practices that impact fish habitat through increased sedimentation, loss of shade (thus higher stream temperature), fish migration barriers at road crossings, and loss of large woody debris. The State and its constituents came to the table for the possibility of negotiating measures that would be important to the Tribe and also provide a degree of long-term certainty under the ESA for: (1) timber harvest in the Salmon and Clearwater basins, and (2) irrigation in the upper Snake River basin.[34] The Settlement includes:

---

32. *See* NOAA, Pacific Salmon and Steelhead, https://www.fisheries.noaa.gov/species/pacific-salmon-and-steelhead.

33. For a discussion of the relation between flow and the salmon and steelhead life cycle, see Barbara Cosens, *Truth or Consequences: Settling Water Disputes in the Face of Uncertainty*, 42 Idaho L. Rev. 717 (2006), for a description of the scientific information and modeling that goes into this type of determination.

34. *Id.*

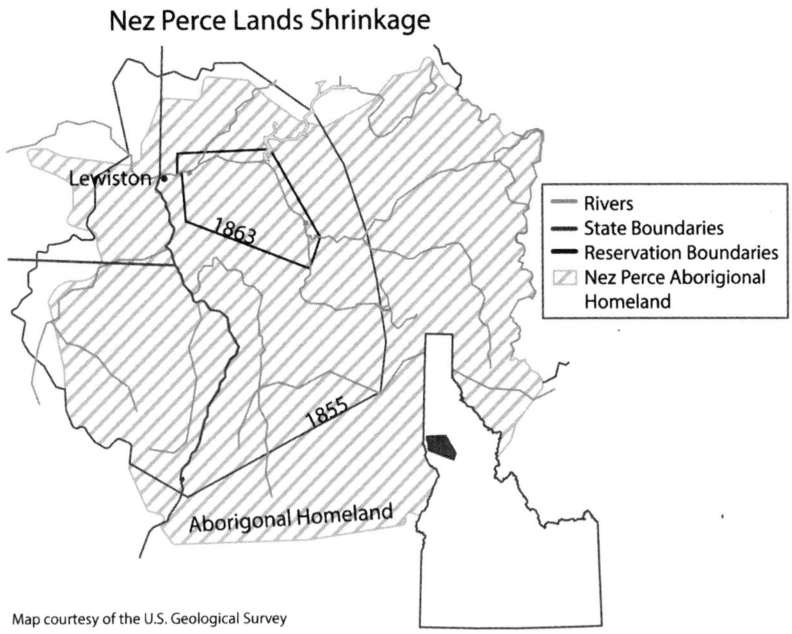

Figure 27.4 Map illustrating the reduction in Nez Perce lands from their aboriginal territory to the 1855 Treaty, to the current reservation with substantial land in non-Indian ownership due to allotment and associated homesteading.

> ... funding for habitat restoration; voluntary measures in a forest practice program (Idaho Forestry Program) that is supplemental to the Idaho Forest Practices Act to improve and protect riparian corridors on salmon spawning streams; flow augmentation from Reclamation projects on the Snake River in the amount identified as necessary by the U.S. Fish and Wildlife Service (FWS) and National Oceanic & Atmospheric Administration ...; and transfer of aspects of fish hatchery management to the Tribe.[35]

The Settlement also designated instream flows on 212 stretches of streams in the Salmon and Clearwater basins upstream of the Reservation to be held by the State under the instream flow program you learned about in Part V.[36] Figure 27.4 shows the current reservation in relation to the Salmon and Clearwater basins and the aboriginal territory of the Tribe. The parties used what is referred to as the "reverse approach" to instream flow quantification.[37] This will be described below under the Yellowstone National Park Compact, where it was first used.

35. *Id.*

36. Mediator's Term Sheet, April 20, 2004, at Article II and Appendix I, available at: Native American Water Rights Settlement Project, UNM Digital Repository: https://digitalrepository.unm.edu/nawrs/94/

37. *See* Barbara Cosens, *Truth or Consequences: Settling Water Disputes in the Face of Uncertainty*, 42 IDAHO L. REV. 717 at 738–747 (2006), for a description of the scientific information and modeling that goes into this type of determination.

Yellowstone National Park-Montana Compact[38] *(YNP):* The settlement between the State of Montana and the United States National Park Service for reserved water rights for the portion of Yellowstone National Park located in Montana included a unique approach to quantification of instream flow and to protection of a groundwater resource with high uncertainty associated with its scope and connection to other water resources.

A major difficulty with quantification of instream flows in snowpack-dominated watersheds (like those surrounding YNP) is the high variability in seasonal flow and the dependence of fish and wildlife habitat on that variability. While it is scientifically possible to come up with quantifications for different levels of flow, implementation is difficult. Peak flow does not arrive on the same date every year and levels may fluctuate with daytime temperature. When do you place a call on junior water rights? And for how long? With the current low level of development adjacent to YNP on streams that flow into YNP from the north or border it on the west, the parties agreed to a method that would preserve the natural hydrograph while avoiding a politically volatile "call" on what are primarily domestic and municipal water rights. The Compact provided for quantification of an amount of future use outside YNP on these shared watersheds, followed by closure of the source to new permits. Thus, the "reverse approach" quantifies use, rather than the instream flow.[39]

Efforts to develop hot springs north of YNP at the time of negotiations led to concerns about the protection of the iconic hydrothermal system. While no federal court ruling on reserved rights to groundwater was available at that time, *Cappaert,* a case you read in Part IV, had recognized the connection between surface and groundwater. *Cappaert* protected what the Court found to be a reserved surface water resource against external groundwater pumping, whereas YNP negotiations required protection of groundwater against external development of springs and groundwater. The documents reserving YNP, however, include express reference to its geysers and hot springs, allowing the parties to agree to the reserved right. The parties agreed to use State law to establish a Controlled Ground Water Area adjacent to YNP.[40] Due to the economic value of YNP tourism to the State of Montana, the parties took a conservative approach to initial regulations within the YCGWA by erring on the side of protection. The parties also recognized the high uncertainty associated with the hydrothermal system. These aspects are reflected in the Statement of Intent for setting up the YVGWA:

> Yellowstone National Park was reserved for the express purpose of "preservation, from injury or spoliation, of all timber, mineral deposits, natural curiosities, or wonders within said park, and their retention in their natural condition." 17 Stat. 32. The parties agree that Congress reserved water necessary to

38. The Compact for Yellowstone National Park is included in the United States National Park Service-Montana Compact, codified at Mont. Code Ann. 85-20-401.

39. Mont. Code Ann. 85-20-401, Article III. G.

40. Mont. Code Ann. 85-20-401, Article IV.

preserve the hydrothermal features within the reserved land of YNP. These reserved water rights have priorities as of the date on which the land was reserved.

The parties understand that knowledge of the interrelationship of hydrothermal features within YNP, the hydrothermal system that supports those features, and groundwater in surrounding areas of Montana will benefit from increased study. The parties agree that the hydrothermal features of YNP are a unique and irreplaceable resource and represent one of the few undisturbed hydrothermal systems in the United States.

This Compact does not recognize a reserved water right to groundwater outside the boundaries of the reserved land of YNP. However, the parties agree that restrictions shall be placed on the development of groundwater adjacent to YNP to the extent necessary to prevent adverse effect on the reserved water right to groundwater within YNP. The parties agree that the goal of establishment and administration of the Yellowstone Controlled Groundwater Area shall be to allow no impact to the hydrothermal system within the reserved land of YNP.[41]

The Compact then used an adaptive management approach to adjustment of regulations as new information was developed. Adjustments would be made by a Technical Oversight Committee established by the following language:

J. Modification of the Yellowstone Controlled Groundwater Area

1. Technical Oversight Committee: Establishment and Authority

a. A joint federal-state Technical Oversight Committee is hereby established to review scientific evidence related to the Yellowstone Controlled Groundwater Area; to advise the Department on administration of the Area, including review of applications to appropriate water of 60°F. or more; to consult with the [Montana Water Bureau within the Department of Natural Resources and Conservation] on inventory and sampling; and to recommend modification of boundaries and restrictions.

b. The committee shall consist of five qualified scientists with experience related to hydrothermal systems. The committee members shall be appointed within six months following the effective date of this Compact: one appointed by the National Park Service; one appointed by the United States Geological Survey; one appointed by the Department; one appointed from the Montana University system by the Montana State Geologist; and one selected by the other four members. Appointments and selections shall be made, to the extent possible, to ensure that three of the qualified scientists with experience related to hydrothermal

41. Mont. Code Ann. 85-20-401, A.

> systems also have experience in (1) geochemistry; (2) geophysics; and (3) hydrogeology.[42]

Federal funding was provided for well inventory and metering within the YCGWA.[43]

Notes & Questions

1. Terms. What does "wet" water mean in contrast to "paper rights"? What does it mean to find a physical solution to a water right dispute?
2. What is the "reverse approach" method to quantifying water rights for instream flow? How does it preserve the natural hydrograph?
3. You are legal counsel for an Indian tribe and you have been asked to provide a list of the pros and cons of settlement versus litigation. Provide that list. Consider that you were asked a similar question on comparing litigation and settlement above. This time you have a specific client. How does that change your answer?
4. Can you identify some of the legal and/or scientific uncertainty that made each of the solutions described possible?

---

42. MONT. CODE ANN. 85-20-401, Article IV. J.1.
43. *See* MONT. CODE ANN. 85-20-402.

Chapter 28

Post Adjudication Administration of Tribal Water Rights

Introduction

Once adjudication and/or settlement is complete, the question arises: who has jurisdiction to administer the tribal water right? Water is one of the key natural resources associated with land, thus integral to territorial sovereignty. It is also closely aligned with economic security as well as individual health and welfare and, as a result, control over water rights is viewed as an essential attribute of sovereignty. As you have learned, many reservations have substantial non-Indian fee land ownership within reservation boundaries. In addition, those boundaries ignore watershed and aquifer boundaries, resulting in numerous water sources shared by a reservation and neighboring water users outside the reservation. As a result, there has long been a struggle among tribes, states, and federal governments over the management and administration of water resources in the West.

The U.S. Supreme Court held in *United States v. Wheeler* that, as sovereigns, tribal nations retain authority "over both their members and their territory...."[1] Since the 1981 case of *Montana v. United States,* the general rule has been that tribes do not have authority to control non-Indian conduct taking place on reservation lands owned in fee by non-Indians, subject to two exceptions. First, "[a] tribe may regulate, through taxation, licensing, or other means, the activities of nonmembers who enter consensual relationships with the tribe or its members, through commercial dealing, contracts, leases, or other arrangements."[2] Second, "[a] tribe may also retain inherent power to exercise civil authority over the conduct of non-Indians on fee lands within its reservation when that conduct threatens or has some direct effect on the political integrity, the economic security, or the health or welfare of the tribe."[3] Is the focus on the connected water resource, such that *Wheeler* might apply, or on the people using it, such that *Montana* might apply? Is water essential to the "political integrity, the economic security, or health or welfare of the tribe," such that the second Montana exception applies?

1. United States v. Wheeler, 435 U.S. 313, 323 (1978).
2. Montana v. United States, 450 U.S. 544, 565 (1981).
3. *Id.* at 566.

Another option is that water has its own legal category in which these general rules do not control. Interstate rivers adjudicated in federal district court (as previously mentioned, the Truckee, Carson, and Walker Rivers shared by California, Nevada, and several Native American Reservations), are administered by a water master appointed by the adjudication court. Does the same process apply when the adjudication is by state court? Does the McCarran Amendment cover this?

This Chapter explores the interrelationship between tribal and state jurisdiction over water rights. It begins by exploring the federal court rulings prior to any state rulings, then explores the ambiguity provided by the McCarran Amendment, and the one series of state rulings on the scope of state jurisdiction over tribal reserved water rights—*Big Horn* (*I* and *III*).[4] Finally, it explores settlement solutions. This section will use the example of the Fort Hall Reservation in Southeastern Idaho, in which settlement provided for tribal administration of reserved water use on the reservation to explore the development of a tribal water code. It will conclude with the joint water entity created by the Compact between the Confederated Salish and Kootenai Tribes (CSKT) of the Flathead Reservation and Montana.

Federal Court Rulings

You read excerpts from *Colville Confederated Tribes v. Walton* and *United States v. Anderson* covering the purpose of the reserved water rights in Part III. You also read *Colville* in the context of the homeland standard in the previous Chapter. These cases also addressed the interrelationship between state and tribal regulatory jurisdiction over non-Indian water use within allotted Indian reservations. While these cases only address the situation created by allotment, the reasoning has value when we turn to the state court ruling in the context of adjudication.

Colville Confederated Tribes v. Walton

United States Court of Appeals, Ninth Circuit
647 F.2d 42 (1981)

Opinion

WRIGHT, Circuit Judge:—... The Colville Confederated Tribes initiated this case a decade ago. They sought to enjoin Walton, non-Indian owner of allotted lands, from using surface and ground waters in the No Name Creek basin....

I. BACKGROUND

[Review the facts of the case, which are recounted in Chapters 10 and 12.]

---

4. In re General Adjudication of All Rights to Use Water in the Big Horn River System (Big Horn I), 753 P.2d 76 (Wyo. 1988); In re General Adjudication of All Rights to Use Water in the Big Horn River System (Big Horn III) 835 P.2d 273, 282–283 (Wyo. 1992).

...

III. THE TRIBE'S WATER RIGHTS

[The Court found that the purposes for the creation of the Colville Reservation included both the development of an agrarian society as well as the maintenance of their traditional fishing rights. Accordingly, the Court found the Confederated Tribes were entitled to water rights for both irrigation and instream flows to support their fishery.]

V. STATE PERMITS

Finally, we consider Walton's claim to water rights based on state water permits. We hold that the state has no power to regulate water in the No Name System, and the permits are of no force and effect.

A.

State regulatory authority over a tribal reservation may be barred either because it is pre-empted by federal law, or because it unlawfully infringes on the right of reservation Indians to self-government. Although these barriers are independent, they are related by the concept of tribal sovereignty. "The tradition of Indian sovereignty over the reservation and tribal members must inform the determination whether the exercise of state authority has been pre-empted by operation of federal law." *Bracker*, 100 S.Ct. at 2583.

Indian tribes are unique aggregations possessing attributes of sovereignty over both their members and their territory.

> The sovereignty that the Indian tribes retain is of a unique and limited character. It exists only at the sufferance of Congress and is subject to complete defeasance. But until Congress acts, the tribes retain their existing sovereign powers. In sum, Indian tribes still possess those aspects of sovereignty not withdrawn by treaty or statute, or by implication as a necessary result of their dependent status.

United States v. Wheeler, 435 U.S. 313, 323 (1978).

A tribe's inherent power to regulate generally the conduct of non-members on land no longer owned by, or held in trust for the tribe was impliedly withdrawn as a necessary result of its dependent status. *Montana v. United States*, ___ U.S. ___, 101 S.Ct. 1245, 1257 (1981). Exceptions to this implied withdrawal exist. A tribe retains the inherent power to exercise civil authority over the conduct of non-Indians on fee lands within its reservation when that conduct threatens or has some direct effect on the health and welfare of the tribe. This includes conduct that involves the tribe's water rights. *See id.* at n.15.

A water system is a unitary resource. The actions of one user have an immediate and direct effect on other users. The Colvilles' complaint in the district court alleged that the Waltons' appropriations from No Name Creek imperiled the agricultural use of downstream tribal lands and the trout fishery, among other things.

Regulation of water on a reservation is critical to the lifestyle of its residents and the development of its resources. Especially in arid and semi-arid regions of the West, water is the lifeblood of the community. Its regulation is an important sovereign power.

Although we need not decide whether this power resides exclusively in the tribe or the federal government, or whether it may be exercised by them jointly, its importance forms the backdrop for our consideration of the pre-emption issue.

B.

We hold that state regulation of water in the No Name system was pre-empted by the creation of the Colville Reservation. The geographic facts of this case make resolution of this issue somewhat easier than it otherwise might be. The No-Name system is non-navigable and is entirely within the boundaries of the reservation. Although some of the water passes through lands now in non-Indian ownership, all of those lands are also entirely within the reservation boundaries.

The Supreme Court has held that water use on a federal reservation is not subject to state regulation absent explicit federal recognition of state authority. *Federal Power Commission v. Oregon*, 349 U.S. 435 (1955).[5] Thus, in creating the Colville Reservation, the federal government pre-empted state control of the No Name system.

In *United States v. McIntire*, 101 F.2d 650, 654 (9th Cir. 1934), we held that state water laws are not controlling on an Indian reservation:

> (T)he Montana statutes regarding water rights are not applicable, because Congress at no time has made such statutes controlling in the reservation. In fact, the Montana enabling act specifically provided that Indian lands within the limits of the state, 'shall remain under the absolute jurisdiction and control of the Congress of the United States.'

Identical language appears in the Washington Enabling Act.

We adhere to this holding because we find no indication Congress intended the state to have this power. In a series of Acts culminating in the Desert Lands Act of 1877, Congress gave the states plenary control of water on the public domain. Based on this and other legislation, the Supreme Court concluded that Congress almost invariably

5. [15] The FPC had licensed construction of a dam on federal property. The lands that would have been flooded were held by the federal government. They had been reserved either as an Indian reservation or for power generation. The flow of the river would have been undiminished below the dam.

This court held the licensee had to obtain state approval because of the state's control over non-navigable waters on the public domain.

The Supreme Court reversed. It held that congressional acts giving the states control of water on the public domain were inapplicable on a federal reservation.

> It is a familiar principle of public land law that statutes providing generally for disposal of the public domain are inapplicable to lands which are not unqualifiedly subject to sale and disposition because they have been appropriated for some other purpose (I)t is enough for the instant case, to recognize that these Acts do not apply to this license, which relates only to the use of waters on reservations of the United States.

349 U.S. at 448.

defers to state water law when it expressly considers water rights. *United States v. New Mexico,* 438 U.S. 696 (1978).

This deference is not applicable to water use on a federal reservation, at least where such use has no impact off the reservation. *FPC v. Oregon*, 349 U.S. at 448. The usual policy stems in part from the need to permit western states to fashion water rights regimes that are responsive to local needs, and in part from the "legal confusion that would arise if federal water law and state water law reigned side by side in the same locality." *California v. United States*, 438 U.S. 645, 653–54 (1978).

Neither rationale is applicable here. Where land is set aside for an Indian reservation, Congress has reserved it for federal, as opposed to state needs. Because the No Name System is located entirely within the reservation, state regulation of some portion of its waters would create the jurisdictional confusion Congress has sought to avoid.

. . .

Finally, we note that the state's interest in extending its water law to the reservation is limited in this case. Tribal or federal control of No Name waters will have no impact on state water rights off the reservation.

Thus, we conclude that Walton's state permits are of no force and effect.

Notes & Questions

1. What is the rule articulated by the court regarding the scope of tribal civil authority over non-member activity on non-Indian lands within the reservation? According to the court, are the Confederated Colville Tribes entitled to regulate under that general rule? Does the court rely on any of the *Montana* exceptions to the presumption of state control over non-Indian water use within the Reservation?
2. What is the rule the court cites regarding the scope of state civil authority within the reservation? What law did the court look to in order to determine that state water law had been preempted within the No Name Basin of the Colville Reservation?
3. Why does the court note that "[t]he geographic facts of this case make resolution of this issue somewhat easier than it otherwise might be." Given the court's broader holdings in the case, do you think that the geographic characteristics of the No Name Basin were the dispositive factor in this case? Or do you think that the rules dictate that tribes have broad jurisdiction over water within their reservations to the exclusion of the states?

The question of whether the Ninth Circuit's language suggesting that its recognition of tribal jurisdiction in *Walton* is limited to watersheds that lie wholly within a reservation will become an actual limitation when tribes share a water course with state-based water users outside reservation boundaries came before the same court three years later in *United States v. Anderson*.

United States v. Anderson

United States Court of Appeals, Ninth Circuit
736 F.2d 1358 (1984)

J. BLAINE ANDERSON, Circuit Judge—The United States of America appeals a district court's determination that water rights appurtenant to certain reservation lands which passed out of trust status but which have subsequently been reacquired by the Spokane Tribe of Indians are entitled to a priority date as of the date of reacquisition by the Spokane Tribe. The Spokane Tribe also appeals, urging that the district court erred in holding that the State of Washington had regulatory jurisdiction over use of water by non-Indians on non-Indian land within the Spokane Indian Reservation. We affirm in part and reverse in part and remand for further proceedings in accordance with this decision.

I. BACKGROUND

[Review the facts of the case, which are recounted in Chapter 12.]

I. DISCUSSION

...

B. *State Regulatory Jurisdiction*

In the case before us, the district court determined that it was permissible for the State of Washington to exercise regulatory jurisdiction over non-Indian use of excess Chamokane Basin waters on lands owned by non-Indians within the Spokane Indian Reservation. The Spokane Tribe takes issue with this determination, arguing that it, not the state, has jurisdiction by virtue of our decision in *Colville Confederated Tribes v. Walton.* We agree with the rationale of the district court in its unpublished Memorandum and Order, C.R. 252 at 22–28, and find that *Walton* is not controlling.

Regulatory jurisdiction of a state over non-Indian activities on a tribal reservation "may be barred either because it is pre-empted by federal law, or because it unlawfully infringes on the right of reservation Indians to self-government." *Walton,* 647 F.2d at 51. These barriers to regulation, although independent, are related by the concept of tribal sovereignty....

In 1980 the Supreme Court set forth a specific rule for analyzing preemption claims in general and in cases involving non-Indians on reservations in particular.

> [Where] a state asserts authority over the conduct of non-Indians engaging in activities on the reservation [the court must make a] particularized inquiry into the nature of the state, federal and tribal interests at stake, an inquiry designed to determine whether, in the specific context, the exercise of state authority would violate federal law.

White Mountain Apache Tribe v. Bracker, 448 U.S. at 145, 100 S.Ct. at 2584. The Supreme Court further stated in *Bracker* that "[t]he tradition of Indian sovereignty over the reservation and tribal members must inform the determination whether the exercise of state authority has been pre-empted by operation of federal law." 448 U.S. at 143, 100 S.Ct. at 2583 (citations omitted).

Of course, tribal sovereignty is not absolute. In particular, the power to regulate generally the conduct of nonmembers on land no longer owned by or held in trust for the tribe is impliedly withdrawn as a necessary result of tribal dependent status. *Montana v. United States,* 450 U.S. 544, 564, 101 S.Ct. 1245, 1257, 67 L.Ed.2d 493 (1981);.... Some exceptions to this implied withdrawal of tribal regulatory authority do exist.

> A tribe may regulate, through taxation, licensing or other means, the activities of nonmembers who enter consensual relationships with the tribe or its members, through commercial dealing, contracts, leases, or other arrangements.... A tribe may also retain inherent power to exercise civil authority over the conduct of non-Indians on fee lands within the reservation when that conduct threatens or has some direct effect on the political integrity, the economic security, or the health or welfare of the tribe.

Montana v. United States, 450 U.S. at 565–66, 101 S.Ct. at 1258–59 (citations omitted) [1981]. This civil authority over non-Indians which the tribe retains, "derives not only from the tribe's inherent power necessary to self-government and territorial management, but also from the power to exclude nonmembers from tribal land." *Babbitt Ford, Inc. v. Navajo Indian Tribe,* 710 F.2d 587, 592 (9th Cir.1983)....

Recent case law has affirmed tribal exercise of civil jurisdiction over nonmembers. Where nonmembers have transacted business with the tribe or entered onto the tribal lands for other purposes, the Supreme Court has upheld the imposition of taxes or the assessment of special fees. *See Merrion v. Jicarilla Apache Tribe* (severance tax on non-Indian mining operation on reservation lands) and *Montana v. United States* (exclusion of nonmembers from hunting on tribal lands). Likewise, this circuit has upheld tribal economic, health and welfare regulations. *See Cardin v. De La Cruz,* 671 F.2d 363 (9th Cir.) (building, health and safety regulations applied to nonmember business located on fee lands within the reservation), *cert. denied,* 459 U.S. 967, 103 S.Ct. 293, 74 L.Ed.2d 277 (1982); *Confederated Salish and Kootenai Tribes v. Namen,* 665 F.2d 951 (9th Cir.) (regulation of riparian rights of non-Indians), *cert. denied,* 459 U.S. 977, 103 S.Ct. 314, 74 L.Ed.2d 291 (1982)

In *Montana,* the Court permitted the Crow Tribe to regulate hunting by nonmembers on tribal lands but did not permit the Tribe to prohibit nonmembers from hunting on reservation lands owned in fee by nonmembers. *Montana v. United States,* 450 U.S. at 566–67, 101 S.Ct. at 1258–59. Three reasons were offered for this distinction.

> First, the non-Indians, who were hunting and fishing on non-Indian fee lands, had not "[entered into] any agreements or dealings with the Crow Tribe so as to subject themselves to tribal civil jurisdiction." Second, there had been no suggestion that the hunting and fishing activities on non-Indian fee land so "[threatened] the Tribe's political or economic security as to justify tribal reg-

> ulation." Finally, the complaint had failed to allege that such activities "[imperiled] the subsistance [sic] or welfare of the Tribe."

Babbitt Ford, Inc. v. Navajo Indian Tribe, 710 F.2d at 592 (citations omitted).

Applying these standards, we conclude that the State, not the Tribe, has the authority to regulate the use of excess Chamokane Basin waters by non-Indians on non-tribal, i.e., fee, land. Our review reveals no consensual agreement between the non-Indian water users and the Tribe which would furnish the basis for implication of tribal regulatory authority. We find no conduct which so threatens or has such a "direct effect on the political integrity, the economic security, or the health or welfare of the Tribe," as to confer tribal jurisdiction. *Montana v. United States,* 450 U.S. at 566, 101 S.Ct. at 1258. The water rights adjudication which furnishes the basis for the instant inquiry quantifies and preserves tribal water rights. The district court appointed a federal water master whose responsibility is to administer the available waters in accord with the priorities of all the water rights as adjudicated. *See Jicarilla Apache Tribe v. United States,* 601 F.2d 1116, 1122 (10th Cir.1979). The district court recognized the importance of the tribal fishery and has awarded non-consumptive water rights to preserve it. The tribe is, of course, entitled to utilize its water for *any* lawful purpose. *Colville Confederated Tribes v. Walton,* 647 F.2d 42, 48 (9th Cir.1981). If the tribe chooses to use water reserved for irrigation in a non-consumptive manner, it does not thereby relinquish any of its water rights to state permittees or subject the exercise of its rights to state regulation. The state may regulate only the use, by non-Indian fee owners, of excess water. Any permits issued by the state would be limited to excess water. If those permits represent rights that may be empty, so be it.

It is evident, however, that the political and economic welfare of the Tribe will not suffer adverse impact from the state-regulated use of surplus waters by nonmembers on non-Indian lands. Instead the factual situation points in favor of state regulation. First, no direct federal preemption of state regulation has occurred. No federal statute or regulatory scheme expressly or impliedly governs water use by non-Indians on the Spokane Reservation. Second, the balance of interest weighs most heavily in favor of the state.

The instant situation is contrary to that addressed by this circuit in *Colville Confederated Tribes v. Walton,* 647 F.2d 42 (1981). In *Walton,* we determined that state regulation of the water system was preempted when viewed in light of the Colville's right to self-government. The *Walton* decision recognized the general rule of deference to state water law. *Walton* rested on a determination that "deference is not applicable to water use on a federal reservation, at least where such use has no impact off the reservation." *Id.* (citing *FPC v. Oregon,* 349 U.S. 435 at 448). Although recognizing that the usual policy of deference

> stems in part from the need to permit western states to fashion water rights regimes that are responsive to local needs and in part from the "legal confusion that would arise if federal water law and state water law reigned side by side in the same locality,"

the *Walton* court found neither rationale applicable to the matter. In accordance with its determination that neither of the policy considerations supporting deference to state jurisdiction would be fulfilled by permitting state regulation of the No Name System, the *Walton* court held such jurisdiction preempted by the creation of the Colville Reservation.

The *Walton* decision was compelled by the geography and hydrology of the No Name Basin and its relationship to the Colville Reservation. The reservation lands in question were allotted, not opened for entry and settlement. *Id.* at 53. The No Name hydrological system is non-navigable and is located *entirely* within the reservation. *Id.* at 52. Validation of the state-issued permits claimed by Walton could have jeopardized the agricultural use of downstream tribal users as well as the existence of the tribal fishery. *Id.* In essence, the interest of the Tribe in regulation of the waters of the No Name Basin was "critical to the lifestyle of its residents and the development of its resources." *Id.*

The district court noted, and we agree, that because water per se lies within the exterior boundaries of an Indian reservation does not necessarily negate a state's interest in overseeing its usage along with the other in-state water systems. Washington is obligated to regulate and conserve water consumption for the benefit of all its citizens, including those who own land within a reservation in fee. *See* 25 U.S.C. § 349. Therefore, the state's special concern is shared with, not displaced by, similar tribal and federal interests when water is located within the boundaries of both the state and the reservation. The weight of the state's interest depends, in large part, on the extent to which waterways or aquifers transcend the exterior boundaries of Indian country.

In *Walton,* the stream in question was small, non-navigable, and located entirely within the reservation and, as noted, water use by non-Indians would impact tribal agriculture and fisheries. Thus, even though some portion of the creek was found to be surplus to the tribe's requirements, state regulation of the remaining supply could create jurisdictional confusion and violate tribal sovereignty. In contrast, Chamokane Creek arises outside of the Spokane Indian Reservation and its course, for a good deal of its length, continues outside of that reservation. When the creek comes to the reservation, it forms the eastern *boundary,* and much of the reservation land with state water rights is immediately adjacent to the creek. The creek then separates from the reservation boundary, flowing into the Spokane River and eventually into the Columbia River and to the Pacific Ocean.

The facts in this case are readily distinguishable from the facts in the *Walton* decision. By weighing the competing federal, tribal and state interests involved, it is clear that the state may exercise its regulatory jurisdiction over the use of surplus, non-reserved Chamokane Basin waters by nonmembers on non-Indian fee lands within the Spokane Indian Reservation. Central to our decision is the fact that the interest of the state in exercising its jurisdiction will not infringe on the tribal right to self-government nor impact on the Tribe's economic welfare because those rights have been quantified and will be protected by the federal water master. Additionally, in view of the hydrology and geography of the Chamokane Creek Basin, the State of Washington's interest in developing a comprehensive water program for the allocation of surplus waters weighs heavily in favor of permitting it to extend its regulatory authority to the excess waters, if any, of the Chamokane Basin. State permits issued for any such excess water will be subject to all preexisting rights and those preexisting rights will be protected by the federal court decree and its appointed water master. We do not believe there is any realistic infringement on tribal rights and protected affairs. If there is any intrusion, it is minimal and permissible under all of the circumstances of this case.

Notes & Questions

1. Why does the court look to *Montana* to determine the scope of *state* jurisdiction within the Spokane Reservation? What factors led the court to conclude that state law was not preempted?
2. Given the broad holding in *Walton*, do you agree that with the court's conclusion that "no direct federal preemption of state regulation has occurred?"
3. Do you agree with the court's conclusion that "the balance of interests [over the regulation of excess water within the Spokane Reservation] weighs most heavily in favor of the state?" Should that matter?
4. How does the court distinguish *Walton*? Given the broad holding in *Walton*, do you find the court's reasoning persuasive?

State Court Rulings

The McCarran Amendment provides that:

> Consent is given to join the United States as a defendant in any suit (1) for the adjudication of rights to the use of water of a river system or other source, or (2) for the administration of such rights, where it appears that the United States is the owner of or is in the process of acquiring water rights by appropriation under State law, by purchase, by exchange, or otherwise, and the United States is a necessary party to such suit.[6]

You learned in Chapter 26 that the U.S. Supreme Court interpreted the language in clause (1) to allow the United States to be joined in a state court general adjudication, including in its role as trustee over tribal water rights. Administration is the subject of clause (2). Does that language allow a state court responsible for the adjudication to administer tribal water rights, or is it limited to state-based rights (such as those for a Reclamation project)? What if the state relies on an agency rather than the court to administer water rights?

The Wyoming Supreme Court addressed this portion of the McCarran Amendment as part of the State of Wyoming's Big Horn Adjudication. As you learned in the previ-

---

6. Act of July 10, 1952, Pub. L. No. 495, § 208, 66 Stat. 549, 560 (codified at 43 U.S.C. § 666 (2012)).

ous Chapter, where you read an excerpt from *Big Horn I*, that adjudication included the reserved water rights of the Wind River Tribes. The excerpt below from *Big Horn I* addresses the role of the adjudication court and the state engineer in administering those reserved water rights.

In re the General Adjudication of All Rights to Use Water in the Big Horn River System

Wyoming Supreme Court
753 P.2d 76 (1988)

Before BROWN, C.J., and THOMAS, CARDINE, and MACY, JJ., and HANSCUM, District Judge

...

VIII MONITORING OF THE DECREE BY THE STATE ENGINEER

The issue of whether the state engineer may monitor the decree is a controversy conferring jurisdiction upon this court. A letter from Wyoming to Judge Johnson which referred to "[t]he federal government's residual dissatisfaction with Judge Joffe's ruling that the State Engineer shall have primary regulatory responsibility" indicates previous disputes as to the propriety of the ruling....

...

Federal law has not preempted state oversight of reserved water rights. In *Arizona v. San Carlos Apache Tribe of Arizona*, the Court merely reiterated that Indian water rights in state adjudications must be judged by federal law. In *Cappaert v. United States*, the Court said: "Federal water rights are not dependent upon state law or state procedures and they need not be adjudicated only in state courts." The procedures referred to are state procedures for perfecting state water rights, not monitoring of already decreed federal water rights.... *United States v. Rio Grande Dam and Irrigation Company* dealt only with interference with a navigable stream, and *United States v. McIntire* held a state appropriation of reserved water to be invalid. In *Colville Confederated Tribes v. Walton* the court indicated that state administration of the No Name System was inappropriate because the system was entirely within the reservation, but conceded that state regulation may be appropriate in some circumstances. The ninth circuit later conceded that the State could assume some regulatory authority on the reservation. *United States v. Anderson*.... The decree entered in the instant case does not require application of state water law to the Indian reservation. The decree recognizes reserved water rights based on federal law. The role of the state engineer is thus not to apply state law, but to enforce the reserved rights as decreed under principles of federal law. This court is also cognizant of the fact that exercise of the reserved water rights are intimately bound up with the state water rights of off-reservation users. The state water appropriators are not in a position to jeopardize the decreed rights of the Tribes. The decree only requires the United States and the Tribes first to turn to the state engineer to exercise his authority over the state users to protect their reserved water rights before they seek court assistance to enforce their rights; it does not preclude access to the courts. Incidental monitoring of Indian use to this end has carelessly been termed "administration" of Indian water by the state engineer. Should the state engineer find that it is the Tribes who are violating the decree, it is clear that he must then turn to the courts for enforcement of the decree against the United States and the Tribes and that he cannot simply close the headgates. Any fear that the state engineer may be unfair must be dispelled by Article 1, § 31 of the Wyoming Constitution which provides that the State "shall equally guard all of the various [water] interests involved." The state engineer has sworn to uphold this constitution. Thus it is readily apparent that the provisions authorizing the state engineer to monitor reserved water rights contemplate neither the application of state law nor the authority to deprive the Tribes of water without the assistance of the courts in a suit for the administration of the decree.

The argument that the instant decree can be administered only by the court in a separate suit for administration under the McCarran Amendment must fail in light of the admission that an independent water master might properly be appointed at this time to administer the decree and in light of the state engineer's limited authority. The Treaty of 1868 prohibits only unauthorized persons from entering the reservation, but the state engineer would be an authorized person upon his appointment to monitor the decree and could properly enter the reservation.

The district court did not err in including provisions giving the state engineer authority to enforce the decree against state appropriators.

Notes & Questions

1. According to the Wyoming Supreme Court, what is the scope of the State of Wyoming's jurisdiction to administer the reserved water rights on the Wind River Reservation?
2. What is the legal basis for that jurisdiction? Would the state have any jurisdiction in the absence of the McCarran Amendment?

Following the quantification of reserved water rights using the PIA method in *Big Horn I*, the Shoshone and Northern Arapaho Tribes of the Wind River Reservation sought to change some of their undeveloped water rights to an instream flow water right to maintain a minimum flow in the Wind River for Tribal fisheries. In describing the process, Professor Robison states:

> The tribes undertook a number of measures to this end, adopting a tribal water code, creating a water resources control board, and subsequently issuing a tribal instream flow permit in April 1990 that dedicated a prescribed amount of water from the Wind River for instream flow purposes [citations omitted].... When the tribes later requested curtailment of appropriative rights

held by Midvale Irrigation District, the State Engineer refused to honor this request on the ground that it was unlawful[7]

The decision of the State Engineer set the stage for another trip to the Wyoming Supreme Court in *Big Horn III.*[8] The issue would be whether PIA is merely a quantification method or a restriction on use. The U.S. Supreme Court had addressed this issue in *Arizona II,* which is the issuance of the decree from *Arizona v. California*. After listing the quantities of water for the five *Indian* reservations, the Decree states:

> The foregoing reference to a quantity of water necessary to supply consumptive use required for irrigation ... shall constitute the means of determining quantity of adjudicated water rights but shall *not* constitute a restriction of the usage of them to irrigation or other agricultural application.[9] [emphasis added]

The Wyoming Supreme Court opinion in *Big Horn III*[10] is anything but a model of clarity with a majority, one concurring, one concurring on one issue and dissenting on another, and two dissenting opinions. The district court had:

> (1) decreed that the Shoshone and Northern Arapaho Tribes on the Wind River Indian Reservation may change the use of their reserved water right as they deem advisable without regard to Wyoming water law; and (2) substituted the tribal water agency for the state engineer as the administrator of both reserved and state-permitted water rights within the Wind River Indian Reservation.[11]

Justice Macy's opinion achieves a majority on various issues only through the concurring and dissenting opinions, and it is impossible to find a majority rationale. The dissent of Justice Gordon spares you the effort of navigating this yourself by providing a roadmap to the various opinions. Four justices (J. Macy, Cardine concurring, and Brown and Golden dissenting) agree that use of water for instream flow is a beneficial use; however, Justice Cardine would limit the ability to change a water right to an instream use to water first developed for irrigation, and Justices Macy and Thomas would apply state, not federal, law to change in use. State law in Wyoming is similar to that of Idaho, allowing only the state to hold an instream flow right. Three justices, (J. Macy, Thomas concurring, Brown dissenting) agree that the "State engineer should administer all water rights on the reservation, turning to the courts for enforcement authority"[12]—i.e., the "monitoring" limit imposed on the State Engineer in *Big Horn I.* Professor Robison summarizes the result:

---

7. Jason A. Robison, *Wyoming's* Big Horn *General Stream Adjudication*, 15(2) Wyo. L. Rev. 243, 289 (2015).

8. In re General Adjudication of All Rights to Use Water in the Big Horn River System (Big Horn III) 835 P.2d 273, 282–283 (Wyo. 1992).

9. Arizona v. California (*Arizona II*), 439 U.S. 419, 422 (1979).

10. In re the General Adjudication of All Rights to Use Water in the Big Horn River System and All Other Sources, 835 P.2d 273 (Wyo. 1992) (*Big Horn III*).

11. *Big Horn III* at 275.

12. *Big Horn III,* dissenting opinion of J. Golden *at* 300–304.

> In sum, although the Wyoming Supreme Court issued a splintered opinion to resolve the instream flow and administrative conflicts in *Big Horn III*, its upshot was that (1) the tribes were not authorized to dedicate water afforded by their reserved right to instream flows, and (2) the State Engineer was responsible for administering all water rights on the Wind River Indian Reservation.[13]

Fear of an unfavorable U.S. Supreme Court ruling that would extend this to reservations in all states led the Shoshone and Northern Arapaho to forego an appeal to the U.S. Supreme Court.[14] To avoid a student revolt, we will not ask any questions on this "fractured" opinion.

Settlement Solutions

As you learned in the last Chapter, the new "settlement era" focused on reserved water rights has led to novel solutions. These solutions include administration and enforcement of the reserved water right. Most settlements provide for Tribal administration of the reserved water right with some mechanism for coordination with the state and its water users on shared resources. Tribal administration requires development of a tribal water code and establishment of an administrative entity.

This section will use the settlement between the Shoshone-Bannock Tribes of the Fort Hall Reservation and the State of Idaho as an example of the development of a Tribal Water Code in the implementation stage. We will then turn to the Compact between the Confederated Salish and Kootenai Tribes of the Flathead Reservation and Montana, to illustrate the novel approach of a joint administration and enforcement entity when a reservation includes significant non-Indian fee land within its borders. The actual water codes are included in your online materials with brief summaries provided here. *Notes & Questions* require reference to the online materials.

Shoshone-Bannock Tribes of the Fort Hall Reservation Tribal Water Resources Code of 2007

The Fort Hall Reservation is home to the Shoshone-Bannock Tribes, and is located in the Eastern Snake Plain of Idaho, described in Chapter 23. The settlement arose in the context of the SRBA. Reservation land is 97% held by the Tribes or Tribal members. The major water sources, including the Snake and Blackfoot Rivers and the Eastern Snake Plain Aquifer, are shared with state-based water use off the reservation. The 1990 Fort Hall Water Rights Agreement addresses administration with the following language:

---

13. Jason A. Robison, *Wyoming's* Big Horn *General Stream Adjudication*, 15(2) Wyo. L. Rev. 243, 293 (2015).

14. *Id.*

> 8.1 The Parties recognize and respect the sovereignty of the Tribes, the State, and the United States, as well as the powers and limitations accompanying the sovereignty of each government. In order to strike a balance among these sovereign interests, the parties ... agree to cooperate in administration of water resources to protect the use of all water rights decreed in the SRBA.
>
> 8.2 Except for the Snake River and the Blackfoot River, the parties agree to administer water rights within the Reservation as follows:
>
> .1 The Tribes shall administer the distribution of all Tribal water rights within the Reservation.
>
> ...
>
> .3 The Tribes shall adopt and submit a Tribal Water Code to the Secretary for approval....
>
> ...
>
> .5 Consistent with Article 8.2.1, the United States shall administer the distribution of the Fort Hall Indian Irrigation Project water rights and the Fort Hall Agency water rights from the point the water is delivered to the project facilities.
>
> .6 The State shall administer the distribution of those rights acquired under state law within the Reservation that are not a part of the Fort Hall Agency, Tribal or Fort Hall Indian Irrigation Project Water Rights.[15]

Separate provisions provide for administration of water from the Snake and Blackfoot Rivers pursuant to the SRBA Decree.

The Shoshone-Bannock Tribes have been managing water resources on the Fort Hall Reservation pursuant to a tribal water code since 2007. In addition to the settlement, the code was authorized as part of the 1990 Fort Hall Water Rights Settlement Act (the bill ratifying the settlement).[16] The code is provided in your online materials. Note how the code is similar to but distinct from the prior appropriation doctrine we have already learned about. Use the following *Notes & Questions* to guide you through the Code.

Notes & Questions

1. What is the division of responsibilities between the Shoshone-Bannock Tribal Water Resources Department and the Water Resources Commission? What does the Commission do? What does the Department do?

---

15. The University of New Mexico, "Special Master's Term Sheet for Nez Perce Tribe Water Rights," Digital Repository, https://digitalrepository.unm.edu/nawrs/94/. 1990 Fort Hall Water Rights Agreement, Article 8 Administration of Water Rights, also available at: Native American Water Rights Settlement Project.

16. 104 Stat. 3059 (1990).

2. Do water permit holders have similar property rights to their water use as state-law water right holders have under the prior appropriation doctrine? How is it different? What are the advantages and disadvantages of these differences?
3. How does the Code handle water allocation in times of shortage? How does this differ from the state system of prior appropriation?
4. What are the differences between a water permit and a water license in the code? For what types of uses can a water permit be issued?
5. Who is tasked with investigation of a permit application? What goes into that investigation?
6. Who is tasked with approval of a new water permit? What is the basis for approval or denial?
7. Under what circumstances may a validly acquired water permit be lost? What happens to the water allocated under the permit if that permit is revoked?
8. What acts are prohibited under the water code? What is the consequence for engaging in a prohibited activity?
9. May water permits be transferred? Under what circumstances? Are there limits on water transfers?
10. What decisions may be appealed? What is the process? What is the standard of review for appeals of decisions by the Engineer? What is the standard of review for appeals of decisions by the Commission?
11. Tribal constitutions that were created pursuant to the Indian Reorganization Act require new code provisions to be approved by the Secretary of the Interior. In 1975, the Secretary instituted a moratorium on the approval of new tribal water codes in the absence of a settlement or an adjudicated water right. Tribal constitutions not created under the IRA do not require secretarial approval for new code provisions. The Navajo Nation, which rejected the Indian Reorganization Act, adopted a water code for on-reservation uses in 1984, without seeking the approval of the Secretary of the Interior. The moratorium was recently lifted in 2022 and the Secretary is working to implement criteria for the approval of new water codes.

Confederated Salish and Kootenai Tribes of the Flathead Reservation (CSKT)—Montana Compact[17]

The Flathead Reservation in Montana includes considerable private fee land held by non-Indians.

The 2015 settlement among the CSKT, State of Montana, and the United States established a joint Tribal/State entity for the administration of water with the following language in Article IV, Implementation of Compact:

---

17. Mont. Code Ann. 85-20-1901, 1902.

I. Administration: Establishment of Flathead Reservation Water Management Board.

1. Establishment of Board. There is hereby established the Flathead Reservation Water Management Board. Upon the Effective Date, the Board shall be the exclusive regulatory body on the Reservation for the issuance of Appropriation Rights and authorizations for Changes in Use of Appropriation Rights and Existing Uses, and for the administration and enforcement of all Appropriation Rights and Existing Uses. The Board shall also have exclusive jurisdiction to resolve any controversy over the meaning and interpretation of the Compact on the Reservation, and any controversy over the right to the use of water as between the Parties or between or among holders of Appropriation Rights and Existing Uses on the Reservation.... The jurisdiction of this Board does not extend to any water rights whose place of use is located outside the exterior boundaries of the Reservation.

2. Membership.

a. Voting Members. The Board shall consist of five voting members: two members selected by the Governor of the State ..., after consultation with holders of Water Rights Arising Under State Law located on the Reservation; two members appointed by the Tribal Council; and one member selected by the other four members....[18]

To govern the authority and process of the Board, the State and Tribe passed parallel implementing legislation that includes provisions similar to other water use acts that you learned about in Part V.[19] The Ordinance to be adopted by both the State and the Tribe is in your online materials for this Chapter and should be used to answer the following questions.

Notes & Questions

1. Unlike the Shoshone-Bannock Water settlement that divides jurisdiction among the Tribes, the United States, and the State, the Flathead Compact and the Unitary Administration and Management Ordinance creates a joint entity. What advantages does the Flathead Ordinance provide over the Shoshone-Bannock Water Code? Are there disadvantages? Consider that the Flathead Reservation has a high level of non-Indian ownership of private land. In contrast, the Fort Hall Reservation is almost entirely held in trust for the Shoshone-Bannock Tribes and its members. How does that difference in reservation population come into play in these two choices for water administration?

---

18. Mont. Code Ann. 85-20-1901, Article IV, I.1 and 2.
19. The State's parallel legislation can be found at Mont. Code Ann. 85-20-1902.

2. What is the scope of the Board's authority? What is the division of responsibilities between the Flathead Water Board and the Reservation Engineer?
3. What types of uses are water permits available for? What information must a new appropriator provide with their application? What must a new appropriator show before they may receive a permit to use water or change their water use? What happens if the Engineer determines that mitigation is necessary?
4. What is the enforcement process in times of shortage?
5. Is there a prohibition against waste? What enforcement powers does the Board have to prevent or rectify waste?
6. Under what circumstances may a water right be declared abandoned? What is the process for declaring a water right abandoned?
7. What decisions may be appealed? What is the process? What is the standard of review for appeals of decisions by the Engineer? What is the standard of review for appeals of decisions by the Commission?

Table of Cases

Index

G

H

I

S

T

U

W